T0351171

Web Engineering
Advancements
and Trends:
Building New Dimensions
of Information Technology

Ghazi Alkhatib
Princess Sumaya University of Technology, Jordan

David Rine
George Mason University, USA

INFORMATION SCIENCE REFERENCE

Hershey · New York

Director of Editorial Content:	Kristin Klinger
Director of Book Publications:	Julia Mosemann
Development Editor:	Julia Mosemann
Publishing Assistant:	Kurt Smith
Typesetter:	Carole Coulson
Quality control:	Jamie Snavely
Cover Design:	Lisa Tosheff
Printed at:	Yurchak Printing Inc.

Published in the United States of America by
Information Science Reference (an imprint of IGI Global)
701 E. Chocolate Avenue
Hershey PA 17033
Tel: 717-533-8845
Fax: 717-533-8661
E-mail: cust@igi-global.com
Web site: http://www.igi-global.com/reference

Library of Congress Cataloging-in-Publication Data

Web engineering advancements and trends : building new dimensions of information technology / Ghazi Alkhatib and David Rine, editors.
       p. cm.
  Includes bibliographical references and index.
  Summary: "This book examines integrated approaches in new dimensions of social and organizational knowledge sharing with emphasis on intelligent and personalized access"--Provided by publisher.
  ISBN 978-1-60566-719-5 (hardcover) -- ISBN 978-1-60566-720-1 (ebook) 1.
Web site development. 2. Web services. 3. Information technology--
Technological innovations. I. Alkhatib, Ghazi, 1947- II. Rine, David C.
  TK5105.888.W3728 2010
  006.7'6--dc22
                                    2009035426

British Cataloguing in Publication Data
A Cataloguing in Publication record for this book is available from the British Library.

Advances in Information Technology and Web Engineering (AITWE) Series

ISBN: 1948-7983

Editor-in-Chief:
Ghazi I. Alkhatib, Applied Science University, Jordan
David C. Rine, George Mason University, USA

Integrated Approaches in Information Technology and Web Engineering: Advancing Organizational Knowledge Sharing

Ghazi I. Alkhatib, Applied Science University, Jordan & David C. Rine, George Mason University, USA
Information Science Reference * copyright 2009 * 361pp * H/C (ISBN: 978-1-60566-418-7)

With the increasing proliferation of information technology and Web-based approaches to the implementation of systems and services, researchers, educators, and practitioners worldwide are experiencing a rising need for authoritative references to enhance their understanding of the most current and effective engineering practices leading to robust and successful solutions.

Integrated Approaches in Information Technology and Web Engineering: Advancing Organizational Knowledge Sharing presents comprehensive, research-driven insights into the field of Web engineering. This book collects over 30 authoritative articles from distinguished international researchers in information technology and Web engineering, creating an invaluable resource for library reference collections that will equip researchers and practitioners in academia and industry alike with the knowledge base to drive the next generation of innovations.

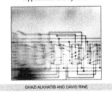

Agent Technologies and Web Engineering: Applications and Systems

Ghazi I. Alkhatib, Applied Science University, Jordan & David C. Rine, George Mason University, USA
Information Science Reference * copyright 2009 * 361pp * H/C (ISBN: 978-1-60566-618-1)

In recent years, the emerging field of agent technologies has become mainstream in Web engineering. With constant field developments and updates, a reference source is needed that reflects the increased scope of agent technology application domains and development practices and tools.

Agent Technologies and Web Engineering: Applications and Systems presents the latest tools and applications addressing critical issues involved with information technology and Web engineering research. Covering topics such as next-generation networks, XML query processing, and Semantic Web services, this book provides cutting-edge research for practitioners and academicians involved in agent technology and Web engineering fields.

The Advances in Information Technology and Web Engineering (AITWE) Book Series aims to provide a platform for research in the area of Information Technology (IT) concepts, tools, methodologies, and ethnography, in the contexts of global communication systems and Web engineered applications. Organizations are continuously overwhelmed by a variety of new information technologies, many are Web based. These new technologies are capitalizing on the widespread use of network and communication technologies for seamless integration of various issues in information and knowledge sharing within and among organizations. This emphasis on integrated approaches is unique to this book series and dictates cross platform and multidisciplinary strategy to research and practice. The Advances in Information Technology and Web Engineering (AITWE) Book Series seeks to create a stage where comprehensive publications are distributed for the objective of bettering and expanding the field of web systems, knowledge capture, and communication technologies. The series will provide researchers and practitioners with solutions for improving how technology is utilized for the purpose of a growing awareness of the importance of web applications and engineering.

Hershey • New York
Order online at www.igi-global.com or call 717-533-8845 x 100 –
Mon-Fri 8:30 am - 5:00 pm (est) or fax 24 hours a day 717-533-8661

Editorial Advisory Board

Table of Contents

Section 1
Semantics and Ontologies

Section 4
Applications

Detailed Table of Contents

Section 1
Semantics and Ontologies

Chapter 1

Hahn Huu Hoang, Vienna University of Technology, Austria
Tho Manh Nguyen, Vienna University of Technology, Austria
A. Min Tjoa, Vienna University of Technology, Austria

Formulating unambiguous queries in the Semantic Web applications is a challenging task for users. This chapter presents a new approach in guiding users to formulate clear requests based on their common nature of querying for information. The approach known as the front-end approach gives users an overview about the system data through a virtual data component which stores the extracted metadata of the data storage sources in the form of an ontology. This approach reduces the ambiguities in users' requests at a very early stage and allows the query process to effectively perform in fulfilling users' demands in a context-aware manner. Furthermore, the approach provides a powerful query engine, called context-aware querying, that recommends the appropriate query patterns according to the user's querying context.

Chapter 2

Maria Indrawan, Monash University, Australia
Seng Loke, La Trobe University, Australia

The debate on the effectiveness of ontology in solving semantic problems has increased recently in many domains of information technology. One side of the debate accepts the inclusion of ontology as a suitable solution. The other side of the debate argues that ontology is far from an ideal solution to the semantic problem. This chapter explores this debate in the area of information retrieval. Several past approaches were explored and a new approach was investigated to test the effectiveness of a generic ontology such as WordNet in improving the performance of information retrieval systems. The test and the analysis of the experiments suggest that WordNet is far from the ideal solution in solving semantic problems in the information retrieval. However, several observations have been made and reported in this chapter that allow research in ontology for information retrieval to move in the right direction.

Chapter 3

This chapter introduces a new framework for intelligent Semantic Web services that overcomes previous drawbacks. Such a framework is based on the graphical autonomous intelligent virtual agents (GAIVAs), virtual agents that exhibit a human-like appearance and behaviour. The agents are completely autonomous, that is, they are able to take decisions and perform actions in order to provide services without human intervention. In addition, those decisions must be intelligent from the point of view of a human observer. To this aim, the framework comprises a collection of powerful artificial intelligence techniques described in this chapter. The framework also incorporates a powerful graphical user interface (GUI) that allows the users to interact with the system in a graphical and very natural way. The authors believe that these advanced features are very helpful to encourage people to use a Web service system. Further, Web service providers and developers might greatly benefit from considering this approach.

Chapter 4

A Semantic Web service composition system can be considered as a multi-agent system, in which each of the component service is considered as an agent capability. This chapter presents a multi-agent system based Semantic Web service composition approach. The proposed approach deals with some of the untouched issues and uses cognitive parameters and quality of service (QoS) parameters in service-provider selection. Education planning, a new application area for Semantic Web technology that involves planning the admission process for higher education courses has been introduced and the proposed approach and models are applied to it.

Chapter 5

Advances in image acquisition and storage technology have led to tremendous growth in very large and detailed image databases. These images, once analysed, can reveal useful information to our uses. The focus for image mining in this chapter is clustering of shoe prints. This study leads to the work in forensic data mining. The authors of this chapter cluster selected shoe prints using k-means and EM (Expectation Maximization). The authors analyse and compare the results of these two algorithms.

Chapter 6

In this chapter, the development and evolution of Web Applications is viewed from an engineering perspective that relies on and accommodates the knowledge inherent in patterns. It proposes an approach in the direction of building a foundation for pattern-oriented Web Engineering. For that, a methodology for pattern-oriented Web Engineering, namely POWEM, is described. The steps of POWEM include selection of a suitable development process model, construction of a semiotic quality model, namely PoQ, and selection and mapping of suitable patterns to quality attributes in PoQ. To support decision making and to place POWEM in context, the feasibility issues involved in each step are discussed. For the sake of is illustration, the use of patterns during the design phase of a Web Application are highlighted. Finally, some directions for future research, including those for Web Engineering education and Social Web Applications, are given.

Section 2
User Interface

Chapter 7

This study tried to examine how cell phone users who undergo a technology leap acquire their procedural knowledge of operating a cell phone and to find out which factors can improve their device competency. Using interviews, usability tests, and a questionnaire, this study found out that many respondents use unstructured means such as asking other cell phone users or rote learning in gaining their procedural knowledge. Some factors influencing users' device competencies that were found in this study are classified into three categories: user interface design, culture, and the users themselves. In order to improve users' device competency, elements in those three categories must be integrated. One realization of such integration is the attempt of localizing user interface through the user's culture, not the culture where the cell phone is designed and manufactured.

Chapter 8

This chapter proposes an application of emotion recognizer system in telecommunications entitled voice driven emotion recognizer mobile phone (VDERM). The design implements a voice-to-image conversion scheme through a voice-to-image converter that extracts emotion features in the voice, recognizes them, and selects the corresponding facial expression images from image bank. Since it only requires audio transmission, it can support video communication at a much lower bit rate than the conventional videophone. The first prototype of VDERM system has been implemented into a personal computer. The coder, voice-to-image converter, image database, and system interface are preinstalled in the personal computer. This chapter presents and discusses some evaluations that have been conducted in supporting this proposed prototype. The results have shown that both voice and image are important for people to correctly recognize emotion in telecommunications and the proposed solution can provide an alternative to videophone systems. The future works list some modifications that can be done to the proposed prototype in order to make it more practical for mobile applications.

Chapter 9

This chapter proposes a methodology to create test suites for a GUI. The proposed methodology organizes the testing activity into various levels. The tests created at a particular level can be reused at higher levels. This methodology extends the notion of modularity and reusability to the testing phase. The organization and management of the created test suites resembles closely to the structure of the GUI under test.

Chapter 10

Software engineers and human computer interaction engineers have come to the understanding that usability is not something that can be "added" to a software product during late stage, since to a certain extent it is determined and restricted by architecture design. Cost effectively developing a usable system must include developing an architecture, which supports usability. Because software engineers in industry lacked support for the early evaluation of usability, the authors defined a generalized four-step method for software architecture level usability analysis called SALUTA. This chapter reports on a number of experiences and problems we observed when performing architecture analysis of usability at three industrial case studies performed in the domain of Web-based enterprise systems. Suggestions or solutions are provided for solving or avoiding these problems so organizations facing similar problems may learn from the authors' experience.

Section 3
Testing and Performance Evaluation

Chapter 11

N. Gupta, Birla Institute of Technology, India
D. Saini, King Saud University, College of Science, Saudi Arabia
H. Saini, Higher Institute of Electronics, Libya

Object-oriented programming consists of several different levels of abstraction, namely, the algorithmic level, class level, cluster level, and system level. This chapter discusses a testing technique to generate test cases at class level for object-oriented programs. The formal object oriented class specification is used to develop a test model. This test model is based on finite state machine specification. The class specification and the test model is analyzed to select a set of test data for each method of the class, and finally the test cases can be generated using other testing techniques like finite-state testing or data-flow testing.

Chapter 12

J. Miller, University of Alberta, Canada
L. Zhang, University of Alberta, Canada
E. Ofuonye, University of Alberta, Canada
M. Smith, University of Calgary, Canada

The construction and testing of Web-based systems has become more complex and challenging with continual innovations in technology. One major concern particularly for the deployment of mission critical applications is security. In Web-based systems, the principal vulnerabilities revolve around deficient input validation. This chapter describes a partially automated mechanism, the tool InputValidator, which seeks to address this issue through bypassing client-side checking and sending test data directly to the server to test the robustness and security of the back-end software. The tool allows a user to construct, execute and evaluate a number of test cases through a form-filling exercise instead of writing bespoke test code.

Chapter 13

Jijun Lu, University of Connecticut, USA
Swapna S. Gokhale, University of Connecticut, USA

Considering the fact that modern Web servers can typically process multiple requests concurrently, this authors of this chapter propose the use of an M/G/m queue to model the performance of a Web server. The performance metric of interest is the response time of a client request. The authors validate the model for deterministic and heavy-tailed workloads using experimentation. Results indicate that the M/G/m queue provides a reasonable estimate of the response time for moderately high traffic intensity. While being an accurate representation of the characteristics of modern Web servers, the model is conceptually simple, requires the estimation of few parameters, and is hence easy to apply.

The social aspects pertaining to a service provided by an organization are at least as significant as the technical aspects. The issue of credibility is a growing concern for the consumers of (persuasive) Web Applications in a variety of domains. Therefore, understanding the notion of credibility and addressing it systematically is crucial for an organization's reputation. In this chapter, based on a given taxonomy of credibility, an approach to address one class of credibility, namely the Active Credibility, of Web Applications is considered. To that regard, a viewpoint-oriented framework for the active credibility engineering of Web Applications is proposed, and the managerial, societal, and technical viewpoints of it are analyzed in some detail. A few directions for extending the framework are outlined.

Section 4
Applications

The fundamental aim of this research is to design and develop a framework for Scenario-driven Decision Support Systems Generator (SDSSG). The focus of the framework is to align the Decision Support Systems (DSS) with the scenario management process that supports usage of scenario as a core component of decision making. Though traditional DSS provide strong data management, modelling and visualisation capabilities for the decision maker, they do not explicitly support scenario management appropriately. Systems that purport to support scenario planning are complex and difficult to use and do not fully support all phases of scenario management. This research presents a life cycle approach for scenario management. The proposed process helps the decision maker with idea generation, scenario planning, development, organisation, analysis, execution, and the use of scenarios for decision making. This research introduces scenario as a DSS component and develops a domain independent, component-based, modular framework and architecture that supports the proposed scenario management process. The framework and architecture have been implemented and validated through a concrete prototype.

Data Grids are currently solutions suggested to meet the needs of scale large systems. They provide highly varied and geographically distributed resources of which the goal is to ensure fast and effective data access. This improves availability, and tolerates breakdowns. In such systems, these advantages are not possible without the use of replication. The use of the technique of replication poses a problem in regards to the maintenance of the consistency of the same data replicas; the strategies of replication of the data and scheduling of jobs were tested by simulation. Several grid simulators were born. One of the most interesting simulators for this study is the OptorSim tool. In this chapter, the authors present an extension of the OptorSim by a consistency management module of the replicas in Data Grids; they propose a hybrid step which combines the economic models conceived for a hierarchical model with two levels. This suggested approach has two vocations, the first allowing a reduction in response times compared to an pessimistic approach, the second gives the good quality of service compared to optimistic approach.

Chapter 17

This chapter characterizes the requirements of Geographic Information Systems (GIS) middleware and its components for dynamic registering and discovering of spatial services specifically for collaborative modeling in environmental planning. The chapter explores the role of Web services with respect to implementation standard and protocols and identifies implementation features for exposing distributed GIS business logic and components via Web services. In particular, the chapter illustrates applications of the interoperability specifications of Open GIS Consortium's (OGC) Web Mapping Service and (WMS), Web Processing Standards (WPS) with respect to implementation feature. The chapter demonstrates a prototype implementation of collaborative environmental decision support systems (GEO-ELCA- Exploratory Land Use Change Assessment) where Web service-enabled middleware adds core functionality to a Web mapping service. The application demonstrates how individual workspace-based namespaces can be used to perform Web mapping functionality (such as spatial analysis in visualization) through the integration of environmental simulation models to explore collective planning scenario. Built on OGC compliant connector and supports WMS and WPS, the system includes interactive supports for geospatial data query, mapping services and visualization tools for multi-user transactions.

Preface

INTRODUCTION

This book is the latest sequel of two previous books: Book I was entitled 'Agent Technologies and Web Engineering: Applications and Systems;' book II was entitled 'Integrated Approaches in Information Technology and Web Engineering: New Dimensions of Social and Organizational Knowledge Sharing.' In this book we include this introductory chapter to reflect on future dimensions of Information Technology and Web Engineering (ITWE). We expand on the two major themes of the first two books to emphasize intelligence, provisioning, and personalization of Web engineering utilizing technologies for the advancement of ITWE applications. Such applications include: E-Cultures, E-Sciences, E-Businesses, and E-Governments. An important technology in Web engineered systems is the social and organizational Web agents.

As to technologies, four important technologies of Web engineered intelligent integrated approaches to Information Technology (IT) and Social and Organizational Knowledge Sharing are Web Ontology, Semantic Web, Dublin Core, and Cloud Computing.

As we shall see in the material that follows, there are many new dimensions appearing in ITWE. Many previously developed and Web engineered systems failures are caused by an incorrect understanding of the intelligent sharing of knowledge. Within the evolution of ITWE, a new form of intelligent sharing and personalization of news and information creation and distribution arises.

Moreover, it is also important to understand the latest contemporary approaches to ITWE investment payoffs. Such ITWE investment payoffs include but are not limited to these elements:

- IT Investment and Organizational Performance
- Qualitative and Quantitative Measurement of ITWE Investment Payoff
- Integrated Approaches to Assessing the Business Value of ITWE
- Relationships Between Firms' ITWE Policy and Business Performance
- Investment in Reusable and Reengineered ITWE and Success Factors
- Modeling ITWE Investment
- Understanding the Business Value of ITWE.

For the reader to better understand each of these fundamental concepts incorporated in the chapters of the book material, an introductory overview of these concepts is in order. While the materials in these chapters do not include all of these new dimensions in applications and technologies, we hope that researchers will embark on these dimensions in the near future. This introductory chapter and the material in the following chapters will be especially helpful for the advanced student or professional who has not followed closely these developments in ITWE.

WEB ENGINEERING

The World Wide Web (http://en.wikipedia.org/wiki/Web_Engineering) has become a major delivery platform for a variety of complex and sophisticated enterprise applications in several domains. In addition to their inherent multifaceted functionality, these Web applications exhibit complex behavior and place some unique demands on their usability, performance, security and ability to grow and evolve.

However, a vast majority of these applications continue to be developed in an ad-hoc way, contributing to problems of usability, maintainability, quality and reliability. While Web development can benefit from established practices from other related disciplines, it has certain distinguishing characteristics that demand special considerations. In recent years, there have been some developments towards addressing these problems and requirements. As an emerging discipline, **Web engineering** actively promotes systematic, disciplined and quantifiable approaches towards successful development of high-quality, ubiquitously usable Web-based systems and applications.

In particular, Web engineering focuses on the methodologies, techniques and tools that are the foundation of Web application development and which support their design, development, evolution, and evaluation. Web application development has certain characteristics that make it different from traditional software, information system, or computer application development.

Web engineering is multidisciplinary and encompasses contributions from diverse areas: systems analysis and design, software engineering, hypermedia/hypertext engineering, requirements engineering, human-computer interaction, user interface, information engineering, information indexing and retrieval, testing, modeling and simulation, project management, usability engineering, and graphic design and presentation.

Web engineering is neither a clone, nor a subset of software engineering, although both involve programming and software development. While software engineering traditionally focuses upon the development of programs that execute on computers and Web engineering focuses upon the development of programs that execute on the Internet, there is more to differences between the two. While Web Engineering uses software engineering principles, it encompasses new approaches, methodologies, tools, techniques, and guidelines to meet the unique requirements of Web-based applications.

INFORMATION TECHNOLOGY AND WEB ENGINEERING

Information technology (IT), (http://en.wikipedia.org/wiki/Information_Technology) (as defined by the Information Technology Association of America (ITAA), is "the study, design, development, implementation, support or management of computer-based information systems, particularly software applications and computer hardware." IT deals with the use of electronic computers and computer software to convert, store, protect, process, transmit, and securely retrieve information, i.e. IT focuses upon the use of information to improve the quality of human work and life.

Today, the term information technology has ballooned to encompass many aspects of computing and technology, and the term is more recognizable than ever before. The information technology umbrella can be quite large, covering many fields. IT professionals perform a variety of duties that range from installing applications to designing complex computer networks and information databases. A few of the duties that IT professionals perform may include data management, networking, engineering computer hardware, database and software design, as well as the management and administration of entire systems.

When computer and communications technologies are combined so as to leverage the use of information to improve the work and life of humans, the result is information technology, or "infotech". Information

Technology (IT) is a general term that describes any technology that helps to produce, manipulate, store, communicate, and/or disseminate information. Presumably, when speaking of Information Technology (IT) as a whole, it is noted that the use of computers and information are associated.

WEB AND E-SCIENCE

Web Science Research Initiative (WSRI) or Web Science (http://en.wikipedia.org/wiki/Web_Science) was energizing more recently with a joint effort of MIT and University of Southampton to bridge and formalize the social and technical aspects of collaborative applications running on large-scale networks like the Web. It was announced on November 2, 2006 in MIT. Tim Berners-Lee is leading a program related to this effort that also aims to attract government and private funds, and eventually produce undergraduate and graduate programs. This is very similar to the ISchool movement.

Some initial areas of interest are:

- Trust and privacy
- Social Networks. See for example the video "The month ahead: Social networks to shake things up in May," about the use of Twitter, Facebook, and MySpace for creating social networks. (http://news.zdnet.com/2422-13568_22-292775.html?tag=nl.e550) Accessed 4/29/2009
- Collaboration, using Web 2.0 for example. One research suggested the use of case-based reasoning to encourage participation and collaboration of users to update and communicate using Web 2.0. (He, et. al., 2009)

The term **e-Science** (or **eScience**) (http://en.wikipedia.org/wiki/E-Science) is used recently to describe computationally intensive science that is carried out in highly distributed network environments, or science that uses immense data sets that require grid computing; the term sometimes includes technologies that enable distributed collaboration, such as the Access Grid. Traditionally e_Science would refer to the use of Internet technology as a platform for either scientific computations or applying the scientific methodologies. The recent term was created by John Taylor, the Director General of the United Kingdom's Office of Science and Technology in 1999 and was used to describe a large funding initiative starting in November 2000. Examples of this kind of science include social simulations, Web and Internet – based particle physics, Web and Internet – based earth sciences and Web and Internet – based bio-informatics. Particle physics has a particularly well developed e-Science infrastructure due to the need since the 1960's for adequate computing facilities for the analysis of results and storage of data originating in the past from Particle In Cell (PIC) plasma physics simulations for electronics designs and astrophysics in the national/international laboratories and more recently from the CERN Large Hadron Collider, which is due to start taking data in 2008.

WEB APPLICATION DOMAINS

E-Business

Electronic Business, commonly referred to as **"eBusiness"** or **"e-Business"**, (http://en.wikipedia.org/wiki/E-business) may be defined as the utilization of information and communication technologies (ICT) in support of all the activities of business and traditionally refers to the use of Internet technology as a platform for doing business. Commerce constitutes the exchange of products and services between businesses, groups and individuals and hence can be seen as one of the essential activities of any business. Hence, electronic commerce or eCommerce focuses on the use of ICT to enable the external activities and relationships of the business with individuals, groups and other businesses. Some of these e-business activities have been popularized by order entry, accounting, inventory and investments services.

Louis Gerstner, the former CEO of IBM, in his book, 'Who Says Elephants Can't Dance?', attributes the term "e-Business" to IBM's marketing and Internet teams in 1996.

Electronic business methods enable companies to link their internal and external data processing systems more efficiently and flexibly, to work more closely with suppliers and partners, and to better satisfy the needs and expectations of their customers.

In practice, e-business is more than just e-commerce. While e-business refers to more strategic focus with an emphasis on the functions that occur using electronic capabilities, e-commerce is a subset of an overall e-business strategy. E-commerce seeks to add revenue streams using the World Wide Web or the Internet to build and enhance relationships with clients and partners and to improve efficiency using the Empty Vessel strategy. Often, e-commerce involves the application of knowledge management systems.

E-business involves business processes spanning the entire value chain: electronic purchasing and supply chain management, processing orders electronically, handling customer service, and cooperating with business partners. Special technical standards for e-business facilitate the exchange of data between companies. E-business software solutions allow the integration of intra and inter firm business processes. E-business can be conducted using the Web, the Internet, intranets, extranets, or some combination of these.

e-Government

e-Government (from **electronic government**, also known as **e-gov**, **digital government**, **online government** (http://en.wikipedia.org/wiki/E-Government) (or in a certain context **transformational government**) refers to the use of Internet technology as a platform for exchanging information, providing services and transacting with citizens, businesses, and other arms of government. e-Government may be applied by the legislature, judiciary, or administration, in order to improve internal efficiency, the delivery of public services, or processes of democratic governance. The primary delivery models are Government-to-Citizen or Government-to-Customer (G2C), Government-to-Business (G2B) and Government-to-Government (G2G) & Government-to-Employees (G2E). Within each of these interaction domains, four kinds of activities take place:

- Pushing information over the Internet, e.g.: regulatory services, general holidays, public hearing schedules, issue briefs, notifications, etc.
- Two-way communications between the agency and the citizen, a business, or another government agency. In this model, users can engage in dialogue with agencies and post problems, comments, or requests to the agency.
- Conducting transactions, e.g.: lodging tax returns, applying for services and grants.
- Governance, e.g.: online polling, voting, and campaigning.

The most important anticipated benefits of e-government include more efficiency, improved services, better accessibility of public services, and more transparency and accountability. While e-government is often thought of as "online government" or "Internet-based government," many non-Internet "electronic government" technologies can be used in this context. Some non-Internet forms include telephone, fax,

PDA, SMS text messaging, MMS, wireless networks and services, Bluetooth, CCTV, tracking systems, RFID, biometric identification, road traffic management and regulatory enforcement, identity cards, smart cards and other NFC applications; polling station technology (where non-online e-voting is being considered), TV and radio-based delivery of government services, email, online community facilities, newsgroups and electronic mailing lists, online chat, and instant messaging technologies. There are also some technology-specific sub-categories of e-government, such as m-government (mobile government), u-government (ubiquitous government), and g-government (GIS/GPS applications for e-government).

There are many considerations and potential implications of implementing and designing e-government, including disintermediation of the government and its citizens, impacts on economic, social, and political factors, and disturbances to the status quo in these areas.

In countries such as the United Kingdom, there is interest in using electronic government to re-engage citizens with the political process. In particular, this has taken the form of experiments with electronic voting, aiming to increase voter turnout by making voting easy. The UK Electoral Commission has undertaken several pilots, though concern has been expressed about the potential for fraud with some electronic voting methods.

Governments are adapting Enterprise Service Bus (ESB), a message passing program among disparate datacenter that functions on top of Service Oriented Architecture paradigm. The following links are for different ESB applications in respective countries:

- **USA:** (http://www.oreillynet.com/xml/blog/2006/08/esb_adoption_in_government.html)
- **Ireland:** (http://www.renault.com/SiteCollectionDocuments/Communiqu%C3%A9%20de%20presse/en-EN/Pieces%20jointes/19579_03042009_PRAlliance_Irish_government_EN_E8032F3B.pdf), (http://www.rte.ie/news/2009/0416/esb.html)
- **Vietnam:** (http://www.esb.ie/main/news_events/press_release217.jsp),
- **Jordan:** (http://www.customs.gov.jo/library/633400494578802642.pdf)

A maturity model for e-government services includes integration (using WS and ESB) and personalization through push and pulls technologies (using data mining and intelligent software agents) as the last two stages. (Alkhatib, 2009) This is very critical for e-government systems since they generate and store voluminous amount of data spreading throughout countries and the world and accessed by a huge number of users, businesses, inter-government agencies access, and government managers. Retrieving relevant data and information over the Web dictates the need for integrating various repositories of data and information, as well as personalizing access over the Web to improve quality of service to citizens, business, and inter-government agencies knowledge sharing.

There are many new dimensions appearing in ITWE. Much of these new dimensions have to do with these elements:

- Global shift of business and government enterprises
- Mobility of stakeholders in social, business and government enterprises
- Evolution of prior IT enterprises such as news, education and intelligence
- Evolution of social cultures in the emerging third world communities
- Evolution of technologies beyond traditional information and Web technologies.
- Failure of ITWE technologies that cause firms to fail.

One author (Wang, 2009) notes that "Analysis of the once highly popular concept enterprise resource planning (ERP) suggests that (1) the popularity of ERP was influenced positively by the prevalence of highlighted business problems that ERP had claimed to solve; (2) ERP's popularity was influenced negatively by the prevalence of related innovation concepts; and (3) these influences largely disappeared after ERP passed its peak popularity."

However, ERP systems still play major rule in enterprises as their backbone application supporting back office operations. The new ERP research emphasizes usability and integration of different databases through middleware technologies such as service oriented architectures and portals. Also, for effective utilization of these ERP systems, many vendors, such as Oracle and SAP, moved their applications to Internet and cloud computing platform. Furthermore, ERPII links Intranet-based ERP to customer and supplier. We note one research on customer relationship management field based on the Internet (eCRM). (Chen, 2007)

In this book, chapter 4 of section 2 contains an analysis ERP usability issues. Other chapter in section 4 presents studies on localized user interface for improving users' devise competency of cell phones, mobile phone voice driven emotion recognizer, and testing methodology for graphic user interface

It is still true today of the observations made by (Christensen, 1997) regarding the ITWE innovator's dilemma attesting to new information technologies causing firms to fail. These include the following:

- Disruptive technological changes
- Technologies that do not match stakeholders' needs or requirements
- Mismatch of an enterprise's size to the market size
- Technology mismatch to emerging markets
- Technology performance provided, market demand and product life cycles
- Mismanagement of disruptive technological change.

Many of these failures are caused by an incorrect understanding of the sharing of knowledge. **Knowledge sharing** (http://en.wikipedia.org/wiki/Knowledge_Sharing) is an activity through which knowledge (i.e. information, skills, or expertise) is exchanged among people, friends, or members of a family, a community (e.g. Wikipedia) or an organization. Consider the present failures and lack of understanding in the news enterprises. Fewer news stake holders now read the traditional newspaper as presented by the traditional writing of news reporters and editors, in part due to the lack of completeness, unbiased reporting and participation within the stake holders' communities. Electronic – digital newspaper presented by email or on the Web pages or TV channels, while allowing broader and cheaper circulation still contains these three failure elements. Yet consider the rise of news interactive sharing communities and blogging to complement traditional news reporting and editing, wherein even global and cross cultural communities interactively share their news information and intelligence insights with one another, eliminating some of three failures within the traditional reporting and editing. Hence, within the evolution of ITWE a new form of news creation and distribution arises. Therefore, this new form of news forms a valuable knowledge asset.

Organizations such as the emerging news sharing communities are recognizing that knowledge constitutes a valuable intangible asset for creating and sustaining competitive advantages. Knowledge sharing activities are generally supported by knowledge management systems. However, as with news organizations, such knowledge management systems are evolving from the traditional hierarchical publisher-reporter-editor model to a wide global distributed community's networks model. However, information and Web technology constitutes only one of the many factors that affect the sharing of knowledge in organizations, such as organizational culture, trust, and incentives. The sharing of knowledge constitutes a major challenge in the field of knowledge management because some employees tend to resist sharing their knowledge with the rest of the organization. Since there are a number of obstacles that can hinder knowledge sharing, one of the obstacles stand out. This obstacle is the notion that knowledge is property and ownership is very important. In order to counteract this notion, individuals must be reassured that they will receive credit for a knowledge product that they created. However, there is a risk in knowledge sharing. The risk is that individuals are most commonly rewarded for what they know, not what they share. If knowledge is not shared, negative consequences such as isolation and resistance to ideas occur. To promote knowledge sharing and remove knowledge sharing obstacles, the organizational culture should encourage discovery and innovation. This will result in the creation of organizational culture trust. Such should be the case within the future domain of news knowledge. Since organizations generate a huge amount of knowledge, intelligent and personalized knowledge sharing becomes necessary to insure effective utilization of knowledge throughout the enterprise. In addition, another related research area is knowledge verification and validation, especially of the type tacit knowledge. This will ensure that only verified and valid knowledge is included in knowledge repositories.

- Removes ambiguity (includes scope notes and parenthetical qualifiers)
- Provides context (terms can be viewed hierarchically (Broader Terms [BT], Narrower Terms [NT], and Related Terms [RT])
- Terms can be viewed alphabetically as well
- Selected terms can be incorporated in a search argument
- Have an intelligent interface

In order to achieve maximum use of Web engineered systems, Section 3: Testing and Performance Evaluation contains chapters related to:

- A methodology for testing object oriented systems
- A theory and implementation of a specific input validation testing tool
- Performance of Web servers
- A framework for incorporating credibility engineering in Web engineering application

WEB ENGINEERING TECHNOLOGIES

Ontologies and Thesauri

Ontology tools, of more recent origin, are similar to machine assisted indexing software, but are far more complex to build. Ontology tools are designed to work on specific knowledge domains and require the collaboration of domain experts and ontology specialists to develop. They are further intended to be comprehensive with regard to the chosen domain. The experience to date with this class of tools suggests that the building of the ontology for a specific domain is a long and expensive process.

A technical thesaurus (as opposed to the Roget kind of thesaurus) is a formalized method of representing subject terms in a given domain. Most of the formal thesauri in use today conform to a standard format (e.g., NISO Z39.19).

There are several compelling reasons to use a technical thesaurus to enhance information retrieval, especially through an interactive interface:

The **Web Ontology Language (OWL)** (http://en.wikipedia.org/wiki/Web_Ontology_Language) is a family of knowledge representation languages for authoring ontologies, and is endorsed by the World

Wide Web Consortium. This family of languages is based on two (largely, but not entirely, compatible) semantics: OWL DL and OWL Lite semantics are based on Description Logics, which have attractive and well-understood computational properties, while OWL Full uses a novel semantic model intended to provide compatibility with RDF Schema. OWL ontologies are most commonly serialized using RDF/XML syntax. OWL is considered one of the fundamental technologies underpinning the Semantic Web, and has attracted both academic and commercial interest.

In October 2007, a new W3C working group was started to extend OWL with several new features as proposed in the OWL 1.1 member submission. This new version, called OWL 2, has already found its way into semantic editors such as Protégé and semantic reasoning systems such as Pellet and FaCT++.

Semantic Web

The **Semantic Web** (http://en.wikipedia.org/wiki/Semantic_Web) (is an evolving extension of the World Wide Web in which the semantics of information and services on the Web is defined, making it possible for the Web to understand and satisfy the requests of people and machines to use the Web content. It derives from World Wide Web Consortium director Sir Tim Berners-Lee's vision of the Web as a universal medium for data, information, and knowledge exchange.

At its core, the semantic Web comprises a set of design principles, collaborative working groups, and a variety of enabling technologies. Some elements of the semantic Web are expressed as prospective future possibilities that are yet to be implemented or realized. Other elements of the semantic Web are expressed in formal specifications. Some of these include Resource Description Framework (RDF), a variety of data interchange formats (e.g. RDF/XML, N3, Turtle, N-Triples), and notations such as RDF Schema (RDFS) and the Web Ontology Language (OWL), all of which are intended to provide a formal description of concepts, terms, and relationships within a given knowledge domain.

Other research relating semantic Web to XML could be found at (http://www.wiley.com/legacy/compbooks/daconta/sw/), and to ontologies (http://www.aifb.uni-karlsruhe.de/WBS/Publ/2001/OLf-SW_amasst_2001.pdf)

Section one with 6 chapters contains research in the areas of context-aware semantic Web and intelligent semantic Web for improving query formulation and information retrieval, the impact of ontologies on information retrieval using multiagent technology, clustering image mining, and integrating patterns in Web engineering applications.

Dublin Core

The **Dublin Core** is a product of the World Wide Web Consortium (W3). It is a standard set of 15 fields, some of which can contain qualifiers, to describe virtually any resource that can be accessed over the WWW (although it is not limited to resources found on the Web). The 15 Dublin Core elements may be thought of as dimensions (or facets) that are the most useful for getting of quick grasp of the resource in question. The 15 core elements (with optional qualifiers in parentheses) are:

- **Identifier:** A unique identifier
- **Format (Extent, Medium):** Description of physical characteristics
- **Type:** Conceptual category of the resource
- **Language:** The language in which the resource is written
- **Title (Alternative):** The title of the resource
- **Creator:** Person primarily responsible for the intellectual content

- **Contributor:** Cecondary contributors to the work
- **Publisher:** Organization responsible for publishing the work
- **Date (Created, Valid, Available, Issued, Modified):** Date as qualified
- **Coverage (Spatial, Temporal):** Locates the content in space and time
- **Subject:** Topics covered, free-form or from a controlled list
- **Source:** From which the resource is derived
- **Relation (Is Version Of, Has Version, Is Replaced By, Replaces, Is Required By, Requires, Is Part Of, Has Part, Is Referenced By, References, Is Format Of, Has Format):** Relationship of the resource to the source cited
- **Rights:** To use or reproduce
- **Description (Table of Contents, Abstract):** Content as qualified or full text of the resource

Each one of the Dublin Core elements can have multiple values.

The following link shows the list of elements as of 2008-01-14. (http://dublincore.org/documents/dces/)

The **Dublin Core** metadata (http://en.wikipedia.org/wiki/Dublin_Core) element set is a standard for cross-domain information resource description. It provides a simple and standardized set of conventions for describing things online in ways that make them easier to find. Dublin Core is widely used to describe digital materials such as video, sound, image, text, and composite media like Web pages. Implementations of Dublin Core typically make use of XML and are Resource Description Framework based. Dublin Core is defined by ISO in 2003 ISO Standard 15836, and NISO Standard Z39.85-2007.

A new announcement on 1 May 2009 from the Dublin Core on Interoperability Levels for Dublin Core Metadata was published as DCMI Recommended Resource: (http://catalogablog.blogspot.com/2009/05/interoperability-levels-for-dublin-core.html) "Interoperability Levels for Dublin Core Metadata" has been published as a Recommended Resource. The document discusses modeling choices involved in designing metadata applications for different types of interoperability. At Level 1, applications use data components with shared natural-language definitions. At Level 2, data is based on the formal-semantic model of the W3C Resource Description Framework (as in Linked Data). At Levels 3 and 4, data also shares syntactic constraints based on the DCMI Abstract Model. The document aims at providing a point of reference for evaluating interoperability among a variety of metadata implementations. The authors expect this document to evolve as the trade-offs and benefits of interoperability at different levels are explored and welcome feedback from its readers."

Dublin Core could be improved by incorporating intelligent and personalized interface for more effective and efficient information access.

XML

XML (eXtensible Markup Language) is a standard Internet protocol for representing a broad variety of Internet resources. It is derived from SGML (Standard General Markup Language) but is considerably simpler. It is also related to HTML, but goes well beyond it in flexibility and uniformity. In the space of a few years, XML has become the lingua franca of the Internet, especially for exchanging information between two otherwise radically different forms of representation.

XML compatibility is proposed for whatever solution is adopted by NASA to enhance its lessons learned capability. The use of XML will essentially allow source systems that generate potentially useful information for the lessons learned repository to remain unchanged and unaffected. The final architecture will include an XML format into which source materials can be mapped and exported. The new lessons learned facility will then be able to import these materials into a standard environment.

It should also be noted here that the Dublin Core can be easily represented in XML format.

An interesting new dimension that applies an advanced form of XML has appeared in the latest of the IEEE standards and related products about IEEE StandardsWire^(TM) - November 2008. In the IEEE StandardsWire™ the featured p product is the Language for Symbolic Music Representation Defined in a New Standard. A new IEEE standard represents the first collective step toward the improvement of both sub-symbolic and symbolic music coding and processing, music communication, and capabilities of individuals and companies.

IEEE 1599-2008™, "IEEE Recommended Practice for Definition of a Commonly Acceptable Musical Application using the XML Language," offers a meta-representation of music information for describing and processing music information within a multi-layered environment, for achieving integration among structural, score, Musical Instrument Digital Interface (MIDI), and digital sound levels of representation.

The Language for Symbolic Music Representation defined this IEEE standard represents the first collective step toward the improvement of both sub-symbolic and symbolic music coding and processing, music communication, and capabilities of individuals and companies.

IEEE 1599-2008^(TM), "IEEE Recommended Practice for Definition of a Commonly Acceptable Musical Application using the XML Language," offers a meta-representation of music information for describing and processing music information within a multi-layered environment, for achieving integration among structural, score, Musical Instrument Digital Interface (MIDI), and digital sound.

XML is the backbone for developing Internet applications through Service Oriented architecture (Web services and Enterprise Bus) linking loosely coupled applications. Two options are available: standard-based and XML-native based. In the first method, three standards are used to deploy a platform independent Web service as software service exposed on the Web and accessed through SOAP, described with a WSDL file, and registered in UDDI. (http://www.startvbdotnet.com/Web/default.aspx) (For more information on the three standards, see http://Webservices.xml.com/pub/a/ws/2001/04/04/Webservices/index.html). In the latter approach, a native XML-based WS is platform dependent, such as Oracle Web Services. (http://download.oracle.com/docs/cd/B28359_01/appdev.111/b28369/xdb_Web_services.htm).

Here is what IBM is doing currently on XML-related research as of 24 November 2008 (http://domino.research.ibm.com/comm/research_projects.nsf/pages/xml.index.html)

"Researchers at several of our labs are completing the infrastructure for the Web to complete its move to XML as its transport data encoding and for much of its data persistence, providing a foundation for Service-Oriented Architecture, Web 2.0 and Semantic Web Technologies, as well as Model-Driven Development. Current focus areas include scalability and performance, and improved programmability. Aspects of our work:

- A modular XHTML system that integrates SMIL (multimedia), XForms, MathML, P3P (controlled disclosure of private information) into HTML
- Ability to separate information content and information rendering, and put them together again using the powerful XSL style sheet language (and thus support accessibility, personalization, collaboration, search and Mobile Computing, and integrate Multimedia on the Web). This includes approaches to integrating style sheets with Java Server Pages.
- Ability for application or industry specific markup vocabularies, described with XML Schema language and queried with XML Query Language (One result: Your program or agent works equally well querying a database or repository as querying a Web site).

- Standard and powerful approaches to linking, metadata, Web Ontologies, and search and filtering (see mineXML).
- Web Services descriptions and message protocols so that code written in any language can interact with server functions written in any language, while preserving the debugging advantages of human readable messages; and use of Web Services by portals
- Extensible Digital Signature model
- DOM API
- The ability to select whether transformations are performed at the client, at edge nodes, or at the server
- Supporting use of XML Processing Languages against non-XML information, via Virtual XML
- Very high quality formatting for text, diagrams, equations
- Multi-modal user interaction abstractions and tools that support new types of interaction and novel devices
- Storing XML documents in databases and querying them efficiently
- The ability for Web sites to hand-off a Web-form initiated transaction while passing the customers information (CP Exchange) in support of e-Commerce.
- An infrastructure for Semantic Web (Introduction to Semantics Technology, W3C Semantic Web)
- An infrastructure for Services Computing
- Experiments in improving the way the Java language can be used in handling XML information (see XJ)"

Another area of IBM research as of 11 August 2008 is Virtual XML. (http://domino.research.ibm.com/comm/research_projects.nsf/pages/virtualxml.index.html)

Virtual XML

Virtual XML is the ability to view and process any data–whether XML or non-XML–as though it is XML, and in particular allow use of XML processing languages, such as XPath and XQuery, on the data. In the Virtual XML project we couple this with special access functions that make it possible to write scripts that "mix and match" XML and non-XML data, and advanced analysis and adaptation technology to ensure that the Virtual XML processing is efficient even on large data collections.

Why?

More and more structured data is converted into XML documents, either for transmission and processing that follow various standards like the Web services standards or for combination with semi-structured data such as HTML documents. Sometimes the original structured data is replaced with the converted data; sometimes it is converted "on the fly." Both approaches pose problems: If the original data is converted, then legacy applications depending on the old format must be rewritten. Converting data on the fly, on the other hand, imposes a significant performance penalty because the standard XML format requires significant overhead for generating or parsing XML character sequences.

Virtual XML solves these problems by:

- Keeping everything in the native format most natural for the data, and
- Providing thin "on-demand" adapters for each format in a generic abstract XML interface corresponding to the XML Infoset as well as the forthcoming XPath and XQuery Data Model."

Cloud Computing (CC)

Cloud computing (http://en.wikipedia.org/wiki/Cloud_Computing) is a style of architecture in which dynamically scalable and often virtualized resources are provided as a service over the Internet. The concept incorporates infrastructure as a service (IaaS), platform as a service (PaaS) and software as a service (SaaS).

More recently two SaaS are announced: Security-as-a-service (http://news.zdnet.com/2422-13568_22-291742.html?tag=nl.e539) accessed 5/12/2009, and PC 'security as a service' offered free by Panda anti-virus. (http://blogs.zdnet.com/Gardner/?p=2920&tag=nl.e539) accessed 4/29/2009.

In another issue, increased maintenance and support costs may force Enterprises to adapt software-as-a-service (SaaS) models to reduce cost and achieve flexibility. (http://blogs.zdnet.com/BTL/?p=17796&tag=nl.e539) accessed 5/12/2009

Comparisons

Cloud computing is often confused with grid computing ("a form of distributed computing whereby a 'super and virtual computer' is composed of a cluster of networked, loosely-coupled computers, acting in concert to perform very large tasks"), utility computing (the "packaging of computing resources, such as computation and storage, as a metered service similar to a traditional public utility such as electricity") and autonomic computing ("computer systems capable of self-management").

Indeed many cloud computing deployments as of 2009 depend on grids, have autonomic characteristics and bill like utilities — but cloud computing can be seen as a natural next step from the grid-utility model. Some successful cloud architectures have little or no centralised infrastructure or billing systems whatsoever, including peer-to-peer networks like BitTorrent and Skype and volunteer computing like SETI@home.

Architecture

The majority of cloud computing infrastructure, as of 2009, consists of reliable services delivered through data centers and built on servers with different levels of virtualization technologies. The services are accessible anywhere that has access to networking infrastructure. *The Cloud* appears as a single point of access for all the computing needs of consumers. Commercial offerings need to meet the quality of service requirements of customers and typically offer service level agreements. Open standards are critical to the growth of cloud computing and open source software has provided the foundation for many cloud computing implementations.

Characteristics

The customers engaging in cloud computing do not own the physical infrastructure serving as host to the software platform in question. Instead, they avoid capital expenditure by renting usage from a third-party provider. They consume resources as a service, paying instead for only the resources they use. Many cloud-computing offerings have adopted the utility computing model, which is analogous to how traditional utilities like electricity are consumed, while others are billed on a subscription basis. Sharing "perishable and intangible" computing power among multiple tenants can improve utilization rates, as servers are not left idle, which can reduce costs significantly while increasing the speed of application development. A side effect of this approach is that "computer capacity rises dramatically" as customers do not have to engineer for peak loads. Adoption has been enabled by "increased high-speed bandwidth" which makes it possible to receive the same response times from centralized infrastructure at other sites.

Economics

Cloud computing users can avoid capital expenditure on hardware, software and services, rather paying a provider only for what they use. Consumption is billed on a utility (e.g. resources consumed, like electricity) or subscription (e.g. time based, like a newspaper) basis with little or no upfront cost. Other benefits of this time sharing style approach are low barriers to entry, shared infrastructure and costs, low management overhead and immediate access to a broad range of applications. Users can generally terminate the contract at any time (thereby avoiding return on investment risk and uncertainty) and the services are often covered by service level agreements with financial penalties

Companies

IBM, Amazon, Google, Microsoft and Yahoo are some of the major cloud computing service providers. It is being adopted by individual users through large enterprises including General Electric and Procter & Gamble

Political Issues

The Cloud spans many borders and "may be the ultimate form of globalization." As such it becomes subject to complex geopolitical issues: providers must satisfy myriad regulatory environments in order to deliver service to a global market. This dates back to the early days of the Internet, where libertarian thinkers felt that "cyberspace was a distinct place calling for laws and legal institutions of its own"; author Neal Stephenson envisaged this as a tiny island data haven called Kinakuta in his classic science-fiction novel Cryptonomicon.

Despite efforts (such as US-EU Safe Harbor) to harmonize the legal environment, as of 2009 providers such as Amazon Web Services cater to the major markets (typically the United States and the European Union) by deploying local infrastructure and allowing customers to select "availability zones." Nonetheless, there are still concerns about security and privacy from individual through governmental level, e.g., the USA PATRIOT Act and use of national security letters and the Electronic Communications Privacy Act's *Stored Communications Act*.

Legal Issues

In March 2007, Dell applied to trademark the term "cloud computing" (U.S. Trademark 77,139,082) in the United States. The "Notice of Allowance" it received in July 2008 was canceled on August 6, resulting in a formal rejection of the trademark application less than a week later.

On September 30, 2008, USPTO issued a "Notice of Allowance" to CGactive LLC (U.S. Trademark 77,355,287) for "CloudOS". A *cloud operating system* is a generic operating system that "manage[s] the relationship between software inside the computer and on the Web", such as Microsoft Azure. Good OS LLC also announced their "Cloud" operating system on December 1st, 2008.

In November 2007, the Free Software Foundation released the Affero General Public License, a version of GPLv3 designed to close a perceived legal loophole associated with Free software designed to be run over a network, particularly software as a service. An application service provider is required to release any changes they make to Affero GPL open source code.

Risk Mitigation

Corporations or end-users wishing to avoid not being able to access their data — or even losing it — should research vendors' policies on data security before using vendor services. One technology analyst and consulting firm, Gartner, lists seven security issues which one should discuss with a cloud-computing vendor:

- **Privileged user access:** Inquire about who has specialized access to data and about the hiring and management of such administrators
- **Regulatory compliance:** Make sure a vendor is willing to undergo external audits and/or security certifications
- **Data location:** Ask if a provider allows for any control over the location of data
- **Data segregation:** Make sure that encryption is available at all stages and that these "encryption schemes were designed and tested by experienced professionals"
- **Recovery:** Find out what will happen to data in the case of a disaster; do they offer complete restoration and, if so, how long that would take
- **Investigative Support:** Inquire whether a vendor has the ability to investigate any inappropriate or illegal activity
- **Long-term viability:** Ask what will happen to data if the company goes out of business; how will data be returned and in what format

Key Characteristics

- **Agility** improves with users able to rapidly and inexpensively re-provision technological infrastructure resources.
- **Cost** is greatly reduced and capital expenditure is converted to operational expenditure. This lowers barriers to entry, as infrastructure is typically provided by a third-party and does not need to be purchased for one-time or infrequent intensive computing tasks. Pricing on a utility computing basis is fine-grained with usage-based options and minimal or no IT skills are required for implementation.
- **Device and location independence** enable users to access systems using a Web browser regardless of their location or what device they are using, e.g., PC, mobile. As infrastructure is off-site (typically provided by a third-party) and accessed via the Internet the users can connect from anywhere.
- **Multi-tenancy** enables sharing of resources and costs among a large pool of users, allowing for:
  Centralization of infrastructure in areas with lower costs (such as real estate, electricity, etc.)
  Peak-load capacity increases (users need not engineer for highest possible load-levels)
  Utilisation and efficiency improvements for systems that are often only 10-20% utilised.
- **Reliability** improves through the use of multiple redundant sites, which makes it suitable for business continuity and disaster recovery. Nonetheless, most major cloud computing services have suffered outages and IT and business managers are able to do little when they are affected.
- **Scalability** via dynamic ("on-demand") provisioning of resources on a fine-grained, self-service basis near real-time, without users having to engineer for peak loads. Performance is monitored

and consistent and loosely-coupled architectures are constructed using Web services as the system interface.

- **Security** typically improves due to centralization of data, increased security-focused resources, etc., but raises concerns about loss of control over certain sensitive data. Security is often as good as or better than traditional systems, in part because providers are able to devote resources to solving security issues that many customers cannot afford. Providers typically log accesses, but accessing the audit logs themselves can be difficult or impossible.
- **Sustainability** comes about through improved resource utilisation, more efficient systems, and carbon neutrality. Nonetheless, computers and associated infrastructure are major consumers of energy

Types of Cloud Computing

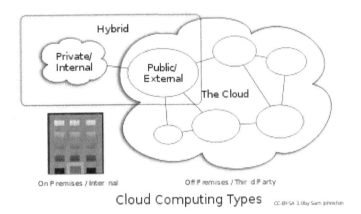

Cloud Computing Types   CC-BY-SA 3.0 by Sam Johnston

Public Cloud

Public cloud or *external cloud* describes cloud computing in the traditional mainstream sense, whereby resources are dynamically provisioned on a fine-grained, self-service basis over the Internet, via Web applications/Web services, from an off-site third-party provider who shares resources and bills on a fine-grained utility computing basis.

Hybrid Cloud

A *hybrid cloud* environment consisting of multiple internal and/or external providers "will be typical for most enterprises". A recent article makes a case for hybrid clouds such as Cisco's recent announcement of an on-premise extension to the rebranded WebEx Collaboration Cloud. (http://blogs.zdnet.com/ SAAS/?p=758&tag=nl.e539) accessed 5/7/2009

Private Cloud

Private cloud and *internal cloud* are neologisms that some vendors have recently used to describe offerings that emulate cloud computing on private networks. These (typically virtualisation automation) products claim to "deliver some benefits of cloud computing without the pitfalls", capitalising on data security, corporate governance, and reliability concerns. They have been criticised on the basis that users "still have to buy, build, and manage them" and as such do not benefit from lower up-front capital costs and less hands-on management, essentially "[lacking] the economic model that makes cloud computing such an intriguing concept".

The First International Cloud Computing Expo Europe 2009 to be held in Prague, Czech Republic, May 18 - 19, 2009 lists the following topics (http://www.cloudexpo-europe.com):

- Getting Ready for Cloud Computing - IT Strategy, Architecture and Security Perspective
- IT Security Delivered from the Cloud
- Application Portability in a Multi-Cloud World
- Load Balancing and Application Architecture in the Cloud
- The Federated Cloud: Sharing Without Losing Control
- Cloud Science: Astrometric Processing in Amazon EC2/S3
- Practical Strategies for Moving to a Cloud Infrastructure
- Cloud Infrastructure and Application – CloudIA
- The Darker Sides Of Cloud Computing: Security and Availability
- The Nationless Cloud?

In yet another important development, National Science Foundation had a Press Release 09-093, (May 8, 2008) that "Nimbus" Rises in the World of Cloud Computing, the cloud computing infrastructure developed by Argonne National Lab shows that cloud computing's potential is being realized now. For more information see link below. (http://www.nsf.gov:80/news/news_summ.jsp?cntn_id=114788&govDel=USNSF_51)

Current research directions in the area of cloud computing are:

- Standards development: Developing standards for cloud computing so organizations and enterprises adapting cloud computing will be able to determine how CC meets their requirements. (http://www.australianit.news.com.au/story/0,24897,25502520-5013040,00.html) accessed May 19, 2009.
- Virtualization: Linking virtualization with CC to optimize data center operations using the Web. Industries deploying virtualization include auto makers, and oil and gas. The following figure shows how one company deploys virtualization and CC: (http://blogs.zdnet.com/BTL/?p=18410&tag=nl.e539) accessed May 20, 2009.

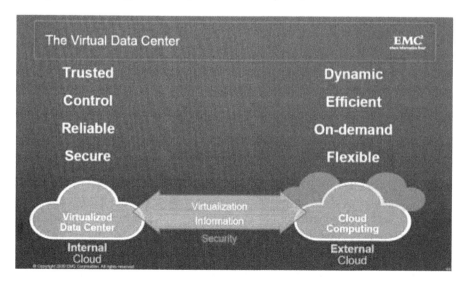

FUTURE NEW DIMENSIONS FOR ITWE SOFTWARE

Global Internet Technology crosses many social and cultural boundaries. Use of Internet (ITWE) Technology raises many ethics and values issues. There is further need for effective and efficient ethics and values identification methods and tools to assist Internet technology workers in businesses, governments and societies in selecting and using cultural features that are both common and distinct in solving global social information infrastructure conflict problems. The proposed research will examine ethics and values contexts that influence and are influenced by Internet technology. Future ITWE research will use approaches to identify and develop the needed ethics and values identification tools to assist workers in solving ethics and values problems that arise in the global application of Internet technology. These problems arise from cultural and social differences in ethics and values about the Internet.

First, in order to investigate ethics and values identification approaches to solve problems based on social conflicts or isolation one needs a cross-cultural means for evaluating communicated ethics and values views about Internet technology. New research combines the speaker typology with ones speech interests within an analysis system of logic formulae. It is possible to design Internet ethics and values identification models for social change by developing software products based on forms or logic types. Doing so allows one to build computer models and solve problems, for example, in Internet communications, Internet social sciences, Internet psychology, Internet education, Internet public policy, and Internet conflict resolution. **Second**, our proposed speaker and speech analyses logic-based method will examine the foundation of speech and speaker typology. This method and tools will be validated using samples of communications about Internet technology written by persons from different cultural and social backgrounds. The method and tools resulting from the research should be more efficient than current alternative approaches to ethics and values identification. **Third**, our proposed Internet Speaker and Speech Analyses logic-based method will examine the foundation of intuitive key-interests sense of speech and speaker through a focus on psychological, sociological and political dimensions which reflects the speech's logical formula and the speaker's typology. **Fourth**, logic forms principles have already been shown to be a fundamental framework for studying commonalities between different features of human beliefs and cultures. Therefore, we will research how to use ethics and values identification computer technology of Unilogic forms, types, classification and clustering to investigate selected social and cultural problems about the use of Internet technology that can be formulated by deriving common beliefs and features between various human beliefs and cultures. **Fifth**, there are seven transformational Steps in the logic form of computer automated reasoning. Step1. Identify the set of potential social conflict problems to be evaluated (e.g. belief or policy systems about use of Internet technology under investigation) as the domain, and describe them informally using logic forms. Step2. Using natural language analysis on these forms, based upon features identification and extraction, transform the result of Step1 into equivalent formal logic computer language. Step3. Using a computer modeling language whose grammar is based upon a given type theory, transform the result of Step2 into an equivalent domain modeling language. Step4. Computer domain model the written specifications from Step1 using the result from Step3. Step5. Select a particular focus of investigation in the domain identified, ethics and values about the use of Internet technology, and analyze this formal computer domain model using new methods, for example, analysis of commonalities between several global belief or policy systems, and analysis of differences. Step6. Set up a computer simulation involving interactions of simulated beings in this focus area. Step7. Execute the computer simulation to assist in identifying and understanding the common human thought concepts about Internet technology expressed within the universe of discourse identified in Step1. **Sixth,** the long term objective of this research in Unilogic Form Ethics and Values Identification is to explore how one can provide a computer ethics and values identification method and tools to extract the universal 'rhythm' from different social interest entity knowledge bases of (business, culture, government, etc.) spoken and written communications about Internet technology, to reuse this universal rhythm in the service of more inclusive dynamic management of, e.g., conflict, to find short or inexpensive ways to administer complex Internet-based social systems, and to provide a predicative logic unityped interest relation of any given entity in the system. The benefits of such basic science research in the long term includes support for decision and policy makers at the levels of organizations, markets, personalities, families, societies, religions, churches, groups of populations nations, states, government agencies, education institutes, etc. **Seventh,** in the short term the objective of logic Form Ethics and Values Identification is to provide computer science and information systems research a global method and tools to analyze and remodel existing information about Internet technology in the forms of spoken and written communications, and to reuse them in new but similar domains. This is related to reuse of unityped interest comprised of relation behavior for any defined entity. For example, reuse of communications information about an isolated system's entities in order to reform them into coexisting system's entities requires ability to discover the interest roots of that isolated system and to remodel it for coexistence system entities. To do this, the researcher needs knowledge of logic forms and the ability to control the unitype predicates to decipher and remodel the communications information.

To find 'Ethics and Values' held about the use of Internet Technology one must examine various issues, such as:

- Privacy of content used
- Type of content used
- Integrity of content used
- Security of content used
- Selective dissemination of content used

These issues represent different kinds of concerns persons from various cultures have about the use of Internet Technology. These concerns are interpreted differently as one moves between global cultures. The policies and beliefs applied to Internet technology regarding Privacy of content used, Type of content used, Integrity of content used, Security of content used, and Selective dissemination of content used vary as one moves across different global cultures. Since Internet Technology bridges between different global cultures, policies and beliefs about the use of Internet Technology change as the Internet crosses different cultures. In order to develop a meaningful global set of policies and beliefs about the use of Internet Technology one must both identify and integrate these different global cultural policies and beliefs.

FUTURE NEW DIMENSIONS FOR ITWE APPLICATIONS

Human exploration and development of space will involve opening the space frontier by exploring, using and enabling the development of space through information technology, while expanding the human experience into the far reaches of space. At that point in time we assert that the current primitive World Wide Web (Web) will be replaced and dramatically expanded into an Interstellar Space Wide Web (SWW) (Rine, 2003). The current state-of-the-art low orbits communications satellites constellations will be dramatically expanded to higher orbits and to orbits supporting work on other remote human colonies. This will be necessary in order to furnish in a human-friendly way the necessary software and information that will be needed in support of Interstellar Space Wide Information Technologies. Many of the problems encountered in conceiving of, modeling, designing and deploying such a facility will be different from those problems encountered in today's Web. Future research and development work will be to identify some of these problems and to conceptually model a few of their solutions.

Twenty-first Century Space Wide Web (SWW) distributed component-based software applications will dwarf today's increasingly complex World Wide Web (WWW) environments, supported by Earth-bound low orbit satellite constellations, and will represent a far more significant investment in terms of development costs, deployment and maintenance (Rine, 2003). As we now move into the twenty-first century part of the cost will come in the effort required to develop, deploy and maintain the individual software components. Many of these components will be on remote, numerous satellites. As now, part of this effort will include implementing the required functionality of components, implementing the required interactions for components and preparing components to operate in some remote runtime environment. One way to reduce the cost of component development will continue to be reuse of existing commercial software components that meet the functional requirements.

The need for an adaptive Web-based configuration language is motivated by considering a future scenario involving planetary and deep space satellites. Assume that there are several teams of researchers scattered across Mars, and that communication between these researchers is supported by a constellation of low-orbit communication satellites, like the present LEOS. Further, suppose that there is a deep space probe exploring the asteroid zone between Mars and Jupiter. Scientists on both Mars and Earth would like to be able to dynamically access data from this probe, via a relay between their low-orbit constellations and a ground or space based relay station. This access can include running different sets of measurements, changing sensor configuration, etc. Further, appropriate Earth scientists would like to share results with their Mars colleagues using Push technology, and vice versa. Finally, scientists will want to run their experiments on the deep space probe by writing and then loading the equivalent of a Java-like applet onto the probe.

The above scenario raises a number of technological challenges (Rine, 2003). First, the Earth-based and the Mars-based scientists may have quite different capabilities in terms of the type and amount of data they can receive from the probe. It may even be desirable to first send the data to Earth, have it processed, and then sent back up to Mars. Second, all space-based communication is costly in terms of power consumption, available bandwidth and round trip propagation delay. Finally, the dynamics of this situation change due to factors such as changing orbits and relative positions. For instance, it may be better for the probe at times to send to Mars, or to Earth, or both. These routing decisions are based upon both the needs of the application and the physical configuration of the communication satellites. In order to make appropriate use of minimal bandwidth and limited power, it is desirable that these semantics are directly reflected from the application down to the network layer. The challenge is to do this in a way that both does not unduly burden the application writer (i.e., the scientist writing the satellite applet) and also makes appropriate usage of network resources. This is possible by developing the SWW-XML and by placing communication control in the appropriate adapters.

To support a space Web (e.g. SWW), a futuristic spacecraft (satellite) orbiting a distant planet or moon needs to robustly self-adapt to its target environment. Sometimes this self-adaptation will be needed in order to respond to SWW user commands from Earth or from another space colony, and sometimes this self-adaptation will be needed as a satellite reconfigures itself to allow it to perform more effectively or efficiently in a new physical environment. Let us imagine a satellite orbiting a different planet or a different orbit around the same planet for a period of time (e.g. a month). Environmental factors can be different versions of sunlight, temperature, magnetic field, gravity, and solar wind. These diverse environments may be uncertain and different for different planets. Suppose a satellite supporting SWW in this proposal supports imaging. Let us use a client-server model. Suppose the client is the ground station on earth and the server is this satellite. Suppose there are three software subsystems embedded in this satellite: command and data handling (CD), flight control, and payload control. Each of these software subsystems runs on a different processor. The CD is basically for receiving up-link commands and routing them through constellations to a given satellite and to a given processor. The flight control software is mainly for the attitude determination and attitude control system (ACS). The payload interface processor (PIP) is for controlling the imaging camera and sending images back to client. We illustrate an idea of an adaptive ACS. In the future, this idea can be applied to adaptive PIP software.

In the last section, we included three chapters on Web applications: Scenario driven Decision support system, market economy approach for managing data grids, and interoperability of Web-based Geospatial applications.

Finally, we develop a multilayered framework for linking all new dimensions in information technology and Web engineering as follows:

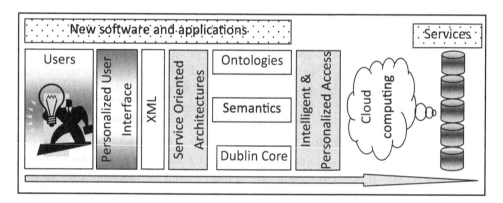

REFERENCES

Alkhatib, G. (2009). A presentation to the "Workshop on Developing and Re-engineering Workflows in e-Government Services." Organized by Datamatix, February 2009, Dubai, UAE.

Chen, H-M., Chen, Q., & Kazman R. (2007). The Affective and Cognitive Impacts of Perceived Touch on Online Customers' Intention to Return in the Web-based eCRM environment. *Journal of Electronic Commerce in Organizations, 5*(1), 69-93.

Christensen, C. (1997). *The Innovator's Dilemma: When New Technologies Cause Great Firms to Fail.* Boston, MA: Harvard Business School Press.

He, W., Xu, L., Means, T., & Wang, P. (2009). Integrating Web 2.0 with the case-based reasoning cycle: A systems approach. *Systems Research and Behavioral Science, 9.*

Rine, D. (2003). Human exploration and development of space: using XML database Space Wide Web. *Information Science: an International Journal, 150*, 123-151.

Wang, P. (2009). Popular Concepts beyond Organizations: Exploring New Dimensions of Information Technology Innovations. *Journal of the Association for Information Systems, 10*(1).

Section 1
Semantics and Ontologies

Chapter 1
A Semantic Web–Based Approach for Context–Aware User Query Formulation and Information Retrieval

Hanh Huu Hoang
Vienna University of Technology, Austria

Tho Manh Nguyen
Vienna University of Technology, Austria

A. Min Tjoa
Vienna University of Technology, Austria

ABSTRACT

Formulating unambiguous queries in the Semantic Web applications is a challenging task for users. This article presents a new approach in guiding users to formulate clear requests based on their common nature of querying for information. The approach known as the front-end approach gives users an overview about the system data through a virtual data component which stores the extracted metadata of the data storage sources in the form of an ontology. This approach reduces the ambiguities in users' requests at a very early stage and allows the query process to effectively perform in fulfilling users' demands in a context-aware manner. Furthermore, the approach provides a powerful query engine, called context-aware querying, that recommends the appropriate query patterns according to the user's querying context.

MOTIVATION

The Semantic Web and ontologies have created a promising background for applying the intelligent techniques in information systems, especially in personal information management

(PIM) systems. In PIM systems, effectively retrieving information from a huge amount data of an individual is a challenging issue. The virtual query system (VQS) (Hoang, Andjomshoaa, & Tjoa, 2006) of the SemanticLIFE framework is an approach of using semantic Web techniques with a user-oriented method in order to tackle this challenge.

The SemanticLIFE project (Ahmed, Hoang, Karim, Khusro, Lanzenberger, Latif et al., 2004) is an effort to realize Vanevar Bush's vision of Memex (Bush, 1945) by providing a general semantic PIM system. The SemanticLIFE system integrates a wide variety of data sources and stores them in an ontological repository. In the VQS-enhanced SemanticLIFE, the user is supported in issuing imprecise queries to retrieve the rich semantic information from the user's historical personal data. However, users themselves often do not actually know or remember the specific qualities of what they are looking for, but have some awareness of other things related to the desired items (Quan, Huynh, & Karger, 2003). The VQS supports users in this nature when querying the information from the huge ontological repository effectively not only in the initial phase with offered "virtual information" but during the query process with the "context-based" querying features.

Furthermore, as mentioned above, the user's nature of asking questions is that the user often does not know what the user is looking for; but the user remembers some concepts about related information the user is looking for. This leads us to a way of querying (browsing/navigating) the system by using redefined query templates (patterns) based on the user's querying context. This would help the user not to be embarrassed in a new phase of query formulation.

The difficulty of query formulation appears not only in the initial phase but it continues in the query process or query refinement. During the query process, the user is asked for new requests using the new knowledge to get the information of interest. In order to ease the user from thinking of new constraints of their queries, we propose a new way based on the users' nature, that is, preferring to customize the query patterns to make new queries. We trace the context of the user's query process and recommend to the user the appropriate query patterns matching up the user's query context.

Our approach originates from the user-side manner in trying to formulate unambiguous requests as early as possible during the querying process. The principle of the approach follows "better known, clearer request" and "customizing than creating." If users are aware of what information they possess, they could ask precise queries against their stored data. This helps the query refinement process of the system by eliminating ambiguities at a very early stage of the query process. These approaches resulted in our query system, the VQS for the SemanticLIFE framework, with a query language called the virtual query language, and with a new way of query formulation entitled *pattern-based* and *context-aware* querying process.

The remainder of this article is organized as follows. The related work to our research is mentioned in Section 2. An overview of the SemanticLIFE project and the VQS is underlined in Section 3. Section 5 describes the details of the "virtual data component." Section 6 presents the VQS's innovative feature for query formulation and information retrieval. Main points of the VQS implementation are pointed out in Section 8. A summarized example is presented in the Section 9. Finally, the article is concluded with a sketch of the intended future work in Section 10.

RELATED WORK

Research activities in ontology-based search/query systems could be classified in to variant categories (Hoang & Tjoa, 2006). In this section we only present two related issues: (a) ontology-enhanced search strategies and (b) query formulation.

Ontology-Enhanced Search Strategies

With the help of ontology technique, OntoLoger (Stojanovic, Gonzalez, & Stojanovic, 2003) builds a query mechanism by recording the user's behaviors in an ontology and recalling it. OntoLoger, similarly to its general version of the Library Agent (Stojanovic, 2003), is a query system based on usage analysis in the ontology-based information portals. Its query mechanism is based on usage-data in form of an ontology, so-called semantic log file. The structure of the ontology reflects the users' needs. By using this, OntoLoger supports the user in fine-tuning of the user's initial query. Moreover, during the refinement process, the system also uses this log ontology for ranking query results and refinements according to the user's needs.

GeoShare (Hübner, Spittel, Visser, & Vögele, 2004) uses ontologies for describing vocabularies and catalogs as well as search mechanisms for keywords to capture more meaning. During the search process, the user narrows a search space's size by selecting specific domain (thematic, spatial, or temporal model). Then the user picks the appropriate concepts from these models and application ontologies, covering all available concepts, to define the concrete query. After that, the user can parameterize the user's query to concertize the retrieval process. In the sequel, the system processes the query and transforms it into the ontology language for the terminological part, where the system looks for equivalent concepts and subconcepts. After processing the query, the system composes a ranked list of relevant information providers based on the weightings of a specific reasoning process.

Semantic Web data consist of ontological and instance data. The actual data the user is interested in are entities belonging to a class, but the domain knowledge and relationships are described primarily as class relationships in the ontology, and this is exemplified in the SHOE search system (Heflin & Hendler, 2000). In SHOE, the user is first provided a visualization of the ontology, and the user can choose the class of instances the user is looking for. The possible relationships or properties associated with the class are then searched, and the user constrains the instances by applying

keyword filters to the various instance properties. A similar approach is also applied in some versions of the SEAL portal (Maedche, Staab, Stojanovic, Studer, & Sure, 2001) and Ontobroker (Decker, Erdmann, Fensel, & Studer, 1998).

However, there are some differences between these systems in their usage ontologies. In SHOE, providers of information can introduce arbitrary extensions to a given ontology. Furthermore, no central provider index is defined. In contrast, Ontobroker relies on the notion of an Ontogroup (Decker et al., 1998) and domain specific ontology defining a group of Web users that agree on an ontology for a given subject.

In a further effort of the above approaches, the authors of Haystack (Huynh, Karger, & Quan, 2002) based their user interface paradigm almost completely on browsing from resource to resource (Quan et al., 2003). This is affirmed by scientific results of a search behavior research (Teevan, Alvarado, Ackerman, & Karger, 2004) that actually most human beings seek information via a process they call "orienteering" rather than carefully formulating a query that precisely defines the desired information target. Users often prefer to start from a familiar location, or a vague search, and "home in" on the desired information through a series of associative steps (Karger, Bakshi, Huynh, Quan, & Vineet, 2005).

Query Formulation

There are two main approaches to reduce the difficulty in formulating queries from user-side. The first trend is going to design a friendly and interactive query interfaces to guide users in generating the queries. The high-rated examples for this trend are geographical RQL (GRQL) (Athanasis, Christophides, & Kotzinos, 2004) and SEWASIE (Catarci, Di Mascio, Franconi, Santucci, & Tessaris, 2003).

GRQL relies on the full power of the RDF/S data model for constructing on the fly queries expressed in RQL (Karvounarakis, Alexaki,

Christophides, Plexousakis, & Scholl, 2002). More precisely, a user can first graphically navigate through the individual RDF/S class and property definitions, then transparently generate the required RQL path expressions required to access the resources of interest. These expressions accurately capture the meaning of its navigation steps through the class (or property) subsumption and/or associations. Additionally, users can enrich the generated queries with filtering conditions on the attributes of the currently visited class by specifying the resource's class(es) appearing in the query result.

Another graphical query generation interface is SEWASIE. As a starting point, the user is provided some preprepared domain-specific patterns to choose from as a starting point, which the user can then extend and customize. The refinements to the query can either be additional property constraints to the classes or a replacement of another compatible class in the pattern such as a subclass or superclass. This is performed through a clickable graphic visualization of the neighborhood ontology of the currently selected class.

The second approach of reducing complexity is the effort in creating much lighter query languages than expressive RDF query languages. Following this trend, the approach by Guha and McCool (2003), known as GetData query interface, is a typical example. GetData query interface of TAP[1] expresses the need of a much lighter weight interface for constructing complex queries. The idea of GetData is to design a simple query interface which allows to present network accessible data as directed labeled graph. This approach provides a system which is very easy to build, and supports both type of users, data providers, and data consumers.

THE SEMANTICLIFE DIGITAL MEMORY FRAMEWORK

"SemanticLIFE"

In the physical world, entities are usually interconnected, either by physical or by semantic means; in the latter case, the semantic meaning is added by human interaction (in an abstract sense) with the physical world. Life items in the system proposed can be understood as information entities (in some cases they are representations of such physical entities) stored according to ontologies in a semantic database, which are connected to other information entities according to their semantic meaning. Also ontologies "live" in a way, as they develop and modify permanently during the system- and user-lifetime.

Current (Web) technologies are highly efficient in processing data for human reception; that is, the transformation from data to information, the "generation of meaning" is up to the human. A great deal of effort has already been made, and work is still going on to represent semantics explicitly on the Web. This is required to give computer systems the capability to enhance preprocessing of huge amounts of data for the user. It becomes more important as the "awareness radius" of the contemporary knowledge worker and consumer is continuously increasing. These results from the observation; those users do not limit their information search to specific data repositories, like searching for an address or an event in a calendar. The availability of databases under common or similar interfaces (like Web pages) creates the demand to express more complex queries demanding information aggregated from many different systems using different semantic concepts.

The proposed PIM systems can significantly contribute in overcoming the common inherent human problems such as limited short term memory, memory loss, forgetfulness, high complexity of data, and so forth. Therefore, it is useful for the system to be able to define and capture the user's life-related events and take or trigger appropriate action(s) for it. This process involves the following subprocesses:

1. Capture events and associated information.
2. Process action associated with events (e.g., in the sense of an active database system).
3. Extract metadata from the event, or allow the user to enrich the data manually with semantic meaning.
4. Store the data including semantic context as ontology in an efficient manner.
5. Allow the user to query the data or support the user directly via associated applications and tools with context-sensitive information or action.

Additionally as described by Dolog, Henze, Nejdl, and Sintek (2003), the system is able to adjust to new user features derived from user interactions with the system or from the information being fed. Thus each user may have individual views and navigational possibilities

for working with the system. From the technology perspective, new technologies emerge and older ones fade out. If a system has a too tight coupling with some technology, it may become obsolete with the change in technology. A layered approach that provides some extent of separation from the technology is more suitable, making the overall structure still work if there is a change in the technology or even in the case of replacement by the newer ones.

The SemanticLIFE Framework

The SemanticLIFE framework is developed on a highly modular architecture to store, manage, and retrieve the lifetime's information entities of individuals. It enables the acquisition and storage of data while giving annotations to e-mail messages, browsed Web pages, phone calls, images, contacts, life events, and other resources. It also provides intuitive and effective search mechanism based upon the stored semantics, and the semantically enriched user interfaces according to the user's needs. The ultimate goal of the project

Figure 1. The architecture of the SemanticLIFE framework

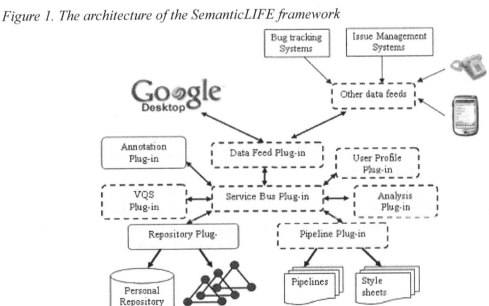

is to build a PIM system over a human lifetime using ontologies as a basis for the representation of its content.

The whole SemanticLIFE system has been designed as a set of interactive plug-ins that fit into the main application and this guarantees flexibility and extensibility of SemanticLIFE platform. Communication within the system is based on a service-oriented design with the advantage of its loosely coupled characteristics. To compose complex solutions and scenarios from atomic services which are offered by SemanticLIFE plug-ins, the service oriented pipeline architecture (SOPA)[2] has been introduced. SOPA provides a paradigm to describe the system-wide service compositions and also external Web services as pipelines. SOPA provides some mechanisms for orchestration of services and transformation of results.

The SemanticLIFE's system architecture overview is depicted in Figure 1. Data with user annotation is fed into the system using a number of dedicated plug-ins from variety of data sources such as Google Desktop[3] captured data, communication logs, and other applications' metadata. The data objects are transferred to the analysis plug-in via the message handler. The analysis plug-in contains a number of specific plug-ins which provides the semantic mark-up by applying a bunch of feature extraction methods and indexing techniques in a cascaded manner.

The semistructured and semantically enriched information objects are then ontologically stored via the repository plug-in. In the SemanticLIFE system, data sources are stored in forms of RDF[4] triples with their ontologies and metadata. This repository is called a metastore.

A set of query processing and information visualization tools provides the means for information exploration and report generation. The analysis module and metadata extraction capabilities make associations between the lifetime items/objects and the lifetime events based on user annotation, user profiles, and the system ontologies.

THE VIRTUAL QUERY SYSTEM

An Overview

Formulating nonambiguous queries is always a too demanding task to users as they do not have the awareness of the semantics of the stored information. The goal of the VQS is to overcome this problem by providing an ontology-based virtual information view of the data available in the system. If the user can "be aware of" what is inside of the system the use can clearly specify the queries on the "real" data stored in the repository.

The VQS system is primarily based on the reduction of semantic ambiguities of the user

Figure 2. The components and architecture of the virtual query system

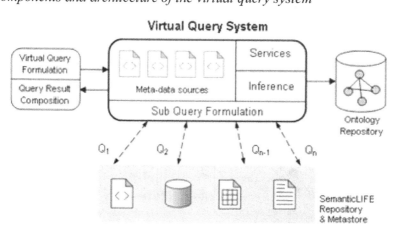

query specifications at the very early stage of the retrieving process. The most important point in the VQS approach is that it provides an image of the real system data sources to the user. The user is aware of the data stored in the system when the user generates the queries. As a result, the ambiguities in the user's requests will be much reduced.

As depicted in Figure 2, with the support of a virtual data component containing metadata of real data sources, the user can generate the virtual query against the virtual data. The VQS then analyzes the virtual query based on a common ontology mapped from local ontologies of data sources and user ontology. As the result, subqueries from initial query are generated for the specific underlined data sources. Finally, the results of subqueries are aggregated and represented to the user with regarding the user's profile.

VQS Main Components

The Virtual Data Component

The virtual data component (VDC) contains the metadata of storage sources. This VQS crucial module acts as a virtual information layer to be delivered to the user. It enables the user to be aware of the semantics of the data sources stored and to specify more precise queries.

The VQS collects metadata from data sources in the metadata repository of the SemanticLIFE system. An analysis process is carried out on these metadata sources to get the semantic information. Then the processed information is stored in this module as a *context ontology*. Furthermore, this part is also referred as an image of the system database in further query processing, so-called the *context-aware querying,* which is discussed in detail later on.

The VQS system, with the organization of the "virtual data component" as a context ontology, will guide its users through the system by intelligently recommended query patterns based on the current query context, so-called query space, and that context ontology (the virtual data). In our "front-end" approach, this is the most crucial feature that is different to the current ontology-based query systems (Hoang & Tjoa, 2006a).

The rational behind the idea of this approach is that when users are aware of their data then they could formulate more unambiguous requests. This ultimately leads to the reduction of the query refinement process complexity. Additionally, this VDC plays as a context ontology. This makes the SemanticLIFE system very flexible as the system can adapt to a new scenario by simply changing the context ontology

The VQS Services

- **Ontology Mapping:** This service deals with mapping concepts from the system ontology to the context ontology, including the instances. It can deal with new data sources added with their respective ontologies, so that these ontologies are mapped or integrated to the global ontology. In our approach, we do not reinvest to develop a new ontology mapping framework. Instead, we use the mapping framework (MAFRA) (Maedche, Motik, Silva, & Volz, 2002) for our mapping tasks.
- **Inference:** The ontology-based inference service provides a basis for the deduction process on the relationships (rules) of concepts of the ontologies specified. Inference tasks are performed on the foundation of the ontologies and the data described by them. This service helps the system to analyze and evaluate the user's virtual queries in the process of generating subqueries based on the inference ontology.

Subquery Formulation

Subqueries formulation is another essential part of the VQS. From the user's initial virtual query, this part parses it into the subqueries (Q_i in the

Figure 2) based on the global ontology for specific data sources. This module does not only transform the virtual query to subqueries for specific data sources but additionally perform inference on the user's request in order to create more possible subqueries afterward.

Query Refinement

This is the interactive way (semiautomated) for the VQS dealing with user's ambiguous queries, which is based on incrementally and interactively (step-by-step) tailoring a query to the current information needs of a user (Quan et al., 2003). This VQS service is a semiautomated process, that is, the user is provided with a ranked list of refinements, which leads to a decrease of some of these ambiguities.

THE VIRTUAL DATA COMPONENT

The Goals

From the user perspective, the VDC plays an important role in the process of query generation in the VQS approach. The core of the VDC is the module containing the metadata storage sources (MSS). This module acts as a virtual information

Figure 3. A fragment of the SemanticLIFE's datafeeds ontology

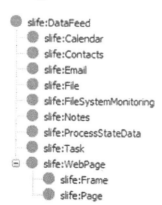

layer allowing the user to be aware of the meaning of the stored data sources and the user can then specify more precise queries as the result.

The VDC harvests the metadata of the data sources within the SemanticLIFE metadata repository. An analysis process and a statistical computation are carried out on these metadata sources to get the semantic information which is then stored in the VDC and will be delivered to the user query generation interface. This component is also referred as an "image" of the system database in further query processing.

Virtual Information Collecting

In the SemanticLIFE metastore, there are different data sources' ontologies that exist along with the instances. The SemanticLIFE system manages a huge range of data from common personal information such as contacts, calendar, tasks, notes, documents, files, phone calls, instant messaging logs, and so on, to general data such as maps and weather information (Ahmed et al., 2004).

Figure 3 presents the data feeds covered by the SemanticLIFE framework in the current prototype. The data feeds are about the personal data of an individual's diary. From this ontology and the underlined instances, a VDC service is called to extract the metadata, perform some statistical computation, and store the information in a new ontology, called the context ontology. This ontology is used in the VDC to provide semantic information on the corresponding data sources to the users.

As mentioned, the core of the VDC is a synthesis ontology which is formed from these variety datafeeds ontologies. This task has been done by using MAFRA ontologies merging framework, with "semantic bridge concept" (Maedche et al., 2002), as the mapping service to merge the ontologies. The process consists of aligning the schemes and merging the instances as well.

Context-Based Support of the VDC

The loosely-coupled organization of the metadata storage sources (an ontology of the "virtual information") reflects the flexibility of the virtual query system as well as the SemanticLIFE system. Based on this ontology, the context-based query templates are also categorized according to the concepts. We can apply the VQS or the SemanticLIFE system in different contexts by simply making changes of this ontology.

The metadata storage sources are constructed as an ontolog,y namely context metadata or context ontology. By doing the taxonomy and reasoning on the concepts and also on the instances, the metadata could be classified into the categories and the data are arranged into the relevant ontology dependent on the context that the SemanticLIFE framework is used for.

Figure 4 shows the ontology constructed by mapping data sources' schemes and the instances. The ontology in the figure is an ontology for a personal diary recording the daily activities of an individual who works in some projects. The extracted metadata will be fetched from system datafeeds ontologies and put into the VDC's context ontology and conformed to its hierarchy. For example, the "Place" class is an abstract concept and formed from classes "Contact," annotations, maps, and their instances. This makes the semantic information to become more contextual, and we call this process the concept contextualization.

Definition 1: *A concept contextualization, Con, in VQS is a transformation of concept (class) C of system ontology, O_1, to the context ontology, O_2. The relationships between C and other concepts in O_2 will be reformed.*

$$Con: \langle C, O_1 \rangle \mapsto \langle C, O_2 \rangle$$

Hence, the context ontology could be redefined based on the concept contextualization as follows:

Figure 4. An example of the virtual data component ontology

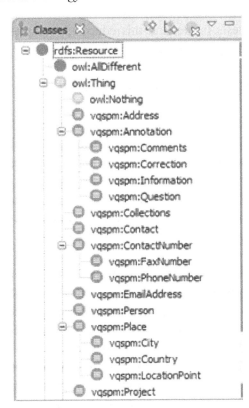

Definition 2: *The concept ontology, CO, of the VDC is:*

$$CO = \bigcup_{i=1}^{n} Con_i$$

where, n is the number of concepts.

The metadata in the VDC's context ontology ("context ontology" in short) is still associated to the "real" metadata in the system ontology. The metadata in the new context is used for the VQS's purposed in rendering information for presentation and reasoning during the querying process.

Additionally, the VDC contains the summary information for each data sources over the customized timelines such as total items and the number of items for each data sources. This provides the user with a very good awareness about the user's data in the system. As a result, the user can query the necessary statistic information.

The VDC is the typical feature of our system compared with the other systems mentioned by

Hoang and Tjoa (2006a). The basic idea behind it is quite simple: if the user is aware of the user's data, then the user could generate more unambiguous requests. In one hand, this reduces the complexity of the query refinement process.

The Virtual Query Language

The VQL (Hoang & Tjoa, 2006b) is designed for the VQS. The VQL aims to be a lighter weight query language which supports "semantic" queries on the ontological RDF-based storages. VQL is very easy to build and use and to be supported. In context of the VQS, the aims of VQL are as follow:

- VQL helps the clients in making queries without the knowledge of RDF query languages. The user just gives basic parameters of request information in VQL, and would receive the expecting results.
- VQL assists users in navigating the system via semantic links/associations, categorized context queries provided in the powerful query operators based on ontologies.

An example of VQL queries is depicted in Listing 1 in which the VQL query is called "RE-LATED-WITH" query (Hoang & Tjoa, 2006b). This query retrieves the related information from data sources of E-mail and Contact to the e-mail address hta@gmx.at.

The VQL is modeled in extensible markup language (XML)[5] with three supported types: data query type, schema query type, and embedded query types for their own goals. The "data" queries are used to retrieve the data from the SemanticLIFE metastore. The "schema" queries are used to get information from the system's ontologies. The "embedded" queries contain the RDF query statements, which are preprocessed to make the query items unambiguous, transfer them to the execution unit to be executed, and get the results back.

The VQL is designed to help the user easily generate requests according to their nature: *minimum of words, maximum of results*. In order to fulfill this principle, the VQL defines the *virtual query operators* which allow the user to simplify the complex queries:

- *GetInstances* operator is the common form of VQL data queries. The operator retrieves the appropriate information according to the criteria described in the parameters, sources, and constraints of the query.
- *GetInstanceMetadata* operator assists the user in easily retrieving all metadata properties and correspondent result instances. This query operator is very useful when the

Listing 1. An example of the VQL GetRelatedData query operator

```xml
<query type="data">
<params>
 <param name="p1:emailTo" show="0">hta@gmx.at</param>
 <param name="p2:RELATED-WITH" show="1"/>
</params>
<sources>
 <source name="email">Email</source>
 <source name="contact">Contact</source>
</sources>
<relations>
 <relation id="1" param="p1" source="email"/>
</relations>
<resultformat>xml</resultformat>
</query>
```

user does not know exactly what properties of data instances are.

- *GetRelatedData* operator provides the accessible related information to the current found information. In Semantic Web applications, particularly in the SemanticLIFE system, finding relevant or associated information plays an important role.

- *GetLinks* operator operates using the system's ontology and RDF graph pattern traversal to find out the associations/links between the instances and the objects.

For instance, we query for a set of instances of eimails, contacts, and appointments. Normally, we receive these data separately and what we expect here is that the associations between the results are provided additionally. The links are probably properties of e-mail addresses (i.e.,, name of the persons and locations).

- **GetFileContent operator:** The SemanticLIFE system covers a large range of data sources, from personal data such as contacts, appointments, and e-mails to files stored in the user's computer, for example, the office docu-

ments, PDF files, and media files. Therefore, this operator is about getting the contents of these files for further processing.

CONTEXT-AWARE QUERY FORMULATION IN THE VQS

In the VQS, the user is not only supported in the query formulation by the "virtual" information, but also during the user's querying process by a load of features, which are introduced as follows.

The VQL Query Template

A *VQL query template* (VQL-QT) is an abstract query pattern which is attached with a specific VQL query, containing the concepts and resources for the user querying process.

VQL-QTs are classified on these concepts and resources so that the appropriate template will be recommended to the user based on the user's querying context. VQL-QTs help the user in generating clear requests by only replacing the values into the selected query pattern.

VQL Query Template Syntax

In the VQS, the VQL query templates, so-called VQL query patterns (VQL-QPs), are defined to assist the user in formulating unambiguous queries. The query templates contain the VQL queries with the necessary parameters and the associated data sources. A VQL-QT or VQL-QP mainly consists of:

- Λ VQL query in form of a *query file name*
- *Parameters* containing the values from the user's input
- *Resources* involved in the querying process

and two optional parts:

Figure 5. The schema of the VQL query template

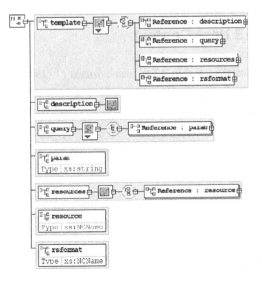

Listing 2. A VQL query template example

```
<template type="vql">
<description>Finding a location of webpage browsed by a person using Googl search engine</
description >
<query name="webpersonse.vql">
 <param>?location</param>
 <param>?tiemStamp</param>
 <param>?person</param >
</query>
<resources>
 <resource>Webpage</resource>
 <resource>Location</resource>
 <resource>Person</resource>
</resources>
<rsformat>xml</rsformat>
</templates>
```

- *Description* of the VQL-QT which is used for display to users
- *Query result format* to specify the dedicated format of the results

The structure of a VQL query template is illustrated in Figure 5, in which the components of the VQL query template are shown in a hierarchical tree.

Listing 2 is an example of a VQL query template. That VQL query template is about retrieving the locations of all Web pages found by Google search engine[6] and these Web pages have been browsed by a given person in a period of time. The related sources for the retrieving process are mentioned in the <resources> part. The parameters are put in subparts <param> and these parameters could be changed or added by the user according the information of interest.

VQL Query Template in Use

The VQL query templates are classified on the concepts of the VDC's context ontology as well as their involved data sources, so-called resources. The concepts of the VDC's context ontology are reflected in parameters of the VQL-QPs. Based on this classification, the VQS will match the VQL-QTs with the user query context and the appropriate VQL-QP will be delivered to the user as a recommendation. When the template is in use, the attached VQL query will be loaded and its variables are then replaced by the template's parameters. The VQL query could be continually edited by the user afterward dependent on the user's interest.

Furthermore, during the VQS user's querying process, a new VQL-QT could be also created. The new VQL-QTs creation can be carried out in two ways: first, it comes from an analysis based on the querying context of the user; second, from the editing of an existing VQL-QT (the user could need to save for later use in the form of another VQL-QT).

VQS User Context

Definition 3: *The VQS user context (VQS-UC) is a set of requested concepts from the context ontology linked to the system ontologies and associated resources, as well as the properties that are in action. Let call U is a VQS-UC, we have:*

Con: $\langle C, R, P \rangle$

where C is the set of the underlying concepts, R is a set of associated resources, and P is a set of queried properties.

In general, in order to formulate a VQS-UC, an analysis process is carried out based on the objects in the querying process. The analysis process counts on the following metadata:

- Querying concepts, their associated resources (based on the system ontologies), and the querying properties.
- The detected semantic links (obtained from VQL's *GetLinks* operator) would help in terms of finding the relationships of the information.
- The query results the last execution of the user's querying process.

A VQS-UC is used to keep the user's querying concepts and querying space, that is, about how the concepts and query results are associated. From that, the new knowledge will be deducted for ideas of further requests.

VQS Query Map

A *VQS query map* (VQS-QM) is a network of VQL query templates, in which the nodes are the VQL query templates and the connections are the related concepts and their properties. $M = \langle T, C, P \rangle$ is a VQS-QM, where T is the set of VQL-QTs, C is the set of concepts of the underlying resources, and P is the set of querying properties.

Generally, with the associated data sources and the VDC's context ontology, the VQL query template creates a *query map* to make the connection network among the templates and underlined resources.

According to the connections between the templates, when a VQL-QT is chosen for making the new queries, the system also recommends the linked VQL-QTs. Besides, when the user selects one or more properties to generate a query, the system could also recommend the relevant templates to the user based on the query map. The connections in the query map are used to determine which templates could be used.

Context-Aware Querying Process

The virtual data component also enhances the query process by a "context-based" querying feature, that is, the query patterns will be proposed by the system according to the context where the user is in. However, a user's query context not only contains all the queried objects and the querying concepts but they are also associated to each other based on the context ontology.

How could the VDC recommend the relevant templates to the user? During context-based information retrieval process, the VDC will do following steps:

1. Keeping track on the concepts queried by the user.
2. From these queried concepts, a context of the user's querying process will be formed. The context is a graph of queried and querying concepts.
3. When the user asks for a new template from the user's querying context through an interactive interface, then a match of the query map in the virtual data component and the user's querying context will be made.
4. The query patterns/templates will be collected and offered to the user.

For example, the context query being applied is about project management which contains the concepts of project, person, document, publication, partner, time, location, and so on. The user's query context could be a graph of *person, location*, and *Web search for project* as depicted in Figure 6. In this case a query template such as *"finding a person I have contacted in Vienna in a related project found by Google search engine"* will be proposed.

This feature is applied in the VQS's interactive interface, in which the user can right click on the results objects, instance,s or virtual data objects and the system will show dedicated templates based on the user's context.

Figure 6. An example of context-based querying

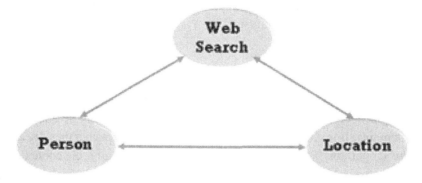

Context-Aware Query Results Representation

The query results back to the VQS according to the schema the SemanticLIFE metastore. Therefore, for the user's information consuming, the results is put into the "context" of the query concerning the VDC's ontology before presenting to the user as depicted in Figure 7.

As described in the figure, the results from the SemanticLIFE metastore are based on the system ontologies; therefore, via the VDC, the query results are contextualized with the VDC's context ontology. Moreover, based on the VDC's ontology, the related information associated to the relationships within its hierarchy is also presented as the recommendation to the user.

SEMANTIC NAVIGATION WITH THE VQS

VQS Semantic Traces

The traces are to keep tracing on successful querying sessions. VQS keeps traces in form of query pipelines with annotation and classification, that is, every trace is attached with pipelines, used resources, and annotation of each pipeline.

Definition 4: *A trace is an extended pipeline with the user's annotation and the context applied. Let us call T as a trace and we have:*

$$T = \{P_i, CT_i\}_{i=1-n}$$

where T is an n-element ordered set with P_i is the ith query pipeline and CT_i is the attached i^{th} context, which is a finite set of m concepts:

Figure 7. The process of returning query results in the VQS

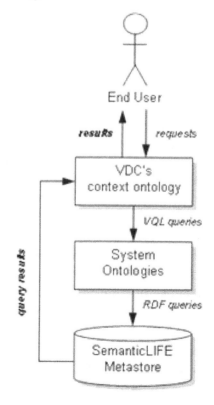

$$CT = \{C_k\}_{k=1-m}$$

where C_k is a concept.

Based on these traces, the users could resume and restore last querying sessions. Moreover the traces could be used as the guidelines for the new querying processes as the recommendations.

Context-Aware System Navigation

The VQS is aiming at not only information retrieval aspects, but in inventing a new way of query and processes the query results for the next round. With help of the VQS-UC, VQS-QTs, VQS semantic traces, the feature of system navigation by semantics (*semantic navigation*) is realized.

Initially, the VQS's user would generate a new query based on the virtual information of the VDC. The user could also select from the commonly used VQL-QTs and customize according the user's interest. After this initial phase, the user enters the process of retrieving information; the

system helps the user for the next query formulation. This could be done based on many VQS's features such as the user's querying context, the user's query map, the query patterns in form of the VQL-QTs, as well as the query results, especially the results of the VQL operators which is rich of semantics.

In addition of the semantic traces, the VQS supports the user through the system by navigating source-by-source and concept-by–concept, which would entertain the user by suggestions and offered query patterns associated with the user's querying space (query context and query map).

THE VQS IMPLEMENTATION

VQS Workflow

The detailed workflow of the VQS is described in the UML sequence diagram depicted in Figure 8. Here, at first, is a process of fetching metadata from the SemanticLIFE metastore and organized then

Figure 8. VQS workflow in its UML sequence diagram

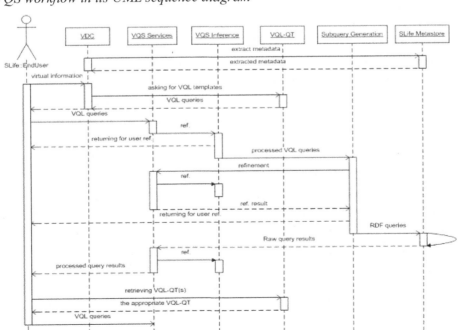

into the VDC of the VQS as the context ontology. This process only run once and it would be updated if the ontologies of metastore are changed.

First, as described in the Figure 8 in the phase of query formulation, the user could use the VQL query templates which are predefined query patterns of the VQS. This helps the users in the first steps. The VQL-QTs could be retrieved directly by the user with(out) referring to the selective information of the VDC. Moreover, after the initial phase, the VQL-QTs would be offered automatically based on the user query context.

Next, the VQL queries delivered to the subqueries generation phase are semantically clarified based on the system ontologies. The query refinement is performed semiautomatically. Referring to the VQS services to detect the ambiguities during this phase, the generated subqueries are updated by the user if necessary as a feedback to finalize the execution of the RDF queries. Finally, the query results are again "contextualized" by VQS services before representing to the user.

The Used Techniques

In the VQS implementation, we have taken the SemanticLIFE architecture as the baseline and inherited the innovative features of the Eclipse platform. We have used the Java open-source frameworks in form of the Semantic Web applications, the ontology engineering, and the Web services.

The Eclipse Platform

The Eclipse platform gives a technical background not only for developing the basic SemanticLIFE architecture, but also its modules as plug-ins using Eclipse PDE. In the development of the VQS and its components, the help of PDE, RCP, and SWT is very valuable.

The Semantic Web Framework

The Semantic Web framework is mainly used in our development is the Jena Semantic Web Framework[7] of HP Labs. Jena is a leading Java framework in the area of building Semantic Web applications. Jena provides a programmatic environment for RDF, RDFS, OWL, and SPARQL, and includes a rule-based inference engine. Jena is open source and grown out of work with the HP Labs Semantic Web research[8].

With the new releases (since version 2.4), Jena has integrated the Lucene index engine[9] to provide a powerful full-text searching feature for the SPARQL query language. This help to increase the precision in searching documents in the SemanticLIFE framework.

The Ontology Mapping Framework

MAFRA is a conceptual description of the ontology mapping process. Ontology mapping is the process where semantic relations are defined between two ontologies at the conceptual level which in turn are applied at data level transforming source ontology instances into target ontology instances.

The MAFRA toolkit[10] implements a specific architecture for MAFRA. The architecture of the system is based on the notion of service which represents not only the system transformation capabilities, but also the expertise in the manipulation of specific semantic relations.

The Web Services Framework

Finally, for the backbone of the whole system, which connects the services extensions offered and invokes the services or related tasks, the Apache Web Services frameworks[11] have been used in our SemanticLIFE development. The VQS service development inherits from the baseline system for its service extension development.

Figure 9. The declaration of the query execution plug-in

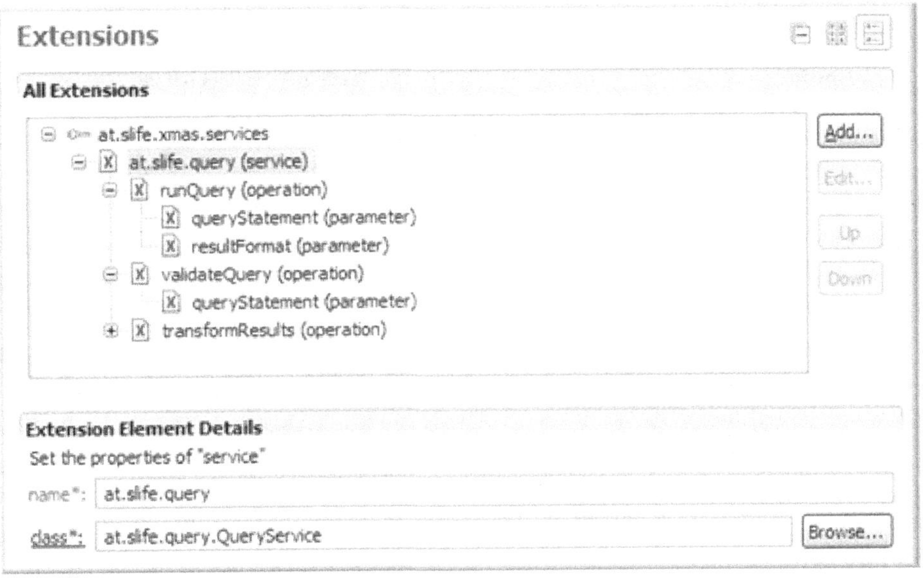

Figure 10. The declaration of the VQS components plug-in

The XML Parser

A XML parser is an essential part in our approach and development. Our VQL queries, VQL query templates, query pipelines, and traces are coded in XML-format. With the enhanced features, we choose DOM4J[12] as our XML parser in the VQS development.

The VQS Plug-ins

The VQS implementation has been developed with three plug-ins: the core query execution unit, the VQS components, and the VQS query GUI plug-ins.

Query Execution Plug-In

This plug-in is the lowest component in the VQS architecture as it works directly with the back-

Figure 11. The declaration of the query interface plug-in

end database. The query execution unit contains internal service extensions such as the query execution, the query results transformation (e.g., transforming the query results to the specific format such as XML, JSON, RDF graphs, or formatted text), and an aggregated query invocation that consists of the query execution and results transformations. The declaration of this plug-in into the SemanticLIFE master service is shown in the Figure 9.

VQS Components Plug-In

This plug-in is the main implementation of our query system which contains the main features of the VQS. The services are mostly for internal use of the VQS querying process; however, some service extensions are offered to other external uses such as getting the "virtual" information, retrieving the VQS-UC, executing VQL queries, and getting the VQL-QT(s). The declaration of the VQS components plug-in into the SemanticLIFE framework is shown in Figure 10.

VQS User Interface Plug-In

This plug-in is the top layer in the VQS architecture as it works interactively with the SemanticLIFE's users. The query interface plug-in consists of functional windows (views) built on Eclipse RCP ViewParts and SWT widgets. These components are then organized in a separate Eclipse perspective associated with the main SemanticLIFE perspective. The declaration of the query interface plug-in into the "backbone" of the SemanticLIFE framework is shown in the Figure 11.

With the above declarations, each plug-in needs an interface to "plug" (register) into the SemanticLIFE plug-in infrastructure so that when the main application runs, all registered plug-ins will automatically be loaded.

The Virtual Data Component

As mentioned in the previous section, the VDC contains the virtual information stored in a context ontology. The context ontology can be customized by the usage of the system and the user. For

Figure 12. Project management context ontology diagram

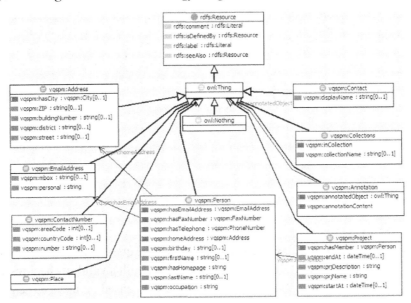

Figure 13. The graphical user interface of the virtual data component

example, the system could have been used in use case of personal project management system; therefore the VDC's context ontology would reflect the scenario as depicted in Figure 12.

The VDC interface displays the virtual information aggregated from the data of SemanticLIFE metastore with reference to the context ontology and the system ontology. Figure 13 is a screenshot of the VQS interface containing the VDC component.

In the Figure 13, the VDC component is reflected in two views: the first one is the left-upper

Figure 14. UML sequence diagram of the VQS context-based query

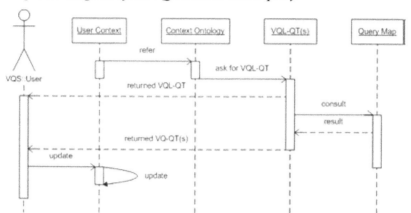

views which contain the context ontology, and the second one is the middle view with tab entitled "Query Home." This view shows the virtual information extracted from the SemanticLIFE metastore in the form of the summary information of the personal data. In this "home" window, there are two tabs for presenting the virtual information: the basic and advanced level. The basic view is just for basic information of the user's personal data and the advanced view presents additional information such as time-based statistical information, last ten items stored, and last ten queries executed.

Other modules of the VQS are also depicted in Figure 13. The VQL-QT(s) is listed in the right-upper view, and the traces are kept in the right-lower window. The middle-lower part is used for results presentation. Finally, the query pipelines are shown in the left-lower view of the main interface window.

THE CONTEXT-AWARE QUERYING FEATURE

VQL Query Templates

As the VQL-QTs are coded in XML that means any party could create and edit the VQL-QTs outside the system. This could lead to syntactical errors

during the query template processing. Therefore, we have built a validity checking mechanism for VQL-QTs based on its XSD schema.

There are two cases of performing this check. First, when the VQS system starts, all VQL-QTs are checked for their validity. Second, this checking procedure will be called upon and a VQL-QT is loaded for using.

The Context-Based Querying

Figure 14 shows the sequence diagram of the VQS context-based querying feature. We make it clear that this feature would be initialized after the first query is successfully executed. First, based on the VQS-UC the necessary resources for the next query are obtained with respect to the context ontology; VQS then retrieves the VQL-QT repository to get the appropriate VQL-QT upon the resources.

The VQL-QT is then returned to the user for editing. Continuously, a procedure of the VQS would consult to the current query map and recommend the relevant VQL-QT(s) to the user.

After execution of the VQL query from the selected VQL-QT, the system will update the VQS-UC for the next round of the querying process. This process will reflect in the change of the VQL-QT view in the VQS GUI main window. The updated

VQL-QT view contains only the VQL-QT(s) for the current VQS-UC. Nevertheless, there is an option to see all VQL-QTs at this time.

During the querying process, the user could temporarily save the queries in the form of "traces" shown in the "Traces" window in the main GUI screen. In addition, the user can save the traces into permanent query pipelines for later use because the traces will be removed for the next start of the system. The user could also add, change, or delete the inappropriate VQL-QT(s) to improve the user's query effectiveness.

THE SUMMARIZED EXAMPLE

After having introduced the VQS approach for the ontology-enhanced querying of SemanticLIFE, we want to illustrate in this article by means of an application scenario how our approach could be practically applied and what benefits it offers. This section is a summary of the examples segmented into the previous sections.

Personalized Project Management

A scientist works for several projects at the same time with different roles. Everyday the scientist has a lot of work to do such as reading and sending a lot of e-mails to projects' members, making many phone calls, processing digital documents, browsing the Web sites for tasks, reading the paper/articles, and coding at times. Generally, the scientist often makes annotation on what the scientist has done.

The scientist wants the SemanticLIFE system to organize the scientist's large repository in a semantic way in order to retrieve effectively. Searching information in a "mountain" of data of working projects is a challenging task for the scientist. The scientist would like to have the support through the SemanticLIFE's query mechanism, the VQS, to simplify the task of information retrieval.

VQS Contextualization

First, the SemanticLIFE will deal with the issues related to storing data semantically with the user's annotation. A range of covered data could be e-mail messages, contacts (persons), calendar for storing appointments, tasks for keeping projects' tasks and progresses, digital documents, call logs, IM logs, Web browsing sessions, and external publication databases. All these data are kept in the SemanticLIFE metastore with underline ontologies.

Second, the main focus of the example is about the information retrieval in the context of the SemanicLIFE's VQS. This task is divided into two subparts. First, the query formulation should be simple to the user so that the user could have the supportive feeling during the user's information retrieval sessions. The second point is the capabilities of the VQS in returning the aggregated, exact results has the user's interest as well as associated information that may be helpful for the user. It means the VQL-QTs are oriented to the subject of scenario, and the query results must be based on the context ontology for suggesting the information as relevant as possible.

CONCLUSION AND FUTURE WORK

Starting from the idea of users' awareness about their stored data which could help in asking for information, our front-approach—the virtual query system for the SemanticLIFE framework—offers many features based on the well-organization of the collected metadata from the SemanticLIFE metastore. These metadata are organized as the *virtual information* and stored in an ontology, that is, the *context ontology*.

With VQS, the SemanticLIFE's user is not only supported in the query formulation at the initial phase of querying process, but also in getting help from the VQS during the process. Based on the user context of querying and the

VQS's context ontology, the VQS analyzes the user's query space—known as VQS query map—for the new knowledge, and tries to match with the predefined query patterns—known as VQL query templates—and then recommends the most appropriate query patterns to the user. We have considered this feature as an innovative approach to support users in complex query formulation.

As the next steps, we plan to focus on user modeling research for applying them into the VQS's approach to improve the personal aspect of the SemanticLIFE's aims. This would enable the VQS to work towards a more user-oriented future.

ACKNOWLEDGMENT

This work has been generously supported by ASEA-UNINET.

REFERENCES

Ahmed, M., Hoang, H. H., Karim, S., Khusro, S., Lanzenberger, M., Latif, K., et al. (2004). *'SemanticLIFE' - a framework for managing information of a human lifetime.* Paper presented at the 6th International Conference on Information Integration and Web-based Applications and Services. Jarkarta: OCG Books.

Athanasis, N., Christophides, V., & Kotzinos, D. (2004). Generating on the fly queries for the Semantic Web: The ICS-FORTH graphical RQL interface (GRQL). In S. A. McIlraith, D. Plexousakis, & F. van Harmelen (Eds.), *International Semantic Web Conference* (LNCS 3298, pp. 486-501). Springer.

Bush, V. (July 1945). As we may think. *The Atlantic, 176*(1), 101-108.

Catarci, T., Di Mascio, T., Franconi, E., Santucci, G., & Tessaris, S. (2003). An ontology based visual tool for query formulation support. In R. Meersman, & Z. Tari (Eds.), *OTM Workshops* (LNCS 2889, pp. 32-43). Springer.

Decker, S., Erdmann, M., Fensel, D., & Studer, R. (1998). *Ontobroker: Ontology based access to distributed and semi-structured information.* Paper presented at the The IFIP TC2/WG 2.6 Eighth Working Conference on Database Semantics-Semantic Issues in Multimedia Systems (pp. 351-369). Deventer, The Netherlands: Kluwer.

Dolog, P., Henze, N., Nejdl, W., & Sintek, M. (2003). *Towards the adaptive Semantic Web.* Paper presented at the International Workshop on Principles and Practice of Semantic Web Reasoning (LNCS 2901, pp. 51-68). Springer.

Guha, R., & McCool, R. (2003). TAP: A Semantic Web platform. *International Journal on Computer and Telecommunications Networking, 42*(5), 557-577.

Heflin, J., & Hendler, J. (2000). *Searching the Web with SHOE.* Paper presented at the AAAI Workshop (pp. 35-40). AAAI Press.

Hoang, H. H., & Tjoa, A. M. (2006a). *The state of the art of ontology-based query systems: A comparison of current approaches.* Paper presented at the IEEE International Conference on Computing and Informatics.

Hoang, H. H., Andjomshoaa, A., & Tjoa, A. M. (2006). *VQS: An ontology-based query system for the SemanticLIFE digital memory project.* Paper presented at the 2th IFIF WG 2.14 & 4.12 International Workshop on Web Semantics - OTM06 (LNCS 4278, pp. 1796-1805). Montpellier: Springer.

Hoang, H. H., & Tjoa, A. M. (2006b). *The virtual query language for information retrieval in the SemanticLIFE framework.* Paper presented at the International Workshop on Web Information Systems Modeling - CAiSE06 (pp. 1062-1076). Luxembourg.

Hübner, S., Spittel, R., Visser, U., & Vögele, T. J. (2004). Ontology-based search for interactive digital maps. *IEEE Intelligent Systems, 19*(3), 80-86.

Huynh, D., Karger, D., & Quan, D. (2002). *Haystack: A platform for creating, organizing and visualizing information using RDF.* Paper presented at the International Workshop on the Semantic Web.

Hyvönen, E., Saarela, S., & Viljanen, K. (2003). *Ontogator: Combining view- and ontology-based search with Semantic browsing.* Paper presented at the XML Finland Conference: Open Standards, XML and the Public Sector.

Karger, D. R., Bakshi, K., Huynh, D., Quan, D., & Vineet, S. (2005). *Haystack: A general purpose information management tool for end users of semistructured data.* Paper presented at the 2nd Biennial Conference on Innovative Data Systems Research (pp. 13-26).

Karvounarakis, G., Alexaki, S., Christophides, V., Plexousakis, D., & Scholl, M. (2002). *RQL: A declarative query language for RDF.* Paper presented at the Eleventh International World Wide Web Conference (pp. 591-603). ACM Press.

Kerschberg, L., Chowdhury, M., Damiano, A., Jeong, H., Mitchell, S., Si, J., et al. (2004). *Knowledge sifter: Ontology-driven search over heterogeneous databases.* Paper presented at the 16th International Conference on Scientific and Statistical Database Management.

Maedche, A., Motik, B., Silva, N., & Volz, R. (2002). *MAFRA: An ontology mapping framework in the Semantic Web.* Paper presented at the 12th International Workshop on Knowledge Transformation.

Maedche, A., Staab, S., Stojanovic, N., Studer, R., & Sure, Y. (2001). *SEAL: A framework for developing Semantic Web portals.* Paper presented at the 18th British National Conference on Databases (pp. 1-22). London: Springer.

Quan, D., Huynh, D., & Karger, D. R. (2003). *Haystack: A platform for authoring end user Semantic Web applications.* Paper presented at the 12th International World Wide Web Conference (pp. 738-753).

Teevan, J., Alvarado, C., Ackerman, M. S., & Karger, D. R. (2004). *The perfect search engine is not enough: A study of orienteering behavior in directed search.* Paper presented at the SIGCHI Conference on Human Factors in Computing Systems (pp. 415-422). New York: ACM Press.

ENDNOTES

[1] TAP Infrastructure, http://tap.stanford.edu/

[2] JAX Innovation Award 2006 Proposal, http://www.jax-award.com/

[3] Google Desktop, http://desktop.google.com/

[4] Resource Description Framework, http://www.w3.org/RDF/

[5] eXtensible Markup Language, http://www.w3.org/XML/

[6] Google, http://www.google.com/

[7] http://jena.sourceforge.net/

[8] http://www.hpl.hp.com/semweb/

[9] http://lucene.apache.org/

[10] http://mafra-toolkit.sourceforge.net/

[11] http://ws.apache.org/

[12] http://dom4j.org/

This work was previously published in International Journal of Information Technology and Web Engineering, Vol. 3, Issue 1, edited by G. Alkhatib and D. Rine, pp. 1-23, copyright 2008 by IGI Publishing (an imprint of IGI Global).

Chapter 2
The Impact of Ontology on the Performance of Information Retrieval:
A Case of WordNet

Maria Indrawan
Monash University, Australia

Seng Loke
La Trobe University, Australia

ABSTRACT

The debate on the effectiveness of ontology in solving semantic problems has increased recently in many domains of information technology. One side of the debate accepts the inclusion of ontology as a suitable solution. The other side of the debate argues that ontology is far from an ideal solution to the semantic problem. This article explores this debate in the area of information retrieval. Several past approaches were explored and a new approach was investigated to test the effectiveness of a generic ontology such as WordNet in improving the performance of information retrieval systems. The test and the analysis of the experiments suggest that WordNet is far from the ideal solution in solving semantic problems in the information retrieval. However, several observations have been made and reported in this article that allow research in ontology for the information retrieval to move towards the right direction.

INTRODUCTION

Semantic understanding is crucial to the success of many information technology applications. Much information technology research is still battling to solve the problem of semantic understanding for their research domain. Ontology adoption is currently the most popular approach taken by many researchers. The proliferation in the use of ontology to support semantic analysis has been found in many domains of information technology such as context awareness (Rack, Arbanowski, & Steglich, 2000; Yan & Li, 2006), service oriented computing (Bramantoro, Krishnaswamy, & Indrawan, 2005; Jingshan, Hunhns, 2006), and Semantic Web (Caliusco, Galli, & Chiotti,

2005; Dou, LePendu, Kim, & Qi, 2006). Some of the researchers adopt a specific built ontology whereas others investigate the use of a general purpose ontology, such as WordNet.

WordNet is an English lexical referencing system built in the early 1990s at Princeton University. Since its introduction, many researchers have used this lexical system for different purposes, such as multimedia retrieval (Benitez, Chang, & Smith; 2001), text summarization (Hachey & Grover, 2004), and automatic creation of domain-based ontology (Chen, Alahakoon, & Indrawan, 2005; Khan & Luo, 2002). In information retrieval research, the impact of WordNet has been investigated by a number of researchers. WordNet has been used to improve the performance of information retrieval systems by way of query expansion (Voorhees, 1993), semantic distance measure (Richrdson & Smeaton, 1995), and semantic indexing (Wang & Brookes, 2004) to name a few. The results showed by these studied are varied. Voorhees (1993) and Richrardson and Smeaton (1995) report that the recall and precision of the retrieval decreased with the inclusion of WordNet. Wang and Brookes (2004), on the other hand, report the opposite. We were encouraged by Wang and Brookes' report and decided to investigate further since we perceived a further improvement can be applied to their model. In addition, we also would like to explore the debate over the impact of WordNet in information retrieval researches. At the end of the investigation we would like to enrich the debate by reporting our experience and observations during the investigation. In order to achieve this, we organize this article as follows. In the next section, the article presents a short description of WordNet for those readers unfamiliar with this lexical system. In the third section, we lay out the current debate on the impact of WordNet in information retrieval. We introduce our improvement to Wang and Brookes' model in the forth section. The following section presents the experiment design and results. We conclude our discussion in the last section.

WordNet

The main construct of WordNet as a lexical system is the synonym set or synset. The synsets are divided into four major speech categories of noun, verb, adjective, and adverb. Within each of these categories, several semantic relations between synsets are defined. Included in the noun category are the *hypernym, hyponym, meronym,* and *holonym.*

Definition 1: *Semantic Relations of Synsets*

- Let assume synsets $S=\{s_i, s_j, ..., s_n\}$ and $L=\{l_i, l_j, ..., l_n\}$ exist in the WordNet.
- *Hypernym:* S is considered to be hypernym of L, if every L is a (kind-of) S.
- *Hyponym:* S is considered to be a hyponym of L, if every S is a (kind-of) L.
- *Meronym:* S is considered to be a meronym of L, if every S is a part-of L.
- *Holonym:* S is considered to be a holonym of L, if every L is a part-of S.
  □

In an example of taxonomy of synsets depicted in Figure 1, a *canine* is considered to be a hyponym of *carnivore* and a hypernym of *dog.*

Figure 1. A hypernym/hyponym relations

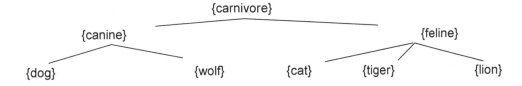

Figure 2. Holonym/meronym relations

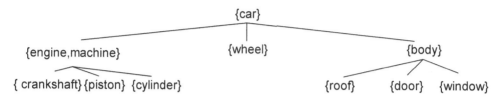

Figure 2 shows that an *engine* is a meronym of a *car* and a holonym of a *piston*. The hypernym/hyponym relations are often referred as *hyponomic* relations. The meronym/holonym relations are referred as *part-whole* relations.

WORDNET FOR INFORMATION RETRIEVAL SYSTEMS

WordNet has been used in several capacities to improve the performance of information retrieval systems. In this section, we explore the research problems in information retrieval and a WordNet-based model that was proposed to solve the problems. First, we present problems associated with information retrieval systems and possible techniques that may solve the problems. Subsequently, we present how the possible techniques can be developed using WordNet.

Information Retrieval Systems Limitations

Information retrieval systems are built to help users find the documents that are relevant to their information need. The information need is represented by queries posed to the system. There are a number of drawbacks inherent in the information retrieval systems. In this section, we present some of these problems and review the role of ontology in resolving these problems.

In most information retrieval systems, the queries are represented as a list of keywords. Some systems may allow users to submit a natural language query; however, in most cases, the natural language query is then processed through an indexing process resulting in a set of indexed terms. Using keywords or indexed terms for the retrieval limits the set of retrieved documents to those with the matching terms. It showed the drawback of the approach because it is possible that a document that does not contain any matching term to the query to be relevant. It is possible that the document uses synonyms of the indexed term. To avoid this problem, information retrieval researches suggest adding similar terms such as synonyms or other terms that are relevant to the document, such as hypernyms. This method is called query expansion.

Performance of information retrieval is usually measured by the precision or accuracy and recall or coverage. The recall may be improved by the query expansion as suggested earlier. To improve the precision, information retrieval needs to deduce the context of the terms used in the query since it is possible that one word has many meaning depending on the context. For example, the word *window* can mean an architectural part of a building or a name of an operating system. Without knowing the precise *sense* of the term *window* in the query, the systems will retrieve both sets of documents on *buildings* and *operating systems* while the users usually want only one set. This drawback leads to poor precision. To solve this problem, *sense disambiguation* can be employed.

Information retrieval task can be considered as finding documents that have the shortest *semantic distance* to the query. A number of distance measures have been developed, such as *cosine similarity* in vector space model. In this model, the matching of the terms in the documents and query is calculated based on finding the matching terms and the frequency analysis of the importance of the terms in discriminating the documents (*tf*idf weighting*). It can be perceived that the semantics of the terms is given mainly by its frequency analysis rather than *linguistic* analysis. There are a number of *semantic distance* measurements that have been developed in the natural language researches (Budanitsky, 1999). It is possible that adopting the semantic distance that is based on linguistic instead of frequency analysis may lead to a better search because it may partially solve the two previous drawbacks.

Most information retrieval systems base there operation on word- or term-level matching. There are attempts in using phrases with aim to improve precision. Similar to word matching, phrases matching can be improved by query expansion and sense disambiguation.

Having presented the problem inherent in the information retrieval systems, the next sections present the discussion on the ontological approaches that have been investigated in order to eliminate the problems.

Query Expansion

Voorhees (1994) suggests that WordNet can be used in information retrieval for query expansion. Query expansion is considered to be one of the techniques that can be used to improve the retrieval performance of short queries. Most of the indexing and retrieval methods are based on statistical methods; short queries posed challenges to this model due to the limited amount of information that can be gathered during its processing.

In expanding the query, Voorhees suggests the used of synonyms, hypernyms, hyponyms, and their combinations. The results showed that the used of synonyms, hypernyms, and hyponyms are significant in the retrieval performance for short queries, but little improvement when they are applied to the long query.

A more comprehensive study was conducted by Smeaton and Berrut (1995). They incorporated both the word sense disambiguation and query expansion into the information retrieval. However, they reported a decrease of performance instead of improvement.

The shortcoming of WordNet in supporting query expansion is also reported by Mandala, Tokunaga, and Tanaka (1999, 1998). To overcome the limitation, additional thesauri are added to complement WordNet. The results showed that the combined thesauri produced much higher recall and precision in comparison to using WordNet alone. This observation is supported by Hsu, Tsai, and Chen (2006). Their findings suggest that WordNet can improve the performance of the retrieval if the specific terms that represent the topic are found in WordNet. They called these terms as kernel words.

The impact of WordNet in query expansion shows more prominent results in the phrase-based retrieval as reported by Liu, Liu, Yu, and Meng (2004). The works previously discussed in this section base their retrieval on term or word-level. In the word-level retrieval, the query expansion based solely on WordNet does not give substantial improvement in the precision and recall.

Word Senses Disambiguation

A word may have a number of different meanings depending on its context. For example the word *arms* could mean *limbs* or *weaponry*. In WordNet, the word context is called *sense*. In most information retrieval systems, the *sense* of the words or terms is ignored during the retrieval. Researchers adopted this approach with the premise that ignoring the senses may broaden the search results which in turn will improve the recall. The increase of the recall in some cases may lead to the decrease in precision. In view to disambiguate senses for information retrieval, Voorhees (1993) proposed the use of WordNet. The proposed model used the *hyponomic* relations to determine the sense of an indexed word. Each of the indexed word were assigned a weight (*tf**idf weight) and a sense type. During the retrieval, an indexed document term and a query term were considered similar only if they belonged to the same sense type. Hence, two terms that were usually considered to be similar in many retrieval systems may be considered to be different in this model. In other words, Voorhees's model may return relevant documents higher in the raking, that is, better precision, compared to the system without sense disambiguation. However, at the same time, it may not necessarily find all the relevant documents because the similarity matching is done with one extra condition, which is the sense type.

Indeed, their results showed that the simple stem-based retrieval without any sense disambiguation performed better than sense-based retrieval, in particular for short queries. The observations showed that short queries have very limited context information and can lead to an incorrect sense resolution. They observed that making incorrect sense resolution created deleterious affect on performance compared to making spurious matches. Hence the cost of improving the precision is not justified by the amount of degradation in the recall.

Moldovan and Milhacea (2000) propose a combination of query expansion and sense disambiguation for the Internet search. They report positive findings. However, it is difficult to directly compare their results to those of Voorhees (1994) due to the different nature of the query and data used in the experiments. Moldovan and Milhacea's sample queries are of the question and answer (Q&A) nature where users expect a specific answer. Hence the nature of *relevance* in their experiment would be different from the typical information retrieval systems. In an information retrieval system that is not Q&A, the relevance is perceived as something very broad rather than specific.

Semantic Distance

Richardson and Smeaton (1995) propose the use of *word semantic distance* in measuring similarity between documents and queries. As previously stated, most of the indexing techniques adopted by the information retrieval systems are based on the frequency analysis of the word occurrence in the document and collection. Hence, the distance between two terms are measured based on this frequency analysis rather than their actual semantic analysis. Unlike traditional systems, Richardson and Smeaton's system base the similarity measure on the word's semantic distance. To do this, they created the system as a controlled vocabulary system. WordNet was used a knowledge based containing the controlled vocabulary. Their experiments showed that the performance of their model was worst than the traditional systems based on the frequency analysis.

Semantic Indexing

In this section, we present another approach of using WordNet to improve the performance of information retrieval systems. It is similar in principle to word sense disambiguation. It attempts to infer the relations among indexed words in a query or a document. However, instead of using the sense type to represent context, it uses the weights of the indexed terms to represent the context. All terms that are related in a context are given higher weights. For example the words *plant, leaves, root, fruit*, and *flower* are related terms for a concept *flora* and are part of a lexical taxonomy. Therefore they should be given higher weights in comparison to other nonrelated words in the document. In other words, an inference is made that the document discussed the concept of *flora*.

In this model, the authors assume that the semantic content of a document would be adequately represented by the closely related terms according to a given lexical taxonomy. There could be other words that occur many times in the document, hence they may have scored high in a frequency analysis (*tf*idf* weights), however, they should not be considered to be semantically important because they lack support from other words of similar concept.

Unlike the sense disambiguation approach, the semantic weighting approach does not restrict the notion of similarity between a query and a document term to only those with similar senses. For this reason, the problem of over-fitting the model towards precision will not occur. Based on this idea Wang and Brookes (2004) propose a novel approach to semantic indexing by using WordNet to infer semantics between terms in the document. The results of the semantics inference are used to modify the term weights which were normally calculated solely based on *tf*idf*. They provide a hypothesis that words that semantically close in distance most likely represent the meaning of the document. For example, the words *car, engine, wheel,* and *brakes* may occur in a document and they are semantically close according to WordNet, then it can be assumed based on the occurrence of these words that the document contains the discussion on *automobile* or *car*. Distinct to the previous attempts in semantic indexing, such as latent semantic indexing (LSI) (Deerwester, Dumain, Furnas, Landauer, & Harshman, 1990), the semantic weight approach does not suffer from high computational expenses. Research in LSI shows that the model can improve the performance of the retrieval, but computationally, it is very expensive.

In a semantic weights model, the weights of the words or terms in a document is derived using the combination of two matrices: the document-term matrix (*W*) and the term-term matrix (*T*).

The document-term matrix (*W*) represents the *tf*idf* weight of a term in a given document. In a formal way, the document-term matrix can be represented as followed:

Definition 2. Document-Term Matrix (W): *Let i be a term in a document j, m be the total number of documents in the corpus, and n to be the total number of known term in the corpus.*

$$W = (w_{ij})_{mxn},$$

where, w_{ij} represent the tf*idf weight of the term i in document j.

Definition 3. Term-Term Matrix (T): *Let P be a set of known terms in the WordNet's hyponomic relations, $P = \{p_a, p_b, ..., p_z\}$.*
Let Q to be a set of known terms in the corpus, $Q = \{q_k, q_l, ..., q_n\}$.
Let X to be a taxonomy tree that has nodes made of synsets S_x.

$$T = (r_{qkql}) \text{ where}$$

$$r_{xy} = \begin{cases} 1 \ if \ k = l \\ 1 \ if \ \exists q_k, q_l \ in \ X. \\ 0 \ otherwise \end{cases}$$

According to the definition of the term-term matrix, the first condition determines the values of the diagonal elements in the matrix. The values of the diagonal elements are always 1 because the distance for a term from itself is always 1 regardless whether the terms exist in WordNet. Included in the second condition is a weaker condition, q_k, $q_l \in S_x$, that is, the two terms are synonyms.

Definition 4. Final-Weight Matrix: *The final weights of all the terms in all documents in the collection are given by the product of the matrix W and T.*

$$Z = W \times T$$

Wang and Brookes reported that the retrieval performance in the ADI and TIME collection is improved. Intuitively, we consider that assigning a binary value to represent an association between terms may not be optimal. Hence, we investigate the possibility of assigning an exact distance measure between terms to the element in the term-term matrix. In the forth section, we present two different possible semantic distance measures that can be adopted to improve Wang and Brookes' model.

Debate on the Role of WordNet in Information Retrieval

The impact of WordNet in improving the performance of information retrieval found to be inconsistent in the reviewed works. Table 1 shows that most of the research on query expansion and sense disambiguation in the word-level retrieval does not improve the performance, and if any, it is not significant (Mandala et Al., 1998; Richardson & Smeaton, 1995; Smeaton & Berrut, 1995; Voorhees, 1993, 1994). Improvement is achieved by either adding additional thesauri, such is that of Mandala et al. (1999), or using phrase-based retrieval (Liu et al., 2004).

The type of ontology employed may influence the performance of the retrieval. Hsu et al. (2006) compared the use of WordNet and ConceptNet (ConceptNet, n.d) and concluded that WordNet is more appropriate in finding a kernel word, that is, a specific term that is highly relevant to the topic, whereas ConceptNet is useful in finding more general words for expansion. They suggested that both ontologies will complement each other when used for retrieval. However, they never directly measured the retrieval performance; hence it is still debatable whether it will be the case since some authors have suggested that one of the main reasons that WordNet does not improve the performance is due to its lack of domain-specific terms (Mandala et al., 1998).

In supporting the linguistic analysis, research that uses WordNet as ontology has shown mixed results. Richardson and Smeaton (1995) show little

improvement, while Wang and Brookes (2004) report significant improvement. We hypothesize that further improvement can be made to Wang and Brookes' model by measuring the exact semantic distance measure between terms in the term-term matrix instead of only assigning the values of 1 or 0. We present our model and discussion on the experimental results in the forth section.

USING SEMANTIC DISTANCE MEASURE IN THE TERM-TERM MATRIX

Measuring semantic relatedness or distance between words of a natural language has played an important role in many natural processing tasks such as word sense disambiguation, text summarization, speech recognition, and so forth. The most natural way of measuring the similarity of two concepts in taxonomy, given its graphical representation, is to calculate the path distance between the two compared nodes. WordNet is a lexical system with clear taxonomy; hence the path length calculation can be adapted to measure the semantic distance between two words.

There are many semantic distance measures (Budanitsky, 1999) and in this research as initial investigation, we choose two distance measures: the edge counting method and the Leacock-Chodorow (LCH) method. The edge counting is considered to be a straightforward distance measures whereas LCH is more sophisticated because it considers the depth of the tree when calculating the distance between two words. We would like to investigate whether the increase of sophistication in the level of measurement will influence the retrieval performance. Next, these two measures will be discussed in detail.

Edge Counting

The edge counting method (Budanitsky, 1999) assumed that the number of edges between terms in taxonomy is a measure of conceptual distance

Table 1. Information retrieval systems with WordNet

Researchers	Techniques	Ontology	Results
Voorhees (1993)	Sense disambiguation	WordNet	• Improve in precision for short query. • Degradation of recall.
Voorhees (1994)	Query expansion	WordNet	• Improve the performance of short query, but not for long query.
Smeaton and Berrut (1995)	Query expansion	WordNet	• Decreased in performance.
Richardson and Smeaton (1995)	Linguistic analysis	WordNet	• Little improvement for extra effort of creating the knowledge base.
Mandala et al. (1998)	Query expansion	WordNet + automatically constructed thesauri.	• Little improvement when only WordNet is used. • Up to 98.2% improvement when WordNet is used in conjunction with other automatic generated thesauri.
Mandala et al. (1999)	Query expansion and sense disambiguation	WordNet and Roget's thesaurus	• Little improvement is achieved when either the WordNet or Roget's thesaurus is used in isolation. • Big improvement is achieved when two of the thesauri are used.
Moldovan and Mihalcea (2000)	Query expansion and sense disambiguation	WordNet	• The experiments were not conducted in the traditional test bed. • Q&A system. • Positive findings.
Liu et al. (2004)	Query expansion and sense disambiguation	WordNet	• The retrieval is based on phrases rather than word. • Improve the precision.
Wang and Brookes (2004)	Linguistic analysis	WordNet	• Improve the precision and recall.
Hsu et al. (2006)	Query expansion	WordNet and ConceptNet	• WordNet is useful in finding kernel words. • ConceptNet is useful in finding cooperative concepts words.

between terms. Following from Definition 3, p_a and p_b are two terms in the WordNet taxonomy. Let n_{edge} be the total number of edges between p_a and p_b.

The related distance of these terms is represented as:

$$dist_{edge}(p_a, p_b) = \min(n_{edge}) \qquad (1)$$

This method is simple to calculate; however, it has a problem because it does not consider the depth of the tree hence it will be sensitive to the granularity of the concept representation in the taxonomy.

Leacock-Chodorow

The Leacock-Chodorow method (Budanitsky, 1999) includes the tree depth into the calculation to remove the sensitivity to the granularity of the concept representation. The related distance of two terms p_a and p_b is measured by:

$$dist_{LCH}(p_a, p_b) = -\log\left(\frac{dist_{edge}(p_a, p_b) + 1}{2xD}\right) \qquad (2)$$

In the calculation of the minimum path, this method uses the number of nodes instead of edges. This is to avoid singularities, so that synonyms are 1 unit of distance apart. The number of nodes in graph theory can be calculated as the total number of edges plus one, and hence taking Equation 1 as a base, the distance measured can be formulated as Equation 2. The D represents the maximum depth of the taxonomy.

Table 2. Experiments settings

	Exact Term Run	**Substring Term Run**
Collection	ADI[1]	ADI [1]
No of documents	82	82
No of queries	35	35
Stop List	SMART stop list	SMART stop list
Stemming	Porter's stemming in SMART.	No stemming
Ontology	WordNet 1.7	WordNet 1.7
Retrieval Model	Cosine similarity in SMART.	Cosine similarity in SMART
Weights		
Traditional	Augmented *tf*idf* in SMART	Augmented *tf*idf* in SMART
Wang and Brookes	As the definition in this article.	As the definition in this article.
Edge counting	As the definition in this article.	As the definition in this article.
LCH	As the definition in this article.	As the definition in this article.

Term-Term Matrix with Semantic Distance

Based on Definition 3, Equation 1, and Equation 2, the new term-term matrix T for the edge counting and LCH methods can be represented as:

$$T_{edge} = (r_{qkql})_{nxn}$$

where

$$r_{xy} = \begin{cases} 1 \; if \; k = l \\ dist_{edge} \; if \; \exists q_k, q_l \; in \; X \\ 0 \; otherwise \end{cases} \quad (3)$$

$$T_{LCH} = (r_{qkql})_{nxn}$$

where

$$r_{xy} = \begin{cases} 1 \; if \; k = l \\ dist_{LCH} \; if \; \exists q_k, q_l \; in \; X \\ 0 \; otherwise \end{cases} \quad (4)$$

In this approach, instead of assigning value of 1 to two related terms, the exact distance measure between the two terms is calculated and is used to populate the term-term matrix.

EXPERIMENTS AND RESULTS

We tested the performance of four different term weights: the traditional *tf*idf*, the Wang and Brookes', the edge counting, and the LCH. The SMART retrieval system was used to tokenize and identify the indexed words. The stop list and stemming were applied to all cases of term weights. In calculating the semantic distance, the WordNet 1.7 was used. We used the vector space retrieval model with cosine similarity for the retrieval. The WordNet is used to measure the semantic distances of the indexed terms in the corpus. We used the hyponomic relations of the noun speech in WordNet. The test is conducted in the ADI collection. Table 2 shows the setup of the two runs across 35 queries in ADI collection.

One issue that we encountered in using the WordNet to calculate the distance measure is the treatment of the stemmed word. We used SMART's stemming module which is based on Porter's stemming algorithm, hence the result of stemming is not necessarily a proper English word. In this case, it is possible that two words are not associated because the system could not find the matching string that represents the stemmed word in WordNet taxonomy, although the proper

Figure 3. Exact term matching results

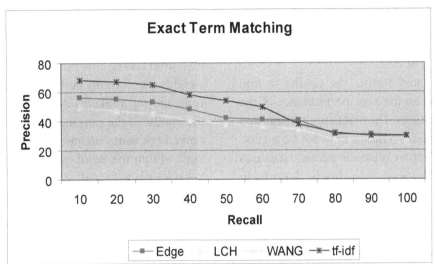

Figure 4. Substring term matching results

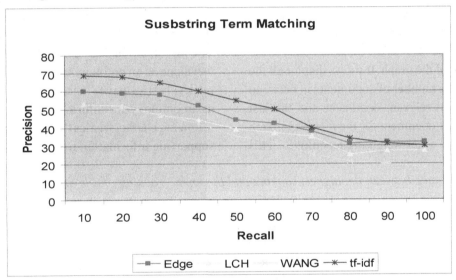

word may actually exist in the taxonomy. We try to reduce the impact of the stemming by using the substring matching instead of the full-word matching in the WordNet. Using this approach we managed to reduce the number of false non-matching cases. Figure 3 and Figure 4 show the results of the experiments.

It is interesting to observe that the nonsemantic weight, *tf*idf* weighting, outperforms all the semantic indexing techniques, including the Wang and Brookes' technique. To the best of our knowledge we have followed exactly the model described in their work (Wang & Brookes, 2004); however, we never managed to get the same results during the experiments. In order to make the comparison objective, we use our implementation of the Wang and Brooke's results in our discussion. We made sure that all the parameters such as stemming algorithm, stop list, and *tf*idf* weights for the document-term matrix were kept the same.

The results were not as anticipated. We expected that the semantic weightings would perform better than the traditional *tf*idf* weighting.

Moreover, we also expected that the LCH would outperform the edge counting technique due to its normalization on the tree depth. The results depicted in both Figure 3 and 4 place the *tf*idf* approach to be the best.

We investigated further the results to find the explanation on the poor performance of the semantic weightings. The first thought suggested that the semantic weighting may not be a good technique to improve precision because it causes the relevant documents to be closely clustered in the ranking. To observe this possibility, we calculate the distance between the position of the first relevant document and the last relevant document in the ranking. This data can show the spread of relevant documents in the ranked output. Figure 5 shows the distance of the relevant documents for a sample of 12 queries in the ADI collection.

The graph shows that the Wang and the edge models have the value of the distance closer to the central point of the graph. It shows that for all the 12 queries, the number of documents in between the first found relevant document and the last found relevant document for the *tf*idf* approach is greater than other weighting techniques. This

observation shows that the semantic weighting creates a closer cluster of relevant documents compared to the output of the *tf*idf*. The cluster is created around the middle of the ranking. From this observation, it is possible that the semantic weights may actually pull the relevant documents from the top ranked into a lower rank around the middle of the ranking and pull out the lower ranked relevant documents towards the middle ranks. From the point of view of retrieval, this behaviour is not ideal.

CONCLUSION

The impact of ontologies, such as WordNet, on the performance of information retrieval has been investigated and possible improvement to the semantic indexing model has been proposed. The investigation suggests that the use of Word-Net alone as an ontology to improve information retrieval performance is not appropriate. WordNet as an ontology for information retrieval has the following characteristics that may not be ideal for supporting information retrieval tasks:

Figure 5. Distance between the highest ranking and the lowest ranking of relevant documents

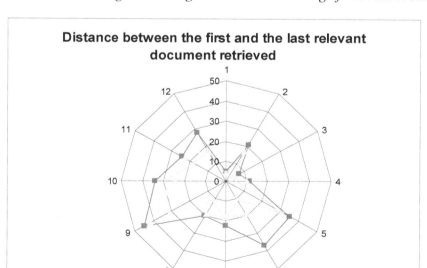

- WordNet contains mainly general English terms. Domain-specific terms or proper names are not represented. Hence many of the retrievals that contain domain-specific terms or proper names will not improve.
- Relations between terms are limited to a single speech. It is not possible to find relation of an adjective and a noun in WordNet. Hence, in the semantic indexing, it is not possible to derive the relation between the color "green" with the concept of "forest" for example.

The first problem stated above is exacerbated by the fact that ADI collection is a small and confined collection. There are many specific computing terms that cannot be found in WordNet. In a small collection such as ADI, improving recall has less negative impact to the level of precision. Hence, a traditional retrieval model based on Porter's stemming algorithm and vector space model produces good results without additional semantic processing using WordNet. This observation has been reported by all related work reviewed in this article. The use of WordNet to improve precision does not provide significant improvement, if not any.

Does this mean that an ontology does not have any role in information retrieval? The answer is no. Ontologies can still play a role in improving the performance of information retrieval, provided the following considerations are observed:

- The ontology used in the retrieval has to be domain or collection specific. WordNet can be used as a starting point and needs to be either combined with other ontologies or be expanded with domain-specific entries.
- Traditional test collections such as ADI, CACM, and MEDLINE tend to favor a model that has a very high recall due to its small size and narrow topic scope. The nature of information retrieval has slightly changed with the introduction of the Internet. The number of possible matching documents is very large, and hence, having a very high recall may not be necessary. It is possible that the user will be satisfied with looking at only 2% of the total matching documents. However, the user will expect that this 2% be highly relevant. Hence, we may need to investigate further in the future a way to report the results of experiments in information retrieval. Recall may not be an important factor in searching information on the World Wide Web.

The debate on the impact of ontology in information retrieval will continue; however, without finding an appropriate test bed and a way of reporting the results, the true potential of ontology in improving the performance of information retrieval may not be ever realized. It is a challenge for the information retrieval community to find a new way of reporting the results according to the evolution in the nature of the way users use the World Wide Web to find information.

REFERENCES

Benitez, A. B., Chang, S. F., & Smith, J. R. (2001, October). *IMKA: A multimedia organization system combining perceptual and semantic Knowledge*. Paper presented at the *ACM Multimedia*, Ottawa, Canada.

Bramantoro, A., Krishnaswamy, S., & Indrawan, M. (2005). *A semantic distance measure for matching Web services*. Paper presented at the Web Information Systems Engineering – WISE 2005 Workshops (pp. 217-226).

Budanitsky, A. (1999). *Lexical semantic relatedness and its application in natural language processing* (Tech. Rep. CSRG-390). University of Toronto, Computer Systems Research Group.

Caliusco, M. L., Galli, M. R., & Chiotti, O. (2005, October 31-November 2). Contextual ontologies for the Semantic Web: An enabling technology. In *Proceedings of the Third Latin American Web Congress (LA-WEB)* (p. 98). Washington, D.C.: IEEE Computer Society.

Chen, S., Alahakoon, D., & Indrawan, M. (2005). *Background knowledge driven ontology discovery.* Paper presented at the 2005 IEEE International Conference on e-Technology, e-Commerce and e-Service (EEE '05) (pp. 202-207).

Deerwester, S., Dumais, S. T, Furnas, G. W., Landauer, T. K., & Harshman, R. (1990). Indexing by latent semantic analysis. *Journal of the American Society for Information Science, 41*(6), 391-407.

Dou, D., LePendu, P., Kim, S., & Qi, P. (2006, April 3-7). Integrating databases into the semantic Web through an ontology-based framework. In *Proceedings of the 22nd International Conference on Data Engineering Workshops (ICDEW'06)* (Vol. 00, p. 54). Washington, D.C.: IEEE Computer Society.

Hachey, B., & Grover, C. (2005, June 6-11). Automatic legal text summarization: Experiments with summary structuring. In *Proceedings of the 10th International Conference on Artificial intelligence and Law* (ICAIL '05), Bologna, Italy, (pp. 75-84). New York: ACM Press.

Hsu, M. H., Tsai, M. F., & Chen, H. H. (2006, October 16-18). Query expansion with ConceptNet and WordNet: An intrinsic comparison. In *Proceedings of the Third Asia Information Retrieval Symposium*, Singapore, (LNCS 4182, pp. 1-13).

Huang, J., Dang, J., & Huhns, M. N. (2006, September 18-22). Ontology reconciliation for service-oriented computing. In *Proceedings of the IEEE International Conference on Services Computing* (pp. 3-10). Washington, D.C.: IEEE Computer Society.

Khan, L., & Luo, F. (2002). Ontology construction for information selection. In *Proceedings 14th*

IEEE International Conference on Tools with Artificial Intelligence (pp. 122- 127).

Liu, S., Liu, F., Yu, C., & Meng, W. (2004, July). An effective approach to document retrieval via utilizing wordNet and recognizing phrases. In *Proceedings of the 27th Annual International ACM SIGIR Conference*, Sheffield, UK, (pp. 266-272).

Mandala, R., Tokunaga, T., & Tanaka, H. (1998). The use of WordNet in information retrieval. In S. Harabagiu (Ed.), *Use of WordNet in Natural Language Processing Systems: Proceedings of the Association for Computational Linguistics Conference,* Somerset, NJ, (pp. 31-37).

Mandala, R., Tokunaga, T., & Tanaka, H. (1999). Complementing WordNet with Roget and corpus-based automatically constructed thesauri for information retrieval. In *Proceedings of the Ninth Conference of the European Chapter of the Association for Computational Linguistics*, Bergen.

Moldovan, D. I., & Mihalcea, R. (2000). Using WordNet and lexical operators to improve Internet searches. *IEEE Internet Computing, 4*(1), 34-43.

Rack, C., Arbanowski, S., & Steglich, S. (2006, July 23-27). *Context-aware, ontology-based recommendations.* Paper presented at the International Symposium on Applications and the Internet Workshops.

Richardson, R., & Smeaton, A. F. (1995). *Using WordNet in a knowledge-based approach to information retrieval* (Tech. Rep. CS-0395). Dublin City University, School of Computer Applications.

Smeaton, A. F., & Berrut, C. (1995). Running TREC-4 experiments: A chronological report of query expansion experiments carried out as part of TREC-4. In *Proceedings of the Fourth Text Retrieval Conference (TREC-4)*. NIST Special Publication.

Voorhees, E. M. (1993, June 27-July 1). Using WordNet to disambiguate word senses for text retrieval. In R. Korfhage, E. Rasmussen, & P. Willett (Eds.), *Proceedings of the 16th Annual international ACM SIGIR Conference on Research and Development in information Retrieval* (SIGIR '93), Pittsburgh, (pp. 171-180). New York: ACM Press.

Voorhees, E. M. (1994, July 3-6). Query expansion using lexical-semantic relations. In W. B. Croft & C. J. van Rijsbergen (Eds.), *Proceedings of the 17th Annual International ACM SIGIR Conference on Research and Development in information Retrieval*, Dublin, Ireland, (pp. 61-69). New York: Springer-Verlag.

Wang, B., & Brookes, B. R. (2004). *A semantic approach for Web indexing* (LNCS 3007, pp. 59-68).

www.conceptnet.org

Yan, Z., Li, Q., & Li, H. (2006). *An ontology-based model for context-aware*. Paper presented at the 1st International Symposium on Pervasive Computing and Applications (pp. 647-651).

ENDNOTE

[1] The ADI used comes as part of SMART retrieval system, ftp://ftp.cs.cornell.edu/pub/smart/

This work was previously published in International Journal of Information Technology and Web Engineering, Vol. 3, Issue 1, edited by G. Alkhatib and D. Rine, pp. 24-37, copyright 2008 by IGI Publishing (an imprint of IGI Global).

Chapter 3
A New Framework for Intelligent Semantic Web Services Based on GAIVAs

Andrés Iglesias
University of Cantabria, Spain

ABSTRACT

The Semantic Web has been recently developed to provide end users with suitable tools and strategies to process information from their Web pages. The Intelligent Semantic Web Services is a new approach aimed at extending Semantic Web capabilities for Services by applying Artificial Intelligence techniques while maintaining the good properties of the standard Semantic Web schemes. However, many current Web services neither consider this approach nor include a powerful user-interface and, consequently, are very limited and difficult to use. This paper introduces a new framework for Intelligent Semantic Web Services that overcomes these drawbacks. Our approach is based on the Graphical Autonomous Intelligent Virtual Agents (GAIVAs), virtual agents that exhibit a human-like appearance and behaviour and are able to take intelligent decisions and perform actions without human intervention. To this purpose, the framework comprises a collection of powerful Artificial Intelligence techniques along with a natural and intuitive Graphical User Interface.

INTRODUCTION

If we might summarize our current world in just a few keywords, one of them would likely be "information." Today's society is often labelled as the "information society." The extraordinary advances in hardware and software, the wide availability of computers and other electronic devices and the rapid development of Internet and its rich collection of tools and resources have opened the door to new ways to store, query, retrieve, and manipulate information. Nowadays, we can easily access to huge amounts of information just surfing at the Web from link to link, querying sophisticated search engines, or just attempting to reach a site by using its domain name, to mention just a few examples. And perspectives are even much better: it is expected that the number of services available on the Web will increase dramatically for the next years.

There is, however, a "bottleneck" in this process: the conversion of all this resulting information into useful knowledge. In just a few minutes, we might become literally collapsed by an impractical load of information coming from hundreds of thousands of Web pages. Thus, even the pre-processing of all this information may typically require several weeks in order to make it suitable for knowledge processing and acquisition.

Several approaches have been described to overcome this limitation. Perhaps the most promising one is Semantic Web. First introduced by Tim Berners-Lee, it represents a step further in order to provide the users with suitable tools and strategies to process information from their Web pages. In words of Berners-Lee, Hendler, and Lassila (2001), the core of Semantic Web is "to bring structure to the meaningful content of Web pages, creating an environment where software agents roaming from page to page can readily carry out sophisticated tasks for users."

Behind this approach is the underlying problem that, while the Web pages may be appealing for humans, for the software they are not more than a string of random characters. Because the meaning of a sentence or paragraph embedded into a Web page cannot be determined automatically by software, this task has been progressively assigned to users and programmers. But this is a very hard, tedious, and time-consuming process. Of course, there are specific tools (mostly based on HTML or XML tags or similar approaches) to deal with this problem. However, they still provide particular and incomplete solutions and are very prone to errors. Consequently, the programmers are getting more and more involved in the process to assign meaning to the Web page contents (in other words, to "capture" the semantics of those pages). Unfortunately, this strategy generates new problems: some desirable features such as information confidentiality and privacy and

other security issues are missed. Furthermore, the subjectivity inherent to the human processes becomes evident here: the meaning assigned by two programmers might be drastically different. In addition, we would expect such tasks to be done automatically. In fact, it has been remarked, "the potential of the semantic Web, however, goes well beyond information discovery and querying. In particular, it encompasses the automation of Web-based services as well." (Bryson, Martin, McIlraith, & Stein, 2003). However, this automation requires specific tools to convert the current Web contents into information understandable by the machines.

These and other problems were already envisioned some years ago. As a consequence, several appropriate mechanisms and strategies to solve them have been suggested during the last few years. Among them, the Semantic Web is complementary to the World Wide Web and consists of machine-readable information. Its goal is to develop standards and technologies to help machines to understand information on the Web (not the natural language, as it will be remarked later on) so that they can support features such as data integration, navigation, automation of tasks, and services or declaration of the kind of information one might trust. The last step in this semantics-oriented software development process is given by the intelligent Semantic Web services, a new approach aimed at extending the Semantic Web capabilities for services by applying artificial intelligence techniques while maintaining the good properties of the standard Semantic Web schemes. As it will be described in the next sections, this work presents a novel approach that falls into this last category.

On the other hand, we noticed that many Web services require a degree of technical comprehension on the user's part. In fact, this is one of the most common complaints of any user: the service can work very well, but the user interface is quite complex to use. Very often the users fail to achieve the service successfully just because of their inability to realize how the system works (in most cases, even simply to understand what is the input of such a service). Fortunately, much research work has recently been done on the development of graphical user interfaces (GUIs) for the Web. Recent approaches include multimodal interfaces (Feiner & McKeown, 1991; Oviatt, 1999), conversational models (Takeuchi & Nagao, 1993; Prevost, Hodgson, Cook, & Churchill, 1999; Thorisson, 1996), virtual humans (Caicedo & Thalmann, 2000; Monzani, Caicedo, & Thalmann, 2001; Thalmann & Monzani, 2002; Luengo & Iglesias, 2003; Iglesias & Luengo, 2004; Iglesias & Luengo, 2005; Iglesias & Luengo, 2007) and embodied agents (Cassell & Vilhjalmsonn, 1999; Cassell, Bickmore, Campbell, Vilhjalmsson, & Yan, 2001), to quote just a few examples. In addition, there has been an increasing interest on the analysis of their potential advantages and limitations in comparison to text-based approaches. In short, it has been shown that these GUIs provide a higher bandwidth of communication that would otherwise be possible. This issue—that will be discussed in detail later on, in the evaluation and validation section—encouraged us to improve the efficiency of our system by incorporating a powerful GUI based on virtual agents. This is actually the motivation of this article and—in our opinion—one of its most interesting and useful contributions.

The structure of this article is as follows: in the next section we summarize our main contributions that will be described in detail throughout the article. Then, some related work is briefly described. The article also provides our readers with a gentle overview about the Semantic Web, its goals and capabilities. Some previous developments for the Semantic Web and Web services are also briefly described. Then, our new framework for intelligent Semantic Web services based on GAIVAs is introduced. The section presents a brief description of the main components of the framework (world, actions, agents, and services). Then, the framework architecture and its simulation flow and imple-

mentation are described. The performance of this proposal is discussed by means of an illustrative example. We also offer a comparison of the present work with some previous—similar—approaches. Then, the evaluation and validation of our system is discussed. In particular, we try to explain what the benefits are for Web users and developers in adopting our approach as well as its main requirements and limitations. The article closes with the main conclusions of this work and some future lines of research.

MAIN CONTRIBUTIONS

This article describes a new framework for intelligent Semantic Web services based on graphical autonomous intelligent virtual agents (GAIVAs), a new concept also introduced in this article. The framework is aimed at fulfilling a twofold objective:

- On one hand, it is a new proposal for intelligent Semantic Web services based on agents. In our approach, the users can invoke Web services whose semantics is interpreted by means of a sophisticated based-on-artificial-intelligence kernel. This kernel combines the strengths of OWL and Prolog for the semantics specification and the behavioural animation tasks, respectively. All "intelligent" tasks are performed by virtual agents that simulate human beings evolving within a virtual 3D world associated with the current Web service. These agents are autonomous in the sense that they are able to take decisions and perform actions without human intervention. In addition, we require those decisions to be intelligent from the point of view of a human observer. For these purposes, the framework comprises a collection of artificial intelligence techniques that will be described in detail in the framework architecture section.

- On the other hand, the framework incorporates a powerful GUI that allows the users to interact with the system in a graphical and very natural way. Once a Web service is requested, the user is prompted through the Web into a virtual world that is actually a replica of the real environment associated with the service. The interplay between the users and the system is accomplished via those virtual agents, which are represented graphically in this virtual world and behave in a human-like way. Up to our knowledge no other approaches have considered this feature in the context of Semantic Web for services.

We think that these two new features do represent a significant contribution in the field of Semantic Web approaches for services. In our opinion, this work is not merely another proposal for an alternative Semantic Web implementation. It is also a framework for Web services that provides a lot of new features that current Semantic Web lacks of. For example, it has been pointed out that the Semantic Web is not about teaching the machines to understand human words or process natural language (see: The Semantic Web—for Web Developers, available online at: http://logicerror.com/semanticWeb-webdev). In other words, the Semantic Web just provides the tools to add support to the databases in a machine-readable form, not tools for understanding natural language. In contrast, we pursue both goals at once. Some additional advantages also discussed in this article—such as the open architecture of the system and its modularity and versatility—greatly improve the efficiency and performance of the system. Although our project is not finished yet, we think it has now reached a stage of development that justifies its publication.

RELATED WORK

Several research groups have worked in behavioural animation of virtual agents during the last few years. Some of them have focused on creating architectures to integrate the set of different techniques involved in this task. Badler et al. (2000) developed the so-called smart avatars, which use the parameterised action representation (PAR) to handle action selection and animation (Badler et al., 2000; Bindiganavale, Schuler, Allbeck, Badler, Joshi, & Palmer, 2000). These PARs allow the programmers to represent either primitives or complex actions, being able to control the motion generators of the virtual agents. Granieri defined the parallel transition network as a network to provide the system with some predicates and conditions in order to handle the different processes involved in the motion routines (Granieri, Becket, Reich, Crabtree, & Badler, 1995). A similar approach is given in Moltenbrey (1999): simple behaviours can be combined altogether into networks that describe behaviours and motions graphically. Daniel Thalmann and his group at the Swiss Institute of Technology put the emphasis on giving the virtual actors a higher degree of autonomy without losing control (Bordeux, Boulic, & Thalmann, 1999; Caicedo & Thalmann, 2000; Monzani, Caicedo, & Thalmann, 2001). Their approach is based on the BDI (beliefs, desires, and intentions) architecture described in (Ingrand, Georgeff, & Rao, 1992; Rao & Georgeff, 1991). The former scheme was later improved in (Monzani et al., 2001) to integrate a set of different techniques to simulate behaviours of virtual humans. In particular, they considered a separation of simulated physical functionalities (low-level modules) and the logical management of behaviours (high-level modules). For the low-level tasks the authors developed the so-called ACE (agents common environment), implemented in C++ and combined with a Python layer for user-interaction, which comprises a set of commands to control the simulation. In ACE each agent is running in a separate process or thread so that they have independent interactions with the environment. For the high-level structures they considered an IVA (intelligent virtual agent) module similar to that described in Caicedo and Thalmann (2000). Both levels are interconnected via a TCP/IP protocol. With this combined architecture the authors obtained convincing simulations of many human behaviours evolving in carefully chosen scenarios, such as a journal office.

Another line of research is given by Brooks (1985), Brooks (1991), Maes (1994), Minsky (1985), and others leading to the school of behavioural-based artificial intelligence (BBAI). This field has been supported by some works published in the early 90s about the application of neural networks and other artificial intelligence techniques to the animation and control of physics-based models (Grzeszczuk & Terzopoulos, 1995; Grzeszczuk, Terzopoulos, & Hinton, 1998). Recent developments in this field include the analysis of the behaviour of crowds (Raupp & Thalmann, 2001), the interaction with objects in an intelligent way (Goncalves, Kallmann, & Thalmann, 2001) or the control of virtual agents with PDAs (Gutiérrez, Vexo, & Thalmann, 2003).

A different approach is given by some works focused on human conversation analyzed from different points of view (Cassell & Vilhjalmsonn, 1999; Takeuchi & Nagao, 1993; Lester, Voerman, Towns, & Callaway, 1997; Cassell et al., 2001). The system Olga has distributed client-server architecture with separate modules for language processing, interaction management, and others via a central server (Beskow & McGlashan, 1997). Olga is event-driven, meaning that is able to react to user's input but unable to generate output on its own (Beskow, Elenius, & McGlashan, 1997). Takeuchi and Nagao (1993) used a different architecture in which the modules are independent and actually compete with one another to see which behaviour is active at a particular moment. Lester et al. (1997) emphasized the agents' gestures and expressions as a function of the objects referred

to and the proximity of those objects to the animated agent. Another similar approach was that of "animated conversation" (Cassell et al., 1994) in which the system produces non-verbal propositional behaviours according to the speech's content. However, the system was not designed to interact with the users, and did not run in real time. More recent approaches are also given in Thorisson (1996) and Prevost et al. (1999).

Another recent approach is given by the multimodal interaction systems (Cohen, Johnston, & McGee, 1997; Neal & Shapiro, 1991; Oviatt, 1999). These systems offer the possibility to combine natural input modes in a coordinated manner with multimedia system output. Clearly, they represent a new—and not sufficiently explored yet—field for Internet systems. Its potential applications to Web services do justify further research on this topic for the next years.

SEMANTIC WEB

What Is the Semantic Web?

As aforementioned, the Semantic Web has been recently introduced to provide the computers—and not only the users—with a reliable way to process the semantics of the Web pages. Although current software is able to find a Web service without human intervention, it is still a challenge for the computers to interpret how to use it or even to realize what the kind and purpose of such a service are. While for us it is a trivial task to say: "I will close this link; it's not about the kind of information I'm interested in" or "this link goes to the personal page of my boss," there is no way for the computers to automatically doing so. The Semantic Web provides programmers with tools and strategies for incorporating these nice features into their current programs for the Web. From this standpoint, the Semantic Web is an extension (arguably the most powerful one ever developed) of the World Wide Web.

The counterpart is that the Semantic Web is not comprised of well-organized, carefully chosen ontologies built by skilled programmers and/or artificial intelligence experts. Instead, the Semantic Web still preserves most of the classical Web features: in addition to its universality (in author's opinion, the most remarkable property of the Web), the Semantic Web is also a chaotic mixture of different small ontological components and tools developed by Web users in a very similar way that earlier Web contents were created. This feature (which is indeed a trademark of the Web itself) is not necessarily bad; even those that rejected such kind of unorganized growth have finally recognized the applicability of the Web tools and the nice properties of its open architecture, not to mention the prompt development of powerful search engines and other complementary tools. The attempts to standardize the Semantic Web are at the earlier stage yet. In fact, no single approach can safely argue it is going to become a standard "de facto" for the Semantic Web so far.

PREVIOUS DEVELOPMENTS FOR SEMANTIC WEB AND WEB SERVICES

Today, virtually every company, university, government agency, group, and even individuals can easily create a Web page, make it available to others by simply uploading it, insert hyperlinks to other pages, add applets, communicate with databases, ask for services, design complex data structures for use in large computer networks, and all the other tasks that make the Web so fascinating and revolutionary.

However, these developments are very recent, dating back to late 80s. The story began with the pioneering work by Tim Berners-Lee for creating the World Wide Web (see, for instance, http://www.w3.org/History.html for an overview about the history of the Web). He is also the "father" of relevant tools for the Web such as URIs, HTTP, and HTML, which definitely changed the world

(see: World Wide Web Consortium: http://www.w3.org/). In addition, powerful search engines and other sophisticated technologies opened the Web to the general media.

At the very beginning, these capabilities were much more limited—basically static tools for Internet—but, after a very short span, a number of dynamic tools (UDDI, WSDL, BPEL, SOAP, WSFL, WSIF, PBML, XIANG) were developed. They are often referred to as Web services (McIraith, Son, & Zeng, 2001). A major problem for Web services was the interoperativity on the Web—to provide protocols and descriptions so that different programs running on different platforms can communicate and collaborate together in an effective manner. This is a critical step in business-to-business applications, an emerging sector whose growth rate has been more than impressive during the last few years. For instance, Gartner group said "using Web services will help to reduce costs and improve the efficiency of IT projects by 30%" (Hendler, Berners-Lee, & Miller, 2002).

Several attempts to standardize this process have been presented during the last recent years. For instance, SOAP (simple object access protocol, http://www.w3.org/TR/soap/), an XML-based protocol aimed at providing tools to allow a program invoking other programs on the Web, UDDI (universal description, discovery, and integration, http://www.uddi.org/), a tool that depends on the functionality of the content language (and, hence, not well suited for advanced features), WSDL (Web services description language, http://www.w3.org/TR/wsdl), a XML grammar for specifying properties of Web services, or BPEL (business process execution language for Web services, http://www.oasis-open.org/committees/tc_home.php?wg_abbrev=wsbpel). However, the semantic description of those services still remained a challenge for the tools existing at that time. Neither UDDI nor WSDL support semantic description of services. Other approaches such as BPEL do not provide a well-defined semantics either.

As soon as the users realized about the limitations of the Web to understand the semantics of Web pages (and, consequently, to perform searches efficiently, among other tasks) some Semantic Web tools such as DAML (DARPA agent markup language, http://www.daml.org/) became a reality. Two major technologies for this issue are XML (extensible markup language, http://www.w3.org/XML/) and RDF (resource description framework, http://www.w3.org/rdf). XML allows users to create their own tags for Web pages or section annotations on a page. By means of adequate scripts, programmers can use those tags in many—sophisticated—ways. In other words, programmers can add arbitrary structure to their documents—regardless what such a structure actually means. However, XML is designed for documents, not data. In fact, it includes some features (such as attributes and entities) that, while working properly for document-oriented systems, are problematic for data expression tasks. In addition, XML codes exhibit some ambiguity, as there are many ways to express the same thing in this language.

On the other hand, RDF expresses meaning as a sequence of triples, each being rather like the subject, verb, and object of a typical sentence. Such triples, which can be written in standard XML tags, inform us about subjects (Web pages, users) that have some properties (the verb) with some values (another Web page or user, for instance). RDF uses the universal resource identifier (URI, http://www.w3.org/Addressing/URL/URI_Overview.html) for the triple components. Those URIs ensure the concepts to be linked to a single definition on the Web. This simple idea allows us to write most of the data processed by machines. In addition, triples are simple things that prevent users from the confusing hybrid tree structure of XML. Furthermore, the composition of two triples is a triple as well, while the merging of two XML documents might be no longer a well-formed XML document.

The next milestone is given by the Semantic Web services (Cowles, 2005; Hendler, 2001).

Since two different databases or services can use different identifiers to mean the same thing, we need some tools to realize both terms and concepts are actually the same one. The solution for this problem is given by the ontology. During the last few years, a number of research groups have developed languages to express the ontology of the Web in a machine-readable form and provide suitable services based on such ontologies. For instance, the OWL (Web ontology language, http://www.w3.org/2004/OWL/) is an expressive markup language with a well-defined semantics for ontology. In addition, some efforts have been conducted in order to define a standard for Semantic Web, such as the U.S. Defense Advanced Research Projects Agency (DARPA) that released DAML. Subsequent versions have been carried out by the Joint U.S./EU Committee on Agent Markup Languages by launching the modification called DAML+OIL (http://www.daml.org/language/), also based on RDF.

If we think about Semantic Web as an extension of World Wide Web, Semantic Web services are, at its turn, an extension of Web services. Figure 1 summarizes the most important developments for Semantic Web and Web services. The vertical axis (from bottom to top) represents the transition from the static to dynamic information, while the horizontal axis represents the evolution over the time, from the initial non-semantic developments to the able-to-deal-with-semantic approaches. The last step so far would be represented by the so-called intelligent Semantic Web services. They are based on the use of artificial intelligence techniques for ontology.

NEW FRAMEWORK FOR INTELLIGENT SEMANTIC WEB SERVICES BASED ON GAIVAS

In this section we introduce a new framework for intelligent Semantic Web services based on agents. By a framework we mean a defined support structure in which another software project can

Figure 1. Scheme of the developments for Semantic Web and Web services (based on Figure 1 of [Cowles 2005])

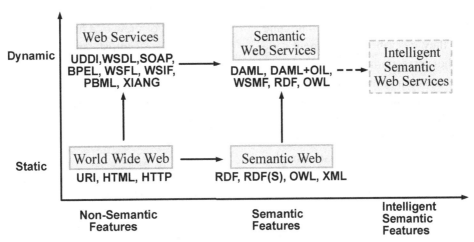

be organized and developed. As it will be shown later on, the open architecture of our system implies that we are not subjected to any particular semantic approach. In fact, our framework can support many different semantic schemes without modifying the underlying structure. In addition, the system has been modularized so that the output of each module is independent and can be used for external purposes as well as for input of the subsequent module. This role of modularity has been emphasized as "a key technique for simplifying software" (Bryson et al., 2003). It also contributes to the ease of maintenance and reusability of resources. All these features make the system especially attractive for Web programmers and developers. In this section, we give a brief description of our framework in terms of the world, actions, objects, agents, and services. Then, its architecture and simulation flow are also discussed.

Framework Description

Our framework for intelligent Web services is based on two concepts introduced in this article: the information platform and the graphical autonomous intelligent virtual agents (GAIVAs). These concepts and their respective components are briefly described in the next paragraphs.

The information platform is given by a triple (W,Φ,I), its components being respectively:

- A virtual world, W (see next paragraphs for details),
- A set, Φ, of S-functions describing the actions performed by the agents, and
- The information itself, I.

The World

Each Web service is represented by means of a virtual world. From the user's viewpoint, such a world is basically a 3D graphical environment associated with the particular service user is asking for. In our opinion, this way to present information to users is very convenient for many reasons: on one hand, it is generally accepted that graphical information can be processed more efficiently than that presented as a sequence of strings, tables, or in other ways. On the other hand, it greatly simplifies the understanding of the sequence of actions. Further, those actions are hereby independent on user's language. This feature is especially important in our approach, since we are interested to preserve the universality of the Web. In our framework, the virtual world, W, is comprised of four components:

1. Environment: it consists of different classes, I_E, which include routines for the description of the geometry and the rendering and animation of the three-dimensional scene

2. Objects: they describe environment's elements. The corresponding classes, I_O, handle the representation of physical objects, their geometry, location, motion and animation, and possible interaction among all objects and agents. Objects in the scene are generated and stored into a database. Roughly, virtual world's objects can be classified into two groups: static objects and smart objects. By smart objects we understand those objects whose shape, location, or status can be modified over time, as opposed to the static ones. This concept has shown to be extremely helpful to define the interactions between virtual agents and objects. We point out that saying that an object is static does not mean it has null influence on agents' actions. For instance, trees and walls are static objects but they must be considered for tasks such as collision avoidance and path planning.

3. Agents: they are comprised of classes for agents' description (one class for each agent) and agents' behavioural information, such as beliefs, desires, intentions, and behaviours. Our scheme falls into the category of based-on-agents Web service framework. In this approach, the agents are responsible to perform actions in order to provide services. Once a new service is requested, the agents responsible for that service are prompted into the 3D environment. Users can insert virtual agents into the virtual world at any time. In this article, we introduce what we call graphical autonomous intelligent virtual agents (GAIVAs). They are virtual agents created to simulate realistically the appearance and behaviour of human beings. These agents are expected to exhibit a high degree of autonomy, so that they can evolve freely, with a minimal user's input.

In addition, their behaviour is expected to be realistic; in other words, virtual agents must behave according to reality from the point of view of a human observer. To this purpose, sophisticated artificial intelligence tools have been implemented. Because of that, our agents can be labelled as intelligent. Lastly, the agents live and evolve within a graphical environment, so no need to explain why we also label them as graphical.

A very common architecture for deliberative agents for the Semantic Web is the belief-desire-intention (BDI) model (Cohen & Levesque, 1987; Cohen & Levesque, 1990; Georgeff & Ingrand, 1989; Rao & Georgeff, 1990; Ingrand et al., 1992). It builds agents consisting of sets of:

- Beliefs: they account for the knowledge about the world
- Desires: the goals that agent wants to achieve or fulfill
- Intentions: the goals or subgoals that agent is currently pursuing
- Behaviours: the actions that agent is able to take

This approach is intended to pull agent's tools and applications into closer collaboration, while designing the architecture to interoperate with the emerging standards and tools of the Semantic Web. However, because of its drawbacks (mostly related to the non-reversibility of the processes and other limiting factors), in this article we consider an extension that includes: (1) a categorization of beliefs, which are no longer associated with agents themselves (instead, they are assigned to the behavioural kernel), (2) the inclusion of semantic memory, (3) the consideration of internal states for agents, (4) the reliability on trust so that agents trust each other, and (5) the inclusion of alternatives into the evolution plans via service composition routines.

4. Services: they include the basic operations for combining different services in a new (composite) service. Let us suppose we consider two services performed by two different agents A_i, i=1,2. In our framework, there are three basic operations for our agent-based services:

a. Composition of services: by A_1oA_2 we represent the composite service of both services. In other words, the composition is an operator for sequence, meaning that the service consists of the service performed by A_1 followed by the service performed by A_2.

b. Choice of services: this operation allows the service to perform either the service by A_1 or that by A_2. Note that, once one of them is chosen and performed, the other one is automatically skipped, so the corresponding service is never performed. This service will be represented by $A_1 \| A_2$, where $\|$ means the operator for choice.

c. Concurrence of services: this operation allows the service to perform both services by A_1 and A_2 independently. This service will be denoted by $A_1 \otimes A_2$, where $\otimes$ means the operator for concurrence.

The Actions

To comply user's request, agents must perform different actions, described by the so-called S-functions. For each S-function, a single computation step of an individual agent is called a move, M, of this agent. We also define a run or execution, R, as a triple consisting of: (1) a collection of moves, (2) the set of S-functions associated with those moves, and (3) a set of states. For a run to be well defined, we impose the following additional conditions:

1. R is a partially ordered set of moves, each having a finite number of predecessors;

2. The S-functions associate agents with moves such that moves of a single agent are totally sorted;

3. Each state is associated with one or several moves.

With this terminology, we consider the actions as a collection of runs designed to perform a specific task. We can, for instance, talk about actions for locomotion, which include all motion routines required for displacement from point A to point B. From this point of view, the reader can easily associate each agent's movement with what we call a move, while the action is the whole displacement from A to B.

Framework Architecture

Figure 2 displays the architecture of the proposed framework. It consists of the following modules (described in detail in the next paragraphs):

- An initial (inbox) module for the semantics: it is comprised of a DAML-S translator, a knowledge database, and an OWL reasoner,

- The graphical module: intended to create the virtual world,

- The behavioural module: it is the kernel of our framework. It is responsible for the interpretation, evaluation, and execution of user-requested services making use of reasoning, memory, learning, and other artificial intelligence features included in this module, and

- The execution module (outbox): it eventually provides the user with the Web service.

The first component of the inbox module is a DAML-S translator. DAML-S (where S stands for services, http://www.daml.org/services/) is a set of ontologies marked up in DAML+OIL to set up a framework to host a description of Web services

Figure 2. Our framework for intelligent Semantic Web services

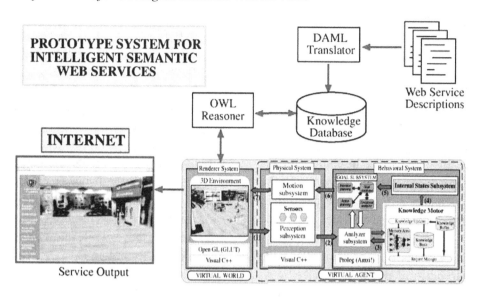

by following a semantic approach. In particular, DAML-S considers that Web services are composed of three elements, called service profile, process model, and grounding, respectively. The service profile describes what the service does. To this purpose, it requires the specification of the input and output types, preconditions and effects. The process model tells us how the service works. Each service is an atomic process, a simple process, or a composite process. An atomic process is executed directly and its output is returned in a single step with a grounding. A simple process is quite similar to an atomic one: they involve single-step executions with no grounding. Finally, composite processes are constructed from other atomic, simple, or composite processes and include conditions and process components. The last component is the grounding, which tells us how the service is used. In particular, it contains the details of how an agent can access a service by using a communication protocol (RPC, HTTP-FORM, CORBA, SOAP, RMI, KQML). It can also include some service-specific details, such as port numbers or so. In short, the service profile and the process model are abstract specifications, while

the grounding provides concrete specification of implementation details.

The ontological information written in DAML-S is converted into RDF triples that are subsequently loaded to the knowledge database. The inference engine is an OWL reasoner built in Prolog and connected to the knowledge motor of virtual agent's behavioural system via the analyzer (see Figure 2). Both subsystems (the OWL reasoner and the knowledge motor) are responsible for information management and its conversion into knowledge. Note that, although the OWL reasoner includes inference rules for deduction, it is designed to deal with the specification of the semantics only (i.e., the inference rules are exclusively applied to semantic purposes). This means that the remaining "intelligent" tasks are actually performed by the knowledge motor, as will be explained.

The second module is responsible of all graphical tasks. Because this is not actually the subject of this article, we do not describe this module here. However, for the sake of completeness, and just for interested readers, we give some implementation details in the next section.

Figure 3. Scheme of the knowledge motor

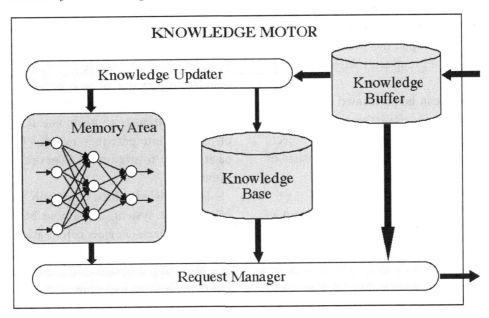

On the contrary, the third module is especially relevant in this article, since it contains all artificial intelligence "machinery" required for our work. Once new information from the OWL reasoner is attained and processed by the analyzer, the knowledge motor then retrieves it. This knowledge motor is actually the "brain" of our system; its main components are depicted in Figure 3. Firstly, current information is temporarily stored into the knowledge buffer, until new information is attained. At that time, previous information is sent to the knowledge updater (KU), the new one being stored into this knowledge buffer and so on. This KU updates both the memory area and the knowledge base.

The memory area is a neural network that will be applied to learn from data. A neural network consists basically of one or several layers of computing units, called neurons, connected by links. Each artificial neuron receives an input value from the input layer or the neurons in the previous layer. Then it computes a scalar output $y=f(\Sigma\ w_{ik}\ x_k)$ from a linear combination of the received inputs $x_1, x_2,..., x_n$ using a set of weights w_{ik} associated with each of the links and a given

scalar function f (the activation function), which is assumed to be the same for all neurons—see Haykin (1994) and Hertz, Krogh, and Palmer (1991) for a gentle introduction to the field.

Among many interesting properties of a neural network, one of primary importance is its ability to learn from the environment and to improve its performance through learning. Such an improvement is achieved through an iterative process based on adjusting the free parameters of the network (the weights). In this article, we consider the unsupervised learning, in which the data is presented to the network without any external information and the network must discover by itself patterns, or categories. In particular, we use an auto-associative scheme, since the inputs themselves are used as targets. In other words, the network tries to learn the identity function, which is a far from trivial problem as the network contains less neurons than the input/output layers, and hence, it must perform dimensionality reduction. What the network attempts is to subdivide the data space into clusters in order to associate each data with a specific neuron, the nearest one in our case. To this end, we try to minimize the sum of the squared within-groups residuals, which are basically the distances of the data locations to the respective group centroids. When a new data is received as input, the whole structure is recomputed and the group centroids are relocated accordingly.

This strategy can be performed by applying the K-means least-squares partitioning algorithm, a procedure to divide a collection of n objects into K groups. The basic algorithm consists of two main steps:

1.   Compute cluster centroids and use them as new cluster seeds
2.   Assign each data to the nearest centroid.

Let us suppose now that we have a neural network with k neurons and that n data vectors x_1, x_2,..., x_n, (with k<n) will eventually be received at different times. To update the memory area, we employ a K-means procedure for competitive networks, which are a popular type of unsupervised network architectures widely used to automatically detect clusters within the available data. A simple competitive neural network is formed by an input and an output layer, connected by feed forward connections. Each input pattern represents a point in the configuration space (the space of inputs) where we want to obtain classes.

This type of architecture is usually trained with a winner takes all algorithm, so that only the weights associated with the output neuron with largest value (the winner) are updated. The procedure is based on the following strategy: at the initial stage, all the neurons are available to store new data. Therefore, the first k data vectors are sequentially assigned to these neurons, that is, data x_i is learned by neuron i, $1 \leq i \leq k$. Simultaneously, time for neuron i is initialized to the moment at which data x_i is learned. Once the next data x_{k+1} is received, it is assigned to the neuron j such that

$$d(x_j, x_{k+1}) \leq d(x_i, x_{k+1}), \ i=1,...,k, \ i \neq j$$

When this condition is satisfied by several neurons simultaneously, the new data is assigned to that storing the oldest information. Interesting enough is the way in which the neuron stores the new information: instead of replacing the old data by the new one, what is actually stored is a combination of both data. The basic idea behind this formulation is to overcome the limitation of having more data than neurons by allowing each neuron to store more than one data at the same time.

The knowledge base is actually a based-on-rules expert system, containing both concrete knowledge (facts or evidence) and abstract knowledge (inference rules). Of course, the number of rules and the design of the inference engine mostly determine the complexity of this system. Additional subsystems for tasks like learning, coherence control, action execution, and others have also been incorporated. In particular, our expert system has been designed according to (Castillo & Alvarez, 1991; Castillo, Gutierrez, & Hadi, 1997). Finally, the request manager is the component that, on the basis of the information received from the previous modules, provides the information requested by the goal definition subsystem, which is the component devoted to perform the actions in order to comply user's request (i.e., the Web service).

Finally, the outbox module returns the requested service to user in a graphical way. The corresponding instructions can be written in either HTTP or using WSDL descriptions, according to the kind of output and service involved. We remark, however, that alternative tools may also be applied to this issue without modifying the other components at all.

Simulation Flow

In this section, we describe the simulation flow of our framework. It is worthwhile to mention that in this article, we are not actually concerned on the description of the internal processes per-

Figure 4. Simulation flow scheme. On the left, the different processes involved. On the right, user's tasks

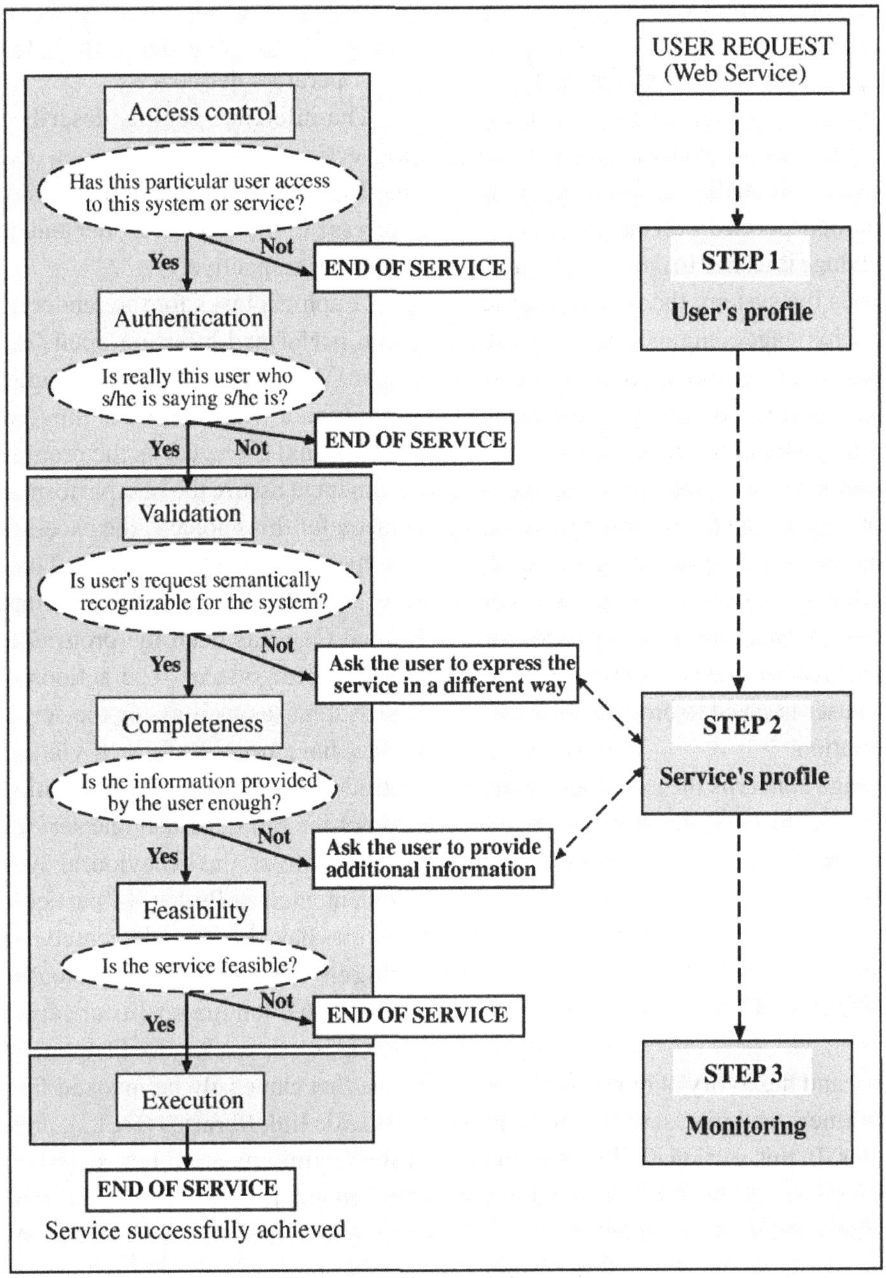

formed at the rendering engine. Therefore, we have intentionally omitted any detail about the graphical tasks.

The simulation flow consists of three stages, as shown in Figure 4: system access, service request, and execution. This classification is based on the kind of processes involved and user's tasks for

each stage. In short, the stages account for the definition of user's profile, service profile, and service execution, respectively.

The first stage corresponds to system access. It is comprised of two processes: access control and authentication. Firstly, the system asks the user about his/her profile. Based on this information, the system determines whether or not the user has the privileges to access to the system (access control). Then, cryptographic tools are applied for user's authentication. Note that this first stage is created to provide users with a reliable and safe access to the system. To this purpose, the most typical security features, such as access control, authentication, confidentiality, and non-repudiation have been incorporated into our system.

The second stage is related to the service. Once the user accesses the system, the service profile must be given. This stage contains three different processes labelled as validation, completeness, and feasibility. The first two steps try to make a decision about the semantic correctness and completeness of user's request: Are user's sentences semantically recognizable for the system? If so, is the information provided by the user enough in order to achieve the service? If the answer to both questions is yes, the system checks for the feasibility of the service at the current time. Otherwise, the user is asked to provide some additional information.

The third stage concerns the execution of the service. Since the processes involved are user-independent, user's tasks reduce to monitoring the service status.

IMPLEMENTATION

The modularity and flexibility of our framework allows programmers to build several different implementations. In this section we describe one of them—not necessarily the best one—that has proved to perform well in our computer experiments. Our prototype is comprised of five main components: a composer, an inference engine, a graphical system, a behavioural system, and a security module. The composer is a user interface that includes the workflow editor—where user declares the input for the service—and the scene renderer—for graphical purposes. Regarding the implementation, user's input is interpreted by us-

ing DAML-S instructions (according to version 0.7, released in 2002) for the DAML translator. The editor can handle the different kind of services (atomic, single, and composite) via the composition operators defined.

The inference engine, described in detail in the section devoted to the framework architecture, has been implemented in Prolog and in Microsoft Access (for the OWL reasoner and the knowledge database respectively).

Graphical tasks for the renderer system have been performed by using open GL with GLUT (open GL utility toolkit) for the higher-level functions (windowing, menus, or input) while we have used Visual C++ v6.0 as the programming environment to assure the best performance. Another reason for this choice is the excellent integration of Open GL with the C++ layer. This combination has also been used for the user interface, while visual C++ has been the programming tool for the physical system. The actions of this physical system (as well as for the service execution stage) have been performed via the S-functions introduced above and the composition operators—except for atomic and single services.

In contrast, the behavioural system has been implemented in Prolog. In particular, all Prolog routines have been implemented in the programming environment "Amzi! Prolog" (developed, at its turn, in C language). In our experience, Amzi! Prolog is an excellent tool to generate optimized code that can easily be invoked from C/C++ via dynamic link libraries (DLLs), providing an optimal communication between the physical and the behavioural systems. Furthermore, this choice provides a good solution for several communication protocols for distributed environments.

The simulation framework described in this article can be implemented on a single CPU platform by creating a dynamic list of classes associated with the virtual agents. The communication between those classes and the behavioural system is achieved via DLLs to optimize the running speed. For virtual scenarios containing a large number

Figure 5. Four screenshots of the virtual shopping center example

of agents, objects and services, the alternative of distributed systems that associate each processor with a particular agent (or group of them) could lead to a substantial saving of time. Note also that many artificial intelligence techniques, such as the neural networks, are especially suited for parallelization. The combination of parallel computing and distributed environments provides the best rates of efficiency in terms of time and computational requirements.

Once the service has been successfully achieved, the output is available on the Web via a Web browser. Simple instructions written in HTTP and commercial software for Web applications are used in this step.

Finally, the security module has not been implemented by the authors. Instead, we reused some cryptographic code freely available on the Web for simple security purposes, while the communication is performed via HTTPS. In fact, security is one of the most critical limitations of current system and should be improved in future versions (see the last section for further details about our future lines).

ILLUSTRATIVE EXAMPLE

In this section we discuss a very simple yet illustrative example, aimed at showing the proposed framework. Our example is a virtual shopping center that mirrors a real mall where users go to do shopping. This scenario has been primarily chosen because it reflects one of the most typical services on the web—e-commerce—and provides users with a potentially large number of possible agent-object and agent-agent interactions. The shopping center (the 3D world according to the previously introduced terminology) consists of a squared-shape gallery of shops, restaurants, and offices, with a playground and some video-game machines at the center of the square and resting areas and drinking machines all around. The most usual services of any shopping center are available in this virtual world. The different shops in this virtual environment can easily be associated with real shops. To this aim, the only programmer's needs are the basic information to be provided to the DAML-S tools, namely, what the services do, how they work, and how they are used, as aforementioned. This information is stored into a database of services. Pointers to this database allow users to navigate through different services associated with the shops, compare prices and items and carry out the most usual tasks of any similar real environment.

The graphical environment is created by just taking still pictures of the shops and pasting them in the virtual world as textures (see Figure 5 for four screenshots of this virtual shopping center), by applying rough texture mapping. Prolog reasoner includes a based-on-rules expert system for making appropriate choices of items, based on user's requests and preferences. Those preferences are included as rules, and the inference engine performs the deductive processes. The system asks users about services via the user interface. The aforementioned semantic tools are then applied to interpret user's choices and proceed accordingly. The final output is returned to the user via a Web browser. Users may do shopping from their home, office, or anywhere else, and get all services currently available in real shopping centers at will. For instance, you can perform any banking service (such as paying a bill, checking your balance account, or modifying your client's profile) by simply creating an agent that goes to the virtual bank office and asks for those services. Security issues are performed in the usual manner through HTTPS secure pages and standard cryptographic procedures. However, security issues can easily be improved in the future, as they are performed by a module independent on the general framework.

The number of possible services available in this environment is extremely huge. For example, you can go to the music shop and listen to the last hit in your own computer, go to the supermarket to buy your weekly food, get the list of prices of a particular plug at the electronics store, or order your take-out meal at the Chinese restaurant. The usual online help of computer programs is now replaced by the information desk. If a particular user, let's say Peter, wants to get some information

Figure 6. Two examples of Web services: (left) buying a drink at a drinking machine; (right) playing with a videogame machine

about any issue related to the shopping center, he proceeds in a similar way he does in real life: after the access control and authentication steps, the virtual agent representing Peter explores the environment in order to find the information desk. Once there, Peter writes the question in a specific window of the inbox user interface at the Web and the system looks for an available virtual assistant at the information desk (say Lucy). She asks Peter to wait for the answer while she inputs graphically the question into a computer terminal at the information desk. Of course, Lucy's actions are actually a metaphor of those happening internally at the system: the string of characters that Peter wrote is retrieved by the DAML translator and converted into a semantically understandable sequence. Then, the system queries the answer at the knowledge database. Eventually, Lucy provides Peter with the answer either by audio (if an external program, such as Via Voice or similar, is available) or as plain text on the screen.

Other examples are shown in Figure 6: on the left, the agent goes directly to the drinking machine and gets one drink. This service provides the user with the list of hot and cold drinks, their prices, and availability at this time. On the right, the user wants to play with a video-game machine. The agent created for this service goes towards the video-game machine, inserts a coin and the game is available at user's console via the Web browser. Simultaneously, the amount for the payment is automatically charged to user's bank account or credit card.

Of course, interactions with other agents (e.g., users asking for similar or different services in the same environment) are also possible. Users can get information (or services) from them or perform tasks in a collaborative manner. For example, if you buy a drink from the drinking machine, one person located in front of the real machine can immediately get such a drink. If you ask for the take-out Chinese meal, you will receive it at home some minutes later.

COMPARISON WITH OTHER APPROACHES

Perhaps the closest works to our approach are Espinoza (2003), Espinoza and Hamfors (2003), and Sirin, Parsia, and Hendler (2004). In fact, the architecture of those systems is quite similar—although not exactly the same—to that described in this article. Differences come from the fact that the spirit and motivation of those papers are not similar to ours. For instance, the proposal in Espinoza and Hamfors (2003) is that end-users themselves can also be service providers. To this aim, they present ServiceDesigner, a tool based on a previous system called sView and intended for creating new services for end-users as providers. Although their orientation is quite different, most of the technical modules—especially those related to the Semantic Web tasks—can actually be incorporated into our implementation. It is worthwhile to mention that in Espinoza and Hamfors (2003) it has been pointed out the need for a graphical user interface (step 2 of their development). That interface is subsequently combined with a specification of the functional components into an sView compatible service. Although the system seems to work well, the user interface presented there is very much limited in comparison with ours.

On the other hand, the general structure of the system prototype in Sirin et al. (2004) inspired us to consider some of their components, such as those of the inbox module described in this article. Note also that, as opposed to our architecture, neither the graphical nor the behavioural modules have been considered in that work. In fact, such modules have never been described in Web service literature yet. Moreover, the approach in Sirin et al. (2004) does not care about the user interface, the focus being placed upon the interactive composition of services and the filtering of the possibilities thereafter by using semantic descriptions and directly executing the services through WSDL. We believe that these differences are very important to determine the degree of originality of this article in comparison with previous approaches.

EVALUATION AND VALIDATION

This section discusses some issues concerning the evaluation and validation of our approach. To this purpose, it is important to realize about the difference between the framework itself—which is rather a theoretical and general approach—and any of its feasible implementations. We do not claim that the implementation described in this article is necessarily the best one or that the readers should follow. In fact, it is basically a prototype, not the final release. Subsequent versions will likely contain a lot of changes with respect to this version, but we do not expect the proposed framework to vary significantly. Consequently, the conclusions of this evaluation process refer to the framework rather than to its current implementation. In this evaluation process, we pose three fundamental questions:

What Are the Benefits for Web Service Users and Developers in Adopting Our Framework?

In software development, there is a general agreement that a powerful user interface is a key factor for the success of products for Web users. In addition to good design principles of navigation and information architecture, the most useable sites also include a powerful graphical design. This issue becomes increasingly important for semantic applications designed to provide services on the Web. Today, most companies and organizations, government agencies, private corporations, and even individuals want to make their Web sites widely marketable and accessible to diversely abled populations. Creating user-friendly, intuitive, graphical interfaces for those Web sites

ensures that inexperienced users can access to Web services in an effective manner.

Besides, it has been pointed out that graphical interfaces have a beneficial effect for all users, even for those who are already familiar with Web services. This statement has been supported by some recent papers that analyzed the interface agents from users' viewpoint. For instance, Koda and Maes (1996) and Takeuchi and Naito (1995) studied users' responses and reactions to interfaces with static and animated faces. They concluded that users found them to be more engaging and entertaining than functionally equivalent interfaces without a face. Another experiment performed by Andre, Rist, and Muller (1998) found that users prefer interfaces with agents and rate them as more entertaining and helpful than an equivalent interface without the agent. Similar results have been obtained in Cassell and Vilhjalmsonn (1999). Agent's physical appearance is also very important: in Sproull, Subramani, Kiesler, Walker, and Waters (1996) and Kiesler and Sproull (1997), authors reported that users were more likely to be cooperative with an interface agent when it had a human face (as opposed to a dog image or anything else).

All these studies have emphasized the expressive power of the graphical virtual environments for user interfaces. Furthermore, they give a clear indication that the inclusion of virtual agents having a human-like appearance and behaviour greatly improves the efficiency of the communication channel and encourages people to use the system. Our framework provides an effective way to include all those features in standard software tools for Web services. Further, the implementation described in this article evidences the technical feasibility of our proposal.

Another remarkable advantage of the present contribution is the inclusion of autonomy for the virtual agents. Most graphical interfaces based on agents—such as the graphical chat systems—do use virtual agents, but those agents are not autonomous. Therefore, the user is forced to switch between controlling agent's behaviour and carrying out other actions. While the user is busy with those actions, the virtual agent keeps motionless or repeats a sequence of prescribed movements. This kind of answer causes misleading and conflicts between what users expect from the system and what they really get. This is a very important—and not sufficiently analyzed yet—issue for Web services. In our approach, the autonomy is provided by the knowledge motor via a combination of different artificial intelligence techniques. Agents are able to evolve freely without human intervention. As far as we know, this is the first Semantic Web approach that includes this feature. Some potential applications include the analysis of the behaviour of crowds under extreme conditions (e.g., in case of fire in the shopping center), online multiplayer video games, and many others.

The fact that virtual agents are autonomous is nice, but not enough. If agents do not take reasonable decisions according to human thinking, users become uncomfortable when using the system and, even worst, their trust is lost. In addition to autonomy, the implementation of intelligent behaviour for virtual agents is a must. This task falls deep into the artificial intelligence techniques incorporated in our approach. Of course, there are other Web service applications using them for semantic recognition purposes, but our approach goes far beyond: those techniques are also applied to realistic behavioural simulation of virtual agents performing services. We do not have knowledge about any other approach addressing this issue.

In our framework, agents are responsible to take decisions and perform actions. Such decisions are based on information: (1) previously stored into the system, (2) acquired from the environment, and (3) provided by users. This decision process is performed at two different levels so that it becomes completely transparent to user. What he/she actually sees on the screen is some virtual agents evolving in the virtual 3D world while performing user's services (the interface or

outer level). At the inner level, there is the Web service application.

Let Us Suppose that a Company or Organization Is Willing to Move into this Approach. How Expensive Could It Be? What Are the Main Requirements and Limitations?

First of all, this new approach is more expensive than only constructing a Web service site—but not too much. This is because creating that site is just a part of the final project. Costs for the additional software modules might vary very much according to the kind of specific requirements the company or organization has. Roughly, the framework is quite easy to design, but expensive to develop because of the software complexity: the whole system requires a lot of different software tools, which immediately translates into several month/person costs. Fortunately, the software tools involved in this process are quite standard. Moreover, the framework architecture is very flexible and allows external modules to be plugged into the system without affecting the other modules. This feature becomes especially attractive if some commercial software is applied to create the virtual environment. Today, there are several commercial software packages allowing programmers to construct virtual worlds for the Web in just a few minutes. The basic input is the geometric data of the real environment, which is often easily available. These nice features make the development more affordable that it could seem at first sight.

Because of its Web service-oriented profile, our proposal is mostly intended for companies and organizations. In fact, the framework is especially well suited for environments offering a large number of different services, such as a mall or similar. In these cases, the implementation and maintenance do not represent a large investment for those companies. In our opinion, the accessibility and ease of use of the resulting Web site will compensate these additional costs in just a few months, provided that the Web site is reasonably publicized.

One possible limitation is user's Internet connection bandwidth. Depending on the environment complexity, the number of services and users and other factors, the Internet resources required for this framework might exceed those commonly available for some users. Consequently, they would need to upgrade their bandwidth in order to access to all services. Also, companies would need a relatively high bandwidth to prevent the possibility of a bottleneck when a huge number of users are connected and using the system at the same time. Although this is a real problem that must be taken into account, future perspectives are getting better: telecommunication operators have begun offering access speed and bandwidth capacity options that match by large those required for this kind of services. While the current price rates are not so affordable for individual users—especially for the occasional ones—the current tendency for prices to decline is a favourable argument for the next future.

What about the Validation of the System?

Inspired by Narayanan and McIlraith (2002) and Narayanan and McIlraith (2003), the implementation described in this article has also been validated by interactive simulation with Petri nets (Iglesias & Kapcak, 2007; Gálvez, Iglesias, & Corcuera, 2007). To this aim, we considered several hypothetical cases for simulation and checked the corresponding results. In general, those results were according to our expectations—the Web services we tested behave quite well—but some limitations became evident during the process. The most important ones have been, on one hand, the security access and authentication and, on the other hand, the integrity and correctness of some data. However, they are two problems of

a completely different nature: the first problem lies on the framework layer, and can be explained by the fact that no specific modules have been designed for this issue. We are currently working to improve this drawback, as detailed in the next section. On the contrary, the limitations about the integrity and correctness lie on the implementation layer—actually, they were mostly due to some improper declarations at different parts of the code—meaning that they do not affect the general picture of the framework.

CONCLUSION AND FUTURE LINES

In this article, we have introduced a new framework for intelligent Semantic Web services based on graphical autonomous intelligent virtual agents (GAIVAs). Once a Web service is requested, the user is prompted through the Web into a virtual world that mirrors the real environment associated with the service. The interplay between users and the system is accomplished via those virtual agents that exhibit a human-like appearance and behaviour. The agents are completely autonomous, that is, they are able to take decisions and perform actions in order to provide services without human intervention. In addition, we require those decisions to be intelligent from the point of view of a human observer. To this aim, the framework comprises a collection of powerful artificial intelligence techniques also described in this article. The framework also incorporates a powerful GUI that allows users to interact with the system in a graphical and very natural way. We think that these advanced features are very helpful to encourage people to use a Web service system. Further, Web service providers and developers might greatly benefit from considering our approach.

In Espinoza and Hamfors (2003), the authors categorized the services into four different classes: being built from scratch, being constructed from a template, being combined from components, or a combination of these. Our approach belongs to the third category, meaning that many new services can be built by combining other services and connecting them to create new functionality. In fact, the architecture presented here is very versatile and able to adapt to many different services by changing the framework components (environments, agents, and others) in a very simple and user-friendly way. Although the power of this approach has not yet been exploited to bring its full potential, the preliminary results in this line are very promising.

Of course, the present scheme can be improved in several directions. After all, what is presented here is just a computer prototype, not the final system running for real purposes and services. However, we think that, as soon as we solve some current limitations of the system, it has a great potential of possible applications. It is our opinion that the advanced features of our graphical user interface and the inclusion of powerful artificial intelligence techniques for reasoning, learning, and cognitive processes do represent a major step in the Information technology field.

Future lines of research will also include some improvements related to security issues—a particularly critical point for commercial purposes and e-business. This field has been recently explored in some papers, such as Kagal, Paolucci, Denker, Finin, and Sycara (2004). We think that their proposals could also be applied to our framework in order to improve system's security and privacy. Other future tasks are the interconnection of the system with real stores and services, the inter-cooperation between different services, and the definitions of some semantic features that have shown to be troublesome at this time. We hope that the recently released version of OWL-S (formerly DAML-S) v1.1 will help us in tasks such as service execution, interoperation, composition, and execution monitoring. Once improved, our next step is to link the system with real applications on the Web. The obtained results will be reported elsewhere.

ACKNOWLEDGMENT

The author is thankful to the three anonymous referees for their constructive comments and suggestions, which greatly contributed to improve the draft version of this manuscript. He also thanks the IJITWE editors-in-chief for their kind assistance and encouraging comments. Financial support from the Spanish Ministry of Education and Science, Project Ref. #TIN2006-13615 and the University of Cantabria is also acknowledged.

REFERENCES

Andre, E., Rist, T., & Muller, J. (1998). Integrating reactive and scripted behaviours in a life-like presentation agent. In Proceedings of AGENTS'98 (pp. 261-268).

Badler, N., Bindiganavale, R. Allbeck, J., Schuler, W., Zhao, L., Lee, S. J. et al. (2000). Parameterized action representation and natural language instructions for dynamic behaviour modification of embodied agents. In Proceedings of AAAI Spring Symposium (pp. 36-40).

Berners-Lee, T., Hendler, J., & Lassila, O. (2001). The semantic web. Scientific American, 284(5), 34-43.

Beskow, J., Elenius, K. & McGlashan, S. (1997). Olga—a dialogue system with an animated talking agent. In Proceedings of EUROSPEECH'97. Rhodes, Greece.

Beskow, J., & McGlashan, S. (1997). Olga: a conversational agent with gestures. In Proceedings of the IJCAI'97 workshop on Animated Interface Agents— Making them Intelligent (pp. 1651-1654). Nagoya, Japan.

Bindiganavale, R., Schuler, W., Allbeck, J. Badler, N., Joshi, A., & Palmer, M. (2000). Dynamically altering agent behaviors using natural language. In Proceedings of Autonomous Agents 2000 (pp. 293-300).

Bordeux, C., Boulic, R., & Thalmann, D. (1999). An efficient and flexible perception pipeline for autonomous agents. Computer Graphics Forum (Proc. of Eurographics '99), 18(3), 23-30.

Brooks, R. A. (1985). A robust layered control system for a mobile robot. Cambridge, MA: MIT AI Lab.

Brooks, R.A. (1991). Intelligence without representation. Artificial Intelligence, 47, 139–159.

Bryson, J. J., Martin, D., McIlraith, S. A., & Stein, L. A. (2003). Agent-based composite services in DAML-S: The behaviour-oriented design of an intelligent semantic web. Web Intelligence, Springer-Verlag, Berlin Heidelberg, 37-58.

Caicedo, A., & Thalmann, D. (2000). Virtual humanoids: let them to be autonomous without losing control. In D. Plemenos (Ed.), Proceedings of the Fourth International Conference on Computer Graphics and Artificial Intelligence (pp. 59-70). University of Limoges, Limoges.

Cassell, J., Bickmore, T., Campbell, L., Vilhjalmsson, J., & Yan, H. (2001). More than just a pretty face: conversational protocols and the affordances of embodiment. Knowledge-Based Systems. 14, 55-64.

Cassell, J., Pelachaud, C., Badler, N,., Steedman, M., Achorn, B., Becket, T., et al. (1994). Animated conversation: rule-based generation of facial expression, gesture and spoken intonation for multiple conversational agents. In Proceedings of ACM SIGGRAPH '94 (pp. 413-420).

Cassell, J., & Vilhjalmsson, J. (1999). Fully embodied conversational avatars: Making communicative behaviours autonomous. Autonomous Agents and Multi-Agent Systems, 2(1) 45-64.

Castillo, E.,& Alvarez, E. (1991). Expert systems. Uncertainty and learning. London and New York: Elsevier Applied Science and Computational Mechanics Publications.

Castillo, E., Gutierrez, J. M. & Hadi, A. S. (1997). Expert systems and probabilistic network models. New York: Springer Verlag.

Cohen, P. R., & Levesque, H. J. (1987). Persistence, intention and commitment. In Proceedings of the 1986 Workshop on Reasoning about Actions and Plans (pp. 297-340). San Mateo, CA: Morgan Kaufmann Publishers.

Cohen, P. R., & Levesque, H. J. (1990). Intention is choice with commitment. Artificial Intelligence, 42(3), 213-261.

Cohen, P., Johnston, M., & McGee, D. (1997) Quickset: Multimodal interaction for distributed applications. In Proceedings of the Fifth ACM International Multimedia Conference (pp. 31–40). ACM Press.

Cowles, P. (2005). Web service API and the semantic web. Web Services Journal, 2(12), 76-82. Available online at: http://webservices.sys-con.com/read/39631.htm

Espinoza, F. (2003). Towards individual service provisioning. In Proceedings of the 2003 International Conference on Intelligent User Interfaces (IUI 2003) (pp. 239-241). ACM Press.

Espinoza, F., & Hamfors, O. (2003). ServiceDesigner: A tool to help end-users become individual service providers. In Proceedings of the Thirty-Sixth Annual Hawaii International Conference on System Sciences (IEEE) (Track 9, Vol. 9, pp. 296.1-10).

Feiner, S., & McKeown, K. (1991). Automating the generation of coordinated multimedia explanations. IEEE Computer, 24(10) 33-41.

Gálvez, A., Iglesias, A., & Corcuera, P. (2007). Representation and analysis of a dynamical system with petri nets. In Proceedings of International Conference on Convergence Information Technology, ICCIT'2007, Gyeongju (Korea) (pp. 2009-2015) IEEE Computer Society Press.

Georgeff, M. P., & Ingrand, F. F. (1989). Decision-making in an embedded reasoning system. In Proceedings of the International Joint Conference on Artificial Intelligence (pp. 972-978). Detroit, MI.

Goncalves, L. M., Kallmann, M., & Thalmann, D. (2001). Programming behaviours with local perception and smart objects: An approach to solve autonomous agent tasks. In Proceedings of SIGGRAPI'2001 (pp. 143-150).

Granieri, J. P., Becket, W., Reich, B. D., Crabtree, J., & Badler, N. I. (1995). Behavioral control for real-time simulated human agents. In Proceedings of Symposium on Interactive 3D Graphics (pp. 173-180). ACM Press.

Grzeszczuk, R., & Terzopoulos, D. (1995). Automated learning of muscle-actuated locomotion through control abstraction. In Proceedings of ACM SIGGRAPH'95 (pp. 6-11).

Grzeszczuk, R., Terzopoulos, D., & Hinton, G. (1998). NeuroAnimator: fast neural network emulation and control of physics-based models. In Proceedings of ACM SIGGRAPH'98 (pp. 9-20).

Gutiérrez, M., Vexo, F., & Thalmann, D. (2003). Controlling virtual humans using PDAs. In Proceedings of 9th International Conference on Multi-Media Modeling (MMM'03) (pp. 27-33). Taiwan.

Haykin, S. (1994). Neural networks. A comprehensive foundation. Englewood Cliffs, NJ: Macmillan Publishing.

Hendler, J. (2001). Agents and the semantic web. IEEE Intelligent Systems, 2(16), 30-37.

Hendler, J., Berners-Lee, T., & Miller, E. (2002). Integrating applications on the semantic web. Journal of the Institute of Electrical Engineers of Japan, 122(10), 676-680.

Hertz, J., Krogh, A., & Palmer, R. G. (1991). Introduction to the theory of neural computation. Reading, MA: Addison Wesley.

Iglesias, A., & Kapcak, S. (2007) Symbolic computation of petri nets. Lectures Notes in Computer Science, 4488, 235-242.

Iglesias, A., & Luengo, F. (2004). Intelligent agents for virtual worlds. In Proceedings of CyberWorlds (CW'2004) (pp. 62-69). IEEE Computer Society Press.

Iglesias, A., & Luengo, F. (2005). New goal selection scheme for behavioral animation of intelligent virtual agents. IEICE Transactions on Information and Systems [Special Issue on "CyberWorlds"] E88-D(5), 865-871.

Iglesias, A., & Luengo, F. (2007) AI framework for decision modeling in behavioral animation of virtual avatars. Lectures Notes in Computer Science, 4488, 89-96.

Ingrand, F. F., Georgeff, M. P., & Rao, A. S. (1992). An architecture for real-time reasoning and system control. IEEE Intelligent Systems, 7(6), 34-44.

Kagal, L., Paolucci, M., Denker, G., Finin, T., & Sycara, K. (2004). Authorization and privacy for semantic web services. IEEE Intelligent Systems, 19(4), 50-56.

Kiesler, S., & Sproull, L. (1997). Social human-computer interaction. In Human Values and the Design of Computer Technology, 199, CSLI Publications, Stanford, CA. 191.

Koda, T., & Maes, P. (1996). Agents with faces: the effects of personification of agents. In Proceedings of Fifth IEEE International Workshop on Robot and Human Communication (pp. 189-194).

Lester, J. C., Voerman, J. L., Towns, S. G., & Callaway, C. B. (1997). Cosmo: a life-like animated pedagogical agent with deictic believability. In Proceedings of IJCAI'97.

Luengo, F., & Iglesias, A. (2003) A new architecture for simulating the behavior of virtual agents. Lectures Notes in Computer Science, 2657, 935-944.

Maes, P. (1994). Agents that reduce work and information overload. Communications of the ACM, 37(7), 31-40,146.

McIlraith, S., Son, T. C., & Zeng, H. (2001). Semantic web services. IEEE Intelligent Systems, 16(2), 46-53.

Minsky, M. (1985). The society of mind. New York: Simon and Schuster Inc.

Moltenbrey, K. (1999). All the right moves. Computer Graphics World, 22(10), 28-34.

Monzani, J. S., Caicedo, A., & Thalmann, D. (2001). Integrating behavioural animation techniques. In Proceedings of the Computer Graphics Forum (EUROGRAPHICS'2001) 20(3), 309-318.

Narayanan, S., & McIlraith, S. (2002). Simulation, verification and automated composition of web services. In Proceedings of the Eleventh International World Wide Web Conference-WWW2002. ACM Press.

Narayanan, & S., McIlraith, S. (2003). Analysis and simulation of web services. Computer Networks, 42, 675-693.

Neal, J. G., & Shapiro, S. C. (1991). Intelligent multi-media interface technology. In Proceedings of Intelligent User Interfaces (pp. 11-43). ACM Press.

Oviatt, S. (1999). Ten myths of multimodal interaction. Communications of the ACM, 42(11) 74-81.

Prevost, S., Hodgson, P., Cook, L., & Churchill, E. F. (1999). Face-to-face interfaces. In Proceedings of CHI'99 (pp. 244-245). ACM Press.

Rao, A. S., & Georgeff, M. P. (1991). Modeling rational agents within a bdi-architecture. In Proceedings of the Third International Conference on Principles of knowledge Representation and Reasoning (pp. 473-484). San Mateo, CA: Morgan Kaufmann.

Raupp, S., & Thalmann, D. (2001) Hierarchical model for real time simulation of virtual human crowds. IEEE Transactions on Visualization and Computer Graphics, 7(2), 152-164.

Sirin, E., Parsia, B., & Hendler, J. (2004). Filtering and selecting semantic web services with interactive composition techniques. IEEE Intelligent Systems, 18(4), 42-49.

Sproull, L., Subramani, R., Kiesler, S., Walker, J., & Waters, K. (1996). When the interface is a face. In Proceedings of Human-Computer Interaction (Vol. 11, pp. 97-124).

Takeuchi, A., & Nagao, K. (1993). Communicative facial displays as a new conversational modality. In Proceedings of ACM/IFIP INTERCHI '93 (pp.187-193). ACM Press.

Takeuchi, A., & Naito, T. (1995). Situated facial displays: towards social interaction. In Proceedings of CHI'95 (pp. 450 – 455). ACM Press.

Thalmann, D., & Monzani, J. S. (2002) Behavioural animation of virtual humans: What kind of law and rules? In Proceedings of Computer Animation 2002 (pp. 154-163). IEEE Computer Society Press.

Thorisson, K. (1996). Communicative humanoids: A computational model of psychosocial dialogue skills. MIT Media Laboratory PhD thesis, MIT, Cambridge, MA.

This work was previously published in International Journal of Information Technology and Web Engineering, Vol. 3, Issue 4, edited by G. Alkhatib; D. Rine, pp. 30-58, copyright 2008 by IGI Publishing (an imprint of IGI Global).

Chapter 4
An Agent–Enabled Semantic Web Service Composition Framework

Sandeep Kumar
Institute of Technology - Banaras Hindu University (IT-BHU), India

Kuldeep Kumar
University Institute of Engineering & Technology - Kurukshetra University, India

Ankita Jain
National Institute of Technology, India

ABSTRACT

A Semantic Web service composition system can be considered as a multi-agent system, in which each of the component service is considered as an agent capability. This chapter presents a multi-agent system based Semantic Web service composition approach. The proposed approach deals with some of the untouched issues and uses cognitive parameters and quality of service (QoS) parameters in service-provider selection. Education planning, a new application area for Semantic Web technology that involves planning the admission process for higher education courses has been introduced and the proposed approach and models are applied to it.

1. INTRODUCTION

Semantic Web Services (SWSs) are web services with well-defined semantics, having their own properties and capabilities described in an unambiguous and computer-interpretable way, and thus providing inter-operability between them (Mcllraith et al., 2001). These are self-contained, reusable software components, which can be used independently to fulfill a need or can be combined with other SWSs to carry out a complex aggregation. SWSs have modular structure and can be published, located, or called through the web. The different services can be combined with other homogeneous or heterogeneous services to form complex web applications. So, the interfaces, properties, capabilities, and effects of SWSs are encoded in a machine-understandable form to allow an easy integration of heterogeneous services. This process of generating aggregated service by the integration of independent available

DOI: 10.4018/978-1-60566-719-5.ch004

component services for satisfying a client-request that can not be satisfied by any single available service is called as SWS Composition.

A Multi-Agent System (MAS) consists of a team or organization of software agents, collectively performing a task, which could not be performed by any individual agent. This paper is based on the understanding that a SWS composition system can be considered as a MAS, where each component service is considered as an agent capability implemented as a self-contained software component. Some of the issues in composition process are there, which are not discussed till now. We have presented a detailed overview of these issues and also proposed a MAS based SWS composition process, which can handle these issues. A detailed evaluation and comparison with the existing similar works has also been presented in the paper. We have used the two mathematical models for service-provider selection, which assess cognitive parameters, and Quality of Service (QoS) parameters in selection. A novel model has been presented for providing the cognitive parameters based selection. This model is an enhancement of a previous work, Hybrid Selection Model (HSM) (Kumar & Mishra, 2008). The work has also been extended by applying the proposed models for education planning. The main contribution of the presented work includes:

- A novel Multi-Agent System based Semantic Web Service Composition approach.

- A novel cognitive-parameters based model for dynamic selection of agents. The model not only considers the past performance of the agent for its selection, but also provides dynamic selection by providing a feedback system.

- Introducing a new domain area of education planning as an application of semantic web based systems. The presented semantic web service composition system has

been successfully applied on this problem of education planning.

The paper has been structured as follows. Apart from Introduction in Section-1, some of the related works has been presented in the Section-2. Section-3 presents a novel MAS based SWS composition approach. Section-4 presents a novel selection-model based on cognitive parameters. A brief introduction to HSM has also been presented in this section. Evaluation of the presented composition approach and its validation and comparison with existing similar works has been presented in Section-5. Section-6 introduces a new area of application i.e. education planning and deals with the issues involved in the implementation of proposed service composition approach and service selection models. Finally, the paper has been concluded in section-7, with some discussion on the future work.

2. RELATED WORKS

From the last decade, a lot of researchers are involved in the research on SWS composition. Among other, some of reported works on SWS composition are (Gomez-Perez et al., 2004; Sell et al., 2004; Wu et al., 2003; Lecue & Leger, 2005; Arpinar et al., 2004; Chen et al., 2003; Pistore et al, 2004; Vallee et al, 2005; Kungas & Matskin, 2006; Agarwal et al., 2004; McIlraith & Son, 2002; Kvaloy et al., 2005; Ermolayev et al., 2004; Charif & Sabouret, 2005; and Wu et al., 2006). But, a little attention has been paid to the field of multi-agent based service composition. Out of the above listed works, (Vallee et al, 2005; Kungas & Matskin, 2006; Ermolayev et al., 2004) have presented the use of MAS in SWS composition.

A P2P based multi-agent environment providing SWS composition has been presented by the Kungas & Matskin (2006). They have mainly discussed the issues pertaining to the P2P networks and MAS environments. In their presented MAS, agents cooperatively apply the distributed symbolic reasoning to discover and compose SWSs. Vallee et al. (2005) have proposed an approach enabling dynamic and context-aware composition of SWSs in ambient intelligence environments by combining multi-agent techniques with SWSs. The benefits that ambient intelligence can get from the coupling of service-oriented approach and multi-agent systems are also discussed by them. According to them, it enables more appropriate interactions with the users. In the works by Kungas & Matskin (2006) and Vallee et al. (2005), agent's capabilities are not representing the SWS components, but they are only supporting in the composition of available SWS components. A work using agent capability as an SWS component has been presented by Ermolayev et al., (2004). They have presented an agent-enabled cooperative dynamic SWS composition approach. They have used a mediation framework for agent-enabled service provisioning targeted to dynamic composition of SWSs. They have also presented a SWS selection model which is based upon the capability and credibility assessment of the various candidate SPAs.

Similar to these existing works, our work also presents an agent-enabled SWS composition framework. The presented work is based upon the similar understanding, as in (Ermolayev et al., 2004), of using the agent capability as a SWS component. A multi-agent based SWS composition approach dealing with some of the untouched issues has been presented. The work presents a SWS selection model based upon the cognitive parameters based rating of candidate services. This model considers a broad range of cognitive parameters such a trust, reputation, capability, desire, intention, commitment etc. in its selection process and a formal modeling has been presented for each of the parameters. The work has also been evaluated. A service composition system has also been implemented for the education planning problem.

3. MAS BASED SWS COMPOSITION APPROACH

In this section, we have presented a novel MAS Based SWS Composition Process (MABSCP). MABSCP is based on the concept of using an independent dedicated coordinator agent for controlling the various activities in composition process. A layout of the MABSCP is shown in Figure 1(a) and 1(b). The system mainly consists of following three types of agents:

- Service Requester Agent (SRA)
- Coordinator Agent (CA)
- Service Provider Agent (SPA)

SRA has the responsibility to perform the request to CA. The request by SRA is then specified in the term of ontology, which is then used by the CA. An intelligent CA has following properties and capabilities:

- CA is a modular, self-contained software component, wrapping coordination services, with ontological service description.
- It has the capability of validating the constraints, preferences, and other higher level parameters of the SRA's input-request.
- It has the capability of validating if the input activity is atomic or complex. In case it is complex, interpreting it as a task comprising of various atomic activities of varying granularity and decomposing it into atomic tasks according to their ontology description.
- It can evaluate and assess the SPAs using their cognitive and Quality of Service (QoS) parameters.
- It can negotiate with the SPAs as well as SRA to adjust activity input, SRA preferences and constraints, and to obtain matching common IOPE (Inputs, Outputs, Preconditions, and Effects) in order to satisfy the ultimate request.

Figure 1.

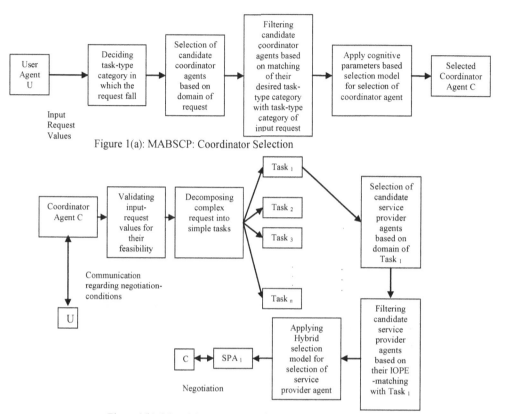

Figure 1(a): MABSCP: Coordinator Selection

Figure 1(b): MABSCP: SPAs Selection and Composition

• It makes arrangement for outsourcing the activity to SPAs based on FIPA Contract Net Protocol (Smith & Davis, 2008) and agent's communication interface built upon FIPA-ACL (FIPA Architecture Board, 2008).

An intelligent SPA has following properties and capabilities:

• SPA is a self-contained, modular agent, wrapping services in the form of software components, with the corresponding ontological service description.
• The purpose of SPA is decided by the services it wraps.
• It is able to understand the meaning of activity, it is to perform.
• SPA joins the composition process, only for the time its service is required.

Layouts of MABSCP are shown in Figures 1(a) and 1(b), for CA and SPA selection respectively. The system has novelty in the following aspects:

• In the practical scenario, it is not always the case that the negotiation can be performed freely between SRA and CA or SPA and CA. Because, there can be following conditions:
  ◦ Some of the request parameters, constraints, or preferences are so rigid that they are not negotiable.
  ◦ All of the constraints, preferences, and parameters specified by the customer are such that they are not negotiable.
  ◦ Customer is not at all interested in performing the negotiation. Avoiding these conditions may cause un-necessarily wasting the negotiation efforts.

If the first condition is there, then the system can avoid those particular parameters for the negotiation process. For example, in some cases, the time constraint may be very rigid and not meeting it may cancel the request. To the best of our knowledge, no literature on MAS based SWS composition handling this issue is there. MABSCP has handled this problem by communicating with the SRA regarding negotiation conditions, before starting the actual composition process.

- Various different requests from SRAs, even falling in same domain, can not be treated in the same manner. The performance of an agent may vary depending on some parameters of requests. For example, in famous travel-planning scenario, one agent may be performing better in handing the problems of travel-planning in Europe region, while the other may be performing for Asia region. It may also be the case that an agent is desirous of performing with only some particular parameters for some particular time-period, while with some other parameters for other time-period. To the best of our knowledge, no literature on MAS based SWS composition is there, which is handling this issue. MABSCP is handing this problem by dividing the requests falling in the same domain into multiple categories. It decides the category into which input-request should fall, based on various parameter-values in the request. It further assesses only those agents for their possible selection, who desires in performing for the decided category of input-request, at the time of their selection. We have only applied this procedure for the selection of CA. However, it can be applied to the selection of SPAs in the similar fashion. But as the request to CA is in the form of a complex task, so there is more chances that

it can be properly categorized, so this concept seems to fit in this case in better way.

- Request from SRA may contain such parameters, constraints, or preferences which seem infeasible or within specified constraints the satisfaction of request seems near to impossible. So, the composition will fail at the end, when even after negotiation between SPAs and CA, the constraints will not be satisfied. MABSCP handle this problem by placing validation on these parameters of requested task by the CA, before proceeding further in the process.

- MABSCP uses a proposed Cognitive Parameters Based Selection Model (CPBSM) for selection of CA. The model calculates an Index of Selection (IoS) for each candidate CA using their different cognitive parameters like capability, desire, commitment, intention, trust, and reputation, which works as basis for agent selection. These parameters also take into account the past performance of the agent. The reputation parameter takes into account the past experience of given SRA as well as other similar SRAs regarding the performance of candidate CA. The model provides dynamicity in the selection process by updating the past reputation factor of selected CA after taking its services, based on a feedback value decided from its present performance. Detailed discussion on CPBSM is presented in forthcoming sections. MABSCP uses HSM (Kumar and Mishra, 2008) for selection of SPAs. HSM provides service-selection based upon both cognitive parameters and QoS parameters. It calculates an Index of Selection (IoS) using a combination of two indexes: Cognitive Index (CI) and Quality Index (QI). CA calculates CI for each of the SPAs using their different cognitive parameters like capability, desire, commitment, intention, trust, and reputation, which are further based on their past performance. QI is calculated by the CA for each of SPAs using their QoS parameters like cost of service, response time, execution time, reliability, penalty etc.

MABSCP involves sending a request from the SRA, user agent U, to the system, which is then represented in the term of ontologies. The parameters in the request are used to decide the domain and further the task-type category within the domain of the request. The domain of the request is used to discover all the candidate CAs by matching from their published ontological service profiles. The candidate CAs are further filtered based on the matching that if the task-type category of the input-request is matching with any of the category mentioned in the set of desired task-type categories of the candidate CA or not. The matchmaking here can be performed either using semantic matching (Paolucci et al., 2002) based on ontology profiles like in DAML-S (The DAML Services Coalition, 2008), OWL (McGuinness & Harmelen, 2008) or using any other service matching method. Various techniques of discovery (Stollberg & Haller, 2005) can be applied here like keyword matching, controlled vocabulary matching, semantic matchmaking etc. The system can be made to proceed with the exact match, plug-in match, subsumption match, or intersection match as required in the process. IoS is then calculated for each of the filtered CAs using CPBSM and the CA with maximum IoS is selected as the coordinator C for given composition problem. At this stage, U can perform negotiation with C based on FIPA Contract Net Protocol (Smith & Davis, 2008). C accepts task from U by means of agent's communication interface built upon FIPA-ACL (FIPA Architecture Board, 2008). All further activities remaining in the MABSCP are coordinated by C; however, it can perform negotiation with U during the process, if required and allowed. C acquires the conditions of negotiation from U by means of agent's communication interface built upon FIPA-ACL (FIPA

Architecture Board, 2008). Now, C performs a validation over the parameters, preferences, and constraints to check their feasibility. Further, it determines from the input-request that it is an atomic activity or complex one. In case the input request is complex task, then C decomposes it into atomic tasks, $Task_1$, $Task_2$, $Task_3$ ... $Task_n$, of varying granularity. Now, for each atomic task, the candidate SPAs are discovered by using the same process as depicted above for discovery of CA. Filtering over discovered SPAs are performed based on their IOPE (Inputs, Outputs, Pre-conditions, Effects) matching with the required task. The matchmaking at this stage can be performed in the similar way as described above for the CA. IoS is then calculated for each of the filtered SPAs using HSM and the agent with maximum IoS is selected as service provider. Now, negotiation between C and the selected SPA can be initiated, if required and allowed. Figure 1(b) shows this process for $Task_1$ only, however, it is performed for each atomic task in the same manner.

It is to be noted that we have applied CPBSM in selection of CA and HSM in selection of SPAs, however they can be adapted easily to apply interchangeably. So, in the following section, we have used the term SPA in both CPBSM and HSM to refer to the provider agent, which may be either CA providing coordination services or any SPA performing specific activities to fulfill a requirement.

4. SELECTION MODELS

This section presents a novel mathematical model, CPBSM, for selection of SPAs based on their cognitive parameters. A brief summary of HSM has also been provided.

4.1. Hybrid Selection Model (HSM)

HSM (Kumar & Mishra, 2008) performs rating of the agents based on their cognitive and QoS parameters. HSM calculates an Index of Selection

(IoS) for the agent based on its cognitive and QoS parameters. The calculated IoS is used as the basis of selection for best provider agent. The IoS has been defined as the weighted sum of cognitive parameter based rating and QoS based rating of provider agent. Various cognitive parameters are capability, desire, intention, commitment, trust, reputation etc. and various QoS parameters are cost, response-time, reliability, accuracy, security feature, execution-time, exception handling feature, penalty on breaking service contract etc. HSM can be used by the requester agent for the selection of best performing provider agent. Where, requester agent is any agent which wants to take any type of services from other agent, called provider agent. The details on this model can be referred from (Kumar & Mishra, 2008). In MABSCP, this model is mainly suited for the SPA selection only. In the presented composition process, the input request has been categorized into task-type categories, which are also used in the selection of coordinator agent. But, the HSM provides no provision for it. So, we have presented a new model, CPBSM, which is based on the cognitive parameters and provides the provision for handling task-type categories in the selection of SPAs. The presented model also proposes an enhanced formalism and procedure for measuring desire and reputation of SPAs.

4.2. Cognitive Parameters Based Selection Model (CPBSM)

Cognitive parameters such as reputation, trust, capability, desire, intention etc. can play an important role in SWS selection and composition. One SWS can be chosen out of the discovered SWSs based on its cognitive parameters and it will be finally invoked by the user. The presented Cognitive Parameters Based Selection Model (CPBSM) can be easily integrated with any multi-agent based SWS composition process. CPBSM can be used by any requester agent for rating provider agents based on their past performance, trustworthiness,

and reputation. CPBSM calculates an Index of Selection (IoS) for the agent based on its trustworthiness, and reputation among the requester agents. IoS calculated can be used as the basis of selection for best provider agent. Where, requester agent is any agent which wants to take any type of services from other agent, called provider agent. However, the services can be of coordinating a task or performing a specific task or any other similar activities. So, the IoS can be defined as the weighted sum of trustworthiness and reputation of agent.

$$IoS = \alpha(TI) + (1-\alpha)(RI) \qquad (1)$$

Where $0 \leq TI \leq 1, \ 0 \leq RI \leq 1, \ 0 \leq \alpha \leq 1, \ 0 \leq IoS \leq 1$

where, TI is the Trust Index, representing a value which is measure of the trustworthiness of the agent and RI is the Reputation Index, representing a value which is measure of the reputation of the agent among other similar requester agents and the given requester agent. α is the measure of relative weight given to trustworthiness as compared to reputation of agent in its selection. The calculation for TI and RI is shown in sections below. As RI also includes the reputation value from the present requester agent, so IoS is not only considering its trustworthiness and reputation among other fellow similar requester agents, but also the reputation in view of present requester.

4.2.1. Measuring Trustworthiness of Agent

The trust of an agent on other information source agent is defined as the confidence in the ability and intention of an information source to deliver correct information (Barber & Kim, 2001). We have adapted this definition for the presented MAS based SWS composition system, to define the trust of SRA on the SPA as the confidence in the ability and intention of the SPA to deliver the committed services. So, TI can be defined as:

$$TI = CI * II \quad \text{where}$$
$$0 \leq CI \leq 1, \quad 0 \leq II \leq 1 \quad (2)$$

Where, CI is the Capability Index, representing a value which is measure of the capability of the agent and II is the Intention Index, representing a value which is measure of the intention of the agent to deliver committed services.

Capability is the measure of both capacity and expertise of an agent. An agent can only perform for its committed goal, if it has capability to do so (Padgham & Lambrix, 2000). So, capability of an agent can be judged from its past performance towards the accepted tasks and with how much perfection these were performed. So, CI of an agent can be calculated as follows:

It is to be noted that the performance of an agent may vary depending on the type of task or problem it is handling. So, it will show different capability with different task-type. Consider that a task which is handled by an agent can be categorized into any one of n task-type categories. Also, the capability and perfection-level of an agent can be judged based on these scenarios: task completed successfully within the committed parameters, task completed successfully but with some relaxed parameters, and task not completed. Each scenario will effect differently on the capability-measure of agent. These scenarios also show perfection-level of the agent.

So, with following parameters the capability index (CI_k) of an agent for a task-type T_k can be given by equation (3). Let CI_1, CI_2 ... CI_n be the capability indexes of an agent for task-types T_1, T_2 ... T_n respectively. N_C^k, N_{CR}^k, N_{NC}^k be the number of tasks completed successfully with committed parameters, completed successfully but with relaxed parameters, and not completed respectively, out of total N^k tasks of task-type T_k, where k = 1, 2 ... n. These parameters can be maintained in the ontological service profiles of agent. WC_C, WC_{CR},

WC_{NC} be the capability-weights given to the tasks completed successfully, completed successfully but with relaxed parameters, and not completed respectively. Then, CI_k can be given as:

$$CI_k = \frac{WC_C * N_C^k + WC_{CR} * N_{CR}^k - WC_{NC} * N_{NC}^k}{(WC_C + WC_{CR} + WC_{NC}) * N^k}$$

And following relations should hold:

1. $N^k = N_C^k + N_{CR}^k + N_{NC}^k$
2. $N^1 = N^2 = ... = N^n = 100$, as equation (3) will take percentage values for N_C^k, N_{CR}^k, N_{NC}^k out of total N^k tasks
3. $0 \leq CI_k \leq 1$, as eq. (3) has value normalized by $(WC_C + WC_{CR} + WC_{NC}) * N^k$
4. $WC_C > WC_{CR}$, this will cause greater weight in the capability calculation to the task which is completed successfully within committed parameters than the task completed successfully but with relaxed parameters
5. $WC_{NC} > WC_C$, as is clear from eq. (3) that WCNC is causing the negative effect on the capability of agent, but this relation will cause an extra penalty over the agent for not completing the committed task.
6. Values of WCC, WCCR, WCNC can be taken under any fixed range, but for uniformity, we can take it between 0 and 1.

Now, it is to be noted that from the view of SRA, all the task-types can not be given equal weights. Some task-types may be difficult to perform than the other ones. So, overall CI will be the weighted mean of individual capability indexes for all task-types. If WD_1, WD_2 ... WD_n be the difficulty weights (their value can be in any fixed range, but for uniformity, we can take it between 0 and 1) for task-types T_1, T_2 ... T_n respectively, then overall CI of an agent can be given by the weighted arithmetic mean of the capability indexes of agent for these task-type categories:

$$CI = \frac{\sum_{i=1}^{n} CI_i * WD_i}{\sum_{i=1}^{n} WD_i} \quad \text{where} \quad 0 \le CI \le 1 \quad (4)$$

Intention of an agent tells about the set of plan for the goal it has committed to achieve. Tweedale et al. (2007) have defined intention as "Intention is desire with commitment". So, intention can be defined as the combination of desire and commitment, where desire tells about the internal mental state of the agent, while the commitment tells about the external public state of agent, which even can be written beforehand as an agreement or contract. So, the II of an agent can be calculated as:

$$II = DI * CommI,$$

$$\text{where} \quad 0 \le DI \le 1, \quad 0 \le CommI \le 1 \quad (5)$$

Where, DI is the Desire Index, representing a value which is measure of the performance of the agent for its desired tasks and CommI is the Commitment Index, representing a value which is measure of the commitment of the agent towards accepted work.

Desire of an agent defines the state of the art that needs to be accomplished. It differs from the intention in the point that, desire defines the motivation towards the work, while intention may be seen as an agent's immediate commitment to implementing an action, as is also clear from equation (5) (Pechoucek, 2003). So, if an agent has desire for a task, then ideally it should perform well for that task. Hence, measuring the past-performance of an agent for the tasks presently desired by it can be good measure of its honesty towards its desire. From this, SRA can properly judge, how reference SPA will react for its present desires. We have incorporated a parameter, Performance-to-Desire (PD), which can be defined as the measure of the performance of an agent for the tasks for

which it has shown desire. We will consider this concept of desire for different task-types. Now, if an agent has published its profile for a task of particular domain (like trip planning), then it is obvious that it is desirous of doing tasks of that domain, but may not be of all types. Also, the desired task-types of agent may vary with time. So, the list of desired tasks has to be checked by SRA for each request. This information can be maintained in the published profile of the SPA. Now, let at the time of request, the desire-list of task-types for SPA is $(DT_1, DT_2 \ldots DT_d)$, where $(DT_1, DT_2 \ldots DT_d) \subseteq (T_1, T_2 \ldots T_n)$ and T_r be the requested task-type. Then, the DI of an agent can be calculated as the combination of PD of agent for $(DT_1, DT_2 \ldots DT_d)$ and PD for T_r. It must be noted that, IoS for this reference SPA will be calculated only if $T_r \in (DT_1, DT_2 \ldots DT_d)$. So, using the concepts as described in the calculation of CI, the PD_k for desired task-type DT_k can be calculated as below:

Let $PD_1, PD_2 \ldots PD_d$ be the Performance-to-Desire values of agent for task-types $DT_1, DT_2 \ldots DT_d$ respectively. $ND_C^k, ND_{CR}^k, ND_{NC}^k$ be the number of tasks completed successfully with committed parameters, completed successfully with relaxed parameters, and not completed respectively, out of total ND^k tasks of task-type DT_k, where k = 1, 2 … d. These parameters can be maintained in the ontological service-profiles of agents. $WDs_C, WDs_{CR}, WDs_{NC}$ be the performance-to-desire weights given to the tasks completed successfully, completed successfully but with relaxed parameters, and not completed respectively, for the tasks which are presently desired by agent. Then, PD_k can be given as:

$$PD_k = \frac{WDs_C * ND_C^k + WDs_{CR} * ND_{CR}^k - WDs_{NC} * ND_{NC}^k}{(WDs_C + WDs_{CR} + WDs_{NC}) * ND^k} \quad (6)$$

And following relations should hold:

1. $ND^k = ND_C^k + ND_{CR}^k + ND_{NC}^k$

2. $ND^1 = ND^2 = ... = ND^d = 100$, as equation (6) will take percentage-values for $ND_C^k, ND_{CR}^k, ND_{NC}^k$ out of total ND^k tasks.

3. $0 \leq PD_k \leq 1$, as equation (6) has value normalized by $(WDs_C + WDs_{CR} + WDs_{NC}) * ND^k$.

4. $WDs_C > WDs_{CR}$, this will cause greater weight to the task which is completed successfully within committed parameters than the tasks completed successfully but with relaxed parameters.

5. $WDs_{NC} > WDs_C$, as is clear from equation (6) that WDs_{NC} is causing the negative effect on the PD of agent, but this relation will cause an extra penalty over the agent for not completing the committed task.

6. Values of $WDs_C, WDs_{CR}, WDs_{NC}$ can be taken under any fixed range, but for uniformity, we can take it between 0 and 1.

7. $WDs_C = WC_C, WDs_{CR} < WC_{CR}, WDs_{NC} > WC_{NC}$ this will work as an extra penalty for not performing the task within parameters and not completing task, even though agent shows the desire for it.

As in the case of CI calculation, all desired task-types can not be given equal weights in judging the PD of agent. So, overall PD will be the weighted mean of individual Performance-to-Desire values(9) for each desired task-types. If $WDsD_1$, $WDsD_2$ ... $WDsD_d$ be the difficulty weights (their value can be in any fixed range, but for uniformity, we can take it between 0 and 1) for task-types $DT_1, DT_2 ... DT_d$ respectively, then overall PD of agent can be given by the weighted arithmetic mean of Performance-to Desire values of agent for these task-types:

$$PD = \frac{\sum_{i=1}^{n} PD_i * WDsD_i}{\sum_{i=1}^{n} WDsD_i} \qquad (7)$$

where $0 \leq PD \leq 1$

Now, if PD_r be the Performance-to-Desire for requested task-type T_r, which can be calculated using equation (6), then DI of agent should hold following inequalities:

$$DI \propto PD \text{ and } DI \propto PD_r$$

So, DI will be:

$$DI = PD * PD_r \qquad (8)$$

Commitment of an agent leads it to make plans for its action, based on its intention. It is a conduct-controlling characteristic of agent, which says that if an agent is committed to do something, then it should not consider the actions which are incompatible with so doing (Tweedale et al., 2007). So, commitment of an agent can be judged from the point that how much of its past actions were compatible with its commitments and how much were incompatible. Hence, the $CommI_k$ of an agent for task-type T_k can be given as:

$$CommI_k = \frac{WCm_C * N_C^k - WCm_{CR} * N_{CR}^k - WCm_{NC} * N_{NC}^k}{(WCm_C + WCm_{CR} + WCm_{NC}) * N^k} \qquad (9)$$

Where, $CommI_1$, $CommI_2$ ... $CommI_n$ are the Commitment Indexes of agent for task-types T_1, T_2 ... T_n respectively. WCm_C, WCm_{CR}, WCm_{NC} are the commitment-weights given to the tasks completed successfully, completed successfully but with relaxed parameters, and not completed respectively out of the total tasks which have been committed by the agent.

In addition to the relations shown in calculation of CI, which can be applicable here, following relations should also hold:

1. $WCm_C = WC_C, WCm_{NC} > WC_{NC}$, to give the penalty of not completing the committed task, as this occurred because the actions incompatible to the commitment must have occurred.

2. $WCm_{CR} \leq WC_{CR}$, the negation for WCm_{CR} in equation (9) must be noted. It is to give penalty of not doing task within committed parameters, so ultimately because of the reason that some actions incompatible to the commitment must have occurred.

3. Values of WCm_{C}, WCm_{CR}, WCm_{NC} can be taken under any fixed range, but for uniformity, we can take it between 0 and 1.

Now, in the case of calculation of CommI, the commitment for each task-type can be given same weight. Because in this case, we aim at measuring the commitment of SPA towards assigned tasks either they are difficult or easy, but not the capacity of SPA in doing tasks, which depends on the difficulty-levels of task. So, the CommI of an agent can be defined as the simple arithmetic mean of the commitment indexes of agent for all task-types:

$$CommI = \frac{1}{n} * \sum_{i=1}^{n} CommI_{i} \qquad (10)$$

The values corresponding to $N_{C}^{k}, N_{CR}^{k}, \quad N_{NC}^{k}$ and $ND_{C}^{k}, ND_{CR}^{k}, \quad ND_{NC}^{k}$ are updated in the profiles after taking the services of selected SPA.

4.2.2 Measuring Reputation of Agent

RI measures the trustworthiness of agent in view of the other similar SRAs. RI is the measure of reputation of agent among other agent community. We have adapted the definition of reputation for information source presented in (Barber & Kim, 2001), for considered MAS based SWS composition system. It says that reputation is the amount of trust an SPA has created for itself through interactions with different SRAs.

The reputation of an agent can be calculated using a mechanism of maintaining a separate Reputation Table (RT) by SRAs in their service profile, which has reputation indexes of SPAs from their view. The Reputation Table (RT) is a data structure which is maintained by the SRA and holds reputation indexes of all those SPAs from which the given SRA has used services in past, for all those task-types for which services were used. It must be noted that the reputation of an agent can be different for different task-types from the view of same SRA. Each entry in the proposed RT for requester agent R contains following elements:

i. The Service Provider Agent/Task-type identifier ($\langle P, T \rangle$).

ii. The reputation index from requester agent R for the provider agent P for task type T ($RI_{R \rightarrow \langle P,T \rangle}$).

Now the given SRA may not equally consider the reputation feedback from all the similar SRAs. The reputation feedback from some of the SRAs may be much affecting or reliable for the given SRA than the other ones. So, the overall RI of SPA for the required task-type will be the weighted arithmetic mean of the reputation indexes for the required task-type from all the SRAs including the given SRA itself.

$$RI = \frac{\sum_{i=1}^{n} RI_{i} * WR_{i}}{\sum_{i=1}^{n} WR_{i}}, \; Where \quad 0 \leq RI_{i} \leq 1 \qquad (11)$$

Where, RI_{i} is the reputation index from any service requester agent R_{i} for the concerned SPA for required task-type and WR_{i} is the reputation weight given by the SRA to the reputation feedback of R_{i}. One of definition for WR_{i} can be as follow:

$$WR_{i} = \begin{cases} = 1 & \textit{If } R_{i} \textit{ is the given reference SRA} \\ > 0, \leq 1 & \textit{If } R_{i} \textit{ is any other SRA} \end{cases} \qquad (12)$$

The provision is also there to update the RI of selected SPA in its local RT after using its services, by the given SRA. So, if q is the quality rating given by the reference SRA to the reference SPA based on its recent services and RI' is the existing reputation index of this SPA in the RT of given SRA, then the updated RI can be calculated as:

$$RI = \varepsilon * RI' + \left(1 - \varepsilon\right) * q,$$
$$Where \quad 0 \leq \varepsilon \leq 1, \quad 0 \leq q \leq 1, \quad (13)$$

Where, ε is the relative weight given to the past reputation of SPA as compared to its present quality rating.

5. EVALUATION AND COMPARATIVE ANALYSIS

This section presents the evaluation and validation of proposed MABSCP and CPBSM by comparing these with the existing similar works.

For evaluating the presented service composition approach, MABSCP, the evaluation approach described in the (Feenstra et al., 2007) can be used. Feenstra et al. (2007) have presented an approach for evaluating web service composition approaches. This can also be used to evaluate the composition features of SWS composition approaches. They have described four evaluation criteria for composition methods:

1. Does the method provide support for the multi-actor perspective?
2. Does the method provide the ability to express and evaluate non-functional requirements? Does the method still support the composition process when service properties are unknown?
3. Does the method provide insight into alternative compositions, for example in the case a part of a composition fails?
4. Does the method support the planning or the creation of a shared view on the composition? For example does it provide an overview of

missing services, or services that have to be changed?

The details of these criteria can be referred from (Feenstra et al., 2007).

For a composition process to support multi-actor perspective, the decision regarding the composition of services should be taken within the network containing different actors and all actors should cooperate to realize a common high-level goal (Feenstra et al., 2007). In MABSCP, the decision of composition is taken by the coordinator agent available on the web and the different decomposed tasks are performed by the various SPAs towards achieving a high-level goal of satisfying input-request. Thus, first criterion is satisfied.

A proper formulation has been used by the MABSCP to express the non-functional requirements and properties like QoS aspects. It uses two mathematical models viz. CPBSM and HSM for formalizing various non-functional parameters. In this process, the tasks which need to be performed for satisfying input composite-request are not pre-defined, but are decided during the course of action. Thus, the second criterion is also satisfied.

MABSCP ranks the various available SPAs for a task, using HSM. So, it can easily provide the insight into alternative composition. If a selected SPA fails, then the next SPA in the ranking can be invoked to perform the specified task. Hence, the third criterion is also satisfied.

The fourth criterion of planning support is also satisfied by the MABSCP. In MABSCP, during the selection of coordinator agent and SPAs using CPBSM and HSM respectively, a desire-index has been calculated. The desire-index checks the desire of the agent to perform services. Thus, availability of the services has been checked before applying selection on them. Also, as the selections of SPAs are performed in parallel for different decomposed tasks, so after the selection is over, the realization of composition process can be easily checked. Thus, all the four criteria of evaluating the service composition approaches proposed by Feenstra et al. (2007) are satisfied by the presented MABSCP.

Further evaluation of MABSCP is also performed by comparing it with existing similar works. Large numbers of different SWS composition approaches have been reported in the literature. Although Gomez-Perez et al. (2004), Sell et al. (2004), Wu et al. (2003), Lecue & Leger (2005), Arpinar et al. (2004), Chen et al. (2003), Pistore et al. (2004), Agarwal et al. (2004), McIlraith & Son (2002), Kvaloy et al. (2005), Charif & Sabouret (2005), and Wu et al. (2006) have presented various SWS composition approaches, but none of them presents MAS based composition of SWSs. In the literature, only a little work was reported, which uses the MAS in SWS composition. Vallee et al. (2005), Kungas & Matskin (2006), and Ermolayev et al. (2004) have used the concept of MASs in SWS composition. But, the works by (Vallee et al., 2005) and (Kungas & Matskin, 2006) do not provide the similar understanding of considering each component service as an agent capability. (Kungas & Matskin, 2006) have presented a P2P based multi-agent environment for SWS composition. They have presented a MAS, where agents cooperatively apply distributed symbolic reasoning for discovering and composing SWSs. In their work, agent's capabilities are not representing the SWS components, but they are supporting in the composition of available SWS components. Their work mainly emphasizes the issues regarding P2P network and MAS environment and a very limited discussion has been provided on the SWS composition and its various activities like discovery, selection etc.

In their work on MAS for dynamic service composition, Vallee et al. (2005) have claimed to propose an approach for combining multi-agent techniques with SWSs to enable dynamic, context-aware service composition in ambient intelligence environments. They also discuss how ambient intelligence gets benefited from the coupling of service-oriented approach and multi-agent systems, towards more appropriate interactions with users. However, the work mainly discusses the possibility of using MASs in ambient intelligence environments for SWS composition, and a very limited discussion has been provided on its architectural details and processes involved.

The conceptual idea, in MABSCP, of using agent capability as an SWS component is not originally new and has also been argued by the work in (Ermolayev et al., 2004). However, the framework for intelligent dynamic service composition using the concept of independent coordinator agent to control the composition process and with the provision to handle various issues involved in the composition process discussed earlier within this paper, has not been worked out before. Ermolayev et al. (2004) have presented an agent-enabled cooperative dynamic service composition approach for SWSs. They have proposed a mediation framework for agent-enabled service provision targeted to dynamic service composition. A discussion on the SPA selection based on their capability and credibility assessment has also been presented. But, their architecture does not provide any provision to handle the various issues raised in section-2 such as handling different negotiation conditions, difficulty-levels of input request, and validation of input request. Further, the selection-model in their architecture is based on the credibility and capability assessments only. Thus, the proposed MABSCP is more efficient model for SWS composition. The tabular comparison in table 1, summarizing the comparison of our proposed SWS composition approach, MABSCP, with other similar works discussed above, also supports this argument.

To our knowledge, no work has been reported in the literature which provides a formal way of measuring the cognition based rating of agents in SWS composition. The presented CPBSM fulfills the same purpose. In a previous work, Kumar & Mishra (2008) have presented a cognition based rating as part of HSM, but CPBSM is

Table 1. Comparison of MABSCP with other similar approaches

Feature	SWS Composition Approach in (Ermolayev et al., 2004)	SWS Composition Approach in (Vallee et al., 2005)	SWS Composition Approach in, (Kungas & Matskin, 2006)	Proposed SWS Composition Approach, MABSCP
Use of Multi-Agent Technology in SWS composition	Yes	Yes	Yes	Yes
Considering each component SWS as an agent capability	Yes	No	No	Yes
Using coordinator agent for controlling composition process	An agent mediation layer is used.	No	No	Yes
Communication with SRA regarding negotiation conditions	No	No	No	Yes
Providing consideration to difficulty-level of input-request	No	No	No	Yes
Validating input-request values	No	No	No	Yes
Providing consideration to QoS parameters of SPAs in their selection	No	No	No	Yes
Providing consideration to cognitive parameters of SPAs in their selection	Only capability and credibility assessment is provided	No	No	A large range of parameters are assessed
Formulations and mechanisms for measuring various cognitive and QoS parameters	Mechanisms are provided for only updating the capability and credibility values, not for measurement.	No	No	Yes

more efficient. It is due to the reason that it also considers the difficulty levels of input-request in calculation of the final index of selection. In addition to enhanced formulation for different cognitive parameters, the calculation of desire index and reputation index has also been completely revised. In the CPBSM, calculation of reputation-index presents richer data-structure for the reputation table. In their work on agent-enabled SWS composition, Ermolayev et al. (2004) have presented a cognition based rating, but it only considers capability and credibility assessment of the SPA. For capability estimation, they have used a Fellow's Capability Expectations Matrix. Each row of this matrix represents the capability estimations of an SPA for different activities. Each element C_i^j of the matrix representing estimation of the SPA_i for activity a^j has been described as: $C_i^j = (q_i^j, p_i^j)$. Where, q_i^j is the quantity of recorded negotiations with fellow agent SPA_i

concerning activity a^j, and p_i^j is the capability expectation. p_i^j is further a recursive function depending on the q_i^j and result of negotiation. But, no discussion has been provided on formalizing any relationship between q_i^j and p_i^j to result the exact value for C_i^j. Further, no discussion has been found to calculate the initial value of p_i^j to get result from the described recursive relation for p_i^j. It is also seen that the capability estimation using this approach is ultimately depending on the quantity of negotiations and result of negotiations only. Similar observations have been made for the credibility assessment described by them. For credibility assessment also, a recursive relation has been presented with no discussion on its initial measurement. So, these relations can only be used for updating the capability and credibility values, but not for their initial measurement. Whereas, the proposed CPBSM not only considers more cognitive parameters like trust, reputation, capability, desire, intention etc., but also presents a formal method of measuring each, using different basic parameters which depends upon the general task-performances of SPAs. In addition, our proposed model also considers difficulty level of input-request in the calculation of index of selection. A distributed approach of measuring the reputation of SPA among the agent community has also been presented by the model. In contrast to the centralized way of maintaining the reputation record, this approach will be faster, as it will enable parallel requests to SRAs for their feedback about reputation of a SPA. Further, the distributed approach is also in line with the distributed nature of semantic web. Hence, the presented cognition based rating will result in more reliable results.

6. IMPLEMENTATION OF SWS COMPOSITION SYSTEM FOR EDUCATION PLANNING

We have implemented a SWS composition system based on the MABSCP. It uses CPBSM and HSM in the selection of coordinator and SPAs respectively. The implementation also shows the application of presented model to the problem of education planning. Education planning is the problem of planning the complete process of securing admission in some higher education program. It involves various activities such as counseling and preparation for entrance examination, choosing the appropriate institute, getting funds, completing admission formalities, and arranging transportation to join. Thus, it involves activities requiring expert-advice. So, a semantic web based system can be helpful in this regard.

The profiles of both coordinator and other task-specific agents are developed using Jena (HP Labs Semantic Web Programme, 2008) in OWL (McGuinness & Harmelen, 2008). These profiles are then published on the web and can

be accessed or manipulated by the SWS composition system. Structure of a profile prepared using Jena Ontology APIs and observed in Altova SemanticWorks (Altova, 2008) for a coordinator agent for education planning is shown in Figure 2. Figure 2 also shows that the ontology in the profile is well-defined under OWL-Full RDF/OWL level. The reasoning in the system is performed using Jena's *OWLReasoner*. The system implemented using Java and related tools easily access the service profiles. It uses the Jena APIs for interrogating, manipulating, or querying the profiles. The querying support provided by the Jena APIs, which is internally implemented in query language SPARQL (Prudhommeaux & Seaborne, 2008), is used for querying over the profiles. The implemented system mainly uses the exact-match approach in discovery process. The composite input ontology in the system mainly have three components: Qualification Input like course in which admission is sought, entrance examination score, qualifying examination score; Additional Admission Requirements like session of admission, date of birth, gender; and Preference and Constraints like finance needed or not, map needed or not, budget constraint, travel class constraint etc. The steps of applying the domain based filtering, agent's desire based filtering, and rating using CPBSM to finally select the coordinator agent are shown in Figure 3.

The first table in Figure 3 shows the agents after applying domain-based filtering. Second table lists only those agents which have a matching current desired task-type with the required task-type. Calculation of IoS for these filtered agents using the different equations of CPBSM has also been shown in the second table. As shown, the agent 'Get-Educated Education Services' has maximum index of selection and hence it is selected as coordinator agent.

Further, the selection of SPAs is performed for all simple tasks obtained from the decomposition of composite request. It follows the process depicted in MABSCP involving domain based

Figure 2. Sample coordinator agent profile

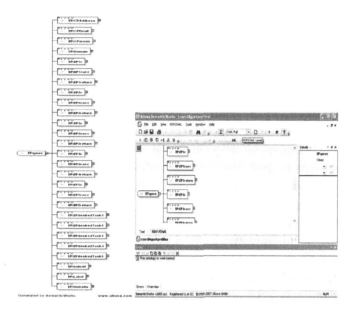

filtering, IOPE filtering, and selection using HSM model. It also involves the validation of input and communication with user-agent regarding negotiation conditions.

The different steps of selecting a 'Counseling and Preparation Agent' are shown in Figure 4. First table of Figure 4 lists the agents after ap-plying the domain based filtering. These are the available agents capable of providing 'Counseling and Preparation' services. Second table shows the agents obtained after applying input-output matching. The result of applying HSM on these agents is shown in the third table of Figure 4. As shown, the SPA 'ABC Counsellors' with highest

Figure 3. Coordinator agent selection

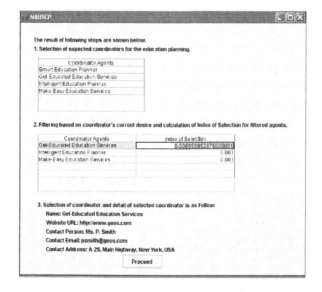

index of selection calculated using HSM, finally got selected as the 'Counseling and Preparation Agent'.

Figure 5 shows the result of MABSCP in the form of blocks, representing different selected agents for various activities such as counseling and preparation service, institute tracker service, admission consulting service, transportation service, financing service, and map & weather information service involved in the education planning request.

Figure 4. Counseling and preparation agent selection

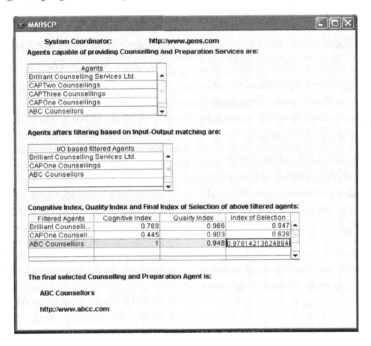

Figure 5. Layout of a composed system

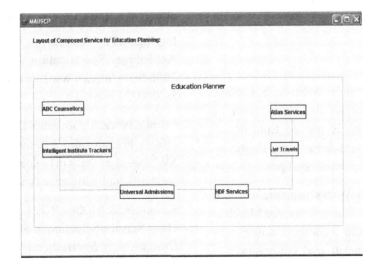

7. CONCLUSION

The work presented a semantic web service composition approach based on multi-agent systems. The presented approach handles some important issues like handling the practical negotiation conditions, categorizing input-request based on difficulty-levels and checking efficiency of service providers corresponding to specific required category, providing validation of input-request to decide the next move in composition process, and providing more accurate selection of service providers by considering their cognitive and QoS parameters. The proposed mathematical model for service-selection provides a novel formalization of various cognitive parameters. This model considers a large range of parameters for service-selection and also considers difficulty-levels of input-requests by categorizing them into task-type categories. Thus, it can give more accurate and reliable results. The work has been validated by providing an evaluation and comparison with existing similar works and more reliability has been reported. The work also introduced a new area of applicability, education planning, for semantic web based systems. Our future work will involve exploring further the education planning as an application of semantic web technology and to enhance the presented service composition process and selection models.

REFERENCES

Agarwal, S., Handschuh, S., & Staab, S. (2004). *Annotation, Composition and Invocation of Semantic Web Services*. Retrieved from http://www.uni-koblenz.de/~staab/Research/Publications/2004/web-service-annotation.pdf.

Altova (2008). SemanticWorks Semantic Web tool - Visual RDF and OWL editor. Retrieved March 1, 2008 from http://www.altova.com/products/semanticworks/semantic_web_rdf_owl_editor.html.

Arpinar, I. B., Aleman-Meza, B., Zhang, R., & Maduko, A. (2004). Ontology-driven web services composition platform. In *Proc. of IEEE International Conference on E-Commerce Technology, CEC'04* (pp. 146-152). San Diego, California, USA, IEEE Press.

Barber, K. S., & Kim, J. (2001). Belief Revision Process Based on Trust: Agents Evaluating Reputation of Information Sources. (LNCS 2246).

Charif, Y., & Sabouret, N. (2005). An Overview of Semantic Web Services Composition Approaches. *Electronic Notes in Theoretical Computer Science, 85*(6), 1–8.

Chen, L., Shadbolt, N. R., Goble, C., Tao, F., Cox, S. J., Puleston, C., & Smart, P. R. (2003). Towards a Knowledge-based Approach to Semantic Service Composition (LNCS 2870, pp. 319-334).

Ermolayev, V., Keberle, N., Kononenko, O., Plaksin, S., & Terziyan, V. (2004). Towards a Framework for agent-enabled semantic web service composition. *International Journal of Web Services Research, 1*(3), 63–87.

Feenstra, R. W., Janssen, M., & Wagenaar, R. W. (2007). Evaluating Web Service Composition Methods: the Need for Including Multi-Actor Elements. *The Electronic .Journal of E-Government, 5*(2), 153–164.

FIPA Architecture Board. (2008). Foundation for Intelligent Physical Agents, FIPA Communicative Act Library Specification. Retrieved on Feb 12, 2008 from http://www.fipa.org/specs/fipa00037/SC00037J.html.

Gomez-Perez, A., Gonzalez-Cabero, R., & Lama, M. (2004). Framework for design and composition of SWS based on Stack of Ontologies. American Assn. for Artificial Intelligence (www.aaai.org), 1-8.

Kumar, S., & Mishra, R. B. (2008). A Hybrid Model for Service Selection in Semantic Web Service Composition. *International Journal of Intelligent Information Technologies, 4*(4), 55–69.

Kungas, P., & Matskin, M. (2006). Semantic Web Service Composition through a P2P-Based Multi-Agent Environment (LNCS 4118, pp. 106-119).

Kvaloy, T. A., Rongen, E., Tirado-Ramos, A., & Sloot, P. (2005). Automatic Composition and Selection of Semantic Web Services (LNCS 3470, pp. 184-192).

Labs Semantic Web Programme, H. P. (2008). *Jena- A Semantic Web Framework for Java.* Retrieved on March 01, 2008 from http://jena. sourceforge.net/.

Lecue, F., & Leger, A. (2005). *A formal model for semantic Web service composition.* Paper presented at the 5th International Semantic Web Conference, Athens, Georgia.

McGuinness, D. L., & Harmelen, F. V. (2008). *OWL Web Ontology Language Overview.* Retrieved on Feb 13, 2008 from http://www.w3.org/TR/owl-features/.

McIlraith, S., & Son, T. C. (2002). Adapting Golog for composition of Semantic Web services. *In Proc. of the Eighth International Conference on Knowledge Representation and Reasoning (KR2002),* Toulouse, France (pp. 482–493).

McIlraith, S. A., Son, T. C., & Zeng, H. (2001). Semantic Web Services. *IEEE Intelligent Systems, 16*(2), 46–53. doi:10.1109/5254.920599

Padgham, L., & Lambrix, P. (2000). *Agent Capabilities: Extending BDI Theory.* American Association for Artificial Intelligence.

Paolucci, M., Kawamura, T., Payne, T., & Sycara, K. (2002). Semantic Matching of Web Service Capabilities. In *Proc. Of Int. Semantic Web Conference (ISWC, 2002), Italy.*

Pechoucek, M. (2003). *Formal Representation for Multi-Agent Systems. Gerstner Laboratory.* Czech Technical University in Prague. Retrieved from http://agents.felk.cvut.cz/teaching/33ui2/bdi.pdf.

Pistore, M., Bertoli, P., Cusenza, E., Marconi, A., & Traverso, P. (2004). *WS-GEN: A Tool for the Automated Composition of Semantic Web Services.* Paper presented at the Int. Semantic Web Conference (ISWC, 2004).

Prudhommeaux, E., & Seaborne, A. (2008). *SPARQL Query Language for RDF.* Retrieved March 1, 2008 from http://www.w3.org/TR/2008/REC-rdf-sparql-query-20080115/

Sell, D., Hakimpour, F., Domingue, J., Motta, E., & Pacheco, R. (2004). Interactive Composition of WSMO-based Semantic Web Services in IRS-III. In *Proc. of the AKT workshop on Semantic Web Services* (AKT-SWS04).

Smith, & Davis (2008). *Foundation for Intelligent Physical Agents. FIPA Contract Net Interaction Protocol Specification.* Retrieved on Feb 12, 2008 from http://www.fipa.org/specs/fipa00029/SC00029H.html.

Stollberg, M., & Haller, A. (2005). *Semantic Web Services Tutorial.* Paper presented at the 3rd International Conference on Web Services (ICWS 2005).

The DAML Services Coalition. (2008). *DAML-S: Semantic Mark-up for Web Services.* Retrieved on Februrary 13, 2008 from http://www.daml.org/services/daml-s/2001/10/daml-s.pdf

Tweedale, J., Ichalkaranje, N., Sioutis, C., Jarvis, B., Consoli, A., & Phillips-Wren, G. (2007). Innovations in multi-agent systems. *Journal of Network and Computer Applications, 30*(5), 1089–1115. doi:10.1016/j.jnca.2006.04.005

Vallee, M., Ramparany, F., & Vercouter, L. (2005). A Multi-Agent System for Dynamic Service Composition in Ambient Intelligence Environments. In *Proc. Third International Conference on Pervasive Computing, PERVASIVE* (pp. 175-182).

Wu, D., Parsia, B., Sirin, E., Hendler, J., & Nau, D. (2003). Automating DAML-S Web Services composition using SHOP2. In *Proc. of the 2nd International Semantic Web Conference, ISWC 2003, Sanibel Island, Florida, USA.*

Wu, Z., Ranabahu, A., Gomadam, K., Sheth, A. P., & Miller, J. A. (2006). *Automatic Semantic Web Services Composition.* Retrieved from http://www.cs.uga.edu/~jam/papers/zLSDISpapers/zixin.doc

Chapter 5
Image Mining:
A Case for Clustering Shoe Prints

Wei Sun
Monash University, Australia

David Taniar
Monash University, Australia

Torab Torabi
La Trobe University, Australia

ABSTRACT

Advances in image acquisition and storage technology have led to tremendous growth in very large and detailed image databases. These images, once analysed, can reveal useful information to our uses. The focus for image mining in this article is clustering of shoe prints. This study leads to the work in forensic data mining. In this article, we cluster selected shoe prints using k-means and expectation maximisation (EM). We analyse and compare the results of these two algorithms.

INTRODUCTION

With the improvement of computer technology, such as multimedia data acquisition and storage techniques, the application of multimedia information becomes more and more prevalent. Therefore, the demand for discovering patterns from a great deal of multimedia data is becoming more relevant in many applications (Ordonez & Omiecinski, 1998; Zaine et al, 1998). In this article, we focus on clustering shoe prints. The work presented in this article is part of a larger project on forensic data mining focusing on multimedia data.

The main objectives of this work are (i) to cluster shoe prints, (ii) to analyse the results of each clustering algorithm, (iii) to use a visualisation tool to see how the clusters are affected by changes of input variables, and (iv) to examine the differences in the distributions of variables from cluster to cluster. Our experiments were conducted to cluster a series of shoe prints by using clustering algorithms in Weka.

PRELIMINARY

Figure 1 shows an overview of the shoe prints mining processes described in this article. The shoe

DOI: 10.4018/978-1-61520-694-0.ch005

Figure 1. Shoe prints clustering process

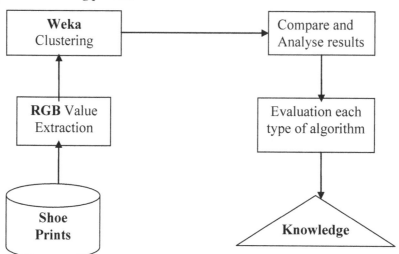

prints from image database are first processed to extract the RGB information. With these RGB data, Weka is used to cluster the extract RGB values of the selected shoe prints. The results are then evaluated and interpreted to obtain the final knowledge, which can be applied to forensic applications.

Figure 2 shows some sample clustered shoe prints. Obviously, we can see there are some commonalities in each group of shoe prints. Actually, the contrast values of images in group two are the lowest. On the other hand, the contrast values in group three are the highest, containing of only black and white colour. In addition, the red colour in group four is very remarkable. Finally, the last group has no similarity with the other groups, so it is separated to another cluster. Each shoe print has its own characteristics; these are reflected from their colour, texture, contrast value, homogeneity, and so forth. To find their colour characteristics, our focus is to group them and analyse the results.

For the experiment, we will use Weka to cluster the shoe prints, where the sample shoe prints are the selected 29 images. To make the experiment more convincible, the RGB values of images chosen are quite close, so the images are not as identifiable as those in Figure 2.

Clustering Techniques

Image clustering is usually performed in the early stages of the mining process. Feature attributes that have received the most attention for clustering are colour, texture, and shape. Generally, any of the three, individually or in combination, could be used. There is a wealth of clustering algorithms available (Han & Kamber, 2006): density based clustering algorithms (e.g., Dbscan and Optics), partition-based algorithms (e.g., EM), mixture-resolving (e.g., Make Density Based Clusterer) and mode-seeking algorithms (e.g., Cobweb), and nearest neighbour clustering (e.g., *k*-means and Farthest First). Once the images have been clustered, a domain expert is needed to examine the images of each cluster to label the abstract concepts denoted by the cluster (Ashley, 1996). In this article, we use the partitioning-based clustering algorithms, namely *k*-means and expectation maximisation (EM).

k-Means

The classic *k*-means algorithm forms clusters by partitioning numerical instances into disjoint clusters. This is a simple and straightforward technique that has been used for several decades.

Figure 2. Sample shoe print clusters

Group 1.

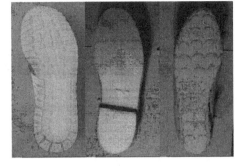

Group 2.

Group 3.

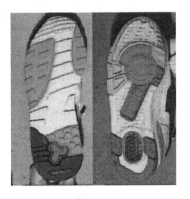

Group 4.

Using the *k*-means method (Han & Kamber, 2006), first, we specify in advance how many clusters are being sought; this is the parameter *k*. Then, *k* points are chosen at random as cluster centres. Instances are assigned to their closest cluster centre according to the ordinary Euclidean distance function. Next the centroid, or mean, of all instances in each cluster is calculated; this is the 'means' part. These centroids are taken to be new centre values for their respective clusters. Finally, the whole process is repeated with the new cluster centres. Iteration continues until the same points are assigned to each cluster in consecutive rounds, at which point the cluster centres have stabilised and will remain the same thereafter.

Expectation Maximisation (EM)

The EM algorithm extends the *k*-means paradigm in a different way. Instead of assigning each ob-

ject to a dedicated cluster, it assigns each object to a cluster according to a weight representing the probability of membership (Han & Kamber, 2006). In other words, there are no strict boundaries between clusters. Therefore, new means are computed based on weighted measures.

THE PROCESSES

The first step is to preprocess the shoe prints. Our program takes the bitmap files and produces colour histograms (8 bit quantised histogram), grey level histogram (by weighted or unweighted calculation), colour moments (mean, standard deviation, and skewness), and the output colour histogram texture information (based on horizontal scan). Figure 3 shows the interface of the image extraction program. is the most commonly used colour feature representation. The colour histogram

Figure 3. Image extraction interface

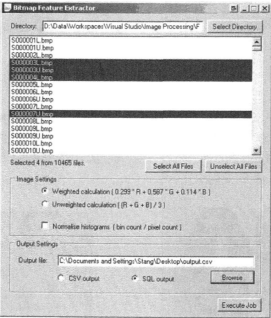

is computed by discretising the colours within the image and counting the number of pixels of each colour in terms of R (red), G (green), and B (blue). To overcome the quantisation effects in colour histograms, colour moments were used. The mathematical foundation of this approach is that any colour distribution can be characterised by its moments.

Most of the information is concentrated on the low-order moments, so only the first moment (mean), and the second and third central moments (variance and skewness) are typically extracted as colour features. If the value of the ith colour channel at the jth image pixel is pij, then the colour moment index entries related to this colour channel are given by the following:

- The 1st moment (mean) average colour:

$$E_{i=} \frac{1}{N} \sum_{j=1}^{N} p_{ij}$$

- The 2nd central moment (standard deviation):

$$\sigma_i = \left(\frac{1}{N} \sum_{j=1}^{N} \left(p_{ij} - E_i \right)^2 \right)^{\frac{1}{2}}$$

- The 3rd central moment (skewness):

$$s_i = \left(\frac{1}{N} \sum_{j=1}^{N} \left(p_{ij} - E_i \right)^3 \right)^{\frac{1}{3}}$$

By following this process, it will be simple to map the images into numeric data. To achieve this by using the developed system, the following steps have been followed. First, input the directory of the file and then select the image files. Second, choose the image settings, weighted or unweighted calculation. Finally, choose the output format (e.g., .csv files). The experimentations were done with real data sets containing 5,612 images from manufacturer shoe soles. The extracted features are stored in several .csv files.

EXPERIMENTAL RESULTS

In the experimentations, we applied six clustering algorithms. The clustering algorithm was implemented using two groups of dataset. One is single colour histogram (R, G, or B) and the other is integrating colour histogram RGB together.

K-Means Results

Two types of experiments were conducted: the first on individual colour elements and the second on RGB.

K-Means Clusters (Individual Colours)

In this experiment, the red means attribute of 29 images are compared. By analysing the mean of each cluster, then we assign each image to its cluster. After clustering the 29 images with $k=2$ (refer to Table 1), it is obvious that Weka finds the boundary between S000004L and S000003L. In Figure 4, the X and Y axes are all mean red for the purpose of ease of visualisation, where the two clusters are easily shown. The small window points to S000004L image with a mean red of 146.4202595. We can see that it seems the k-means method divides these points in the middle and also the largest distance is not always used to cluster. Further experimentations were carried out for different number of clusters. Figure 5 show the results for $k=7$.

The difference between clusters is not very distinct because the attribute used is one of the three colour histograms, namely red means. As shown in Figure 6, we can see the five images, which belong to Cluster 2, are quite different. However, because their value of red mean is very close, in which they have the least amount of red colour among those 29 images.

Similarly, the value of the red mean of each image of Cluster 0 when $k=7$ are very close. Even though the differences are not apparent, we still can find some similarities. The same experiments

Table 1. k-means results with k=2

Cluster 1

Image	Mean
S000026L.bmp	96.87684028
S000022L.bmp	111.219566
S000001U.bmp	115.8457949
S000015L.bmp	117.1832246
S000017L.bmp	120.2657552
S000008L.bmp	129.966684
S000005L.bmp	130.8865797
S000013L.bmp	132.8192969
S000009L.bmp	137.3344792
S000011L.bmp	138.3883594
S000010L.bmp	138.5785938
S000028L.bmp	138.9737587
S000020L.bmp	140.4979514
S000023L.bmp	141.6563802
S000016L.bmp	141.8979601
S000001L.bmp	144.2282465
S000004L.bmp	146.4202595

Cluster 2

Image	Mean
S000003L.bmp	149.9640972
S000025L.bmp	156.3013368
S000019L.bmp	157.2241319
S000007L.bmp	157.9359549
S000018L.bmp	159.1205208
S000014L.bmp	160.0049913
S000029L.bmp	164.1852344
S000002L.bmp	169.7494358
S000021L.bmp	176.4560563
S000012L.bmp	176.7394444
S000024L.bmp	184.7721875
S000006L.bmp	194.7869097

Figure 4. Visualising mean red for k=2

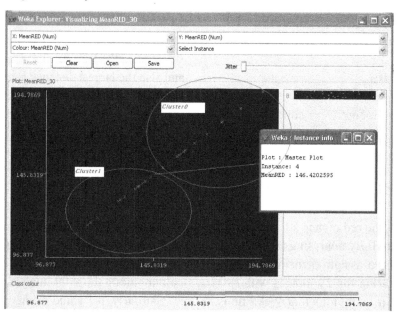

Figure 5. Visualising mean red for k=7

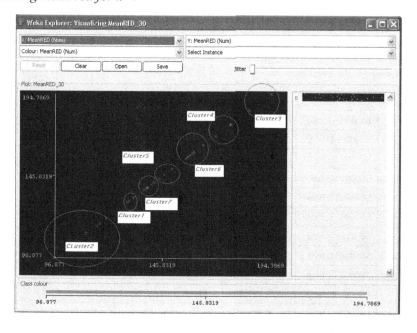

were conducted for the green mean and the blue mean. As mentioned earlier, the output includes not only the first moment (mean), but also the second and third central moments (variance and skewness). To avoid the repeated testing processes, we chose colour histogram.

K-Means Clusters (RGB)

The chart in Figure 7 shows the three RGB values of all the 29 images. In this section, clustering RGB will be analysed. When *k*=2, the Cluster 1 and 0 are the same as the cluster in single attribute

Figure 6. Cluster 2 members

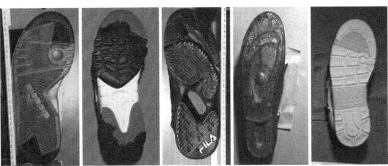

red mean, except the three image S0000016L, S000001L, and S000004L (refer to Figure 8) move to Cluster 0. As the difference between these two groups is not apparent, further testing was done. Table 2 shows the relationship between the mining results of single colour and RGB.

As we can see from Ttable 2, the results of RGB take each colour result into consideration and try to balance the results, although not absolutely evenly. For example, when k=2, the results of red are 12 and 17 and the results of green and blue are 16 and 13. Therefore, the result of RGB stands in the middle (e.g., 15 and 14)

EM Results

Like those of k-means, for the EM method, we conducted testing for individual colours, as well as RGB.

EM Clusters (Individual Colours)

As we can see from Figure 9, when k=2, the EM method clusters these points into the same clusters as those of k-means, however, the cluster sequence number is the opposite, and the mean and standard deviation calculated by EM and k-means are different.

The EM clustering algorithm computes probabilities of cluster memberships based on one or more probability distributions, which include:

Cluster 1:
   Mean = 131.5594 StdDev = 14.2791
Cluster 0:
   Mean = 166.5382 StdDev = 14.0073

After six iterations, k-means assigns each case to cluster to maximise the differences in means for continuous variables and calculate these number as:

Cluster 0:
   Mean/Mode: 167.27 StdDevs: 13.4173
Cluster 1:
   Mean/Mode: 130.767 StdDevs: 13.7975

As shown in Figure 10, when k=3, the points are totally redistributed to different clusters. The goal of EM clustering is to estimate the means and standard deviations for each cluster so as to maximise the likelihood of the observed data (distribution). Put it into another way, the EM algorithm attempts to approximate the observed distributions of values based on mixtures of different distributions in different clusters.

When the parameter k is changed from 3 to 4, we can see that these points are redistributed again (refer to Figure 11). The points, which belong to Cluster 1 (k=3), now become Cluster 3. Nonetheless, these points are still together as a cluster. From here, noticeably, we can see that although the clustering result may be similar, the calculation processes of EM are different from those of

Figure 7. Visualising RGB values

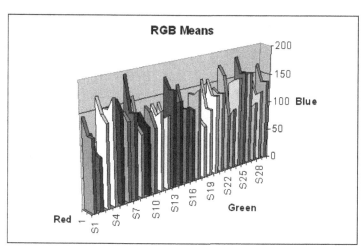

Figure 8. These are the three images where the results for RGB clustering is different from that of single colour clustering (for k=2)

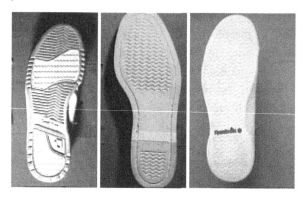

k-means. In *k*-means, Cluster 2 is unchanged when the parameter *k* is changed from 3 to 7, and the next clustering results are always based on the previous clustering results. For example, when *k* changes from 3 to 4, Cluster 1 splits into Cluster 1 and 0. When *k* changes from 4 to 5, Cluster 1 splits into Cluster 1 and 0 as well. The other clusters did not change.

On the other hand, EM takes the entire 29 images into consideration and therefore the clusters are always changed. For example, when parameter *k* changes from 3 to 6, Cluster 1 changes to Cluster 3 (*k* from 3 to 4), and then changes to 4 (k from 4 to 5), and splits to two clusters: 4 and 5 (k from 5 to 6). In EM, all points being clustered are shuffled again when k changes. The result is still the same

as that of k-means, but when k is greater then 4, the difference starts to appear.

When k=6 and 7 (refer to Figure 12), using k-means, Cluster 2 still is unchanged. No matter how small the other clusters are, the size of optimum cluster is temporarily fixed. Unlike k-means, EM deals with these numbers differently. Noticeably, the size of Cluster 1 is becoming even larger when k value is increased. This definitely does not happen in k-means.

Instead of using classifications, EM uses classification probabilities. The results of EM clustering are different from those computed by k-means clustering. The latter will assign observations to clusters to maximise the distances between clusters. The EM algorithm does not compute actual assignments of observations to clusters, but computes classification probabilities. In other words, each observation belongs to each cluster with a certain probability. Nevertheless,

as a final result we can usually review an actual assignment of observations to clusters, based on the (largest) classification probability.

Table 2. k-means comparison

K	RED	GREEN	BLUE	RGB
2	0 12 (41%) 1 17 (59%)	0 16 (55%) 1 13 (45%)	0 16 (55%) 1 13 (45%)	0 15 (52%) 1 14 (48%)
3	0 11 (38%) 1 13 (45%) 2 5 (17%)	0 9 (31%) 1 11 (38%) 2 9 (31%)	0 11 (38%) 1 7 (24%) 2 11 (38%)	0 11 (38%) 1 5 (17%) 2 13 (45%)
4	0 7 (24%) 1 12 (41%) 2 5 (17%) 3 5 (17%)	0 7 (24%) 1 9 (31%) 2 4 (14%) 3 9 (31%)	0 8 (28%) 1 7 (24%) 2 6 (21%) 3 8 (28%)	0 8 (28%) 1 5 (17%) 2 13 (45%) 3 3 (10%)
5	0 9 (31%) 1 4 (14%) 2 5 (17%) 3 2 (7%) 4 9 (31%)	0 4 (14%) 1 3 (10%) 2 9 (31%) 3 9 (31%) 4 4 (14%)	0 8 (28%) 1 4 (14%) 2 5 (17%) 3 7 (24%) 4 5 (17%)	0 7 (24%) 1 5 (17%) 2 13 (45%) 3 3 (10%) 4 1 (3%)
6	0 9 (31%) 1 3 (10%) 2 5 (17%) 3 2 (7%) 4 3 (10%) 5 7 (24%)	0 4 (14%) 1 2 (7%) 2 9 (31%) 3 5 (17%) 4 4 (14%) 5 5 (17%)	0 5 (17%) 1 4 (14%) 2 4 (14%) 3 5 (17%) 4 5 (17%) 5 6 (21%)	0 4 (14%) 1 5 (17%) 2 8 (28%) 3 3 (10%) 4 1 (3%) 5 8 (28%)
7	0 7 (24%) 1 3 (10%) 2 5 (17%) 3 2 (7%) 4 3 (10%) 5 3 (10%) 6 6 (21%)	0 3 (10%) 1 2 (7%) 2 9 (31%) 3 3 (10%) 4 4 (14%) 5 5 (17%) 6 3 (10%)	0 4 (14%) 1 4 (14%) 2 4 (14%) 3 4 (14%) 4 5 (17%) 5 6 (21%) 6 2 (7%)	0 4 (14%) 1 5 (17%) 2 8 (28%) 3 2 (7%) 4 1 (3%) 5 4 (14%) 6 5 (17%)

Figure 9. Visualising mean red when k=2 (EM)

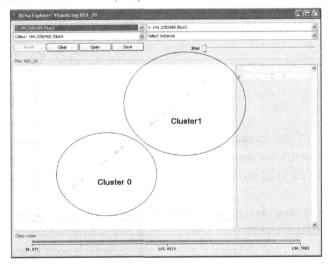

Figure 10. Visualising mean red when k=3 (EM)

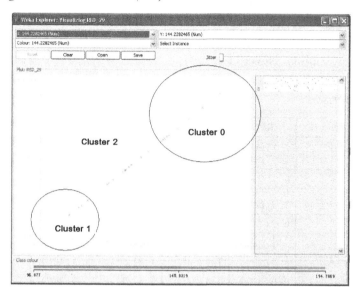

Figure 11. Visualising mean red when k=4 (EM)

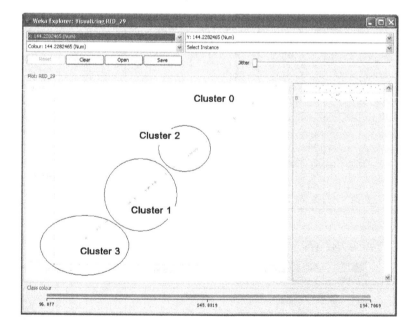

EM Clusters (RGB)

To consider the integrity of the image, cluster images based on three colours are used. First, we will compare the mean of RGB attributes of 29 images.

When *k*=2, the clustering result is the same as the *k*-means. It starts to differentiate after *k*=2. In comparison with k-means, the only difference is

that EM places image S000017L into Cluster 2. It shows again that k-means cluster these points based on previous clustering results. It actually splits a bigger cluster into smaller ones in order to fulfil the k condition and it is based on the image sequence to cluster. For Clusters 1, 2, and 0, the mean value is increasing gradually. Comparatively, EM reorganises the points based on the probability distributions. It reassigns each point to its most feasible cluster.

Figure 12. Visualising mean red when k=7 (EM)

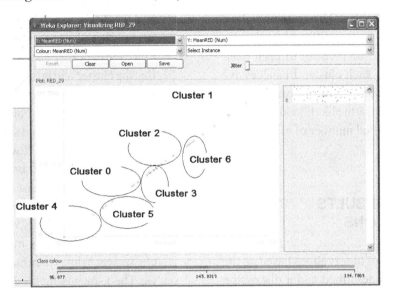

When k=4, there are two differences when compared with k-means. The first difference is that image S000017L has moved to Cluster 2 which was the same variance when k=3. The second difference is that image S000021L has moved into Cluster 3. Interestingly, image S000021L was separated as a cluster by using k-means when k=5. At the time when k=5, the only similar clustering result is Cluster 3 which contains images S000012L.bmp, S000024L.bmp, and S000006L. bmp. The other clusters are all different. The most significant change in comparison with k-means is that EM splits Cluster 2 into Cluster 0 and 2 when k increases from 4 to 5.

When k increases to 6, Clusters 1 and 3 have changed to Cluster 1, 3, and 0. For images S000017L to S000019L, EM still clusters them into two clusters but the boundary has changed. When k=7, for images S000017L to S000019L, EM clusters them into three clusters, Cluster 4, 2, and 3, respectively. The other clusters remain the same.

After clustering these images from 2 to 7, the cluster that keeps the same images as the parameter k changes is the optimum cluster. For example, in this case, the cluster which contains images S000026L, S000022L, S000001U, and S000015L (the smallest 4 instances) are unchanged when k changes from 3 to 7. Comparatively, the optimum cluster in k-means contains one more image S000017L.

Analysis of EM

The EM algorithm extends the basic approach to clustering in three important ways:

1. Instead of assigning cases, or observations, to clusters to maximise the differences in means for continuous variables, the EM clustering algorithm computes probabilities of cluster memberships based on one or more probability distributions. The goal of the clustering algorithm then is to maximise the overall probability or likelihood of the data, given the last clusters.

2. Unlike the classic implementation of k-means clustering, the general EM algorithm can be applied to both continuous and categorical variables (note that the classic k-means algorithm can also be modified to accommodate categorical variables).

3. The EM algorithm can also accommodate categorical variables. The method will at first randomly assign different probabilities (weights, to be precise) to each class or category, for each cluster. In successive iterations, these probabilities are refined (adjusted) to maximise the likelihood of the data given the specified number of clusters.

ANALYSIS OF RESULTS AND APPLICATIONS

In this section, some of observations based on the experiments will be described and a discussion of challenging aspects and applications of image mining processes will be presented.

Discussions

Based on the above experiments, we can conclude the following points:

1. The *k*-means method cannot separate numbers evenly; in fact, it is based on certain unregulated distance rule. It is used especially when you do not have a clear idea of your initial data. Moreover, there is no shortcut to find optimum cluster. To increase the chance of finding a global minimum, the only way is to repeat the whole algorithm several times with different starting points and then choose the best.

2. In the iterative distance-based method, the original choice of a value for *k* determines the number of clusters that will be found. If this number does not match the natural structure of the data, this technique will not obtain good results. We probably want to experiment with different values for k. Each set of clusters must then be evaluated. In general, the best set of clusters is the one that does the best job of keeping the distance between members of the same cluster small and the distance between members of adjacent clusters large.

3. Once the data are clustered, it does not mean that the cluster will be stable. Actually, it definitely will change due to the changes of the parameters. Only the optimum cluster, say Cluster 2, is unchanged within a constraint k value from 3 to 7. However, the stabled cluster, Cluster 2, will break up in order to fulfil the requirement of k parameters.

4. In k-means, if we have a close review of all the images, interestingly, certain points, such as point 149.96 keeps moving to different clusters each time when the parameter changes. The k-means method chooses it as the borderline to separate clusters. Obviously, this point is based on the Euclidean distance function and it is not cluster based.

5. EM uses classification probabilities. The results of EM clustering are different from those computed by k-means clustering. The latter will assign observations to clusters in order to maximise the distances between clusters. The EM algorithm does not compute actual assignments of observations to clusters, but classification probabilities. In other words, each observation belongs to each cluster with a certain probability. Therefore, EM algorithm makes clustering more objective and integrating.

6. It is difficult to see the variance between the images of each cluster by eye because the experiment already quantifies the shoe prints and the selected RGB values are quite close.

7. The preprocessing phase plays an indispensable role in our experiments. If the preprocessing is done well, it can be decisive whether clusters could be discovered well. Therefore, this phase still requires a lot of techniques to optimise. For example, the output of our feature extractor program can only reflect the colour histogram, homogeneity, and contrast value. Therefore, the

experiment can only be conducted one aspect at a time. It would be better for this extractor to set up a data reduction function so that we can take the whole picture as a consideration.

Applications to Forensic

Having to review the forensic evidence, particularly about footwear evidences, we can apply shoe prints evidence into forensic.

Clustering large number of image collections. Large numbers of images have been collected and often put in a data warehouse (Rusu, Rahayu, & Taniar, 2005). In the context of shoe image from crime scene, it is then very important and necessary to determine and prove that a particular person or persons may or may not have been present at the crime scene. For this reason, the crime scene investigators have to collect and analyse the crime scene evidences through scientific and advance gadgets such as camera, chemical solutions, and so forth (Chen et al, 2004). Thus, there are many different types of physical evidence accumulated in the forensic database such as fingerprints, tool marks, footwear evidence, tire marks, blood stains, and so on. Henceforth, the large amounts of images with robust information lead to the possibility of applying image mining techniques in order to discover some hidden patterns.

Purpose of selecting shoeprints. Although the shoeprints are sometimes being overlooked or destroyed due to the improperly secured and disorganised crime scenes, this type of evidence can be greatly important to crime scene investigators in proving or disproving the presence of a suspect (Ashley, 1996). This is because footwear evidences are able to tell not only the identification of the brand and style of a particular shoe, but we could also know some information such as the size of the shoes, the direction of gait, the path through and away of the crime scene, the numbers of suspects, and so on.

Knowledge discovered served as future reference. With image mining techniques, the hidden knowledge could be served as future reference in crime scene investigations. The use of image mining techniques is not intended to take over the vital role played by the forensic experts of crime scene investigators (Oatley, Zeleznikow, & Ewart, 2004). In fact, this technique gives the domain experts another perception and understanding of their database. Perhaps with these new perceptions, it could help in solving cases efficiently and effectively.

No focus on images in existing crime data mining. The existing crime data mining is focusing on alphanumeric data, thus forensic images are not treated as major source of data in crime data mining. Several existing work focuses on 'soft' forensic evidence, where only alphanumeric data regarding the behaviour of criminals and cases are used (Zeleznikow, Oatley, & Ewart, 2005). We need to consider images together with the supported alphanumeric information in finding patterns in shoeprints database. We also need to look at how ontology information may be used (Flahive, Rahayu, Taniar, & Apduhan, 2004).

CONCLUSION AND FUTURE RESEARCH

Experience shows that no single machine learning scheme is appropriate to all data mining problems. As we have emphasised, real datasets vary, and to obtain accurate models the bias of the learning algorithm must match the structure of the domain. In this article, we experimented with k-means and EM to cluster shoe print images. The k-means method gives an overview analysis of the whole structure of the data and helps to group data in a simple way. The EM algorithm extends the *k*-means paradigm in a different way. Instead of assigning each object to a dedicated cluster, it assigns each object to a cluster according to a weight representing the probability of membership.

The work carried out in the article is merely a minor research in the area of clustering colour data, as there are many related topics that need further investigation. Some possible future studies that may be conducted in the area of image mining include the experimentations on other image elements such as textures, shape, and so forth. It will also be interesting to explore hidden relationships among images. For example, intensive and extensive exploratory pattern analysis involved in the existing shoeprints systems in footwear evidence database can be very useful. The main focus and purpose is to classify footwear evidence, identify the evidence, and relate some unsolved cases, thus helping in solving crime cases.

ACKNOWLEDGMENT

The research presented in this article has partly been financially supported by the Victorian Partnership for Advance Computing (VPAC) eResearch Grant Round 8 on the "Forensic Image Mining: A Case for Mining Shoe Marks in Crime Scenes" project (EPANMO161.2005).

REFERENCES

Ashley, W. (1996). What shoe was that? The use of computerized image database to assist in identification. *Journal of Forensic Science International, 82,* 7-20. Ireland: Elsevier Science.

Chen, H., et al. (2004). Crime data mining: A general framework and some examples. *IEEE Computer, 37*(4), 50-56.

Flahive, A., Rahayu, J. W., Taniar, D., & Apduhan, B. O. (2004). A distributed ontology framework for the grid. In *Proceedings of the 5th International Conference on Parallel and Distributed Computing: Applications and Technologies (PD-CAT'2004)* (pp. 68-71).

Han, J., & Kamber, M. (2006). *Data mining, concepts and techniques* (2nd ed.). Morgan Kaufmann.

Oatley, G. C., Zeleznikow, J., & Ewart, B. W. (2004). Matching and predicting crimes. In *Proceedings of the 24th SGAI International Conference on Knowledge Based Systems and Applications of Artificial Intelligence (SGAI'2004)* (pp. 19-32).

Ordonez, C., & Omiecinski, E. (1998). *Image mining: A new approach for data mining* (Tech. Rep. GIT-CC-98-12). Georgia Institute of Technology, College of Computing.

Rusu, L. I., Rahayu, J. W., & Taniar, D. (2005). A methodology for building XML data warehouses. *International Journal of Data Warehousing and Mining, 1*(2), 23-48.

Zaiane, O. R., et al (1998). Multimedia-miner: A system prototype for multimedia data mining. In Proceedings of the *1998 ACM-SIGMOD Conference on Management of Data.*

Zeleznikow, J., Oatley, G. C., & Ewart, B. W. (2005). *Decision support systems for police: Lessons from the application of data mining techniques to 'soft' forensic evidence.* Retrieved December 20, 2007, from http://www.aic.gov.au/conferences/occasional/2005-04-zeleznikow.html

This work was previously published in International Journal of Information Technology and Web Engineering, Vol. 3, Issue 1, edited by G. Alkhatib and D. Rine, pp. 70-84, copyright 2008 by IGI Publishing (an imprint of IGI Global).

Chapter 6
On the Prospects and Concerns of Pattern-Oriented Web Engineering

Pankaj Kamthan
Concordia University, Canada

ABSTRACT

In this chapter, the development and evolution of Web Applications is viewed from an engineering perspective that relies on and accommodates the knowledge inherent in patterns. It proposes an approach in the direction of building a foundation for pattern-oriented Web Engineering. For that, a methodology for pattern-oriented Web Engineering, namely POWEM, is described. The steps of POWEM include selection of a suitable development process model, construction of a semiotic quality model, namely PoQ, and selection and mapping of suitable patterns to quality attributes in PoQ. To support decision making and to place POWEM in context, the feasibility issues involved in each step are discussed. For the sake of is illustration, the use of patterns during the design phase of a Web Application are highlighted. Finally, some directions for future research, including those for Web Engineering education and Social Web Applications, are given.

INTRODUCTION

The engineering of non-trivial Web Applications presents various challenges (Zheng, 2008). The reliance on available expertise (including knowledge, skills, and discretion) derived from past practical experience can help meet those challenges. In this chapter, the interest is in one such body of knowledge, namely patterns.

The ideas behind the notion of a pattern originated in the mid-to-late 1960s, largely motivated by the pursuit for a systematic approach to solving recurring structural problems in the urban architectural and design aspects of civil engineering. The term *pattern* itself was formally coined in the late 1970s (Alexander, 1979; Alexander, Ishikawa, & Silverstein, 1977). It has since then been found useful in other engineering domains of interest (Rising, 2000) including Web Engineering.

DOI: 10.4018/978-1-60566-719-5.ch006

The interest in this chapter is highlighting the prospects and concerns in the deployment of patterns, particularly from the viewpoint of quality. From the empirical studies that have been reported (Ivory & Megraw, 2005), it can be concluded that a lack of attention towards the pragmatic quality of Web Applications is an increasing concern. This chapter builds on previous work (Kamthan, 2008a; Kamthan, 2008b; Kamthan, 2008c) of using patterns for orienting the development of (Mobile) Web Applications aiming for 'high-quality.'

The organization of the rest of the chapter is as follows. First, the background and state-of-the-art related to the evolution of Web Applications and patterns necessary for the discussion that follows is outlined. This is followed by the presentation of a methodology for pattern-oriented Web Engineering, namely *POWEM* (pronounced as "poem"), for systematically addressing the quality of Web Applications. POWEM consists of a sequence of steps that include selection of a suitable development process model, construction of a semiotic quality model, namely PoQ, and selection and mapping of suitable patterns to quality attributes in PoQ, along with the feasibility of each of these steps. Then, the use of patterns during macro- and micro-architecture design of a Web Application is illustrated. Next, challenges and directions for future research, including those for Social Web Applications, are discussed. Finally, the concluding remarks are presented.

BACKGROUND AND RELATED WORK

In this section, the background and previous work on the need for a systematic approach to the development of Web Applications from the perspective of quality and the role of patterns is briefly presented.

For the sake of this chapter, a *Web Site* is defined as a collection of resources that reside in a distributed computing environment enabled by the technological infrastructure of the Internet. Furthermore, a *Web Application* is defined as a Web Site that behaves like an information-intensive interactive software system specific to a domain and typically requires a non-trivial infrastructure for development. This infrastructure may include a disciplined and systematic development process, a team with high-level of knowledge and skills, deployment of additional software on the client- and/or server-side, and a schedule comprising of several weeks or months from inception to completion.

Identifying Characteristics for the Directions of the Evolution of Web Applications

It is admittedly difficult to make (any) predictions of a rapidly growing field. However, based on the knowledge of the past decade, the following characteristics identify the pivotal directions of evolution in the development of Web Applications: [C-1] Computing Environment-Neutral, [C-2] Domain-Specific, [C-3] Human-Centered, [C-4] Information Interaction-Intensive, [C-5] Model-Driven, [C-6] Open Environment-Based, [C-7] Pattern-Oriented, and [C-8] Quality-Sensitive.

Figure 1 depicts [C-1] − [C-8] and their (non-transitive) interrelationships of dependencies. The interest in this chapter is in a confluence of [C-1] − [C-8], especially in the interplay between [C-7] and [C-8]. This is implicit in the sections that follow; however, for consideration of space, a detailed treatment of each of these individually is suppressed. [C-1] − [C-8] together determine the *velocity* of development: a *sensitivity to quality* implies that the issue of quality is taken into consideration in all activities and could determine the 'speed' of development, and an *orientation due to patterns* implies that it is patterns that determine the *direction* taken by development.

It is important to note that certain characteristics, such as standards-conforming, even though desirable, are not among the current directions of

Figure 1. The characteristics of evolution of Web Applications and their interrelationships of dependencies

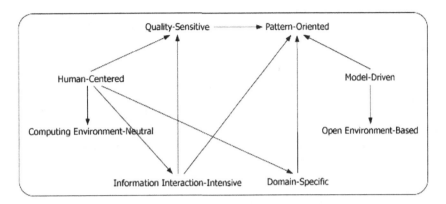

evolution of Web Applications. There is a plethora of examples of Web Applications that violate International Organization for Standardization (ISO)/International Electrotechnical Commission (IEC) standards and/or World Wide Web Consortium (W3C) recommendations and, as a result, can be perceived as being of 'poor' quality by their stakeholders.

Patterns and Web Applications

In this section, the fundamental terminology related to patterns and the implications of patterns towards Web Applications are discussed.

An Overview of the Pattern Space

There is currently no 'standard' for terminology related to patterns. Therefore, for the definition of the members in the *pattern space*, this section relies on selected publications (Meszaros & Doble, 1998; Buschmann, Henney, & Schmidt, 2007b) that can be considered as authoritative.

For the sake of this chapter, a *pattern* is an empirically proven solution to a recurring problem that occurs in a particular context. There are a number of possible views of a pattern. From an epistemological perspective, a pattern is kind of a posteriori and conceptually reusable knowledge.

This knowledge can be made explicit and organized (for example, classified and structured) in number of ways. It is the richness of the structure associated with patterns that makes them more than a mere collection of 'problem-solution' pairs and unique among expert bodies of knowledge such as principles, guidelines (Fowler & Stanwick, 2004; Wesson & Cowley, 2003), and heuristics.

The description of a pattern typically (Meszaros & Doble, 1998) comprises of an ordered list of labeled elements. For instance, the elements relevant to this chapter are: (pattern) name, author, context, problem, forces, solution, examples, and related patterns. The *name* element of a pattern is often an evocative, pronounceable, noun-phrase metaphor that reflects the nature of the *solution*; the *author* element gives the identity of the *pattern author*(s); the *context* element provides the situation or pre-conditions in which the *problem* occurs; the *forces* element lists the constraints that are balanced to arrive at the *solution*; the *solution* element provides an abstract, general, and conceptually reusable solution to the *problem*; the *examples* element demonstrates the *solution* in practice; and, finally, the *related patterns* element outlines any other pattern(s) to which the given pattern is related to in some way. The actual labels may vary across community and domain, and other (optional) elements, such as those related to metadata, may be included to enrich the description. A pattern is usually referred to by its name. In this chapter, the name of a pattern is presented in uppercase in order to distinguish it from the surrounding text.

A collection of patterns, if related, have special implications towards development. A set of related patterns is commonly referred to as a *pattern catalog*, a *pattern system*, or a *pattern language* (Buschmann, Henney, & Schmidt, 2007b), depending on the nature of relationships among patterns. In the following, the aforementioned distinctions between sets of patterns are suppressed unless otherwise stated.

It is not automatic that every solution to a given problem is 'good.' An *anti-pattern* suggests a 'negative' solution to a given problem. It usually occurs when the context of the problem is not understood or the underlying forces are not optimally balanced. In it original appearance, an anti-pattern was termed as a *misfit* (Alexander, 1964); in recent years, it has been termed as a *dysfunctional pattern* (Buschmann, Henney, & Schmidt, 2007b).

Patterns and Quality

The relationship between a pattern and quality has been known since the notion of a pattern was first introduced. It was then suggested (Alexander, 1979) that the use of a pattern during urban architecture and design leads to 'Quality Without A Name' (QWAN) or 'wholeness' (among a number of other synonyms) in the construction of living spaces.

The interest in this chapter is in the *product* quality, the product being the Web Application. If used justifiably, a pattern can also aid in the development of high-quality software systems in general and Web Applications in particular. This can be explained as follows. For a given problem (that is, functional requirement of a Web Application) in some stated context, there is usually more than one solution (that is, design). The selection of

a specific solution is based on the resolution of a subset of a number of forces that have the highest priority as determined by the context. These forces can be viewed as non-functional requirements, including quality requirements of the Web Application. If the realization (implementation) of the design is carried out appropriately, then the Web Application can attain the quality attributes with high-priority. However, as discussed in detail in later sections, this is neither trivial nor automatic since, in general, the relationship between quality and patterns is equivocal.

Related Work on Pattern-Oriented Development of Web Applications

It is well-known that software systems developed in an ad-hoc, casually, or haphazard manner can lead to a variety of issues, including economic problems (such as budget-overruns), management problems (such as delays), and technical problems (such as unfavorable impact on software quality). Indeed, the macro-architecture of such systems can be succinctly described by the BIG BALL OF MUD pattern.

The need for introducing a systematic process in the development of Web Applications involving patterns has been realized since the late 1990s, initially from the hypermedia engineering community and more recently impetus from information systems engineering and software engineering communities. As a result, a number of efforts have been made that are discussed briefly and chronologically next.

For using the patterns in urban architecture and design (Alexander, Ishikawa, & Silverstein, 1977), a procedure has been outlined. It suggests starting by selecting a pattern that most closely matches the project at hand, and then subsequently selecting related patterns that are hierarchically lower in the pattern language. However, this procedure is simplistic in the sense that it does not taken into consideration challenges involved in selecting a pattern from multiple sets of patterns, intricacies of the relationship between quality and patterns, and the issue of feasibility.

The Object-Oriented Hypermedia Design Method (OOHDM) is a hypermedia design methodology that has been applied to the developmental life cycle of Web Applications (Schwabe & Rossi, 1998). It has been suggested that the patterns for navigation design (Rossi, Schwabe, & Lyardet, 1999) could be integrated in OOHDM. However, there are certain outstanding issues with OOHDM including that it does not address feasibility concerns, does not explicitly and systematically approach quality concerns, and lacks broad tool support for some of the design notations it suggests.

The Web Modeling Language (WebML) (Ceri, Fraternali, & Bongio, 2000) is a model-driven approach to specifying Web Applications. Although WebML has been used to express the *solution*s of certain design patterns (Fraternali, Matera, & Maurino, 2002) as conceptual models, the precise impact of these patterns on quality attributes and the relationship between patterns and quality attributes is not shown.

The Agile Web Engineering (AWE) (McDonald & Welland, 2001) is a lightweight process developed to tackle short development life-cycle times; small multidisciplinary development teams; and delivery of bespoke solutions integrating software and data. AWE encourages more focus on requirements analysis, including business needs; better testing and evaluation of deliverables; and consideration of the issues associated with the evolution of Web Applications. However, the discussion on the quality is limited to usability and the use of patterns is not taken into consideration.

The Web Application Extension (WAE) (Conallen, 2003) is a methodology for building Web Applications based on the Unified Modeling Language (UML). WAE includes a (non-standard) extension of UML via profile mechanism and includes support for some macro- and micro-architecture design patterns. However, the selection

of patterns does not appear to be rationalized and their relationship to quality is not discussed.

A pattern-based software development process based on case-based reasoning (CBR) has been discussed and applied to an Internet chat application (Wentzlaff & Specker, 2006). However, it does not explicitly suggest any implications towards quality and does not discuss the significance of the context in which a problem occurs and the forces that its solution resolves.

The Oregon Software Development Process (OSDP) (Schümmer & Lukosch, 2007) has been applied to the development of groupware. OSDP encourages participatory design involving end-users, piecemeal growth, and diagnosis, all of which are guided by patterns. For example, a collection of patterns become a 'language of communication' among stakeholders. However, it appears that OSDP does not use any process patterns in its definition, and currently it lacks maturity and broad community support to be deemed suitable for the development of Web Applications.

Crystal Orange Web (Cockburn, 2007) is part of Crystal Methods and is an agile methodology that was created to delivering code to the Web in a continual stream: it deals with a continuous stream of initiatives that require programming and with each initiative's results being merged with the growing code base being used by the public. However, Crystal Orange Web is currently in trial run, and the quality-related concerns of Web Applications and the use of patterns are not discussed.

The integration of patterns for accessibility in a model-driven approach to the development of Web Applications, namely UML-based Web Engineering (UWE), has been suggested (Jeschke, Pfeiffer, & Vieritz, 2009). However, an accessibility model is not given, the proposed patterns are not mature, and the feasibility issues are not considered.

Finally, a method for integrating patterns in the development of interactive television (iTV) applications has been proposed (Kunert, 2009).

Figure 2. An abstract and high-level model of pattern-oriented Web engineering

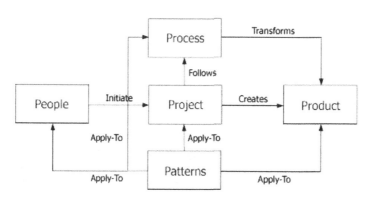

This method places a strong emphasis on the context of use of a user of an iTV application. However, besides usability, this method does not take other quality attributes into consideration and the feasibility of integrating the proposed patterns is not considered.

A THEORETICAL AND PRACTICAL PERSPECTIVE OF PATTERN-ORIENTED WEB ENGINEERING

In this section, the interplay of theoretical and practical aspects of pattern-oriented Web Engineering is considered. In that regard, essentially all concerns in the development of a Web Application, including quality assurance and evaluation, are studied from the viewpoint of patterns.

A View of Pattern-Oriented Web Engineering

The discipline of Web Engineering can be viewed from a number of viewpoints. A pattern viewpoint leads to a *problem solving* view of Web Engineering. Figure 2 depicts the People, Project, Process, Product, and Patterns (5P) model of pattern-oriented Web Engineering.

From the 5P model, it follows, for example, that there can be use of patterns for project management, patterns for handling team structure

and dynamics, patterns for selecting and carrying out activities in a development process (and other cognate processes), and patterns for different (by-)product deliverables (such as use case model, requirements specification, design description, implementation, inspection report, test documentation, and license). Any pattern-oriented approaches to Web Engineering are specialized/refined instances of the 5P model.

Towards Pattern Maturity

As per the 5P model, '*pattern-ness*' or the degree of sophistication of use of patterns (and absence of anti-patterns) by an organization could itself be an indicator of the maturity of that organization. For the sake of this chapter, such an organization is an entity involved in Web Engineering. This in turn calls for a definition and establishment of a *Pattern Maturity Model (PMM)* in general and, for Web Applications, *PMM-WA* in particular.

PMM-WA could have multiple levels and sub-levels corresponding to each level. Table 1 presents a preliminary instance of PMM-WA that correlates higher (sub-)level with the higher the level of use of patterns in the organization. It is evident that other sub-levels are possible. For example, there can be sub-levels for Sub-Level 0: Web Architecture Patterns and Sub-Level 5': Formal Specification Patterns. Further discussion of this aspect is beyond the scope of this chapter.

Table 1. An example of a pattern maturity model for Web Applications

Pattern Maturity Level	Pattern Maturity Sub-Level
Level 5: Organization Patterns	
Level 4: People Patterns	
Level 3: Project Patterns	
Level 2: Process Patterns	
Level 1: Product Patterns	Sub-Level 6: Conceptual Modeling Patterns Sub-Level 5: Requirements Patterns Sub-Level 4: Inspection Patterns Sub-Level 3: Test Patterns Sub-Level 2: Design Patterns Sub-Level 1: Implementation Patterns
Level 0: No Patterns	

A Situational Methodology for Integrating Patterns in the Engineering of Web Applications

For the sake of this chapter, a *methodology* is defined as a documented approach presented as a collection of sequence of related and rationalized steps, each involving certain activities, for achieving some constructive goal. Furthermore, a methodology should be used as a guideline rather than as a strict set of instructions.

This section presents a summary of a methodology for pattern-oriented Web Engineering, namely POWEM, for systematically addressing the quality of Web Applications and the role of patterns in addressing it. In its different appearances (Kamthan, 2008a; Kamthan, 2008b; Kamthan, 2008c), POWEM has gone through customizations.

POWEM is a projection of the 5P model. POWEM is inspired by situational method engineering (Kumar & Welke, 1992) in the sense that it is motivated by characteristics unique to Web Applications, and acknowledges that each Web Application is different. The use of a pattern is dependent on the context outlined in the description of that pattern. The context is used to prioritize the forces of a pattern and thereby arrive at the solution that pattern proposes. It is this context of use that makes POWEM *situational*.

Figure 3 presents an abstract, ontological view of POWEM.

The realization of the three main elements in Figure 3, namely process, quality, and patterns, is made concrete in the following sequence of non-atomic and non-mutually exclusive steps:

Figure 3. A high-level view of the development of Web Applications within POWEM

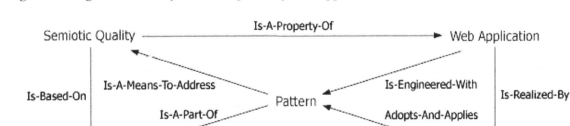

- **[S-1]** Selecting the development process model.
- **[S-2]** Identifying and organizing semiotic quality concerns in a model.
- **[S-3]** Acquiring, selecting, and applying suitable patterns.

The steps [S-1] to [S-3], upon execution, need to take certain feasibility issues under consideration. By reference, these feasibility issues also determine the scope and limitations of POWEM.

Selecting the Development Process Model

The inclusion of patterns in the development of Web Applications can not be ad-hoc. Indeed, POWEM must be deployed within the auspices of a suitable process model, the deployment of which rests on the following hypothesis:

H-1. An improvement in the *process* for development can bring about improvement in the quality of the *product*, namely the Web Application itself (Nelson & Monarchi, 2007).

It has been articulated (Lea, 1994) that a pattern-oriented process for the development of urban architectures relies on the following principles: Collective Development, Participatory Design, Responsibility, Decentralization, Integration of Roles, Integration of Activities, and Stepwise Construction. It is understood that a process model used in POWEM must embody these principles.

The selection and adoption of a process model depends on several criteria, including the following non-mutually exclusive primary factors:

1. **Intrinsic flexibility:** It is well-known that the development of Web Applications is uniquely sensitive to changes in the market, evolution of technologies, and other uncertainties (Ziemer & Stålhane, 2004). This requires that the development process of Web Applications is specified so as to be flexible. The desired flexibility can be achieved by several means including by allowing revisitations of previous phases and by facilitating parallel development. This makes the development process non-linear (iterative and incremental) in nature.

2. **Human-centricity:** This is a reaffirmation of [C-3]. The development of Web Applications is prone to risks, and one approach for mitigating risks is to involve users as an integral part of the process from the outset. In general, Web Applications are inherently interactive in nature, and the users (and their computing environments) vary broadly in their capabilities. Therefore, any selection and adoption of a process model must especially be sensitive to the users. Indeed, this 'empowering' of users is aligned with *participatory design* approach inherent to the original inception of patterns.

3. **Support for quality:** This is a reaffirmation of [C-7] and [C-8]. There must be an explicit provision in the development process specification for assurance of the quality of the underlying Web Application, specifically, using patterns. The process must address quality concerns during early phases of its execution. In addition, the process must have a provision for evaluation (such as inspections and testing).

The aforementioned criteria are not found universally. For example, a recent extension of WebML (Brambilla et al., 2006) does not satisfy the second criterion.

The secondary criteria in the selection and adoption of a process model could be: its alignment with the organizational vision; its openness, for example, availability for public use along with non-restrictive licensing conditions; its economy, for example, the learning curve; its level of familiarity with the engineers; its maturity demonstrated by successful/proven use; and cost-effective, broad, and readily available tool support for it.

The process environments satisfying the aforementioned primary criteria and could be used in POWEM are Extreme Programming (XP) (Wallace, Raggett, & Aufgang, 2002) for small-to-medium size projects, and the Rational Unified Process (RUP) (Kappel et al., 2006), OpenUP, and Web OPEN (Henderson-Sellers, Lowe, & Haire, 2002) for large size projects. (It is not the intention of POWEM to unreservedly advocate or endorse a certain process or a method and these are mentioned only as suggestions.)

Remarks

Standards for development process. The implications of adopting a standard for a development process are significant. The IEEE Standard 1074-1997, ISO/IEC 12207:2008 Standard, and ISO/TR 18529:2000 Standard provide a high-level meta-description of (human-centric) development processes. It is known that both XP and RUP conform, to a certain extent, to the ISO/IEC 12207:2008 Standard.

Patterns for development process. In practice, there are several possible paths through a process and, based on experience, some better than others. In light of H-1 and H-3, the underlying process must be carried out effectively. To strengthen these hypotheses, the use of patterns can be made *throughout* the development process (Ambler, 1998; Coplien & Harrison, 2005; Dumas, van der Aalst, & ter Hofstede, 2006), a consequence of the 5P model. In particular, there are patterns available for putting agile methodologies in general and XP in particular into practice (Bergin, 2005; Hansen, 2002). There are patterns available also for creating agile documentation and for the development of process artifacts, namely elicitation of use cases and specification of requirements. The use of these patterns in turn can strengthen H-1. Further discussion of this aspect is beyond the scope of this chapter.

Web for unification of development process. It is critical that a process be visible, and one way to accomplish that is to record its proceedings. Indeed, the *maturity* of software documentation (Huang & Tilley, 2003) can depend on whether it is interactive (say, hyperlinked) and documents the use of patterns (if any). For example, if a design pattern reflects a predefined design decision (Kruchten, 2004), then the design documentation can rationalize the selection of patterns that in turn becomes part of the higher-level rationale behind implementation decisions.

If the descriptions of any patterns used in either the process or the product are themselves available on the Web, then they could be pointed to (for example, hyperlinked) from the process workflow artifacts. Thus, the Web becomes a *unifying* environment for the development of Web Applications that is unique in the sense that the process workflow artifacts (for example, models or documents), the resources (for example, patterns) used, and the final product can all reside in the same environment, namely the Web. Figure 4 depicts this confluence of process, resources, and product.

Feasibility of Development Process Model

It is acknowledged that there can always be exceptional cases which simply may not fit into a 'fixed' process model or for which a given process model may have to be customized to suit the development.

The use of any process model for the development of a Web Application will entail costs. For example, RUP is inherently commercial. It is not automatic that these costs can be absorbed or sustained by an organization. In general, agile methodologies have shown to be cost-effective for projects with certain types of uncertainties (Liu, Kong, & Chen, 2006) and, according to surveys (Khan & Balbo, 2005), been successfully applied to certain kinds of Web Applications. The

Figure 4. An exemplar of the Web as a unifying environment for the process workflow artifacts, the corresponding Web Application, and the patterns used therein

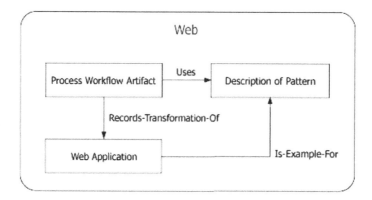

benefits and drawbacks of agile and disciplined approaches to development have been pointed out and a heterogeneous combination that balances agility and discipline is suggested (Boehm & Turner, 2004).

The adoption of any process model for the development of a Web Application and the realization of the activities recommended therein will evidently depend on the organizational process maturity. These can be determined by the appropriate level in the Capability Maturity Model for Software (CMM), by the assessment based on the Excellence Model of the European Foundation for Quality Management (EFQM), or the deployment of ISO/IEC 15504 series of standards. For the sake of this chapter, PMM-WA Level 1 (especially Sub-Level 2 for a later illustration) and Levels 2–4 are also relevant.

Identifying and Organizing Quality Concerns in a Model

From a semiotics (Shanks, 1999) viewpoint, a representation of a Web Application can be viewed on six interrelated levels: physical, empirical, syntactic, semantic, pragmatic, and social. In this section, the discussion is restricted to the pragmatic level where the interest is in the utility of a representation to its stakeholder(s).

Stakeholders of a Web Application

Using a systematic approach (Sharp, Galal, & Finkelstein, 1999), two major classes of stakeholders can be broadly identified: a *producer* (that can have sub-classes such as a owner, manager, or engineer) is the one who is responsible in different ways at different times at different stages of the Web Application, and a *consumer* (that can have sub-classes such as a novice and expert end-user) is the one who interacts the Web Application for some purpose.

For the sake of this chapter, a user and an end-user are interchangeable. Figure 5 depicts this classification of stakeholders in a UML Class Diagram.

There are patterns to assist in the aforementioned role-based stakeholder classification. Following the DOMAIN EXPERTISE IN ROLES pattern (Coplien & Harrison, 2005), the stakeholder classification is based on the *role* of a stakeholder in relationship to a Web Application. For example, both the engineer and the end-user could be the same person, but their roles with respect to the Web Application are different. The number of roles is kept to the necessary minimal by using the FEW ROLES pattern (Coplien & Harrison, 2005). The stakeholders can themselves be related in different ways; however, this aspect is suppressed.

Figure 5. A classification of stakeholders of a Web Application

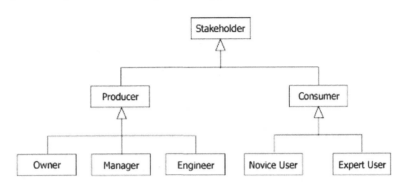

There are patterns for team formation. For example, the producers using XP can organize themselves using the OLD PEOPLE EVERYWHERE pattern (Alexander, Ishikawa, & Silverstein, 1977) and the APPRENTICESHIP and DEVELOPING IN PAIRS patterns (Coplien & Harrison, 2005).

A Model for the Semiotic Quality of a Web Application

The relationship between quality and value is historical. It is known that there are a number of possible views of quality. These, in turn, drive the process of constructing a quality model. The quality modeling in POWEM rests on the following hypothesis:

H-2. For an understanding of quality of a Web Application, the notion of quality needs to be decomposed into a manageable number of attributes (Fenton & Pfleeger, 1997).

The construction of PoQ is as follows. For consideration of space, the focus is on pragmatic quality only.

- **PoQ: Step 1.** It is assumed that quality in general and pragmatic quality in particular is a multifaceted concept. Using that and H-2, pragmatic quality is decomposed into *granular* levels that consist of quality attributes that can be addressed directly or indirectly. The relevance of the quality attributes extenuating their inclusion is based on current literature on the quality of Web Applications (Mendes & Mosley, 2006) and is discussed in later sections.

- **PoQ: Step 2.** These quality attributes could for example manifest themselves as non-functional requirements (NFRs) of a Web Application and should be specified accordingly in a requirements specification. (For consideration of space, the quality attributes outlined here are not defined.) For the definitions of most of these quality attributes, (international) standards such as the IEEE Standard 1061-1998, the ISO 9241-11:1998 Standard, the ISO/IEC 9126-1:2001 Standard, and the ISO 9241-171:2008 Standard could be referred.

- **PoQ: Step 3.** To address quality attributes (in the decomposition from Step 1), patterns are assigned as preventative means. For example, let **W** be the set of Web Applications, **Q** be the set of quality attributes, and **P** be the set of patterns. Then, for a given W in **W**, to aid a Q in **Q** during the development of W, a pattern P in **P** is assigned.

The result of the construction is summarized in Table 2.

Table 2. A subset of elements and a partial view of PoQ, a model for the semiotic quality of a Web Application

Semiotic Level	Quality Attributes	Means for Quality Assurance
Social Quality Concerns		
Pragmatic	[Tier 3] [Maintainability] [Usability]	Patterns
	[Tier 2] [Performance] [Reliability] [Understandability]	
	[Tier 1] [Attractiveness] [Availability] [Efficiency] [Familiarity] [Readability]	
Physical, Empirical, Syntactic, and Semantic Quality Concerns		

Remarks

Comparison of PoQ and standard quality models. The proposed quality model PoQ differs from conventional quality models for software systems. The structure of PoQ is an acyclic graph rather than a hierarchy. The focus in Table 2 is non-functional rather than functional requirements. Therefore, even though functionality as a quality attribute is present in the ISO/IEC 9126-1:2001 Standard, it is not a candidate for Table 2. The focus in Table 2 is to emphasize preventative means. Therefore, even though the ISO/IEC TR 9126-3:2003 Standard maps a set of metrics to quality attributes, this is not done in the last column of Table 2.

Evolvability of PoQ. The quality attributes in Table 2 are necessary but there is no claim of their sufficiency. The tiers in Table 2 and the list of quality attributes therein are open-ended. They are prone to evolution for a number of reasons including as the Web and the stakeholder expectations of a Web Application evolve. For example, Tier 1 could be extended by including quality attributes such as *interoperability*, Tier 2 could be extended by including quality attributes such as *findability*, and Tier 3 could be extended by including quality attributes such as *dependability*. Therefore, PoQ is based on the 'Open World Assumption' so that it can evolve.

Relationships between quality attributes in PoQ. The quality attributes in Table 2 are not

mutually exclusive. Indeed, the quality attributes in Tier 3 depend on that in Tier 2, and those in Tier 2 in turn depend on the quality attributes in Tier 1. For example, in order to use or maintain a Web Application, one must be able to understand it, and in turn be able to read (the resources in) it. Similarly, for a Web Application to be reliable, it must be available.

The quality attributes within the same tier in Table 2 are also not necessarily mutually exclusive. For example, attractiveness can impact the perception and reception of the resource being read, or the steps taken towards improving reliability (say, fault tolerance) may lead to inclusion of redundant source code or data (that can be unfavorable to maintainability) but enable ease-of-use (that can be favorable to usability).

The Pragmatic Quality: Stakeholder Relationships

The relevance of quality attributes at the pragmatic level of Table 2 varies with respect to stakeholder types (Kamthan, 2008a). For the sake of argument, consider the case of an end-user and an engineer:

- **PoQ: Pragmatic level-tier 1.** The quality attributes of direct concern to an end-user are attractiveness (similar to, but not synonymous with, aesthetics), availability, familiarity, and readability (similar to, but not synonymous with, legibility). The quality attribute of direct concern to an engineer are (space and time) efficiency and readability. It is important to note that a user that is typically concerned with a dynamic view and an engineer with a static view of a Web Application. Therefore, readability concerns of each with respect to the Web Application can be different.

- **PoQ: Pragmatic level-tier 2.** The quality attributes of direct concern to an end-user are performance, reliability, and understandability. The quality attribute of direct concern to an engineer is understandability. It is important to note that the understandability concerns of a user and an engineer with respect to the Web Application can be different.

- **PoQ: Pragmatic level-tier 3.** The quality attribute of direct concern to an end-user is usability. For simplicity, accessibility is viewed as a special case of usability. The quality attribute of direct concern to an engineer is maintainability. For simplicity, modifiability, portability, and reusability are considered as special cases of maintainability.

Finally, it could be noted that the significance of each quality attribute will vary across different kinds of Web Applications. For example, the quality needs of a Web Application providing auction services will have some similarity with a shopping application (as both are related to sales) but will differ substantially from an application providing periodically-updated news in real-time on a natural disaster.

Feasibility of Quality Attributes

Any commitment to quality has associated costs including time, effort, personnel, and other resources. Therefore, in order to be realistic, the expectations of improving the quality attributes of a Web Application must be feasible.

There are pragmatic quality attributes in Table 2 that can not (at least mathematically) be quantified or *completely* satisfied. For example, an a priori guarantee that a Web Application will be attractive, accessible, or usable to *all* end-users at *all* times in *all* computing environments that the end-users deploy, is not realistic. Therefore, the quality assurance plan and in turn the quality requirements of a Web Application must both reflect the fact that certain attributes can only be *satisficed* (Alexander, 1964; Simon, 1996).

Acquiring, Selecting, and Applying Suitable Patterns

The deployment of patterns in POWEM rests on the following hypothesis:

H-3. A preventative approach to quality assurance is at least as significant as a curative approach (Dromey, 2003).

Acquisition of Patterns

There is currently no centralized location per se for acquiring all the patterns that may be desirable for the development of Web Applications. The availability of patterns relevant to the development of Web Applications varies significantly across multiple dimensions: medium (print, electronic), publishing avenue (book, event proceedings, mailing list, newsgroup, periodical, thesis, Wiki), cost (commercial, free-of-cost/'open content'), and so on.

For example, while some patterns, pattern systems, and pattern languages are only available commercially in print form such as books, others are available commercially via some means of electronic archival such as a compact disc (CD), and yet others are available either commercially through membership subscription of an organization that publishes event proceedings or free-of-cost via a portal on the Web. There are (partial) indices and (by necessity, time- and cost/benefit ratio-dependent) surveys (Henninger & Corrêa, 2007) that also inform the existence of patterns.

Selection of Patterns

In the beginning (Alexander, 1979; Alexander, Ishikawa, & Silverstein, 1977), there was only one set of patterns (indeed, a unique pattern language) for any domain. The path through this language was preset. Therefore, the issue of *selection* of patterns did not arise. The situation, however, has changed considerably in the ensuing decades.

In general, the relationship between the set of quality attributes and the set of patterns is many-to-many. This in turn *necessitates* selection of a pattern from a set of candidates, a process that is largely manual and subjective. It has also become non-trivial due to a number of reasons including (1) the rapid growth in the number of available patterns and (2) the variations in the level of support from the pattern author's side for selecting a pattern.

In case there are multiple candidate patterns with different *problem* and *context*, then the selection of a desirable pattern can be based on a number of factors:

The role of the meta-description in selecting a pattern. In some cases (Gamma et al., 1995), the guidance for selecting a pattern from a given set of patterns is provided explicitly and independently *external* to the descriptions of patterns as well demonstrated by a case study. However, in general, that is not the case. In these situations, the engineer (for example, a designer) needs to make a personal decision (or a collective decision, if in a team) that may or may not coincide with the original intent of the pattern author.

The role of relationships in selecting a pattern. In some cases, the set of patterns to select from may be constrained due to certain reasons such as the relationship of a given pattern to other patterns. For example, the deployment of a specific macro-architecture design pattern may necessitate the use of a predetermined collection of micro-architecture design patterns. These relationships should be made explicit in the description of a pattern (Meszaros & Doble, 1998) by the pattern author. However, upon publication of new patterns, potentially new relationships to a given pattern, say P, can arise. If the description of P has not evolved since its original publication, then it will not reflect these new relationships. For example, this is more likely to happen in print than in electronic medium.

The role of the description in selecting a pattern. In some cases, checking the maturity of the pattern (indicated by an associated confidence rating) if available and/or reading and understanding (at least) the examples included in the description of a pattern can help towards the decision of selecting a pattern (Meszaros & Doble, 1998). In other cases, guidance for using the pattern is embedded in the description of a pattern (Tidwell, 2005). In any case, the impact of each candidate pattern on a quality attribute (in Table 2) has to be assessed. The quality of the description of a pattern (and, by reference, the reputation of the author(s) of the pattern) plays an imperative role in these cases.

In case there are multiple candidate patterns each with the same *problem* and *context*, the selection of the desirable pattern can, in certain situations, be made by a decision analysis approach based on the aforementioned factors (Taibi, & Ngo, 2002). The lack of a standard for describing patterns and consequently the presence of descriptions of patterns in different pattern forms and presentation styles can pose a challenge in comparing patterns.

Application of Patterns

The main non-mutually exclusive concerns in the application of patterns are (1) an understanding of the pattern description, (2) the order in which patterns are applied, which includes an understanding of the relationships (if any) between patterns, and finally, (3) acceptability of the result upon a composition of patterns in some sequence.

If the end result is unsatisfactory, the selection itself and/or the composition may need to be revisited and revised. This is in agreement with the creative and experimental nature of development that aims to seek alternatives and the iterative and incremental nature of the development process that enables it (for example, through prototyping).

Composition of Patterns and Pattern Sequences

There are certain essentially invariant constraints that come into play in the development of a set of patterns targeted for Web Applications that an aspiring pattern author need to consider before embarking on such an endeavor. It is known that the nature of a non-trivial Web Application can be inherently heterogeneous (Kamthan, 2009a). For example, the knowledge of the Internet and the Web in particular is intrinsic. In addition, there can be different modalities of information that in turn can be made available in different media types in a Web Application. In other words, the knowledge in the development of a Web Application can span *multiple* domains. Furthermore, the individual phases of a Web Application (including but not limited to those dealing with conceptual modeling, requirements engineering, designing, and testing) themselves are large constitute sub-disciplines of Web Engineering.

Therefore, the development of a single set of patterns that can be used to build any arbitrary Web Application is simply impractical: (1) it would require an extraordinarily large-scale collaboration of experts in a number of domains (that is already difficult as-is) and, even if that is feasible, (2) it would result in a single monolithic set of patterns, the evolution of which would be prohibitive to manage. Indeed, the decision not to label the collection of object-oriented software design patterns (Gamma et al., 1995) as a 'pattern language' is intentional. This in turn suggests that a given single set of patterns is insufficient

for developing non-trivial software systems and necessitates the presence of multiple sets of patterns. The existence of multiple patterns in a pattern language and the existence of multiple pattern languages are analogous to the existence of, for example, multiple use cases in a use case model, multiple (software) requirements in a (software) requirements specification, and so on. This inevitably leads to the need for composing patterns from *different* sets that are likely authored by different people in different times.

In applying patterns, the issue of composition of patterns is especially critical. There can two possibilities:

1. **Intra-pattern set composition.** In this case, there is a composition from a single set of patterns. In an intra-pattern set composition, the temporal order in which the patterns are to be applied is predetermined (specified a priori) if they belong to a pattern system or a pattern language.

2. **Inter-pattern set composition.** In this case, there is a composition from multiple sets of patterns. In an inter-pattern set composition, the temporal order in which the patterns are to be applied is not predetermined.

A pattern-oriented Web Application may use a specific collection of patterns from a single or multiple sets of patterns and compose them in some order. This order leads to a *pattern sequence*. The case of pattern sequences in an inter-pattern set composition based on an arbitrary set of patterns (that are not predetermined but selected by the engineer) is especially challenging and intrinsically depends on the expressiveness of the descriptions of patterns (Porter, Coplien, & Winn, 2005; Zdun, 2007)..

The instance or concrete realization of the actual pattern sequence followed is a *pattern story*. (This is similar to the relationship between a use case and a scenario.) The rationale for selecting patterns and the pattern stories need to be docu-

Figure 6. An abstract view of a design sequence (shown in bold lines) that traverses through different sets of interrelated patterns (shown as solid circles)

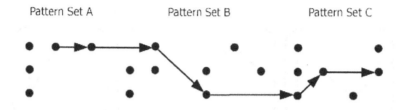

mented in the appropriate process artifacts (such as in Figure 4) so as to be useful in the future for activities such as maintenance and project retrospectives.

An Example of Pattern-Oriented Development of Web Applications

It follows from the 5P model that patterns are applicable to any phase of a process. However, for considerations of space, this chapter is limited to addressing the role of patterns in the design phase of a Web Application.

The purpose of design is to find alternative solutions to a problem. A pattern if described appropriately includes both the advantages and limitations of the proposed solution. Therefore, the benefit of a pattern-oriented design for the design team is being able to *discuss* the strengths and weaknesses of each alternative.

As depicted in Figure 6 and evident from the discussion that follows, the patterns presented here form a skeleton sequence that traverses through a number of existing sets of patterns, eventually terminating in the preferred design of a Web Application.

In the following sections, the macro-architecture and the micro-architecture design of a Web Application are considered. For consideration of space, the details of design decision and design rationale that are associated with pattern sequences are not given.

Macro-Architecture Design of Web Applications

The macro-architecture design model is the place where high-level design decisions, independent of any paradigm or technology, are made. These decisions may be inspired by a variety of factors including organizational and technical considerations.

The macro-architecture design patterns suggested from an organizational viewpoint are based on the fact that a Web Application will implicitly or explicitly target some area of public service such as education, commerce, entertainment, and so on. For example, the choice of the domain name (such as .org or .net) does not always or automatically reveal the nature of the area of public service. The SITE BRANDING pattern (Van Duyne, Landay, & Hong, 2003) is a means for the engineers to make the genre of a Web Application explicit, which in turn contributes to familiarity for an end-user.

The macro-architecture design patterns suggested from a technical viewpoint are based on the fact that a Web Application belongs to the class of distributed request-response-type interactive systems. In particular, the applicable patterns are the CLIENT-SERVER pattern (Schmidt et al., 2000) followed by the APPLICATION SERVER pattern (Manolescu & Kunzle, 2001), which in turn is followed by the MODEL-VIEW-CONTROLLER (MVC) pattern (Buschmann et al., 1996; Buschmann, Henney, & Schmidt, 2007a). Figure 7 depicts an assembly of these architectural design patterns.

Figure 7. An abstract illustration of solutions of a set of architectural design patterns in the development of Web Applications

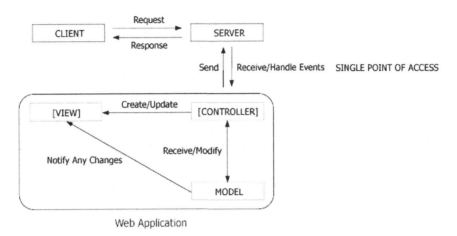

Web Application

The CLIENT-SERVER pattern supports modifiability and reusability. For example, a server or resources on the server-side could be modified without impacting the client. Also, a single server can support multiple clients simultaneously, or a client could make simultaneous requests for resources residing on multiple servers. For instance, an Extensible Markup Language (XML) document could be located on one server, while an ECMAScript script on another server, and a Cascading Style Sheet (CSS) or Extensible Stylesheet Language Transformations (XSLT) document on yet another.

The APPLICATION SERVER pattern also supports maintainability. It isolates the Web Application from other aspects on the server-side. This separation allows the Web Application to evolve independently. Using the SINGLE ACCESS POINT (Yoder & Barcalow, 1997) pattern, the Web server becomes the unique point of access between the consumer and the Web Application.

The MVC pattern advocates the separation of structure of a document from both its logic and its presentation, which leads to three semantically-different components: model, view, and controller. The (theoretical) minimization of the coupling between these components contributes towards

the modifiability of a Web Application. Since a model is normally not aware of the views and controllers attached to it, the *same* model in a MVC could be used with multiple views and multiple controllers, which in turn contributes towards the reusability of a Web Application. For example, the same information could be adapted (repurposed or transformed) and delivered to different situations (like different user agent environments or consumer needs). Figure 6 shows the possible presence of multiple controllers by [CONTROLLER] and of multiple views by [VIEW].

As a Web Application becomes increasingly sophisticated (with functionalities such as dynamic delivery of resources, personalization, and so on), the implementation of MVC faces a number of challenges that can be tackled with the use of other special-purpose patterns (Fowler et al., 2003). For example, to invoke different user interface styles in a Web Application, there may be a need to have multiple controllers. As the number of controllers increase, this can lead to redundancy that in turn is prohibitive to maintainability. In such a case, the common logic could be extracted via the APPLICATION CONTROLLER pattern.

The delivery of resources in a Web Application can be either static or dynamic. In case of static delivery, a single model, view, and controller may suffice. A Web Application is relatively more complex in case of dynamic delivery and would typically require multiple views and multiple controllers. There are patterns available to realize this (Fowler et al., 2003). For example, the PAGE CONTROLLER pattern assigns one controller to each dynamically-generated document in a Web Application.

In response to a request to a Web Application, there may be several tasks that need to be performed and these tasks may have overlapping aspects. The distribution of the behavior of the input controller across multiple objects can lead to redundancy, which in turn is exorbitant to maintainability. The FRONT CONTROLLER pattern suggests a consolidation of all request-handling by channeling requests through a single handler object.

A dynamic delivery of resources could be viewed as a transformation pipeline: the data is usually archived in some normative format (with preferably no presentation semantics) and, upon request, goes through a sequence of transformations at the end of which it is delivered in some renderable format. For simple cases (where there is a need for one transformation), this can be realized in practice via a combination of TEMPLATE VIEW pattern that allows interweaving of programming language code and markup (and therefore not favorable to modifiability), and the TRANSFORM VIEW pattern; for complex cases (where there is a need for two transformations), we could deploy the TWO-STEP VIEW pattern.

It can be noted that one of the patterns that can be seen as competing with MVC is the PRESENTATION-ABSTRACTION-CONTROL (PAC) pattern (Buschmann et al., 1996; Buschmann, Henney, & Schmidt, 2007a). However, PAC as opposed to MVC supports multiple interaction paradigms and is therefore not suitable for the computing environment of a typical Web Application.

Micro-Architecture Design of Web Applications

The micro-architecture design model is the place where low-level design decisions are cast. Although at this stage complete independency with respect to a paradigm or technology is difficult, the aim is to allow the possibility of multiple implementations.

In an object-oriented approach to micro-architecture design, the DOMAIN MODEL pattern (Fowler et al., 2003) provides a way to construct an object model of the micro-architecture that incorporates both structure and behavior. The separation of model, view, and controller suggested by the MVC pattern can be achieved with the help of micro-architecture design patterns (Gamma et al., 1995) such as COMPOSITE, OBSERVER, and STRATEGY, that a separation is achieved.

In the following, the focus is only on the design aspects that impact pragmatic quality. As such, the attention is geared towards client-side concerns. For the purpose of illustration, three interaction design aspects of a Web Application, namely information design, navigation design, and presentation design, independent of any specific domain, are considered. These incidentally are also part of W2000 (Baresi et al., 2006), a model-driven approach and notation for Web Applications.

Information Design

The information in Web Applications, particularly those targeted for the Social Web, can often be aggregated from multiple sources and thereby become heterogeneous. The recent evolution of mashups is a prime example.

The patterns related to information architecture can help organize information in a predictable manner. The entry point to a Web Application can be made explicit to an end-user via the HOME PAGE pattern (Graham, 2003), and contributes to usability. The information in it can be organized as a hierarchy of objects via the WHOLE-PART pattern (Buschmann et al., 1996). Since each of these objects can be modified or replaced independently, the WHOLE-PART pattern supports maintainability. Also, since a 'part' can correspond to more than one 'whole,' the WHOLE-PART pattern also supports reusability. However, multiple indirections stemming from client requests and responses for fulfilling them can lead to a loss of performance, particularly when each 'part' itself is structured as WHOLE-PART.

The information organization patterns, when use appropriately, aid readability, understandability, and usability. The information in a single document could be organized into a grid of rows and columns where every atomic information element is made to fit within this grid via the GRID LAYOUT pattern (Van Duyne, Landay, & Hong, 2003), and even organized further based on some criterion like alphabetical or chronological via the ALPHABETICAL ORGANIZATION and CHRONOLOGICAL ORGANIZATION patterns, respectively.

A Web Application may contain images for presenting some information such as the corporate logo or product pictures. The FAST-DOWNLOADING IMAGES pattern (Van Duyne, Landay, & Hong, 2003) suggests creation of images optimized for color and size in an appropriate format, and thus aids accessibility and performance. The REUSABLE IMAGES pattern (Van Duyne, Landay, & Hong, 2003) suggests caching images that appear at multiple places in a Web Application, and thereby aids performance. The ACCESSIBLE IMAGES pattern (Vora, 2009) provides guidance to aid the accessibility of any images used.

Navigation Design

There are different means for finding information (Morville, 2005) on the Web, one of which is navigation. Within the context of the Web, navigation is traversal through space for some purpose like casual or targeted browsing for information or complementing a reading sequence. The journey can become increasingly challenging if the path is nonlinear. Therefore, an appropriate design of the information graph that can optimize the end-user experience of the journey is critical. It is known that there are differences between search strategies of novice and expert end-users (Chevalier & Kicka, 2006).

The navigation patterns, when use appropriately, aid findability (and therefore usability). The BREADCRUMBS pattern (Van Duyne, Landay, & Hong, 2003) or its extensions such as LOOK-AHEAD BREADCRUMBS can inform an end-user of the location of the resource that has been accessed relative to the entry point of the Web Application. The CLEAR ENTRY POINTS pattern (Tidwell, 2005) can restrict the navigation to a specific category and make it task-oriented. The FLY-OUT MENU pattern (Marks & Hong, 2006) suggests a 'compound' menu where each menu item itself has a sub-menu that expands only upon end-user interaction. This allows large amount of navigation information to be presented at different levels of abstraction, thereby improving both (spatial) efficiency and readability. The navigation information itself may be organized horizontally or vertically as suggested by the HORIZONTAL NAVIGATION or VERTICAL NAVIGATION patterns (Marks & Hong, 2006), respectively.

There are navigation design patterns that aid understandability (Tidwell, 2005). For example, the WIZARD pattern leads an end-user through the interface in a stepwise manner for carrying out tasks in a prescribed order. However, it can have a negative impact on the performance of an expert user. The RESPONSIVE DISCLOSURE pattern starts with a very minimal interface, and guides an end-user through a series of steps by exposing more of the interface as an end-user completes each step. These two patterns could, for example, be used for providing a registration process.

Any navigation design must take exceptional behavior into consideration to support usability. The SESSION pattern (Weiss, 2003) can help

Figure 8. An abstract illustration of solutions of a set of interaction design patterns in the development of Web Applications

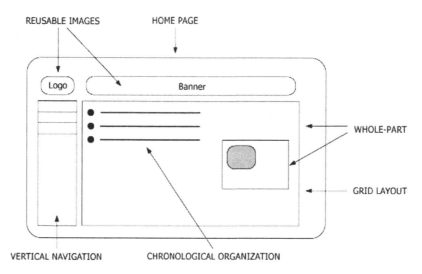

maintain the state of the Web Application in the event of an interruption of navigation flow. The MISSING LINK pattern (German & Cowan, 2000) informs an end-user that certain hyperlink does not exist and suggests alternatives.

Presentation Design

It is known that end-users value the attractiveness or the 'look-and-feel' of a Web Application. Furthermore, the information included a Web Application not only needs to be structured but also appropriately presented to used optimally. For that, a variety of patterns could be used.

The end-users of a Web Application can vary in their (physical and mental) capabilities and preferences, and may find one view of information to be more usable than another. The MIRRORWORLD pattern (German & Cowan, 2000) provides two or more views of the same information. Specifically, information in these views could be presented in TWO-PANEL SELECTOR pattern (Tidwell, 2005) when two different views that are to be presented simultaneously, or CLOSABLE PANELS or CARD STACK patterns (Tidwell, 2005) when several different views are to be presented in such as way that only one view is visible at a

time in each panel or stack, respectively.

It is known that colors can have a positive impact both cognitively and contribute to attractiveness if used appropriately. Using patterns like FEW HUES, MANY VALUES or COLOR-CODED SECTIONS (Tidwell, 2006) a Web Application could be given a unique 'identity.' It is common to use tables to structure information in two dimensions. However, readability becomes inversely proportional to the number of rows, particularly for a table with a large number of rows and multiple columns. To enable the separation of the entries visually, the backgrounds of the table rows could be alternately colored using two similar shades as suggested by the ROW STRIPING pattern (Tidwell, 2006). The ACCESSIBLE TABLES pattern (Vora, 2009) provides guidance to aid the accessibility of any tables used.

Figure 8 depicts an abstract view of solutions of some of the patterns mentioned previously. It is not representative since the modality of the solution of a pattern need not be entirely visual and may include behavioral aspects.

The resulting design could be evaluated in some informal, semi-formal, or formal manner. For example, an inspection is a common approach for a formal evaluation of design. In doing so, instead of the conventional guidelines-based checklist, a pattern-based checklist could be used.

Remarks

'Imperfection' of Pattern-Oriented Development. It can seem natural that in practice there is no 'perfect' design (of a Web Application). However, a pattern-oriented approach to design can highlight the origins of the limitations and reasons for their existence. There may be more than one solution to a given problem of a pattern. The selection of a specific solution is based on the resolution of forces that have the highest priority as determined by the particular context. In doing so, some forces may only be partially resolved and other forces may not be resolved at all. The application of other patterns may or may not resolve some of these forces (either partially or completely). Therefore, at the end of the design process, there can be an optimal design but that design may not resolve all the forces (either partially or completely).

Evolvability of Pattern-Oriented Development. The list of patterns outlined in the previous section is by no means complete and is subject to evolution. It is evident that there are certain aspects of design such as search design that are not covered and can not be covered in their entirety due to consideration of space. However, more importantly, there are consequences of applying (the solution of) any pattern. The use of each pattern places the design of a Web Application in a new state (context) that can lead to new problem(s). To solve those problem(s), a new set of pattern(s) may have to be applied, assuming that such pattern(s) are available.

In the previous section, the WIZARD pattern solves a problem but leads to other problems(s) such as the need to support a user in case help is necessary, the need to save data from previous steps in case of an (unforeseen) interruption, and so on. For example, the presence of a context-sensitive help aids usability and could be included

at appropriate places in a Web Application via the CONTEXTUAL HELP pattern (Vora, 2009). It is evident that the use of the CONTEXTUAL HELP pattern in turn places the design of a Web Application in a new state (context) that can lead to new problem(s). For example, a context-sensitive help must itself be available to be useful.

In principle, this recursive sequence is essentially unlimited. However, stopping criteria can be set based on a number of conditions such as that the cost of acquiring, selecting, and applying new patterns outweighs the benefits.

Relationship between Patterns and Quality. It should be apparent from the previous section that the relationship between patterns and quality is not one-sided. In particular, it is not automatic that the *solution* of a given pattern will lead to the improvement of all quality attributes in a given quality model such as PoQ. In fact, the use of a pattern may have a positive impact on one quality attribute but may have a negative impact on another. This is in agreement with the findings of empirical studies elsewhere (Khomh & Guéhéneuc, 2008; Wendorff, 2001). Furthermore, the 'degree' of impact in either direction may vary.

There are a number of possible reasons for this including the following: (1) the description of the pattern is inappropriate (the pattern has not been evaluated and (as a result or otherwise) it does not satisfy the expected properties of a pattern), (2) a pattern in general or one of its crucial elements such as the *problem*, *context*, or *solution* in particular is not understood and (as a result or otherwise) misapplied, (3) the construction of the quality model (to which the quality attribute belongs) for the domain is inappropriate, (4) the *solution* of the pattern does not present a sufficient condition for assuring a quality attribute, (5) the quality attribute in question can not be (completely) quantified and (as a result or otherwise) there are differences in the understanding of it (by stakeholders, particularly the evaluators), and (6) it is not possible to implement the pattern as expected in the underlying selected technology.

Feasibility of Acquiring, Selecting, and Applying Patterns

The benefits that entail in using patterns are not automatic. Therefore, the approach for using patterns in any development should be circumspect. The adoption and subsequent deployment of patterns in Web Applications needs to be viable, to which there are a variety of challenges:

- **Availability:** For a pattern-oriented approach to the development of Web Applications, it is important that design and implementation patterns sufficiently 'map' the solution space. However, currently such a mapping does not exist: the difference of the desirable set P_D of patterns and the union P_A of all available patterns and pattern languages can still consists of 'holes', that is, $P_D - P_A \neq \varphi$. Therefore, there is no *a priori* guarantee that for a given quality attribute, there exist suitable patterns (if any).
- **Locatability:** Even when it is ascertained that for a given problem a pattern does exist, that pattern needs to be located. There is currently no unique way of classifying, indexing, or representing patterns, all of which can pose obstacles in locating desirable patterns. Even though there may be patterns in other domains (say, interaction design) that are relevant to Web Applications, they are not always explicitly classified as such. Usually, patterns are not classified by quality attributes, a factor relevant that is relevant to Table 2. The name of a pattern is a common way for locating patterns; however, the association between a name and a pattern is not unique. For example, there are several variants of the MVC and BREADCRUMBS patterns. This makes the process of locating desirable patterns cumbersome and somewhat arbitrary.
- **Cost:** There is cost in terms of time and effort in learning and adapting any

conceptually reusable knowledge, including patterns. For example, the descriptions of patterns can be unclear about their target audience and, as a result, not all patterns are described in a manner that they can be easily read and understood. Indeed, as highlighted in a number of studies (Henninger & Corrêa, 2007; Manolescu et al., 2007; Segerståhl & Jokela, 2006), lack of communicability of patterns continues to be a concern in their proper use.

DIRECTIONS FOR FUTURE RESEARCH

The work presented in this chapter can be extended in a few other directions. These are briefly discussed next.

Evaluation of POWEM

The feasibility of POWEM can be checked from practical realizations of it in different situations, specifically in academic, governmental, and industrial contexts. These experiences, upon project retrospectives, could provide valuable lessons including a better understanding of the mapping between theory and practice, increasingly accurate cost estimates of deploying POWEM, and so on.

For example, patterns contain the knowledge that can be used to develop a pattern management system (PMS). Figure 9 depicts the symbiotic relationship between a pattern and the Web: a pattern assists the evolution of the Web by encapsulating the knowledge needed to develop high-quality Web Applications (such as a PMS) and, conversely, the Web presents an environment to assists with a number of activities related to a pattern. The academic experience of developing a PMS called *Patterns for Web, Web for Patterns (P4W4P)* has been described elsewhere (Kamthan, 2008a) and lessons learnt from it have been reported.

Figure 9. (a) A pattern can help in the evolution of the Web and (b) the Web can help provide an environment for a pattern

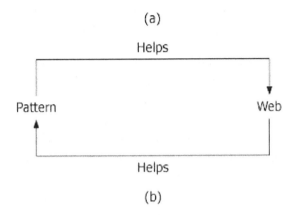

(a)

POWEM in a Metamodel

An initiative towards establishing a theoretical basis for POWEM can be useful. This, for example, could be carried out by situating POWEM within the universe of development methodologies. In particular, an investigation into the alignment of POWEM with metamodels for development methodologies, such as the ISO/IEC 24744:2007 Standard, is of research interest.

Extensions of PoQ

PoQ can be extended in a number of ways. In particular, Table 2 could be populated in both the 'horizontal' and the 'vertical' directions.

A possible extension of Table 2 is increasing the granularity of the quality attributes at the level Pragmatic Level-Tier 1, and thereby adding another level (say, Tier 0) underneath it. In that case, for example, fault tolerance and recoverability could be candidate quality attributes that belong to the level Pragmatic Level-Tier 0. Some patterns for fault tolerance and recoverability have been suggested (Ahluwalia & Jain, 2006). Similarly, consistency (on which familiarity depends) could be a candidate for the level Pragmatic Level-Tier 0.

Pattern-Oriented Social Web Applications

The Social Web, or as it is more commonly referred to by the pseudonym Web 2.0 (O'Reilly, 2005), is the perceived evolution of the Web in a direction that is characterized by user participation, openness, and network effects; driven by 'collective intelligence;' and realized by information technology. The Social Web is a result of the confluence of conventional social networks and contemporary technological networks.

There are a number of potential benefits of the Social Web. It has been posited (Shneiderman, 2007) that the Web empowers individuals, invigorates collaboration, and unleashes social creativity: the Social Web is a manifestation of this spirit. There are evident similarities (in technical aspects) as well as differences (in human and social aspects) between the nature of Social Web Applications and that of 'conventional' Web Applications. The apparent socialization of the Web enables the consumers to play the role of co-producers and, as a result, brings additional set of issues relevant to all stakeholders.

In light of the Social Web or even otherwise, another possible extension of PoQ is the use of patterns for addressing other, particularly higher-level, semiotic quality concerns. At the social level, the interest is in the manifestations of social interaction among stakeholders with respect to a representation.

The relevant social quality attributes that Table 2 could incorporate are credibility, legality, privacy, and security. These quality attributes can be organized in multiple different tiers, with credibility placed at a higher tier than legality, privacy, and security. There are patterns, for example, for writing information, reputation, and warranty policies (Kaluscha & Grabner-Kräuter, 2003) and for licensing (Perry & Kaminski, 2005), that in part address credibility and legal concerns, respectively. For instance, the CONTACT US pattern (Kaluscha & Grabner-Kräuter, 2003) is a means for the engineers to render help or to solicit feedback from the end-users, thereby contributing to the credibility of a Web Application (Kamthan, 2007) using the Wiki environment. There are also patterns for privacy (Hafiz, 2006) and security (Schumacher et al., 2006), some of which apply to the development of Web Applications.

The aforementioned extensions of PoQ would, however, require that the aspects of micro-architecture design to which the patterns are applied, are essentially different than those dealt with in this chapter. For example, in case of applying patterns for privacy and security, the attention would be more on the server-side rather than on client-side components. Furthermore, since steps taken towards the aforementioned social quality concerns are not always favorable to maintainability and/or usability, care would need to be taken in selecting and applying these patterns in the development of Web Applications. The converse is also possible: patterns introduced to aid usability can adversely impact privacy or security. For instance, personalization aims to aid usability and there are patterns available for personalization of different services offered by Web Applications (Rossi, 2001; Rüping, 2006; Vora, 2009). In particular, the ACCOUNT SETUP pattern (Marks & Hong, 2006) allows reuse of an end-user's personal information and can assist in realizing the efficacy of the SELECTABLE KEY-WORDS or EXPLOIT SOCIAL INFORMATION patterns discussed previously, especially on Web Portals. However, personalization is often achieved at the cost of privacy as the end-user and/or the client-side information is exposed deliberately or inadvertently. Similarly, the use of any input form (such as the STRAIGHTFORWARD SEARCH FORMS) can make the interface vulnerable, and thus require extra security effort (like checks for the presence of shell meta-characters).

Metrics for Pattern-Oriented Web Applications

PoQ could be extended even further. It can be seen that patterns provide a qualitative assurance of quality and metrics provide a quantitative evaluation of quality. Therefore, Table 2 could be extended to include a column after the last column containing metrics for measuring *some* of the aforementioned quality attributes of pattern-oriented Web Applications.

In this regard, there are a number of initiatives (Dhyani, Ng, & Bhowmick, 2002; Freire et al., 2008; Guéhéneuc et al., 2007; Mendes & Mosley, 2006; Vigo et al., 2007) that introduce, define, organize, and map a metric to a quality attribute that belongs to a (express or implied) quality model. A metric can be used as an *indicator* of deterioration of the corresponding quality attribute that is analogous to the presence of (the solution of) an anti-pattern.

However, the underlying basis of a metric (such as those in a metric-based quality model) tends to be subjective rather than objective. This is because the expression of metric is often derived from empirical data that is usually collected from ethnographic research at a specific time rather than proven mathematically. In turn, this can render a metric to be limited essentially only to the study in which it is originally introduced. Thus, prior to adoption and use, validity of a metric must be established and (since a validation of a metric also tends to be empirical) the conclusions drawn from the numerical results it supplies should be treated with circumspection.

Refactoring to Pattern-Oriented Web Applications

POWEM, as presented in this chapter, is oriented towards the development of *new* Web Applications. However, there is an increasingly large base of *existing* (or legacy) Web Applications that could benefit from being pattern-oriented, if done so appropriately.

There are cases in which a fragment (say, program or markup) of a Web Application indicates the presence of a 'smell' or a situation in which there is a deterioration of a quality attribute. For example, ad-hoc modifications made to a markup language fragment over time could leave it virtually unreadable by a human. In general, the existence of an anti-pattern indicates the presence of a smell (Brown et al., 1998).

The purpose of *refactoring* (Fowler et al., 1999) is eradication of smell(s) in a system in a manner that is transparent to the user of the system. To do that, refactoring involves steering (modifying) the structure of a 'bad' solution to a 'good' solution by means of a sequence of behavior-preserving transformations (namely, the *refactoring methods*). The 'good' solution usually belongs to that of a desirable pattern. Thus, there is a close relationship between an anti-pattern, smell, refactoring, and a pattern (Kerievsky, 2005).

The refactoring methods specific to Web Applications are beginning to appear (Harold, 2008) and a study of refactoring to patterns for Web Applications could strengthen POWEM. It is evident that such a study should also consider the situations in which refactoring will not lead to any notable improvements of the structure of a Web Application or to lead to improvements to a point where the costs outweigh the benefits of refactoring. This, for example, is the case where the issues are at the macro-architecture level or deterioration at the micro-architecture level is significant to the point of being irreversible.

Support for Patterns in Web Engineering Education

From a pedagogical perspective, patterns, if described adequately, can be useful as a learning aid (Gamma et al., 1995). For example, instead of simply following a given design 'template', a student new to design can learn the reasons behind one macro-architecture design model being better than other choices in a given situation before embarking on a new design. This naturally leads to the issue of support for patterns in Web Engineering education.

There is potential for deployment of patterns in Web Engineering education, both inside and outside the classroom. For example, during lectures, teachers could demonstrate the use of patterns in the design of Web Applications. The students could be asked to compare and contrast between a given set of competing patterns for a specific problem. They could also be, as seen examples in the previous section, asked to make use of a pre-selected collection of patterns in their course project.

However, the current state of education on patterns and their relation to quality in academic institutions such as Universities and training schools is inadequate. The coverage of patterns is usually limited to a few lectures (if at all) in courses. Even though patterns can be applied to all aspects of development, the scope of patterns in these courses is usually limited to design. A mere addition of patterns to a course outline does not reflect that the patterns are being used to their full potential (Wallingford, 2000).

There have been a few isolated efforts towards a methodical approach to Web Engineering education. A pedagogical model for Web Engineering education has been proposed (Hadjerrouit, 2005), however, there is no mention of patterns at any level in it. The significance of accessibility, privacy, security, and usability in a course on 'Web Design' based on a student survey has been emphasized (Krunić et al., 2006), however, the means for addressing them are limited to the use of guidelines or a specific low-level technology rather than patterns. In 2009, the Web Standards Project introduced a WaSP InterAct curriculum for educating the next generation of professionals; however, it is essentially focuses on technologies pertaining to the Web, and does not include any coverage of Web Engineering or patterns.

The assimilation of patterns in Web Engineering education needs to be conducted in a systematic manner and in line with the teaching strategies and learning theories, and is of research interest. There are a few obstacles to inclusion of patterns in Web Engineering curriculum, including the lack of the availability of proper guidance on using patterns and a lack of standard effort towards defining the knowledge areas and the basic body of knowledge in Web Engineering education. If [C-7] and [C-8] are to be realized in the development of Web Applications, then there needs to be a cultural change to the foundation of Web Engineering education.

Support for Patterns in Standards for Web Engineering

Even though patterns themselves are not standards per se, an explicit support for patterns in international standards is crucial for their broad exposure and acceptance. This is especially the case for standards that cater to the development of information-intensive software systems such as Web Applications.

There is currently no single, standard body of knowledge dedicated to Web Engineering. There are international standards such as the ISO/IEC 23026:2006 Standard and the ISO 9241-151:2008 Standard that are directly relevant to the development of Web Applications. There are also initiatives from the World Wide Web Consortium (W3C) such as the Web Accessibility Initiative Accessible Rich Internet Applications Suite (WAI-ARIA) Best Practices that is directly relevant to the development of Web Applications aiming for accessibility and usability. However, the current support for patterns in these standards is limited. An investigation into the use of patterns that is consonant with the adoption of aforementioned standards is of research interest.

CONCLUSION

A sustainable evolution of the Web rests on attention to its in-depth analysis and synthesis that manifests in form of Web Science and Web Engineering, respectively. It is crucial that these disciplines take into consideration, learn from, and build upon the past history of the Web as it relates to its successes as well as failures in human, social, and technical aspects.

There are multiple directions of evolution available to Web Applications. The velocity of evolution intrinsically depends on the long-term quality of service a Web Application provides to its stakeholders. The reliance on the knowledge and skills garnered from past experience can be crucial for the development of high-quality Web Applications.

A pattern-oriented methodology such as POWEM, if carried out within the periphery of its scope, provides a preventative and practical means to develop Web Applications aiming for high-quality and hoping for acceptance by their stakeholders. At the same time, it should be acknowledged that initiatives towards the development of high-quality Web Applications are neither trivial nor free-of-cost. For long-term benefit, the adoption of a pattern-oriented methodology should be a part of the overall organizational vision, including the organization's capability to change, and needs to be planned in advance, taking the feasibility issues into consideration.

REFERENCES

Ahluwalia, K. S., & Jain, A. (2006). *High Availability Design Patterns*. Paper presented at the Thirteenth Conference on Pattern Languages of Programs (PLoP 2006), Portland, USA, October 21-23, 2006.

Alexander, C. (1964). *Notes on the Synthesis of Form*. Harvard University Press.

Alexander, C. (1979). *The Timeless Way of Building*. Oxford University Press.

Alexander, C., Ishikawa, S., & Silverstein, M. (1977). *A Pattern Language: Towns, Buildings, Construction*. Oxford University Press.

Ambler, S. W. (1998). *Process Patterns*. Cambridge University Press.

Baresi, L., Colazzo, S., Mainetti, L., & Morasca, S. (2006). W2000: A Modeling Notation for Complex Web Applications. In E. Mendes & N. Mosley (Eds.), *Web Engineering* (pp. 335-364). Springer-Verlag.

Bergin, J. (2005). *Patterns for Extreme Programming Practice.* Paper presented at the Tenth European Conference on Pattern Languages of Programs (EuroPLoP 2005), Irsee, Germany, July 06-10, 2005.

Boehm, B., & Turner, R. (2004). *Balancing Agility and Discipline: A Guide for the Perplexed.* Addison Wesley.

Brambilla, M., Stefano, C., Fraternali, P., & Manolescu, I. (2006). Process Modeling in Web Applications. *ACM Transactions on Software Engineering and Methodology, 15*(4), 360–409. doi:10.1145/1178625.1178627

Brown, W. J., Malveau, R. C., McCormick, H. W., & Mowbray, T. J. (1998). *AntiPatterns: Refactoring Software, Architectures, and Projects in Crisis.* John Wiley and Sons.

Buschmann, F., Henney, K., & Schmidt, D. C. (2007a). *Pattern-Oriented Software Architecture, Volume 4: A Pattern Language for Distributed Computing.* John Wiley and Sons.

Buschmann, F., Henney, K., & Schmidt, D. C. (2007b). *Pattern-Oriented Software Architecture, Volume 5: On Patterns and Pattern Languages.* John Wiley and Sons.

Buschmann, F., Meunier, R., Rohnert, H., Sommerlad, P., & Stal, M. (1996). *Pattern Oriented Software Architecture, Volume 1: A System of Patterns. John Wiley and Sons.*

Ceri, S., Fraternali, P., & Bongio, A. (2000). *Web Modeling Language (WebML): A Modeling Language for Designing Web Sites.* Paper presented at the Ninth International World Web Conference (WWW9), Amsterdam, The Netherlands, May 15-19, 2000.

Chevalier, A., & Kicka, M. (2006). Web Designers and Web Users: Influence of the Ergonomic Quality of the Web Site on the Information Search. *International Journal of Human-Computer Studies, 64*(10), 1031–1048. doi:10.1016/j.ijhcs.2006.06.002

Cockburn, A. (2007). *Agile Software Development: The Cooperative Game* (2nd Ed.). Addison-Wesley.

Conallen, J. (2003). *Building Web Applications with UML* (2nd Edition). Addison-Wesley.

Coplien, J. O., & Harrison, N. B. (2005). *Organizational Patterns of Agile Software Development.* Prentice-Hall.

Dhyani, D., Ng, W. K., & Bhowmick, S. S. (2002). A Survey of Web Metrics. *ACM Computing Surveys, 34*(4), 469–503. doi:10.1145/592642.592645

Dromey, R. G. (2003). Software Quality - Prevention Versus Cure? *Software Quality Journal, 11*(3), 197–210. doi:10.1023/A:1025162610079

Dumas, M., van der Aalst, W. M., & ter Hofstede, A. H. (2006). *Process-Aware Information Systems: Bridging People and Software through Process Technology.* John Wiley and Sons.

Fenton, N. E., & Pfleeger, S. L. (1997). *Software Metrics: A Rigorous & Practical Approach.* International Thomson Computer Press.

Fowler, M., Beck, K., Brant, J., Opdyke, W., & Roberts, D. (1999). *Refactoring: Improving the Design of Existing Code.* Addison-Wesley.

Fowler, M., Rice, D., Foemmel, M., Hieatt, E., Mee, R., & Stafford, R. (2003). *Patterns of Enterprise Application Architecture.* Addison-Wesley.

Fowler, S., & Stanwick, V. (2004). *Web Application Design Handbook: Best Practices for Web-Based Software.* Morgan Kaufmann.

Fraternali, P., Matera, M., & Maurino, A. (2002). *WQA: An XSL Framework for Analyzing the Quality of Web Applications*. Paper presented at the Second International Workshop on Web-Oriented Software Technology (IWWOST 2002), Malaga, Spain, June 10-11, 2002.

Freire, A. P., Fortes, R. P. M., Turine, M. A. S., & Paiva, D. M. B. (2008). *An Evaluation of Web Accessibility Metrics based on their Attributes*. Paper presented at the Twenty Sixth Annual ACM International Conference on Design of Communication (SIGDOC 2008), Lisbon, Portugal, September 22-24, 2008.

Gamma, E., Helm, R., Johnson, R., & Vlissides, J. (1995). *Design Patterns: Elements of Reusable Object-Oriented Software*. Addison-Wesley.

German, D. M., & Cowan, D. D. (2000). *Towards a Unified Catalog of Hypermedia Design Patterns*. Paper presented at the Thirty Third Hawaii International Conference on System Sciences (HICSS 2000), Maui, USA, January 4-7, 2000.

Graham, I. (2003). *A Pattern Language for Web Usability*. Addison-Wesley.

Guéhéneuc, Y.-G., Guyomarc'h, J.-Y., Khosravi, K., & Sahraoui, H. (2007). Design Patterns as Laws of Quality. In J. Garzás & M. Piattini (Eds.), *Object-Oriented Design Knowledge: Principles, Heuristics and Best Practices* (pp. 105-142). Hershey, PA: IGI Global.

Hadjerrouit, S. (2005). Designing a Pedagogical Model for Web Engineering Education: An Evolutionary Perspective. *Journal of Information Technology Education, 4*, 115–140.

Hafiz, M. (2006). *A Collection of Privacy Design Patterns*. Paper presented at the Thirteenth Conference on Pattern Languages of Programs (PLoP 2006), Portland, USA, October 21-23, 2006.

Hansen, K. M. (2002). *Agile Environments - Some Patterns for Agile Software Development Facilitation*. Paper presented at the First Scandinavian Conference on Pattern Languages of Programs (VikingPLoP 2002), Højstrupgård, Denmark, September 20-22, 2002.

Harold, E. R. (2008). *Refactoring HTML: Improving the Design of Existing Web Applications*. Addison-Wesley.

Henderson-Sellers, B., Lowe, D., & Haire, B. (2002). OPEN Process Support for Web Development. *Annals of Software Engineering, 13*(1-4), 163–201. doi:10.1023/A:1016549527480

Henninger, S., & Corrêa, V. (2007). *Software Pattern Communities: Current Practices and Challenges*. Paper presented at the Fourteenth Conference on Pattern Languages of Programs (PLoP 2007), Monticello, USA, September 5-8, 2007.

Huang, S., & Tilley, S. (2003). *Towards a Documentation Maturity Model*. Paper presented at the Twenty First Annual International Conference on Documentation, San Francisco, USA, October 12-15, 2003.

Ivory, M. Y., & Megraw, R. (2005). Evolution of Web Site Design Patterns. *ACM Transactions on Information Systems, 23*(4), 463–497. doi:10.1145/1095872.1095876

Jeschke, S., Pfeiffer, O., & Vieritz, H. (2009). Using Web Accessibility Patterns for Web Application Development. The 2009 ACM Symposium on Applied Computing (SAC 2009), Honolulu, USA, March 9-12, 2009.

Kaluscha, E. A., & Grabner-Kräuter, S. (2003). *Towards a Pattern Language for Consumer Trust in Electronic Commerce*. Paper presented at the Eighth European Conference on Pattern Languages of Programs (EuroPLoP 2003), Irsee, Germany, June 25-29, 2003.

Kamthan, P. (2007). Towards a Systematic Approach for the Credibility of Human-Centric Web Applications. *Journal of Web Engineering, 6*(2), 99–120.

Kamthan, P. (2008a). A Situational Methodology for Addressing the Pragmatic Quality of Web Applications by Integration of Patterns. *Journal of Web Engineering, 7*(1), 70–92.

Kamthan, P. (2008b). A Methodology for Integrating Patterns in Quality-Centric Web Applications. *International Journal of Information Technology and Web Engineering, 3*(2), 27–44.

Kamthan, P. (2008c). Towards High-Quality Mobile Applications by a Systematic Integration of Patterns. *Journal of Mobile Multimedia, 4*(3/4), 165–184.

Kamthan, P. (2009a). A Model for Characterizing Web Engineering. In M. Khosrow-Pour (Ed.), Encyclopedia of Information Science and Technology, Second Edition (pp. 3631-2637). Hershey, PA: IGI Global.

Kamthan, P. (2009b). A Framework for Integrating the Social Web Environment in Pattern Engineering. *International Journal of Technology and Human Interaction, 5*(2), 36–62.

Kappel, G., Pröll, B., Reich, S., & Retschitzegger, W. (2006). *Web Engineering*. John Wiley and Sons.

Kerievsky, J. (2005). *Refactoring to Patterns*. Addison-Wesley.

Khan, A., & Balbo, S. (2005). *Agile versus Heavyweight Web Development: An Australian Survey*. Paper presented at the Eleventh Australian World Wide Web Conference (AusWeb 2005), Gold Coast, Australia, July 2-6, 2005.

Khomh, F., & Guéhéneuc, Y.-G. (2008). *Do Design Patterns Impact Software Quality Positively?* Paper presented at the Twelfth European Conference on. Software Maintenance and Reengineering (CSMR 2008), Athens, Greece, April 1-4, 2008.

Kruchten, P. (2004). *An Ontology of Architectural Design Decisions in Software-Intensive Systems.* Paper presented at the Second Gröningen Workshop on Software Variability Management: Software Product Families and Populations, Gröningen, The Netherlands, December 2-3, 2004.

Krunić, T., Ružić-Dimitrijević, L., Petrović, B., & Farkaš, R. (2006). Web Design Curriculum and Syllabus Based on Web Design Practice and Students' Prior Knowledge. *Journal of Information Technology Education, 5*, 317–335.

Kumar, K., & Welke, R. J. (1992). Methodology Engineering: A Proposal for Situation-Specific Methodology Construction. In W. W. Cotterman & J. A. Senn (Eds.*), Challenges and Strategies for Research in Systems Development* (pp. 257-269). John Wiley and Sons.

Kunert, T. (2009). User-Centered Interaction Design Patterns for Interactive Digital Television Applications. Springer-Verlag.

Lea, D. (1994). Christopher Alexander: An Introduction for Object-Oriented Designers. *ACM SIGSOFT Software Engineering Notes, 19*(1), 39–46. doi:10.1145/181610.181617

Liu, L., Kong, X., & Chen, J. (2006). *An Economic Model of Software Development Approaches.* Paper presented at the Twelfth Australian World Wide Web Conference (AusWeb 2006), Australis Noosa Lakes, Australia, July 1-5, 2006.

Manolescu, D., Kozaczynski, W., Miller, A., & Hogg, J. (2007). The Growing Divide in the Patterns World. *IEEE Software, 24*(4), 61–67. doi:10.1109/MS.2007.120

Manolescu, D., & Kunzle, A. (2001). Several Patterns for eBusiness Applications. The Eighth Conference on Pattern Languages of Programs (PLoP 2001), Monticello, USA. September 11-15, 2001.

Marks, M., & Hong, D. (2006). Web Design Patterns Collection Technical Design. Center for Document Engineering (Technical Report CDE2006-TR09). University of California, Berkeley, USA.

McDonald, A., & Welland, R. (2001). *Agile Web Engineering (AWE) Process* (Tech Rep TR-2001-98). University of Glasgow, Glasgow, Scotland.

Mendes, E., & Mosley, N. (2006). *Web Engineering*. Springer-Verlag.

Mendes, E. M., Mosley, N., & Counsell, S. (2001). Web Metrics - Estimating Design and Authoring Effort. *IEEE MultiMedia, 8*(1), 50–57. doi:10.1109/93.923953

Meszaros, G., & Doble, J. (1998). A Pattern Language for Pattern Writing. In R. C. Martin, D. Riehle, & F. Buschmann (Eds.), *Pattern Languages of Program Design 3* (pp. 529-574). Addison-Wesley

Morville, P. (2005). *Ambient Findability: What We Find Changes Who We Become*. O'Reilly Media. 2005.

Nelson, H. J., & Monarchi, D. E. (2007). Ensuring the Quality of Conceptual Representations. *Software Quality Journal, 15*(2), 213–233. doi:10.1007/s11219-006-9011-2

O'Reilly, T. (2005). *What Is Web 2.0: Design Patterns and Business Models for the Next Generation of Software*. O'Reilly Network, September 30, 2005.

Perry, M., & Kaminski, H. (2005). *A Pattern Language of Software Licensing*. Paper presented at the Tenth European Conference on Pattern Languages of Programs (EuroPloP 2005), Irsee, Germany, July 6-10, 2005.

Perzel, K., & Kane, D. (1999). *Usability Patterns for Applications on the World Wide Web*. Paper presented at the Sixth Conference on Pattern Languages of Programs (PLoP 1999), Monticello, USA, August 15-18, 1999.

Porter, R., Coplien, J. O., & Winn, T. (2005). Sequences as a Basis for Pattern Language Composition. *Science of Computer Programming, 56*(1-2), 231–249. doi:10.1016/j.scico.2004.11.014

Rising, L. (2000). The Pattern Almanac 2000. Addison-Wesley.

Rossi, G. (2001). *Patterns for Personalized Web Applications*. Paper presented at the Sixth European Conference on Pattern Languages of Programs (EuroPLoP 2001), Irsee, Germany, July 4-8, 2001.

Rossi, G., Pastor, O., Schwabe, D., & Olsina, L. (2008). *Web Engineering: Modelling and Implementing Web Applications*. Springer-Verlag.

Rossi, G., Schwabe, D., & Lyardet, F. (1999). *Improving Web Information Systems with Navigational Patterns*. Paper presented at the Eighth International World Wide Web Conference (WWW8), Toronto, Canada, May 11-14, 1999.

Rüping, A. (2006). *Web Content Management - Patterns for Interaction and Personalisation*. Paper presented at the Eleventh European Conference on Pattern Languages of Programs (EuroPLoP 2006), Irsee, Germany, July 5-9, 2006.

Schumacher, M., Fernandez-Buglioni, E., Hybertson, D., Buschmann, F., & Sommerlad, P. (2006). *Security Patterns: Integrating Security and Systems Engineering*. John Wiley and Sons.

Schümmer, T., & Lukosch, S. (2007). *Patterns for Computer-Mediated Interaction*. John Wiley and Sons.

Schwabe, D., & Rossi, G. (1998). An Object Oriented Approach to Web-Based Application Design. *Theory and Practice of Object Systems, 4*(4).

Segerståhl, K., & Jokela, T. (2006). *Usability of Interaction Patterns*. Paper presented at the CHI 2006 Conference on Human Factors in Computing Systems, Montréal, Canada, April 22-27, 2006.

Shanks, G. (1999). *Semiotic Approach to Understanding Representation in Information Systems.* Paper presented at the Info. Systems Foundations Workshop, Sydney, Australia, September 29, 1999.

Sharp, H., Galal, G. H., & Finkelstein, A. (1999). *Stakeholder Identification in the Requirements Engineering Process.* Paper presented at the Tenth International Conference and Workshop on Database and Expert Systems Applications (DEXA 1999), Florence, Italy, August 30-September 3, 1999.

Shneiderman, B. (2007). Web Science: A Provocative Invitation to Computer Science. *Communications of the ACM, 50*(6), 25–27. doi:10.1145/1247001.1247022

Simon, H. (1996). The Sciences of the Artificial (Third Edition). The MIT Press.

Taibi, T., & Ngo, C. L. (2002). *A Pattern for Evaluating Design Patterns.* Paper presented at the Sixth World Multiconference on Systemics, Cybernetics and Informatics (SCI 2002), Orlando, USA, July 14-18, 2002.

Tidwell, J. (2005). *Designing Interfaces: Patterns for Effective Interaction Design.* O'Reilly Media.

Van Duyne, D. K., Landay, J., & Hong, J. I. (2003). *The Design of Sites: Patterns, Principles, and Processes for Crafting a Customer-Centered Web Experience.* Addison-Wesley. Vigo, M. Arrue, M., Brajnik, G., Lomuscio, R., & Abascal, J. (2007). *Quantitative Metrics for Measuring Web Accessibility.* Paper presented at the 2007 International Cross-Disciplinary Workshop on Web Accessibility (W4A 2007), Banff, Canada, May 7-8, 2007.

Vora, P. (2009). *Web Application Design Patterns.* Morgan Kaufmann.

Wallace, D., Raggett, I., & Aufgang, J. (2002). *Extreme Programming for Web Projects.* Addison-Wesley.

Weiss, M. (2003). *Patterns for Web Applications.* Paper presented at the Tenth Conference on Pattern Languages of Programs (PLoP 2003), Urbana, USA, September 8-12, 2003.

Wendorff, P. (2001). *Assessment of Design Patterns during Software Reengineering: Lessons Learned from a Large Commercial Project.* Paper presented at the Fifth European Conference on Software Maintenance and Reengineering (CSMR 2001), Lisbon, Portugal, March 14-16, 2001.

Wentzlaff, I., & Specker, M. (2006). *Pattern Based Development of User Friendly Web Applications.* Paper presented at the Workshop on Model-Driven Web Engineering (MDWE 2006), Palo Alto, USA, July 10, 2006.

Wesson, J., & Cowley, L. (2003). *Designing with Patterns: Possibilities and Pitfalls.* Paper presented at the Second Workshop on Software and Usability Cross-Pollination, Zürich, Switzerland, September 1-2, 2003.

Yoder, J., & Barcalow, J. (1997). *Architectural Patterns for Enabling Application Security.* Paper presented at the Fourth Conference on Pattern Languages of Programs (PLoP 1997), Monticello, USA, September 3-5, 1997.

Zdun, U. (2007). Systematic Pattern Selection using Pattern Language Grammars and Design Space Analysis. *Software, Practice & Experience, 37*(9), 983–1016. doi:10.1002/spe.799

Zheng, G. (2008). A Historical Perspective of Web Engineering. In G. D. Putnik & M. M. Cunha (Eds.), *Encyclopedia of Networked and Virtual Organizations.* Hershey, PA: IGI Global.

Ziemer, S., & Stålhane, T. (2004). *The Use of Trade-offs in the Development of Web Applications.* Paper presented at the First International Workshop on Web Quality (WQ 2004). Munich, Germany. July 27, 2004.

Section 2
User Interface

Chapter 7
Localized User Interface for Improving Cell Phone Users' Device Competency

Lucia D. Krisnawati
Duta Wacana Christian University, Indonesia

Restyandito
Duta Wacana Christian University, Indonesia

ABSTRACT

This study tried to examine how cell phone users who undergo a technology leap acquire their procedural knowledge of operating a cell phone and to find out which factors can improve their device competency. Using interviews, usability tests, and a questionnaire, this study found out that many respondents use unstructured means such as asking other cell phone users or rote learning in gaining their procedural knowledge. Some factors influencing users' device competencies that were found in this study are classified into three categories: user interface design, culture, and the users themselves. In order to improve users' device competency, elements in those three categories must be integrated. One realization of such integration is the attempt of localizing user interface through the user's culture, not the culture where the cell phone is designed and manufactured.

INTRODUCTION

The use of cellular (cell) phones has been increasing sharply in recent years. Even the number of cellular phone subscribers exceeded the number of the fixed-line phone subscribers as reported by the International Telecommunication Union (ITU) in 2002. The rate of cell phone users will continuously rise in the coming years as the cell phone manufacturers are steering their sale growth in densely populous countries such as China, India, and Indonesia (Diryo, 2006). With a population 222 million, in which 178.8 million have the potential to be cell phone users, Indonesia becomes one of the promising market targets.[1]

As a consequence of becoming a potential market, Indonesia has undergone a surprisingly significant growth of cellular phone subscribers. According to ITU data (2006), there were only 3.6 million subscribers in 2000 and 6 million subscribers in 2001, but it grew to approximately 30 million in 2004 and 46.9 million in the middle of 2005. With this rate, the teledensity of cell phone subscribers in 2005 was 21.6 cell phones per one hundred inhabitants. In contrast to this fantastic growth, the growth rate of the fixed-line phone subscribers escalated insignificantly. In 2000, there were 6.6 million subscribers of the fixed-line phones. In 2001, it increased to 7.2 million, 9.9 million in 2004, and 12.7 million in the middle of 2005 (Diryo, 2006). This shows that the percentage of fixed-line phone subscribers in 2005 was about 12 % of the total telephone subscribers. The teledensity of fixed-line phone in 2005 reached 5.73 fixed-line phones per one hundred inhabitants. According to ITU (2006), the numbers of the main phone line subscribers have also included the public payphones and ISDN channels.

Scrutinizing the statistical data above, it can be seen that there lie some interesting phenomena. The 12% rate of the fixed-line phone subscribers implies two facts. First, only a few people living in cities and their surroundings are able to take advantages of the fixed-line phone technology. Second, the infrastructure of the fixed-line phone has not been widely spread and well established. In contrast to this rate, the 78% of the cell phone subscribers signify that the use of cell phones in Indonesia as a developing country replaces the use of the fixed-line phone. Only for a small number of subscribers, the cell phone functions as a supplementary communication device. Therefore, there are many cell phone users who have no or little experience in operating the fixed-line telephone. Based on these phenomena, this study tries to examine the usability aspects of cell phones for certain groups of users in Yogyakarta, Indonesia and tries to find out factors that influence their

device competency. The result of this study is not intended to give a generalization about cell phone users in Indonesia, but rather to present a description about the device competency of the majority of cell phone users in time of the global market and international user interface design. This study considers also the fact that the cell phones which are widely marketed in Indonesia have been localized at the superficial level only through language.

THEORETICAL FOUNDATION

Culture and Interface Design

In today's increasingly global market, market behavior analysts agree that the expectation of homogenization and internalization can be misleading. Forced by the global competition and the demand of increasing their sale rate, many multinational firms have to develop new marketing strategies and new products that consider the local culture where the products are sold. This principle works also for the user interface design. Some research on the importance of localizing user interface design has been made and concluded that localized user interface could enhance the usability (e.g., Khaslavsky, 1998; Kondratova & Goldfarb, 2005; Marcus, 2001 & Vatrapu et al., n.d.). But what might "localized user interface" mean?

Localized user interface means adapting the interface design to local culture and sensibilities. Kondratova and Goldfarb (2005) review three models that have been proposed by researchers for integrating cultural aspects in user interface design. The most outstanding model is the cultural dimension (*n*-factor) model. Cultural dimension models attempt to measure and compare different cultures using a number of cultural factors. The number of factors varies from five, as can be found by Hofstede's (n.d.) five-factor model, to nine, as in Khaslavsky's model. Among the cultural dimension models, Hofstede's model is widely cited. Based on interviews with IBM employees in 64 countries, Hofstede derived five independent dimensions of culture that manifest themselves in a culture's choices of symbols, heroes/heroines, rituals, and values. His five dimensions of culture are a) power-distance, b) collectivism vs. individualism, c) femininity vs. masculinity, d) uncertainty avoidance, and e) long- vs. short-term orientation (orientation to the past, present, and future). Khaslavsky's nine-factor model is a combination of Hofstede's and other models.

The second model is known as a cultural markers model which was introduced by Barber and Badre as reported by Kondratova and Goldfarb (2005). In his work, Badre (2001) provides a list of cultural markers corresponding to Web design elements such as color, spatial organization, fonts, icons, metaphors, geography, language, flags, sounds, motion, preferences for text vs. graphics, directionality of how language is written, help features, and navigation tools. The third model is named "cultural attractor" and lists a smaller number of cultural design elements: colors, color combinations, banner adverts, trust signs, use of metaphor, language cues, and navigation controls. Apart from three models mentioned earlier, Marcus (2001) proposes five components of user interface, whether for the Web or for other technologies, that can be integrated with local culture. Marcus's five user interface components are metaphor, mental model, navigations, interaction, and appearance.

Culture and Usability

Khaslavsky (1998) describes the impact of culture on usability and design. Since culture is a system of shared meanings that form a framework for problem solving and behavior in everyday life, a person's perception on the system affordance of a cell phone is influenced much by that person's cultural framework. Further, she emphasizes issues in localization of design so that a user in-

terface is not a merely translation of an American interface. The goal of this localization is to make systems or software easy to use and easy to learn (i.e., usability).

Another study worth mentioning here is the one done by Kim and Lee (2005). Kim and Lee attempt to clarify the relation between cultural traits and mobile phone interface in term of the icon styles. They classify icon styles into three groups, namely abstract, semi abstract, and concrete. In their usability testing, they employed 20 participants that comprised of 10 Americans and 10 Koreans. The results show that Koreans performed significantly better in concrete icons, while Americans performed better to the opposite tendencies. They argue that there is possibility of cultural impact on icon recognition according to the level of abstraction.

RESEARCH OBJECTIVES AND HYPOTHESIS

The facts described in the introduction section disclose a reality of the cell phone users in Indonesia: that there is a group of users who undergo a technology leap. The worst is that the number of this group is quite large. Furthermore, not only do they lack experience in operating fixed-line phones, but they also have no or little contact to modern communication technologies such as computers. In this study we assume that the order of technology someone needs to follow is fixed-line phones, computer, then cell phone. Since metaphor, icons, icon referents, navigation, and other interface elements in cell phones are similar to those in computers, someone who has no contact to computers and fixed-line phones could be considered as a user experiencing a technology leap. This study concentrates on this group of cell phone users. The objectives are first trying to examine how this group of users gains their procedural knowledge of operating their cell phones, and second to see the role of local culture in improving their device competency. The cultural elements emphasized in this study are Hofstede's cultural dimension on individualism vs. collectivism, some elements in cultural markers model such as icon recognition, icon referents, and language, and two components from Marcus's model, namely mental model and metaphor.

In this study, the usability tests were administered to get the accuracy rate of recognizing icons, their referents of function, and the success rate of completing four frequently-used tasks in a cell phone. The goal of the test is to achieve a description on the degree of cultural impact on elements of user interface and factors that may improve users' device competency. Therefore, hypothesis related to this test are as follows:

1.   Users with no prior knowledge of operating cell phone have more difficulties in recognizing icons and their referents.
2.   Users with no prior knowledge of operating system have a lower rate of icons and their referents compared to users with exposure to communication technologies.
3.   Users with no prior knowledge about communication technology gain their device competency by unstructured learning.

METHODOLOGY

There were three main phases in conducting this study. First, the library and online research were conducted to gather some demographic data on cell phone usage. Second, tools used in the field studies were prepared by simulating two cell phones and by writing a semistructured interview script. Third, the field studies were conducted by exposing the cell phone simulations to the respondents, by testing and interviewing them. In doing the test, the participants were asked to think aloud or to verbalize what they think. If they sat amazed in front of the computer and said nothing, the interviewer would actively pose questions to

dig out what they thought. The interviews and tests were recorded on tapes which later were examined to elaborate and to verify data noted during interviews.

The field studies were carried out in two periods of time. The first field studies were conducted in six different places in Yogyakarta, Indonesia. In each place, three preliminary questions are posed to the volunteers to know which group they belong to. After that, they were asked to do device a competency test and interview. Each participant accomplished four phases of tasks which were done in four different posts in the following order:

1.   Each participant was openly interviewed. This aimed to gather demographic data, and data concerning participants' behaviour in using cell phones.
2.   Moving to the second post, each participant was faced with a simulation of Nokia 2112. In this phase, each participant completed four tasks. First, the participant had to identify nine icons on the top level of Nokia's hierarchical menu and their functions. Second, the participant had to add a new name and phone number in the list of contacts. Third, the participant had to set the alarm. And fourth, the participant had to set a new personal identification number (PIN) for the security of the participant's cell phone.
3.   The third phase had the same tasks as the second one, but participants did it for a Sony-Ericsson (SE) K700i. Instead of nine icons, participants needed to recognize 12 icons and their functions in SE.
4.   Each participant completed a questionnaire posing post-task questions which measured subjectively their competency in operating the simulation of the two cell phones above.

The second field studies were conducted in public places such as an under-construction building, parking area, auditorium, or food center where many people gather. Owing to the cultural background, there were no difficulties both for interviewer and interviewees having this study in open places. The difference from the first field studies was that each participant accomplished three phases of tasks only but there were no differences on the first and the last phases of the tasks. The difference was set on the usability test, where in recognizing icons and its function, participants performed a simulation of either Nokia 2112 or SE k700i. Thus, each participant did only one out of two cell phone simulations. We added one task to be completed in this phase, namely making calls. In other words, participants had to complete four tasks: making calls, adding new names and number in the phone book, setting the alarm, and changing the PIN. The last task was accomplishing a questionnaire. Many respondents had difficulties in completing the questionnaire. We lent our hands by explaining the questions and wrote down the answers. In this case, the questionnaires transformed themselves to be a post-task interview.

Sampling Method

As explained before, the field studies were carried out in two periods of time. The first was conducted during July and August of 2006, and the second was done during January and February of 2007. Since we announced our need of respondents before the first field studies began, volunteers came to our posts for interviews and usability tests, and we stopped after the number of respondents reached 40. In contrast, the second period of field studies applied the following procedures for selecting samples: 1) identifying all elements in the sampling population; 2) deciding the number of population strata (k) into 3 categories (i.e., nonusers, users with no prior knowledge of operating computers but might have no or little contact to fixed-line phones, and users with exposure to communication technologies such as computers and fixed-line phones); 3) placing elements in Step 1 in each stratum and adding two samples of cell

phones in each stratum, and 4) deciding the total sample size (n) and the number of sample in each stratum, where n=48, k=3 with 16 respondents in each stratum, 8 for Nokia 2112, and 8 for Sonny Ericsson k700i. Based on the procedures above, the sampling strategy applied in the second period of field studies can be said as making use of a proportionate stratified sampling method. This sampling method emphasizes the equal number of samples for each stratum in the population.

This study used three preliminary questions as its method for selecting participants who voluntarily gave their time for the interview and usability test. The first question asked volunteers whether they were cell phone users or not. If they were not cell phone users, then they were classified in the first stratum. If they were, then the next two questions asked whether they had experiences in operating fixed-line phones and computers. If they did not, then they were classified in the second stratum; if they did, then they were classified into the third stratum. Those who had little contact with fixed-line phone in public payphones but had no experiences for operating computer were classified in the second stratum. The reason is that their encounter with fixed-line phone is very rare and the operator of the public payphone helps them in dialing the destination number. A total of 12 participants were excluded from the second stratum since they had intensive contacts with fixed-line public payphones.

Participants

A total of 88 respondents were interviewed and were asked to do the usability test for this study. Forty of them were obtained from the first period of field study and 48 were attained during the second one. They were grouped into three strata as mentioned in the previous section. From the first field studies, the percentage of the first group is 21%, 42.5% for the second, and the last is 45%. The percentage of each stratum in the second field studies is equal, that is, 33% for both Nokia 2112 and SE k700i. The rate of the third stratum from the first field studies is high enough due to different perception and concept on the "exposure" to these two technologies between respondents and the researchers. By this concept, we mean that respondents actively use and own these two technologies. The facts show that three users in the second stratum had experiences in operating a fixed-line phone but their encounter with fixed-line phones takes place in public payphones or on their work. This indicates that they were not active fixed-line users. A handful of respondents did have fixed-line phones for a short period of time (e.g., 2 or 4 years). The same thing happens to those having a background in operating computer. Twenty-five percent of the participants had learned a computer before and they had learned it in school with DOS as its operating system. After their graduation, they lacked access to computers. In term of gender, 74% of participants were male and 26% were female. The unequal gender composition is due to cultural aspects, that men take more initiatives to be volunteers in our study. Some excuses given by the women for being volunteers are that they were shy or afraid of making mistakes. The age range of participants was about 30-65 years. We set the minimum age limit to 30 for reasons of easiness in finding respondents for the second stratum. This study assumes that the chance of having contact to computer technologies for someone above 30 is less than those who are younger. Most persons below 30 years have received at least computer lessons when they were in school. As for education background, 3.4% participants are illiterate, 21.5% participants have completed elementary school, 25% graduated from junior high school, 44.4% are senior high school graduates, and 5.6% have completed undergraduate programs in universities. Since this study emphasizes the stratum of cell phone users, the education background was ignored in recruiting respondents. The percentage of education background of respondents that were randomly chosen might describe the real education background of Indonesian society, where only a handful of them have university degrees.

Material and Equipments

The simulation of two cell phones were developed using Macromedia Flash Player 7.0 r14. We chose Nokia 2112 to represent the CDMA system and cell phones with hierarchical menu display, while Sonny-Ericsson K700i to represent the GSM system and those with nonhierarchical menu display. The hardware features of the simulation were employed by capturing the models displayed by sponsors in the Internet. The simulation was presented on a Compaq and a Toshiba laptop running windows XP and on an Apple laptop running Panther, Mac OS 10.x.

An overall field studies script was developed, including a semistructured interview script and a post-task, Likert-scaled questionnaire that was administered to gather subjective evaluation from participants. In addition, seven post-task questions were developed to measure participants' competency in operating the two cell phones above.

RESULTS AND DISCUSSION

Using mixed approaches, this study collected both qualitative and quantitative data. Qualitative data were obtained from reviewing the interview notes and playing back the cassettes. The quantitative data were derived from participants' performance on completing the tasks, from participants' subjective evaluation acquired from questionnaire, and from the effort of quantifying the qualitative data. The results of this study can be seen below and the interconnection among data are presented in the discussion section.

Recognition Rate

In the usability test, participants were asked to identify pictures shown by icons and to predict their referents of functions. From experiment using Nokia 2112, they needed to recognize 9 icons and 12 icons from an experiment using SE k700i. From both periods of field studies, it can be seen that a user's background of technology exposure plays an important role in identifying the icons. Users with prior exposure to communication technology, especially computers, have mostly higher rates of icon recognition. The exception falls in the menu icons for Message (M1) and Setting (M4) in Nokia and menu icon for Internet Service (M2) in Sony Ericsson. In recognizing Nokia's icons for Message which is depicted by a picture of an envelope and for Setting depicted by screwdriver and a cell phone, nonusers' rate of icon recognition is higher than users with prior exposure to communication technology. The lowest rate was achieved by users with no background of communication technology. In SE k700i, the highest score of icon recognition for Internet Service (M2) falls to the second stratum, that is, users with no background of communication technology, and the lowest falls to the first stratum of nonusers. Figure 1 shows the icon recognition rate for the three strata in Nokia 2112 and SE k700i.

The number labels on the X axis for Nokia 2112 both in Figures 1 and 2 stand for the following: M1 for Message, M2 for Call Register, M3 for Profiles, M4 for Setting, M5 for Voice, M6 for Organizer, M7 for Games, M8 for Mini Browser, and M9 for Flexi Menu. The numbers on the X axis for SE k700i represent the following menu items: M1 for Sonny Ericsson, M2 for Internet Service, M3 for Games, M4 for Radio, M5 for Message, M6 for Camera, M7 for File Manager, M8 for Phone Book, M9 for Media player, M10 for Setting, M11 for Organizer, and M12 for Connectivity menu. For the next discussion, this study tends to ignore the success rate of menu #9 in Nokia and menu #1 in SE 700i with a reason that the Flexi menu (#9) and the Sonny-Ericsson menu (#1) are vulnerable to change according to the brand of cell phone and SIM card used.

In recognizing the referents of function in Nokia 2112, users classified in the third stratum, those with prior exposure to communication

Figure 1. The accuracy rate of icon identification in Nokia and SE K700i

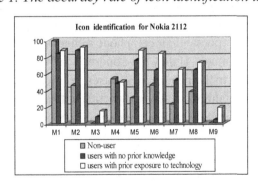 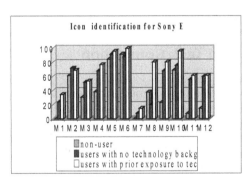

Figure 2. The accuracy rate of feature function identification

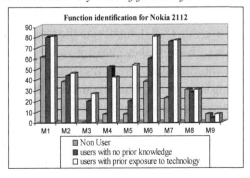 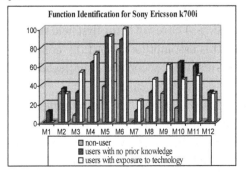

technology, still dominate the highest rank of recognition. Only in recognizing the function of icon that is symbolized by screwdriver (M2), users with no background of technology have the highest score. In contrast to the rate of function recognition in Nokia, the highest ranks of function recognition rate in SE k700i are distributed to users in the second and third strata with 58.3% for users with prior exposure to communication technology and 41.7% for users with no technology background. This is surprising that users in the second stratum could identify the function of the menu for Internet Service (M2), Setting (M10), Organizer (M11), and Connectivity (M12) in SE. This is due to biases done on the third phase of the usability test in the first field studies where participants had to accomplish simulation tasks with two models of cell phones. In the previous phase, the interviewers could not help in explaining the functions and icons in Nokia when participants in the second stratum asked for it after knowing that they had failed. The new knowledge acquired from interviewers and testers was directly applied to understand icons in SE as they moved to the third phase of test.

The Rate of Task Completion

The first field studies assigned participants three tasks: adding a new entry in the phone book, setting alarm, and altering the PIN. One reason for assigning these three tasks is that cell phones in the second stratum are used by passive users, meaning that they operate their cell phones mostly for making calls and sending SMS. This study had assumed that they knew how to make a call and to send SMS. The result of the first field study proved that this assumption is not fully correct. Based on this result, the second field studies added one more task, making a call.

Figure 3 shows the result of task completion from both periods of field studies, except for the task of making calls. Users who were the focus of this study have averagely low rate of task

completion. The highest rate is 67.7% for adding new names and numbers in the phone book. The success rate of making calls reaches 56.25%. This result is quite astonishing since making calls ranked second on the frequently-used functions. This rate should be higher. Based on the interview results, the reason for this low rate is that many users in this stratum often accept calls more than they make calls. Some users (i.e., 5 persons) never made calls themselves. They asked their children or relatives to dial the destination number, and then they just spoke and turned it off.

Methods Used for Gaining Procedural Knowledge of Operating Cell Phone

Most participants have interesting methods for solving operational problems, recognizing icons, and their referents of function. The results of the first and second periods of field studies show that there is no significant difference in these methods. The results show that 77.9% users from the first field study and 71.8% users from the second field studies prefer asking other users about how to operate their cell phone rather than consulting manuals. If they have operational problems, they go to their children, spouses, relatives, friends, or neighbors. Even two participants acknowledged that they frequently go to cell phone service centers and one participant goes to the salesman who sold him a cell phone for solving the operational problems. What we mean by operational problems here are problems concerning purely how to operate cell phones and those which exclude the dysfunctional problems. Also, 19.3% users from this group (77%) memorize the tips and instructions given. If they make a call, then they just count how many times they need to hit specific buttons, ignoring the hierarchical depth of menu shown on the screen. Furthermore, 17.5% of users from the first field studies like to do trial and error by reading the system affordance. Only 5% users from the first field studies and 15% users

Figure 3. The accuracy rate of task completion in Nokia 2112 and Sony Ericsson k700i

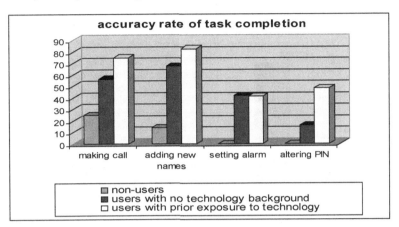

from the second field studies prefer looking up manuals. Figure 4 shows this result.

The habit of gaining device competency through asking influences many participants' way of recognizing icons and their referents of functions. They tended to pose many questions during the simulation and usability tests and thus ignored some elements of user interface. In Nokia, 41.6% participants tended to ignore the icons, but focused their attention on the labels which denotes the referents of functions; only if they meet labels denoting incomprehensible concepts such as Mini

Browsers tend to see the icons. In contrast, most participants doing simulation with SE k700i tended to ignore the labels and focused their attention on the icons in SE. Only 28% participants read the labels together with the icons. This is understandable enough because in SE, the label was placed on the top of the screen and 12 icons are spread under it. In other words, SE displays all 12 icons for its menu at once in one screen. But in Nokia, the icons are hierarchically displayed; one icon per screen and the label is placed directly above each icon. Nokia's menu structure proves to be helpful for users who fail to grab the significance of the icons. Since an icon is too abstract to understand, they are able to recognize its function through the labeling addressed to it.

Cell Phone-User Ratio and the Frequently-Used Task

This study found out that many participants (66.3%) use one cell phone for the whole family whose members vary from 2 to 6. Even five participants share 3-4 cell phones for the whole extended family (i.e., the family of parents, sisters, and brothers). The cell phone-user ratio mean is 1:3, meaning that one cell phone is operated by three persons. This ratio correlates positively to the variety of applications being frequently operated. Some participants with cell phone-user ratio more than or equal to three operate their cell phone not only for making calls or sending SMS but also for taking pictures, setting the alarm, or taking pictures if their cell phone is completed with such features.

Apart from the cell phone-user ratio, most participants use their cell phones for primary functions such as making calls and sending SMS. The most frequently-used function is sending SMS with the rate of 41.6%, then followed by making call with the rate of 38.9%. Also, 8.8% participants make use of the games on their cell phone, and the rest rate is for camera, radio, or alarm. Figure 5 shows the results of the most frequently used features in cell phones. Along with this study, a survey done by *Kompas*, a leading daily newspaper in Indonesia, stated that

Figure 4. Methods used for gaining procedural knowledge of operating cell phones

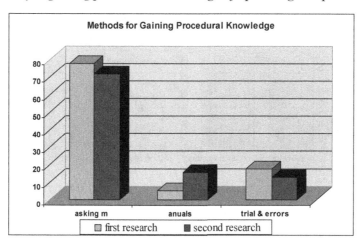

the use of cell phones has not been maximized. The survey that was conducted in Yogyakarta in December 2006 gave results that are similar with the result of this study. The majority of users are not accustomed to using other technologies such as searching the Internet or utilizing Bluetooth technology that are provided with a cell phone. They use their cell phone mostly for primary functions, such as making calls and writing SMS ("Ponsel," 2006).

Discussion

As it is widely known, good user-interface design has an effect on users' device competency or the

usability of a product. This study found out some factors that can enhance users' device competency in terms of icon design. The first factor is the choice of objects to represent a function. For most users in Indonesia, especially users having no background of computer and fixed-line phone technology, concrete objects from their surrounding will work better. This explains the high rates of function recognition for Message that is represented by a picture of an envelope both in Nokia and SE, and for Camera in SE. Kim and Lee's arguments (2005) on the icon style work partly here, since users in this study are able to recognize abstract icons better than those classified in the semiabstract group. Figure 6 and 7

Figure 5. Functions that are frequently used in this study

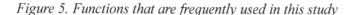

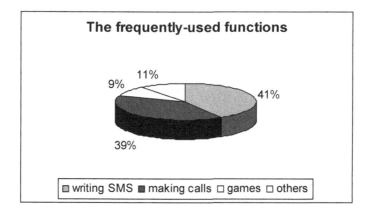

show the percentage of function recognition for users that are the focus of this study. Their better recognition on the Register that is more abstract is supported by another factor in icon design, that is, animation. The animation in Voice and Minibrowser does not help much since the objects are not concrete enough and unavailable in users' surrounding. Some users identify a smiley for menu Voice as a rooster's head, hence it refers to Alarm function that wakes people up from their sleep. In contrast, the animation in Register is used to move arrows going into and out of the cell phone. This abstract concept along with its animation is better understood since arrows are commonly used for showing direction in communal events such as burial and so forth.

If Nokia uses animation to improve its usability, SE uses icon highlight. An icon that is highlighted will be bigger, and shows different stages of an object or icon elements. For example, if Message is highlighted, then the icon of a closed envelope will transform into an open one. Highlighting icons work well with users having computer background but not for users undergoing a technology leap. It becomes a hindrance in comprehending the referents of function and makes them more confused since one icon has two different manifestations. This explains that the mean of accurate rate for function recognition is about 30%, except for Message and Games in SE.

The fourth factor is labeling. Putting a label of function directly under or above an icon helps

increase users' device competency. Users tend to perceive labels and icons as an inseparable group, in which the icon is a visual form for the concept mentioned by the label. Gestalt laws of perceptual organization works here (Preece, 1994; Preece et al., 2002). This is proved by the icon and function recognition for Game. Nokia uses a handset and tic-tac-toe animation as icons for Games. Tic-Tac-Toe is not a common game in Indonesia, therefore only 64% participants recognized its icon. However, 76% participants could guess its referent of function correctly due to the label above it. The labeling in SE is against the principle of proximity as it is placed above 12 icons and appears only if an icon is highlighted. Users tend to see 12 icons as a group and the label above them as a separated element.

User Interface design per se is insufficient for increasing users' device competency. There is a factor that influences much user interface but it is often ignored. This factor is culture. Culture is almost inseparable from metaphors and objects chosen for designing user interface of cell phones. Most cell phones available in Indonesian markets use metaphors and objects from western culture. This, of course, presents some usability problems when user interface built in western cultural context must be understood in eastern cultural context. As an example, a desktop metaphor in SE is not well understood. The rate of function recognition for file manager reaches 12%, since it uses a picture of a folder as its icon. To lessen

Figure 6. Sets of mobile phone menu

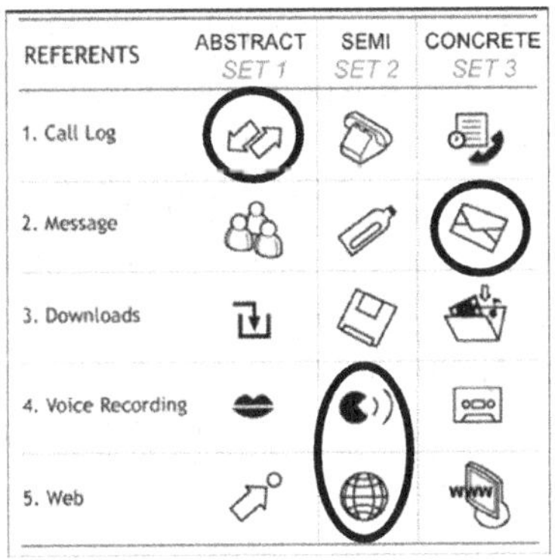

Figure 7. Icon used by Nokia 2112 and the function recognition

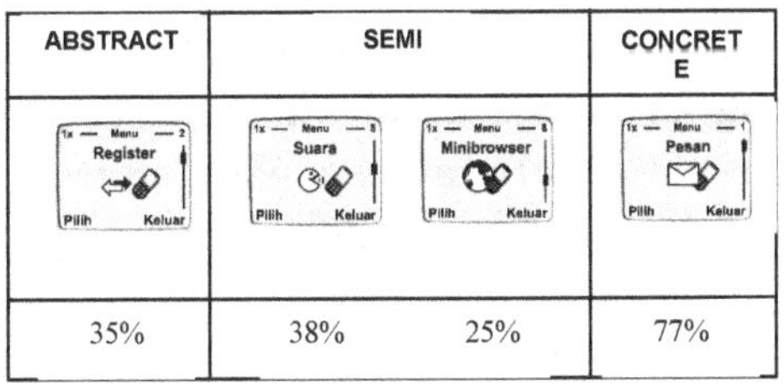

ABSTRACT	SEMI		CONCRETE
35%	38%	25%	77%

Figure 8. Providing a context of an icon

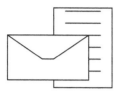

these usability problems, the metaphors used can be localized by using metaphors that are relevance to users' cultural environment, as suggested by Shneiderman (1998). The office desk metaphor for the concept of file and storage could be replaced with "house metaphor" which uses a picture of a cupboard, a cabinet, or a wardrobe. The tic-tac-toe can be replaced with the local game such as *dakon*. Users' device competency will probably improve since they are familiar with these objects and metaphors. Another localization strategy can be done by providing context in which an icon is being used. In spite of its high rate of recognition, some users identified the function of the icon of an envelope as an object to keep or store money. This perception is influenced by the culture of using an envelope as a covering when someone presents money as a gift. To lead users to come to the intended meaning, a context that is a picture of a sheet of full-written paper can be added as a background to the Message menu. Figure 8 illustrates this solution.

Culture also influences the ways used to gain the procedural knowledge of operating cell phones. As explained in the previous section, most users prefer learning to operate their cell phone by asking other users rather than doing trial and error or looking up the manuals. This is a typical characteristic of a communal society. Hofstede (n.d.) ranks Indonesia as one of the lowest world ranking for individualism with a 14. The total score is 100, and the average Asian score is 23. Hofstede's score for individualism indicates that Indonesian society tends to be collectivist as compared to individualistic. Anthropologists agree that collectivity manifests in a close long-term

commitment to the member "group," that is, a family, extended family, or extended relationship. The tendency to consult other users for operational problems functions more as fostering the strong relationship where the more capable users take responsibility for enhancing capability of their fellow members on operating cell phones. In addition to fostering the relationship, the habit of asking shows that users are still attaching themselves to the oral tradition in acquiring their procedural knowledge. Besides, sharing a cell phone between several users emphasizes the cultural dimension of collectivism.

In contrast to individualism score, Indonesia has a high ranking for uncertainty avoidance (UAI) at 48. According to Hofstede, a high uncertainty avoidance indicates the society's low level of tolerance for uncertainty. As a result, the society does not readily accept change and is very risk adverse [4]. The high UAI is reflected on the participants' behavior in choosing the cell phone. In our interview, we tried to dig out the history of cell phone usage and pose a question on which brand of cell phone will be bought if participants have an opportunity to buy the new one. Seventy-two percent of participants from the whole strata (users and nonusers) stated their preferences on Nokia. Their main reason for buying Nokia is that Nokia provides a simple menu structure and it is easy to operate. The perception of the system's ease of use and simplicity is a reason that comes up to the surface. But deep inside, they are unaware of the cultural dimension defined by Hofstede as UAI. In our opinion, the real reason is that they are not ready to accept change if they buy brands other than Nokia, since most participants in this study (85%) operate Nokia. Only a handful of them use Siemens, Motorola, and SE. Some participants (5 persons) did acknowledge their reluctance to learn a new device if they bought other brands of cell phone. This is one of the difficulties faced in this study that many participants, intending to be polite and to cover their making mistakes, tend to tell things indirectly. This is a part of the local culture. In this case, the interviewers should pose tricky questions in order to get the real information.

User interface design and culture are external factors that can be manipulated to improve users' device competency. One factor that is as important as those two major factors is the internal one, that is, users themselves. In trying to examine this internal factor, this study found out that education influences users' device competency. Most participants in the third stratum acquire their procedural knowledge on operating computers by learning it in schools, an academy, or by joining short computer courses offered by vocational training institutions. In short, they learned how to use a device through structured means. Such learning helps users create strong schema, which is a network of general knowledge based on previous experience (Preece, 1994). These schemata will be activated if they face new devices based on computer technology, such as cell phones. The stored schemata which are dynamically constructed at a specific moment assumed to form a mental model (Preece, 1994). In doing the tasks in the usability test, participants on the third stratum are not influenced much by the mental model of their cell phone, since they have various schemata on operating a device and their education background enables them to adapt to a new device quickly. This explains why their rate of task completion is higher than other users in this study.

Unlike users in the third stratum, most users having no background of computer technology acquire their knowledge on how to operate cell phones through unstructured means such as asking other users and rote learning. Thus their mental model of a cell phone is limited to one that they own. Many users in this category (53%) still attached themselves on the mental model of their current or previous cell phone as they did four tasks in the usability test. This mental model is so strong that it influences their performance and the time duration of completing the tasks. The

average time for completing the tasks is longer compared to the time spent by users in the third stratum. Their success rate of task completion is lower enough, as for example, their accuracy rate of making call reaches 56%. Even two participants gave up the test since they could not find the menu for setting alarm. In their cell phone, the submenu for setting alarm is included in the Setting menu and placed in the second node of the menu hierarchy. In Nokia 2112, it is placed in the Organizer menu and displayed on the sixth node of the menu hierarchy. In this case, it can be seen how strong the role of mental model in improving one's device competency is. A further study on the deconstruction of users' mental model of their previous cell phone and how to design user interface that is able to deconstruct such strong mental model need to be done.

SUMMARY

In tracking the device competency of cell phone users, this study found out that many cell phone users in Indonesia undergo a technology leap, and therefore their device competency is quite low. Further, many participants in this study (77%) acquired their device competency through unstructured means such as asking their relatives and friends, and memorizing the tips given by either other users sharing the same cell phone or users with more expertise in operating a cell phone. The structured means significantly proves to be a factor that can improve device competency as shown by the correlation between the education background and the high accuracy rate in completing the tasks. In addition to the methods of gaining the procedural knowledge, this study identifies three major factors that can enhance users' device competency. These are user interface design, culture, and users themselves. The user interface elements comprise designing icon and its referent of function, the use of animation, highlighting, and labeling. The local culture should be integrated in choosing the metaphors and in providing context for objects chosen to be icons.

Scrutinizing the results of this study, we come to some suggestions on how to improve the device competency of cell phone users who use unstructured means for gaining their competency and who undergo technology leap. The first one is to design a simple, easy-to-use cell phone with minimal features or functions, but such cell phones should not be apparently distinguishable from others to hinder a feeling of discrimination. However, we perceive that the cell manufacturers dislike this idea because it will make them less competitive in international markets for new innovation. Secondly, it is recommended to keep the consistency of menu order in various products from one vendor. The new features or functions can be added after the old ones. For example, if Nokia 2112 has eight menus and puts Minibrowser in the last order (here we discount the Flexi menu which was added by the SIM card Provider in Nokia 2112), then the menu in the next series of Nokia which has Camera as an additional feature would have the same order. The Camera menu could be put in the ninth order after Minibrowser. The consistency should include also the submenus or items put under the top level menu. Such menu order consistency would be very helpful for users who operate their cell phones by rote learning. The third suggestion is based on the habit of acquiring the procedural knowledge for operating cell phones and the fact that altering the habits of cell phone users is less popular. Then it is better to use an oral method to increase the device competency for most cell phone users in Indonesia. It will be wiser if cell phone manufacturers or distributors organize learning centers or gatherings where cell phone users can gather, learn how to use a new device, and share their experiences. The learning centers can function also as a means of promoting new products. In such centers, both users and distributors can obtain very precious benefits.

ACKNOWLEDGMENT

This research was supported by the department of Information Technology, Duta Wacana Christian University, Yogyakarta, Indonesia. The authors would like to give thanks to Agnes Febrina, David Surya Pratama, Elisa and Mardi Tamma who have spent their valuable time in helping them conduct the field studies.

REFERENCES

Badre, A. (2001) The effects of cross cultural interface design on World Wide Web user performance. *GVU tech reports*. Retrieved January 10, 2007, from http://www.cc.gatech.edu/gvu/reports/2001

Chipchase, J. (2005) Understanding non-literacy as a barrier to mobile phone communication. *Nokia research center*. Retrieved August 15, 2006, from http://research.nokia.com/buesky/non-literacy-001-2005/index.html

Diryo, A. D. (2006). Prospek Bisnis Telekomunikasi Di Indonesia. *Economic Review*, 204.

Hofstede, G. (n.d.). *Geert-HofstedeTM vultural dimensions*. Retrieved January 23, 2007, from http://www.geert-hofstede.com/ hofstede_indonesia.shtml

Huang, S. C., Chou, I-F., & Bias, R. G. (2006) Empirical evaluation of a popular cellular phone's menu system: Theory meets practice. *Journal of Usability Studies*, *2*(1), 91-108.

Khaslavasky, J. (1998). Integrating culture into interface design. *ACM CHI*, 365-366.

Khaslavsky, J. (1998). Culture and international software design. *ACM CHI*, 387.

Kondratova, I., & Goldfarb, I. (2005). Cultural visual interface design. In *Proceedings of the EDMedia, World Conference on Educational Multimedia, Hypermedia & Telecommunications*. Montreal, (pp. 1255-1262).

Kim, J. H., & Lee, K. P. (2005). Cultural difference and mobile phone interface design: Icon recognition according to level of abstraction. *Mobile HCI*, 19-22.

Lee, Y.S., et al. (n.d). *Usability testing with cultural groups in developing a cell phone navigation system*. Retrieved August 10, 2006, from uweb. txstate.edu/~yr12/Papers/HCII2005_Submission_Cultural.pdf

Marcus, A. (2001). Cross-cultural user-interface design. In M. J Smith & G. Salvendy (Eds.), *Proceeding of the Human-Computer Interface Internat (HCII) Conference* (Vol. 2, pp. 502-505). New Orleans: Lawrence Erlbaum Association.

Ponsel Masih Lebih Banyak Untuk Telpon. (2006, December 11). *Kompas*. Jogja edition, 1.

Preece, J. (1994). *Human-computer interaction*. New York: Addison-Wesley.

Preece, J., et al. (2002*). Interaction design: Beyond human-computer interaction*. New York: John Wiley & Sons.

Shneiderman, B. (1998*). Designing the user interface: Strategies for effective human-computer interaction*. Reading: Addison-Wesley.

Statistik Indonesia. (2007). Retrieved February 28, 2007 from www.datastatistik-Indonesia.com

Vatrapu, R., & Perez-Quinones, M. (2006). Culture and international usability testing: The effects of culture in structure interviews. Unpublished masters' thesis. *Digital library and archives: Formerly the scholarly communication project*. Retrieved August 11, 2006 from http://scholar.lib.vt.edu/theses/available/etd-09132002-083026/

World Telecommunication/ICT Indicators: Cellular Subscribers. (2006). *International telecommunication union*. Retrieved August 10, 2006, from http://www.itu.int/ITU-D/statistics/at_glance/cellular05.pdf

Ziefle, M., & Bay, S. (2004). Mental models of a cellular phone menu. Comparing older and younger novice users. In Brewster & Dunlop (Eds.), *Mobile human-computer interaction*. Berlin: Springer.

ENDNOTE

[1] Data were taken from United Nations Population Division. Retrieved in August 09, 2006 from http://esa.un.org/unpp/ index. asp? panel=3.

This work was previously published in International Journal of Information Technology and Web Engineering, Vol. 3, Issue 1, edited by G. Alkhatib and D. Rine, pp. 38-52, copyright 2008 by IGI Publishing (an imprint of IGI Global).

Chapter 8
Voice Driven Emotion Recognizer Mobile Phone:
Proposal and Evaluations

Aishah Abdul Razak
Multimedia University, Malaysia

Mohamad Izani Zainal Abidin
Multimedia University, Malaysia

Ryoichi Komiya
Multimedia University, Malaysia

ABSTRACT

This article proposes an application of emotion recognizer system in telecommunications entitled voice driven emotion recognizer mobile phone (VDERM). The design implements a voice-to-image conversion scheme through a voice-to-image converter that extracts emotion features in the voice, recognizes them, and selects the corresponding facial expression images from image bank. Since it only requires audio transmission, it can support video communication at a much lower bit rate than the conventional videophone. The first prototype of VDERM system has been implemented into a personal computer. The coder, voice-to-image converter, image database, and system interface are preinstalled in the personal computer. In this article, we present and discuss some evaluations that have been conducted in supporting this proposed prototype. The results have shown that both voice and image are important for people to correctly recognize emotion in telecommunications and the proposed solution can provide an alternative to videophone systems. The future works list some modifications that can be done to the proposed prototype in order to make it more practical for mobile applications.

INTRODUCTION AND MOTIVATION

Nonverbal communication plays a very important role in human communications (Komiya, Mohd Arif, Ramliy, Gowri, & Mokhtar, 1999). However, in telephone systems, only audio information can be exchanged. Thus, using telephony, the transmission of nonverbal information such as one's emotion would depend mostly on the user's conversation skills. Although the importance of nonverbal aspects of communication has been recognized, until now most research on nonverbal information concentrated on image transmission such as transmission of facial expression and gesture using video signal. This has contributed to the emergence of a videophone system, which is one of the most preferred ways to exchange more information in communication. Such services, however, require a wide bandwidth in order to provide real time video that is adequate for a natural conversation. This is often either very expensive to provide or difficult to implement. Besides, in a videophone system, the user has to be fixed in front of the camera at the correct position during the conversation, so that the user's image can be captured and transmitted correctly. This limitation does not happen in the normal telephone system.

Another approach is to use model-based coding (Kidani, 1999). In this approach, instead of transmitting video signals containing an image of the user, only the human action data such as the facial expressions, movement of the mouth, and so on acquired using a microphone, a keypad, and other input devices, are transmitted over the network. When these data are received by the receiver, the polygon coordinate data for each facial feature is recalculated in accordance with the displacement rules and the person's expression is synthesized.

Our approach is similar to the second approach in a sense that a synthesize image is used for the facial expression reconstruction at the receiver side. However, the difference is that only voice is transmitted and the emotion data is extracted from the received voice tone at the receiving side. This is based on the idea that, voice, besides for communication, it is also an indicator of the psychological and physiological state of a speaker. The identification of the pertinent features in the speech signal may therefore allow the evaluation of a person's emotional state. In other words,

by extracting the emotion information from the voice of the speaker, it is possible to reconstruct the facial expression of that speaker. Thus, based on this voice-to-image conversion scheme, we propose a new system known as voice driven emotion recognizer mobile phone (VDERM), as seen in Figure 1. This system uses a voice-to-image converter system at the receiver side that identifies the emotional state of the received voice signal and selects the corresponding facial expression of that particular emotion from the image bank to be displayed. Using this approach, only audio transmission is required. Therefore, the existing second generation (2G) mobile phone infrastructures can be used. Another advantage is that the user does not need to be fixed in front of the camera during the conversation because there is no need for image transmission.

VOICE TO IMAGE CONVERSION

Referring to Figure 1, the voice-to-image conversion for this system is done at the receiving side. The conversion scheme can be divided into two parts: the emotion recognition and facial expression reconstructor. These two processes are done by the voice-to-image converter.

Emotion Recognition

Before we come out with the emotion recognizer design, first we have to deal with these three issues:

1.   What kind of emotion to be recognized?

How many and what types of emotional states should be recognized by our system is an interesting yet difficult issue. Besides, there is no widely accepted definition and taxonomy of emotion; it should also be kept in mind that a single emotion can be uttered in different ways. Scherer (1986) distinguishes different categories in a single

Figure 1. Basic block diagram of VDERM system

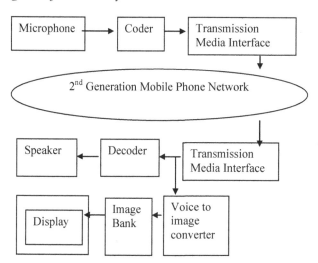

emotion, for instance, the category "cold anger/ irritation" and the category "hot anger/rage." In our study, we have chosen to consider emotions as discrete categories (Ekman, 1973; Izard & Carroll, 1977; Plutchik, 1980). Six basic emotions defined by Cornelius (1996), that is, happiness, sadness, anger, fear, surprise, and disgust, have been chosen as the emotions to be recognized and reconstructed.

2.   What are the features to represent emotion?

Determining emotion features is a crucial issue in the emotion recognizer design. This is because the recognition result is strongly dependant on the emotional features that have been used to represent the emotion. All the studies in this area point to the pitch (fundamental frequency) as the main emotion feature for emotion recognition. Other acoustic features are vocal energy, frequency, spectral features, formants (usually only one or the first two formants F1 and F2 are considered), and temporal features (speech rate and pausing) (Banse & Scherer, 1996). Another approach to feature extraction is to enrich the set of features by considering some derivative features, such as linear predictive coding cepstrum (LPCC) parameters of signal (Tosa & Nakatsu, 1996). Our study has adopted this approach and uses linear

Table 1. Speech features and description

No	Feature	Symbol used	Description
1	Energy	e	Average energy of the speech signal
2	LPC Coefficient	$a_1, a_2, a_3, \ldots a_{14}$	The weighting coefficient used in the linear prediction coding analysis.
3	Duration	d	Duration of the speech signal
4	Pitch	f_0	Fundamental frequency (oscillation frequency) of the glottal oscillation (vibration of the vocal folds).
5	Jitter	jt	Perturbation in the pitch

predictive analysis (Rabiner & Schafer, 1978) to extract the emotion features. A detailed analysis has been done on selected emotion parameters (Aishah, Izani, & Komiya, 2003a, 2003b, 2003c). Based on these analyses, a total of 18 features (as in Table 1) have been chosen to represent the emotion features. The 18 features are pitch (f_0), jitter (jt), speech energy (e), speech duration (d), and 14 LPC coefficients (a_1- a_{14}). The LPC coefficients are included because we intended to use LPC analysis for the extraction algorithm. Besides, it represents the phonetic features of speech that are often used in speech recognition

3.   What technique to be used for recognition?

There are many methods that have been used for emotion recognition/classification. For instance, Mcgilloway, Cowie, Douglas-Cowie, Gielen, Westerdijk, and Stroeve (2000) have compared and tested three classification algorithms, namely linear discriminant, support vector machine (Schölkopf, Burges, & Smola, 1998), and quantization (Westerdijk & Wiegerinck, 2000). Others are using fuzzy model, K-nearest neighbors, and neural networks (Petrushin, 1999). Among all, perhaps the most common and popular method of emotion recognition is neural network. However, the configuration of the networks differs from one researcher to another, as discussed by Morishima and Harashima (1991), Nakatsu, Nicholson, and Tosa (1999), Petrushin (1999), and Tosa and Nakatsu (1996). In this article we applied neural network configuration as described by NETLAB (Nabney, 2001) for the recognition technique. It uses a 2-layer multilayer perceptron (MLP) architecture with 12-18 elements in the input vector which correspond to the speech features, 25 nodes in the hidden layer, and 6 nodes in the output layer which correspond to the six elements of output vector, the basic emotions. This configuration is illustrated in Figure 2.

The weights are drawn from a zero mean, unit variance isotropic Gaussian, with variance scaled by the fan-in of the hidden or output units as appropriate. This makes use of the MATLAB function RANDN and so the seed for the random weight initialization can be set using RANDN ("STATE," S) where S is the seed value. The hidden units use the TANH activation job.

During the training, the weights are adjusted iteratively using a scaled conjugate gradient algorithm (Fodslette, 1993) to minimize the error function, which is the cross-entropy function with softmax as the output activation function. In our experiment, 1,000 iterations are found to be sufficient to achieve an acceptable error rate.

Once our network is trained, we test the network using test samples and calculate the recognition rate. The speech features from test samples are fed into the network and forward propagate through the network to generate the output. Then, the resulted classification performance for the predicted output (output which is recognized by the network) is compared to the target output and displayed in the confusion matrix table. A detail discussion on the result of our experiment using neural network approach is presented by Aishah, Azrulhasni, and Komiya (2004). It is found that an emotion recognition rate of 60% is achievable

Figure 2. The neural network configuration

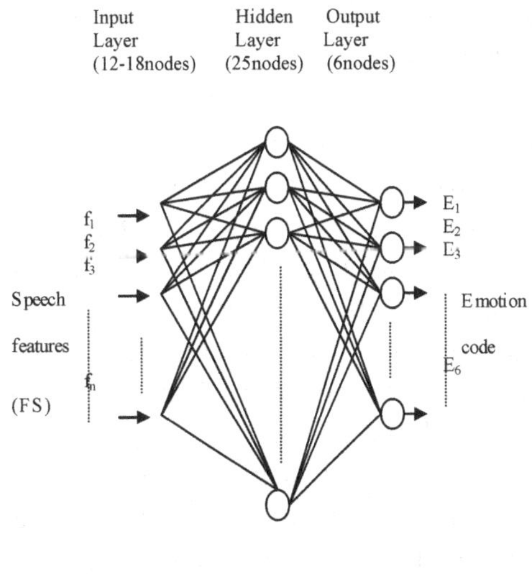

Figure 3. Block diagram of emotion recognition process

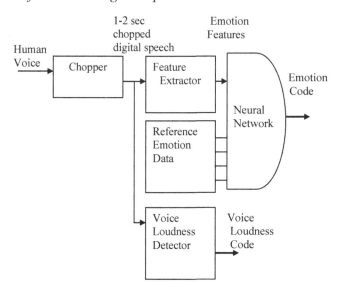

using the neural network method and this result is sufficient based on a human recognition rate done on the same experiment data.

Once we have dealt with the above issues, we come out with an emotion recognition process as shown in Figure 3. Basically this part extracts the emotion content of the speech received from the transmitting user and recognizes it. In addition to emotion, we also identify the voice loudness level of the speech so that it can be used to control the opening of the mouth shape on the facial images later on.

First, the continuous human voice would be chopped into 2 second speech and undergo preprocessing where it is normalized by its maximum amplitude and the d.c. component is removed. Next, it will go through a feature extractor process where the sample is segmented into 25 msec frames with a 5 msec overlap. LPC analysis is then carried out on these series of frames and the outputs are the 14 LPC coefficients, first reflection coefficient, and energy of the underlying speech segment and energy of the prediction error. Using these outputs, the remaining parameters are determined in the next stage. Speech duration is determined by first classifying the speech frames as voiced or unvoiced using the prediction error signal by simply setting a threshold. The first frame that is classified as voiced will mark the begin-

ning of the speech period. After the beginning of the speech period, if the frame is classified as unvoiced for few consecutive frames, the speech is decided to be ended. The length of the speech period is calculated to get the speech duration. The pitch period for each frame that lies within the speech period is calculated using the cepstrum of the voiced prediction error signal. If an abrupt change in the pitch period is observed, that period is compared to previous pitch periods, and then low-pass filtered (or median filtered) to smooth the abrupt change. With the perturbation in the pitch, jitter is then calculated using pitch perturbation order 1 method, which is obtained by taking the backward and forward differences of perturbation order zero. All the calculation is developed using MATLAB with the use of speech processing and synthesis toolbox (Childers, 1999).

It should be noted that the features extracted so far are based on frame-by-frame basis. As a result, for each sample, it might have many sets of features depending on the number of frames that lie within the speech period of that particular sample. Since we need to standardize the entire sample to have only one feature set, the average of each feature over the frame size is calculated for each sample. The final feature set (FS) for sample n (s_n), consisting of 18 elements is given as

FS for $s_n = (e_n, a_{1n}, a_{2n}, a_{3n} \ldots a_{14n}, d_n, f_{0n}, jt_n)$ (1)

On the other hand, a copy of the chopped digital speech will be sent to the voice loudness level detector to detect the loudness level. The outputs of this emotion recognition process are emotion code (from the neural network) and voice loudness code (from the voice loudness detector).

Facial Expression Reconstructor

Figure 4 shows the process involved in facial expression reconstructor. First, the code processor will process the emotion code and voice loudness code and convert it to the equivalent image ID used in the database. The code conversion would also depend on which image the user would like to use represented by the model ID.

For the first prototype of this system, we have used Microsoft Access for the image database and Visual Basic is used as its interface. For each images stored in the database, there is a unique ID tagged to it. The ID is generated sequentially by the system automatically whenever an image is uploaded into the system. Before starting the conversation, the user must first choose which image to be used (for example, male or female model) and once the image is selected, the code

processor will make necessary conversions on the received emotion code and voice loudness code to match the ID range for that image. Accordingly, the ID number is sent to the image database, and the image with a matching ID retrieved from the database is then displayed. This image database by default consists of 24 images of female models and 24 images of male models. For each model, the images consist of six basic emotions and each emotion has four levels of voice presented by the opening of mouth shape. In addition we also include different eye shapes which are generated randomly among the four levels.

System Interface

Figure 5 shows the main interface of the facial expression reconstructor system. It consists of a display displaying the facial expression images and buttons for the user to select which model to be used, such as a male or female model. If they click on the "Male" button, the image of male model will be used. Similarly, when they click on the "Female" button, the female image will be displayed, as shown in Figure 5.

In addition to the prestored male and female model, users can also use their own images by using the "Upload own Image" button. When a

Figure 4. Block diagram of facial expression reconstructor process

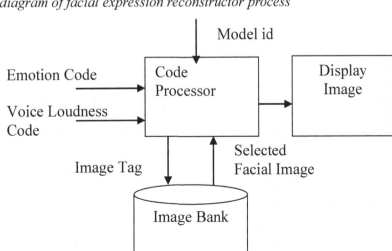

Figure 5. Main interface of facial expression re-constructor

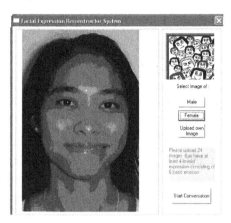

Figure 6. Interface for uploading new image

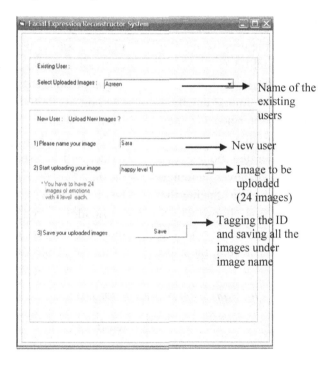

user clicks on it, a second interface that is shown in Figure 6 will pop up. It has the buttons that show the name of the users that already have their own images uploaded and stored in the system. For new users who want to upload their own image, they can type in their name or any name that will represent them. This will act as the name of the folder which will store all the 24 images of the person. Then users can start to upload their own images which consist of all the six basic emotions which are happiness, sadness, anger, disgust, fear, and surprise with four levels each. The user must have all the 24 images in order to have a complete set of images. At this section, once the user chooses, for example "happy level 1," it will pop up a dialog box and the user will search and upload the appropriate image and save it. Each of the newly uploaded images will be tagged accordingly with an image ID. After all the 24 images are completely uploaded, users have to click on the "Save as" button for the final step. This is the part where all the images will be put under the folder that has been created and the image ID range for this image name will be recorded and saved for future use. Once this is done, the user can use it by selecting the name from the "uploaded images" box.

EVALUATIONS

Preliminary Evaluations

There are three preliminary evaluations conducted in the process of completing our first prototype. The details of the evaluations are discussed in the next subsections.

PE I

The main objective of this evaluation are to select good quality of emotional voice samples for our voice database. The samples would later be used for training and testing our neural network model for emotion recognition. The second objective is to see how accurate a person can recognize the emotion content in a speech by just listening to the speech/voice. The result of this human recognition rate will be used as a guide for the recognition rate expected to be achieved by our recognition system later on. The evaluation involves two steps:

1.   Collecting voice sample

Four short sentences frequently used in everyday communication that could be expressed in all emotional states without semantic contradictions are chosen as the utterance. The sentences are: "Itu kereta saya" (In Malay language), "That is my car" (In English), "Sekarang pukul satu" (In Malay language), and "Now is one o'clock" (In English). Two languages are used for the utterance because we want to compare the emotional parameters for both languages and determine how much difference in language could influ-

ence the way emotions are expressed. Then, we asked acting students to utter the same utterance 10 times, each for different emotional states and also in neutral voice as a reference.

2.   Listening test

The emotionally loaded voice samples are then randomized and each sample is repeated three times within short intervals followed by a 30 second pause. The series of stimuli are presented via headphones to 50 naive listeners to evaluate the emotional state within seven categories: happiness, sadness, anger, fear, disgust, surprise, and not recognizable emotional state.

PE II

The main objective of this evaluation is to detect the most appropriate and highly recognizable facial expressions images that can be used to represent the six basic human emotions for our image database. Another objective is to see how accurate humans can detect emotion based on only the facial expression images, without any audio support. The evaluation also involves two steps:

1.   Image collection

For this purpose we have selected three male models and three female models. The facial expressions of the six basic human emotions, which are happy, sad, angry, surprise, disgust, and fear, portrayed by each model are captured, focusing from the neck and above. The background used is a blank white wall with natural daylight so that the model image is clear and focused. The size of images taken are 1000x1600, using a Sony Cyber shot digital camera. The images are then cropped and resized to 6x4 inches size.

2.   Viewing test

All the images are randomized and presented to 20 assessors consisting of 10 males and 10 females volunteers. The images are displayed for 2 seconds each with a 3 second gap between images. The assessors are asked to identify the emotion of the given images and then the recognition rates for each image and emotion state are calculated.

PE III

The main objective of this experiment is to verify that the combination of voice and image can improve the capability of humans to correctly recognize an emotion and thus justify the importance of a VDERM system.

For the purpose of this evaluation, we have selected three emotional voice samples for each emotion and matched it with the corresponding images. Around 50 assessors have participated in this evaluation and the recognition rate is calculated and analyzed. They are also asked to answer some questions to reflect the importance of voice and facial expressions in effective communications.

System Evaluation

The main objective behind this system evaluation is to evaluate the reliability and feasibility of the idea of a VDERM system using the developed prototype. This evaluation tries to get some feedback from the user on how efficient the system can improve the message conveyed during a conversation, is the displayed image synchronous with the intended emotion of the speech, and how can the interface be further improved according to the user's specification. Responses from the assessors on their perception of the VDERM system are important to determine better research direction for the proposed system. For this initial evaluation, the prototype of the VDERM system has been implemented into a personal computer. The coder, voice-to-image converter, image database, and system interface are preinstalled in the personal computer.

Experimental Set-Up

A subjective assessment technique is chosen due to the practicability and suitability. A total of 20 assessors consisting of experts and nonexperts take part in the evaluation test. Assessors first went through a demo on the idea behind a VDERM system and followed with a briefing about the evaluation form contents and the way evaluation must be done. The list of evaluation item is given in Table 2. A sample of a 40 second one-way conversation was played, first using a female model and then a male model with a 15 second gap. The facial expression images switched between different emotions and mouth shapes depending on the emotion content and loudness level of the conversation at every two seconds. Assessors were asked to pretend that they were having a conversation with the model and then they were required to rate the quality of each of the evaluation items based on the scale given in Table 3. Then, they were asked to give comments and suggestions on the grade given for each evaluation item.

Table 2. List of evaluation item for preliminary system evaluation

No.	Item
1	Overall
2	Image accuracy in displaying the facial expression
3	Image synchronization with the speech
4	Features and interface
5	Quality of the images
6	Emotion recognition capability

Table 3. Grading scale

Scale	Quality
0	Worse
1	Average
2	Good
3	Best

RESULTS AND ANALYSIS

PE I

From this evaluation, we have achieved an average recognition rate of 62.33%. The average recognition rate is in line with what has been achieved by other studies using different languages (i.e., around 55-65%) (Morishima & Harashima, 1991; Nakatsu et al., 1999; Petrushin, 1999). This result has proven that even a human is not a perfect emotion recognizer. This is because recognition of emotions is a difficult task due to the fact that there are no standard ways of expressing and decoding emotion. Besides, several emotional states may appear in different scale and have very similar physiological correlates, which result the same acoustic correlates. In an actual situation, people solve the ambiguities by using the context and/or other information. This finding indicates that we shall not try to have our machine to achieve a perfect recognition rate. The human recognition rate is used as a guideline towards achieving the satisfactory rate for computer recognition. Table 4 shows the confusion matrix table that is achieved in PE I. The confusion matrix table of PE I suggests how successful the actors were in expressing the intended emotion and which emotions are easy or difficult to realize. We see that the most easily recognizable emotion based on this experiment is disgust (77%) and the least easily recognizable category is anger (46%). A high percentage of confusion occurs in sad-fear (18%) and anger-sad (21%).

A total of 200 samples which have the highest recognition rate are selected for each emotion. This has resulted in 1,200 samples for the whole voice database.

PE II

From the results in Table 5, it is concluded that among all the facial expression images of emotion, the easiest expressions detected by assessors is happy. This is due to the fact that happiness is the most common emotion shown publicly by humans and it is usually expressed with a smile and bright eyes. Thus it is not difficult to identify a happy face even without an audio support. The least recognizable emotion is found to be disgust (40%) and it is often confused with anger (35%). This is because the expressions for both of these emotions are very similar, shown through the "hostile" face; the tight line of the mouth and the squinting eyes. Another thing to note is that based on image, the diversification of confusion in a particular emotion is less compared to recognition based on voice only.

We have also done some analysis on the images which are highly recognizable, and together with the feedback from the assessors, we have identified some main facial gestures which significantly contribute to the recognition of certain emotion. This is summarized in Table 6. Based on the results of Human

Table 4. Confusion matrix table of PE I

Intended emotion	Response from the assessors					
	Happy	Sad	Anger	Disgust	Fear	Surprise
Happy	**68**	2	5	8	12	5
Sad	7	**61**	9	3	18	2
Anger	4	21	**46**	11	7	11
Disgust	4	1	5	**77**	7	6
Fear	9	12	5	15	**54**	5
Surprise	8	1	5	8	10	**68**

Table 5. Confusion matrix table of PE II

Intended emotion	Response from the assessors					
	Happy	Sad	Anger	Disgust	Fear	Surprise
Happy	**90**	0	0	0	0	10
Sad	0	**80**	0	5	15	0
Anger	0	0	**60**	35	0	5
Disgust	0	0	35	**40**	0	15
Fear	0	5	0	5	**60**	30
Surprise	10	0	0	0	30	**60**

Evaluation II, we have identified 1 male and 1 female model which have the highest recognizable images to be our model. Then the images of six emotions are recaptured according to the significant facial gestures and each emotion is further developed into four levels of mouth shape, resulting in 24 images for each models.

PE III

From the confusion matrix Table 7, it is illustrated that the recognition rate for all emotions are quite high (70%-87%). According to assessors, fear is difficult to recognize (70%) compared to other emotions as the expression accompanying the voice of fear can be confused or sad. The most easily recognizable emotion is happy (87%), as the cheerful voice is supported by the smiling face.

Figure 7 compares the recognition rate achievable in all the three preliminary evaluations. On average, PE I achieved an average recognition rate of 62.33% with individual recognition rates ranging between 46% and 77%. PE II shows a slightly higher average recognition rate (65%) compared to PE I with a wider range of individual recognition rate (between 40% and 90%). A significant increase in average and individual recognition is clearly seen in PE III with an average recognition of 78.3% and individual recognition concentration between 70% and 87%. The results have clearly illustrated that PE III has the most percentage of correctness in emotion identification by assessors. This shows that combination of both what we hear (voice) and what we see (image) can greatly improve human capability of identifying the emotions. Thus, this result has justified the importance of the proposed system, which is to combine the image and voice to improve the naturalness and efficiency of telecommunication.

On top of the recognition rate presented above, below we have summarized the findings that were collected from the assessors feedback.

Table 6. Summary of facial gestures according to emotions

EMOTION	FACIAL GESTURES
Happy	Smile, laughter
Sad	Down turned mouth and eyes, tears
Angry	Eyes bulging, mouth tighten
Disgust	Wrinkled nose, lowered eyelids and eyebrow, raised upper lip
Fear	Eyes squinting
Surprise	Eyes bulging, raised eyebrows, mouth shaped "O"

Table 7. Confusion matrix table of PE III

Intended emotion	Response from the assessors					
	Happy	Sad	Anger	Disgust	Fear	Surprise
Happy	**87**	0	0	0	0	13
Sad	0	**78**	0	0	22	0
Anger	0	0	**82**	18	0	0
Disgust	0	6	15	**79**	0	0
Fear	0	16	7	0	**70**	7
Surprise	26	0	0	0	0	**74**

Figure 7. Comparison between recognition rate achieved in PE I, II and III

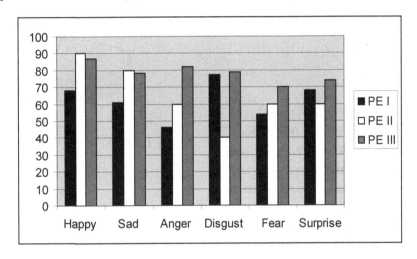

1. Comfortable way to express and detect emotion

For emotion expression (Figure 8), 45% agreed that facial expression is the most comfortable way to express emotion, followed by voice tone (34%), and body gesture (21%).

The pattern is also the same for emotion detection (Figure 9) but the percentage for emotion detection by facial expression is higher at 64%. This is followed by voice tone at 30% and body gesture at 6%.

2. Medium of communication

The results in Figure 10 show that telephone/ mobile phones are the most popular medium of communication nowadays with 48% as the majority, followed by Internet instant messenger (40%) and short messages service (SMS) (12%). This is because telephones are the most convenient and widely available medium of communication.

3. Importance of audio (voice tone) and video (facial expression) information for effective communication

The result in Figure 11 show that 98% agreed that both audio and video information are important for effective communication.

4. Reliability of emotion extraction from voice

Figure 8. Comfortable way to express emotion

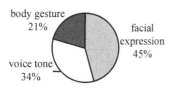

Figure 10. Popular medium of communication

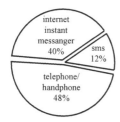

Figure 9. Preferable way to detect emotion

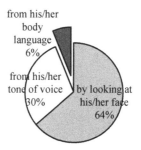

Figure 11. Importance of audio (voice tone) and video (facial expression) information for effective communication

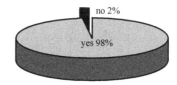

Figure 12. Reliability of emotion extraction from voice

The result in Figure 12 show that 64% have agreed that it is reliable to extract emotion from voice.

The result of human emotion recognition based on audio, video, and both highlights two important points. The first one is that emotion recognition is a difficult task and humans can never perfectly recognize emotion. This is because the way people express and interpret emotion might differ from one another, even though some researches have found that it does follow some standard pattern (Cosmides, 1983). The second point is that the ability of humans to correctly recognize emotion is increased to more than 70% when both audio and video information of the speaker are present.

It is also found that facial expression is the most comfortable way for people to express and detect emotion during communication. Thus the presence of facial expressions is very important in communication.

Overall, the results of the preliminary evaluations highlight the importance of facial expressions in providing effective communication, and thus, it is very important to incorporate facial expressions in today's telephone system, as proposed in the VDERM system.

System Evaluation

An average score of each evaluation item was calculated and a bar chart was plotted to represent the results. The preliminary evaluation results are illustrated in Figure 13. From the chart, it is shown that the quality of the images used have the highest scale average with value of 2.85. This shows that the assessors are happy with the quality of the images used, which are clear and focused. This level of quality is not achievable when using a videophone system because the image is transmitted real time and thus subject to transmission quality and the position of the user during the conversation. The next highest scale average is on the emotion recognition capability. This is expected because this system provides both audio and visual information of the speaker which help the assessors to recognize the emotion more easily compared to just having the audio information, as in the case of normal phone conversation.

The third highest score item goes to features and interface design. Overall the assessors think that the system is user friendly because the system has a straight forward design that does not confuse a user, even if the user is not familiar with a computer system. Another point is that the interface buttons have direct and clear instructions to be followed by the user. Moreover, most of the assessors find that the feature to upload their own image is very interesting because it gives the user customization to make the system personal to them. However, a few are concerned with the image database size as more images are being uploaded, and the difficulty of having a set of 24 images before can use their own image. Some also suggested that the features can be improved by having interactive interface using JAVA and personalized skins for the background.

The average score for overall system performance is 1.85. Many of the assessors agreed that this system can improve the efficiency of telecommunication system because the presence of both audio and visual have given them more clues on the emotions being conveyed. Besides they also found that having both elements made the conversation more fun and interesting. In addition, the automatic detection of emotion from voice is also an interesting attempt because most of the currently available chat/Web cam applications require the user to manually select the emotion to be/being conveyed. However, the assessors believed that the system still has a lot of room for improvement, especially in the aspect of image accuracy and image synchronization.

As shown on the chart, image accuracy in displaying the facial expression and image synchronization with the speech has an average score of less than 1.5. The main reason for this is that the level of image for each emotion currently used is only four, which has resulted in switching between images which seems less smooth and the lip movement does not appear to be synchronized with the speech. This is an important issue to address because if the images and voice do not synchronize, the user might not be able to catch the emotion being conveyed. By having more levels for a particular emotion, switching between different emotion states can be smoother, thus the user can have more time to identify the emotion of the images.

Figure 13. Result for system evaluation

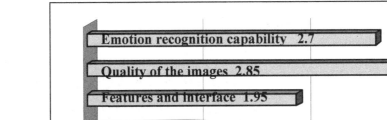

FUTURE DESIGN ISSUES

The main improvement in the system is concerned with the accuracy of the images being displayed. Since our intention is to provide real time visual images as in video conferencing, it is very important that the image switching appears to be smooth and synchronized with the speech and emotion content of the speech. One simple modification is to have more levels to represent the voice loudness. However, increasing the level means increasing the number of images needed and consequently can increase the size of our database, which is not desirable.

One possible solution to this is to have the personal images of the user deleted after the call is terminated. However, the problem with this is that the user might need to upload their image every time before the user can start a conversation, which can be time consuming and not practical.

The other advanced alternative for facial expression reconstruction is to use a 3D artificial face model, which can generate facial expressions based on the coded emotion, instead of switching between still pictures. This method is more advanced and complicated but it can provide a more natural facial expressions. For this method, software will be used to convert a person's photo into a face model and a program will be developed to generate the facial expressions on the model based on the emotion code and voice loudness. Using this technique, there is no need for a large image database, which might be more appropriate for application on a mobile phone.

CONCLUSION

In general, based on the results, the system has achieved its main objective, that is, to improve telecommunication by providing voice together with facial expressions and provide an alternative to videophone systems. However it still has a lot of room for improvement in the aspect of inter-

face design and the accuracy of the images being displayed. The evaluation that we have conducted so far was tested on a personal computer. In order to apply the system on a mobile phone, the issues pertaining to the image database size should be thoroughly dealt with.

REFERENCES

Aishah, A. R., Azrulhasni, M. I., & Komiya, R. (2004). A neural network approach for emotion recognition in speech. In *Proceedings of the 2nd International Conference on Artificial Intelligence in Engineering and Technology (ICAIET2004)* (pp. 910-916).

Aishah, A. R., Izani, Z. A., & Komiya, R. (2003a). A preliminary analysis for recognizing emotion in speech. In *Proceedings of IEEE Student Conference On Research and Development (SCOReD 2003)*.

Aishah, A. R., Izani, Z. A., & Komiya, R. (2003b). Emotion pitch variation analysis in Malay and English voice samples. In *Proceedings of the 9th Asia Pacific Conference on Communications (APCC2003)* (Vol. 1, pp. 108-112).

Aishah, A. R., Izani, Z. A., & Komiya, R. (2003c). Towards automatic recognition of emotion in speech. In *Proceedings of the IEEE International Symposium on Signal Processing and Information Technology (ISSPIT2003)*.

Banse, R., & Scherer, K. R. (1996). Acoustic profiles in vocal emotion expression. *Journal of Personality and Social Psychology, 70*, 614-636.

Childers, D. G. (1999). *Speech processing and synthesis toolboxes*. New York: John Wiley & Sons.

Cornelius, R. R. (1996). *The science of emotion: Research and tradition in the psychology of emotion*. Upper Saddle River, NJ: Prentice-Hall.

Cosmides, L. (1983). Invariance in the acoustic expression of emotion during speech. *Journal of Experimental Psychology: Human Perception and Performance, 9*, 864-881.

Ekman, P. (1973). *Darwin and facial expression: A century of research in review.* New York: Academic Press.

Fodslette, M. M. (1993). A scaled conjugate gradient algorithm for fast-supervised learning. *Neural Networks, 6*, 525-533.

Izard, & Carroll, E. (1977). *Human emotions.* New York: Plenum Press.

Kidani, Y. (1999). Video communication system using portrait animation. In *Proceedings of the IEEE Southeastcon '99* (pp. 309-314).

Komiya, R., Mohd Arif, N. A., Ramliy, M. N., Gowri Hari Prasad, T., & Mokhtar, M. R. (1999). A proposal of virtual reality telecommunication system. In *Proceedings of the WEC'99* (pp. 93-98).

Mcgilloway, S., Cowie, R., Douglas-Cowie, E., Gielen, C. C. A. M., Westerdijk, M. J. D., & Stroeve, S. H. (2000). Approaching automatic recognition of emotion from voice: A rough benchmark. In *Proceedings of the ISCA Workshop on Speech and Emotion* (pp. 207-212).

Morishima, S., & Harashima, H. (1991). A media conversion from speech to facial image for intelligent man-machine interface. *IEEE J. on Selected Areas in Comm., 9*(4), 594-600.

Nabney, I. (2001). *Netlab: Algorithms for pattern recognition, advances in pattern recognition.* London: Springer-Verlag.

Nakatsu, R., Nicholson, J., & Tosa, N. (1999). *Emotion recognition and its application to computer agents with spontaneous interactive capabilities.* Paper presented at the International Congress of Phonetic Science (pp. 343-351).

Petrushin, V. A. (1999). Emotion in speech recognition and application to call centers. In *Proceedings of the ANNIE '99.*

Plutchik, R. (1980). *Emotion: A psycho-evolutionary synthesis.* New York: Harper and Row.

Rabiner, L. R., & Schafer, R. W. (1978). *Digital processing of speech signals.* Eaglewood Cliffs, NJ: Prentice-Hall.

Scherer, K. R. (1986). Vocal affect expression: A review and a model for future research. *Psychological Bulletin, 99*, 43-165.

Schölkopf, C. J. C., Burges, A. J., & Smola (1998). *Advances in kernel methods: Support vector learning.* Cambridge, MA: MIT Press.

Tosa, N., & Nakatsu, R. (1996). Life-like communication agent-emotion sensing character MIC and feeling session character MUSE. In *Proceedings of the IEEE Conference on Multimedia* (pp. 12-19).

Westerdijk, M., & Wiegerinck, W. (2000). Classification with multiple latent variable models using maximum entropy discrimination. In *Proceedings of the 17th International Conference on Machine Learning* (pp. 1143-1150).

This work was previously published in International Journal of Information Technology and Web Engineering, Vol. 3, Issue 1, edited by G. Alkhatib and D. Rine, pp. 53-69, copyright 2008 by IGI Publishing (an imprint of IGI Global).

Chapter 9
A Graphical User Interface (GUI) Testing Methodology

Zafar Singhera
ZAF Consulting, USA

Ellis Horowitz
University of Southern California, USA

Abad Shah
R & D Center of Computer Science, Pakistan

ABSTRACT

Software testing in general and graphical user interface (GUI) testing in particular is one of the major challenges in the lifecycle of any software system. GUI testing is inherently more difficult than the traditional and command-line interface testing. Some of the factors that make GUI testing different from the traditional software testing and significantly more difficult are: a large number of objects, different look and feel of objects, many parameters associated with each object, progressive disclosure, complex inputs from multiple sources, and graphical outputs. The existing testing techniques for the creation and management of test suites need to be adapted/enhanced for GUIs, and new testing techniques are desired to make the creation and management of test suites more efficient and effective. In this article, a methodology is proposed to create test suites for a GUI. The proposed methodology organizes the testing activity into various levels. The tests created at a particular level can be reused at higher levels. This methodology extends the notion of modularity and reusability to the testing phase. The organization and management of the created test suites resembles closely to the structure of the GUI under test.

INTRODUCTION

Graphical user interfaces (GUI) are an important part of any end-user software application today and can consume significant design, development, and testing activities. As much as half of the source code of a typical user-interaction intensive application can be related to user interfaces (Harold, Gupta, & Soffa, 1993; Horowitz & Singhera, 1993). GUIs provide an easier way of using various functions of the application by organizing them in a hierarchy of options and presenting only the options which make sense in the current working context. GUIs help users concentrate on the problem instead of putting efforts in remembering all the options provided by the software application that is being used to solve the problem, or searching for the right option from a huge list of options provided by the application. Graphical user interfaces organize the standard user actions and working paradigms into various components that are presented graphically to the user during various usage and application contexts. GUIs enhance the usability of an application significantly. However it also makes application development, testing and maintenance significantly more difficult (Myers, 1993; Wittel & Lewis,1991). The nature of GUI applications, their asynchronous mode of operation, nontraditional input and output, and hierarchical structure for user interaction make their testing significantly different and difficult from the traditional software testing.

Functional and regression testing of graphical user interfaces is significantly more complex than testing of traditional non-GUI applications because of the additional complexities mentioned in the previous paragraph. A number of commercial tools, like Mercury Interactive's WinRunner, XRunner and Segue Software's SilkPerformer, are used in the industry to test graphical user interfaces. These tools provide capture/replay capabilities to test a graphical user interface. Although functionality provided by these tools is sufficient for typical recored/replay scenarios but they lack an underlying model that can provide more information about the test coverage or to determine the quality of the user interface from a particular functional or implementation perspective. These tools also do not provide a framework that assists in organized and modular testing. The methodology presented in this article uses user interface graphs (UIG) as a framework for organization of test scripts, generation of modular test suites, and coverage analysis of a test execution.

In this article, we propose a methodology for regression testing of graphical user interfaces, with and without a formal specification of the applica-

tion under test. The remainder of this article is organized as follows: Section 2 highlights some of the best practices and recommendations that help in testing a GUI application in an organized fashion, improve efficiency and effectiveness of testing, reduces possibility of errors, and minimizes repeated work. Section 3 describes the major steps of the proposed methodology. It also introduces a sample X application, called Xman, which is used to demonstrate the effectiveness of the suggested strategy. Section 4 demonstrates the testing methodology when formal specifications of the application under test are not available. Section 5 illustrates the proposed testing methodology when the formal specifications of the application under test are available. This section also describes the way statistics are collected during a testing activity and how those can be used to improve the quality of the testing. Section 6 points out the situations when a modification to the application under test might require tuning or recapturing of some of the test scripts. Section 7 concludes the article by summarizing our contribution and providing hints about the future related work.

GUI TESTING: BEST PRACTICES AND RECOMMENDATIONS

In this section, we highlight some of the sought features, well-knows best practices and recommendations for planning a testing activity for a graphical user interface.

- Every element of the GUI should be considered as an object uniquely identifiable by a name. The objects should have a well-defined set of parameters and their response to the outside events should also be well defined.
- The testing activity should be planned carefully around a formal model of the application under test. This model should be powerful enough to provide automatic test generation and coverage analysis.

- Testing of a GUI should be performed in a layered fashion. The list of objects to be tested at a particular level, is either built dynamically while testing at lower levels or from the specifications of the application under test. The list of objects for the lowest level is the basic widget, supported by the underlying toolkit. While testing the highest level, it considers the entire application as a single object. The decision about the number of testing levels and the qualifying criteria for a particular testing level must be made before creating any tests.

- The tests should be organized as a hierarchy of scripts, that is, files containing commands to simulate user actions and verify results. This hierarchy should closely correspond to the object hierarchy of the application under test. Each directory in the hierarchy holds scripts that are related to a particular object and its descendents. The individual scripts should be as small as possible and should test one particular feature of each object. However, if the features are related and simple, then they can be grouped together in the same script.

- Each script should begin with a cleat and precise description of the intended purpose of the script and the state of the application required for its proper execution. A script should be divided into three sections. The first section of the script builds the environment required to test the particular feature of the application, the script is intended for. The second section of the script tests the intended feature of the application being tested by the script. The third section restores the state of the AUT and the operating environment, to a point that existed before entering the script.

- A script should be created in such a way that some or all the sections of the script can be executed by calling the script from another script. It provides reusability feature in testing also.

- Instead of manually capturing or replaying the test scripts, a tool should be used to perform these functions automatically and verify the behavior of the application under test. The tool should be capable of addressing an object in the GUI by its symbolic name, instead of its location, dimensions or any other contextual information.

- The data for the result verification should be captured in terms of object attributes when possible and only those attributes should be captured which are critical to verify the functions of the application, being tested by the current script. If image comparisons are unavoidable, then the images should be captured with reference to the smallest enclosing object and area of the captured images should not be more than absolutely required. The number of verifications should also be kept to an absolute minimum especially when image comparisons are involved.

- The script commands to simulate user actions during the replay and the data for verification of the AUT behavior should be kept separately. This separation is required because the verification data might change depending on the environment while the script commands should be independent of the environment and should be valid across multiple platforms. If script commands and verification data are stored separately, then it is easier to port a test suite across multiple platforms. In fact, a good tool should automatically perform the porting from one hardware platform to the other.

Proposed Methodology for GUI Testing

This section proposes a methodology for the testing of a graphical user interface (GUI). This proposed methodology is suitable particularly when one has a tool similar to Xtester (Horowitz & Singhera, 1993). It follows the recommendations provided in the previous section. The methodology works in the following two scenarios:

i. Testing without formal specifications/model of the application under test
ii. Testing with a formal model of the application.

Both these scenarios are described in the following subsections.

Testing Without a Formal Model

Creation of formal specifications of a GUI application for its testing purposes is a difficult task and requires a significant amount of effort. It is also not feasible to invest resources in creating the formal specifications of the application; hence the testing has to be performed without it. The best thing that can be done in such a situation is to incrementally build a test hierarchy for the application, by capturing-user sessions in an organized way. Automatic test generation or coverage analysis is not possible without formal specifications of the application under test. The major steps of the proposed methodology to test an application without a specification are given below:

Step 1: Initialization

Make basic decisions about the testing activity. Some of the most important decisions, which must be taken at this point, are:

- The number of testing levels and criteria to build list of objects for a particular level.
- Initialize a list of objects for each level that holds the names and some information about the objects of the user interface. The information includes the way the object can be mapped on the screen, the mechanism to unmap it from the screen, and if it has been tested or not.
- The location of the test suite and its organization.
- The application resources that will be used during this testing activity should be listed.

Step 2: Building the Initial Object List

Go through the documentation of the application under test and find all the top-level windows, which might appear as starting windows of the

Figure 1. Strategy for testing without specifications

```
Display the_ object on the screen and verify its appearance;
If the object has sub-objects
        Add its immediate sub-objects at the top of the list;
If the object qualifies for a higher testing level
Add it to the list of objects for the higher level;
Send expected events to the object and verify its response;
If a new object appears in response to the event
if the new object is not listed as a tested object
        Add it to the end of the list;
        Pop down the object from the screen;


Mark the object in the list as tested;
```

application. These windows and, their related information is added to the list of objects for the first testing level and marked as tested.

Step 3: Building Test Suite

Take the first object from the top of the object list, which has not been tested, and create test scripts for it. The procedure for creating test scripts for a particular object is given in Figure 1. The sub-objects of the object under test are added to the list of objects by scanning the object from left to right and top to bottom. Keep on taking objects from the top of the object list and testing them until all the objects in the list are marked as tested. When the list associated with a particular level has no untested object, start testing objects from the list, associated with the next higher level. This process continues until all the levels are tested.

Step 4: Creating Script Drivers

Write higher level scripts for all the top level windows for any other complex objects, each of the testing levels and for the entire test suite. These scripts will replay all the scripts related to the object and its descendents. The highest-level script driver should replay each and every script in the suite.

Step 5: Testing the Test Suite

Make sure that all the scripts and script drivers work properly and cover all the features of the application, which needs to be tested. One cannot do much automatically to determine the quality of a test suite, in the absence of a formal model of the application under test. After the creation of the test suite, run the highest-level script driver

Figure 2. Main windows of Xman

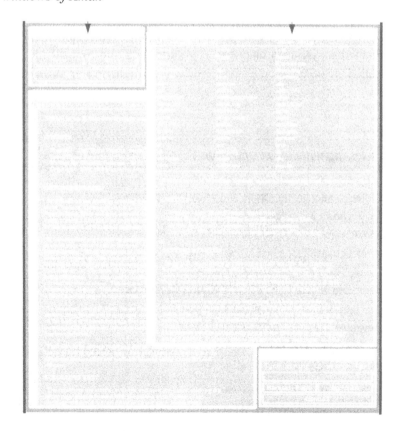

to verify that all the scripts in the suite are capable of properly replaying and trying to match the features covered by the test suite with those included in the test requirements or application documentation

Testing with a Formal Model

The strategy to build test scripts without a formal specification, discussed in the previous subsection, puts a lot of responsibility on the person creating those scripts. The strategy also requires that the application under test should be running reliably before the capturing of script is even started. The scripts created without any formal specification are also vulnerable to any modification in the application, which affects its window hierarchy. It requires that after making any changes to the application under test, the affected scripts should be located manually and recaptured or tuned to offset the modification in the application. It is also not possible to create test scripts automatically or to get a coverage measure after running a set of test suites. To overcome these drawbacks and get access to advanced features like automatic test generation and coverage analysis, one has to invest some effort to formally specify the application under test. This section provides a methodology to test an application when its formal specification is provided or resources are available to build such a specification. The following are the major steps of the testing methodology when a formal specification of an application under test is available.

Step 1: Building the Model

Build a user interface graph of an application under test. When resources permit, the very first step in testing the application should be to build a formal model of the application under test. XTester provides such a formal model, called *user interface graph (UIG)*. UIG provides information about the object hierarchy of the application. It also provides information about the nature of a

particular object and the effects of an event in an object to the other objects in the user interface. A UIG can be built manually by creating a user interface description language (UIDL) file, or it can be created semi-automatically by steering through the application under test and filling in the missing information about the objects (see Horowitz & Singhera, 1993) for more details on syntax of UIDL and UIG).

Step 2: Initialization

Make basic decisions about the testing activity. Some of the most important decisions, which must be taken at this point, are listed as follows:

- The number of testing levels and qualifying criteria for each testing level.
- The location of the test suite and its organization.
- The application resources that will be used during this testing activity.

Step 3: Build Object Lists

Build a list of objects for each testing level. After building the formal model, it is possible to build the object lists for all testing levels. The procedure for building those lists is to start from the root of the UIG and perform a post-order walk of the object hierarchy. Add each visited node to the object lists associated with the levels, for which it qualifies.

Step 4: Building Test Suite

The strategy for capturing scripts without any formal specification, which has been discussed in the previous section, can also be used for capturing scripts when the application has been specified formally. However, capturing scripts with formal specifications provides us some additional advantages over the scripts which have been captured without any specification. These advantages include an overall picture of the application under test, and hence a more efficient test suite, a test suite which is less affected by the changes in the application, automatic test generation, and coverage analysis.

Step 5: Creating Script Drivers

Write higher level scripts for all the top level windows or any other complex objects, each of the testing levels and for the entire test suite. These scripts will replay all the scripts related to the object and its descendents. A highest-level script driver should replay each and every script in the suite. These scripts can also be created automatically.

Step 6: Coverage Analysis

Once a test suite has been created; it should be replayed in its entirety to determine the coverage provided by the test suite. This coverage should be performed at each level, that is, the coverage criteria for level-I should be the verification of all the objects in the application that have been created, mapped, unmapped and destroyed, at least once and every event expected by an object, has been exercised on it at least once. The criteria for higher levels is to make sure that all the interactions and side effects among objects which make a composite object at the corresponding level, has been verified.

AN INTRODUCTION TO XMAN

In this section, we introduce the application Xman, which is used to demonstrate the effectiveness of the methodology, discussed in the previous section. Xman is a small application which is distributed with the standard X release. It provides a graphical user interface to the UNIX *man* utility. It has been developed using the Athena widget set and some of its windows are shown in Figure 1. The following

paragraphs briefly describe the functionality of Xman.

When Xman is started, it displays its main window, called Xman, by default. This main window contains three buttons: Help, Manual Page and Quit. Clicking on the manual page button, it displays a window, called manual page. A Help window is displayed when the help button is clicked. The quit button is used to exit from Xman.

The manual page window is organized into various sections. A breathe top of the window contains two menu buttons, options and sections, in the left half and a message area in the right. The rest of the area below the bar, called text area, is used to display the names of the available manual pages in the currently selected section, and the contents of the currently selected manual page. Both the names and contents portions of the text area are resizable and have vertical scrollbars on the left.

The Options menu contains the following entries:

- **Display Directory:** It displays names of manual pages in the entire text area.
- **Display Manual Page:** It displays contents of the currently selected manual page in the entire text area.
- **Help:** It displays a help window.
- **Search:** It displays a dialog box to enter the name of a manual page to search for.
- To show both screens, the area is vertically divided into two halves, with the upper half showing the directory contents of currently selected man page section and the lower half showing the contents of the currently selected manual page. This option toggles to Show One Screen and also disables menu entries Display Directory and Display Manual Page.
- **Remove This Manpage:** It removes the Manual Page window from the screen.

- **Open New Manpage:** It creates another Manual Page window.
- **Show Version:** It displays the current version of Xman in the Message area
- **Quit:** exits from the Xman application.

The Sections menu contains one option for each manual page section available on the system. The standard options are User Commands, System Calls, Subroutines, Devices, File Format, Games, Miscellaneous, and System Administration.

The Help window displays a limited version of the Manual Page window. The window has exactly the same structure as the Manual Page window but the Sections menu button and the first five options in the Opt ions menu are disabled. It displays man page for Xman itself. No more than one Help window can exist at a time while an arbitrary number of Manual Page windows can be created.

The testing of Xman has been organized in three layers. The first layer verifies the behavior of individual GUI objects. The second layer verifies the inter-object effects among objects belonging to the same top level window. The third layer verifies the inter-object effects among objects belonging to different top level windows. The following sections provide details of this testing activity.

TESTING WITHOUT FORMAL SPECIFICATIONS

This section provides a demonstration for the testing of Xman, when no formal model is available for it. The following subsections demonstrate each step of the methodology, described in Section 2.

Initialization

- **Number of testing levels:** As Xman is a fairly small and simple application, so the

testing activity is organized in three (3) levels. The first level tests the individual objects in Xman. The second and third levels verify the interactions and side effects of the objects which belong to the same top level window and different top level windows, respectively.

- **Location of the test suite:** Suppose that the root directory for the test suite being captured, is Xman Test. This directory contains resource file(s) used during testing, and the result files are created in the directory, by default. It also has three subdirectories, that is, *Level-1*, *Level-2* and *Level-3*, one for each testing level.
- **Object list:** A list of objects, called *Obj List*, is initialized. This list contains information about the objects and is initialized to be empty.
- **Application resources:** ~/XmanTest/Xman. Defaults is the file which contains the default application resources of Xman for this testing activity and these resources always remains the same.

Building the Initial Object List

By default, Xman starts with a top *box,* called Main Window in Figure 2. However, a command line option, -notopbox, is available which can be used to bypass the Main Window and display the Manual Page window directly. As Main Window and Manual Page window are the only windows, which can appear when Xman is started, so the initial object list contains only these two objects.

Building the Test Suite

This section provides the details on building all the three testing levels for Xman. To make things simple, we only discuss the creation of test suites related to the Main Window of Xman. We ignore any keyboard accelerators to which Xman responds. The test suites for other windows can

Figure 3. Test Suite Hierarchy of Xman

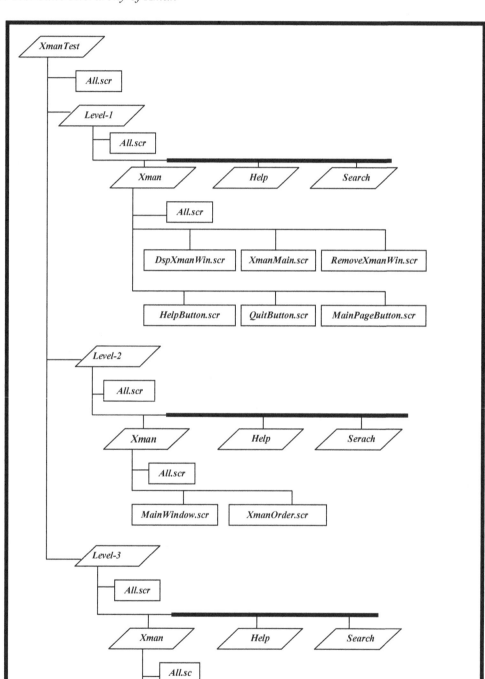

be created in a similar way. Figure 3 provides the hierarchy of scripts related to the Main Window for all the three testing levels.

First Level

Suppose that the initial object list is built in such a way so that Xman **Main Window** is on the top of the list. We select it as the object under test and create a new directory, called ~/**Xman Test/ Leve1-1/Xman** to build test scripts related to the first level testing. The scripts related to XMan Main window object display itself the window on the screen, exercise all the window manager operations on it, and then finally pop-down the window. **DspXmanWin.scr** script pop-up the Xman window and verifies that looks right RemoveXman Win.scr pops down the Xman window. The script XmanMain.scr ruses DspXmanWin.scr in its entering section to display the Xman window. It verifies the window manager operations in its core section and then uses RemoveHelp Win.scr script in its leaving section to pop-down the Xman Window. As soon as the Xman window pops up on the screen, we see that it contains *four* objects, i.e., Manual

Browser Label, Help

There are buttons which are **Quit** and **Manual Page**. **Manual Browser** label is a static piece of text and does not respond to any user actions, so we do not need a script for it. The other three (3) objects are active objects and respond to user events so we create one script for each of them. The entering section of each one of these scripts calls DspXmanWin.scr to display the Xman Main Window on the screen. The ending section of each of these scripts call RemoveXmanwin. scr to remove the Xman Main Window from the screen. The core section of **Help** Button.scr script verifies the behavior of **Help** button in Xman Main Window when it is clicked on by a mouse button. The core sections of **QuitButton.**

scr and **ManPageBut** ton.scr scripts verify the same thing for Qui t and Manual Page buttons in Xman Main Window.

Second Level

The object list of the second level contains all the top level windows of Xman. As we are considering the **Main Window** only in this discussion so we assume that it is at the top of the list and is selected for the testing. There is not much interaction going on in the objects which belong to the Xman **Main Window**. The only interaction is the disappearance of **Main Window**, in response to click on the Quit button. So there will be only one script related to the Main **Window** which will verify that a click on the Quit button actually destroys the Main **Window** of Xman. This script is called **MainWindow.**scr and is located in ~/**XmanTest/ Level2/.** This script is also used DspXmanWin. scr and RemoveXman.scr script to display and remove the Main Window from the screen. Another potential script, let us call it XmanOrder. scr, related to the Main Window verifies that the order in which **Help** or Manual Page buttons are pressed is insignificant. No matter the Help button is pressed before or after the Manual **Page** button, it displays the Help window properly. The same is also true for the Manual Page button.

Third Level

The object list of the third level includes the root object only, and tests any interactions among the top level windows of Xman can be done. Such interactions which involve the Main Window of Xman include display of the Help window and thc Manual Page window in response to mouse clicks on the Help and the Manual page buttons, respectively. Similarly, it also includes disappearance of all the windows related to Xman in response to a click on the Quit button. The three scripts provided at this level, that is, Help.scr, ManualPage.scr and Quit.scr, verify the behavior, related to the corresponding button, mentioned above. This level might also include scripts which verify application behavior, like multiple clicks on the Help button and do not create more than one Help windows while each click on the Manual Page button create a new Manual Page window.

Creating Script Drivers

Once all the scripts for Xman has been captured, we need driver scripts so that all the scripts in the entire suite, all the scripts in a particular testing level or all the scripts related to a particular object can be executed automatically in the desired sequence. For example, we create a script driver, at each testing level, which executes all the scripts created for testing Xman Main Window and its descendents, at that particular level. These scripts are ~/XmanTest/Level-l/Xman/All.scr,-/XmanTest/Level-2/Xman/All. scr, and ~/XmanTest/Level-3/Xman/All. scr, respectively. The script ~/ XmanTest/Level-l/All.scr

drive all the scripts created for the first testing level and similarly the other two drivers execute scripts related to the other two levels. The script ~/XmanTest/All.scr drives all the scripts in all the three levels of the test suite.

Testing the Test Suite

After the creation of the test suite, it is necessary to replay all the scripts in the suite and verify if they work properly and also to make sure that they cover all the features which need to be tested. Although, without a formal specification, it is impossible to perform any reasonable automatic coverage analysis but at least the replayed events and the objects which appear during the replay, can be matched against application documentation to determine if any object or event has not been covered by the generated test suite.

Figure 4. User interface graph built for Xman

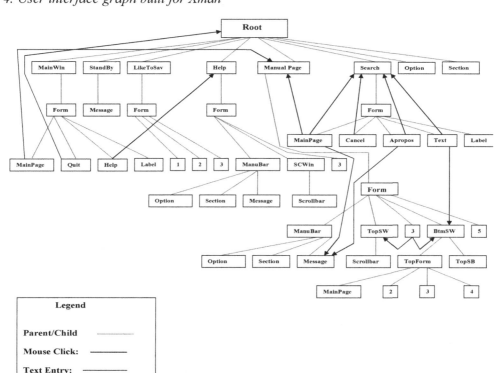

TESTING WITH FORMAL SPECIFICATIONS

This section demonstrates the testing of Xman when we have enough resources to build a formal model for Xman. The following subsection illustrates each step of the methodology, described in Section 2.2.

Building the Model

When the resources permit, the first step for testing is building a formal model for the application under test. Figure 4 displays a User Interface Graph built for Xman. The Root node of the graph represents the root window of the screen. The children of the Root node represent the six top level windows of Xman. The nodes at lower levels in the graph represent the descendents of the top level windows. Let us take the main window of Xman as an example. It is represented as MainWin node in the User Interface Graph. The child of the MainWin node is the Form node which acts as a container widget for the buttons and the label in the main window. The ManPage, Quit and Help nodes represent the Manual. Page, Quit and Help command buttons in the main window, respectively. The label node represents the Manual Browser label in the main window. The dark black arc from the Manpage noqe to the Manual Page node represents the fact that clicking a mouse button over the Manpage button in the main window affects the top level window, called Manual Page. The arc from the Quit node to the Root node represents that a click on the Quit button affects all the top level windows of Xman. The type of event represented by an arc is reflected by the drawing pattern of the arc. The two arcs mentioned above have the same pattern and represent button clicks. An arc with a different pattern is the arc from the Text node to the search node. This pattern represents text entry and the arc represents that entering text in the Text node affect the search dialog box.

Initialization

All the decision and actions taken at the initialization step, that is, the number of testing levels and their organization, the location of the test suite and the application default resources, is kept the same as for testing without a formal specification, described in Section 4.1.

Building Object Lists

After building the user interface graph for Xman, it is possible to build object lists for all levels of testing. This can be done either manually or automatically by scanning each and every node in the User Interface Graph and verifying if it qualifies to be tested on a particular testing level. All the objects in Xman qualify for the first testing level and hence are placed on the list associated with it. The qualifying criterion for the second level is that the object must be a top level window, that is, its corresponding node must be a child of the root of the user interface graph. Some of the objects which qualify for the second testing level are Xman Main Window, Manual Page window, Help window, Search dialog box and so forth. The third level treats the entire Xman application as a single object, and its corresponding node, the root, is the only object which qualifies for the third level of testing.

Building Test Suite

The strategy for capturing scripts without any formal specifications, discussed in Section 4.3, can be used for capturing scripts when the application has been specified formally. However, capturing scripts with formal specifications also provides us the capability to write the test scripts manually or generate test scripts automatically by using the formal model and the test requirements. All of these three techniques for building a test suite are explained in the following section.

Capturing Scripts

A tool can be used for capturing user sessions for building a test suite, in exactly the same way as for capturing without a formal model, as mentioned in Section 4.3. However, the presence of a formal model makes the generated scripts more robust and easy to follow and debug. A formal model also provides the flexibility that the captured scripts can be executed in any order without any conflict in window names. It becomes easier to modify the test suite in case of a modification to the application under test. In fact in most cases the modification can be reflected in the specification file and the test suite remains valid without making any changes.

Writing Scripts Manually

The formal specifications of the application, under test, also allows the user to write scripts manually, even for the first level of testing. This feature is particularly helpful when the test scripts need to be created in parallel with the application development in order to reduce the total development time. The way it can be organized is to formally specify the graphical user interface of the application once the design is complete. The developers and testers agree on this formal specification and any future changes are properly communicated between the two groups. Having the formal specification of the graphical user interface at hand, the testers can develop the scripts manually in parallel with the application development. Once the object hierarchy and the behavior of the objects is known, the manual writing of test scripts is as easy as writing a UNIX shell script.

Automatic Test Generation

The formal specifications of an application under test also provide capabilities to generate test scripts automatically. A tool can be developed, which will read the specifications of an application and create test scripts for a particular level of testing or the entire test suite. Similar tools can be developed and used to generate test scripts to test all the objects of a particular type or all the user actions of a particular type. For example, such a tool can generate test scripts to exercise clicks on each command button in an entire application. A similar tool can generate a suite of test scripts to verify that all windows in an application under test are displayed on the screen at least once. Another tool might generate scripts to individually select all the options of each menu in the application and verify that the application responds in the expected manner. There can be another tool that will create scripts for the selection of multiple menu options and/or command buttons in different sequences to verify the application response. All the mentioned tools will only create scripts and validation data that have to be captured by replaying these scripts and by using **caprep** (Horowitz & Singhera, 1993) or a similar tool to replay these scripts in **Update** mode.

The logic behind these automatic test generation tools is the same as it is used in Section 5 for manual creation of test suites. The tool starts at the root of the UIG and builds a list of GUI elements by performing a pre-order walk of the UIG. During this walk only the arcs that represent parent-child relationships are considered. After building this list, its entries are taken one by one to create test scripts for them. If the current GUI element, taken from the list, is a top-level window, then a separate directory is created for it and the scripts for the element and all of its descendents are created in that directory. If the currently selected element belongs to the category for which a script is required, then following the arcs that represent user actions on the element creates one. Figure 4 shows the pseudo code for such an automatic test generator.

Coverage Analysis

No testing activity is useful unless it provides some coverage measures/analysis. This cover-

Figure 5. Pseudo code for automatic test generator

```
Build the User Interface Graph of the application under
test;
Build an object list by a pre-order traversal of the User
Interface Graph using parent-child relationship arcs.
for each "element on the list
do
    If the element is a top level window
        Create a new directory and change to the
      directory.
        Display the element on the screen.
    fi
    if the element accepts any user events
        Create a script for the element
        for each kind of user event accepted by the
    element
        do
            Add commands in script to
                Generate the event on the element;
                Verify the effect of that event;
                Undo the effect of the event;

            done
    fi
done
```

age measure reflects the quality of the testing activity. The UIG provides us with a framework to determine such a coverage. During capture or replay of scripts, XTester keeps track of the user actions and their effects on individual objects. This information is available in a .stt file at the end of the testing activity. Currently, the information captured in .stt about a particular object includes the number of times it was created, mapped, unmapped, and destroyed. It also accumulates the number of times a mouse button or keyboard key was pressed or released over the object. This information helps the user to locate any particular objects in the application which have not been created, destroyed, mapped, unmapped, or received a user event. These statistics can also be used for improving the efficiency of the test suite by removing the repetitive testing of the same characteristics, whenever possible. Figure 6 shows a file created by XTester after replaying a certain

test suite for Xman. The legend is displayed at the top of the file to describe acronyms for various actions. The next line after the legend provides the heading for the table. Each line in the table provides statistics about a particular object. For example, the very first line of the table provides statistics about the Main Window of Xman, named Xman. This particular line shows that the object named Xman was created once, never destroyed, mapped twice on the screen and unmapped once, by the corresponding test script. It also shows that the corresponding test suite never exercised a button press/release or key press/release events on the Xman object.

Tools can be developed to extract information from a .stt file. Analysis tools are developed that take a .uidl file to build a UIG of the application under test, and a .stt file to get statistics collected from a particular test run. The tool maps the collected statistics on to the object hierarchy and produces an annotated graph. Queries can be run on this annotated graph to determine the effectiveness of the test suite. For example, one can see how many nodes and arcs in the object hierarchy have not been exercised by this particular test suite, or see the objects and inter-object arcs to determine objects that did not receive an expected user action. Similarly, one can filter out the objects that did not receive an expected user event to create an annotated graph that satisfies a particular criterion.

INVALIDATION OF TEST DATA

XTester captures information as two entities, script commands and verification data and saves them in different files, .scr and .img, respectively. This section describes the scenario in which created test script(s) might fail and has to be re-captured or re-written. The following scenarios invalidate some of the captured scripts:

- An application is modified in such a way that WM _NAME property of a top-level window is changed. This modification will only affect the scripts that have been captured without a specification and are related to the window whose WM _NAME property was changed. The scripts captured with a formal specification remain unaffected, provided the relevant specifications are also modified to reflect the change in the application.
- The application is changed so that the order or number of children of a particular node is changed. The scripts that are captured without a specification and address objects in the modified hierarchy, are affected and have to be recaptured or tuned. However, the scripts captured with a formal specification remain unaffected provided the specification is also modified accordingly. XTester provides option to build either full or short object names. If the application is modified so that the depth of a hierarchy is

changed, then all the fully qualified names belonging to that hierarchy will no longer be valid names and has to be modified to reflect the change. However, short names that are relative to their immediate parents will still remain valid.

- If object information has been captured as an image, then trying to replay the scripts on another workstation that is incompatible with the workstation on which image was captured will give false alarms. The scripts work fine across multiple platforms, however, verification data is the platform specific in case of images. An easier way of creating verification data for a new hardware platform will be to replay all the scripts in Update mode that replaces the current verification data with the newly available one.

CONCLUSION AND FUTURE DIRECTIONS

In this article, we have suggested guidelines that are useful in planning a testing activity for a graphical user interface (GUI). We have also presented a methodology for testing a GUI, both when specifications of an application under test is not available, and when such specifications are provided or resource code is available to build such a specification. This article also demonstrates the use of the proposed methodology to test a sample X application, Xman, with or without specifications. It also illustrates how the model is helpful in automatic test generation and coverage analysis. In the end, we describe the situations in which the scripts captured by XTester become invalid.

The methodology and the underlying UIG framework discussed in this article can be very effectively used to model and test web sites and web applications. We are actively working to extend this proposed methodology to be used for testing web-based applications and semantic web applications.

Figure 6. Statistics file created by XTester

```
Legend:
CW=Create Window DW=Destroy Window MW=Map Window
UMW=Unmap Window BP=Button Press BR=Button Release
KP=Key Press KR=Key Release
  Object Name               CW DW MW UMWBP BR    KP KR
Xman :                      1   0  2  1  0   0    0  0
Xman*Form :                 1   0  2  1  0   0    0  0
Xman*ManualPage :           1   0  2  1  50  50   0  0
Xman*Quit :                 1   0  2  1  0   0    0  0
Xman*Help :                 1   0  2  1  10  10   0  0
Xman*Label :                1   0  2  1  0   0    0  0
StandBy :                   28  23 2  1  0   0    0  0
StandBy*Message :           28  23 2  1  0   0    0  0
LikeToSave :                1   0  0  0  0   0    0  0
LikeToSave*Form :           1   0  0  0  0   0    0  0
LikeToSave*Message :        1   Q  0  0  0   0    0  0
LikeToSave*Yes :            1   0  0  0  0   0    0  0
LikeToSave*No :             1   0  0  0  0   0    0  0
Help :                      1   0  7  7  0   0    0  0
Help*Form :                 1   0  7  7  0   0    0  0
Help*MenuBar :              1   0  7  7  0   0    0  0
Help*Options :              1   0  7  7  20  2    0  0
Help*Seetions :             1   0  7  7  0   0    0  0
Help*Message :              1   0  7  7  0   0    0  0
Help*TextArea :             1   0  7  7  0   0    0  0
Help*Serollbar :            1   0  7  7  10  10   0  0
Help. Form. 3 :             1   0  7  7  0   0    0  0
Manpage :                   27  23 27 1  0   0    0  0
ManPage*Form :              27  23 27 1  0   0    0  0
ManPage*MenuBar :           27  23 27 1  0   0    0  0
ManPage*Options :           27  23 27 1  92  6    0  0
ManPage*Seetions :          27  23 27 1  18  2    0  0
Manpage*Message :           27  23 27 1  0   0    0  0
ManPage*TextArea :          27  23 27 1  0   0    0  0
ManPage*Serollbar :         27  23 27 1  8   8    0  0
ManPage.Form.3 :            27  23 27 1  0   0    0  0
ManPage*DirArea :           27  23 27 1  0   0    0  0
ManPage*DirList :           27  23 27 1  0   0    0  0
ManPage*List :              27  23 27 1  0   0    0  0
```

REFERENCES

Berstel, J., Reghizzi, S. C., Roussel, G., & San Pietro, P. (2001). A scalable formal method for design and automatic checking of user interfaces. *In Proceedings of the 23rd International Conference on Software Engineering*, (pp. 453-462).

Campos J., & Harrison, M. (2001). Model checking interactor specifications. *Automated Software Engineering, 3*(8), 275-310.

Gamma, E., Helm, R., Johnson, R., & Vlissides, J. (1995). *Design patterns*. Addison Wesley Publishers.

Horowitz, E.& Singhera, Z. (1993). Graphical user interface testing. *In proceedings of the Eleventh Annual Pacific Northwest Software Quality Conference.*

Horowitz, E.& Singhera, Z. (1993). XTester – A System for Testing X Applications. *Technical Report No. USC-CS-93-549*, Department of Computer Science, University of Southern California, Los Angeles, CA.

Horowitz, E. & Singhera, Z. (1993). A Graphical User Interface Testing Methodology. *Technical Report No. USC-CS-93-550,* Department of Computer Science, University of Southern California, Los Angeles, CA.

Harold, M. J., Gupta, R., & Soffa, M. L. (1993). A methodology for controlling the size of a test suite. *ACM Transactions on Software Engineering and Methodology, 2*(3), 270-285.

Mercury Interactive, Mountain View, CA., http://www.mercury.com

Myers, B. A. (1993). Why are human-computer interfaces difficult to design and implement?

Technical Report CS-93-183, Carnegie Mellon University, School of Computer Science.

Myers, B. A., Olsen, D. R., Jr., & Bonar, J. G. (1993). User interface tools. In proceedings of ACM INTERCHI'93 Conference on Human Factors in Computing Systems, Adjunct Proceedings, Tutorials, (p. 239).

Sommervill, I. (2001). *Software engineering* (6th ed.) Addison Wesley Publishers.

Segue Software Inc., Newton, MA, http://www.segue.com

Wittel, W. I., Jr. & Lewis, T. G. (1991). Integrating the mvc paradigm into an object-oriented framework to accelerate gui application development. *Technical Report 91-60-D6,* Department of Computer Science, Oregon State University.

This work was previously published in International Journal of Information Technology and Web Engineering, Vol. 3, Issue 2, edited by G. Alkhatib and D. Rine, pp. 1-18, copyright 2008 by IGI Publishing (an imprint of IGI Global).

Chapter 10
Experiences with Software Architecture Analysis of Usability

Eelke Folmer
University of Nevada - Reno, USA

Jan Bosch
Intuit Inc. - Mountain View, USA

ABSTRACT

Software engineers and human computer interaction engineers have come to the understanding that usability is not something that can be "added" to a software product during late stage, since to a certain extent it is determined and restricted by architecture design. Cost effectively developing a usable system must include developing an architecture, which supports usability. Because software engineers in industry lacked support for the early evaluation of usability, we defined a generalized four-step method for software architecture level usability analysis called SALUTA. In this article, we report on a number of experiences and problems we observed when performing architecture analysis of usability at three industrial case studies performed in the domain of Web-based enterprise systems. Suggestions or solutions are provided for solving or avoiding these problems so organizations facing similar problems may learn from our experiences.

INTRODUCTION

A key problem facing software engineers today is meeting quality requirements, such as maintainability, reliability, and performance. Quality is not something that can be "added" to a software product during late stage, since to a certain ex-

tent it is determined and restricted by *software architecture* design (Bosch, 2000), that is, the fundamental organization of a system embodied in its components, their relationships to each other, and to the environment and the principles guiding its design and evolution (IEEE, 1998). Significantly improving the quality of a software system often requires major changes to the software architecture. For example, using layers (Buschmann, Meunier, Rohnert, Sommerlad, & Stal, 1996) may improve maintainability, but requires a significant amount of restructuring if imposed upon an existing software design and puts restrictions on how components can access each other.

A complicating problem is that most of these qualities can only be measured during deployment. In addition, trying to restructure the architecture during late stage is prohibitively expensive as it affects large parts of the existing source code. The problem boils down to making sure your initial architecture design supports the right amount of quality, since fixing it during the later stages of development is expensive. Software architects have been aware of these constraints and much research effort has been put into the development of architecture analysis methods. A number of methods (see related work section) have been developed, allowing an architect to predict the support for maintainability, performance, or reliability for any given architecture design.

A quality that has previously largely been ignored by software engineers—but which is increasingly recognized as one of the most important qualities—is usability. Providing interaction different from how the user would expect it or requires it is usually detrimental to the commercial success of any software application. Similar to other qualities, usability is restricted by software architecture design. The quintessential example used to illustrate this restriction is adding undo to an application. Undo allows you to reverse actions (such as reversing making a text bold in Word). Undo improves usability as it allows a user to explore, make mistakes, and easily go some steps back; facilitating learning the application's functionality. Experiences with implementing undo to an existing application show that it is very expensive to do since implementations of undo are usually based upon the command pattern (Gamma, Helm, Johnson, & Vlissides,

1995). Similar to using the layers pattern, this requires some significant restructuring and is expensive to retrofit into an existing software design. Several other usability features such as user profiles, visual consistency, and actions for multiple objects have also proven (Bass, Kates, & John, 2001; Folmer, Gurp, & Bosch, 2003) to be architecture "sensitive."

Studies (Pressman, 1992; Landauer, 1995) reveal that a significant large part of the maintenance costs of software systems is spent on dealing with usability issues and we have reason to believe that part of these costs are explained by making expensive changes to an architecture design to support particular usability features. In order to be able to cost effectively develop a usable application we need to make sure that our software architecture design can support such usability features. Yet few software engineers and human computer interaction engineers are aware of this constraint and as a result avoidable rework is frequently necessary.

In order to improve upon this situation we first captured the relevant design knowledge. In Folmer et al. (2003) we describe the software-architecture-usability (SAU) framework, which identifies a number of usability features that are hard to retrofit. Next we developed a method providing architects with a number of steps for performing architecture analysis of usability. In Folmer and Bosch (2002) we provide an overview of usability evaluation techniques. Unfortunately, no architecture assessment techniques have been identified which focus on usability. Based upon successful experiences (Lassing, Bengtsson, van Vliet, & Bosch, 2002) with scenario based assessment of maintainability, we developed a scenario based architecture level usability assessment technique (SALUTA) (Folmer, Gurp, & Bosch, 2004). A number of case studies have been performed with SALUTA to refine it.

This article reports upon a number of experiences and problems encountered when performing architecture analysis of usability. Suggestions are provided for solving or avoiding these problems so organizations that want to conduct architecture analysis facing similar problems may learn from our experiences.

RESEARCH METHODOLOGY

Research in software engineering is fundamentally different from research in other fields of (computer) science. The problem domain of software engineering is that of improving the practice of software manufacturing. Solutions to such problems can be tools, techniques, or methodologies. This context puts limitations on how research can be performed:

- An industrial setting offers little opportunity for established research methods such as experiments.
- Many factors are involved in the success or failure of a software project; making it difficult to model.
- A solution addressing a technical factor sometimes affects the software engineering process; a solution must fit in the overall context of business, organization, process, and organization and must be accepted by the developers.

Many sciences have well-defined research strategies providing guidance on how to perform research, however, software engineering is still a comparatively young discipline, therefore it does not have this sort of well-understood guidance (Shaw, 2002) yet. Researchers in software engineering therefore rely on research methods that have emerged from empirical sciences such as sociology and psychology. In this article, we rely on:

- **Case studies:** for providing us with examples for developing theories and for validating our approaches.

- **Action research:** an applied research strategy (Robson, 1993) which involves cycles of data collection; evaluation, and reflection with the aim of improving the quality or performance of an organization.

In our case, assessing software architectures for usability, no prior research had been conducted, therefore case studies and action research fit well within the flexible "explorative" qualitative research strategy that we adopt. This paper describes experiences with performing software architecture analysis of usability in three cases. Three case studies were performed—rather then relying on a single case study—to make the results more generalizable and avoid the risk of inferring too much from what might be circumstance (Robson, 1993). As an input to the three case studies, we interviewed the software architects and several other individuals involved in the development of these systems. While performing case studies our architecture assessment technique was gradually adjusted and refined based upon input from these individuals.

RELATED WORK

Many authors (Shackel, 1991; Nielsen, 1993; Hix & Hartson, 1993; Preece, Rogers, Sharp, Benyon, Holland, & Carey, 1994; Wixon & Wilson, 1997; Shneiderman, 1998; Constantine & Lockwood, 1999; ISO 9126-1) have studied usability. Most of these authors focus on finding and defining the optimal set of attributes that compose usability and on developing guidelines and heuristics for improving and testing usability. Several techniques such as usability testing (Nielsen, 1993), usability inspection (Nielsen, 1994), and usability inquiry (Nielsen, 1993) may be used to evaluate the usability of systems. However, none of these techniques focuses on the essential relation with software architecture.

Nigay and Coutaz (1997) discuss a relationship between usability and software architecture by presenting an architectural model that can help a designer satisfy ergonomic properties. Bass et al. (2001) give several examples of architectural patterns that may aid usability. Previous work has been done in the area of usability patterns, by Tidwell (1998), Perzel and Kane (1999), and Welie and Trætteberg (2000). For defining the SAU framework we used as much as possible usability patterns and design principles that where already defined and accepted in HCI literature and verified the architectural-sensitivity with the industrial case studies we conducted. The framework based approach for usability is similar to the work done on quality attribute characterizations (Bass, Clements, & Kazman, 2003) in Folmer et al. (2003) the most important differences between their approach and ours are outlined.

The software architecture analysis method (SAAM) (Kazman, Abowd, & Webb, 1994) was among the first to address the assessment of software architectures. SAAM is stakeholder centric and does not focus on a specific quality attribute. From SAAM, ATAM (Kazman, Klein, & Clements, 2000) has evolved. ATAM also uses scenarios for identifying important quality attribute requirements for the system. Like SAAM, ATAM does not focus on a single quality attribute but rather on identifying tradeoffs between quality attributes. Some specific quality-attribute assessment techniques have been developed. In Alonso, Garcia-Valls, & de la Puente (1998) an approach to assess the timing properties of software architectures is discussed using a global rate-monotonic analysis model. The software architecture analysis method for evolution and reusability (SAAMER) (Lung, Bot, Kaleichelvan, & Kazman, 1997) is an extension to SAAM and addresses quality attributes such as maintainability, modifiability, and reusability. In Bengtsson and Bosch (1999) a scenario based architecture-level modifiability analysis (ALMA) method is proposed.

We use scenarios for specification of quality requirements. There are different ways to interpret the concept of a scenario. In object oriented

modeling techniques, a scenario generally refers to use case scenarios: scenarios that describe system behavior. The 4+1 view (Kruchten, 1995) uses scenarios for binding the four views together. In human computer interaction, use cases are a recognized form of task descriptions focusing on user-system interactions. We define scenarios with a similar purpose namely to user-system interaction that reflect the usage of the system but we annotate it in such a way that it describes the required usability of the system.

THE SAU FRAMEWORK

Before we can assess an architecture for its support of usability we need to know how architecture design exactly affects usability. A software architecture allows for early assessment of quality attributes (Kazman, Klein, Barbacci, Longstaff, Lipson, & Carriere, 1998; Bosch, 2000). Specific relationships between software architecture entities (such as - styles, -patterns, -fragments, etc.) and software quality (maintainability, reliability, and efficiency) have been described by several authors (Gamma et al., 1995; Buschmann et al, 1996; Bosch, 2000). Until recently (Bass et al., 2001; Folmer et al., 2003) such relationships between usability and software architecture had not been described nor investigated. In Folmer et al. (2003) we defined the SAU framework that expresses specific relationships between software architecture and usability. The SAU framework consists of an integrated set of design solutions, such as undo or user profiles, that have been identified in various cases in industry, modern day software, and literature surveys (Folmer & Bosch, 2002). These solutions are typically considered to improve usability but have been identified to be hard to retro-fit into applications because they require architectural support. Architectural support implies:

- Structural impact: These solutions are often implemented as new architectural entities (such as components, layers, objects, etc.) and relations between these entities or an extension of old architectural entities. Implementations of undo are usually based upon the command pattern (Gamma et al., 1995). If a software architecture is already implemented then changing or adding new entities to this structure during late stage design is likely to affect many parts of the existing source code.

- Architectural support: Some solutions such as providing visual consistency do not necessarily require an extension or restructuring of the architecture. It is possible to implement these otherwise for example by imposing a design rule on a software system that requires each window to be visually consistent (which is a solution that works if you only have a few windows). However, this is not the most optimal solution; visual consistency, for example, may be easily facilitated by the use of a separation-of-data-from-presentation mechanism such as XML and XSLT (a style sheet language for transforming XML documents). A template can be defined that is used by all screens when the layout of windows needs to be modified, only the template should be changed. In this case the best solution is also driven by other qualities such as the need to be able to modify windows (modifiability).

For each of these design solutions we analyzed the effect on usability and the potential architectural implications. The SAU framework consists of the following concepts:

Usability Attributes

If we want to be able to improve usability we first need to be able to measure usability; therefore the first step in investigating the relationship was to decompose usability into smaller measurable components, for example, usability attributes. A number attributes have been selected from literature that appear to form the most common denominator of existing notions of usability (Shackel, 1991; Nielsen, 1993; Hix & Hartson, 1993; Preece et al., 1994; Wixon & Wilson, 1997; Shneiderman, 1998; Constantine & Lockwood, 1999):

- Learnability—how quickly and easily users can begin to do productive work with a system that is new to them, combined with the ease of remembering the way a system must be operated.
- Efficiency of use—the number of tasks per unit time that the user can perform using the system.
- Reliability in use—the error rate in using the system and the time it takes to recover from errors.
- Satisfaction—the subjective opinions that users form when using the system.

Usability Properties

The next step involves being able to design for usability by following certain heuristics and design principles that researchers in the usability field have found to have a direct positive influence on usability, a set of usability properties have been identified from literature (Rubinstein & Hersh, 1984; Norman, 1988; Ravden & Johnson, 1989; Polson & Lewis, 1990; Holcomb & Tharp, 1991; Nielsen, 1993; Hix & Hartson, 1993; ISO 9241-11; Shneiderman, 1998; Constantine & Lockwood, 1999). Properties are high-level design primitives that have a known effect on usability and typically have some architectural implications. Properties are not the same as attributes. Attributes are used to *measure* the level of usability, for example, time to perform a particular task is an indicator for the efficiency attribute, whereas a property will guide in *designing* a more usable application;

something like "error management" may help the user recover from errors quicker speeding up the efficiency attribute. The usability property consistency is presented in Table 1.

ARCHITECTURE SENSITIVE USABILITY PATTERNS

The third step involves identifying those design solutions that need to be applied during the design of a system's software architecture, rather than during the detailed design stage. We identified a number of solutions and described them as interaction design patterns. Patterns and pattern languages for describing patterns are ways to describe best practices, good designs, and capture experience in a way that it is possible for others to reuse this experience. Each pattern is a three-part rule, which expresses a relation between a certain context, a problem, and a solution and usually a rationale is also provided. Patterns originated as an architectural concept by Christopher Alexander (Alexander, 1977), but patterns in software became popular with the "Gang of four" design patterns book (Gamma et al., 1995). Since then, a pattern community has emerged that has specified patterns for all sorts of domains including interaction design. An interaction design pattern describes

a repeatable solution to a commonly occurring usability problem. Our set of patterns has been identified from various cases in industry, modern software, literature surveys (Shackel, 1991; Nielsen, 1993; Hix & Hartson, 1993; Preece et al., 1994; Wixon & Wilson, 1997; Shneiderman, 1998; Constantine & Lockwood, 1999) as well as from existing usability pattern collections (Tidwell, 1998; Brighton, 1998; Welie & Trætteberg, 2000; PoInter, 2003).

With our set of patterns, we have concentrated on capturing the architectural considerations that must be taken into account when deciding to implement the pattern. For some patterns we do provide generic implementation details in terms objects or classes or small application frameworks that are needed for implementing the pattern. An excerpt of the multilevel undo pattern is shown in table 2.

Relationships in the SAU Framework

Relationships, typically positive, have been defined between the elements of the framework that link architecturally sensitive usability patterns to usability properties and attributes. For example, a wizard needs a particular architecture configuration. It also improves usability because it positively affects guidance which on its term

Table 1. Consistency

Intent:	Users should not have to wonder whether different words, situations, or actions mean the same thing. Consistency might be provided in different ways: • *Visual consistency*: user interface elements should be consistent in aspect and structure. • *Functional consistency*: the way to perform different tasks across the system should be consistent, also with other similar systems, and even between different kinds of applications in the same system. • *Evolutionary consistency*: products should be consistent with regard to functionality & visuals with regard to earlier versions.
Usability attributes affected:	+ **Learnability**: consistency makes learning easier because concepts and actions have to be learned only once, because next time the same concept or action is faced in another part of the application, it is familiar. + **Reliability**: visual consistency increases perceived stability, which increases user confidence in different new environments.
Example:	Most applications for MS Windows conform to standards and conventions with respect to, for example, menu layout (file, edit, view, ..., help) and key-bindings.

Table 2. Multi-level undo

Problem	Users do actions they later want reversed because they realized they made a mistake or because they changed their mind.
Use when	You are designing a desktop or Web-based application where users can manage information or create new artifacts. Typically, such systems include editors, financial systems, graphical drawing packages, or development environments. Such systems deal mostly with their own data and produce only few non-reversible side-effects, like sending of an e-mail within an e-mail application. Undo is not suitable for systems where the majority of actions is not reversible, for example, workflow management systems or transaction systems in general.
Solution	**Maintain a list of user actions and allow users to reverse selected actions.** Each "action" the user does is recorded and added to a list. This list then becomes the "history of user actions" and users can reverse actions from the last done action to the first one recorded.
Why	Offering the possibility to always undo actions gives users a comforting feeling. It helps the users feel that they are in control of the interaction rather than the other way around. They can explore, make mistakes, and easily go some steps back, which facilitate learning the application's functionality. It also often eliminates the need for annoying warning messages since most actions will not be permanent.
Architectural Considerations	There are basically two possible approaches to implementing undo. The first is to capture the entire state of the system after each user action. The second is to capture only relative changes to the system's state. The first option is obviously needlessly expensive in terms of memory usage and the second option is therefore the one that is commonly used. Since changes are the result of an action, the implementation is based on using command objects that are then put on a stack. Each specific command is a specialized instance of an abstract class command. Consequently, the entire user-accessible functionality of the application must be written using command objects. When introducing undo in an application that does not already use command objects, it can mean that several hundred command objects must be written. Therefore, introducing undo is considered to have a high impact on the software architecture.
Implementation	Most implementations of multi-level undo are based on the <u>command</u> (Gamma et al., 1995) pattern. When using the command pattern, most functionality is encapsulated in command objects rather than in other controlling classes. The idea is to have a base class that defines a method to "do" a command, and another method to "undo" a command. Then, for each command, you derive from the command base class and fill in the code for the do and undo methods. The "do" method is expected to store any information needed to "undo" the command. For example, the command to delete an item would remember the content of the item being deleted. The following class diagram shows the basic Command pattern structure: In order to create a multi-level undo, a command stack is introduced. When a new command is created, its "do" function is called and the object is added to the top of the stack if the command was successful. When undoing commands, the "undo" function of the command object at the top of the stack is called and the pointer to the current command is set back.

improves learnability and efficiency. These relationships have been derived from our literature survey (Folmer et al., 2003) and industrial experiences. Defining relationships between the elements serves two purposes:

- Inform design: The usability properties in the framework may be used as requirements during design. For example, if a requirement specifies, "the system must provide feedback," we use the framework to identify which usability patterns should be considered during architecture design by following the arrows in Figure 2.

• Architecture analysis: The relationships are then used to analyze how particular patterns and properties that have been implemented in the architecture, support usability. For example, if undo has been implemented we can analyze that undo improves efficiency and reliability.

SALUTA uses the SAU framework for analyzing the architecture's support for usability. A complete overview and description of all patterns and properties and the relationships between them can be found in Folmer et al. (2003).

Figure 1. Example relationship between attributes, properties, and patterns

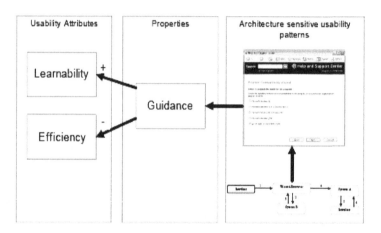

Figure 2. Relationships between attributes, properties, and patterns

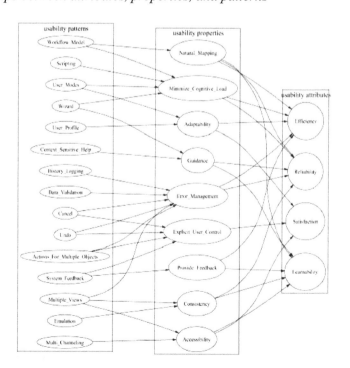

Figure 3. Example usage scenario

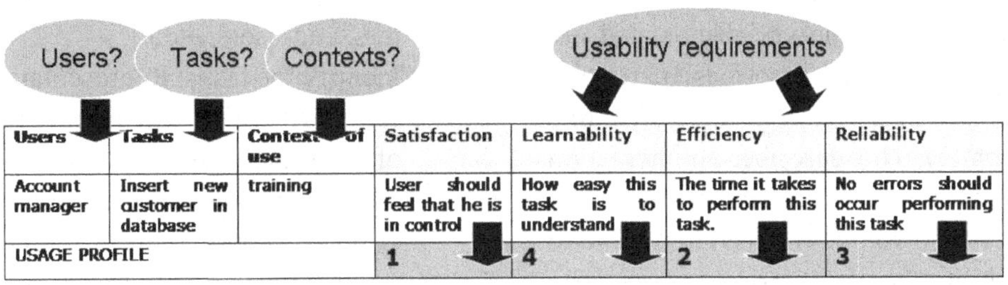

OVERVIEW OF SALUTA

In Folmer et al. (2004) the SALUTA method is presented. SALUTA is scenario based, that is, in order to assess a particular architecture, a set of scenarios is developed that concretizes the actual meaning of that quality requirement (Bosch, 2000). Although there are other types of architecture assessment techniques such as metrics, simulations, and mathematical models (Bosch, 2000) in our experience with scenario based analysis, we have come to understanding that the use of scenarios allows us to make a very concrete and detailed analysis and statements about their impact or support they require. SALUTA has been derived from scenario based assessment techniques such as ALMA (Bengtsson, 2002), SAAM (Kazman et al., 1994), ATAM (Kazman et al., 1998), and QASAR (Bosch, 2000). Although it is possible to use a generic scenario based assessment technique such as ATAM or QASAR, a specialized technique (such as ALMA) usually provides guidelines and criteria for creating specific scenarios and may lead to more accurate assessment results. To assess the architecture, a set of *usage scenarios* are defined. By analyzing the architecture for its support of each of these usage scenarios, we determine the architecture's support for usability. SALUTA consists of the following four steps:

1. Create usage profile; describe required usability.

2. Analyze the software architecture: describe provided usability.

3. Scenario evaluation: determine the architecture's support for the usage scenarios, for example, compare the provided with the required usability.

4. Interpret the results: draw conclusions from the analysis results.

A brief overview of the steps is given in the next subsections, a more detailed elaboration of and motivation for these steps can be found in Folmer et al, (2004).

Usage Profile Creation

Existing usability specification techniques (Nielsen, 1993; Hix & Hartson, 1993; Preece et al., 1994) are poorly suited for architectural assessment (Folmer et al., 2004), therefore a scenario profile (Lassing et al., 2002; Bengtsson, 2002) based approach was chosen. Usability is not an intrinsic quality of the system. According to the ISO definition (ISO 9241-11), usability depends on:

- The users (e.g., system administrators, novice users).
- The tasks (e.g., insert order, search for item X).
- The contexts of use (e.g., helpdesk, training environment).

Usability may also depend on other variables, such as goals of use, and so forth. However, in a usage scenario only the variables stated are included. A usage scenario describes a particular *interaction (task)* of a *user* with the system in a particular *context*. This describes an interaction and not a particular level of usability that needs to be provided. To do that we need to be able to measure usability, therefore we relate our scenario to the four usability attributes defined in the SAU-framework. For each usage scenario, numeric values are determined for each of these usability attributes to determine a prioritization between the usability attributes. For some usability attributes, such as efficiency and learnability, tradeoffs have to be made during design. It is often impossible to design a system that has high scores on all attributes. A purpose of usability requirements is therefore to specify a necessary level for each attribute (Lauesen & Younessi, 1998). For example, if for a particular usage scenario learnability is considered to be of more importance than other attributes (e.g., because a requirement specifies it), then the usage scenario must reflect this difference in the priorities for the usability attributes. Quantitative values will make it easier for the analyst to determine the level of support the architecture provides for that particular scenario. An example usage scenario is displayed in Figure 3.

Usage profile creation does not replace existing requirements engineering techniques. Rather it is intended to transform (existing) usability requirements into something that can be used for architecture assessment. Existing techniques such as interviews, group discussions, or observations (Nielsen, 1993; Hix & Hartson, 1993; Hackos & Redish, 1998; Shneiderman, 1998) typically already provide information such as representative tasks, users, and contexts of use that are needed to create a usage profile. The steps that need to be taken for usage profile creation are the following:

1. Identify the users: Rather than listing individual users, users that are representative for the use of the system should be categorized in types or groups (e.g., system administrators, end-users, etc.).

2. Identify the tasks: Representative tasks are selected that highlight the important features of the system. An accurate description of what is understood for a particular task and of which subtasks this task is composed, is an essential part of this step. For example, a task may be "search for specific compressor model" consisting of subtasks "go to performance part" and "select specific compressor model."

3. Identify the contexts of use: In this step, representative contexts of use are identified. (e.g., helpdesk context or disability context).

4. Determine attribute values: For each valid combination of user, task and context of use, usability attributes are quantified to express the required usability of the system. Defining specific indicators for attributes may assist the analyst in interpreting usability requirements. To reflect the difference in priority, numeric values between one and four have been assigned to the attributes for each scenario.

5. Scenario selection and weighing: Evaluating all identified scenarios may be a costly and time-consuming process. Therefore, the goal of performing an assessment is to evaluate a representative subset only. Different profiles may be defined depending on the goal of the analysis. For example, if the goal is to compare two different architectures, scenarios may be selected that highlight the differences between those architectures. To express differences between scenarios in the profile, properties may be assigned to the scenarios, for example: priority or probability of use within a certain time. The result of the assessment may be influenced by weighing scenarios, if some scenarios are more important than others, weighing these scenarios reflect these differences.

This result of this step is a set of usage scenarios (called a scenario profile) that express the required usability of the system.

Analyze the Software Architecture

In the second step of SALUTA, we need to extract information from the architecture that will allow the analyst to determine the support for each of the usage scenarios. In earlier research we have defined the SAU framework, which establishes a relationship between architecture design and usability. The SAU framework is an integral part of the SALUTA method. In this step we use it to extract relevant information from the architecture. Two types of analysis are performed:

- Identify patterns: Using the list of architecturally sensitive usability patterns we identify whether support for these has been implemented in the architecture.
- Identify properties: The software architecture is the result of a series of design decisions (Gurp & Bosch, 2002). Reconstructing this process and assessing the effect of individual design decisions with regard to usability provides additional information about the intended quality of the system. Using the list of usability properties, the architecture and the design decisions that lead to this architecture are analyzed for these properties.

The quality of the assessment very much depends on the amount of evidence for patterns and property support that can be extracted from the architecture. SALUTA does not dictate the use of any specific way of documenting a software architecture. Initially, the analysis is based on the information that is available, such as architecture designs and documentation used with in the development team. For example, Figure 4 lists a conceptual view (Hofmeister, Nord, & Soni, 1999) that was used to identify the presence of patterns in the compressor case.

Scenario Evaluation

The next step is to evaluate the architecture's support for each of the scenarios in the usage profile. For each scenario, we identify how each implemented pattern or property may affect it. Since the SAU framework relates particular usability patterns to specific usability attributes, we can use it to analyze the support for usability for each scenario. For example, if undo has been implemented we analyze whether it affect that scenario, if so the relationship between undo and usability are analyzed to determine the support. Undo improves error management and error management may improve reliability and efficiency. This step is repeated for each pattern and property affecting that scenario. The number and type of patterns and properties that support a particular attribute of a scenario are then compared to the required attribute values to determine the support for this scenario. See Figure 4 for a snapshot assessment example.

For each scenario, the results of the support analysis are expressed qualitatively using quantitative measures. For example, the support may be expressed on a five level scale (++, +, +/-,-,--). The outcome of the overall analysis may be a simple binary answer (supported/unsupported) or a more elaborate answer (70% supported) depending on how much information is available and how much effort is being put in creating the usage profile.

Interpretation of the Results

After scenario evaluation, the results need to be interpreted to draw conclusions concerning the software architecture. If the analysis is sufficiently accurate, the results may be quantified. However, even without quantification the assessment can produce useful results. If the goal is to iteratively design an architecture, then if the architecture proves to have sufficient support for usability, the design process may be finalized. Otherwise, architecture transformations need to be applied to improve the support for usability. For example,

Figure 4. Compressor architecture

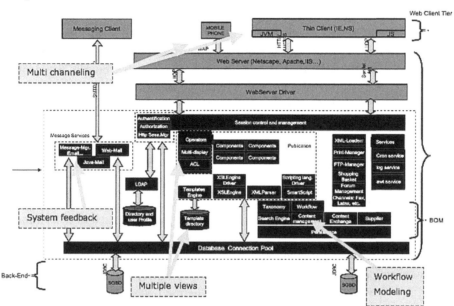

Figure 5. Snapshot assessment example

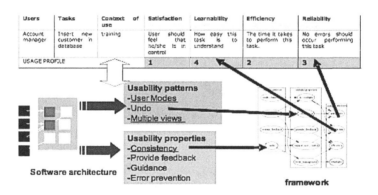

in the e-suite case, the architecture's support for usability was improved by adding three patterns to it. Qualitative information such as which scenarios are poorly supported and which usability properties or patterns have not been considered may guide the architect in applying certain design solutions. An architect should always discuss with a usability engineer, which solutions need to be applied. The SAU framework is then used as an informative source for design and improvement of the architecture's support for usability.

CASE DESCRIPTIONS

In this section we introduce the three systems used in the case studies. The goal of the case studies was to conduct a software architecture analysis of usability on each of the three systems.

As mentioned in the research methodology section, the action research (Argyris, Putnam, & Smith, 1985) methodology was used. Close cooperation and participation which are important aspects of this type of research allowed us to get a more complete understanding of the research issues. The first case study (Folmer et al., 2004) was performed at a software organization which is part of our university. This provided us with valuable insights and made us revise some of the SALUTA steps. The other two case studies were performed at our industrial partners in the STATUS project. STATUS was an IST project (IST-2001-32298) financed by the European Commission in its Information Society Technologies program and studied the relationship between software architecture and the usability of a software system. The partners are Information Highway Group (IHG), Universidad Politecnica de Madrid (UPM), University of Groningen (RUG), Imperial College of Science, Technology and Medicine (ICSTM), LOGICDIS S.A. Between those cases again our method was revised and refined. The last two case studies been published as part of the STATUS deliverables (STATUS).

All case studies have been performed in the domain of *Web-based* enterprise systems. Web-based systems have become an increasingly popular application format in recent years. Web-based systems have two main advantages: Centralization: The applications run on a (central / distributed) Web server, there is no need to install or maintain the application locally. Accessibility: The connectivity of the Web allows anyone to access the application from any Internet connection in the world and from any device that supports a Web browser. From a usability point of view, this is a very interesting domain: anyone with an Internet connection is a potential user. A lot of different types of users and different kinds of usages must therefore be supported. An overview of the differences between the applications (see Table 3) illustrates the scope of applicability of our method. The remainder of this section introduces the three systems that have been analyzed and presents the assessment results.

Webplatform

The Webplatform is a Web-based content management system for the University of Groningen (RuG) developed by ECCOO (expertise centrum computer ondersteunend onderwijs). The Webplatform enables a variety of (centralized) technical and (de-centralized) non technical staff to create, edit, manage, and publish a variety of content (such as text, graphics, video, etc.), whilst being constrained by a centralized set of rules, process and workflows that ensure a coherent, validated Web site appearance. The Webplatform data structure is object based; all data from the definitions of the CMS itself to the data of the faculty, portals or the personal details of a user are objects. The CMS makes use of the Internet file system (IFS)

Table 3. Comparison of system characteristics

Type of system	CMS	E-commerce	ERP
Number of users	> 20.000	> 100	> 1000
Goal of the analysis	Analyze architecture's support for usability / risk assessment: analyze SA related usability issues.	Selection: compare old versus new version of compressor.	Design: iteratively design & improve an architecture.
Types of users	3	3	2
Characterization of interaction	Information browsing and manipulation of data objects (e.g., create portals, course descriptions)	Information browsing (e.g.) comparing and analyzing data of different types of compressors and compressor parts.	Typical ERP functionality. (e.g., insert order, get client balance sheet)
Usage contexts	Mobile / desktop/ helpdesk	Mobile/sesktop/standalone	Mobile/desktop

to provide an interface which realises the use of objects and relations as defined in XML. The IFS uses an Oracle 9i database server implementation with a java based front end as search and storage medium. The java based front-end allows for the translation of an object oriented data structure into HTML. The oracle 9i database is a relational based database. On top of the IFS interface, the Webplatform application has been built. Thus, the CMS consists of the functionality provided by the IFS and the java based front-end. Integrated into the Webplatform is a customised tool called Xopus, which enables a content-administrator to create, edit, and delete XML objects through a Web browser. As an input to the analysis of the Webplatform, we interviewed the software architect, the usability engineer, and several other individuals involved in the development of the system. In addition, we examined the design documentation and experimented with the newly deployed RuG site.

Compressor

The compressor catalogue application is a product developed by the Imperial Highway Group (IHG) for a client in the refrigeration industry. It is an e-commerce application, which makes it possible for potential customers to search for detailed technical information about a range of compressors; for example, comparing two compressors. There was an existing implementation as a visual basic application, but the application has been redeveloped in the form of a Web application. The system employs a three-tiered architecture and is built upon an in-house developed application framework. The application is being designed to be able to work with several different Web servers or without any. The independence of the database is developed through Java database connectivity (JDBC). The data sources (either input or output) can also be XML files. The application server has a modular structure, it is composed by a messaging system and the rest of the system is based on several connectable modules (services)

that communicate between them. This potential structure offers a pool of connections for those applications that are running, providing more efficiency on the access to databases. As an input to the analysis of compressor, we interviewed the software architect. We analyzed the results from usability tests with the old system and with an interface prototype of the new system and examined the design documentation such as architectural designs and requirements specifications.

E-Suite

The E-Suite product developed by LogicDIS is a system that allows access to various ERP (enterprise resource planning) systems, through a Web interface. ERP systems generally run on large mainframe computers and only provide users with a terminal interface. E-Suite is built as a Web interface on top of different ERP systems. Users can access the system from a desktop computer but also from a mobile phone. The system employs a tiered architecture commonly found in Web applications. The user interfaces with the system through a Web browser. A Web server runs a Java servlet and some business logic components, which communicate with the ERP. As an input to the analysis of E-Suite, we interviewed the software architect and several other individuals involved in the development of the system. We analyzed the results from usability tests with the old system and with an interface prototype of the new system and examined the design documentation such as architectural designs and, usability requirements specifications.

Assessment Results

Table 4 lists the results of the assessment. The table lists the number of scenario defined and lists whether these scenarios are strongly rejected, weakly rejected, accepted/rejected, weakly accepted, or strongly accepted. Our impression was that overall the assessment was well received by the architects that assisted the analysis. Based on the assessment results, the E-Suite architecture was improved by applying patterns from the SAU framework. In the other cases, we were not involved during architecture design but the assessments provided the architects with valuable insights till which extent certain usability improving design solutions could still be implemented during late stage without incurring great costs. This emphasized and increased the understanding of the important relationship between software architecture and usability. The results of the assessments were documented and taken into account for future releases and redevelopment of the products.

EXPERIENCES

This section gives a detailed description of the experiences we acquired during the definition and use of SALUTA. We consider SALUTA to be a prototypical example of an architecture assessment technique, therefore our experiences are relevant in a wider context. These experiences will be presented using the four steps of the method. For each experience, a problem description, examples, possible causes, available solutions, and research issues are provided. The experiences are illustrated using examples from the three case studies introduced before.

Usage Profile Creation

In addition to experiences that are well recognized in the domain of SE and HCI such as:

- **Poorly specified usability requirements,** for example: In all cases, apart from the Web platform case (some general usability guidelines based on Nielsen's heuristics [Nielsen, 1993] had been stated in the functional requirements) no clearly defined and verifiable usability requirements had been collected or specified.
- **Changing requirements**, for example: In all case studies we noticed that during development the usability requirements had changed. For example, in the Webplatform case it had initially been specified that the Webplatform should always provide context sensitive help texts, however, for more experienced users this turned out to be annoying and led to a usability problem. A system where help texts could be turned off for more experienced users would be much better.

The following experiences were collected:

Difficult to Transform Requirements

Problem: To be able to assess a software architecture for its support of usability we need to transform requirements into a suitable format. For SALUTA we have chosen to define usage scenarios. For each scenario, usability attributes are quantified to express the required usability of the system, based on the requirements specification. A problem that we encountered is that sometimes it is difficult to determine attribute values for a scenario because usability requirements and at-

Table 4. Assessment results

	No. of scenarios	Strong reject	Weak reject	Accept/reject	Weak accept	Strong accept
Webplatform	11	-	-	-	8	3
Old compressor	14	2	2	8	-	-
New compressor	14	-	-	5	6	3
E-Suite	12	-	-	3	4	3

tributes can be interpreted in different ways.

Example: What do efficiency or learnability attributes mean for a particular task, user, or user context? Efficiency can be interpreted in different ways: does it mean the time that it takes to perform a task or does it mean the number of errors that a user makes? It can also mean both. Usability requirements are sometimes also difficult to interpret for example in the Webplatform case: "*UR1: every page should feature a quick search which searches the whole portal and comes up with accurate search results.*" How can we translate such a requirement to attribute values for a scenario?

Causes: Translating requirements to a format that is suitable for architecture assessment is an activity that takes place on the boundary of both SE and HCI disciplines. Expertise is required; it is difficult to do for a software architect since he or she may have no experience with usability requirements.

Solution: In all of our cases we have let a usability engineer translate usability requirements to attribute values for scenarios. To formalize this step we have let the usability engineer specify for each scenario how to *interpret* a particular attribute. For example, for the Web platform case the following usage scenario has been defined: "*end user performing quick search.*" The usability engineer formally specified what should be understood for each attribute of this task. Reliability has been associated with the accuracy of search results; efficiency has been associated with response time of the quick search, learnability with the time it takes to understand, and use this function. Then the usability requirements (UR1) were consulted. From this requirement we understand that reliability (e.g., accuracy of search results is important). In the requirements, however, it has not been specified that quick search should be performed quickly or that this function should be easy to understand. Because most usability requirements are not formally specified we discussed these issues with the usability engineer that assisted the analysis and the engineer found

that this is the most important aspect of usability for this task. Consequently, high values have been given to efficiency and reliability and low values to the other attributes (see Figure 6). Defining and discussing specific indicators for attributes (such as number or errors for reliability) may assist the interpretation of usability requirements and may lead to a more accurate prioritization of usability attributes.

Research issues: The weakness in this process is that is inevitably some guesswork involved on the part of the experts and that one must be careful not to add too much value to the numerical scores. For example, if learnability has value 4 and efficiency value 2, it does not necessarily mean that learnability is twice as important as efficiency. The only reason for using numerical scores is to reflect the difference in priority which is used for analyzing the architecture support for that scenario. To improve the representativeness of a usage scenario possibly a more fine grained definition of a scenario needs to be developed.

Specification of Certain Quality Attributes is Difficult During Initial Design

Problem: A purpose of quality requirements is to specify a *necessary* level (Lauesen & Younessi, 1998). In the SAU framework, four different usability attributes have been presented which we use for expressing the required usability for a system in a usage scenario. Specifying a necessary level for satisfaction and specifying how satisfaction should be interpreted has proven to be difficult during initial design. In addition, we could not identify specific usability requirements that specify a necessary level for this attribute during initial design.

Example: In the compressor case we defined the following usage scenario: "*Suppliers get the performance data for a specific model.*" What does satisfaction mean for this scenario? What is the necessary level of the satisfaction for this scenario? Attributes such as learnability, efficiency,

Figure 6. Transforming requirements to a usage profile

1	End user	Quick search	4	2	3	1

and reliability are much easier interpreted and it is therefore much easier to specify a necessary level for them.

Cause: Satisfaction to a great extent depends on, or is influenced by the other three usability attributes (efficiency, reliability, and learnability); it expresses the subjective opinions users have in using the system, therefore satisfaction can often only be measured when the system is deployed (e.g., by interviewing users).

Solution: The importance of satisfaction in this context should be reevaluated.

Research issues: Satisfaction has been included in our usability decomposition because it expresses the subjective view a user has on the system. We are uncertain if this subjective view is not already reflected by the definition of usability. Which software systems are not usable but have high values for their satisfaction attributes?

Cost Benefit Tradeoffs

Problem: The number of usage scenarios in the usage profile easily becomes a large number. Evaluating and quantifying all scenarios may be a costly and time-consuming process. How do we keep the assessment at a reasonable size?

Example: For example, for the Web platform case, we initially had identified 68 scenarios. For the compressor case, we identified 58 different usage scenarios.

Cause: The number of scenarios that are identified during the usage profile creation stage can become quite large since many variables are included; users, user contexts, and tasks.

Solutions: Inevitably, tradeoffs have to be made during usage scenario selection, an important consideration is that the more scenarios are evaluated the more accurate the outcome of the assessment is, but the more expensive and time

consuming it is to determine attribute values for these scenarios. We propose three solutions:

- **Explicit goal setting**: allows the analyst to filter out those scenarios that do not contribute to the goal of the analysis. Goal setting is important since it can influence which scenarios to include in the profile. For example, for the Web platform case we decided, based on the goal of the analysis (analyze architecture's support for usability), to only to select those scenarios that were important to a particular user group; a group of content administrators that only constituted 5% of the users population but the success of Webplatform was largely dependent on their acceptance of the system. This reduced the number of scenarios down to a reasonable size of 11 usage scenarios.

- **Pair wise comparison**: For most usage scenarios, concerning expressing the required usability, there is an obvious conflict between attributes such as efficiency and learnability or reliability and efficiency. To minimize the number of attributes that need to be quantified, techniques such as pair wise comparison should be considered to only determine attribute values for the attributes that conflict.

- **Tool support**: It is possible to specify attribute values over a particular task or context of use or for a user group. For example, for the user type "expert users" it may be specified that efficiency is the most important attribute for all scenarios that involve expert users. For a particular complex task it may be specified that learnability should be the most important attribute for all scenarios that have included that task. We consider developing tool support in the future which should assist the analyst in specifying attribute values over contexts, users and tasks and that will automatically determine a final prioritization of attribute values for a usage profile.

Architecture Analysis

Non-Explicit Nature of Architecture Design

Problem: In order to analyze the architecture support for usability, some representation of the software architecture is needed. However, a software architecture has several aspects (such as design decisions and their rationale) that are not easily captured or expressed in a single model or view.

Example: Initially, the analysis is based on the information that is available. In the compressor case, a conceptual architecture description had been created (see Figure 4). However, to determine the architectural support for usability we needed more information, such as which design decisions were taken.

Cause: Because of the non-explicit nature of architecture design, the analysis strongly depends on having access to both design documentation and software architects; as design decisions are often not documented the architect may fill in the missing information on the architecture and design decisions that were taken.

Solution: Interviewing the architect provided us with a list *if* particular patterns and properties had been implemented. We then got into more detail by analyzing the architecture designs and documentation for evidence of *how* these patterns and properties had been implemented. Different views on the system (Kruchten, 1995; Hofmeister et al., 1999) may be needed to access such information. A conceptual view (Hofmeister et al., 1999) on the system of the compressor (see Figure 4) was sufficient for us to provide detailed information on how the patterns (Folmer et al, 2003) system

feedback, multi channeling, multiple views and workflow modeling had been implemented. For the other systems that lacked architecture descriptions, we let the software architects create conceptual views.

Validation of the SAU Framework

Problem: Empirical validation is important when offering new techniques. The analysis technique for determining the provided usability of the system relies on the SAU framework we developed in earlier research (Folmer et al., 2003). Initially, the SAU framework was based on discussions with our partners in the STATUS project and did not focus on any particular application domain. The list of patterns and properties that we had identified then was substantial but incomplete. Even the relation of some of the patterns and properties with software architecture was open to dispute. For particular application domains the framework may not be accurate.

Example: Our case studies have been performed in the domain of Web-based systems. Initially, our SAU framework contained usability patterns such as multitasking and shortcuts. For these patterns, we could not find evidence that they were architecturally sensitive in this domain. Other patterns such as undo and cancel have different meanings in Web-based interaction. Pressing the stop button in a browser does not really cancel anything. Undo is generally associated with the back button. Web-based systems are different from other types of applications.

Causes: the architecture sensitivity of some of our usability patterns depends on its implementation which depends on the application domain.

Solution: The applicability of our analysis method is not excluded to other application domains but the framework that we use for the analysis may need to be specialized for different application domains in the future. The "best implementation" of a particular pattern may depend on several other factors such as which application framework is used or on other qualities such as maintainability and flexiblity. Some patterns do not exist or are not relevant for a particular domain. Some patterns may share similar implementations across different domains these patterns can be described in a generic fashion.

Research issue: Our framework is a first step in illustrating the relationship between usability and software architecture. The list of architecturally sensitive usability patterns and properties we identified are substantial but incomplete, it does not yet provide a complete comprehensive coverage of all potential architecturally sensitive usability issues for all domains. The case studies have allowed us to refine and extend the framework for the domain of Web-based enterprise systems, and allowed us to provide detailed architectural solutions for implementing these patterns and properties (based on "best" practices).

Qualitative Nature of SAU Framework

Problem: Relationships have been defined between the elements of the framework. However, these relationships only indicate positive relationships. Effectively, an architect is interested in how much a particular pattern or property will improve a particular aspect of usability in order to determine whether requirements have been met. Being able to quantify these relationships and being able to express negative relationships would greatly enhance the use of our framework.

Example: The wizard pattern generally improves learnability but it negatively affects efficiency. Until now it is not known how much a particular pattern or property improves or impairs a particular attribute of usability, for example, we only get a qualitative indication.

Causes: Our framework is a first step in illustrating a relationship between usability and software architecture. Literature does not provide us with quantitative data on how these patterns may improve usability.

Solution: In order to get quantitative data, we need to substantiate these relationships and to provide models and assessment procedures for the precise way that the relationships operate. However, we doubt whether identifying this kind of (generic) quantitative information is possible. Eventually we consider putting this framework in a tool and allow architects and engineers to put weights on the patterns and properties that they consider to be important.

Scenario Evaluation

Evaluation Is Guided by Tacit Knowledge

Problem: The activity of scenario evaluation is concerned with determining the support the architecture provides for that particular usage scenario. The number of patterns and properties that support a particular usability attribute required by a scenario, for example, learnability, provide an indication of the architecture's support for that scenario, however, the evaluation is often guided by tacit knowledge.

Example: For example, in the E-Suite case, the following scenario was affected by four usability patterns and six usability properties. The scenario requires high values for learnability (4) and reliability (3). Several patterns and properties positively contribute to the support of this scenario. For example, the property consistency and the pattern context sensitive help increases learnability as can be analyzed from Figure 2. By analyzing for each pattern and property, the effect on usability, the support for this scenario was determined. However, sometimes this has proven to be difficult. How much learnability improving patterns and properties should the architecture provide for deciding whether this scenario is supported?

Cause: Although SALUTA provides the steps for identifying the support, determining whether a scenario is accepted or rejected is still is very

Table 5. E-Suite usage scenario

Novice	Mobile	Insert Order	1	2	4	3

much guided by tacit knowledge, that is, the undocumented knowledge of experienced software architects.

Solution: Our framework has captured some of that knowledge (e.g., the relationships between usability properties and patterns and usability attributes) but it is up to the analyst to interpret these relationships and determine the support for the scenarios.

Research issues: Since evaluating all the scenarios by hand is time consuming, we consider developing a tool that allows one to automatically determine for a set of identified patterns and properties which attributes they support and to come up with some quantitative indication for the support. Although it may not be possible to give an absolute indication of an architectures support for usability, when iteratively designing and evaluating an architecture, we are able to express relative improvements.

Interpretation

Lacked a Frame of Reference

Problem: After scenario evaluation, we have to associate conclusions with these results. However, initially we lacked a frame of reference to interpret the results.

Example: The results of the evaluation of our first case study (Webplatform) were that three scenarios were weakly accepted, and eight were strongly accepted. How should this be interpreted and which actions need to be taken?

Cause: Interpretation is concerned with deciding whether the outcome of the assessment is acceptable or not. The experiences that we have, is at initially, we lacked a frame of reference for interpreting the results of the evaluation of Web-

platform. Were these numbers acceptable? Could we design an architecture that has a better support for usability? The results of the assessment were relative, but we had no means or techniques to relate it to other numbers or results yet. Another issue was that we doubted the representativeness of the usage profile. Did this profile cover all possible usages by all types of users?

Solution: The three case studies have provided us with a small frame of reference. We have seen architectures with significant better and weaker support for usability. This provided us with enough information to judge whether a particular architecture could still be improved. In order to refine our frame of reference more case studies need to be done within the domain of Web-based application. Certain patterns such as multiple views were present in all architectures we examined, whereas other patterns such as user modes were only present in one system. We need more info on which patterns are already integrated in application frameworks such as STRUTS (Mercay & Gilbert, 2002) and which patterns have not.

In addition to the architecture assessment related experiences, the following general experiences were collected.

General Experiences

Some general experiences that are well recognized in the SE and HCI domains which are of cultural and psychological nature have been identified such as:

- **Lack of integration of SE and HCI processes,** for example: Processes for software engineering and HCI are not fully integrated. There is no integration of SE and HCI techniques during architectural design. Because interface design is often postponed to the later stages of development, we run the risk that many assumptions may be built into the design of the architecture that unknowingly may affect interface design and vice versa. The software architecture is seen as an intermediate product in the development process but its potential with respect to quality assessment is not fully exploited.

- **Technology driven design**: Software architects fail to associate usability with software architecture design, for example, the software architects we interviewed in the case studies were not aware of the important role the software architecture plays in fulfilling and restricting usability requirements. When designing their systems the software architects had already selected technologies (*read features*) and had already developed a first version of the system before they decided to include the user in the loop. A software product is often seen as a set of *features* rather then a set of "*user experiences*."

In addition to these experiences, the following experiences were collected:

Impact of Software Architecture Design on Usability

Problem: One of the reasons to develop SALUTA was that usability may unknowingly impact software architecture design, for example, the retrofit problem. However, we also identified that it worked the other way around; architecture design sometimes leads to usability problems in the interface and the interaction.

Example: In the ECCOO case study we identified that the layout of a page (users had to fill in a form) was determined by the XML definition of a specific object. When users had to insert data, the order in which particular fields had to be filled in turned out to be very confusing.

Causes: Because interface design is often postponed until the later stages of design we run the risk that many assumptions are built into the design of the architecture that unknowingly affect interface/interaction design and vice versa.

Solution: Interfaces/interaction should not be designed as last but as early as possible to identify what should be supported by the software architecture and how the architecture may affect interface/interaction design. We should not only analyze whether the architecture design supports certain usability solutions but also identify how the architecture design may lead to usability problems.

Research issues: Usability is determined by many factors, issues such as:

- Information architecture: how is information presented to the user?
- Interaction architecture: how is functionality presented to the user?
- System quality attributes: such as efficiency and reliability.

Architecture design does affect all these issues. Considerable more research needs to be performed to analyze how a particular architecture design may lead to such kind of usability problems.

Accuracy of the Analysis Is Unclear

Problem: Our cases studies show that it is possible to use SALUTA to assess software architectures for their support of usability, whether we have accurately predicted the architecture's support for usability can only be answered after the results of this analysis are compared to the results of final user testing results when the system has been finished. Several user tests have been performed. The results of these tests fit the results of our analysis: the software architecture supports the right level of usability. Some usability issues came up that where not predicted during our architectural assessment. However, these do not appear to be caused by problems in the software architecture.

We are not sure that our assessment gives an accurate indication of the architecture's support for usability. On the other hand, it is doubtful whether this kind of accuracy is at all achievable.

Causes: The validity of our approach has several threats:

- Usability is often not an explicit design objective; SALUTA focuses on the assessment of usability during architecture design. Any improvement in usability of the final system should not be solely accounted to our method. More focus on usability during development in general is, in our opinion, the main cause for an increase in observed usability.
- Accuracy of usage profile: Deciding what users, tasks, and contexts of use to include in the usage profile requires making tradeoffs between all sorts of factors. The representativeness of the usage profile for describing the required usability of the system is open to dispute. Questions whether we have accurately described the systems usage can only be answered by observing users when the system has been deployed. An additional complicating factor is the often weakly specified requirements, which makes it hard to create a representative usage profile.

Solution: To validate SALUTA we should not only focus on measuring an increase in the usability of the resulting product but we should also measure the decrease in costs spent on usability during maintenance. If any usability issues come up which require architectural modifications then we should have predicted these during the assessment.

Research issues: Architectural assessment saves maintenance costs spent on dealing with usability issues. However, at the moment we lack figures that acknowledge this claim. In the organization that participated in the case studies, these figures have not been recorded nor did they have any historical data. To raise awareness and change attitudes (especially those of the decision makers) we should clearly define and measure the business advantages of architectural assessment of usability.

Design Rather than Evaluate

Problem: The usage profile and usage scenarios are used to evaluate a software architecture, once it is there.

Solution: A much better approach would be to design the architecture based on the usage profile, for example, an attribute/property-based architectural design, where the SAU framework is used to suggest patterns that should be used rather than identify their absence post-hoc.

CONCLUSION

Software engineers and human computer interaction engineers have come to the understanding that usability is not something that can be easily "added" to a software product during late stage, since to a certain extent it is determined and restricted by architecture design. Because software engineers in industry lacked support for the early evaluation of usability, we defined a generalized four-step method for software architecture level usability analysis, called SALUTA. This article reports on 11 experiences we acquired developing and using SALUTA. These experiences are illustrated using three case studies we performed in the domain of Web-based enterprise systems: Webplatform, a content management system developed by ECCOO, compressor, an e-commerce application developed by IHG and E-Suite, an enterprise resource planning system developed by LogicDIS. With respect to the first step of SALUTA, creating a usage profile, we found that transforming requirements to a format that can be used for architectural assessment is difficult because requirements and quality attributes can be interpreted in different ways. In addition, specifying a necessary level for certain quality attributes is difficult during initial design since they can often only be measured when the system is deployed. To keep the assessment at a reasonable size we need set an explicit goal for the analysis to filter out those scenarios that do not contribute to this goal, tool support is considered for automating this step. With respect to the second step of SALUTA, architecture analysis, we found that some representation of the software architecture is needed for the analysis however some aspects such as design decisions can only be retrieved by interviewing the software architect. The applicability of SALUTA is not excluded to other application domains but the SAU framework that we use for the architectural analysis may need to be specialized and the relationships quantified for different application domains in order to produce more accurate results. Concerning the third step, scenario evaluation is often guided by tacit knowledge. Concerning the fourth step, interpretation of results we experienced that initially the lack of a frame of reference made the interpretation less certain. In addition, we made some general observations; not only does usability impact software architecture design but software architecture design may lead to usability problems. The accuracy of the analysis and the representativeness of a usage scenario can only be determined with results from final usability tests and by analyzing whether costs that are spent on usability during maintenance have decreased. Rather than identify the absence or presence of patterns post-hoc, we should use the SAU framework to suggest patterns that should be used. In our view, the case studies that have been conducted have provided valuable experiences that have contributed to a better understanding of architecture analysis and scenario based assessment of usability.

ACKNOWLEDGMENT

This work is sponsored by the STATUS project under contract no IST-2001-32298. We would like to thank the companies that enabled us to perform the case studies, that is, ECCOO, IHG, and LogicDIS. We would especially like to thank Lisette Bakalis, Roel Vandewall of ECCOO, Fernando Vaquerizo of IHG, and Dimitris Tsirikos of LogicDIS for their valuable time and input.

REFERENCES

STATUS deliverables, http://lucio.ls.fi.upm.es/status/results/deliverables.html

Alexander, C. (1977). *A pattern language*. Oxford: University Press.

Alonso, A., Garcia-Valls, M., & de la Puente, J. A. (1998). Assessment timing properties of family products. In *Proceedings of Second International ESPRIT ARES Workshop* (pp. 161-169).

Argyris, C., Putnam, R., & Smith, D. (1985). *Action science: concepts, methods and skills for research and intervention*. New York: Jossey-Bass.

Bass, L., Clements, P., & Kazman, R. (2003). *Software architecture in practice* (2nd ed.). Boston: Addison-Wesley.

Bass, L., Kates, J., & John, B. E. (2001). *Achieving usability through software architecture* (Tech. Rep.) http://www.sei.cmu.edu/publications/documents/01.reports/01tr005.html

Bengtsson, P. O. (2002). *Architecture-level modifiability analysis*. Ph.D. thesis, Department of Software Engineering and Computer Science, Blekinge Institute of Technology.

Bengtsson, P. O., & Bosch, J. (1999). Architecture level prediction of software maintenance. In *Proceedings of the 3rd EuroMicro Conference on Software Engineering* (pp. 139-147). IEEE CS Press.

Bosch, J. (2000). *Design and use of software architectures: Adopting and evolving a product line approach.* New York: Pearson Education (Addison-Wesley and ACM Press).

Brighton (1998). *The Brighton usability pattern collection.* http://www.cmis.brighton.ac.uk/research/patterns/home.html

Buschmann, F., Meunier, R., Rohnert, H., Sommerlad, P., & Stal, M. (1996). *Pattern-oriented software architecture: A system of patterns.* New York: John Wiley and Son Ltd.

Constantine, L. L., & Lockwood, L. A. D. (1999). *Software for use: A practical guide to the models and methods of usage-centered design.* New York: Addison-Wesley.

Folmer, E., & Bosch, J. (2002). Architecting for usability; a survey. *Journal of Systems and Software, 70*(1), 61-78.

Folmer, E., Gurp, J. v., & Bosch, J. (2003). A framework for capturing the relationship between usability and software architecture. *Software Process: Improvement and Practice, 8*(2), 67-87.

Folmer, E., Gurp, J. v., & Bosch, J. (2004). Software architecture analysis of usability. In *Proceedings of the 9th IFIP Working Conference on Engineering for Human-Computer Interaction* (pp. 321-339).

Folmer, E., Welie, M. v., & Bosch, J. (2006). Bridging patterns—an approach to bridge gaps between SE and HCI. *Journal of Information and Software Technology, 48*(2), 69-89.

Gamma, E., Helm, R., Johnson, R., & Vlissides, J. (1995). *Design patterns elements of reusable object-orientated software.* New York: Addison-Wesley.

Gurp, J. v., & Bosch, J. (2002). Design erosion: Problems and causes. *Journal of Systems and Software, 61*(2), 105-119.

Hackos, J. T., & Redish, J. C. (1998). *User and task analysis for interface design.* New York: John Wiley and Sons, Inc.

Hix, D., & Hartson, H. R. (1993). *Developing user interfaces: Ensuring usability through product and process.* New York: John Wiley and Sons.

Hofmeister, C., Nord, R. L., & Soni, D. (1999). *Applied software architecture.* New York: Addison Wesley Longman.

Holcomb, R., & Tharp, A. L. (1991). What users say about software usability. *International Journal of Human-Computer Interaction, 3*(11), 49-78.

IEEE Architecture Working Group (1998). Recommended practice for architectural description. Draft IEEE Standard P1471/D4.1, IEEE.

ISO 9126-1 (2000) Software engineering—Product quality—Part 1: Quality Model.

ISO ISO 9241-11 (1994). Ergonomic requirements for office work with visual display terminals (VDTs)—Part 11: Guidance on usability.

Kazman, R., Abowd, G., & Webb, M. (1994). SAAM: A method for analyzing the properties of software architectures. In *Proceedings of the 16th International Conference on Software Engineering* (pp. 81-90).

Kazman, R., Klein, M., Barbacci, M., Longstaff, T., Lipson, H., & Carriere, J. (1998). The architecture tradeoff analysis method. In *Proceedings of the International Conference on Engineering of Complex Computer Systems* (pp. 68-78).

Kazman, R., Klein, M., & Clements, P. (2000). *ATAM: Method for architecture evaluation (CMU/SEI-2000-TR-004).* Pittsburgh: Carnegie Mellon University.

Kruchten, P. B. (1995). *The 4+1 view model of architecture. IEEE Software.*

Landauer, T. K. (1995). *The trouble with computers: Usefulness, usability and productivity.* MIT Press.

Lassing, N., Bengtsson, P. O., van Vliet, H., & Bosch, J. (2002). Experiences with ALMA:

Architecture-level modifiability analysis. *Journal of Systems and Software*, 47-57.

Lauesen, S., & Younessi, H. (1998). Six styles for usability requirements. In *Proceedings of REFSQ'98*, (pp.155–166). Presses universitaires de Namur.

Lung, C., Bot, S., Kaleichelvan, K. K. R., & Kazman, R. (1997). An approach to software architecture analysis for evolution and reusability. In *Proceedings of the 1997 Conference of the Centre for Advanced Studies on Collaborative research* (p. 15).

Mercay, J., & Bouzeid, G. (2002). *Boost struts with XSLT and XML*. http://www.javaworld.com/javaworld/jw-02-2002/jw-0201-strutsxslt-p1.html

Nielsen, J. (1993). *Usability engineering*. Boston: Academic Press, Inc.

Nielsen, J. (1994). Heuristic evaluation. In J. Nielsen & R. L. Mack (Eds.), *Usability inspection methods* (pp. 25-64). New York: John Wiley and Sons.

Nigay, L., & Coutaz, J. (1997). Software architecture modelling: Bridging the worlds using ergonomics and software properties. In Formal Methods in Human-Computer Interaction, Springer-Verlag, ISBN 3-540-76158-6, 1997, Chapter 3, 49-73.

Norman, D. A. (1988). The design of everyday things. New York: Currency- Doubleday.

Perzel, K., & Kane, D. (1999). Usability patterns for applications on the world wide web. In *Proceedings of the Pattern Languages of Programming Conference*.

Polson, P. G., & Lewis, C. H. (1990). Theory-based design for easily learned interfaces. In *Proceedings of the SIGCHI Conference on Human Factors in Computing Systems: Empowering People* (pp. 235-242).

Preece, J., Rogers, Y., Sharp, H., Benyon, D., Holland, S., & Carey, T. (1994). *Human-computer interaction*. New York: Addison Wesley.

Pressman, R. S. (1992). *Software engineering: A practitioner's approach*. New York: McGraw-Hill.

Ravden, S. J., & Johnson, G. I. (1989). *Evaluation usability of human-computer interfaces: A practical method*. New York: Ellis Horwood Limited.

Robson, C. (1993). *Real world research*. Oxford: Blackwell Publishing Ltd.

Rubinstein, R., & Hersh, H. (1984). *The human factor: Designing computer systems for people*. Bedford: Digital Press.

Shackel, B. (1991). Usability—context, framework, design and evaluation, in *human factors for informatics usability*. Cambridge University Press.

Shaw, M. (2002). What makes good research in software engineering? *International Journal on Software Tools for Technology Transfer (STTT)*, 1-7. Springer Berlin / Heidelberg.

Shneiderman, B. (1998). *Designing the user interface: Strategies for effective human-computer interaction*. New York: Addison-Wesley.

Tidwell, J. (1998). Interaction design patterns. In *Proceedings of the Conference on Pattern Languages of Programming*.

Welie, M., & Trætteberg, H. (2000). Interaction patterns in user interfaces. In *Proceedings of the 7th Conference on Pattern Languages of Programming (PloP)*.

Wixon, D., & Wilson, C. (1997) The usability engineering framework for product design and evaluation. In M. G. Helander, T. K. Landauer, & P. V. Prabhu (Eds), *Handbook of human-computer interaction* (2nd ed.). Englewood Cliffs, N.J.: Elsevier Science.

This work was previously published in International Journal of Information Technology and Web Engineering, Vol. 3, Issue 4, edited by G. Alkhatib and D.. Rine, pp. 1-29, copyright 2008 by IGI Publishing (an imprint of IGI Global).

Section 3
Testing and Performance Evaluation

Chapter 11
Class Level Test Case Generation in Object Oriented Software Testing

N. Gupta
Birla Institute of Technology, India

D. Saini
King Saud University, College of Science, Saudi Arabia

H. Saini
Higher Institute of Electronics, Libya

ABSTRACT

Object-oriented programming consists of several different levels of abstraction, namely, the algorithmic level, class level, cluster level, and system level. In this article, we discuss a testing technique to generate test cases at class level for object-oriented programs. The formal object oriented class specification is used to develop a test model. This test model is based on finite state machine specification. The class specification and the test model is analyzed to select a set of test data for each method of the class, and finally the test cases can be generated using other testing techniques like finite-state testing or data-flow testing.

INTRODUCTION

The object-oriented technology has many benefits for parts of the entire software development cycle (analysis, design and implementation phases). The object-oriented development process is iterative, the object-oriented paradigm emphasizes reuse, and the items of interest are always the objects. Thus, engineers and managers want to use this technology in their own field. But, for critical systems, which need a certification, the testing process is an important task. Testing can be done at four different levels of abstraction found in object-oriented systems. These are the method level, class level, cluster level, and system level. The method level considers the code for each operation in a class. The class level is composed of the interactions of methods and data that are encapsulated within a given class. The cluster level consists of the interactions among cooperating classes, which are grouped to accomplish some tasks. The system level is composed of all the clusters (Smith & Robson, 1992)

Testing at the method and system levels is similar to conventional program testing. Many researchers have addressed the class-level testing (Doong & Frankl, 1991, 1994; Harrold, McGregor, & Fitzpatrick, 1992; McGregor & Korson, 1994; Murphy, Townsend, & Wong, 1994). Formal methods can be used in software testing process to improve the quality and effectiveness of the process (Bernot, Gaudel, & Marre, 1991; Carrington & Stocks, 1994; Crnkovic, Filipe, Larsson, & Lau, 2000; Eden & Hirshfeld, 2001). Based on the formal methods we have developed a testing process for object oriented software. In this article we present an object oriented software testing process which can be used to generate test cases systematically and effectively. To generate the test cases for a class, which may have mutable objects (which can be modified after it is created), we will use specification-based testing technique. The purpose of specification-based testing is to derive testing information from a specification of the software under test, rather than from the implementation.

There are various methods of object-oriented software specifications. These may be graphical techniques, decomposition specification techniques, communication specification techniques, functional specification techniques and behavior specification techniques (Wieringa, 1998). In this article we will focus on finite state diagram which is a behavior specification technique, for the generation of test cases. We will consider that classes are instantiated into mutable objects.

CLASS LEVEL TEST CASE GENERATION

A software testing model summarizes how you should think about test development. It tells you how to plan the testing effort, what purpose tests serve, when they're created, and what sources of information you use to create them [17]. Here, we have extracted our test model from the formal specification. In this strategy, class specification is used to obtain class state space, which is partitioned into substates. A test model is composed of a set of states and a set of transitions among the states. Each state is obtained through the state space partition of the class. Each transition consists of a method, which can change the value of an object from source state to target state. The input space of each method, which is the sets of values for the input parameters of the method, is partitioned. The input space partition values are used with test model to obtain the test data. Finally this test data can be used for the generation of test cases. The process of generating test cases at the class level is illustrated schematically in Figure 1.

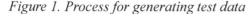

Figure 1. Process for generating test data

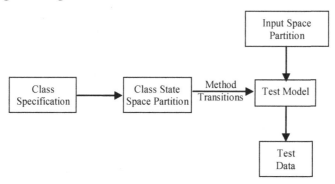

Figure 2. Functional tier of the class account

```
MinimumBalance = 1000
class Account has Balance
        operation GetBalance() returns Balance
        return Balance;
        endoperation
        operation Deposit(Amount X)
        Balance = X + GetBalance();
        endoperation
        operation Charge()
        if 500 <= GetBalance() < 1000 then
                    Balance = GetBalance() –
        10;
        endif
        if 20 <= GetBalance() < 500 then
                    Balance = GetBalance() –
        20;
        endif
        if 0 <= GetBalance() < 20 then
                    Balance = 0;
```

Figure 3. The conditional tier of the class account

```
class Account
invariant {Balance >= 0}.
constructor Account()
ensures {Balance == 0}
method Deposit (Amount X)
requires {X > 0}
ensures {Balance(post-operation) ==
        Balance(pre-operation) + X}
method Withdraw (Amount Y)
requires {Balance(pre-operation) >= Y}
ensures {Balance(post-operation) ==
        Balance(pre-operation) - Y}
```

CLASS SPECIFICATION

Larch (Guttag, Horning, Garland et al.,1993; Wing, 1983) may be thought of as an approach to formal specification of program modules. This approach is an extension of Hoare's ideas for program specification (Hoare, 1969, 1972). Its distinguishing feature is that it uses two "tiers" (or layers). A class specification will consist of two layers: a functional tier and a conditional tier. The functional tier is an algebraic specification, which is used to define the abstract values of objects. An algebraic specification may consist of a number of modules. Each module is used to specify a collection of related types. The properties of the operations (or functions) related to a particular type is specified by a set of equational axioms. In particular, the type for the abstract values of objects of a class is known as a base type of the class.

Figure 2 shows the functional tier of the class Account in pseudo-code form, which specifies

the set of abstract values for objects of this class. Class account has various operations (methods). The operation GetBalance returns the current balance of any Account object. The operation deposit takes some amount X and adds it to previous value of balance. Every account object is supposed to maintain a minimum balance of amount 1,000, otherwise a charge of amount 10 is deducted if balance is between 500 and 1,000. Amount of 20 is deducted if balance found less than 500. The charge is applied on a monthly basis. The next operation withdraw receives some amount Y. If the account has sufficient balance then this amount Y is deducted from current value of balance.

In the conditional tier, the class name, invariant, pre and post conditions of methods of each class are specified. A class is a template for describing the attributes and behavior of its objects. At any certain moment the attribute values of an object assign it to a certain named abstract value, which is called state of an object. An object can change its state by calling mutable operations. A state invariant is a condition, or constraint which is true of all possible states. Each method has its own syntax and pre and post-conditions.

Figure 3 shows the conditional tier of the class Account. The invariant clause specifies an invariant property that must be true of all values of the

Figure 4. The state-space partition of class account

Here, we first consider the partition analysis of state space. Depending upon the valid values of attributes of a class it will have a certain set of states which is called its state space. Since the state space of a class may be very large, making it difficult to test all the states. We can subdivide it into some finite number of substates. For the purpose of testing, these substates will have similar behavior.

> self.Balance < 1000, self.Balance > 1000
>
> Taking into account the clauses in Figure 3, the state space is further partitioned into five substates. In Figure 4, five substates are shown.
>
> self.Balance < 0 (invalid), self.Balance = 0, 0 < self.Balance < 500, self.

Let us consider the class account. The state space of this class is partitioned into following substates: the balance is less than 1000 and the balance is greater than 1,000.

No further partitioning is necessary in this simple example. It is assumed that an object behaves uniformly in each substate. The test model in this example class is a finite-state machine, which describes the state-dependent behaviors of individual objects of the class. The test model will have a set of states and a set of transitions among the states. Each state is obtained through the state-space partition of the class. Each transition between the states consists of a method, which changes the value of an object from the source state to the target state of the transition, and a guard predicate derived from the pre-condition of the method. Also there are two special states: initial and final states. The former represents the state before an object is created and the latter represents the state after an object is destroyed. The test model of class Account is shown in Figure 5. There are seven states:

type (Heffter, 1997). The invariant condition for the Account class is defined by invariant clause. This invariant says here that balance must be non-negative in any state of Account object. The method clause declares syntax for each method. The required clause is used to state a predicate that follows from the precondition. The ensured clause follows the post-conditions of the method. The names pre-operation and post-operation denote the value of the respective attribute before and after calling the method respectively.

CLASS STATE SPACE PARTITION

Partition analysis, that assists in program testing by incorporating information from both a formal specification and an implementation of procedures (Richardson & Clarke, 1981). We will improve this strategy so that it can be applied in class-level testing with formal specifications. Depending upon the values of attributes a class object may acquire various states. All such states form state space (VanderBrug & Minker, 1975) of a class. In our approach, the state space of a class will be partitioned into sub states. For each sub state, the input space of each method will be partitioned into sub-domains. Partition testing or sub domain testing comprises a broad class of software testing methods that call for dividing a program's input domain into sub domains and then selecting a small number of tests (usually one) from each of them (Weyuker & Jeng, 1991).

$S0 = \{unborn\}$, $S1 = \{b = 0\}$, $S2 = \{0 < b < 500\}$, $S3 = \{b = 500\}$, $S4 = \{500 < b < 1000\}$, $S5 = \{b = 1000\}$, $S6 = \{b > 1000\}$

Where S0 is initial state and b denotes the attribute Balance. The transitions are:

$t0 = Account()$, $t1 = Deposit(X)$ $\{0 < X < 500\}$, $t2 = Deposit(X)$ $\{X = 500\}$, $t3 = Deposit(X)$ $\{500 < X < 1000\}$, $t4 = Deposit(X)$ $\{X = 1000\}$, $t5 = Deposit(X)$ $\{X > 1000\}$, $t6 = Deposit(X)$ $\{b + X = 500\}$, $t7 = Deposit(X)$ $\{500 < b + X < 1000\}$, $t8 = Deposit(X)\{b + X = 1000\}$, $t9 = Deposit(X)\{b + X > 1000\}$,

Figure 5. The test model of the class account

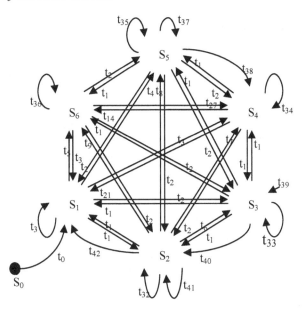

t10=Deposit(X) {500<X<1000}, t11=Deposit(X) {X=500}, t12=Deposit(X) {X>500}, t13=Deposit(X) {b+X=1000}, t14=Deposit(X) {b+X>1000}, t15=Deposit(X) {X>0}, t16=Withdraw(Y) {b-Y=0}, t17=Withdraw(Y) {0<Y<500}, t18=Withdraw(Y) {Y=500}, t19=Withdraw(Y) {b-Y=500}, t20=Withdraw(Y) {0<b-Y<500}, t21=Withdraw(Y) {b-Y=0}, t22=Withdraw(Y) {0<Y<500}, t23=Withdraw(Y) {Y=500}, t24=Withdraw(Y) {500<Y<1000}, t25=Withdraw(Y) {Y=1000}, t26=Withdraw(Y) {b-Y=1000}, t27=Withdraw(Y) {500<b-Y<1000}, t28=Withdraw(Y) {b-Y=500}, t29=Withdraw(Y) {0<b-Y<500}, t30=Withdraw(Y) {b-Y=0}, t31=GetBalance(), t32=GetBalance(), t33=GetBalance(), t34=GetBalance(), t35=GetBalance(), t36=GetBalance(), t37=Charge() {510<b<1000}, t38=Charge() {b=510}, t39=Charge() {500<b<510}, t40=Charge() {b=500}, t41=Charge() {20<b<500}, t42=Charge() {b<=20}.

During partition analysis, we need to distinguish four kinds of methods: (such as deposit (Amount X) and withdraw (Amount Y)), observers (such as GetBalance()), constructors (such as Account ()), and destructors. We need to unfold the complex denotations by introducing

observable contexts (Bernot, Gaudel, & Marre, 1991; Gaudel, 1995). Our test model can be turned into a complete finite-state machine by adding error states, error transitions, undefined states, and undefined transitions.

PARTITION OF INPUT-SPACE

Input space of each method is also required to partition when we partition the state space of the class. The input space is the sets of values for the input parameters of the method. A valid input space for a method is the subset of the input space satisfying the pre-condition of the method. The input space of a method can be partitioned at least into two sub-domains, whether valid or invalid values. Test data can then be drawn from each sub-domain (Chen & Yu, 2002).

While considering the partition the input spaces of methods it becomes important to consider the type of each input variable. In above discussed example of class account, the input space of deposit (Amount X) or withdraw (Amount Y) the type of input is amount. The pre-condition of deposit (Amount X) will give its valid input space

Figure 6. Partition of input-space for each method of account class

---

Input-space partition of Deposit (Amount X)

In State S1:

$p1 = \{0<X<500\}$, $p2 = \{X=500\}$, $p3 = \{500<X<1000\}$, $p4 = \{X=1000\}$, $p5 = \{X>1000\}$

In State S2:

$p6 = \{0<X<500 \text{ and } b+X<500\}$, $p7 = \{0<X<500 \text{ and } b+X=500\}$, $p8 = \{0<X<500 \text{ and } 500<b+X<1000\}$, $p9 = \{X=500 \text{ and } 500<b+X<1000\}$, $p10 = \{500<X<1000 \text{ and } 500<b+X<1000\}$, $p11 = \{500<X<1000 \text{ and } b+X=1000\}$, $p12 = \{500<X<1000 \text{ and } 1000<b+X<1500\}$, $p13 = \{X=1000\}$, $p14 = \{X>1000\}$

In State S3:

$p15 = \{0<X<500\}$, $p16 = \{X=500\}$, $p17 = \{X>500\}$

In State S4:

$p18 = \{0<X<500 \text{ and } 500<X+b<1000\}$, $p19 = \{0<X<500 \text{ and } X+b=1000\}$, $p20 = \{0<X<500 \text{ and } X+b>1000\}$, $p21 = \{X=500\}$, $p22 = \{X>500\}$

In State S5:

$p23 = \{X>0\}$

In State S6:

$p24 = \{X>0\}$

Input-space partition of Withdraw (Amount Y)

In State S2:

$p25 = \{0<Y<500\}$

In State S3:

---

which is applied for the input values of amount. Similarly for the method withdraw (Amount Y), the pre-condition of this method will give its valid input space. Since methods are used to manipulate the states of objects, the input-space partition of each method is also related with the state-space partition of the class. When we do the input-space partition of a method the state or some attributes of the class may be considered as implied parameters of the method. Based on the functional tier, the conditional tier, and the test model in Figures 2, 3, and 5, we can partition the input space of each method as shown in Figure 6.

The test data for each input parameter of a method can be selected from every sub-domain using existing testing techniques. It is important here to make a little assumption. In the simplest manner we can assume that the method under test behaves uniformly in each sub-domain. Based on this assumption, we need to select one value randomly which will work as representative from each sub-domain, and for each method we can obtain a set of test data.

GENERATION OF TEST CASES

The test cases generated in this way have various method sequence invocations utilizing the different sets of test data. The various methods of class interact to change the state of the class object. Thus the generated test cases are actually used to test the various scenarios which are dependent on the change of state which in turn is depending upon the interaction of methods. Here let us first use finite-state testing techniques to generate test cases (Offutt, Liu, Abdurazik, & Ammann, 2003). A test case is generated by traversing the test model from the initial state. Method sequences are derived from the traversed transitions. A set of test cases are required to be generated so that it can cover the test model in the form of state coverage, transition coverage, and path coverage. For example, the test case

Account(), Deposit(600), Deposit(400), With-
draw(700), Deposit(1000)

covers the six states in the following sequence:

S0, S1, S4, S5, S2, S6

We may also use data-flow testing techniques to generate test cases. Then here the test cases will be generated according def-use criteria (Rapps & Weyuker, 1982) of attributes in the test model. Each attribute is classified as being defined or used. It is said to be defined at a transition if the method of the transition changes the value of the attribute and is said to be used at a transition if the method of the transition refers to the value of the attribute. A set of test cases is generated by covering def-use paths with regard to each attribute according to certain data-flow testing criteria. Various testing techniques based on finite-state machines can be found in literature (Cheng & Kumar, 1983; Friedman, Hartman, Nagin, & Shiran, 2002; Naik, 1997).

CONCLUSION

In this article we discussed a technique which can be used to generate the test cases at class level testing for object oriented programs. The testing technique based on class specification is used in this method. This technique provides the test model which can be integrated to other existing techniques to generate the test cases. The generation of test cases, its execution and test

result analysis can be done in a systematic and in an effective way using this test model. Since the test model is generated based on the behavior of the class as specified by the class specification, therefore the actual intended behavior is also represented by the test model.

REFERENCES

Bernot, G., Gaudel, M.C., & Marre, B. (1991). Software testing based on formal specifications: a theory and a tool. *Software Engineering Journal, 6*(6), 387-405.

Carrington, D., & Stocks, P. (1994). A tale of two paradigms: formal methods and software testing. *Proceedings of 8th Annual Z User Meeting (ZUM '94)*, J.P. Bowen and J.A. Hall (eds.), Workshops in Computing (pp. 51-68). Springer-Verlag, Berlin

Chen, T.Y., & Yu, Y.T. (2002). A decision-theoretic approach to the test allocation problem in partition testing. *IEEE Transactions on Systems, Man, and Cybernetics, Part A: Systems and Humans, 32*(6), 733-745.

Cheng, K.T., & Kumar, A. S. K. (1983). Automatic functional test generation using the extended finite state machine model. *Proceedings of the 30th international Conference on Design Automation (Dallas, Texas, United States, June 14 - 18, 1993). DAC '93* (pp. 86-91). New York, NY: ACM Press.

Crnkovic, F., J. K., Larsson, M., & Lau, K. K. (2000). Object-oriented design frameworks: Formal specification and some implementation issues. *Proceedings of 4th IEEE International Baltic Workshop, Vol. 2,* (pp. 63—77).

Doong, R.K., & Frankl, P. (1991). Case Studies in Testing Object-Oriented Software. *Testing, Analysis, and Verification Symposium, Association for Computing Machinery,* (pp. 165 – 177). New York.

Doong, R.K., & Frankl, P. (1994). The ASTOOT approach to testing object-oriented programs. *ACM Transactions on Software Engineering and Methodology, 3*(2), 101-130.

Eden, A. H., & Hirshfeld, Y. (2001). Principles in formal specification of object oriented design and architecture. D. A. Stewart and J. H. Johnson (Eds.), *Proceedings of the 2001 Conference of the Centre For Advanced Studies on Collaborative Research (Toronto, Ontario, Canada, November 05 - 07, 2001)*. IBM Centre for Advanced Studies Conference. IBM Press.

Friedman, G., Hartman, A., Nagin, K., &Shiran, T. (2002, July 22 - 24). Projected state machine coverage for software testing. Proceedings of the 2002 ACM SIGSOFT international Symposium on Software Testing and Analysis (Roma, Italy 2002). ISSTA '02 (pp. 134-143). New York, NY: ACM Press..

Gaudel, M.C. (1995). Testing can be formal, too. *Theory and Practice of Software Development (TAPSOFT '95): Proceedings of 6th International Joint Conference of CAAP/FACE, P.D. Mosses, M. Nielsen, and MI. Schwartzbach (eds.), Lecture Notes in Computer Science,* Vol. 915, (pp. 82-96). Berlin: Springer-Verlag.

Guttag, J. V., & Horning, J. J., Garland, S.J., Jones, K.D., Modet, A., & Wing, J.M. (1993). Larch: languages and tools for formal specification. *Texts and Monographs, Computer Science series* NY: Springer-Verlag.

Harrold, M.J., McGregor, J.D., & Fitzpatrick, K.J. (1992). Incremental testing of object-oriented class structures. *Proceedings of the 14th International Conference on Software Engineering* (pp. 68 – 80.

Heffter, A. P., (1997). Specification and verification of object-oriented programs. Habilitationsschrift, Technische Universitaet Muenchen, 1997. Retrieved from the URL http://wwweickel. informatik.tu-muenchen.de/ persons/poetzsch/

habil.ps.gz.

Hoare, C. A. R. (1969). An axiomatic basis for computer programming. *Comm. ACM, 12*(10), 576-583.

Hoare, C. A. R. (1972). Proof of correctness of data representations. *Acta Informatica, 1(*4), 271-281.

Marick, B. (1999). New models for test development. *Proceedings of International Quality Week, May, 1999.* Retrieved from http://www.testing. com/writings/ new-models.pdf

McGregor, J.D., & Korson, T.D. (1994). Testing the polymorphic interactions of classes. *Technical Report No. TR-94-103*, Clemson University.

Murphy, G.C., Townsend, P., & Wong, P.S. (1994). Experiences with cluster and class testing. *Communications of the ACM, 37*(9), 39 – 47.

Naik, K. (1997). Efficient computation of unique input/output sequences in finite-state machines. *IEEE/ACM Trans. Netw, 5*(4), pp. 585-599.

Offutt, Liu, J., Abdurazik, S., & Ammann, P. A. (2003). Generating test data from state-based specifications. *Software testing verification and reliability, 13*(1), 25-54.

Rapps, S., & Weyuker, E. J. (1982, September 13-16). Data flow analysis techniques for test data selection. *Proceedings of the 6th international Conference on Software Engineering. International Conference on Software Engineering (pp. 272-2780).* Los Alamitos, CA: IEEE Computer Society Press.

Richardson, D. J., & Clarke, L. A. (1981, March 9-12). A partition analysis method to increase program reliability. *Proceedings of the 5th international Conference on Software Engineering (San Diego, California, United States,). International Conference on Software Engineering. (pp. 244-253).* Piscataway, NJ: IEEE Press.

Smith, M.D., & Robson, D.J. (1992). A framework

for testing object-oriented programs. *Journal of Object-Oriented Programming, 5*(3), 45 – 53.

VanderBrug, G. J., & Minker, J. (1975). State-space problem-reduction, and theorem proving—some relationships. *Commun. ACM, 18*(2), 107-119.

Weyuker, E. J., & Jeng, B. (1991). Analyzing partition testing strategies. *IEEE Trans. Softw. Eng., 17*(7), 703-711.

Wieringa, R. (1998). A survey of structured and object-oriented software specification methods and techniques. *ACM Comput. Surv., 30*(4), 459-527.

Wing, J.M. (1983). A two-tiered approach to specifying programs. *Technical Report TR-299*, Mass. Institute of Technology, Laboratory for Computer Science.

This work was previously published in International Journal of Information Technology and Web Engineering, Vol. 3, Issue 2, edited by G. Alkhatib and D. Rine, pp. 18-26, copyright 2008 by IGI Publishing (an imprint of IGI Global).

Chapter 12
Towards Automated Bypass Testing of Web Applications

J. Miller
University of Alberta, Canada

L. Zhang
University of Alberta, Canada

E. Ofuonye
University of Alberta, Canada

M. Smith
University of Calgary, Canada

ABSTRACT

The construction and testing of Web-based systems has become more complex and challenging with continual innovations in technology. One major concern particularly for the deployment of mission critical applications is security. In Web-based systems, the principal vulnerabilities revolve around deficient input validation. This chapter describes a partially automated mechanism, the tool InputValidator, which seeks to address this issue through bypassing client-side checking and sending test data directly to the server to test the robustness and security of the back-end software. The tool allows a user to construct, execute and evaluate a number of test cases through a form-filling exercise instead of writing bespoke test code.

INTRODUCTION

The usage of Web-based applications has significantly expanded and affects our daily lives in a multitude of ways. Internet usage statistics show that as of June 2008 (Internet World Stats, 2008), over 1.4 billion individuals have used the World Wide Web (WWW) for various undertakings ranging from communication (mail, telecommunication), business (buying and selling, stock trading), social events (multimedia, virtual hang-outs, gaming), and information gathering (weather data, news); all from the convenience of their homes and offices.. Constructing an effective Web-based system to satisfy this rising dependence and very demanding non-functional requirements has become increasingly complex and challenging with

DOI: 10.4018/978-1-60566-719-5.ch012

systems typically running on distributed hardware and containing both client-side and server-side components. Incompatibility and associated security issues abound on the client side from the variety of browsers. The problems change with each new software release (Nguyen, 2001), and are compounded with the countless combinations of hardware configurations. On the server side, there is equal complexity derived from the deployment of miscellaneous environments to support Web-applications. The challenges to the testing of Web-based systems has increased given that the server-side software for many companies and global corporations has to be distributed over a number of physical servers, or hosted by third-party Web service providers. Vulnerabilities concerning network reliability, accessibility, security and compatibility are made worse by the simple fact that, of necessity, most Web-based applications are exposed to an unidentified worldwide set of (un-trustworthy) users.

Another challenge to testing such systems is the "Management Factor". The competitiveness of software development and IT industry has pushed companies to shorten their software development life cycle to design, code, test, and deliver products rapidly using development processes such as Extreme Programming and test-driven development, etc (Beck et al., 2008). However this has placed increased pressure on testing and quality assurance activities.

Due to the complexity introduced by the environment and technology factors, as well as the pressure from management, the testing of Web-based systems must be automated to be successful. While some testing tools have been adapted to accommodate Web-based systems (Hower, 2008; Automated Testing Specialists, 2006), these tools tend to be rather generic in nature and do not cover the full spectrum of issues that are unique to Web-based systems.

This paper introduces a new test tool developed to help testing engineers to automatically parse form parameters, generate test cases according to

users' input data, and provide an interface which implements bypass testing (Offutt, 204). The remainder of this paper is as follows. In section 2, testing methods and issues arising from them is defined for two of the most common vulnerabilities: SQL injection and invalid input. In section 3, bypass testing is introduced as a technique to solve these issues; together with how the new tool (the main topic of the paper) can be efficiently used to implement bypass testing. Section 4 illustrates this tool-based testing approach on a real Web site; followed by the final section, Section 5, the conclusion.

CURRENT STATE OF THE ART

There is no common wisdom on how to categorize the very wide range of potential risks or prevention mechanisms found in Web-based systems. Attempting this categorization, Gerrard and Thompson (2002) identified 24 distinct test types; grouped into seven categories. Nguyen (2001) categorizes tests into 14 distinct types. Vijayaraghavan and Kaner (2002) summarize bugs that can happen on (virtual) "shopping carts" into no less than 60 categories! However, no matter how the testing of Web-based systems is sorted, security concerns and their associated testing have drawn much attention and have become extremely critical for Web-based systems; especially for e-commerce applications. The Open Web Application Security Project's (2006) top ten vulnerabilities that need to be addressed through security testing are, in order of importance, invalidated input, broken access control, broken authentication, cross-site scripting, buffer overflows, injection flows, improper effort handling, insecure storage, application denial of service, and insecure configuration management. Although categorized separately, many of the listed vulnerabilities, for example cross-site scripting, injection flows, and buffer overflows, are indirectly a result of insufficient input validation. Thus, validating inputs can be identified as being particularly significant for preventing the majority of serious security flaws.

SQL Injection and Testing

SQL injection, the exploitation of Web-based systems by introducing SQL-reserved characters into SQL queries, is considered one of the most serious types of attacks against Web-based systems (Halfond & Orso, 2005). In these attacks, the malicious user's input is included in the SQL query so that it will be treated as part of the code. If not properly validated, execution of such invalid SQL commands could cause confidential information to be leaked or the database corrupted. SQL injection attacks can be implemented through *select*, *insert*, or SQL server stored procedures (SPI Dynamics, 2002). The most common injection technique is authorization bypass, where the unauthorized user is allowed to access the database after the form-based login authorizations are bypassed. Lists of characters commonly tried by an attacker for bypassing a site's validation can be found in (MSDN, 2004; Offutt, 2004). SQL injection can be prevented by input validation such as filtering the data with a "default-deny" regular expression (SPI Dynamics, 2002). Also taint based approaches (Huang et al, 2004; Halfond et al, 2007) can be used to uncover and prevent common SQL injection vulnerabilities using static analysis of Web application source code.

Invalidated Input Vulnerability and Bypass Testing

Despite SQL injection being the most recognized form of code-based security defects in Web-based systems, it is in fact a sub-component of a wider set of issues – that of invalidated input vulnerabilities. Invalidated input is the result of lack of proper user input validation on either the client-side, or the server-side, or both. Currently, many applications apply input validation (HTML form elements) and enforce input rules on the client side. Client-side

scripting is used to check which fields are required to be filled, the format (such as a URI or an email address), the length or size of input and the set of characters allowed in the input fields. Additionally, often "value comparison" (such as comparing the retyped password to the initially entered one) is utilized to cross-check the validity of the input. This results in preventing invalid or malformed input being sent – reducing the request traffic to the server. However, an attacker can deliberately manipulate any part of an HTTP request and easily bypass all such client side checks.

Bypass testing is simply checking for the correct response from the server by directly sending valid and invalid data via a HTTP request independently of any client-side checking. Offutt et al. (2004) characterizes bypass testing into three types:

1. **Value level** bypass testing is intended to verify the ability of the server to evaluate invalid inputs. Examples of this type of testing include:

    a. Data type and value modification which involve changing the data types associated with input values, *e.g.* using real numbers instead of integers.

    b. HTML built-in length violations where the maximum length of the input string attributed in the HTML tag 'input' is exceeded.

    c. HTML built-in value violation attempts to change the pre-defined value in HTML select, check box or radio buttons.

    d. Value violation which is normally attempted by supplying non-alphabetic or reserved characters.

A more substantial, categorized list of possible invalid inputs can be found in Tappenden et al. (2005).

2. **Parameter level** bypass tests are designed to enumerate possible invalid inputs through customizing and combining input parameter selection and inter-value constraints *e.g.* a postal code text field accepting five chars automatically when users select the U.S. as a country in a registration form, while six must be allowed if Canada is selected. Offutt et al. (2004) proposed an algorithm to derive all possible input patterns in Web applications. However, care needs to be exercised with this approach, as the number of tests cases, in realistic scenarios, often suffers from a computational explosion (Sahil, 2006).

3. **Control flow level** bypass testing is verifying whether the system provides a proper response to an invalid system state that is reached by altering the control flow. The common way to break the normal flow of control involves navigating backwards and forwards, refreshing a page and entering a new URI.

Only value level bypass testing is covered in this paper, as only this form of bypass testing is currently supported by the tool. The authors plan to expand the system to cover completely these other forms of bypass testing in the future.

SUPPORTING BYPASS TESTING

Description of State of the Art Support Tool: HTTPUNIT

Bypassing the browser and directly accessing the server is commonly realized via HTTPUNIT (httpunit.sourceforge.net/); a unit test framework that allows the implementation of automated test scripts for Web applications. HTTPUNIT works by emulating the browser in terms of form submission, frame handling, JavaScript, basic http authentication, cookies, and automatic page redirection. The ease of testing is improved through the use of Java test code to examine returned pages either as text, as XML DOM, or containers of forms, tables, and links (Gold, 2008). Although developed for unit testing, as its name indicates, HTTPUNIT is also a powerful tool for creating test suites to ensure the total end-to-end functionality of Web applications.

HTTPUNIT can emulate an entire session by using a class called *WebConversation* to manage the requests, handle the cookies, and resolve URIs (Scheinblum, 2006). The *WebRequest* class represents requests to a server, while the *WebResponse* class encapsulates the reply. Once a request has been sent successfully, HTTPUnit utilizes several external systems to parse the HTML, XML and JavaScript code responses from the server side (CyberNeko, 2006; APACHE, 2008; Mozilla. org, 2008).

As a browser emulator, HTTPUNIT accepts all client-side input constraints by default, which makes it most suitable for the implementation of automated functional and acceptance tests. However, the default verification can be disabled to allow bypassing of all client-side validations to test the robustness and security of a Web-server directly through calling *WebForm.newunvalidatedRequest()* (to set any values in this request), or changing the original value in the form through

```
<form>.getScriptableOb-
ject().setParameterValue
(<name>,<value>)
```

The New Support Tool *InputValidator*

While *HTTPUnit* supports the bypass testing method, the user is still required to program and create a large number of test cases manually to cover all possible invalid inputs to test a modern Web server; potentially containing hundreds of form fields and requests. The enormity of the possible workload is clearly illustrated by the fact that Offutt et al. (2004) found it necessary to generate and execute 107 value level tests when

Figure 1.The workflow of the automatic bypass testing via InputValidator

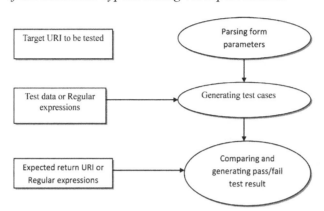

testing a Small Text Information System (STIS) which contained only eight JSPs that processed parameterized requests. *InputValidator* is a value-level bypass testing tool that extends HTTPUnit to ease this construction burden. The workflow of the automated bypass testing, as implemented by *InputValidator*, is described and illustrated in Figure 1. Through a GUI, testing engineers can now simplify the testing process by entering the target URI, the expected return URI and the test data without touching any test code. Further, when compared to Tappenden et al's (2005) approach, there are a number of significant enhancements present in the new *InputValidator* tool: (1) the automatic evaluation of the results; and (2) the ability to apply regular expressions to simulate the returned URI. Table 1 shows the comparison of the major functionalities of HTTPUnit and *InputValidator* when used as automatic bypass testing support systems.

Table 1. The comparison of major features implemented in HTTPUnit and InputValidator

Functionality/Concerns	Test via HTTPUnit	Test via InputValidator
Generate test data	manually	manually
Parse form parameters	manually	automatically
Create test cases	manually	automatically
Accept test data	In test code	Via GUI
Create HTTP request	In test code	Via GUI

Parsing Form Parameters Using *InputValidator*

First, users input the target URI to which the GET or POST HTTP test requests will be sent. A HTML Parser then searches through the specified URI to find all of the forms and their parameters. The results of this search are listed in the Test Suite Frame. For example, if there are two forms in the target HTML page, two test-suite frames (Figure 2A) will be created with the same name as the forms. The user can then double click one of the test suites to open the main window. In the main window (Figure 2B), users can input the prepared test data for each parameter or input a regular expression to specify a generic test pattern. A simple click on *Build test cases* generates the specified test cases without the user being required to generate any test code.

Preparing Test Data and Generating Test Cases Using *InputValidator*

To test the robustness of the server by value level bypass testing, many kinds of invalid data need to be created, for example:

1. System reserved, or non-alphabetic, characters in a string as part of the SQL query;

Figure 2. (A) Test task frame and (B) Mainframe window of the InputValidator tool

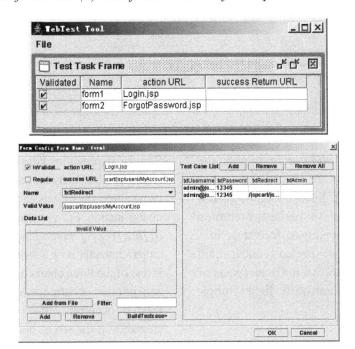

2. Strings exceeding the maximum length limited for a text field; and
3. Using real numbers instead of integers.

Tappenden et al. (2005) provide a detailed definition of the required test patterns. With pre-existing support tools, users need to prepare test data for each field manually and preparing sufficient test data to cover all scenarios is time-consuming. However as discussed above, when using *Inputvalidator* users can also choose to input a regular expression to automatically retrieve relevant test data strings from as associated data files or databases.

As a further example, consider the simple login page found at https://oldWebmail.ualberta.ca/ where valid and invalid data must be generated from each of the form parameters: the User and Password fields, plus the two hidden fields (*SaveUser, DoLogin*). Then a test case must be generated with values for these four HTTP parameters, and subsequently sent to the server directly via HTTPUnit, i.e. bypassing the browser (client).

When using the tool, we view bypass testing as having two components, boundary testing and statistical testing. When the testers can identify boundary situations, they produce test cases and oracles by defining specific examples; both inside (valid) and outside (invalid) the boundary. This clearly allows for the precise evaluation of the correctness and robustness of the system at these critical junctures. Away from these areas, the testers are involved in statistical, or random, testing, where they probe the system with a multitude of examples and check for only a type of response rather than specific values. This second statistical type of testing is implemented via the regular expressions. This allows the tester to generate one or two test patterns, while the system automatically generates (input side) and evaluates (output side) a large number of test cases for a specific input region or category.

Although the above example, with 4 fields in one form, is clearly trivial, we can already see that the number of possible test cases (and evaluations) is escalating; hence the need for the proposed automatic approach is obvious.

Figure 3. Test result

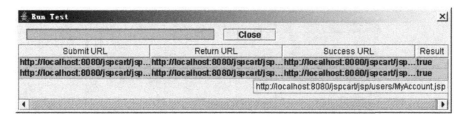

When using *InputValidator* to bypass the browser, HTTP requests are created and sent to the server automatically. Subsequently pass/fail results are identified after comparing the returned URI (expressed in the common format or in a regular expression) to the expected or unexpected one. The result will be shown in Green (pass) or Red (fail) using the common traffic light symbolism (Figure 3).

Using Regular Expressions for Describing Test Patterns

In our system, regular expressions are utilized to express inputs (test data) and to define valid results (test oracles) and to describe test patterns for bypassing testing of Web-based systems. A regular expression is a string (pattern) for describing a set of strings that can be used for matching strings.

Regular expressions consist of normal characters and meta-characters and are formed into a pattern using three operations: alternation, grouping and quantification. For example the regular expression $a | [bcd] f^* b + [^\wedge notme]$ indicates a pattern to match either character *a* or a string whose first character is one of the three characters *b, c or d*, followed by zero or more occurrences of the character *f*, then at least one occurrence of the character *b* with the final character in the string being any (alpha-numeric) character other than *e, m, n, o* or *t*. An example of a regular expression to detect cross-site scripting faults on the input-side is "(<script>)[A-Za-z0-9]+"; which can be used to extract any string starting with "<script>". Table 2 shows the typical special characters and strings that are important for validation of server-side robustness (Tappenden, 2005).

On the output side, regular expressions are utilized for the modeling of returned parameters.

Table 2. Sample input validation patterns

Special Input	Example Symbols	Example Strings
Special Characters	empty string	
XML Reserved Characters	&, <, >, ", '	<xml>
		""
Unix Reserved Characters	;, &, (,), |, *, ?, !	!substitution^
		& background execution
SQL Reserved Characters	(,), ;, [,], ', ", OR, AND	' OR ' '='
		x' AND email IS NULL; --'
Windows Reserved Characters	\, /, |,, ;,, <, >,;	... /
		.abcdefg
Characters with high bit set	þ, ÿ	þÿ
Control Character	NIL, newline	NIL
		newline

For example, if the target test link is Yahoo finance, http://finance.yahoo.com/currency, then after submitting the test data, four parameters (`amt´, `from´, `to´, and `submit´) and their associated values are returned; which can be recognized (defined) through a regular expression such as:

```
".*((amt=[1-9]&?)|(from=USD&?)|
(to=JPY&?)|(submit=Convert&?))
{4}"
```

When the test case is executed, the system parses the returned URI

```
http://finance.yahoo.com/cur-
rency/convert?amt=3&from=USD&to=
JPY&submit=Convert
```

to get the parameters and their values. If they match to the specified regular expression, the test case passes; otherwise, the test case fails.

Deriving Test Cases from Regular Expressions

Regular expressions have been widely used in Computer Science in areas of specifying lexical analyzers for programming languages, controllers for sequential machines, filters for database searching, patterns in image processing and communication protocols (Foster, 1989). Many researchers have studied how to match a regular expression to a string since 1960's (Berry & Sethi, 1986; Thompson, 1968). The general approach is to convert a regular expression into an equivalent finite state automaton. Sequences in a set described by a regular expression are equivalent to the transitions of its finite state machine.

However our requirements are not to produce such a system; in fact we need the inverse operation when testing. Instead, the system is required to generate a random set of strings that satisfy the input constraints defined by the tester as a regular expression. Given that the solution set is probably infinite, there is no obvious optimal approach to this problem. Our initial approach was to view this as a goal-oriented problem and generalize the concept used in other test case generation systems, where attempts are made to satisfy code coverage measures. We had recently published a paper on this type of system, used in an entirely different testing context. The approach blends Genetic Algorithms as the optimization component with rigorous code parsing to supplement the often sparse feature space encountered by the optimization algorithm (Miller et al., 2006). However, our initial attempts in redefining the objective function within the Web-testing context tended to lead to relatively flat, feature-less, search terrains. In addition, as the exact alphabet and operations for the expression of the input description are embedded within the goal-oriented algorithm, an attempt to move this approach into the new environment lacked flexibility. The main problem is that the form of the objective function will be required to be reformulated as Web-based systems evolve; potentially in connection with the adoption of new technologies.

A less obvious, but nevertheless useful approach was used to circumvent the problem and, at the same time, utilize existing resources. We are able to trivially generate large text files with random contents. Given, sufficient numbers of these files, they will clearly contain examples of every possible regular expression. Hence, the problem is now transformed into one of efficiently and effectively searching this text space (the multitude of random files). This reformulation of the problem allows us to utilize the considerable amount of research and systems that exist on this topic. Clearly, standard regular expression matching systems such as lex, awk and grep can be utilized to prove a solution (Levine, 1992; Aho et al. 1988). While, this approach has obvious merit, our investigations are still in their infancy and our trials, to-date, have only been upon small Web-sites requiring only relatively simple regular expressions to be constructed. However, we are still to explore the question of whether this approach scales up if it is required to construct highly complex expressions; potentially with an extended alphabet and operation set. This would potentially require the construction of very large text files and the efficiency of the search strategy may become a bottleneck. To solve these issues, we have started to explore fast regular expression indexing approaches, such as suffix trees (Baeza-Yates & Gonnet, 2006) and multigram indexes (Cho & Rajagopalan, 2002); as well as exploring approaches which take advantage of sub-matches (Laurikari, 2001).

EVALUATION OF THE SYSTEM

In this section, we briefly illustrate the application of bypass testing and *InputValidator* on an open-source shopping cart, JspCart (Version 1.2, downloaded: January 2006) which can be downloaded at: www.neurospeech.com/Products/JspCart.aspx

Due to the volume of data generated by the testing process, we will illustrate the procedure by simply supplying some insightful examples rather than providing the process in its entirety. The test cases are designed based on the value level bypass testing concept and methodologies. In the following subsections, the illustration is demonstrated in the following format:

1. **Test scenario:** Defining the testing purpose against a certain feature/functionality.
2. **Source code:** Client-side code, with or without input restriction. Some source code is simplified for greater readability. Comments are added in bold text. Note: this is the code that we are bypassing when sending responses directly to the server.
3. **Test input:** The test URI, the target (or returned) URI, and values for any input fields which exist. This is the input accepted by the *InputValidator* tool and used to automatically

generate the responses send directly to the server.
4. **Expected test result:** Describing the expected test result.
5. **Actual test result:** Describing the real test result and what errors, if any, are found.

The Test Environment for Evaluating the Robustness of JspCart

We downloaded the source code and setup a local system for testing purposes using a supporting environment of Tomcat 4.1 (tomcat.apache.org/) and the MySQL (www.mysql.com). JspCart provides most of the functionalities common to other commercial shopping carts. Users can register and login to an online shop; the administrator has the privilege to edit and customize all of the information provided to the users. This customization includes editing the product list, email templates, setting preferences for presenting pages, managing orders and user lists. Figure 4 shows the entry page for the online store.

Test Scenario 1: Does the JspCart System Validate the Input Restrictions on the Server-Side?

This test scenario is used to determine whether the JspCart system blocks invalid requests by validating, cross-checking on the server side, the input restrictions imposed by the client-side JavaScript code of the signup page. The signup page utilizes length restrictions, password comparisons, and email formatting when constructing its required fields. Figure 5 shows the page to be tested. Listing 1 is the source code (Signup.jsp provided by the JspCart server) to perform client-side input validation. We have added some commentary (**bolded**) to increase its readability.

Test input. To test how the sign-up page responses are handled by the JspCart server, the tester provides *InputValidator* with the required Test URIs (page's location) and Target URI (successful

Figure 4. Registration page for the on-line store

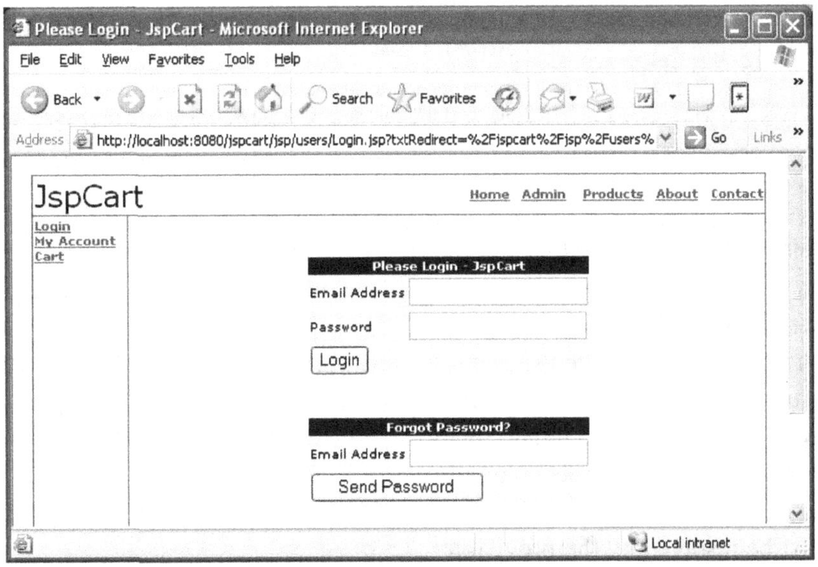

Figure 5. The signup page on JSPCart

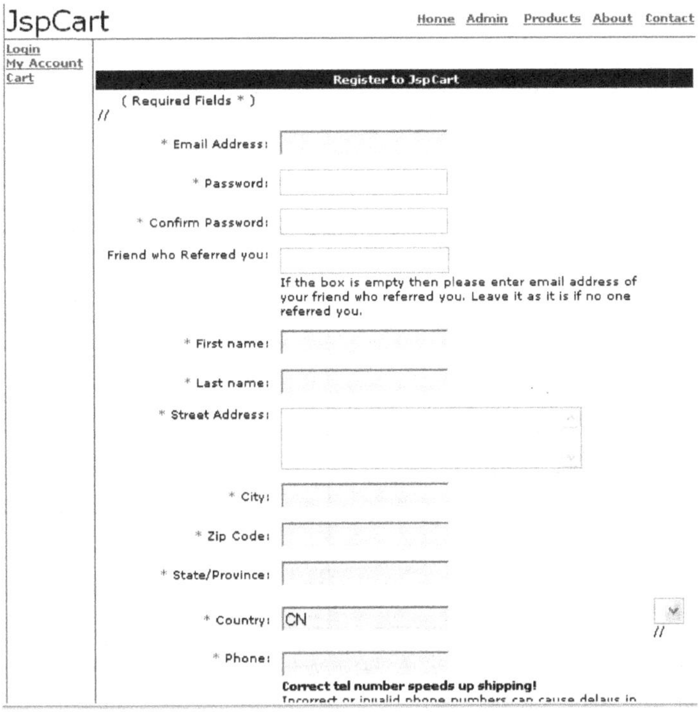

registration response) as shown in Table 3, together with the associated form parameters (Table 4). Note the testers are not required to write any code, they simply provide a set of values. The three supplied

data sets all contain illegal data – and hence should be rejected by the online system.

Expected test result: For this system, the tester expects that when any data set contain-

Table 3. The page's location and the expected output are provided by the tester

Test URI (Input URI)	**http://localhost:8080/jspcart/jsp/users/Signup.jsp?txtRedirect=/jspcart/jsp/ users/MyAccount.jsp**
Target URI	http://localhost:8080/jspcart/jsp/users/Login.jsp?txtMessage=Registration%20 Successful,%20please%20login.&txtRedirect=%2Fjspcart%2Fjsp%2Fusers%2F MyAccount.jsp

ing any invalid elements is supplied, the system rejects the input.

Actual test result: As can be seen from Fig. 6, the three sets of test data are submitted successfully, i.e. all sign ups were found to be successful with the returned URI matching the target URI ("successful login page") despite the input of invalid responses. Thus the testers have found a defect which must be resolved by the provision that additional server side checking be made to ensure that the expected input restrictions are met *e.g.* email format, an empty and inconsistent password. This will ensure that the system remains safe regardless of whether the user supplies this data via the page on the browser (i.e. being processed by the client-side code) or bypasses the client-side

and sends the request directly to the server with the intent of penetrating the system.

Listing 1. The Source Code, Signup. jsp, Provided by the JspCart Server to Perform Client-Side Input Validation

```
<SCRIPT LANGUAGE=javascript>
<!-
//Assign a default value to txt-
Country, i.e. this field should
not be empty document.Signup-
Form.txtCountry.value = "United
States of America"
    alphabets = new String("abcde
fghijklmnopqrstuvwxyz");
```

Table 4. The form parameters input into InputValidator; Blank cells imply empty values

Form Parameters	Client-side Validation	Test Data		
		Set 1	Set 2	Set 3
txtEmailAddress	must contain "@"	tester.@gmail	hello	tester
txtPassword	must not be empty and must be 5 or more chars			
txtPassword2	Must be same as the value of txtPassword			abc
txtReferredBy	n/a			
txtStreetAddress	must not be empty			
txtCity	must not be empty			
txtZipCode	must not be empty			
txtState	must not be empty			
txtPhone	must not be empty			
txtCountry	Default value is US	country?		
txtReference	n/a			
bSendPromotion	n/a			
bNeverSendMail	n/a			
bAgree	must be checked			

Figure 6. The test cases in this figure shows that, despite being sent invalid data, the server could be hoodwinked into allowing a successful registration

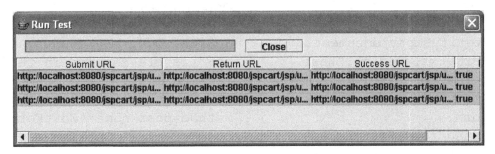

```
   numbers = new
String("0123456789");
//Verify that the value of the
object cannot be empty
   function
verifyEmpty(object,name) {
     if(object.value=="") {
          alert(name + " can
not be empty.")
          object.focus();
          return false;   }
     return true;   }
//Verify that "Password" can not
be empty must be 5 or more char-
acters,
// and that the confirmation
password2 is same as password.
   function
verifyPasswords(pass,pass2) {
     if(!verifyEmpty(pass,"Pass
word"))  return false;
     if(!verifyLength(pass,5,"P
assword"))  return false;
     passString = new
String(pass.value)
     pass2String = new
String(pass2.value)
          if((passString.length
== pass2String.length) &&
(passString.indexOf(pass2String)
==0))                    return
true;
     alert("Both passwords are
not same. Please enter once
```

```
again")
        pass.value = ""; pass2.
value = "";  pass.focus();
        return false;}
//Verify that an email address
must contain "@"
   function verifyMail(object) {

if(!verifyEmpty(object,"Email
Address"))  return false;
     if(!exists(object.val-
ue,"@"))  { alert("Please enter
any valid email address")
          return false;   }
     return true; }
//Call functions to validate
email address, password, and
prohibit empty fields
// of "First name", "Last name",
"Street address", "Zip Code",
// "City", "State/Province",
"Phone", and also validate to
only accept the  // checked
"agree to terms and conditions"
option.
function verifyForm() {
     if(!verityMail(document.Sign-
upForm.txtEmailAddress))  return
false;

if(!verifyPasswords(document.
SignupForm.txtPassword,
document.SignupForm.txtPass-
word2))  return false;
```

```
    if(!verifyEmpty(document.
SignupForm.txtFirstname,"First
name")) return false;
    if(!verifyEmpty(document.
SignupForm.txtLastname,"Last
name")) return false;
    if(!verifyEmpty(document.
SignupForm.
txtStreetAddress,"Street ad-
dress"))
             return false;
    if(!verifyEmpty(document.
SignupForm.txtZipCode,"Zip
Code")) return false;
    if(!verifyEmpty(document.
SignupForm.txtCity,"City")) re-
turn false;
    if(!verifyEmpty(document.
SignupForm.txtState,"State/Prov-
ice")) return false;
    if(!verifyEmpty(document.
SignupForm.txtPhone,"Phone"))
return false;
    if(!document.SignupForm.
bAgree.checked) {
         alert("You must agree
to terms and conditions");
         document.SignupForm.
bAgree.focus()
         return false; }
    return true;   }
//-->
</SCRIPT>·
```

Test Scenario 2: Validation of Values from a Shopping Cart Selection List

The following test seeks to determine whether the system revalidates, on the server side, the values from a selection list (Listing 2). In this test case, the pre-defined country name is to be changed when editing the user's information.

Listing 2. Client-Side Selection List Code

```
Source code: the country name
"AF" is pre-defined in the se-
lection list.
<FORM action='Edit.jsp'
method=post name='EditForm'>
<!--------   Data Area -------
----->
    <TABLE border=0 class=Data
cellspacing=1 >
    <TD>txtEmailAddress</TD>
<TD><INPUT TYPE=TEXT
name='txtEmailAddress' val-
ue='12345@12345'></TD>
<TD>txtCountry</TD>
    <TD><INPUT TYPE=TEXT
name='txtCountry' value='AF'></
TD>
<TD colspan=2><INPUT TYPE=Submit
name='Submit' Value='Submit'></
TD>
</TABLE>
<!--------   End of Data Area
------------>
```

Test input: The test and input URI are shown in Table 5 with the tests on the form parameters shown in Table 6

Expected test result: The invalid country name should not be allowed.

Actual test result: Any string can be input as a country's name when editing a user's information. The actual effect of this defect, identified through testing, on the performance of JspCart was found to be very different than the effect of the defect found in the first test case. Consider the situation where the user has logged in and has added some products into his / her cart, to be purchased. When the user tries to check-out the shopping cart (i.e. buy the goods), a system exception occurs (Figure 7)! Clearly, this type of error is likely to be of serious concern to the

Figure 7. Exception generated, on checkout, as a consequence of the server erroneously accepting an invalid country name during a much earlier user profile change

Table 5. Input from Tester - The start and end points

Test URI (Input URI)	http://localhost:8080/jspcart/admin/users/Edit.jsp?txtEmailAddress=12345@12345
Target URI	http://localhost:8080/jspcart/admin/users/List.jsp

user, especially as they are trying to complete a financial transaction. These sort of errors directly impact the user's perception of the competence and trustworthiness of Web-sites (Ofuonye et al, 2008) and the-is impact could be that they take their business elsewhere.

Test Scenario 3: Cross-Site Scripting Failures

This test case evaluates the sites vulnerabilities to cross-site scripting faults. Listing 3 shows part of the source code: a simple form with a few parameters and some default values. No client-side restrictions are imposed. Table 7 shows the input and target URI, with Table 8 providing the test cases for the form parameters.

Listing 3. The Client-Side Code for the Form Under Test

```
<FORM action="Edit.jsp"
method="POST">
<input type=hidden
```

Table 6. Form parameters for the Test URI – Invalid country

Form Parameter	Test Data
txtEmailAddress	tester.sqa@gmail.com
txtCountry	Afzzzzzzzzzzzz

Table 7. Driver URIs

Test URI (Input URI)	http://localhost:8080/jspcart/admin/preferences/Edit.jsp?txtName=nbp.jspcart.preferences.SignupPage
Target URI	http://localhost:8080/jspcart/admin/preferences/List.jsp

Table 8. Form data inject the problem via txtHeader

Form Parameter	Test Data
txtHeader	<Script> Empty dummy command
txtFooter	hello
txtTitle	

```
name="txtName" value="nbp.jsp-
cart.preferences.SignupPage">
<TD valign><STRONG>txtHeader</
STRONG></TD>
<TD><textarea cols=40 rows=5
name='txtHeader'></textarea></
TD>
<TD valign><STRONG>txtFooter</
STRONG></TD>
<TD><textarea cols=40 rows=5
name='txtFooter'></textarea></
TD>
<TD valign><STRONG>txtTitle</
STRONG></TD>
<TD><textarea cols=40 rows=5
name='txtTitle'>Signup - Jsp-
Cart</textarea></TD>
<TD><input type=submit
value='Save'></TD>
</FORM>
```

Expected test result: "<Script>" should not be accepted by the server if cross-site scripting failures are to be avoided

Actual test result: The set of test data was submitted and the preference was found to be updated successfully in the system. However, the link between the Signup page and the selection event is not created after executing the test case in which "<script>" was entered as the value of txtHeader in any Preferences edit forms. That is, when clicking "Click here" to signup with JspCart, the expected signup page (Figure 5) does not appear, and instead we are presented with a corrupted page! Since, the sign page cannot be completed everyone is locked out of the system.

It is believed that our three boundary-condition test scenarios effectively demonstrate the utility of bypass testing and the support tool *Inputvalidator*. Further, it is believed that the examples are illustrative of a general problem found in many Web-based systems – that of over dependency on client-side processing for input validation. One only needs to look at the entries in popular vulnerability databases, such as the Open Source Vulnerability Database (http://www.osvdb.org/) and Bugtraq (http://www.securityfocus.com/archive/1), to view the multitude of open source, and commercial systems that have large numbers of known vulnerabilities due to inadequate input validation.

CONCLUSION

As their popularity rises, the security of Web-based systems is of increasing concern. A recent study on cyber-attacks shows that 75 percent of attacks occur at the application level (Grossman, 2004). Many Web applications have been discovered to possess various security vulnerabilities; weaknesses in a system that allow an attacker to violate the integrity, confidentiality, access control, availability, consistency or audit mechanism of the system or the data and applications that it hosts. This problem does not only exist in small companies; many of the affected Websites belong to large organizations who have extensive resources to secure their Web-sites. For example, the following high-profile sites have all experienced problems: FBI.gov, CNN.com, Time.com, Ebay, Yahoo!, Apple Computer, and Microsoft (CGISecurity.com, 202).

Researchers have demonstrated that bypass testing can be an effective mechanism in tackling security vulnerabilities, especially vulnerabilities introduced during the implementation phase of the construction process (Offutt et al., 2004; Tpaaneden et al. 2006). HTTPUNIT is the framework in which users can write and run test code to test the Web systems by emulating the browser. Since it emulates the browser, all client-side validation takes effect by default. However, only a very generic, highly manual, form of bypass testing can be implemented using HTTPUNIT through the disabling of default validation using *WebForm.newunvalidatedRequest()*. This process, while possible, is highly inefficient; and fails to support the tester both in analyzing the complexity of a Web-site and in the construction of test cases and oracles. This paper discusses a new tool *Inputvalidator*, which extends HTTPUNIT's capabilities by automating much of the bypass testing process and specifically seeks to address the outlined deficiencies. Specifically, testers can use the tool to automatically extract forms and to fill these forms without resulting to the production of test case code. They can also enter regular expressions to retrieve input data from pre-defined data files to automatically generate multiple test cases from a single test pattern; resulting in the ability to automatically generate test cases and perform the bypass testing rather than looking for each form field manually and writing the test code

by hand. Finally testers can enter output patterns, again using regular expressions, to automatically construct a variety of test oracles.

Using these facilities, it is believed that bypass testing now becomes a highly efficient and effective testing process which will hopefully greatly increase the tester's prospects in finding and locating security vulnerabilities. Several scenarios, based on testing an actual open-source shopping cart, are used to demonstrate the capabilities of the InputValidator tool. Test cases are quickly constructed and executed to find defects that cause a multitude of faults and vulnerabilities; including SQL injection, cross-scripting, hidden form field manipulation, the breaking of input length restrictions, invalidated input formats, and default value manipulations. These scenarios further serve as a demonstration of a common problem with modern Web-based systems – the over reliance on client-side validation and verification. If the next generation of Web-based systems is to be truly designed to be secure then both client-side and server-side verification and validation need to become the norm. In fact, client-side and server-side verification and validation need to become mirror images of each other. It is believed that bypass testing and *InputValidator* have a valid role of the production of this new breed of Web-based system.

REFERENCES

Aho, A. V., Kernighan, B. W., & Weinberger, P. J. (1988). *The AWK Programming Language.* Addison-Wesley

APACHE (2008). *The APACHE XML Project. Xerces2 Java Parser Readme.* Retrieved April 18, 2008 from xerces.apache.org/xerces2-j/index. html.

Automated Testing Specialists. (2006) Web and E-Commerce Testing. Retrieved February 26, 2006 from http://www.sqa-test.com/test.html

Baeza-Yates, R., & Gonnet, G. (1996). Fast text searching for regular expressions or automaton simulation over trees. *Journal of the ACM, 43*(6), 915–936. doi:10.1145/235809.235810

Beck, K., Beedle, M., van Bennekum, A., Cockburn, A., Cunningham, W., Fowler, M., & Grenning, J. Highsmith, J., Hunt, A., Jeffries, R., Kern, J., Marick, B., Martin, R.C., Mellor, S., Schwaber, K., Sutherland, J. & Thomas, D. (2008). Manifesto for Agile Software Development. Retrieved April 18, 2008 from http://www.agilemanifesto.org/

Berry, G., & Sethi, R. (1986). From regular expressions to deterministic automata. *Theoretical Computer Science, 48*, 117–126. doi:10.1016/0304-3975(86)90088-5

CGISecurity.com. (2002). The Cross Site Scripting FAQ. Retrieved February 2, 2006 from http://www.cgisecurity.com/articles/xss.faq.shtml

Cho, J., & Rajagopalan, S. (2002). A Fast Regular Expression Indexing Engine. In *Proceedings of 2002 International Conference on Data Engineering.*

CyberNeko (2006). The CyberNeko HTML Parser. Retrieved February 27, 2006 from people.apache.org/~andyc/neko/doc/html/index.html

SPI Dynamics (2002). SQL Injection: Are Your Web Applications Vulnerable [SPI Dynamics Whitepaper].

Foster, M. J. (1989). Avoiding latch formation in regular expression recognizers. *IEEE Transactions on Computers, 38*(5), 754–756. doi:10.1109/12.24279

Gerrard, P., & Thompson, N. (2002) *Risk-Based E-Business Testing* (1ˢᵗ ed.). Artech House.

Gold, R. (2008). HTTPUnit. Retrieved April 18, 2008 from httpunit.sourceforge.net

Grossman, J. (2004). Thwarting SQL Web Hacks. *VAR Business.*

Halfond, W., Orso, A., & Manolios, P. (2007). WASP: Protecting Web Applications Using Positive Tainting and Syntax-Aware Evaluation. *IEEE Transactions on Software Engineering, 34*(1), 65–81. doi:10.1109/TSE.2007.70748

Halfond, W. G. J., & Orso, A. (2005). Combining Static Analysis and Runtime Monitoring to Counter SQL-Injection Attacks. *Workshop on Dynamic Analysis* (pp. 1 -7).

Hower, R. (2008). Software QA/Test Resource Center. Web Site Test Tools and Site Management Tools. Retrieved April 18, 2008 from http://www.softwareqatest.com/qatweb1.html

Huang, Y., Yu, F., Hang, C., Tsai, C., Lee, D., & Kuo, S. (2004). Securing Web Application Code by Static Analysis and Runtime Protection. In *Proceedings of the 13th international conference on World Wide Web, May-2004* (pp. 40–52).

Internet World Stats (n.d.). World Internet Usage and Population Statistics. Retrieved October 25, 2008 from http://www.internetworldstats.com/stats.htm

Laurikari, V. (2001). *Efficient Submatch Addressing for Regular Expressions.* M.Sc. thesis, Dept. of Computer Science and Engineering, Helsinki University of Technology

Levine, J., Mason, T., & Brown, D. (1992). *Lex and Yacc.* O'Reilly

Miller, J., Reformat, M., & Zhang, H. (2006). Automatic Test Data Generation Using Genetic Algorithm and Program Dependence Graphs. *Journal of Information and Software Technology, 1*(2), 1–24.

Mozilla.org. (2008). *Rhino: JavaScript for Java.* Retrieved April 18, 2008 from http://www.mozilla.org/rhino

MSDN (2004). Injection Testing. Retrieved January 22, 2006 from msdn.microsoft.com/msdnmag/issues/04/09/SQLInjection

Nguyen, H. Q. (2001). *Testing Applications on the Web: test Planning for Internet-Based Systems*. John Wiley & Sons

Offutt, J., Wu, Y., Du, X., & Huang, H. (2004). Bypass Testing of Web Applications. *15th International Symposium on Software Reliability Engineering* (pp. 187-197).

Ofuonye, E., Beatty, P., Reay, I., Dick, S., & Miller, J. (2008). How do we Build Trust into Ecommerce Web Sites? *IEEE Software*, *25*(5), 7–9. doi:10.1109/MS.2008.136

Sahil, T. (2006). Robust Testing for Web Applications. Retrieved from http://www.Weberdev.com/ViewArticle-341.html

Scheinblum, J. (2006). Test entire Web applications with HTTPUNit. Retrieved February 20, 2006 from builder.com.com/5100-6370-1046258.html

Tappenden, A., Beatty, P., & Miller, J. (2005). Agile Security Testing of Web-Based Systems via HTTPUnit. *Agile*, *2005*, 29–38.

The Open Web Application Security Project. (2006). *OWASP Top Ten Most Critical Web Application Security Vulnerabilities*. Retrieved January 7, 2006 from www.owasp.org/documentation/topten.html

Vijayaraghavan, G., & Kaner, C. (2002). *Bugs in your shopping cart: A Taxonomy*. Paper presented in San Francisco QW2002 Paper 4I.

Chapter 13
Performance Analysis of a Web Server

Jijun Lu
University of Connecticut, USA

Swapna S. Gokhale
University of Connecticut, USA

ABSTRACT

With the rapid development and widespread use of the Internet, Web servers have become a dominant source of information and services. The use of Web servers in business and critical application domains imposes stringent performance requirements on them. These performance requirements cast a direct influence on the choice of the configuration options of the hardware and the software infrastructure on which a Web server is deployed. In addition to the selection of configuration options, for a given level of load and a particular hardware and software configuration, it is necessary to estimate the performance of a Web server prior to deployment.

INTRODUCTION AND MOTIVATION

The World Wide Web (WWW) has experienced an exponential growth in the last 10 years and today Web servers are important sources of information and services. Web servers, which are typically based on the HTTP protocol running over TCP/IP, are expected to serve millions of transaction requests per day with acceptable performance, which may be defined in terms of transaction throughput and latency experienced by the users (Van der Mei, Hariharan, & Reeser, 2001). The stringent performance requirements imposed on Web servers have a direct influence on the configuration options of the hardware and software infrastructure used for deployment. Hardware configuration options may include the capacity and the number of processors and caching strategies. Software configuration options may include the number of server threads/processes to serve client requests, the buffer size, and the scheduling discipline. Prior to deployment, for a given level of load, it is necessary to determine the hardware and software configuration options that would provide acceptable server performance.

One of the ways of estimating the performance of a Web server is by conducting actual measurements. While the measurement-based approach may be viable to estimate the performance for a given set of configuration options, it is cumbersome and expensive for "predictive" or "what-if" analysis and for an exploration of a set of alternative configurations. Model-based analysis, which consists of capturing the relevant aspects of a Web server into an appropriate model, validating the model and then using the validated model to predict the performance for different settings is an attractive alternative to the measurement-based approach.

Web servers receive and process a continuous stream of requests. As a result, a vast majority of their time is spent waiting for I/O operations to complete, making them particularly apt to fall under the category of I/O intensive applications (Ling, Mullen, & Lin, 2000). The performance of such I/O intensive applications (responsiveness, scalability, and throughput) can be improved dramatically if they are provided with the capability to process multiple requests concurrently. Thus, modern Web servers invariably process multiple requests concurrently to enhance their performance and to fulfill their workload demands. Considering the concurrent processing capability, we propose the use of a multiserver $M/G/m$ queue to model a Web server with an I/O intensive workload. The performance metric of interest is the response time of a client request. Since there is no known analytically or computationally tractable method to derive an exact solution for the response time of the $M/G/m$ queue, we use an approximation proposed by Sakasegawa (1977). We validate the model for deterministic and heavy-tailed workloads using experimentation. Our results indicate that the $M/G/m$ queue provides a reasonable estimate of the response time for moderately high traffic intensity. The conceptual simplicity of the model combined with the fact that it needs the estimation of very few parameters makes it easy to apply.

The balance of the article is organized as follows: First, we present the performance model of a Web server. We then discuss the workload characteristics used for the experimental validation of the model, followed by a description of the experimental infrastructure used for validation. Subsequently, we present and discuss the experimental results. Research related to the present work is summarized next. Finally, we offer concluding remarks and directions for future research.

PERFORMANCE MODEL

We describe the performance model of a Web server in this section. Towards this end, we first provide an overview of the software architecture of a Web server. Subsequently, we discuss the rationale for modeling a Web server using an $M/G/m$ queue and present an analytical expression to compute the approximate response time.

Web Server Software Architecture

Modern Web servers implement concurrent processing capability using a thread-based, a process-based, or a hybrid approach (Menasce, 2003). An example of a thread-based server is the Microsoft IIS server (Microsoft Corporation, n.d.), a process-based server is the Apache HTTP server 1.3, and a hybrid server is the Apache HTTP server 2.0 (Apache Software Foundation, n.d.).

In both the thread-based and process-based architectures, to avoid the overheads of forking a process/thread for every request, the Web server can fork a pool of processes/threads at start-up. If all these threads/processes are busy, either additional threads/processes can be forked or the request waits in a queue. In the former case, the size of the thread/process pool changes dynamically, whereas in the latter case the size of the thread/process pool is fixed and a new request waits in the queue if all the threads/processes are busy.

Queuing Model

We assume that the Web server consists of a static thread/process pool, with the number of threads/processes in the pool or the pool size, denoted m. Requests arrive at the server according to a Poisson distribution and the request service time is exponentially distributed. In most Web servers, the capacity of the queue to hold requests when all the threads/processes are busy is typically very large to ensure low probability of denying a request. Thus, for the purpose of modeling we assume the queue size to be infinite. The queuing model that coincides with these characteristics of a Web server, capable of processing requests concurrently is an $M/G/m$ queue. We note that since the model is based on the existence of concurrent processing capabilities, and not on the specific implementation of concurrency, it is general and equally applicable to a thread-based, a process-based or hybrid architecture.

Figure 1 shows a pictorial depiction of the $M/G/m$ queue. The arrival process is Poisson with rate and there are m parallel servers serving the requests. The service times of the requests are independent and identically distributed random variables, with a general distribution that has a finite mean μ^{-1} and a finite coefficient of variance

Figure 1. M/G/m queuing model

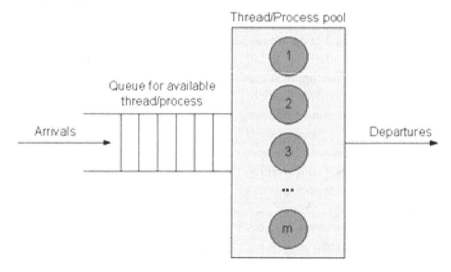

Table 1. Parameters of the M/G/m queuing model

Symbol	Meaning
R	Response time
m	Number of servers
λ	Arrival rate
μ	Service rate
c_s	Coefficient of variance of service time (ratio of standard deviation to the mean)
ρ	Traffic intensity $\rho = \lambda/(m\mu)$

c_s (the ratio of standard deviation to the mean). Specifically, for deterministic service times, $c_s = 0$; for exponential service times, $c_s = 1$; and for heavy-tailed service times, $c_s \to \infty$ (Lipsky, 1992). Let $\rho = \lambda/(m\mu)$ denote the traffic intensity, also known as utilization factor (Lipsky, 1992). For a stable system $\rho < 1$ and the queuing discipline is first-come-first-served (FCFS). Table 1 summarizes the parameters of the *M/G/m* model.

The performance metric of interest is the expected or the average response time of a client request denoted R. Except for certain special cases, there is no known analytically or computationally tractable method to derive an exact solution for the response time of the *M/G/m* queue. Several approximations have been proposed (Hokstad, 1978; Kimura, 1983; Sakasegawa, 1977; Yao, 1985) and among these we consider the one by Sakasegawa (Sakasegawa, 1977) since it requires very few parameters and involves straightforward computations. Using this approximation, the mean number of requests in the queue for the *M/G/m* model is given by:

$$L_q \approx \frac{(1+c_s^2)}{2} \frac{\rho^{\sqrt{2(m+1)}}}{1-\rho} \qquad (1)$$

Equation (1) indicates that the queue length increases as ρ increases. Further, for a service time distribution with high variability (where c_s is high), such as in the heavy-tailed distribution (Crovella, Taqqu, & Bestavros, 1998), the queue length will increase very rapidly.

Using Equation (1), the mean response time for the *M/G/m* queue as per Little's law (Kleinrock, 1976) is:

$$R_{M/G/m} \approx 1/\mu + \frac{L_q}{\lambda} =$$
$$1/\mu + \frac{(1+c_s^2)}{2\lambda} \frac{\rho^{\sqrt{2(m+1)}}}{1-\rho} \qquad (2)$$

Since a single server queue is commonly used to model a Web server (Cao, Anderson, Nyberg, & Kihl, 2003; Nossenson & Attiya, 2004; Squillante, Yao, & Zhang, 1999), we compare the mean response time of a multiserver *M/G/m* queue to the response time of a single-server *M/G/1* queue, which is given by:

$$R_{M/G/1} = 1/\mu + \frac{(1+c_s^2)}{2\lambda} \frac{\rho'^2}{1-\rho'} \qquad (3)$$

where $\rho' = 1/\mu = m\rho$. Notice that $R_{M/G/1} > R_{M/G/m}$ holds for $\forall m \geq 2$.

WORKLOAD CHARACTERISTICS

We consider service scenarios where each request is for a single static file and the server responds to the client with the file. Since the file size is demonstrated to be heavy-tailed (Crovella et al., 1998), we consider two types of workloads, namely, deterministic and heavy-tailed, which are described next.

Deterministic Workload

For a deterministic workload, all the requests are for the same file size in a single experiment. We consider four deterministic workloads with file sizes of 64 KB, 128 KB, 256 KB, and 512 KB. The smallest size considered is 64 KB due to the measurement granularity, which is 10 *msec* for our test bed (described in the next section). We note that even for a deterministic workload, in which the file size in every request is the same, the service time on an experimental test bed/real system will fluctuate (Lipsky, 1992), implying that $c_s \neq 0$ in Equation (1). Since the magnitude of these fluctuations is expected to be small compared to the actual service time, we use the term *deterministic workload* to indicate a relatively stable workload compared to the heavy-tailed one described next.

233

Heavy-Tailed Workload

In this section we discuss how the heavy-tailed workload was generated based on the Pareto distribution, which has been widely used to model such characteristics in a variety of phenomena including inter-arrival times (Paxson & Floyd, 1995), burst sizes (Charsinski, 2000), topological properties (Faloutsos, Faloutsos, & Faloutsos, 1999), workload properties (Crovella et al., 1998), and error rates (Goseva-Postojanova, Mazimdar, & Singh, 2004).

The Pareto distribution is characterized by a shape parameter α and a scale parameter k. The probability density function (pdf) of the Pareto distribution is given by:

$$f(x) = \alpha k^{\alpha} x^{-\alpha-1} \tag{4}$$

where $\alpha, k > 0$ and $x > k$. The cumulative distribution function (CDF) of the Pareto distribution is given by:

$$F(x) = 1 - k^{\alpha} x^{-\alpha} \tag{5}$$

When $\alpha > 1$, the Pareto distribution has a finite mean which is given by:

$$E[X] = \frac{\alpha k}{\alpha - 1} \tag{6}$$

A series of numbers following the Pareto distribution can be generated by computing the inverse of the CDF presented in Equation (5) as below (Jin & Bestavros, 2005):

$$x = F^{-1}(u) = k(1-u)^{-1/\alpha} \tag{7}$$

In Equation (7), if α and k are known, then for random variates u_i's generated from the uniform distribution $U(0,1)$, $\{x_i\}$'s following the Pareto distribution can be generated. Note here $x_i > k$ for every i. It is expected that most $\{x_i\}$'s will have values close to k, with a small number being extraordinary high. When the shape parameter α of the Pareto distribution is fixed, the scale parameter k for a given mean $E[X]$ can be obtained as follows:

$$k = E[X] (1 - 1/\alpha) \tag{8}$$

We set the value of the shape parameter α to 1.36, based on prior research (Crovella, Taqqu & Bestavros, 1998). Four different mean file sizes, namely, 120 KB, 150 KB, 180 KB, and 200 KB were considered, and for each mean file size, using the preselected shape parameter α, the scale parameter k was obtained using Equation (8). Using the (α, k) pair, the CDF F_{S_i} of file size S_i is obtained. The probability of each file size is then computed as:

$$P_{S_i} = F_{S_i} - F_{S_{i-1}} \tag{9}$$

Table 2. File size distribution (P_{S_i}) in heavy-tailed workload

File size (S_i)	Mean file size $\overline{S}_i$			
	120KB	150KB	180KB	200KB
64 KB	0.6099	0.4776	0.3305	0.2274
128 KB	0.2381	0.3189	0.4086	0.4716
256 KB	0.0928	0.1242	0.1592	0.1837
512 KB	0.0361	0.0484	0.0620	0.0716
1 MB	0.0141	0.0189	0.0242	0.0279
2 MB	0.0055	0.0073	0.0094	0.0109

Table 3. System configuration parameters

Machine	Hardware	Software
Server	Dell OptiPlex GX260 (Intel Pentium 4 processor at 2.4GHz, 1GB of RAM, 40GB hard driver and Intel PRO 1000 MT network adapter)	Microsoft Windows XP Professional SP2, Microsoft IIS 5.1
Client	IBM ThinkPad T40 (Intel Pentium-M processor at 1.5GHz, 1GB of RAM, 40GB hard driver and Intel PRO 100 VE network adaptor)	Microsoft Windows XP Professional SP2

The individual file sizes considered are 64 KB, 128 KB, 256 KB, 512 KB, 1 MB, and 2 MB and the distributions of these file sizes in the four workloads are reported in Table 2.

EXPERIMENTAL INFRASTRUCTURE

In this section, we describe the experimental infrastructure used for model validation. We also describe the process used to estimate the mean service time for each file size.

Test Bed Description

The experimental infrastructure comprises of a single server and a single client, with configurations summarized in Table 3. Both computers are connected via a 100M Ethernet across a LAN.

In a multithreaded server, as the size of the thread pool increases, each thread may experience some performance degradation. However, when the thread pool size is below a threshold, this degradation is negligible (Xu & Bode, 2004). As

Table 4. Web server configurations

Parameter	Value
CPU	1
Thread	2
Web caching	No
Network Bandwidth	100 Mbps
Maximum queue length	3000

a rule of thumb, to ensure negligible degradation, the size of the thread pool should be twice the number of CPUs on the host machine (Ling et al., 2000; Richter, 2000). Thus, for the single processor server in our test bed, the size of the thread pool is set to 2. The configurations of the Web server used in the experiments are summarized in Table 4. Since the maximum queue length used is very large as compared to the number of threads, the assumption of infinite queue length needed to apply the *M/G/m* model is reasonable.

Service Time Estimation

To compute the mean response time of a workload based on the *M/G/m* model using Equation (2), the mean service time for the workload needs to be obtained. The mean service time of a workload will depend on the distribution of the file sizes in the workload and the mean service time for each of those file sizes. Thus, to obtain the mean service times of the workloads, the mean service times of the file sizes in the workload need to be obtained.

To obtain the mean service time for a single file size, client requests at a very low arrival rate such that the traffic intensity is low (less than 0.4%) were presented to the server. For each file size, the average response time was computed using response time measurements for 200 requests. The low traffic intensity causes negligible queuing delay and the response time mostly consists of the service time. Thus, the mean service time was approximated by the response time under very low load, which for each file size is summarized in Table 5.

Table 5. Mean service time of each file size (msec)

File size (S_i)	Service time ($\bar{T}_{S_i}$)
64 KB	10.00
128 KB	16.25
256 KB	32.85
512 KB	69.13
1 MB	133.03
2 MB	286.38

RESULTS AND DISCUSSION

In this section we present and discuss the results of the experimental validation of the *M/G/m* model. Several experimental scenarios for both deterministic and heavy-tailed workloads were considered, with each scenario comprised of a single workload (deterministic or heavy-tailed). For the deterministic workload, all the client requests were for the same file size. For the heavy-tailed workload, requests were generated according to the file size distribution for a given mean file size. In each scenario, request arrivals were generated according to a Poisson distribution with varying rates, chosen to maintain the condition ρ < 1 necessary for a stable system. Due to the high variability of the arrival rates of the Poisson process and for the file size distribu-

tions, the steady state mean queue length given by Equation (1) increases with ρ (Lipsky, 1992). The traffic intensity is considered to be low for ρ < 0.3, medium for 0.3 ≤ ρ ≤ 0.5, and high for ρ ≥ 0.5 (Lipsky, 1992; Nossenson & Attiya, 2004).

For each arrival rate, using the measured response times of 200 requests, the average response time was obtained. The mean response times were computed for the *M/G/m* model from Equation (2) and *M/G/1* model from Equation (3) using MAT-LAB. For each workload, the traffic intensity ρ for each arrival rate is also reported.

Deterministic Workload

The measured and the computed response times along with the traffic intensities for deterministic workloads of 64 KB, 128 KB, 256 KB, and 512 KB are reported in Tables 6, 7, 8, and 9, respectively. The results indicate that the response time predicted by the *M/G/m* model is very close to the measured response time for low to moderately high loads, with value of ρ around 0.5. The predicted response time is lower than the measured, and the deviations are within 7–8% for low and medium traffic intensities. As the traffic intensity increases, greater deviations occur. However, the deviation is within 10% even for high traffic intensities, with ρ close to 0.6. For the arrival rates and file

Table 6. Deterministic workload (S_i = 64KB) (msec)

$1/\lambda$	ρ	$R_{measure}$	$R_{M/G/m}$	$R_{M/G/1}$
2000	0.0024	10.07	10.00	10.03
1000	0.0049	10.17	10.01	10.05
500	0.0098	10.36	10.06	10.10
200	0.0243	10.55	10.14	10.26
100	0.0463	10.80	10.30	10.56
50	0.1067	11.05	10.79	11.25
40	0.1283	11.72	11.32	11.67
30	0.1743	12.74	12.03	12.50
20	0.2953	13.46	12.64	15.00
15	0.5405	16.88	15.41	--

Table 7. Deterministic workload (S_i = 128KB) (msec)

$1/\lambda$	ρ	$R_{measure}$	$R_{M/G/m}$	$R_{M/G/1}$
2000	0.0045	17.07	16.26	16.32
1000	0.0083	17.20	16.33	16.38
500	0.0182	17.80	16.71	16.82
200	0.0446	18.11	17.08	17.17
100	0.0861	18.63	17.37	17.83
50	0.1764	20.38	17.13	20.16
40	0.2614	23.35	21.97	21.81
30	0.3485	24.47	22.72	25.85
20	0.5650	27.26	24.84	--

size distributions, the system is already heavily loaded when $\rho \geq 0.5$ (Nossenson & Attiya, 2004) which cause these deviations.

The results also indicate that the response time predicted by the *M/G/1* model is always higher than the response time predicted by the *M/G/m* model. As the arrival rate increases, the rate at which the predicted response time increases is much higher for the *M/G/1* model as compared to the *M/G/m* model. Further, as the arrival rate λ approaches service rate μ while maintaining $\lambda < \mu$, the response time predicted by the *M/G/1* model deviates significantly from the measured response time. When $\mu < \lambda < 2\mu$, the response time of the single-server *M/G/1* model is not meaningful since it leads to $\rho' > 1$, resulting in an unstable system. The *M/G/m* model, however, still represents a stable system for $0.5 < \rho < 1$ and hence provides meaningful predictions of response time. Thus, a single-server queue is not adequate to represent a Web server equipped with concurrent processing capabilities.

Heavy-Tailed Workload

To compute the average response time for a heavy-tailed workload using Equation (2), the mean service time for the workload with a given mean file size can be computed using:

$$\overline{T}_{\overline{S}_i} = \sum \sum_i \overline{T}_{S_i} P_{S_i} \qquad (10)$$

where S_i denotes the file size, $\overline{T}_{S_i}$ the mean service time of file size S_i, P_{S_i} the probability of requesting a file of size S_i, and $\overline{T}_{\overline{S}_i}$ the mean service time of a workload with mean file size $\overline{S}_i$. As discussed earlier, the mean file sizes considered are 120KB, 150KB, 180KB, and 200KB. The mean service times of these workloads computed using the service times and probabilities reported in Table 2 and Table 5 respectively, are summarized in Table 10.

The measured and the computed response times for the heavy-tailed workload for different mean file sizes are summarized in Tables 11, 12, 13, and 14. The trend in the deviation between the predicted and measured response times in this case is similar as in the case of the deterministic workload. The predicted and the mean response times are within 10%, with the predicted one being lower than the measured for low and medium traffic intensities ($\rho < 0.5$). As indicated earlier, for the arrival rate and file size distributions, the system is already heavily loaded when $\rho < 0.5$ (Nossenson & Attiya, 2004) which cause these deviations. We note, however, that the difference between the computed and measured response time is around 12% even for moderately high traffic intensity with ρ close to 0.6. The response times predicted by the M/G/1 model follow similar trends as in the case of deterministic workload.

RELATED RESEARCH

Several efforts have focused on Web server and workload performance modeling and analysis. Slothouber (1996) proposes to model a Web server as an open queuing network. Heidemann, Obraczka, and Touch (1997) present analytical models for the interaction of HTTP with several transport layers. Van der Mei et al. (2001) present an end-to-end queuing model for the performance of Web servers, encompassing the impact of client workload characteristics, server hardware/software configurations, communication protocols, and interconnect topologies. Kamra, Misra, and Nahum (2004) present a control-theoretic approach that achieves dual objectives, namely,

preventing overload and enforcing absolute response times. Cao et al. (2003) use an *M/G/1/K*PS* queuing model to model the performance of a Web server. Nossenson and Attiya (2004) introduce a new *N-Burst/G/1* queuing model with heavy-tailed service time distribution for Web server performance modeling. Squillante et al. (1999) employ a *G/G/1* queue to model high-volume Web sites. Liu, Heo, and Sha (2005) provide a model of a three-tiered Web services architecture, where each tier is modeled by a multistation queuing center. Kant and Sundaram (2000) present a queuing network model for a multiprocessor system running a static Web workload. Hu, Nanda, and Yang (1999) measure and analyze the behavior of a Web server driven by benchmarks and propose techniques for performance improvement. Hardwick, Papaefstathiou, and Guimbellot (2001) use a performance modeling framework, to create a performance analysis tool for database-backed

Table 8. Deterministic workload ($S_i = 256KB$) (msec)

$1/\lambda$	ρ	$R_{measure}$	$R_{M/G/m}$	$R_{M/G/1}$
2000	0.0082	33.15	32.86	33.12
1000	0.0164	33.75	32.83	33.41
500	0.0329	34.07	32.97	34.01
200	0.0936	36.51	34.76	36.08
100	0.1947	39.25	38.09	40.89
50	0.3912	45.25	43.86	64.31
40	0.4993	50.38	47.45	108.31
35	0.5889	62.11	56.13	--

Table 9. Deterministic workload ($S_i = 512KB$) (msec)

$1/\lambda$	ρ	$R_{measure}$	$R_{M/G/m}$	$R_{M/G/1}$
2000	0.0178	69.25	69.13	70.37
1000	0.0334	69.67	69.34	71.70
500	0.0688	70.53	69.74	74.68
200	0.1738	71.22	71.13	87.39
100	0.3944	90.13	87.45	146.53
80	0.5073	105.65	96.91	--
70	0.5683	110.69	100.26	--

Web sites. Kohavi and Parekh (2003) offer several useful, practical recommendations for supplementary analyses. Iyengar, Challenger, Dias, and Dantzig (2000) present techniques to be used at popular sites to improve performance and availability based on two case studies.

Previous works mostly use a *single* server queue to model a Web server. However, modern Web servers typically have multiple processes/ threads that work independently and simultaneously to service requests. Thus, it is appropriate to consider this system a multiserver system, as in the *M/G/m* model in this article. While being an accurate representation of the characteristics of a modern Web server, the *M/G/m* model is simple to comprehend, needs the estimation of very few parameters, and involves straightforward computations, which makes it easy to apply. Since the model is not tied to a specific implementation of concurrency, it is equally applicable to a thread-based, a process-based, or hybrid architecture.

Table 10. Mean service times of heavy-tailed workload (msec)

Mean file size $(\overline{S}_i)$	Mean service time $(\overline{T}_{S_i})$
120 KB	18.95
150 KB	21.99
180 KB	25.37
200 KB	27.74

CONCLUSION AND FUTURE RESEARCH

In this article we propose the use of an *M/G/m* queue to model the performance of a Web server capable of processing multiple requests concurrently. The performance metric of interest is the response time of a client request. We validate the model experimentally for deterministic and heavy-tailed workloads. Our results indicate that the *M/G/m* queue provides a reasonable estimate of the service response time for low to moderately high traffic intensities. It is a more accurate representation of modern server characteristics, is conceptually simple, requires the estimation of very few parameters, involves straightforward computations, and is hence easy to apply.

Our future research includes extending the methodology to: (i) consider general arrival processes in performance analysis (Nossenson & Attiya, 2004), (ii) apply the methodology to model the performance of an application server in a three-tier Web services architecture, and (iii) consider QoS provisioning and overload control.

REFERENCES

Apache Software Foundation (n.d.). *Apache HTTP server project*. Retrieved June 9, 2008, from http://httpd.apache.org/

Table 11. Heavy-tailed workload ($\overline{S}_i$ = 120KB)

$1/\lambda$	ρ	$R_{measure}$	$R_{M/G/m}$	$R_{M/G/1}$
2000	0.0047	19.65	18.95	19.04
1000	0.0097	20.30	19.34	19.43
500	0.0198	20.60	19.34	19.52
200	0.0534	21.25	19.98	20.04
100	0.1066	23.25	21.93	22.17
50	0.2414	24.25	22.56	24.73
40	0.2875	27.12	24.97	27.48
30	0.3731	31.27	28.92	35.20
20	0.5547	40.39	35.94	--

Table 12. Heavy-tailed workload ($\overline{S}_i = 150KB$)

$1/\lambda$	ρ	$R_{measure}$	$R_{M/G/m}$	$R_{M/G/1}$
2000	0.0053	22.32	22.00	22.11
1000	0.0099	23.05	22.52	22.74
500	0.0255	24.31	23.64	23.80
200	0.0582	26.44	24.50	24.75
100	0.1215	27.31	25.30	25.89
50	0.2253	27.64	25.59	30.62
40	0.2974	29.22	26.97	35.41
30	0.4455	32.78	29.94	52.17
25	0.5631	38.25	34.03	--

Table 13. Heavy-tailed workload ($\overline{S}_i = 180KB$)

$1/\lambda$	ρ	$R_{measure}$	$R_{M/G/m}$	$R_{M/G/1}$
2000	0.0056	25.63	25.37	25.53
1000	0.0117	25.86	25.41	25.70
500	0.0243	27.48	26.35	26.65
200	0.0673	28.69	27.23	27.61
100	0.1291	30.67	29.63	30.68
50	0.2843	33.40	31.90	38.44
40	0.3636	35.02	32.33	47.37
30	0.5303	43.12	39.15	--

Table 14. Heavy-tailed workload ($\overline{S}_i = 200KB$)

$1/\lambda$	ρ	$R_{measure}$	$R_{M/G/m}$	$R_{M/G/1}$
2000	0.0066	28.43	27.74	27.94
1000	0.0136	29.28	28.21	28.64
500	0.0266	30.55	29.01	29.55
200	0.0714	31.17	29.87	30.97
100	0.1553	33.65	31.88	33.06
50	0.3105	37.75	35.08	45.02
40	0.4006	39.66	36.89	59.12
30	0.5637	49.50	44.15	--

Cao, J., Andersson, M., Nyberg, C., & Kihl, M. (2003). Web server performance modeling using an *M/G/1/K*PS* queue. In *Proceedings of the 10th International Conference on Telecommunications* (pp. 1501–1506).

Crovella, M., Taqqu, M. S., & Bestavros, A. (1998). *Heavy-tailed probability distributions in the World Wide Web. A practical guide to heavy tails: Statistical techniques and application.* Boston: Birkhauser.

Faloutsos, M., Faloutsos, P., & Faloutsos, C. (1999). On the power-law relationships of the Internet topology. In *Proceedings of ACM SIGCOMM* (pp. 251–262).

Goseva-Postojanova, K., Mazimdar, S., & Singh, A. (2004). Empirical study of session-based workload and reliability of Web servers. In *Proceedings of the 15th International Symposium on Software Reliability Engineering* (pp. 403–414).

Hardwick, J. C., Papaefstathiou, E., & Guimbellot, D. (2001). Modeling the performance of e-commerce sites. In *Proceedings of the 27th International Conference of the Computer Measurement Group* (pp. 3–12).

Heidemann, J., Obraczka, K., & Touch, J. (1997). Modeling the performance of HTTP over several transport protocols. *IEEE/ACM Transactions on Networking, 5*(5), 616–630.

Hokstad, P.(1978). Approximation for the *M/G/m* queue. *Operations Research, 26*(3), 510–523.

Hu, Y., Nanda, A., & Yang, Q.(1999). Measurement, analysis and performance improvement of the Apache Web server. In *Proceedings of the IEEE International Performance, Computing and Communications Conference* (pp. 261–267).

Iyengar, A., Challenger, J., Dias, D., & Dantzig, P. (2000). High-performance Web site design techniques. *IEEE Internet Computing, 4*(2), 17–26.

Jin, S., & Bestavros, A. (2005). *Generating Internet streaming media objects and workloads* (chap. 1, Recent advances on Web content delivery). Kluwer Academic Publishers.

Kamra, A., Misra, V., & Nahum, E. (2004). Controlling the performance of 3-tiered Web sites: Modeling, design and implementation. In *Proceedings of SIGMETRICS 2004/ PERFORMANCE 2004* (pp. 414–415).

Kant, K., & Sundaram, C. R. M. (2000). A server performance model for static Web workloads. In *Proceedings of the IEEE International Symposium on Performance Analysis of Systems and Software* (pp. 201–206).

Kimura, T. (1983). Diffusion approximation for an *M/G/m* queue. *Operations Research, 31*(2), 304–321.

Kleinrock, L. (1976). *Queueing systems, Volume 1: Theory.* New York: John Wiley & Sons.

Kohavi, R., & Parekh, R. (2003). Ten supplementary analyses to improve e-commerce Web sites. In *Proceedings of the 5th WEBKDD Workshop* (pp. 29–36).

Ling, Y., Mullen, T., & Lin, X. (2000). Analysis of optimal thread pool size. *ACM SIGOPS Operating System Review, 34*(2), 42–55.

Lipsky, L. (1992). *Queueing theory: A linear algebraic approach.* New York: McMillan and Company.

Liu, X., Heo, J., & Sha, L. (2005). Modeling 3-tiered Web applications. In *Proceedings of the 13th IEEE International Symposium on Modeling, Analysis and Simulation of Computer Telecommunications Systems* (pp. 307–310).

Menasce, D. (2003). Web server software architecture. *IEEE Internet Computing, 7*(6), 78–81.

Microsoft Corporation (n.d). *Internet information services (IIS).* Retrieved June 9, 2008, from http:// www.microsoft.com/WindowsServer2003/iis/ default.mspx

Nossenson, R., & Attiya, H. (2004). The N-burst/G/1 model with heavy-tailed service-times distribution. In *Proceedings of the International Symposium on Modeling, Analysis, and Simulation of Computer and Telecommunications Systems* (pp. 131–138).

Paxson, V., & Floyd, S. (1995). Wide area traffic: The failure of Poisson modeling. *IEEE/ACM Transactions on Networking, 3*(3), 226–244.

Richter, J. (2000). *Programming server-side applications for Microsoft Windows 2000.* Microsoft Press.

Sakasegawa, H. (1977). An approximation formula $L_q = \alpha \rho^\beta / (1-\rho)$. *Annals of the Institute of Statistical Mathematics, 29*(1), 67–75.

Slothouber, L. (1996). A model of Web server performance. In *Proceedings of the 5th International World Wide Web Conference.*

Squillante, M. S., Yao, D. D., & Zhang, L. (1999). Web traffic modeling and Web server performance analysis. In *Proceedings of the 38th Conference on Decision and Control* (pp. 4432–4439).

Van der Mei, R. D., Hariharan, R., & Reeser, P. (2001). Web server performance modeling. *Telecommunication Systems, 16*(3–4), 361–378.

Xu, D., & Bode, B. (2004). Performance study and dynamic optimization design for thread pool systems. In *Proceedings of the International Conference on Computing, Communications and Control Technologies.*

Yao, D. (1985). Refining the diffusion approximation for the *M/G/m* queue. *Operations Research, 33*(6), 1266–1277.

This work was previously published in International Journal of Information Technology and Web Engineering, Vol. 3, Issue 3, edited by G. Alkhatib and D. Rine, pp. 50-65, copyright 2008 by IGI Publishing (an imprint of IGI Global).

Chapter 14
A Perspective on the Credibility Engineering of Web Applications

Pankaj Kamthan
Concordia University, Canada

ABSTRACT

The social aspects pertaining to a service provided by an organization are at least as significant as the technical aspects. The issue of credibility is a growing concern for the consumers of (persuasive) Web Applications in a variety of domains. Therefore, understanding the notion of credibility and addressing it systematically is crucial for an organization's reputation. In this chapter, based on a given taxonomy of credibility, an approach to address one class of credibility, namely the Active Credibility, of Web Applications is considered. To that regard, a viewpoint-oriented framework for the active credibility engineering of Web Applications is proposed, and the managerial, societal, and technical viewpoints of it are analyzed in some detail. A few directions for extending the framework are outlined.

INTRODUCTION

The Web continues to evolve since its inception more than a decade and half ago, and the Semantic Web (Hendler, Lassila, & Berners-Lee, 2001) and the Social Web (O'Reilly, 2005) are two of its recent directions being commonly pursued. The Semantic Web provides the technological infrastructure for better knowledge representation, interpretation, and reasoning; the Social Web opens new vistas for interaction, participation, and collaboration. In

spite of the significant prospects offered by these advancements and their confluence (Lassila & Hendler, 2007), there are certain caveats.

The trends in the implementation of certain structural, behavioral, and creational properties in Web Applications present new challenges related to the quality of those Web Applications from a user's viewpoint. There are a number of examples that highlight the problem. The presence of personalized advertisements (such as 'Ads by Google') can, at times, have only peripheral relevance rather than clear benefits to a user; on the other hand, non-personalized interstitial advertisements (such

DOI: 10.4018/978-1-60566-719-5.ch014

as 'Skip This Ad') are usually distracting and uninvited. There is no a priori guarantee that the rating and suggestion of a product or a service by a recommender system is impartial and accurately reflects the interests of a user. For example, an implementation of a recommender system built-in some search engines could, by misuse of meta-information or otherwise, skew the results not necessarily in favor of a user. There is no a priori guarantee that the implementation of a recommender system rates and suggests a product or a service is impartial and accurately reflects the interests of a user. The potential for the distribution of inaccurate medical information from unqualified sources and the presence of implicit advertising of drugs has had an acute impact on the consumer perception of health-related Web Applications (Walther, Wang, & Loh, 2004). It has been observed in recent surveys (Consumer Reports WebWatch, 2005) that uninvited solicitation and misuse of information provided by consumers with little repercussions for the perpetrators is a matter of grave concern.

The situation described above is only exacerbated in the context of a Social Web Application whereby some 'transfer of control,' a consumer becomes a co-producer or 'prosumer.' For example, Wikipedia is one of the projects under the auspices of the Wikimedia Foundation, is based on a Wiki, and is created by contributions of many in an open collaborative global effort. The challenges to the quality of such projects have been of interest in recent studies (Cusinato et al., 2009).

The trustworthiness of information remains one of the critical constants in the evolution of the Web. Indeed, credibility is a necessary condition for trustworthiness of a Web Application in general and information provided by it in particular. It also needs to be approached in a systematic and feasible manner to be achievable. The rest of the chapter is centered on this theme, and is organized as follows. First, the background necessary for later discussion and a brief outline of related work is provided. Next, a viewpoint-oriented framework for the active credibility engineering within the context of Web Applications is introduced. Then, challenges and directions for future research are outlined. Finally, concluding remarks are given.

BACKGROUND AND RELATED WORK

In this section, necessary background on credibility is given and relevant previous work as it pertains for further discussion is reported.

For the sake of this chapter, a *Web Application* is defined as a Web Site that behaves like an interactive software system specific to a domain. It typically has a large-size that requires a non-trivial infrastructure: a systematic development process, a team with high-level of knowledge and skills, deployment of additional software on the client- and/or server-side, and a schedule comprising of several weeks or months from inception to completion. In this chapter, the terms consumer and user are interchangeable unless otherwise stated.

Definition of Credibility and Related Concepts

For the sake of this chapter, *credibility* is considered to be synonymous to (and therefore interchangeable with) believability (Fogg & Tseng, 1999). Even though applicable to more general contexts, for the sake of this chapter, *credibility engineering* in the context of the Web is defined as the discipline of ensuring that a Web Application will be perceived as credible by its stakeholders and doing so throughout the life cycle of the Web Application.

The approach towards credibility engineering of Web Applications in this chapter rests on the following spectrum of theoretical and practical considerations: understanding credibility, assessing the impact of credibility on stakeholders, proposing means for addressing credibility, incorporating credibility in the development process, and managing credibility.

Scope of Credibility

It should be noted that credibility is neither a universal, nor an absolute concern. For example, the credibility of a Web Application is a concern to a consumer if there is an associated cost (say, in terms of lost time, effort, or money) that is outright unacceptable to the consumer. Also, as a quality attribute of a Web Application, the credibility is *satisficed* (Simon, 1996), not satisfied, and therefore needs to be evaluated on a multi-valued set rather than on a binary set. For example, even if a Web Application as a whole is labeled as noncredible, parts of it may still be credible.

There are limits to the responsibility of the producers of a Web Application. For example, the nature of the domain and the information available at the other end of external hyperlinks (destination) from a Web Application (source) is not within the control of the producer of that Web Application. However, if an impression is given (such as by misuse of HTML Frames) that destination is part of the source, then the issue of the credibility of the source Web Application can arise.

The issue of the credibility is not native to human-interaction as it manifests on the Web and is of concern in any human-machine interaction. Furthermore, irrespective of the underlying entity (including, but not limited to, a software system) or the medium with which it is associated, credibility can be related to the context of *persuasion*.

Persuasion, Waptology, and Credibility

It has been recognized that the approach for understanding and addressing credibility needs to be multi-dimensional (Rieh & Danielson, 2007), and persuasion is one of those dimensions. For the sake of this chapter, *persuasion* is defined as an attempt to reinforce, alter, or shape human attitudes or behaviors (or both) without coercion or deception. There are both advantages and disadvantages of persuasion (Fogg, 2003b) and there are various means to persuade (Oinas-Kukkonen & Harjumaa, 2008). The use of a computer as a technology for persuasion has been termed as *human-computer persuasion* (Oinas-Kukkonen & Harjumaa, 2008) and the study of the use of a computer as a technology for persuasion has been termed as *captology* (Fogg, 2003b; Fogg, Cueller, & Danielson, 2008).

For a number of reasons including the pervasiveness and reachability of the Web, the potentially adverse impact of the use of information technology pertaining to it for the purpose of persuading people is especially severe. Therefore, the study of the use of the Web as a technology for persuasion can be termed similarly as *waptology*. From the standpoint of interest to waptology, persuasion belongs to the intersection of at least the following areas: (1) human-computer interaction (HCI) and/or human- information interaction (HII), (2) perceptual psychology, (3) behavioral psychology, and (4) social psychology. For example, the prominence-interpretation theory (Fogg, 2003a) provides one explanation of how people associate 'significance' with (and therefore perceive the credibility of) a Web Application.

Based on the case of a general software system (Oinas-Kukkonen & Harjumaa, 2008), a *persuasive Web Application* can be defined as a Web Application that attempts to reinforce, alter, or shape human attitudes or behaviors (or both) without coercion or deception. For example, for the sake of this chapter, credibility engineering of persuasive Web Applications belongs to the domain of Web Engineering in general and waptology in particular, and is therefore of special interest.

Persuasive Web Application: Example

Figure 1 illustrates a part of the user interface of a Web Application where two downloading options

Figure 1. An example of persuasion on the Web

for a product are given: (1) the Premium Download option is commercial but a user does not have to wait and (2) the Free Download option is free but the user has to wait for the timer to expire.

To draw attention of the user (and thereby, hopefully, persuade the user) to select (1), there is distinctive use of positioning (relative location of buttons) and typography (size and color of button labels, color contrast between foreground and background) to clearly differentiate (1) from (2).

Comparison of Persuasion, Coercion, and Deception: Example

It can be noted that persuasion, coercion, and deception are not synonymous. For the purpose of illustration, consider the following example. Let WA_1 and WA_2 be two Web Applications such that WA_2 is managed by person P_1 at a non-profit educational institution and WA_2 is owned by person P_2 at a commercial bookstore. Furthermore, let there be a book B whose title and corresponding hyperlink L are present on a resource R_1 on WA_1. The Uniform Resource Locator (URL) of L points to a resource R_2 on WA_2 that includes the description of B and the means of purchasing it. If a user U voluntarily visits R_2 from R_1 through L, then there is no persuasion, coercion, or deception. However, L may also include the details on referral that upon purchase of B by U benefit not only P_2 but also P_1. This is an example of persuasion but neither coercion, nor deception. P_1 could 'impose' a visitation of R_2 from R_1 by some means such as using the Hypertext Transfer Protocol (HTTP) Refresh Header. This is an example of coercion but neither persuasion, nor deception. P_1 could

further 'conceal' from U the URL of L by some means such as using a client-side script. This is an example of deception but neither persuasion, nor coercion.

In some cases, however, the boundary between persuasion, coercion, and deception can become blurred. For example, an anti-virus software S presents a dialog D that notifies the user of its expiry. D gives the user options to renew subscription immediately or to be reminded again in the future. However, D does not give the user an option not to be reminded again in the future or not to renew subscription to S. This is an example that borders on persuasion and coercion.

Addressing Credibility of Web Applications

The issue of the credibility of Web Applications has garnered attention in recent years, and has culminated into both theoretical and empirical studies (Danielson, 2006; Fogg, 2003b; Lazar, Meiselwitz, & Feng, 2007; Wathen & Burkell, 2002). These efforts, particularly the surveys, have highlighted both the breadth and depth of the concern for the credibility of Web Applications by their users as well as reinforced the need to address it.

However, these initiatives are limited by one or more of the following aspects: the treatment is prescriptive rather than constructive, and therefore inadequate for Web Engineering; the discussion on credibility is not within the context of any development process; the approach towards ensuring and/or evaluating credibility is not systematic; in addressing credibility, the focus is exclusively on the quality of information even though other

Table 1. A taxonomy of credibility

Credibility			
Active Credibility		Passive Credibility	
Surface Credibility	Experienced Credibility	Presumed Credibility	Reputed Credibility

properties of a software system can be relevant; the proposed means for ensuring credibility is singular (for example, only broad guidelines); and feasibility of the means is not taken into consideration.

The aforementioned issues have been attended to recently. In this chapter, previous work (Kamthan, 2007; Kamthan, 2008c) is extended in part and situated in a larger context of credibility engineering.

TOWARDS A SYSTEMATIC APPROACH FOR UNDERSTANDING AND ADDRESSING ACTIVE CREDIBILITY OF WEB APPLICATIONS

In this section, a classification of credibility is proposed and a specific class, namely the Active Credibility, is addressed in some detail.

A Classification of Credibility

The concept of credibility can be classified (Fogg & Tseng, 1999; Kamthan, 2007; Kamthan, 2008c) based upon the types of consumer interactions with a Web Application. A consumer could consider a Web Application to be credible based upon direct interaction with the application (*Active Credibility*), or consider it to be credible in absence of any direct interaction but based on certain predetermined notions (*Passive Credibility*).

There can be two types of *Active Credibility*, namely *Surface Credibility*, which describes how much a consumer believes a given Web Application based on simple inspection, and *Experienced*

Credibility, which describes how much a consumer believes a given Web Application based on first-hand experience in the past. For example, the Surface Credibility of a shopping system may be perceived as high by a consumer upon 'scanning' through the product catalog. However, the Experienced Credibility of the same shopping system may be perceived as low by the same consumer *after* an experience, such as, selection and purchase of a product from it.

There can be two types of *Passive Credibility*, namely *Presumed Credibility*, which describes how much a consumer believes a given Web Application because of general assumptions that the consumer holds, and *Reputed Credibility*, which describes how much a consumer believes a given Web Application because of a reference from a third party. For example, the Presumed Credibility of an entertainment portal owned by a specific company may be perceived as low by a consumer who has a negative image of business rules and practices of that company. However, the Reputed Credibility of a sports portal owned by a company with a dubious business record may be perceived as high by a consumer (who does not know that portal or the company) due to a recommendation by a relative or indeed by another portal.

The coverage of rest of this chapter is essentially limited to the treatment of Active Credibility. Let C_T be the set of all types of credibility. Table 1 provides a subset of C_T.

Remarks

It can be noted that neither a given consumer, nor the Web Application are necessarily static, and do change over time. It follows that the cred-

Figure 2. A high-level view of a framework for the active credibility engineering of Web Applications

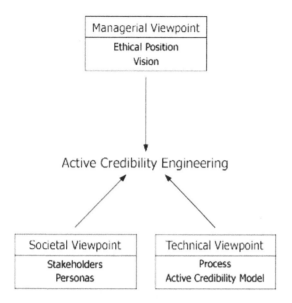

ibility assessments of the same consumer and the Web Application at two different times can be different.

The aforementioned types of credibility in Table 1 are not necessarily mutually exclusive in the sense that the existence of one can impact the other. Let for a large number n there be a sequence of Web Applications $WA_{t(1)}, \ldots, WA_{t(n)}$, t(i) denotes time, that belong to the same genre, say, auction. If collectively the Experienced Credibility of $WA_{t(1)}, \ldots, WA_{t(n-1)}$ is low with respect to U, then, in turn, this (extensive past experience) can impact the Presumed Credibility of $WA_{t(n)}$ with respect to U.

Viewpoints of Active Credibility

There are a number of possible views of quality (Wong, 2006) and, for the sake of this chapter, so also are of credibility. A view conforms to a viewpoint. It is evident that not all possible views or viewpoints are equally relevant for practical purposes.

The proposed viewpoint-oriented conceptual framework for the active credibility engineering of Web Applications, hereafter labeled as $\mathbf{F}_{ACE}$, consists of the following non-mutually exclusive (and therefore non-orthogonal) dimensions: (1) managerial viewpoint, (2) societal viewpoint, and (3) technical viewpoint. It is expected that the managerial viewpoint constraints the scope of the other two viewpoints. Figure 2 provides an illustration of $\mathbf{F}_{ACE}$.

Active Credibility of Web Applications: Managerial Viewpoint

From a managerial viewpoint, a Web Application reflects the ideology of the organization that produces and/or owns it. It is this place where all the administrative and executive decisions are cast. In particular, the organizational vision governs the environment in which a Web Application (during its development, operation, and maintenance) resides. It marks the foundation for any organizational obligation to credibility.

The vision that an organization has for its products (such as a Web Application) is directly influenced by its ethical position and practices. Furthermore, ethical concerns have a strong affinity to quality of which credibility is one attribute (Kamthan, 2008a).

The Software Engineering Code of Ethics and Professional Practice (SECEPP) is a recommendation of the ACM/IEEE-CS Joint Task Force on Software Engineering Ethics and Professional Practices that puts forth principles and clauses that software engineers are expected to adhere to. It is possible to adapt SECEPP to Web Engineering in general and to Web Engineers in particular. Based on that, the vision of an organization for its Web Application could be made explicit. As an example, the Unified Process (UP) suggests that a 'vision document' be produced at the inception of a software project. It is within this context where the level of an organization's commitment to credibility is highlighted.

Active Credibility of Web Applications: Societal Viewpoint

From a societal viewpoint, a Web Application is an interactive system in the ecosystem of stakeholders. The identification and understanding of the stakeholders is critical to addressing human and social perspectives of a Web Application, and thus the underlying credibility concerns.

The possible classes of stakeholders with respect to their roles in relationship to a Web Application can be identified using a systematic approach (Sharp, Galal, & Finkelstein, 1999). For example, two broad classes of stakeholders with respect to their *roles* are: (1) a *producer* (who owns, finances, develops, deploys, or maintains the Web Application), and (2) a *consumer*, (who uses the Web Application for some purpose). The aforementioned classification scheme can be granularized further if necessary.

The goals of stakeholders with respect to the credibility of a Web Application are different. While a consumer would like to assess if the information on the Web Application is credible, a producer would like to engineer 'highly credible' Web Applications in the hope of establishing credibility with the consumer. A major challenge to the assurance of credibility in Social Web Applications is that the line between the producers and the consumers gets blurred with 'user-added' information. In other words, with the socialization of the Web, the assurance of credibility is increasingly becoming a *collective* and *symbiotic* responsibility of both the producers and the consumers.

The consumers are not homogeneous and individual characteristics, such as age (Rieh & Danielson, 2007), can mean different assessments of credibility. To create an understanding of consumers, user models can be constructed. These user models may be based on extrospections of actual usage of a Web Application and/or an analysis of ethnographic studies (such as surveys). Among the possible user models, *personas* (Junior &

Filgueiras, 2005) are the most practical in their applicability as they provide concrete information on consumer background and personal preferences as they relate to the Web Application.

Active Credibility of Web Applications: Technical Viewpoint

From a technical viewpoint, a Web Application is a product that results from a Web Engineering process. Over the last decade, a number of process models for the development of Web Applications have been proposed. Due to the unique nature of the development of Web Applications (Kamthan, 2009), the underlying process needs to be flexible, consumer-centric, evolutionary, mature, and have a broad community and tool support. As an example, Extreme Programming (XP), customizations of the Unified Process (UP) such as the Rational Unified Process (RUP) and OpenUP, and Web OPEN are process environments that, to a large extent, meet those criteria.

To tackle credibility systematically, it needs to be considered as a *mandatory* non-functional requirement that is expressed early and subsequently attended to *throughout* the development process. To do that, the concept of credibility needs to be clarified further.

A Semiotic Quality Model for the Active Credibility of Web Applications

There are a number of approaches for quality modeling (Fenton & Pfleeger, 1997). The Active Credibility of Web Applications can be viewed as a qualitative aspect and addressed indirectly. Table 2 provides an organization of the elements of a model for the Active Credibility of Web Applications, hereafter labeled as M_{AC}. M_{AC} uses semiotics as its theoretical basis for communication of information. It is evident that M_{AC} forms one aspect of a practical realization of F_{ACE}.

Table 2. A high-level view of the model for the Active Credibility of Web Applications from the perspective of semiotics

Semiotic Level	Quality Attributes		Means for Assurance and Evaluation	Decision Support
Social	Credibility		**Process-Oriented:** Inspections, Testing (Acceptance Testing) **Product-Oriented:** Training, Guidance (Principles, Guidelines and Heuristics, Patterns and Anti-Patterns) Metrics	Tools Feasibility
	Layer 1: Aesthetics, Legality, Privacy, Security, Transparency			
Pragmatic	**Layer 3:** Accessibility, Dependability, Usability, Utility			
	Layer 2: Findability, Performance, Reliability, Robustness, Understandability			
	Layer 1: Attractiveness, Availability, Efficiency, Familiarity, Interoperability, Perceivability			

Semiotic Levels

The first column of Table 2 outlines semiotic levels. The theory of semiotics has evolved to become especially relevant to HCI and HII. From a semiotics perspective (Stamper, 1992; Shanks, 1999), a Web Application can be viewed on six interrelated levels: physical, empirical, syntactic, semantic, pragmatic, and social.

The quality concerns at the last two levels only are considered as they directly involve stakeholders. At the *pragmatic level* the interest is in the utility of the representations of a resource in a Web Application to its stakeholders, while at the *social level* the interest is in the manifestations of social interaction among stakeholders with respect to the representations.

Quality Attributes

The second column of Table 2 draws the relationship between semiotic levels and corresponding quality attributes.

Organization of Quality Attributes

The quality attributes in Table 2 are organized in two different ways: (1) by semiotic level and (2) by relationships.

The notions of social quality and pragmatic quality are rather abstract to be tackled directly. Therefore, each semiotic level is decomposed further into quality attributes that are deemed relevant from previous studies (Rieh & Danielson, 2007) or otherwise inspired by conventional information and software quality models. Then, each semiotic level is divided into echelons, and these quality attributes are placed at different echelons (layers).

The quality attributes included in Table 2 are not necessarily mutually exclusive. Indeed, these quality attributes can be related to each other (1) on the same semiotic level, (2) across different echelons on the same semiotic level, and (3) across semiotic levels. In particular, credibility belongs to the social level and depends on the layers beneath it. The rest of the quality attributes are organized as follows:

Relationship between Social Level Layer 1 and Pragmatic Level Layer 3: The quality attributes such as aesthetics, legality, privacy, security, and transparency (of the producer) at the social level depend upon the quality attributes such as accessibility, dependability, usability, and utility (similar to, but not synonymous with, functionality) at the pragmatic level.

Relationship between pragmatic level layer 3 and pragmatic level layer 2: The quality attributes such as accessibility, dependability, usability, and utility at the pragmatic level in turn depend upon other quality attributes such as findability, performance, reliability, robustness, and understandability (similar to, but not synonymous with, comprehensibility) also at the pragmatic level.

Relationship between pragmatic level layer 2 and pragmatic level layer 1: The quality attributes such as findability, performance, reliability, robustness, and understandability again in turn depend upon other quality attributes such as attractiveness, availability, efficiency, familiarity, interoperability, and perceivability (similar to, but not synonymous with, readability) also at the pragmatic level.

The quality attributes at the same level can similarly be related to each other.

Significance of Quality Attributes

The relationship between credibility and the other quality attributes can be illustrated by an example. Let U_1 and U_2 be users of Web Applications WA_1 and WA_2, respectively. Upon accessing the 'Home Page' of WA_1, U_1 receives a 'Document Not Found' message, that is, there is lack of availability. Upon accessing the 'Home Page' of WA_2, U_2 finds that the 'Home Page' of WA_2 states that it is 'Under Construction,' which does not impact accessibility, dependability, or usability, but there is lack of utility. If this phenomenon repeats multiple times over, it can negatively impact the Surface Credibility of WA_1 and WA_2.

The quality attributes included in Table 2 are not necessarily equally significant. The significance associated with a quality attribute can vary with respect to a number of factors including stakeholder preferences, computing environment, and the underlying domain. For example, for the consumers of a library information system as a Web Application belonging to a school for the blind, perceivability may be more significant than attractiveness; for the consumers of an income tax Web Application belonging to a state government, reliability may be more significant than transparency; and for the consumers of a distributed computer game Web Application belonging to an entertainment provider, usability may be more significant than dependability.

Remarks

The IEEE Standard 1061-1998, the ISO 9241-11:1998 Standard, the ISO/IEC 9126-1:2001 Standard, and the ISO 9241-171:2008 Standard could be referred to for the definitions of most of the pragmatic and social quality attributes in M_{AC}. They are not given here and discussed further due to considerations of space.

The quality attributes included in Table 2 are generic, not specific, to the type of information in a Web Application. In general, a Web Application can be heterogeneous in a number of ways (Kamthan, 2009). Therefore, the precise meaning of a quality attribute can depend on the modality of information included in a Web Application. For example, accessibility concerns of an animation can be different from that of an audio.

The relationships among quality attributes can be (1) favorable, (2) unfavorable, or (3) neutral. In other words, in general, the quality attributes of M_{AC} as a collective form a connected acyclic graph, say G. In specific cases, G may also be a directed. A single quality attribute can be described by a subgraph of G.

The quality attributes included in Table 2 are necessary but there is no claim of their sufficiency. For example, the quality attributes such as correctness (accuracy) and (internal or external) consistency belong to other semiotic levels, namely semantic and syntactic levels. In other words, M_{AC} is based on the 'Open World Assumption' so that it can evolve.

Means for Assurance and Evaluation

The third column of Table 2 lists the means for assuring and evaluating Active Credibility. The means can be classified into those that are process-oriented, namely inspections and testing for evaluating the Active Credibility of a Web Application, and the ones that are product-oriented, namely training and guidance (via guidelines or patterns) for assuring the Active Credibility of a Web Application.

The position of this chapter is that a preventative approach is at least as significant as a curative approach. Therefore, due to considerations of space, only an intentionally selected subset of the means of assurance is discussed briefly; further details are available elsewhere (Kamthan, 2007)

Training

It is natural that training is an integral part of any profession. Unfortunately, it appears to be the case that the education related to the Web Applications usually tends to focus on the client- and/ or server-side 'technologies-of-the-day' rather than the fundamentals of analysis and synthesis necessary towards a *systematic* approach to the development of large-scale Web Applications. It should be acknowledged that credibility is a human and social concern, and therefore may not always amenable to a purely technological treatment.

If the support for credibility is deemed necessary, then the pedagogical models for Web Engineering education (Hadjerrouit, 2005) need to evolve accordingly. In particular, they need to include knowledge and learning activities related to a comprehensive technical background as well as non-technical aspects such as understanding consumer preferences and needs; understanding social manifestations of quality; training in cultural-sensitivity for internationalized and/or localized Web Applications; ability of journalistic writing, including the ability of balancing information with other types of media (related to marketing); and basic knowledge of legal issues (such as those related to intellectual property rights (IPR) and licensing).

Guidelines

It is known that guidelines encourage the use of conventions and good practice. They could serve as a checklist with respect to which a Web Application could be heuristically or, to certain extent, automatically evaluated. There are guidelines available for addressing credibility in general (Fogg, 2003b) and accessibility, privacy, security, and usability of Web Applications in particular (Caldwell et al., 2008; Nielsen & Loranger, 2006).

However, there are certain limitations in the use of guidelines. They often are stated as 'context-free', 'absolute,' and 'universal'; are usually stated at a level that is more suitable for an expert than for a novice; do not consider the possible relationships among them; and do not discuss trade-offs of their application. For example, a guideline such as *allow a personalized and tailored experience to users* can not easily be related to a credibility model as it lacks rationale and can not easily be designed and implemented in a Web Application as it is rather general.

Patterns

The reliance on expertise gained from past experience can be useful to any development. In the past decade and a half, patterns have provided conceptually reusable and empirically proven practical solutions to recurring problems in given contexts, both during analysis and synthesis phases of a development process. There are a number of properties, including special structure of their descriptions (Buschmann, Henney, & Schmidt, 2007), that makes patterns uniquely practical over other bodies of knowledge such as principles, guidelines, and heuristics.

There are currently a number of collections of patterns relevant to the development of Web Applications (Van Duyne, Landay, & Hong, 2007; Vora, 2009), some of which are relevant to addressing the quality attributes of Table 2. Indeed, patterns can be systematically integrated in Web Applications (Kamthan, 2008b), and an appropriate use of patterns can address many of the pragmatic and social quality attributes in Table 2.

However, there are certain limitations in the use of patterns. There is an evident cost involved in any reuse, including patterns, related to adaptation and learning; the number of patterns continues to grow nonlinearly that, in absence of proper directions, similarities and overlaps among them, and/or appropriate quality of their descriptions, makes the selection of desirable candidates non-trivial; and there is always a distinct possibility (such as for new domains) that for a given problem, there simply may not be any suitable pattern available.

Decision Support

The last column of Table 2 acknowledges that the activities of credibility assurance and/or evaluation must be realizable in practice. In particular, the producers of Web Applications need to take into account organizational constraints of time and resources (personnel, infrastructure, budget, and so on) and external forces (market value, competitors, and so on). This compels them to make quality related decisions that, apart from being sensitive to credibility, must also be feasible.

For example, an a priori guarantee that a Web Application will be accessible to *all* consumers at *all* times in *all* task-specific or computing environment-specific situations that the consumers can find themselves in, is not practical.

The feasibility analysis is evidently related to multi-criteria decision making and could be a part of the overall Web Application project planning activity. There are well-known techniques such as Analytical Hierarchy Process (AHP) and Quality Function Deployment (QFD) for carrying out feasibility analysis, and further discussion of this aspect is beyond the scope of this chapter.

Remarks

The means for assurance and evaluation are not necessarily mutually exclusive. Indeed, in some cases, they can be used in conjunction to assist each other. For example, it is common for inspections to use guidelines as a checklist for evaluation and, although not common, the same applies to patterns.

The mapping between the pragmatic and social quality attributes in $\mathbf{M}_{AC}$ and the means for addressing them is many-to-many. For example,

there are guidelines and patterns for security; and, conversely, acceptance testing is applicable to both accessibility and usability.

At social and pragmatic levels, the use of metrics and tools is useful but limited. For example, it is not possible to completely automate an auditing process such as inspections that depends on the reading ability of the inspectors or the application of the means for guidance (especially, principles and guidelines) that depends on the interpretation and discretion of the development engineer.

Active Credibility of Web Applications: Example

For an illustration of the impact of quality attributes towards Active Credibility of Web Applications, consider the social level of $\mathbf{M}_{AC}$. (The details of quality attributes in it along with the precise role of patterns are large areas to discuss at any length in this chapter and, therefore, admittedly, the treatment is brief.)

The notion of aesthetics is associated with the philosophies of art and value, and is often culture-specific. The sensitivity part of aural/visual perception is close to human senses, and therefore is strongly related to aesthetics. The artistic expression plays an important role in making a Web Application 'appealing' to its customers beyond simply the functionality it provides. There are patterns available for appropriate use of technological affordances in order to make the user interface of a Web Application appealing but, at the same time, avoiding negative persuasion. For example, the SITE BRANDING pattern (Van Duyne, Landay, & Hong, 2003) is can be used to make a Web Application appear culture- and locale-specific. If carried out, this contributes towards Surface Credibility.

It is also critical that the Web Application as a whole be legal (for example, is legal in the jurisdiction it operates and all components it is comprised of, local or remote, are legal). Furthermore, it is imperative that steps are taken by the producer of the Web Application to respect consumer's privacy (for example, there are controls to minimize, ideally avoid, any abuse or sharing consumer-supplied information without prior permission) and to ensure security (for example, in situations where financial transactions are made). There are patterns available for both privacy and security. Finally, the producer must take all steps to be transparent with respect to the consumer (for example, not include misleading information such as the features of products or services offered, clearly label promotional content, make available their contact information including physical address, policies regarding returning/exchanging products, and so on). There are patterns available for especially for information architecture and design that can aid a producer towards achieving transparency. If carried out, this contributes towards Experienced Credibility.

DIRECTIONS FOR FUTURE RESEARCH

The work presented in this chapter can be extended in a few different directions. In particular, F_{ACE} in general and M_{AC} in particular could be strengthened in a number of ways.

F_{ACE} could benefit from empirical validation for Web Applications aimed for specific domains where the need to establish credibility is relatively urgent. For example, such areas include electronic commerce and portals providing information on matters that impact the daily lives of consumers such as finance, health, housing, shopping, travel, and so on.

The elicitation of real-world examples and non-examples using them for developing a collection of patterns and anti-patterns, respectively, dedicated specifically to credibility can support M_{AC}. For example, such a collection could be useful for the micro-architecture design of (Social) Web Applications for which credibility is a high priority. There are early signs (Vora, 2009) but a lot more needs to be done.

The relationship between credibility, legality,

and ethical practices in Web Applications could be explored further that in turn could strengthen M_{AC}. The case of special interest is the interplay between credibility and transclusion. For example, parts of a resource to which a request is made may be hosted on external servers (say, via 'inlining' images, 'deep linking,' or 'framing') whose bandwidth is used without request. This often seamless integration of external resources in a Web Application when combined with means to 'persuade' consumers (such as advertisements) may be legal but raises the issue of credibility.

There are cognitive and affective aspects to all human interactions: cognitive to assign meaning and affective to assign value (Norman, 2004). Therefore, further investigating the relationship between Active Credibility and affect in general and human emotion in particular, and implications of this the relationship towards the development of Web Applications, is of interest.

Finally, the chapter is exclusive to Active Credibility. An examination into the role of third party audits such as TRUSTe, VeriSign, and WebTrust in enhancing the Reputed Credibility of Web Applications, particularly for small-to-medium enterprises (SMEs) where budget of such audits is an issue, is also of interest.

CONCLUSION

The concerns of credibility and the extent to which they are addressed is likely to remain a key determinant towards the success of the different shapes and forms into which the Web morphs in the future. Although there have been many advances towards enabling the technological infrastructure of the Web in the past decade, there is much to be done in addressing the social challenges, including user perceptions and expectations.

A Web Application is only as useful as the value it provides to its consumers. This value is significantly diminished if the Web Application cannot be trusted. If the issue of credibility not addressed, there is a potential for lost consumer confidence, thereby compromising the benefits and opportunities the Web as a medium offers. At the same time, it is also crucial that any efforts for addressing credibility be systematic and feasible.

For that, a collective effort resulting from the involvement of all stakeholders of a Web Application is called for. This requires initiation, formulation, and execution of a number of steps, both internal and external to the organization, including (1) awareness in the organization, (2) a confluence of people with expertise in different managerial, social, and technical areas, (3) integration of credibility in the development process, (4) implementation of both preventative and curative measures, (5) outreach among public of the organization's position on credibility, and (5) education of consumers in discerning pertinent information.

In conclusion, establishing credibility is imperative for sustaining an organization's reputation, for elevating or restoring consumer confidence, and for building consumers' trust. The producers of Web Applications who hope to change the user perceptions in their favor need to view credibility as a *first-class* concern, and take explicit and systematic steps to ensure and evaluate it. In that regard, credibility engineering needs to be adopted, pursued, and steered on par with the currently more established sub-disciplines of quality engineering such as reliability engineering, security engineering, and usability engineering. F_{ACE} along with M_{AC} present a preliminary step in that direction.

REFERENCES

Buschmann, F., Henney, K., & Schmidt, D. C. (2007). *Pattern-oriented software architecture, Volume 5: On patterns and pattern languages.* John Wiley and Sons.

Caldwell, B., Chisholm, W. Reid, L. G., & Vanderheiden, G. (2008). *Web Content Accessibility Guidelines 2.0.* W3C Recommendation. World Wide Web Consortium (W3C).

Consumer Reports WebWatch. (2005, October 26). *Leap of faith: Using the Internet despite the dangers. results of a national survey of Internet users for consumer reports WebWatch.* A Consumer Reports WebWatch Research Report.

Cusinato, A., Della Mea, V., Di Salvatore, F., & Mizzaro, S. (2009, April 20-21). *QuWi: Quality control in Wikipedia.* Paper presented at the Third Workshop on Information Credibility on the Web (WICOW 2009), Madrid, Spain.

Danielson, D. R. (2006). Web credibility. In C. Ghaoui (Ed.), *Encyclopedia of human-computer interaction.* Hershey, PA: IGI Global.

Fenton, N. E., & Pfleeger, S. L. (1997). *Software metrics: A rigorous & practical approach.* International Thomson Computer Press.

Fogg, B. J. (2003a, April 5-10). *Prominence-interpretation theory: Explaining how people assess credibility.* Paper presented at the ACM CHI 2003 Conference on Human Factors in Computing Systems (CHI 2003), Fort Lauderdale, USA.

Fogg, B. J. (2003b). *Persuasive technology: Using computers to change what we think and do.* Morgan Kaufmann Publishers.

Fogg, B. J., Cueller, G., & Danielson, D. (2008). Motivating, Influencing, and Persuading Users: An Introduction to Captology. In A. Sears & J. A. Jacko (Eds.), *The Human-Computer Interaction Handbook: Fundamentals, Evolving Technologies, and Emerging Applications* (2nd ed., pp. 133-146). Lawrence Erlbaum Associates.

Fogg, B. J., & Tseng, S. (1999, May 15-20). *The elements of computer credibility.* Paper presented at the ACM CHI 1999 Conference on Human Factors in Computing Systems, Pittsburgh, USA.

Hadjerrouit, S. (2005). Designing a pedagogical model for Web engineering education: An evolutionary perspective. *Journal of Information Technology Education*, 4, 115–140.

Hendler, J., Lassila, O., & Berners-Lee, T. (2001). The Semantic Web. *Scientific American, 284*(5), 34–43. doi:10.1038/scientificamerican0501-34

Junior, P. T. A., & Filgueiras, L. V. L. (2005, October 23-26). *User Modeling with Personas*. Paper presented at the 2005 Latin American Conference on Human-Computer Interaction (CLIHC 2005), Cuernavaca, Mexico.

Kamthan, P. (2007). Towards a systematic approach for the credibility of human-centric Web applications. *Journal of Web Engineering, 6*(2), 99–120.

Kamthan, P. (2008a). Ethics in software engineering. In M. Quigley (Ed.), *Encyclopedia of information ethics and security* (pp. 266-272). Hershey, PA: IGI Global.

Kamthan, P. (2008b). A methodology for integrating patterns in quality-centric Web applications. *International Journal of Information Technology and Web Engineering, 3*(2), 27–44.

Kamthan, P. (2008c). A Framework for the Active Credibility Engineering of Web Applications. *International Journal of Information Technology and Web Engineering, 3*(3), 17–27.

Kamthan, P. (2009). A model for characterizing Web engineering. In M. Khosrow-Pour (Ed.), *Encyclopedia of information science and technology* (2nd ed., pp. 2631-2637).

Lassila, O., & Hendler, J. (2007). Embracing "Web 3.0". *IEEE Internet Computing, 11*(3), 90–93. doi:10.1109/MIC.2007.52

Lazar, J., Meiselwitz, G., & Feng, J. (2007). Understanding Web credibility: A synthesis of the research literature. World Scientific.

Nielsen, J., & Loranger, H. (2006). *Prioritizing Web usability*. New Riders.

Norman, D. A. (2004). *Emotional design: Why we love (or hate) everyday things*. Basic Books.

O'Reilly, T. (2005,, September 30). *What Is Web 2.0: Design patterns and business models for the next generation of software*. O'Reilly Network.

Oinas-Kukkonen, H., & Harjumaa, M. (2008, February 10-15). *Towards deeper understanding of persuasion in software and information systems*. Paper presented at the First International Conference on Advances in Computer-Human Interaction (ACHI 2008), Sainte Luce, Martinique.

Pirolli, P. (2007). *Information foraging theory: Adaptive interaction with information*. UK: Oxford University Press.

Rieh, S. Y., & Danielson, D. R. (2007). Credibility: A multidisciplinary framework. *Annual Review of Information Science & Technology, 41*, 307–364. doi:10.1002/aris.2007.1440410114

Shanks, G. (1999, September 29). *Semiotic approach to understanding representation in information systems*. Information Systems Foundations Workshop, Sydney, Australia.

Sharp, H., Galal, G. H., & Finkelstein, A. (1999, August 30-September 3). *Stakeholder identification in the requirements engineering process*. Paper presented at the Tenth International Conference and Workshop on Database and Expert Systems Applications (DEXA 1999), Florence, Italy.

Simon, H. (1996). *The sciences of the artificial* (3rd ed.). The MIT Press.

Stamper, R. (1992). *Signs, organizations, norms and information systems*. Paper presented at the Third Australian Conference on Information Systems, Wollongong, Australia, October 5-8, 1992.

Van Duyne, D. K., Landay, J., & Hong, J. I. (2007). *The design of sites: Patterns for creating winning web sites* (2nd ed.). Prentice-Hall.

Vora, P. (2009). *Web application design patterns*. Morgan Kaufmann.

Walther, J. B., Wang, Z., & Loh, T. (2004). The effect of top-level domains and advertisements on health web site credibility. *Journal of Medical Internet Research*, 6(3), 2004. doi:10.2196/jmir.6.3.e24

Wathen, C. N., & Burkell, J. (2002). Believe it or not: factors influencing credibility on the Web. *Journal of the American Society for Information Science and Technology*, 53(2), 134–144. doi:10.1002/asi.10016

Wong, B. (2006). Different views of software quality. In E. Duggan & J. Reichgelt (Eds.), *Measuring Information Systems Delivery Quality* (pp. 55-88). Hershey, PA: IGI Global.

Section 4
Applications

Chapter 15
A Lifecycle Approach for Scenario Driven Decision Systems

M. Daud Ahmed
Manukau Institute of Technology, New Zealand

David Sundaram
University of Auckland, New Zealand

ABSTRACT

The fundamental aim of this research is to design and develop a framework for Scenario-driven Decision Support Systems Generator (SDSSG). The focus of the framework is to align Decision Support Systems (DSS) with the scenario management process that supports usage of scenario as a core component of decision making. Though traditional DSS provide strong data management, modelling and visualisation capabilities for the decision maker, they do not explicitly support scenario management appropriately. Systems that purport to support scenario planning are complex and difficult to use and do not fully support all phases of scenario management. This research presents a life cycle approach for scenario management. The proposed process helps the decision maker with idea generation, scenario planning, development, organisation, analysis, execution, and the use of scenarios for decision making. This research introduces scenario as a DSS component and develops a domain independent, component-based, modular framework and architecture that supports the proposed scenario management process. The framework and architecture have been implemented and validated through a concrete prototype.

1 INTRODUCTION

Herman Kahn, a military strategist at Rand Corporation, first applied the term scenario to planning in the 1950s (Schoemaker, 1993). Scenarios are constructed for discovering possibilities, leading to a projection of the most likely alternative. Scenarios offer a dynamic view of possible futures (Weinstein, 2007; NIC, 2004). Scenarios are not forecasts (Schwartz, 1991), predictions (Weinstein, 2007), future plans (Epstein, 1998), trend analyses or analyses of the past. It is for strategy identification rather than strategy development (Schoemaker, 1993) and to anticipate and understand risk and to discover new options for action. Ritson (1997) agrees with Schoemaker (1995) and explains that

DOI: 10.4018/978-1-60566-719-5.ch015

scenario planning scenarios are situations planned against known facts and trends but deliberately structured to enable a range of options and to track the key triggers which would precede a given situation within the scenario.

Scenarios explore the joint impact of various uncertainties, which stand side by side as equals. Computed scenarios help the decision makers to understand what they do not know and what they need to know. Usually sensitivity analysis examines the effect of a change in one variable, keeping all other variables constant. Moving one variable at a time makes sense for small changes. However, if the change is much larger, other variables do not stay constant. Decision makers have been using the concepts of scenarios for a long time, but due to its complexity, its use is still limited to strategic decision making tasks. Scenario planning varies widely from one decision maker to another mainly because of lack of generally accepted principles for scenario management. Albert (1983) proposes three approaches for scenario planning. Ringland (1998) identifies three-step scenario planning. Schoemaker (1995) outlines a ten-step scenario analysis process. Huss and Honton (1987) describe three categories of scenario planning. The literature still lacks a suitable approach for planning, developing, analysing, organising and evaluating the scenario using model-driven decision support systems. Currently available scenario management processes are cumbersome and not properly supported by the available tools and technologies. Therefore, we introduce a life cycle approach based scenario management guideline.

Generation of multiple scenarios and sensitivity analysis exacerbate the decision makers problem. The available scenario planning tools are not suitable for assessing the quality of the scenarios and do not support the evaluation of scenarios properly through comparison processes. Considering the significance of scenarios in the decision-making process, this research includes scenario as a decision-support component of the DSS and defines Scenario-driven DSS as an inter-

active computer-based system, which integrates diverse data, models and solvers to explore decision scenarios for supporting the decision makers in solving problems.

Traditional DSS have been for the most part data-driven, model-driven and/or knowledge-driven (Power, Sharda and Kulkarni, 2007; Power 2001, 2002) but have not given due importance to scenario planning and analysis. Some of the DSS have partial support for sensitivity analysis and goal-seek analysis but this does not fulfil the needs of the decision maker. In most cases, the available scenario analysis tools deal with a single scenario at a time and are not suitable for development of multiple scenarios simultaneously. A scenario impacts on related scenarios but currently available tools are not suitable for developing a scenario based on another scenario.

To address the problems and issues raised above we followed an iterative process of observation/evaluation, theory building, and systems development (Nunamaker, Chen and Purdin, 1991; Hevener 2004), wherein we proposed and implemented a flexible framework and architecture for a scenario driven decision support systems generator (SDSSG). It includes scenario as a DSS component, extends the model-driven DSS, and incorporates knowledge- and document-driven DSS (Power, 2001). A prototype was developed, tested and evaluated using the evaluation criteria for quality and appropriateness of scenarios (Schoemaker, 1995) and principles of DSSG frameworks and architectures (Collier, Carey, Sautter and Marjani-emi, 1999; Geoffrion, 1987; Ramirez, Ching, and Louis, 1990). The conceptual framework as well as the prototype was modified on the basis of the findings and the process was continued until a satisfactory result was achieved.

In the rest of this paper, we first introduce a life cycle approach for management of scenarios. We then propose a scenario-driven flexible decision support framework and follow this with a presentation of an n-tiered architecture that details the SDSSG framework. Finally we discuss

Figure 1. Scenario management: A life cycle approach

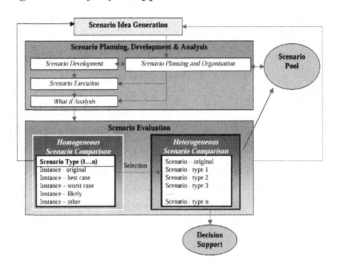

briefly the implementation within which the proposed process, framework, and architecture were validated.

2 SCENARIO MANAGEMENT: A LIFECYCLE APPROACH

Before discussing the management of scenarios it is worth clearly defining what a scenario entails. A scenario is a situation that is comprised of one or more problem instances. A change in one scenario might have chain effects on any related scenarios. The basic structure and behaviour of the scenario is similar to the decision support system components model and solver respectively. A model describes real-life phenomena and solves real-life problems (Gachet, 2004). We define scenario as a complex situation analogous to a model that is instantiated by data and tied to solver(s). A scenario can be presented dynamically using different visualisations. A scenario may contain other scenarios. Hence, a scenario structure is an object that establishes a complex relationship among various models, solvers, visualisations, contained scenarios (if there be any), and related data for integrating them.

The scenario may vary for different problems and domains but a single management approach should support the model-driven scenario analysis process. This research introduces a scenario management process using life cycle approach that synthesises and extends ideas from Ringland (1998, 2002), Schoemaker (1995), Albert (1983), Huss and Honton (1987), van der Heijden, (1996), and Wright, (2000). The proposed life cycle approach for scenario management process addresses a variety of problem types. The life cycle process starts with scenario idea generation and finishes with the usage of scenario for decision support as illustrated in Figure 1.

2.1 Idea Generation

A decision situation can be factual or hypothetical and represented by a combination of previous and current facts and assumptions (Gachet, 2004). The scenario planner foresees the key issues that exist within the scenario and analyses the concerns for identifying the influential driving forces and parameters for the scenarios. In addition, the planner may also use the existing scenarios from the scenario pool. The leading factors, which could be either internal and/or external, could lead to various changes on the system. The decision maker as a domain expert predicts the possible changes of the indicators that would guide to the development of ideas for scenario planning.

2.2 Scenario Planning, Development and Analysis

In this phase, the decision maker will carry out the tasks of scenario planning and organisation, scenario development, scenario execution, and what-if analysis. Existing scenarios could also act as inputs to this phase apart from the ideas generated from the previous phase.

2.2.1 Scenario Planning and Organisation

Scenario planning step mainly focuses on decomposing the whole big scenario into multiple inter-related scenarios that are suitable for development, execution, analysis and evaluation. It also includes scenario structuring and identification of the scenario components.

2.2.1.1 Scenario Structure
The components of the scenario can be either pre-customised or loosely coupled. For a pre-customised scenario, the relationships between data, model, and solver as well as with other dependent scenarios are inflexible. The relationships between data-model, model-solver, and data-model-solver-scenario are defined during scenario planning. For example, a scenario is a collection of data, models, solvers, and scenario(s) in which the relationships among the constituent components are fixed and the model instantiation and model evaluation processes by data and solver are distinct. So the scenario components are tightly integrated and the relationships are not exposed for the decision maker. For a loosely coupled scenario, the scenario components namely, the data, model, solver, and dependent scenarios remain independent within the scenario. The relation-

ships among these components are established at runtime using a mapping component.

2.2.1.2 A Mechanism for Structuring Scenarios
Scenarios are complex and dynamically related to other scenarios. In view of addressing the complexity and inter-relatedness of scenarios, we propose to divide larger scenarios into multiple simple scenarios having independent meaning and existence. In this context we identify three types of scenarios, namely: a) Simple Scenarios – the simple scenario is not dependent on other scenarios but completely meaningful and usable b) Aggregate Scenarios – the structure of different scenarios or results from multiple scenarios are combined/aggregated together to develop a more complex scenario and c) Pipelining Scenarios – one scenario is an input to another scenario in a hierarchical scenario structure. In this type of scenario, lower-level scenario can be tightly or loosely integrated with the higher-level scenario. The decision maker may combine simple as well as complex scenarios together using pipelining and aggregation to develop more complex scenarios.

2.2.1.3 Scenario Organisation
Scenario organisation activities include making availability of already developed scenarios, and storing, retrieving, deleting and updating the scenarios to and from a scenario pool. This scenario pool should support both temporary and permanent storage systems. The temporary storage, termed as a runtime pool, is used for managing scenarios during development, analysis and evaluation. The newly developed and retrieved scenarios are cached in the runtime pool for developing aggregate or pipelining scenarios. The scenario pool also permanently stores scenarios for future use or reference. Both the temporary and permanent storage systems are capable of storing the scenario structure, scenario instance and executed scenarios.

2.2.2 Scenario Development

Scenario planning and scenario development stages are inter-dependent and iterative. Scenario development is the process of conversion and representation of planned scenarios into fully computer based scenarios. Chermack (2003) argues that scenarios have rarely been applied to develop alternative processes. The proposed life cycle approach supports development of alternative process models and scenarios. In this stage, the decision maker organises the related data, model, solver, and dependent scenarios for constituting the relationships among them to develop scenario(s). The decision maker could potentially use pre-customised and/or loosely coupled scenarios and may skip this step if they use previously developed scenarios. The scenarios are developed in mainly two steps. In step 1, the basic scenarios of the domain are developed, and in step 2, scenarios related to what-if (goal seek and sensitivity) analysis are developed.

2.2.3 Scenario Execution

The proposed scenario development process ensures that the scenario can be executed and analysed for determining quality and plausibility. In this step, the models are instantiated with the data, and then the model instance is executed using the appropriate solver(s). Model selection is completely independent while one or more solvers may be used for a model execution. A flexible mapping process bridges the state attributes of the model and solver to engage in a relationship and to participate in the execution process. For a complex scenario, the decision maker may need to apply several models and solvers to analyse various aspects of the scenario. If a scenario contains other scenario instances, execution of the containing scenario will depend on the execution of the contained scenarios. But if the containing scenario contains the structure of the contained scenarios, the execution of the containing scenario depends

on a series of model instantiation and model execution. This process may be pre-customised during the scenario development step or customisable during the execution step. The decision maker can skip this step if they use only the previously stored scenario instances and executed scenarios from the scenario pool.

2.2.4 What-If Analysis

What-if analysis can be divided into two categories, namely sensitivity analysis and goal-seek analysis. Sensitivity analysis allows changing one or more parametric value(s) at a time and analyses the outcome for the change. It reveals the impact itself as well as the impact on other related scenarios. Because a scenario contains other scenarios, each and every change dynamically propagates to all the related scenarios. Goal-seek analysis accomplishes a particular task rather than analysing the changing future. This goal seek analysis is just a reverse or feedback evaluation where the decision maker supplies the target output and gets the required input.

2.3 Scenario Evaluation Process

Scenario evaluation is a challenging task (Chermack, 2002) but some end-states are predetermined dependent upon the presence of an interaction of identified events (Wright, 2000) which can be used to devise an evaluation process. The decision maker can develop many scenarios. The question is – do all these scenarios represent a unique situation? Each scenario might appropriately draw the strategic question; represent fundamentally different issues; present a plausible future; and challenge conventional wisdom. Schwartz (1991) and Tucker (1999) discourage too many scenarios and advocate for the use of best-case scenario, worst-case scenario and most-likely scenario. The evaluation is done through scenario execution and comparison of the executed results. A visualisation object displays results of all the executed scenario instances either as a table or as graph. This presentation helps comparing the computed inputs and outputs including other attributes. The comparison may take place among homogeneous scenarios or heterogeneous scenarios.

2.4 Decision Support

The above described scenario planning, development, and evaluation through comparative analysis results in improved participant learning (Shoemaker, 1995) and help decision makers re-perceive reality from several viewpoints (der Heijden et al., 2002) and thereby better support for decision making. The following section proposes a framework that realises the proposed scenario management process.

3 SCENARIO DRIVEN FLEXIBLE DECISION SUPPORT SYSTEMS GENERATOR FRAMEWORK

A scenario framework offers a variety of scenarios designed to help guide strategic decision making (Drew, 2006). Each scenario covers a range of circumstances that could have a significant impact on the organizational strategies. Few of the DSS frameworks emphasise fully featured scenario planning, development, analysis, execution, evaluation and their usage for decision support. DSS components such as data, model, solver, and visualisation have been extensively used in many DSS framework design but they did not consider scenario as a component of DSS. Scenario plays such an important role in the decision-making process that it is almost impractical to develop a good decision modelling environment while leaving out this component. Scenarios also need to be modelled. Therefore they resemble a model-driven DSS but the scenarios are more complex than models. Therefore, the scenario-driven DSS should add the scenario as an independent component in addition to the

existing decision-support components. The scenario does not have a separate existence without its base components. It means that every scenario is built up from a unique nature of the problem (model) that can have a number of alternative unique attributes (data) and each instance can be interpreted, executed or implemented using one or more alternative methods (solver).

To overcome the problems and address the issues mentioned above we propose a scenario-driven decision support systems generator (SDSSG) framework as illustrated in Figure 2. The SDSSG components are separated into the following three categories: a) Decision-support components (DSC) that include the data, model, solver, scenario and visualisation, b) Integration Components (IC) that include Kernel, Component Set, Mapping, and Validation Component, and c) Component Pools that include data pool, model pool, solver pool, scenario pool, and visualisation pool. Each component of the DSC has a direct relationship with a component pool. In this framework, the DSCs, ICs and Component pools are independent of each other. The DSCs communicate via the kernel component. Mapping component develops the correct path of communication between data and model, and model and solver, while the validation component tests the correct matching of the component interface and the appropriate communication between the components.

The data, model, solver, scenario, and visualisation are stored in different component pools as shown in Figure 2 and the framework allows retrieving these components from the component pools. The related model, data and solver are combined together to develop a scenario. This scenario is saved to the scenario pool for future use. This also allows using the scenario(s) as an input for developing a number of simple, aggregate, and pipelined scenarios. Every instance of the scenario can be termed as a specific decision support system. Therefore, the framework is a generator of scenarios as well as the decision support systems.

Figure 2. Scenario-driven decision support systems generator (SDSSG) framework

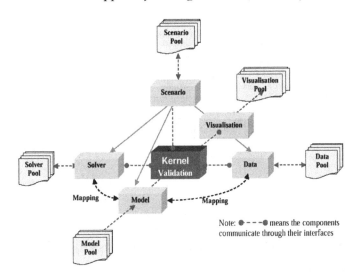

Scenarios can be saved and retrieved to and from the scenario pool and the same can again be customised using separate models and solvers. The scenario instances can be used as complex data for input to the next level of model for further analysis. Different scenarios are computed simultaneously and sensitivity and goal-seek analysis are done using different scenarios. The framework is suitable for analysing internally coherent scenarios or scenario bundles, and examining the joint consequences of changes in the environment for supporting the decision maker's strategy.

4 SDSSG ARCHITECTURE

In order to implement the SDSSG framework we develop a component-based layered architecture as shown in Figure 3 that is suitable for implementation as an n-tiered system. The proposed architecture is comprised of the user services tier, application tier, and component base tier; and the layers are user services, integration, data access, decision support services, application customisation, and component pool. The component pool layer stores data, model, solver, and scenario. A relational database management system or XML

documents can be used as a component layer. The data access layer provides components' management services e.g. addition, retrieval, modification, and removal of a component. The decision support services layer provides the services of DSS components namely, model, solver, scenario, and visualisation. The integration layer provides integration, mapping and validation services through Kernel, Mapping, and Validation components. The kernel arranges communication between data-model, model-solver and scenario-visualisation using the mapping component for model instantiation, model execution, and scenario presentation respectively. It also uses the validation component to validate the proper communication and execution of the components. The Common Component facilitates creation of dynamic graphical user interface (GUI) and presentation layer depending on the decision maker's selection of data, model, solver, scenario, and visualisation components at runtime. This GUI supports decision maker's interactivity with the system for input, mapping, scenario development, execution, analysis, evaluation and presentation.

The architecture also contains an Application Customisation module, which contains Component Container, Framework Template, and Tem-

Figure 3. SDSSG architecture

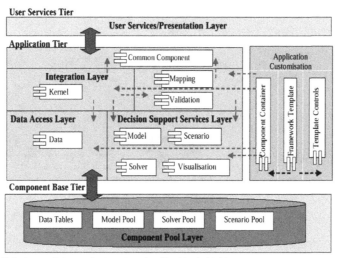

Note: Arrows to be interpreted as "…..using….." e.g. Kernel is using Model

plate Controls. This module facilitates customisation of the SDSSG system with newer components. The Application Customisation module works on top of the other architectural components for their customization. This Framework Template component is the medium of user interaction for customisation of the system. Framework Control component creates controls on the framework template for user interaction with the customisation process of the system. The Component Container contains abstract components and interfaces of all the architectural components.

The architecture separates the decision-support components from the integration components. It supports independent development and use of the components, flexible scenario modelling, scenario manipulation and integration, flexible mapping between different DSS components, flexible integration of DSS components, and finally scenario analysis. Pre-customised and customisable modelling system can be achieved through pre-defined relationships and the mapping component respectively. This mapping component facilitates dynamic communication between model-data, model-solver, and model-visualisation. A further detail of this architectural class diagram has described in Ahmed and Sundaram (2008a).

5 IMPLEMENTATION

The SDSSG framework and architecture can be implemented using any platform that supports component-based development. Since object-orientation and componentisation concepts are the central focus of the SDSSG framework and architecture, C# was used for implementing the SDSSG architecture that leverages Microsoft's .NET Framework. Relational Database Management Systems (e.g. SQL 2000 Server, Microsoft Access) and Extensible Markup Language (XML) were also used in building the system for managing data, model, solver, and scenario components. Ringland (2002) explains that business case should be at the centre of the scenario planning. Therefore the SDSSG framework and architecture have been implemented within the context of a mortgage domain. We implemented base scenarios e.g. affordability scenario, lending scenario (equal instalment, reducing instalment, interest only lending scenarios), payment scenario, etc. An implementation of the SDSSG Framework and Architecture can be seen in Ahmed and Sundaram (2008b). The generalisability of the lifecycle approach for scenario planning, SDSSG framework, and architecture has been proved in other domains and other paradigms.

6 CONCLUSION

Current scenario planning and analysis systems are very complex, not user friendly, and do not support modelling and evaluating multiple scenarios simultaneously. To overcome these problems we propose a scenario management life cycle, and a framework and architecture for scenario driven flexible decision support systems generator that support the lifecycle. The lifecycle as well as the framework and architecture are validated through a concrete implementation of a prototype.

This research also introduces the concepts of scenario structure and their development strategy. It decomposes large complex scenarios into multiple small and executable scenarios and uses the decomposition and re-composition methodology for defining the scenario structure. The proposed life cycle approach for scenario management supports a range of activities from conceptualising and understanding the scenario to final use of the scenario for decision making. Key phases of the life cycle are idea generation, scenario planning, organisation, development, execution, analysis, evaluation, and finally decision support. The process hides external factors and complexities of the scenario and allows seamless combination of decision parameters for appropriate scenario generation.

The research further realises the scenario-driven decision-making processes through extending model-driven decision support systems. This research develops a generic scenario driven flexible decision support systems generator framework and architecture that supports the above-mentioned scenario management processes. It also supports sensitivity and goal-seek analysis. Scenario has been introduced as a new DSS component.

The proposed framework and architecture are domain independent, platform independent, component-based and modular. The architecture is comprised of multiple layers e.g. component pool layer, data access layer, decision support services layer, integration layer, and user services layer. Each layer performs specific functions, which are suitable for implementation of the architecture as an n-tiered system. The implemented system supports customisation for developing semi-automated pre-customised specific DSS.

REFERENCES

Ahmed, M. D., & Sundaram, D. (2007). A framework for sustainability modelling and reporting. *The International Journal of Environmental, Cultural . Economic and Social Sustainability*, *3*(2), 29–40.

Ahmed, M. D., & Sundaram, D. (2008a). Design and implementation of scenario management systems. In M. Khosrow-Pour (Ed.), *Encyclopaedia of Information Science and Technology* (2nd ed., Vol. III, pp. D1-10). Hershey, PA: IGI Publishing.

Ahmed, M. D., & Sundaram, D. (2008b). A framework for scenario driven decision support systems generator. *International Journal of Information Technology and Web Engineering*, *3*(2), 45–62.

Albert, K. J. (1983). *The Strategic Management Handbook*. McGraw-Hill.

AMP. (2001, July 18). AMP Banking Survey – New Zealand home affordability highest for two years. Retrieved on October 10, 2001 from http://www.amp.co.nz.

Chermack, T. J. (2002). The mandate for theory in scenario planning. *Futures Research Quarterly*, *18*(2), 25–28.

Chermack, T. J. (2003). A Methodology for Assessing Performance-Based Scenario Planning. *Journal of Leadership & Organizational Studies*, *10*(2), 55. doi:10.1177/107179190301000206

Collier, K., Carey, B., Sautter, D., & Marjaniemi, C. (1999). A Methodology for Evaluating and Selection Data Mining Software. In *Proceedings of the 32nd Hawaii International Conference on System Sciences*.

Drew, A. W. S. (2006). Building technology foresight: using scenarios to embrace innovation. *European Journal of Innovation Management, 9*(3), 241. doi:10.1108/14601060610678121

Epstein, J. H. (1998). Scenario Planning: An Introduction. *The Futurist, 32*(6), 50–51.

Gachet, A. (2004). *Building Model-Driven Decision Support Systems with Dicodess*. Zurich: VDF.

Geoffrion, A. (1987). An Introduction to Structured Modelling. *Management Science, 33*(5), 547. doi:10.1287/mnsc.33.5.547

Hevner, A. R., March, S. T., Park, J., & Ram, S. (2004). Design Science in Information Systems Research. *MIS Quarterly, 28*(1), 75–105.

Huss, W.R., & Honton, E. J. (1987). Scenario Planning: What Style Should You Use? *Long Range Planning*, April.

NIC (2004). *Mapping the Global Future*. Report on the National Intelligence Council's 2020 Project, December 2004.

Nunamaker, J. F. Jr, Chen, M., & Purdin, T. D. M. (1991). Systems Development in Information Systems Research. *Journal of Management Information Systems, 7*(3), 89–106.

Power, D. J. (2001). Supporting Decision Makers: An Expanded Framework. *Informing Science Conference*, Poland.

Power, D. J. (2002). *Decision support systems: concepts and resources for managers*. Westport, CT: Quorum Books.

Power, D. J., Sharda, R., & Kulkarni, U. (2007*). Understanding Decision Support Systems for Global Enterprises*. 9th International Conference on Decision Support Systems (ICDSS 2007), Kolkata, India.

Ramirez, R. G., Ching, C., & St Louis, R. D. (1990). Model-Data and Model-Solver Mappings: A Basis for an Extended DSS Framework. *ISDSS Conference Proceedings*, (pp. 283-312).

Ringland, G. (1998). *Scenario Planning- Managing for the Future*. John Wiley & Sons.

Ringland, G. (2002). *Scenarios in business*. New York: John Wiley & Sons.

Ritson, N. (1997). Scenario Planning in Action. *Management Accounting, 75*(11), 24–28.

Schoemaker, P. J. H. (1993). Multiple Scenario Development: Its Conceptual and Behavioural Foundation. *Strategic Management Journal, 14*(3), 193–213. doi:10.1002/smj.4250140304

Schoemaker, P. J. H. (1995). Scenario Planning: A Tool for Strategic Thinking. *Sloan Management Review, 36*(2), 25–40.

Schwartz, P. (1991). *The Art of the Long View*. Doubleday.

Tucker, K. (1999). Scenario Planning. *Association Management, 51*(4), 70–75.

van der Heijden, K. (1996). *Scenarios, The Art of Strategic Conversation*. Wiley.

Weinstein, B. (2007). Scenario planning: current state of the art, Manager Update. *Henley-on-Thames, 18*(3), 1.

Wright, A. D. (2000). Scenario planning: A continuous improvement approach to strategy. *Total Quality Management, 11*(4-6), 433–438. doi:10.1080/09544120050007742

Chapter 16
An Approach Based on Market Economy for Consistency Management in Data Grids with OptorSim Simulator

Ghalem Belalem
University of Oran (ES Senia), Algeria

Belabbes Yagoubi
University of Oran (ES Senia), Algeria

Samah Bouamama
University of Oran (ES Senia), Algeria

ABSTRACT

Data Grids are currently solutions suggested to meet the needs of scale large systems. They provide highly varied and geographically distributed resources of which the goal is to ensure fast and effective data access. This improves availability, and tolerates breakdowns. In such systems, these advantages are not possible without the use of replication. The use of the technique of replication poses a problem in regards to the maintenance of the consistency of the same data replicas; the strategies of replication of the data and scheduling of jobs were tested by simulation. Several grid simulators were born. One of the most interesting simulators for this study is the OptorSim tool. In this chapter, the authors present an extension of the OptorSim by a consistency management module of the replicas in Data Grids; they propose a hybrid step which combines the economic models conceived for a hierarchical model with two levels. This suggested approach has two vocations, the first allowing a reduction in response times compared to an pessimistic approach, the second gives the good quality of service compared to optimistic approach.

DOI: 10.4018/978-1-60566-719-5.ch016

1 INTRODUCTION

Data storage and the data-gatherings can be processed by various means. In the history of computing, several memory technologies were presented and are largely widespread today. Starting from the simple places of storage like the main memory of machine, several manners of data distributing are known. A very important factor of memory technologies is the time of data access (Xu, 2002). While based on the various hardware of memory technologies (main memory, hard drive, …), the access time change. In distributed system which holds account of the data distribution at several places of storage and the distribution of the users and thus of the applications, there is always a difference in execution between the local (on the same machine) or remote data of access through network. This difference is related to the access time, to minimize factor, by providing copies (replicas) data in several places. The replicas are not only employed to gain the execution in access time and consequently hide of latencies of access but also to deal with the problems that occur in the distributed systems. However, the use of this technique generates consistency problem. The management and the scheduling of the resources in large scale systems consider many parameters which must be considered and the complex interactions which occur, make the impracticable model analytically.

The work presented in this research contributes to the consistency management of replicas in data grids. It allows proposing an incremental approach to converge replicas towards a global replica of the system by using, for conflict resolution, strategy based on economic market models under the OptorSim grid simulator (Bell, 2003). In Section 2 of this paper, we describe in very short OptorSim simulator of grids. The approaches to consistency management of replicas are described in Section 3. Section 4 presents the proposed process based on market economy model for consistency management in the grid environments. The various preliminary experiments are discussed in section 5. We end this paper with a conclusion and some future directions.

2 OPTORSIM SIMULATOR

Resource management and scheduling of resources in large scale systems are complicated and require sophisticated tools to analyze algorithms before applying them to real systems. Many phenomena cause non-determinism of the test platform. It is customary to simulate what can iterate as necessary experience and see for example the influence of a parameter in particular on the results of simulations. As a result, many tools and standards which are specific to the application have been established. Several simulators have been proposed to study and analyze the behavior of environment types grids and management of their resources, among which, we can cite: Bricks (Takefusa, 1999), SimGrid (Casanova, 2003), GridSim (Buyya, 2002), ChicSim (Ranganathan, 2002), EdgSim (Edgsim, 2003), MicroGrid (Song, 2000), GangSim (Dumitrescu, 2005), OptorSim (Bell, 2003).

The principal motivation of OptorSim was the lack of environment of simulation for data grid treatment applications. The objective of OptorSim is to study the stability and transitory behavior of the replica optimization methods. OptorSim models the interactions of the individual data grid components design (Figure 1) drifts directly of the architecture of the data grid project. OptorSim considers the following concepts:

- The sites provide date processing and/or storage resources
- A Broker Resource for scheduling works
- A router is without treatment or storage resources

Work is carried out on the treatment resources and uses the data stored in the storage resources.

Figure 1. Basic OptorSim architecture

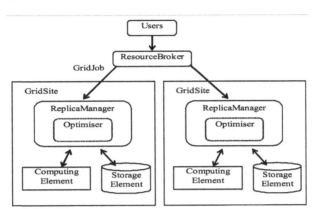

OptorSim allows the description of the network topology by enumerating the bonds between available sites and their bandwidth.

With OptorSim, several replication strategies were compared: no replication, replication without conditions, removing the oldest files if space is insufficient. The width of the available simulators allows various research groups of study various aspects of the grid computing and data grid. The choice of the OptorSim simulator for our work, was motivated (Belalem, 2007b), on the one hand, by the fact that OptorSim is a simulator to study and analyze replication protocols in the data grids and on the other hand by the fact that Optorsim is an Open source written in Java.

3 APPROACHES OF CONSISTENCY MANAGEMENT

Data replica is made up of multiple copies, on separate computers. It is a significant technology which improves availability and execution. But the various replicas of the same object must be coherent, i.e. seem only one copy. There are many models of consistency. All does not offer the same performances and do not impose the same constraints to the application programmers. The consistency management of replicas can be done either in a synchronous way by using algorithms

known as pessimistic, or in an asynchronous way with use of algorithms known as optimistic (Saito, 2005). The synchronous model allows to make an immediate propagation of the updates towards the replicas by blocking the access, whereas the asynchronous model permits a different operation from update propagation, it introduces a certain level of divergence between replicas.

3.1 Pessimistic Approach

The pessimistic approach forbids any access to a replica provided that it is up to data (Belalem, 2007a; Saito, 2005), what gives an illusion to the user to have a single substantial copy. The main advantage of this approach is that all replicas converge at the same time, a fact that allows guaranteeing a strong consistency, then avoiding any problem linked to the stage of reconciliation. This type of approach is well adapted to systems of small and average scales and it becomes very complex to implement for systems with wide scale. So, we can raise three major drawbacks of this type of approach:

- It is very badly adapted to vague or unstable environments, such as the mobile systems or the grids at strong rate of change

- It cannot support the updating cost when the degree of replication is very high
- It is unsuitable for environments which require data sharing such as the collaborative environments

There are several protocols of the pessimistic approaches; we quote (Belalem, 2007a):

a. **Rowa (Read One Write All)** consists in writing all the copies and in reading a single copy. This protocol guarantees that all the copies are identical at any time, but the inconvenience of this protocol is that all the system is going to be blocked, if a node falls out of order until the breakdown is tracked down;

b. **Quorum** is a protocol based on the vote which imposes that a quorum is accessible so that it can make an operation. It requires that most of the part of the replicas agree on the most recent contents. The distribution of the updates is in a synchronous way only on it under all the copies which form the quorum. The copies not a part of the quorum are updated in an asynchronous way. There is often a quorum to read R (Read) and a quorum to write W (Write). The quota to read and quota to write must be assigned in a way that it assures that at least a node is up-to-date in a quorum of read. This condition can be verified. We take for example the quorum to read (N/2) and quorum of writing (N/2+1), where N is the number of replicas in the system.

3.2 Optimistic Approach

This approach authorizes the access to any replica and all the time. In this way, it is then possible to access a replica which is not inevitably coherent (Belalem, 2007a; Saito, 2005). So, this approach tolerates a certain difference between replicas. On the other hand, it requires a phase of detection of the difference between replicas then a phase of correction of this difference by converging the replicas on a coherent state. Although it does not guarantee strong consistency as in the pessimistic case, it possesses nevertheless certain number of advantages which we can summarize as follows (Belalem, 2007a; Belalem, 2007b):

- They improve the availability: because the access to data is never blocked;
- They are flexible as regards the network management which does not need to be completely connected so that the replicas are completely accessible, like the mobile environments;
- They can support large number of replicas by the fact that they do not require not enough synchronization between sites;
- Its algorithms are well adapted to large scale systems;
- They allow the autonomy of sites and users;
- The optimistic algorithms work well over the occasional or unfinished links of network. This allows updates to be exchanged between any pair of nodes. This property is essential in a mobile environment in which nodes can communicate from time to time and in an unpredictable way.

4 CONSISTENCY MANAGEMENT WITH MARKET ECONOMY MODEL

To improve the quality of services (QoS) in the management of consistency replicas in grid environments, we find it valuable to extend the work presented in (Belalem, 2007a; Belalem, 2007b) by an economic model of the market when resolving conflicts between replicas. In the real world market, there exist various economic models for setting the price of services based on supply-and-demand and their value to users. These real world economy models such as commodity market model, market bidding, auction model,

Figure 2. Proposed model for consistency management

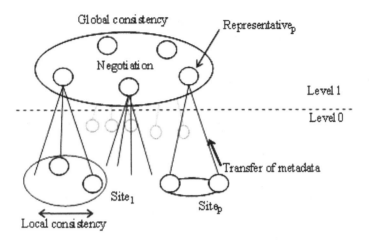

bargaining model etc can also be applied to allocate resources and tasks in distributed computing (Buyya, 2002). In our work, we regard a grid as a distributed collection of computing elements (CE's) and storage elements (SE's).

These elements are entirely dependent on a network to form a Site. This hierarchical model is composed of two levels (Figure 2), level 0 is charged to control and manage local consistency within each site; level 1 consists in ensuring the global consistency of the grid.

The model presented in Figure 2 can be formalized with UML. The corresponding class diagram of UML is illustrated in Figure 3. This figure shows the constituents of our hierarchical model of two levels.

Figure 3. Class diagram for the proposed model

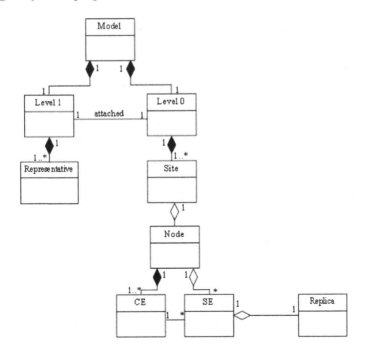

Figure 4. Principal stages of consistency management

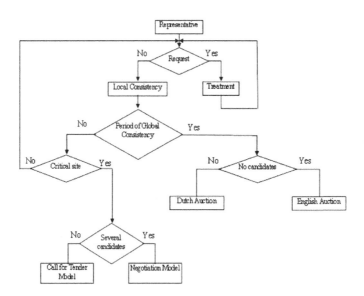

The proposed approach to the management of consistency through three stages:

- Collection of information: to collect information that is a regular on states sites;
- Analysis: permits, based on the information collected, to calculate the various measures to prepare the consistency management process. These measures can inform us about different situations sites from data grid;
- Decision: from measurements calculated, a decision to trigger the process of consistency management.

The principal stages of global process for consistency management of replicas proposed are defined by Figure 4.

4.1 Local Consistency

Local consistency (also called coherence intra-site): we find, in this level, the sites which make the grid. Each site contains CE's and SE's. The retorted data are stored on the SE's and are accessible by CE's via the operations from reading or writing. Each replica attached to additional information is called metadata (Timestamp, indices, versions,…). The control and the consistency management are ensured by representatives elected by a mechanism

Table 1. Measures and their definitions

Measure	Definition
n_i	Number of replicas of same object inside $Site_i$
$D_{local\ i}$	$Version_{max}$ - $Version_{min}$ of replicas inside $Site_i$
τ_i	Rate of number of conflicts inside $Site_i$
σ_i	Standard deviation of $Site_i = \sqrt{1/n_i \sum_{t=1}^{n_i}(V_{it} - \overline{V}_i)^2}$ Where $\overline{V}_i$ is average version inside $Site_i$

of election. The goal of these representatives is to treat the requests of readings and writings coming from the external environment, and also control the degree of divergence within the site, by calculating three measurements (see Table 1): Rate of the number of conflicts per site (τ_i), distance within a site (D_{local_i}), dispersion of version (σ_i).

We detect critical situations of one site to meet of one of the following cases:

- τ_i > Rate of Conflicts number tolerated
- D_{local_i} > Distance tolerated
- σ_i > σ_m tolerance rate for dispersion of versions

4.2 Global Consistency

This level, is also called coherence of inter-sites, is responsible for global coherence of data in the grid. Each site cooperates with the other sites via the representatives who communicate between them. Two situations can be treated, the first situation corresponds to the competing negotiation, started after the presence of a critical situation of a site. This negotiation proceeds between two groups (group of stable representatives who are not in critical situation and a group of representatives in crisis). This is by a call for tender, where a representative in crisis receives offers of the other stable representatives by providing described measurements above. This representative seeks the representative which has measurements close with his algorithm below (Algorithm 1) described the mechanism to this negotiation:

Algorithm 1 CALL FOR TENDER

```
1: Calculate τ_i, D_local_i, σ_i /*
measurements of i^th representa-
tive */
2: candidates ← false, Nbr_can-
didates ← 0
3: for all elements of the group
of sites in crisis do
```

```
4: Representative_a ← representa-
tive of site in crisis
5: j ← 1
6: repeat
7:      Representative_b ← repre-
sentative of the stable site
8:          if (|τ_a - τ_b|< ε)
∨ (|D_local_a - D_local_b|< ε)  ∨ (|σ_a
>σ_b|< ε) then
9:               Nbr_candidates
← Nbr_candidates+1
10:          end if
11:              j ← j +1
12:    until j ≥ Number of el-
ements of the group of stable
sites
13:      if (Nbr_candidates > 1)
then
14:      candidates ← true
15:      Algorithm Negotiation
/* Negotiation of candidates */
16:    else
17:      Propagation of the up-
dates of the stable site to the
sites in crisis
18:    end if
19:  end for
```

If there are two or more representative candidates (candidates = true), (see algorithm 1), being able to put the site in crisis in stable state one passes to a negotiation between these candidates. The best of them is that which is more stable, and will proceed after a to update the site in crisis. The second situation corresponds to the co-operative negotiation between the representatives of each site (see Algorithm 2), started by the exhaustion of the period defined for total coherence.

Algorithm 2 NEGOTIATION

```
1: τ_i , D_local_i, σ_i /* measure-
ments of i^th representative for
stable site */
```

```
2: winner ← first of all sites
stable  /* Candidate supposed
winner */
3: τ_i , D_local_i, σ_i  /* measure-
ments of i^th representative */
4: no_candidate ← false
5: for all representatives - {
candidate_winner } do
6:     if (τ_i <τ_winner) ∧ (D_i <
D_winner) ∧ (σ_i <σ_winner) then
7:            winner ← reprensen-
tative_i
8:        end if
9:     Winner propagates its
updates with the sites in crisis
10:   end if
```

For that, two algorithms inspired by the market economy can be used to put all of the replicas in a coherent state:

Algorithm 3 DUTCH AUCTION

```
1: representativemax ← represen-
tative having the most recent
version
2: version_reserves   /* the av-
erage of all vectors of versions
*/
3: τ_i, D_local_i, σ_i  /* measurements
of i^th representative */
4: no_candidate ← false
5: for all representatives -
{representative_max} do
6:     if (τ_max > τ_i) ∨
(D_local_max > D_local_i) ∨ (σ_max >σ_i)
then
7:            if version_i ≤
version_reserves then
8:                no_candidate ←
true
9:        else
10:                represen-
tative_max ← representative_i
```

```
11:              no_candi-
date ←false
12:        end if
13:    end if
14:  end for
15:   if (no_candidates = false)
then
16:   representative_max propa-
gates the updates with the whole
of representatives
17:   else
18:      Algorithm English
Auction
19:  end if
```

The Dutch auction (Algorithm 3) ensures the quality of service of which the aim is to obtain the most recent replica; it consists in seeking the representative with the largest version and comparing its measurements with those of the other representatives. The aim is to have a representative with less conflicts and divergences, and to compare the version of this representative with the average of all vectors of version. If its version is lower or equal "*no_candidate = true*" (see Algorithm 3), then we proceed to the Algorithm of English Auction.

Algorithm 4 ENGLISH AUCTION

```
1: representative_min ← represen-
tative having the oldest version
2: version_reserves   /* the av-
erage of all vectors of versions
*/
3: τ_i, D_local_i, σ_i  /* measurements
of i^th representative */
4: for all representatives -
{representative_min} do
5:     if (τ_min > τ_i) ∨
(D_local_min > D_local_i) ∨ (σ_min > σ_i)
then
6:            representa-
tive_min ← representative_i
```

Figure 5. Average response time according to requests number

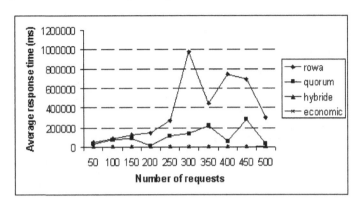

7:        **end if**
8: **end for**
9: representative$_{min}$ propagates
the updates with the whole of
the representatives

The English auction (Algorithm 4) has the same
principle that the Dutch auction except that it is
ascending starting with the representative having the oldest replica and increases according to
measurements calculated within each site.

5 EXPERIMENTAL STUDY

In order to validate and to evaluate our approach
of consistency management of replicas compared
to the traditional (pessimistic and optimistic) approaches, we carried out a series of experiments.
The results and interpretations are covered in
this section.

In order to analyze the results related to the
experimentation of our approach, we used three
metrics to know the response time, the number
of conflicts between replicas.

5.1 Impact of Requests Number

These experiments were carried out with the following parameters of simulation: 5 sites, 50 nodes,
10 data and 10 replicas per data. With regard to
the requests, we considered going number of requests from 50 to 500 per step 50, with a rate of
30% of requests of reading and 70% of requests
of writing. The Figure 5 illustrates the evolution
of the average response time according to the
number of requests.

From this figure, it is clear that the number
of requests has a significant impact on the grid
performance. In pessimistic approaches (Rowa
and Quorum) the average response time of the
requests tends to augment with the increase of
the number of requests. Moreover, this increase
is very significant in Rowa approach compared
to Quorum's approach, which reduces its performance considerably. Based on the results of these
numerical simulations, we were able to assess that
the gain from the approaches Rowa and Quorum
is very significant. For example, we can infer
that the improved performance achieved by our
approach in the order of 98% for Rowa and 93%
for the approach Quorum. We can conclude that
these two approaches are in poor performance
for large-scale systems. We note the Figure 5, in
relation to performance, as for the hybrid approach
proposed in (Belalem, 2007a) is almost identical
(curves are almost together) with our approach
based on market economy.

These experiments allow us to evaluate and
compare the quality of service (QoS) between
our suggested approach and optimistic one, while
holding in account divergences and the conflicts

Figure 6. Average number of conflicts according to requests number

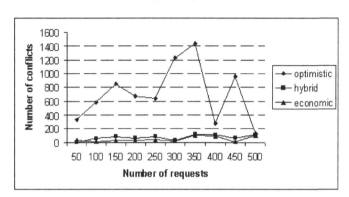

Figure 7. Average response time according to replicas number

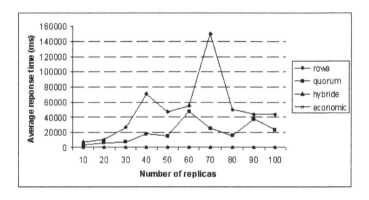

between replicas. The results, presented in Figure 6, show significantly way that the proposed approach solves quickly the divergences and conflicts by using market economy models. We can notice a slight improvement in our approach compared to the hybrid approach proposed in (Belalem, 2007a).

5.2 Impact of Replicas Number

In the second series of experiments, we took the following parameters of simulation: 5 sites, 50 Nodes, 50 requests, band-width of 100Mb/s, 10 data. With regard to sites, we varied the number of replicas from 10 to 100 per step 10 associated each data. For requests, we used a rate of 50% reading and 50% writing requests. In the same way, Figure 7 shows that the proposed approach gives better results compared with the approaches

pessimistic (Rowa and Quorum), an improvement of 98% for Rowa and 94% Quorum approach.

From this figure we can conclude that the pessimistic approaches (Rowa and Quorum) are impassable in the large-scale systems such as grids and P2P. We also note that the curve of our approach is confused with that of the hybrid approach reference. No improvement in performance is achieved with the use of the market economy model.

Figure 8 proves that our approach based on market economy models gives a better QoS optimistic that the approach and the addition of a faster resolves differences and conflicts between replicas in grid by the principle of negotiation.

The statistical study of the numerical results can show an improvement of 91% obtained by our approach compared to the optimistic approach and 3% compared with the hybrid approach reference.

Figure 8. Average number of conflicts according to number of replicas

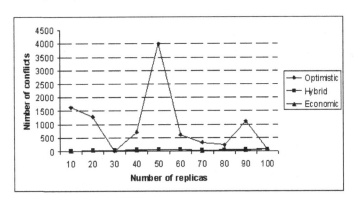

This result shows that the proposed approach solves soon encountered conflicts, which can increase QoS to the clients in the grid.

6 CONCLUSION AND FUTURE WORKS

We tried, through this work, to seek a balance between the performance and the quality of service. This led us to propose an approach of consistency management. Its aim is to improve the performances of the access to retorted data, while maintaining a certain quality of services (reduction of the divergences and conflicts). The approach suggested is articulated around a hierarchical and distributed model which at the same time allows ensuring local consistency for each site of data grid and global consistency of the grid.

The step suggested, for consistency management of replicas based on the models of market economy, follows primarily three phases:

Phase to collect information: it consists in collecting in periodic way information on the states of the various replicas (contents of the vectors of versions) of each site of the data grid;

Phase of analysis: this phase allows to evaluate various measurements of the approach suggested starting from information to collect first phase (calculate D_{local_i}, τ_i and σ_i);

Phase of decision: starting from the phase of analysis, the phase of decision consists in starting or not the local consistency of a site or global consistency of grid.

The results of these experiments are rather encouraging and showed that the objective of compromise between quality of service and performance was achieved. However, the use of economic model has allowed us to obtain a better QoS in terms of conflict resolution.

There are a number of directions which we think is interesting and worth further investigation. We can mention:

- Development of Web service for consistency management of replicas: We propose to integrate our approach in the form of Web service in the Globus environment by using technology WSDL (Foster, 2004)
- Placement replicas: In the current version, we placed replicas randomly. It is worthwhile to explore the possibility of making a static or dynamic placement to improve QoS in the data grid (Haddad, 2007)
- Load balancing: From this point of view, and for improving even more performances and the quality of service of our approach, we propose to extend it by a service of load balancing (Li, 2005; Yagoubi, 2007), which allows to balance the requests on the various sites of Data Grid

REFERENCES

Belalem, G., & Slimani, Y. (2007a). A hybrid approach to replica management in data grids [IJWGS]. *International Journal Web and Grid Services, 3*(1), 2–18. doi:10.1504/IJWGS.2007.012634

Belalem, G., & Slimani, Y. (2007b). Hybrid approach for consistency management in optorsim simulator. [IJMUE]. *International Journal of Multimedia and Ubiquitous Engineering, 2*(2), 103–118.

Bell, W. H., Cameron, D. G., Millar, A. P., Capozza, L., Stockinger, K., & Zini, F. (2003). Optorsim - a grid simulator for studying dynamic data replication strategies. *High Performance Computing Applications, 17*(4), 52–59.

Buyya, R., & Murshed, M. M. (2002). Gridsim: A toolkit for the modeling and simulation of distributed resource management and scheduling for grid computing. [CCPE]. *The Journal of Concurrency and Computation: Practice and Experience, 4*(13-15), 1175–1220. doi:10.1002/cpe.710

Casanova, H., Legrand, A., & Marchal, L. (2003). Scheduling distributed applications: the simgrid simulation framework. In *Proceedings of the Third IEEE International Symposium on Cluster Computing and the Grid (CCGrid'03)*, 138-144, Tokyo, Japan.

Dumitrescu, C., & Foster, I. (2005). Gangsim: A simulator for grid scheduling studies. *In Proceedings of the IEEE International Symposium on Cluster Computing and the Grid (CCGrid'05)* (pp. 1151-1158), Cardiff, UK.

Edgsim (2003). A simulation of the European datagrid. Retrieved from http://www.hep.ucl.ac.uk/ pac/EDGSim/index.html.

Foster, I., & Kesselmann, C. (2004). *The Grid 2: Blueprint for a new computing infrastructure*. Elsevier Series in Grid Computing. Morgan Kaufmann Publishers.

Haddad, C., & Slimani, Y. (2007). Economic model for replicated database placement in grid. In *Proceedings of* Seventh *IEEE International Symposium on Cluster Computing and the Grid (CCGrid'07)* (pp. 283-292). Rio de Janeiro, Brazil.

Li, Y. & Lan, Z. (2005). A survey of load balancing in grid computing. *High Performance Computing and Algorithms* (LNCS 3314, pp. 280-285).

Ranganathan, K., & Foster, I. (2002). Decoupling computing and data scheduling in distributed data-intensive applications. *Eleventh IEEE Symposium on High Performance Distributed Computing (HPDC)* (pp. 138-145). Edinburgh, Scotland.

Saito, Y., & Shapiro, M. (2005). Optimistic replication. *ACM Computing Surveys, 37*(1), 42–81. doi:10.1145/1057977.1057980

Song, H., Liu, X., Jakobsen, D., Bhagwan, R., Zhang, X., Taura, K., & Chien, A. (2000). The microgrid: a scientific tool for modeling computational grids. *In Scientific Programming*, volume 8, 127-141.

Takefusa, A., Matsuoka, S., Nakada, H., Aida, K., & Nagashima, U. (1999). Overview of a performance evaluation system for global computing scheduling algorithms. In *Proceedings of the 8th IEEE International Symposium on High Performance Distributed Computing (HPDC-8)* (pp. 97-104). Redondo Beach, California.

Xu, J., Li, B., & Li, D. (2002). Placement problems for transparent data replication proxy services. *IEEE Journal on Selected Areas in Communications, 7*, 1383–1398.

Yagoubi, B. & Slimani, Y. (2006). Dynamic load balancing strategy for grid computing. *Transactions on engineering computing and technology, 13*, 260-265.

Chapter 17
Web–Based Geospatial Services:
Implementing Interoperability Specifications

Iftikhar U. Sikder
Cleveland State University, USA

Aryya Gangopadhyay
University of Maryland - Baltimore County, USA

Nikhil V. Shampur
Cleveland State University, USA

ABSTRACT

This chapter characterizes the requirements of Geographic Information Systems (GIS) middleware and its components for dynamic registering and discovering of spatial services specifically for collaborative modeling in environmental planning. The chapter explores the role of Web services with respect to implementation standard and protocols and identifies implementation features for exposing distributed GIS business logic and components via Web services. In particular, the chapter illustrates applications of the interoperability specifications of Open GIS Consortium's (OGC) Web Mapping Service and (WMS), Web Processing Standards (WPS) with respect to implementation feature. The chapter demonstrates a prototype implementation of collaborative environmental decision support systems (GEO-ELCA- Exploratory Land Use Change Assessment) where Web service-enabled middleware adds core functionality to a Web mapping service. The application demonstrates how individual workspace-based namespaces can be used to perform Web mapping functionality (such as spatial analysis in visualization) through the integration of environmental simulation models to explore collective planning scenario. Built on OGC compliant connector and supports WMS and WPS, the system includes interactive supports for geospatial data query, mapping services and visualization tools for multi-user transactions.

INTRODUCTION

Both public and private enterprises have recently produced a surge of interest in Web applications for Geographic Information Systems (GIS). In recent years service oriented middleware has emerged as an essential ingredient in distributed systems (Alonso, 2004; Chang & Park, 2006; Chatterjee & Webber, 2004). This has triggered a new wave of

DOI: 10.4018/978-1-60566-719-5.ch017

enthusiasm in composition of complex services in a meaningful way involving not only traditional alphanumeric data but complex geographic data and services (Jones & Taylor, 2004; Sikder & Gangopadhyay, 2003, 2004). In particular, collaborative and groupware researches are being directed towards developing reusable generic model and procedures, which can be made to communicate each other in any distributed system in a heterogeneous environment. Integrating Web service with collaborative Geographic Information Systems (GIS) has triggered new wave of researchers who are composing dynamic services involving complex geospatial objects and models (Balram & Dragic´evic, 2006). The growing need for a service oriented middleware for GIS is especially realized in three main contexts: (1) to access GIS data from anywhere (2) to disseminate spatial information of analysis and exploration of spatial patterns and relationships between disparate GIS datasets and (3) to allow GIS modeling/processing tools and services to be downloaded or uploaded over the internet by remote users to work interactively by using existing Web browsers rather than installing proprietary GIS software locally on their machines (Peng & Tsou, 2003). The recent trend of geospatial computing is a gradual shift of traditional desktop GIS towards distributed GIS (also referred to as GIServices). With technology moving at such a fast pace, the services expected by a GIS user (including mobile ones) are quite demanding. The growing demand for users' need to view relationships between several geographically separate datasets and perform varying degree of analysis and geo-processing would inevitably require service oriented architecture (SOA) of core GIS which would define the use of services to support the requirements of software users. In this context, GIServices may be defined as a self-contained, stateless spatial processing function which accepts one or more requests and returns one or more responses through a well-defined, standard interface. By having such services distributed all over the Internet and accessible in a uniform standard manner, it is possible to envision the integration of several spatial services (chaining of services) to provide higher levels of functionality to existing services (Peng & Tsou, 2003). For example, a typical GIS query "Find the nearest Japanese restaurant along the highway" could possibly be answered by chaining Web services such as geocoding points of interest, integrating transport networks, dynamic segmentation of network, providing routing network, cartographic map rendering, and text-to-voice conversion.

This paper explores the role of Web services and their implementation standards and protocols and characterizes features for distributed GIS for modeling collaborative spatial processes with respect to the current interoperability standards and specifications. In particular the paper the identifies the interoperability requirements of OGC's (Open GIS Consortium) Web Mapping Service and (WMS), Web Processing Standards (WPS) with respect to implementation features. The rest of the paper is organized as follows: section 2 discusses the framework of service integration in distributed GIS; section 3 discusses implementation standard for interoperability-based distributed GIS; section 4 characterizes the essential features of distributed GIS components; and finally section 5 illustrates a prototype implementation of a system for geospatial resource integration in environmental planning.

Progress in Distributed Spatial Services: Related Works

Collaborative GIS have been used in many planning problems for solving semi-structured or loosely structured decision problems in environmental planning (Angelides & Angelides, 2000; Balram & Dragic´evic, 2006; Balram et al.,2003; Kingston et al., Carver, 2000) The Web GIS implementation area mainly includes environmental planning (ISikder & Gangopadhyay, 2002; Tuchyna, 2006), data dissemination (Hu, 1999; Schuurman & Leszczynski, 2006), community planning (Al-Kodmany, 2000; MacEachren et al., 2006; Rao et al., 2007). While researchers continue to argue for an integration and structuring of collaborative mapping and visualization technologies into spatial decision making (Armstrong, 1994; Balram & Dragic´evic, 2006; Jankowski & Nyerges, 2001; MacEachren, 2001; Nyerges & Jankowski, 2001), a Web-based GIS framework designed to integrate stakeholders into the planning process has yet to be realized. One of the major impediments to developing GIServices for collaborative modeling is the lack of interoperable component technologies. Heterogeneity of geo-spatial systems has plagued GIS since its inception (Goodchild et al., 1992; Stoimenov & Djordjevic-Kajan, 2005; Worboys & Deen, 1991). Different agencies had built many different geographic data models and systems, following their native organizational interest and problem domain (Egenhofer & Herring, 1991). The benefit of collective learning has not yet been fully realized, due to a lack of mechanism for reusable service and models in participatory systems.

As a precursor to Web services, CORBA and Microsoft's DCOM or Java-based RMI were often used for distributed access and query of spatial data, sometimes integrated with DSS (Eldrandaly, 2006). However, being "tightly coupled" with native data structure, the broker-based services are unable to make sure that whenever an organization makes changes in their native data structure or services the corresponding change is automatically reflected in all other organizations sharing the same resource. Moreover, middleware-based access through a broker relies on a standard definition of "interfaces." Geo-processing services can become very cumbersome in the absence of such interfaces. From the decision support point of view, having data access at the client's end without robust geo-processing capabilities amounts to little help. In a broker-based solution, the client has to pull massive amounts of data at his/her end and manage it locally. Such approaches assume the client's explicit ability to manipulate server

connections and invoke remote objects. Thus, a frequent spatial process, such as a spatial join between data from two different servers, needs to be coordinated at the client's end. Such object level manipulations of spatial processes often fail to provide a high-level view to the application developer. Paradoxically, in a spatial decision support system the user or decision maker's view on spatial features or geometry needs to be realized at a higher level of abstraction while at the same time maintaining the transparency of system processes (Anderson & Moreno-Sanchez, 2003; Rao et al., 2007; Tait, 2005).

Unlike current component technologies, however, Web Services do not use object model-specific protocols such as DCOM, RMI, or IIOP that require specific, homogeneous infrastructures on both the client and service machines. While implementations tightly coupled to specific component technologies are perfectly acceptable in a controlled environment, they become impractical on the Web. As the set of participants in an integrated business process changes and as technology changes over time, it becomes very difficult to guarantee a single, unified infrastructure among all participants. Web Services take a different approach; they communicate using ubiquitous Web protocols and data formats, such as HTTP and XML. Any system supporting these Web standards will be able to support Web Services (Peng & Tsou, 2003).

In static web mapping the web client is a simple web browser with the capability of handling HTML and Web Forms. A Web Form is a HTML Page with data entry fields for user input. The user inputs are collected and sent by the browser to the server in a HTTP message. The web server receives the message but cannot respond to it. Since it does not understand any requests other than for HTML or other MIME-type documents, it passes the request to a back-end program. The back end program is a traditional server side application that does the actual processing. In the case of web mapping, these back-end programs include map servers and DBMS servers. The web server then returns the results to the client. Here, the web server becomes middleware, connecting the web client and the back end applications(Peng & Tsou, 2003).

Web mapping of GIS applications has evolved from the concept of simple static web publishing of maps on a web page as static map images in appropriate graphic formats (GIF, JPEG, PNG, PDF etc). The client (web browser) makes requests using standard HTTP constructs such as GET and POST to a web server, which returns the requested map image file in appropriate file format. However, an effective Web mapping requires more than just making static making maps; it requires processing queries and doing some limited spatial analysis on the server before presenting the output in a specialized cartographic format on the standard web browser. Historically, the Xerox PARC Map Viewer developed in 1994 was the earliest attempt to distribute GIS using HTTP server and CGI program(Putz, 1994). This was followed by the development of an on-line GIService of GRASSLinks prototype that mimicked traditional GISystem functions, such as map browsing and buffering overlay (Huse, 1995). The Alexandria Digital Library offered a "digital library" metaphor for publishing multimedia content including georeferenced data. Among the commercially available Web service-enabled applications, ESRI's ArcWeb Services offer a way to include GIS content and capabilities, Intranet applications, or ArcGIS—on demand. ESRI's ArcExplorer viewer is designed to support Web services provided through its proprietary ArcIMS server software. Microsoft's MapPoint offers a street-mapping program that includes some demographic overlays. Users can buy the package or access MapPoint Web Services, which can be utilized to integrate other applications: location-based services, GPS car navigation, and decision support systems. MapInfo supports both OpenGIS and the World Wide Web Consortium's Web services standards, including SOAP, WSDL and

UDDI, in products such as its *miAware* software (MapInfo, 2007) (mobile location services platform for MapInfo) for developing location-based services. MapServer, an open environment, supports the creation of maps at the client's side by serving as a map engine to provide database and spatial content through the client's browser. It also supports many OGC's specifications like WMS, non-transactional WFS, WCS, WMC, SLD, and GML (MapServer, 2007).

The concept of dynamic distributed computing paradigm calls for a metaphorical counterpart of the so called LEGO blocks that can be interlocked and stacked to create complex geospatial services (Tsou & Buttenfield, 2002). The GIService and modules like LEGOs can be rearranged and restacked in a different configuration do a different task (Zipf & Jost, 2006). In Web services, a series of protocols such as eXtensible Markup Language (XML); Simple Object Access Protocol (SOAP); Web Service Description Language (WSDL); and Universal Description, Discovery, and Integration (UDDI) - provides standards for communication and collaborative processing capacity among Web-service compliant architecture. A key advantage is that various GIS layers can be dynamically queried and integrated while still maintaining independence in a distributed environment. One of the promises of Web Services in the GIS world is up-to-date information since the data is stored with the service provider and expectedly kept up-to-date when accessed by the GIS web service consumer. From organizational point of view, this may be very appealing, for local governments (such as counties and other organizations) can still independently collect and manage data locally and integrate information and services using Web services. A client, for example, a transportation company, could directly access a local government's base map without maintaining its own. At the same time the client can update local government's data from its own record. As far as data interoperability is concerned, extended collaboration and partnerships using Web Services could provide opportunity to open interfaces and communication mechanisms for distributed computing. Web services extend the use of GIS by making the integration with other applications easier. Despite the promise of GIS Web services, interoperability among GIS programs and data sources is far from seamless. Vendor adoption of GIS Web services is still a work in progress. Interactive Web mapping demands more interactions between the user and the client interface and more client-size processing and functionalities than the static web mapping applications. Also, CGI extensions such as Servlets, ASP, etc. are used to mitigate shortcomings of CGI. Most current interactive Web CGI programs are based on this model (dynamic viewer with CGI extensions). Interactive viewers include 1) DHTML viewer – makes static HTML pages dynamic using client side scripting (VBscript, javascript), DOM and CSS; 2) Java Applets – Executable java code downloaded from the server and executed on the client at runtime. Applets can be integrated inside the web browser; and 3) ActiveX Controls – Modular pieces of software that perform tasks and communicate with other programs and modules over the Internet via OLE.

Implementing Interoperability Standards in Distributed GIS

A suite of emerging Web services standards from the Open GIS Consortium Inc. (OGC) is facilitating the transition of historically standalone GIServices by enabling interoperability. Web services can put relevant GIS applications on the end user's desktop by embedding them within familiar applications. The most intensively used standards include Web Map Service, Web Feature Service and the XML-based Geography Markup Language (GML)(OGC, 2007; Peng & Zhang, 2004; Siyuan, Griffiths, & Paton, 2007); they allow applications to access distributed spatial data across the Internet to any OGC-enabled repository.

Interoperability Requirements of OGC's WMS, WPS Standards

Although interactive mapping programs are popular, they suffer from common problems such as poor performance and limited functions. However the biggest problem is that they are often proprietary and not necessarily interoperable. Different web mapping programs were developed in different database frameworks and use different technologies. Integrating and sharing information among web mapping programs are arduous tasks. Furthermore, migrating technology from one platform to another is very difficult. Open GIS Consortium (OGC) has been making efforts to develop a set of standards to guide the development of web mapping programs so that they can be interoperable. OGC developed Web Map Server (WMS) implementation information specifications that are the first effort towards standardizing the implementations of web mapping programs (Peng & Tsou, 2003).

Web Map Server (WMS) Implementation Specifications

A Web Map Service (WMS) produces maps of spatially referenced data dynamically from geographic information. A "map" is defined to be a portrayal of geographic information as a digital image file suitable for display on a computer screen. The WMS specification stipulates that a mapping service should be able to at least 1) produce a map (as a picture, series of graphical elements, feature data); 2) answer basic queries; and 3) inform other programs about its capabilities (what maps it can produce and which can be queried further)(OGC). OGC initially came up with thin, medium and thick clients in its specification, but abandoned them for they were inherently ambiguous in classifying clients this way. Instead they use the kind of information presented at to web client to categorize web mapping services into three cases:

1. **Picture case**: Here a client's request is answered by a picture of the map
2. **Graphic element case:** Here the web client receives a set of graphic elements (e.g., Scalable Vector Graphics (SVG)). The picture element case may be considered as a subset of graphic element case.
3. **Data or feature case:** Here geographic feature data is sent from the server to the client.

Currently the picture case is the most popular framework adopted by the GIS industry. It provides only for limited map display functions and user interactions. Along with progress of web mapping and information technologies, the data case and the graphic element case have become slightly more popular. WMS-produced maps are generally rendered in a pictorial format such as PNG, GIF or JPEG, or occasionally as vector-based graphical elements in Scalable Vector Graphics (SVG) or Web Computer Graphics Metafile (WebCGM) formats.

Web Map Service operations can be invoked using a standard web browser by submitting requests in the form of Uniform Resource Locators (URLs). The content of such URLs depends on which operation is requested. In particular, when a client requests a map, the URL indicates what information is to be shown on the map, what portion of the Earth is to be mapped, the desired coordinate reference system, and the output image width and height. When two or more maps are produced with the same geographic parameters and output size, the results can be accurately overlaid to produce a composite map. The use of image formats that support transparent backgrounds (e.g., GIF or PNG) allows underlying maps to be visible. Furthermore, individual maps can be requested from different servers. The Web Map Service thus enables the creation of a network of distributed map servers from which clients can build customized maps. A basic WMS classifies its geographic information holdings into "Layers"

and offers a finite number of predefined "Styles" in which to display those layers.

Requirements for a WMS over HTTP

The International Standards defines the implementation of the Web Map Service on a distributed computing platform (DCP) comprising Internet hosts that support the Hypertext Transfer Protocol (HTTP). Thus the online resource of each operation supported by a server is an HTTP URL (Uniform Resource Locator). The URL may be different for each operation, or the same, at the discretion of the service provider. Each URL is implementation-dependent, with only the query portion comprising the service request itself as defined by the International Standard. The HTTP supports two request methods: GET and POST. One or both of these methods may be offered by a server, and the use of the Online Resource URL differs in each case. Support for the GET method is mandatory; support for the POST method is optional. A Web Map Service shall support the "GET" method of the HTTP protocol while the Web Map Service may support the "POST" method of the HTTP protocol.

Operations on Web Map Services

The three operations defined for a Web Map Service are as follows:

1. **GetCapabilities:** The purpose of the mandatory GetCapabilities operation is to obtain service metadata, which is a machine readable (and human-readable) description of the server's information content and acceptable request parameter values.
2. **GetMap:** The GetMap operation returns a map. Upon receiving a GetMap request, a WMS shall either satisfy the request or issue a service exception.
3. **GetFeatureInfo:** GetFeatureInfo is an optional operation. The GetFeatureInfo

operation is designed to provide clients of a WMS with more information about features in the pictures of maps that were returned by previous Map requests. The canonical use case for GetFeatureInfo is that a user sees the response of a Map request and chooses a coordinate (i, j) on that map from which to obtain more information. The basic operation provides the ability for a client to specify which pixel is being asked about, which layer(s) should be investigated, and what format the information should be returned in. Since WMS protocol is stateless, the GetFeatureInfo request indicates to the WMS what map the user is viewing by including most of the original GetMap request parameters. The actual semantics of how a WMS decides what to return more information about or what exactly to return are left up to the WMS provider.

Web Processing Service

Web processing service exposes pre-programmed calculations for geospatial data to the Internet. The Web Processing Service (WPS) interface specifies WPS operations that can be requested by a client and performed by a WPS server. Those operations are as follows:

- **GetCapabilities:** This operation allows a client to request and receive back service metadata (or Capabilities) documents that describe the abilities of the specific server implementation.
- **DescribeProcess:** This operation allows a client to acquire more specific information about an Execute operation provided by the WPS, including the input parameters and formats, and similarly the outputs.
- **Execute:** This operation allows a client to run a specified process of the WPS with qualified input parameters and values.

Implementing GetCapabilites and DescribeProcess through WSDL

These operations have many similarities to other OGC Web Services such as Web Mapping Service (WMS), Web Feature Service (WFS), etc. The GetCapabilites and DescribeProcess are implemented using web services through WSDL which is an XML format for describing Web Services. WSDL describes the public interface to the web service using XML-based service description. It specifies how to communicate using the web service, namely the protocol bindings and message formats required to interact with the web services listed in its directory. The supported operations and messages are described abstractly, and then bound to a concrete network protocol and message format. WSDL is often used in combination with SOAP and XML Schema to provide web services over the Internet (Chang & Park, 2006). A client (program) connecting to a web service can read the WSDL to determine what functions are available on the server. Any special data types used are embedded in the WSDL file in the form of XML Schema. The client can then use SOAP to actually call one of the functions listed in the WSDL. This amounts to achieving the same objectives as OGC WPS operations, GetCapabilities and DescribeProcess.

Characterizations of Components in a Distributed GIService

What follows is the characterization of the component of distributed mapping services of GIS with respect to dynamically distributed GIS. We have seen that that although web server and map server perform important tasks, they cannot directly communicate since each talk different languages. Web servers use HTTP and HTML while map servers have different query structures and formats, so they rely on in-between programs to translate between them. Therefore, for a robust distributed GIservice-oriented middleware should include the following things:

- Establishing connections between web server and map server
- Translating user requests from the web server and passing them to the map server for processing
- Translating output from map server to output expected by the web server (such as HTML) which will be forwarded to the web browser

In addition, GIS middleware performs value added service such as

- Managing concurrent requests, load balancing
- Managing state, transaction management
- Security

There already exists a wealth of business logic that has been implemented for providing various web mapping services. Exposing existing GIS business functionality (geospatial analysis, processing, etc.) via web services is an essential aspect. Web services provide standard interfaces via WSDL needed for a distributed GIS architecture. Server side components can be implemented using any distributed computing framework such as J2EE or .NET. However to provide the necessary standard interface, the functionality must be exposed via web services.

Figure 1 shows the various components typically found in the architecture of a distributed GIS provider. It consists of a web server as the front end and interfaces with the client. The web server communicates with the application server and other related middleware, all of which are responsible for the business login that fulfills the user's request. The map server is responsible for generating the requested maps. The data server is the data store where the geographic data is housed. To provide for higher scalability, we use multiple map servers and multiple web servers. Since many map servers and data servers are involved, we should also include catalog services, data repositories and load balance services. A catalog service is used to keep track of what functions each map server can provide. Data repository is a registration service that keeps track of the data types and location of data sets; it also manages multiple data servers by filtering the right data set from the appropriate data server.

GEO-ELCA: COLLABORATIVE GISERVICE ARCHITECTURE

In this section we illustrate a prototype implementation of a Web-based spatial decision support system for collaborative planning of urban land use change evaluation. GEO-ELCA allows the various features of GIS services on the Web. The system allows dynamic selection of a feature type (i.e., polygon – from land use theme) interactively, so that a user can change attribute items and identify a feature property. A user can initiate a change in land use type by graphically selecting a polygon. The server side application processes the request and makes necessary updates in the database to reflect the corresponding the changes of the pollutant coefficients. Every request to change in land use category results in a recalculation of the mass export of pollutants and corresponding statistics. The processed result is sent back to the Web server and then to the client side. The user decision profile is then input to a simulation model to estimate the yearly pollution load. The system integrates a simulation model commonly used in urban hydrology--the so-called "Simple Method"(Schueler, 1999) for estimating exports of various pollutants runoff from different land uses. The output is then visualized as pollutant distribution in terms of different classification schemes (e.g., standard deviation, plain break, quantile, etc.) with a modified map legend.

Figure 1. Exposing component functionality via Web service

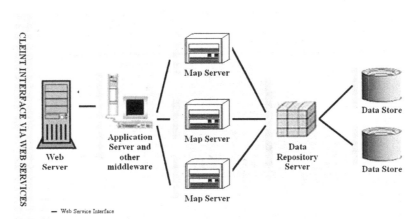

Multi-User Context in Distributed GIS

In view of a decision support framework, collaborative modeling presupposes multiple parties with different perspectives working together in a complex emergent environment. These parties (henceforth termed as "agent, "decision maker", or "stakeholder" interchangeably) must have an integrated data access from heterogeneous sources to integrate with transparent high performance computing resources to compose decision models dynamically. However, in real life situations, it is often difficult to achieve the stakeholders' views or effective patterns of social interactions in the planning process. For example, decisions on how current land use should be changed depend on legal, environmental, regulatory constraints as well as biases and preferences of different group or institutions. In particular, understanding urban land use dynamics involves considerations of the complex behavior of individual decision makers and the interaction of local and regional institutions in multiple scales. Moreover, such decisions are inherently spatial in nature because the change in a particular parcel may have direct or indirect consequences to the neighboring parcels.

For example, EPA's Brownfields development program involves the expansion and redevelopment of urban areas that may be complicated by the potential presence of a hazardous substance, pollutant, or contaminant (EPA, 2007) . While cleaning up and reinvesting in these properties takes development pressures off of undeveloped, open land and improves the environment, evaluating a candidate property to determine if it meets the criteria for redevelopment is inherently a collective decision process. For instance, an individual landowner may act from his or her individual interest; however, in the long run the overall land use scenario may be undesirable to everyone. Moreover, changes in land use may create concern for environmental impact in the surrounding region. While land-use changes are often identified as a major driving force of ecological changes, with the conversion of land use from one category to another there is an overall change of hydrological characteristics resulting from the changes of impervious areas. Consequently, there is an increase of volume and peak flow of possible increase in the concentration of pollutants, which potentially could deteriorate the environment. Hence, a centralized planning process is essentially inadequate to reflect group dynamics. Such group-individual dilemmas make it ideally suited for collaborative planning in a distributed environment, particularly in the seamless integration of Web-services in accessing geospatial data and models for environmental planning.

Figure 2. User specific visualization to change polygon attributes in GEO-ELCA

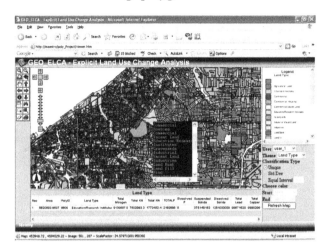

The resulting pollution map can be visualized with multiple theme overlay (Figure 2). A user can review the planning scenario of other users. The system logs individual users' preferences which can be used as input into mediating algorithm (e.g., genetic algorithm) to resolve conflicts among user preferences of land use choice and thereby optimize pollution scenarios.

Distributed Mapping Services

GEO-ELCA offers cartographic representation with a specialized visualization feature aided with dynamic legend rendering and symbol manipulation. The GEO-ELCA's cartographic features include the following:

- A visualization of pollution potential map based on different themes (e.g., total Nitrogen, total BOD etc.)
- Multiple representations and visualizations of the same data based on different statistical classification schemes (Equal Interval, Standard Deviation, etc.)
- Visualization of a user-specified color ramp of customized legend
- Enhanced navigational options for spatial overlay of multiple geographic layers

Figure 2 shows a typical example where users graphically select a polygon and choose a land use category from the pop up list (upon right click) to simulate the "what if" kind of pollution scenario. The simulation model estimates the pollution potential as a result of land use change. For example, users can visualize the pollution characteristics of total Nitrogen or total BOD, etc., of the selected polygon. The changes made in the database by the user (user-1) are completely invisible to other users (e.g., user-2). User-2 has an option to concurrently perform the similar operation independently without being effected by User-1's. The result of the simulation will be different if different options are chosen. The visualization and cartographic representations can be locally customized by users. In each case, the corresponding legends and color rendering services are implemented accordingly.

Service Integration in GEO-ELCA

GEO-ELCA's main feature provides users with a meaningful composition of services to perform an exploratory analysis and assessment of the consequence of users' decisions in environmental planning and compares the results with the collective decision. The system is built on an

Figure 3. Overview of service integration mechanism of GEO-ELCA

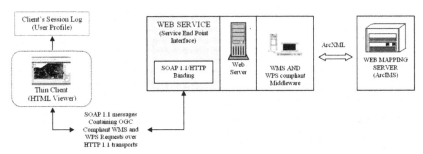

OGC-compliant connector that supports access to WMS and WPS.

The client sends WMS Request (GetMap, GetCapabilities, GetFeatures) and WPS Execute Operation (changeLandUsageType) messages which are XML encoded and enclosed in SOAP 1.1 messages (see Figure 3). The construction of SOAP messages is done using client side scripting such as JavaScript, VBScript and can also makes use of advanced features such as AJAX (Sayar, Pierce, & Fox, 2006). Built on top of the ESRI's ArcIMS, the system uses ArcXML (native XML encoding of spatial object) to communicate between the custom middleware and the Web mapping server. The services offered by the Web Mapping Server are similar to the requirements of OGC's implementation specification for a web map service (WMS). The only difference is that the communication language is ArcXML whereas the OGC international standard defines a more generic XML format. The communication with client and Web server involves ArcXML in both directions, whereas OGC specifies that only response parameters need to be an XML document while request parameters may be in formats such

as Key Value Protocol (KVP) encoding-- commonly used in HTTP GET and POST. It should be noted that a bidirectional mapping of request and response parameters from OGC format to ArcXML format is quite simple and can be achieved by a middleware solutions. Table 1. shows ArcXML equivalent of OGC WMS operation.

The following example illustrates how the services rendered by the customized middleware uses ArcXML to map directly to the operations needed to conform to the OGC standard for a WMS (and a WPS). The operation offered by the WPS which is implemented by our middleware are as follows:

```
void changeLandUsageType(string:
userID, long: minX, long: minY,
long: maxX, long: maxY, int:
newLandType)
```

The operation allows users to change the land type graphically underlying GIS data. The input agreements are as follows:

Table 1. ArcXML equivalent of OGC Web mapping service operations

OGC WMS Operation	ArcXML Request Operation
GetCapabilities	GET_SERVICE_INFO
GetMap	GET_IMAGE
GetFeatures	GET_FEATURES

```
userID - Identifier of the user
(to perform data manipulation on
user specific data)
minX, minY, maxX, maxY - bound-
ing co-ordinates of land whose
land type is to change
newLandType - Identifier of
class of Land Type to which the
land must be changed.
```

For example, a simple request for change of land use is encoded using KVP encoding

```
http://localhost/service?user=te
ster&minX=23.45&minY=24.34&maxX=
45.67&maxY=67.8
OGC Complaint GET MAP Request
(Encoded using KVP Key-Value
Pair and send using HTTP-GET)
http://localhost:8080/poly_Proj-
ect/switchUser?VERSION=1.1&REQUE
ST=GetMap&LAYERS=polygon&STYLES=
None&SRS=None&BBOX=418755.237974
071,4569670.72466017,468691.8843
83251,4608998.26066327&WIDTH=786
&HEIGHT=400&FORMAT=image/gif
```

This is mapped in GEO-ELCA according to the corresponding request to the web mapping server which is in ArcXML. GET_IMAGE Request sent to the web map server (in ArcXML) looks like what follows:

```
<?xml version="1.0"
encoding="UTF-8" ?>
<ARCXML version="1.1">
  <REQUEST>
    <GET_IMAGE>
        <PROPERTIES>
            <ENVE-
LOPE minx="418755.237974071"
miny="4569670.72466017"
maxx="468691.884383251
            "
maxy="4608998.26066327" />
            <IMAGESIZE
height="400" width="786" />


<LAYERS>
                <LAYER
name="polygon" id="0" />
            <LAYERS>
            <LEGEND
title="Legend" font="Arial"
width="170" height="300"
autoextend="true" backgroundcol-
or="255,255,255" />
        </PROPERTIES>
        <LAYER type="acetate"
name="theNorthArrow">
            <OBJECT
units="pixel">
            <NORTHARROW
type="4" size="15" coords="20
35" shadow="32,32,32" angle="0"
antialiasing="True" />
            </OBJECT>
        </LAYER>
        <LAYER type="acetate"
name="theScaleBar">
            <OBJECT
units="pixel">

            <SCALEBAR
screenlength="157" coords="471
3" mode="geodesic" fontcol-
or="0,0,0" fontstyle="Regular"
width="5"  />
            </OBJECT>
        </LAYER>
    </GET_IMAGE>
  </REQUEST>
</ARCXML>
```

GET_IMAGE Response received from Map Server:

```
<?xml version="1.0"
encoding="UTF-8"?>
<ARCXML version="1.1">
   <RESPONSE>
      <IMAGE>
            <ENVELOPE
minx="405084.257055615"
miny="4569670.72466017"
maxx="482362.865301707"
maxy="4608998.26066327" />
            <OUTPUT url="http://
maestro/output/poly_project_MAE-
STRO47223362.jpg" />
            <LEGEND url="http://
maestro/output/poly_project_MAE-
STRO47223363.jpg" />
      </IMAGE>
   </RESPONSE>
</ARCXML>
```

This is mapped to an OGC complaint GET_MAP response. The response to a valid GetMap request must be a map of the georeferenced information layer requested, in the desired style, and have the specified spatial reference system, bounding box, size, and format. Every GET_IMAGE request to the web map server returns the URL of the generated file which has a unique filename. The URL of the image returned by the web map server complies with the expected OGC Complaint GET_MAP Response.

'Virtual' Private User Workspace for Model Preference

In this section we examine the database design which allows the WPS operation to be performed and also allows for collaborative modeling using a single underlying GIS data set. In order to generate multi-use profiles for collaborative modeling,

a relational model was developed providing each user a "virtual private" (note: can you say "virtually private"?) workspace. Each user is associated with a native profile database, while in fact the actual visualization is rendered from a single dataset. The GIS layer includes shapefile--a non-topological data structure commonly used to represent GIS data in polygon features. Every polygon has an associated area, perimeter, and land usage class (represented by class ID and described in human-readable form as a Class Label field). We demonstrate two use case scenarios of the collaborative modeling. In case I, the user performs default services that involve normal backup, replacement, map generation and restoration of data (Figure 4). In case II the user specifies a land change operation, so after the backup, the user's table is updated to reflect the land change request and then the same replace, map generation and restore operations follow, similar to case I. The sequences are as follows:

1. The operations begin with a request from the client sent to the web server (not shown in diagram).
2. The middleware receives the request, backs up the master data (backing up only the required amount of data) into a backup data store.
3. The middleware then updates the spatial layer with user specific data.
4. Then the middleware forwards the request for map to the web map server after converting the request to a format understandable by the web map server. In GEO-ELCA ArcXML is the language of communication with ArcIMS.
5. The web map server queries the data store to retrieve the data it needs to generate the map
6. The records returned consist of current user's data.
7. A map image is generated using the updated (current user's) data and the map image is returned to the middleware solution.

8. The master data is restored to original values by updating records from backup data store

9. The middleware solution returns the map image (or URL) of the newly generated user specific Map.

A change of land type request issued involves a number steps when compared to GetFeatures or GetMap requests. The additional step that is performed by the middleware are steps 3 and 4 updates the user's table to reflect the change in polygon values prior to switching master data contents with user data contents. The changes made by the users are reflected on their respective data table and hence changes can be tracked. We note that the response to a changeLandType request is a Map Image response showing the visualization Map reflecting changed land type on map (see Figure 6).

Figure 5 illustrates the sequence of operations when the user performs a land use change. The sequences are as follows:

1. The operations begin with a request from the client sent to the web server (not shown in diagram).

2. The middleware receives the request, and then it updates the specific user's data.

3. It then backs up the master data (backing up only the required amount of data) into a backup data store.

4. The middleware then updates the spatial layer with user specific data.

5. Then the middleware forwards the request for a map to the web map server after converting the request to a format understandable by the web map server. In our case ArcXML is the language of communication with ArcIMS.

6. The web map Server queries the data store to retrieve the data it needs to generate the map

7. The records returned consist of current user's data.

8. A map image is generated using the updated (current user's) data and the map image is returned to the middleware solution.

9. The master data is restored to original values by updating records from backup data store.

10. The middleware solution returns the map image (or URL) of the newly generated user specific Map.

CONCLUSION

This article presents a conceptual and prototypical implementation of a Web service-based geospatial resource integration scheme. Since Web services avoid problems of tightly coupled distributed object techniques and exposes an application programming interface over the Web, it holds promise for distributed resource sharing and collaborative environmental planning. By wrapping and dynamically integrating remote geo-processing services from multiple sources, one can develop an emergent collaborative system using interoperable standards of XML and SOAP (Chang & Park, 2006). We introduced architecture for Web service-based collaborative modeling applications for environmental planning. The prototype system is based on the conversion of the OGC compatible GIS services to Web Services for flexible collaboration. The prototype architecture offers functionalities to integrate disparate spatial data processing services into meaningful compositions to perform complex exploratory analysis such as the assessment of the environmental consequences of individual decision makers' choices and the collective behavior that results. The significant advantage of the architecture is that it provides a means for self-describing services in which the end user (any WMS/WPS client) can invoke a set of services (e.g., catalog services of spatial map). Specifically the system makes use of OGC's GetCapabilities, GetMap and GetFeaturesInfo to create a user-specific "on-the-fly" map layer from existing spatial data layers. The composition GIS components allow development of collaborative applications (e.g., dynamic user specific plan profiling and customization of cartographic visualization and rendering). In terms of collaborative decision-making, the added advantage is that community based geo-spatial vocabulary and the corresponding modeling semantics can be communicated effectively (e.g., the consequence of user decision can be simulated graphically to estimate the yearly pollution load as a result of individual decisions). Each user's planning profile can finally be compared for further modification. The collaborative model espoused here is geared towards archiving different opinions regarding visualization and negotiation. We have also noted that before GIservices can be wrapped with SOAP API, the generic geo-processing model formalism is needed to link models to the domain specific application. A formal description of the spatial data component and process model will allow better interoperation among heterogeneous systems. Future extension of GEO-ELCA will include an ontology-driven semantic layer for high level communication with geo-processing services.

REFERENCES

Al-Kodmany, K. (2000). Using Web-based technologies and geographic information systems in community planning. *Journal of Urban Technology, 7,* 1–30. doi:10.1080/713684108

Alonso, G. (2004). *Web services: concepts, architectures and applications.* Berlin: Springer.

Anderson, G., & Moreno Sanchez, R. (2003). Building Web-based spatial information solutions around open specifications and open source software. *Transactions in GIS, 7*(4), 447–466. doi:10.1111/1467-9671.00158

Angelides, M., & Angelides, M. C. (2000). Using multimedia database information systems over the internet for enhancing the planning process for dealing with the built heritage. *International Journal of Information Management, 20,* 349–367. doi:10.1016/S0268-4012(00)00028-1

Armstrong, M. (1994). Requirements for the development of GIS-based group decision support systems. *Journal of the American Society for Information Science American Society for Information Science, 45*(9), 669–677. doi:10.1002/(SICI)1097-4571(199410)45:9<669::AID-ASI4>3.0.CO;2-P

Balram, S., & Dragic'evic, S. (2006). Modeling collaborative GIS processes using soft systems theory, UML and object oriented design. *Transactions in GIS, 10*(2), 199–218. doi:10.1111/j.1467-9671.2006.00253.x

Balram, S., Dragicevic, S., & Meredith, T. (2003). Achieving effectiveness in stakeholder participation using the GIS-based collaborative spatial Delphi methodology. *Journal of Environmental Assessment Policy and Management, 5*(3), 365–339. doi:10.1142/S1464333203001413

Chang, Y.-S., & Park, H.-D. (2006). XML Web service-based development model for Internet GIS applications. *International Journal of Geographical Information Science, 20*(4), 371–399. doi:10.1080/13658810600607857

Chatterjee, S., & Webber, J. (2004). *Developing enterprise Web services: an architect's guide.* Upper Saddle River, NJ: Prentice Hall PTR.

Egenhofer, M., & Herring, J. R. (1991). High-level spatial data structures for GIS. In D. J. Maguire, M. F. Goodchild & D. W. Rhind (Eds.), *Geographical information systems: principles and applications* (Vol. 1, pp. 227-237). London: Longman Scientific Publications.

Eldrandaly, K. A. (2006). A COM-based expert system for selecting the suitable map projection in ArcGIS. *Expert Systems with Applications, 31*(1), 94–100. doi:10.1016/j.eswa.2005.09.008

EPA. (2007). *Brownfields cleanup and redevelopment*. Retrieved January 2007, from http://www.epa.gov/brownfields/

Goodchild, M. F., Hanning, R., & Wise, S. (1992). Integrating GIS and spatial data analysis: problems and possibilities. *International Journal of Geographical Information Systems, 6*(5), 407–423. doi:10.1080/02693799208901923

Hu, S. (1999). Integrated multimedia approach to the utilization of an Everglades vegetation database. *Photogrammetric Engineering and Remote Sensing, 65*(2), 193–198.

Huse, S. M. (1995). *GRASSLinks: A new model for spatial information access for environmental planning*. Retrieved from http://www.regis.berkeley.edu/sue/phd/

Jankowski, P., & Nyerges, T. (2001). *Geographic information systems for group decision making: Towards a participatory geographic information science*. New York: Taylor and Francis.

Jones, M., & Taylor, G. (2004). Data integration issues for a farm decision support system. *Transactions in GIS, 8*(4), 459–477. doi:10.1111/j.1467-9671.2004.00196.x

Kingston, R., Carver, S., Evans, A., & Turton, I. (2000). Web-based public participation geographical information systems: An aid to local environmental decision-making. *Computers, Environment and Urban Systems, 24*(2), 109–125. doi:10.1016/S0198-9715(99)00049-6

MacEachren, A. M. (2001). Cartography and GIS: Extending collaborative tools to support virtual teams. *Progress in Human Geography, 25*, 431–444. doi:10.1191/030913201680191763

MacEachren, A. M., Pike, W., Yu, C., Brewer, I., Gahegan, M., & Weaver, S. D. (2006). Building a geocollaboratory: Supporting human-environment regional observatory (HERO) collaborative science activities. *Computers, Environment and Urban Systems, 30*(2), 201–225. doi:10.1016/j.compenvurbsys.2005.10.005

MapInfo. (2007). *miAware2.0 documentation library*. Retrieved May 2007, from http://reference.mapinfo.com/common/docs/mapxtend-dev-web-none-eng/

MapServer. (2007). *MapServer*. Retrieved May 2007, from http://mapserver.gis.umn.edu/

Nyerges, T., & Jankowski, P. (2001). *Geographic Information Systems for Group Decision Making*. London: Taylor & Francis.

OGC. (2007). *OpenGIS. Geography markup language (GML) implementation specification*. Retrieved May 2007, from http://opengis.net/gml/

OGC. *Web map service interface* (No. 03-109r1): OGC.

Peng, Z.-R., & Tsou, M.-H. (2003). *Internet GIS: Distributed geographic information services for the Internet and wireless networks*. Wiley.

Peng, Z.-R., & Zhang, C. (2004). The roles of geography markup language (GML), scalable vector graphics (SVG), and Web feature service (WFS) specifications in the development of Internet geographic information systems (GIS). *Journal of Geographical Systems, 6*(2), 95–116. doi:10.1007/s10109-004-0129-0

Putz, S. (1994). *Interactive information services using World-Wide Web hypertext*. Retrieved 2006 from http://www2.parc.com/istl/projects/www94/mapviewer.html

Rao, M., Fan, G., Thomas, J., Cherian, G., Chudiwale, V., & Awawdeh, M. (2007). A web-based GIS decision support system for managing and planning USDA's conservation reserve program (CRP). *Environmental Modelling & Software*, *22*(9), 1270–1280. doi:10.1016/j.envsoft.2006.08.003

Sayar, A., Pierce, M., & Fox, G. (2006). Integrating AJAX approach into GIS visualization Web services. In *Telecommunications, 2006. AICT-ICIW '06. International Conference on Internet and Web Applications and Services/Advanced International* (pp. 169-169).

Schueler, T. (1999). Microbes and urban watersheds. *Watershed Protection Techniques*, *3*(1), 551–596.

Schuurman, N., & Leszczynski, A. (2006). Ontology-based metadata. *Transactions in GIS*, *10*(5), 709–726. doi:10.1111/j.1467-9671.2006.01024.x

Sikder, I., & Gangopadhyay, A. (2002). Design and Implementation of a Web-based collaborative spatial decision support system: Organizational and managerial implications. *Information Resources Management Journal*, *15*(4), 33–47.

Sikder, I. U., & Gangopadhyay, A. (2003). Distributed data warehouse for go-spatial services. In G. Grant (Ed.), *ERP & data warehouse in organizations: Issues and challenges* (pp. 132-145). IRM Press.

Sikder, I. U., & Gangopadhyay, A. (2004). Collaborative decision making in Web-based GIS. In M. Khosrow-Pour (Ed.), *Advanced topics in information resources management* (Vol. 3, pp. 147-162). Idea Group Publishing.

Siyuan, F., Griffiths, T., & Paton, N. W. (2007). GML for Representing data from spatio-historical databases: A case study. *Transactions in GIS*, *11*(2), 233–253. doi:10.1111/j.1467-9671.2007.01043.x

Stoimenov, L., & Djordjevic-Kajan, S. (2005). An architecture for interoperable GIS use in a local community environment. *Computers & Geosciences*, *31*(2), 211–220. doi:10.1016/j.cageo.2004.09.017

Tait, M. G. (2005). Implementing geoportals: applications of distributed GIS. *Computers, Environment and Urban Systems*, *29*(1), 33–47.

Tsou, M. H., & Buttenfield, B. (2002). A dynamic architecture for distributing geographic information services. *Transactions in GIS*, *6*(4), 355–381. doi:10.1111/1467-9671.00118

Tuchyna, M. (2006). Establishment of spatial data infrastructure within the environmental sector in Slovak Republic. *Environmental Modelling & Software*, *21*(11), 1572–1578. doi:10.1016/j.envsoft.2006.05.014

Worboys, M., & Deen, S. M. (1991). Semantic heterogeneity in distributed geographic databases. *SIGMOD Record*, *20*(4), 30–34. doi:10.1145/141356.141366

Zipf, A., & Jost, M. (2006). Implementing adaptive mobile GI services based on ontologies: Examples from pedestrian navigation support. *Computers, Environment and Urban Systems*, *30*(6), 784–798. doi:10.1016/j.compenvurbsys.2006.02.005

Compilation of References

Agarwal, S., Handschuh, S., & Staab, S. (2004). *Annotation, Composition and Invocation of Semantic Web Services*. Retrieved from http://www.uni-koblenz.de/~staab/Research/Publications/2004/web-service-annotation.pdf.

Ahluwalia, K. S., & Jain, A. (2006). *High Availability Design Patterns*. Paper presented at the Thirteenth Conference on Pattern Languages of Programs (PLoP 2006), Portland, USA, October 21-23, 2006.

Ahmed, M. D., & Sundaram, D. (2007). A framework for sustainability modelling and reporting. *The International Journal of Environmental, Cultural . Economic and Social Sustainability, 3*(2), 29–40.

Ahmed, M. D., & Sundaram, D. (2008). Design and implementation of scenario management systems. In M. Khosrow-Pour (Ed.), *Encyclopaedia of Information Science and Technology* (2nd ed., Vol. III, pp. D1-10). Hershey, PA: IGI Publishing.

Ahmed, M. D., & Sundaram, D. (2008). A framework for scenario driven decision support systems generator. *International Journal of Information Technology and Web Engineering, 3*(2), 45–62.

Ahmed, M., Hoang, H. H., Karim, S., Khusro, S., Lanzenberger, M., Latif, K., et al. (2004). *'SemanticLIFE' - a framework for managing information of a human lifetime*. Paper presented at the 6th International Conference on Information Integration and Web-based Applications and Services. Jarkarta: OCG Books.

Aho, A. V., Kernighan, B. W., & Weinberger, P. J. (1988). *The AWK Programming Language*. Addison-Wesley

Aishah, A. R., Azrulhasni, M. I., & Komiya, R. (2004). A neural network approach for emotion recognition in speech. In *Proceedings of the 2nd International Conference on Artificial Intelligence in Engineering and Technology (ICAIET2004)* (pp. 910-916).

Aishah, A. R., Izani, Z. A., & Komiya, R. (2003). A preliminary analysis for recognizing emotion in speech. In *Proceedings of IEEE Student Conference On Research and Development (SCOReD 2003)*.

Aishah, A. R., Izani, Z. A., & Komiya, R. (2003). Emotion pitch variation analysis in Malay and English voice samples. In *Proceedings of the 9th Asia Pacific Conference on Communications (APCC2003)* (Vol. 1, pp. 108-112).

Aishah, A. R., Izani, Z. A., & Komiya, R. (2003). Towards automatic recognition of emotion in speech. In *Proceedings of the IEEE International Symposium on Signal Processing and Information Technology (ISSPIT2003)*.

Albert, K. J. (1983). *The Strategic Management Handbook*. McGraw-Hill.

Alexander, C. (1964). *Notes on the Synthesis of Form*. Harvard University Press.

Alexander, C. (1979). *The Timeless Way of Building*. Oxford University Press.

Alexander, C., Ishikawa, S., & Silverstein, M. (1977). *A Pattern Language: Towns, Buildings, Construction*. Oxford University Press.

Al-Kodmany, K. (2000). Using Web-based technologies and geographic information systems in community planning. *Journal of Urban Technology, 7*, 1–30. doi:10.1080/713684108

Alonso, A., Garcia-Valls, M., & de la Puente, J. A. (1998). Assessment timing properties of family products. In *Proceedings of Second International ESPRIT ARES Workshop* (pp. 161-169).

Alonso, G. (2004). *Web services: concepts, architectures and applications.* Berlin: Springer.

Altova (2008). SemanticWorks Semantic Web tool - Visual RDF and OWL editor. Retrieved March 1, 2008 from http://www.altova.com/products/semanticworks/semantic_web_rdf_owl_editor.html.

Ambler, S. W. (1998). *Process Patterns.* Cambridge University Press.

AMP. (2001, July 18). AMP Banking Survey – New Zealand home affordability highest for two years. Retrieved on October 10, 2001 from http://www.amp.co.nz.

Anderson, G., & Moreno-Sanchez, R. (2003). Building Web-based spatial information solutions around open specifications and open source software. *Transactions in GIS, 7*(4), 447–466. doi:10.1111/1467-9671.00158

Andre, E., Rist, T., & Muller, J. (1998). Integrating reactive and scripted behaviours in a life-like presentation agent. In Proceedings of AGENTS'98 (pp. 261-268).

Angelides, M., & Angelides, M. C. (2000). Using multimedia database information systems over the internet for enhancing the planning process for dealing with the built heritage. *International Journal of Information Management, 20*, 349–367. doi:10.1016/S0268-4012(00)00028-1

APACHE (2008). *The APACHE XML Project. Xerces2 Java Parser Readme.* Retrieved April 18, 2008 from xerces.apache.org/xerces2-j/index.html.

Apache Software Foundation (n.d.). *Apache HTTP server project.* Retrieved June 9, 2008, from http://httpd.apache.org/

Argyris, C., Putnam, R., & Smith, D. (1985). *Action science: concepts, methods and skills for research and intervention.* New York: Jossey-Bass.

Armstrong, M. (1994). Requirements for the development of GIS-based group decision support systems. *Journal of the American Society for Information Science American Society for Information Science, 45*(9), 669–677. doi:10.1002/(SICI)1097-4571(199410)45:9<669::AID-ASI4>3.0.CO;2-P

Arpinar, I. B., Aleman-Meza, B., Zhang, R., & Maduko, A. (2004). Ontology-driven web services composition platform. In *Proc. of IEEE International Conference on E-Commerce Technology*, CEC'04 (pp. 146-152). San Diego, California, USA, IEEE Press.

Ashley, W. (1996). What shoe was that? The use of computerized image database to assist in identification. *Journal of Forensic Science International, 82*, 7-20. Ireland: Elsevier Science.

Athanasis, N., Christophides, V., & Kotzinos, D. (2004). Generating on the fly queries for the Semantic Web: The ICS-FORTH graphical RQL interface (GRQL). In S. A. McIlraith, D. Plexousakis, & F. van Harmelen (Eds.), *International Semantic Web Conference* (LNCS 3298, pp. 486-501). Springer.

Automated Testing Specialists. (2006) Web and E-Commerce Testing. Retrieved February 26, 2006 from http://www.sqa-test.com/test.html

Badler, N., Bindiganavale, R. Allbeck, J., Schuler, W., Zhao, L., Lee, S. J. et al. (2000). Parameterized action representation and natural language instructions for dynamic behaviour modification of embodied agents. In Proceedings of AAAI Spring Symposium (pp. 36-40).

Badre, A. (2001) The effects of cross cultural interface design on World Wide Web user performance. *GVU tech reports.* Retrieved January 10, 2007, from http://www.cc.gatech.edu/gvu/reports/2001

Baeza-Yates, R., & Gonnet, G. (1996). Fast text searching for regular expressions or automaton simulation over trees. *Journal of the ACM, 43*(6), 915–936. doi:10.1145/235809.235810

Balram, S., & Dragic'evic, S. (2006). Modeling collaborative GIS processes using soft systems theory, UML and object oriented design. *Transactions in GIS, 10*(2), 199–218. doi:10.1111/j.1467-9671.2006.00253.x

Balram, S., Dragicevic, S., & Meredith, T. (2003). Achieving effectiveness in stakeholder participation using the GIS-based collaborative spatial Delphi methodology. *Journal of Environmental Assessment Policy and Management, 5*(3), 365–339. doi:10.1142/S1464333203001413

Banse, R., & Scherer, K. R. (1996). Acoustic profiles in vocal emotion expression. *Journal of Personality and Social Psychology, 70,* 614-636.

Barber, K. S., & Kim, J. (2001). Belief Revision Process Based on Trust: Agents Evaluating Reputation of Information Sources. (LNCS 2246).

Baresi, L., Colazzo, S., Mainetti, L., & Morasca, S. (2006). W2000: A Modeling Notation for Complex Web Applications. In E. Mendes & N. Mosley (Eds.), *Web Engineering* (pp. 335-364). Springer-Verlag.

Bass, L., Clements, P., & Kazman, R. (2003). *Software architecture in practice* (2nd ed.). Boston: Addison-Wesley.

Bass, L., Kates, J., & John, B. E. (2001). *Achieving usability through software architecture* (Tech. Rep.) http://www.sei.cmu.edu/publications/documents/01.reports/01tr005.html

Beck, K., Beedle, M., van Bennekum, A., Cockburn, A., Cunningham, W., Fowler, M., & Grenning, J. Highsmith, J., Hunt, A., Jeffries, R., Kern, J., Marick, B., Martin, R.C., Mellor, S., Schwaber, K., Sutherland, J. & Thomas, D. (2008). Manifesto for Agile Software Development. Retrieved April 18, 2008 from http://www.agilemanifesto.org/

Belalem, G., & Slimani, Y. (2007). A hybrid approach to replica management in data grids [IJWGS]. *International Journal Web and Grid Services, 3*(1), 2–18. doi:10.1504/IJWGS.2007.012634

Belalem, G., & Slimani, Y. (2007). Hybrid approach for consistency management in optorsim simulator. [IJMUE]. *International Journal of Multimedia and Ubiquitous Engineering, 2*(2), 103–118.

Bell, W. H., Cameron, D. G., Millar, A. P., Capozza, L., Stockinger, K., & Zini, F. (2003). Optorsim - a grid simulator for studying dynamic data replication strategies. *High Performance Computing Applications, 17*(4), 52–59.

Bengtsson, P. O. (2002). *Architecture-level modifiability analysis.* Ph.D. thesis, Department of Software Engineering and Computer Science, Blekinge Institute of Technology.

Bengtsson, P. O., & Bosch, J. (1999). Architecture level prediction of software maintenance. In *Proceedings of the 3rd EuroMicro Conference on Software Engineering* (pp. 139-147). IEEE CS Press.

Benitez, A. B., Chang, S. F., & Smith, J. R. (2001, October). *IMKA: A multimedia organization system combining perceptual and semantic Knowledge.* Paper presented at the *ACM Multimedia,* Ottawa, Canada.

Bergin, J. (2005). *Patterns for Extreme Programming Practice.* Paper presented at the Tenth European Conference on Pattern Languages of Programs (EuroPLoP 2005), Irsee, Germany, July 06-10, 2005.

Berners-Lee, T., Hendler, J., & Lassila, O. (2001). The semantic web. Scientific American, 284(5), 34-43.

Bernot, G., Gaudel, M.C., & Marre, B. (1991). Software testing based on formal specifications: a theory and a tool. S*oftware Engineering Journal, 6*(6), 387-405.

Berry, G., & Sethi, R. (1986). From regular expressions to deterministic automata. *Theoretical Computer Science, 48,* 117–126. doi:10.1016/0304-3975(86)90088-5

Berstel, J., Reghizzi, S. C., Roussel, G., & San Pietro, P. (2001). A scalable formal method for design and automatic checking of user interfaces. *In Proceedings of the 23rd International Conference on Software Engineering,* (pp. 453-462).

Beskow, J., & McGlashan, S. (1997). Olga: a conversational agent with gestures. In Proceedings of the IJCAI'97 workshop on Animated Interface Agents—Making them Intelligent (pp. 1651-1654). Nagoya, Japan.

Beskow, J., Elenius, K. & McGlashan, S. (1997). Olga—a dialogue system with an animated talking agent. In Proceedings of EUROSPEECH'97. Rhodes, Greece.

Bindiganavale, R., Schuler, W., Allbeck, J. Badler, N., Joshi, A., & Palmer, M. (2000). Dynamically altering agent behaviors using natural language. In Proceedings of Autonomous Agents 2000 (pp. 293-300).

Boehm, B., & Turner, R. (2004). *Balancing Agility and Discipline: A Guide for the Perplexed.* Addison Wesley.

Bordeux, C., Boulic, R., & Thalmann, D. (1999). An efficient and flexible perception pipeline for autonomous agents. Computer Graphics Forum (Proc. of Eurographics '99), 18(3), 23-30.

Bosch, J. (2000). *Design and use of software architectures: Adopting and evolving a product line approach.* New York: Pearson Education (Addison-Wesley and ACM Press).

Bramantoro, A., Krishnaswamy, S., & Indrawan, M. (2005). *A semantic distance measure for matching Web services.* Paper presented at the Web Information Systems Engineering – WISE 2005 Workshops (pp. 217-226).

Brambilla, M., Stefano, C., Fraternali, P., & Manolescu, I. (2006). Process Modeling in Web Applications. *ACM Transactions on Software Engineering and Methodology, 15*(4), 360–409. doi:10.1145/1178625.1178627

Brighton (1998). *The Brighton usability pattern collection.* http://www.cmis.brighton.ac.uk/research/patterns/home.html

Brooks, R. A. (1985). A robust layered control system for a mobile robot. Cambridge, MA: MIT AI Lab.

Brooks, R.A. (1991). Intelligence without representation. Artificial Intelligence, 47, 139–159.

Brown, W. J., Malveau, R. C., McCormick, H. W., & Mowbray, T. J. (1998). *AntiPatterns: Refactoring Software, Architectures, and Projects in Crisis.* John Wiley and Sons.

Bryson, J. J., Martin, D., McIlraith, S. A., & Stein, L. A. (2003). Agent-based composite services in DAML-S: The behaviour-oriented design of an intelligent semantic web. Web Intelligence, Springer-Verlag, Berlin Heidelberg, 37-58.

Budanitsky, A. (1999). *Lexical semantic relatedness and its application in natural language processing* (Tech. Rep. CSRG-390). University of Toronto, Computer Systems Research Group.

Buschmann, F., Henney, K., & Schmidt, D. C. (2007). *Pattern-oriented software architecture, Volume 5: On patterns and pattern languages.* John Wiley and Sons.

Buschmann, F., Henney, K., & Schmidt, D. C. (2007). *Pattern-Oriented Software Architecture, Volume 4: A Pattern Language for Distributed Computing.* John Wiley and Sons.

Buschmann, F., Meunier, R., Rohnert, H., Sommerlad, P., & Stal, M. (1996). *Pattern Oriented Software Architecture, Volume 1: A System of Patterns. John Wiley and Sons.*

Bush, V. (July 1945). As we may think. *The Atlantic, 176*(1), 101-108.

Buyya, R., & Murshed, M. M. (2002). Gridsim: A toolkit for the modeling and simulation of distributed resource management and scheduling for grid computing. [CCPE]. *The Journal of Concurrency and Computation: Practice and Experience, 4*(13-15), 1175–1220. doi:10.1002/cpe.710

Caicedo, A., & Thalmann, D. (2000). Virtual humanoids: let them to be autonomous without losing control. In D. Plemenos (Ed.), Proceedings of the Fourth International Conference on Computer Graphics and Artificial Intelligence (pp. 59-70). University of Limoges, Limoges.

Caldwell, B., Chisholm, W. Reid, L. G., & Vanderheiden, G. (2008). *Web Content Accessibility Guidelines 2.0.* W3C Recommendation. World Wide Web Consortium (W3C).

Caliusco, M. L., Galli, M. R., & Chiotti, O. (2005, October 31-November 2). Contextual ontologies for the Semantic Web: An enabling technology. In *Proceedings of the Third Latin American Web Congress (LA-WEB)* (p. 98). Washington, D.C.: IEEE Computer Society.

Campos J., & Harrison, M. (2001). Model checking interactor specifications. *Automated Software Engineering, 3*(8), 275-310.

Cao, J., Andersson, M., Nyberg, C., & Kihl, M. (2003). Web server performance modeling using an *M/G/1/K*PS* queue. In *Proceedings of the 10th International Conference on Telecommunications* (pp. 1501–1506).

Carrington, D., & Stocks, P. (1994). A tale of two paradigms: formal methods and software testing. *Proceedings of 8th Annual Z User Meeting (ZUM '94)*, J.P. Bowen and J.A. Hall (eds.), Workshops in Computing (pp. 51-68). Springer-Verlag, Berlin

Casanova, H., Legrand, A., & Marchal, L. (2003). Scheduling distributed applications: the simgrid simulation framework. In *Proceedings of the Third IEEE International Symposium on Cluster Computing and the Grid (CCGrid'03)*, 138-144, Tokyo, Japan.

Cassell, J., & Vilhjalmsson, J. (1999). Fully embodied conversational avatars: Making communicative behaviours autonomous. Autonomous Agents and Multi-Agent Systems, 2(1) 45-64.

Cassell, J., Bickmore, T., Campbell, L., Vilhjalmsson, J., & Yan, H. (2001). More than just a pretty face: conversational protocols and the affordances of embodiment. Knowledge-Based Systems. 14, 55-64.

Cassell, J., Pelachaud, C., Badler, N,., Steedman, M., Achorn, B., Becket, T., et al. (1994). Animated conversation: rule-based generation of facial expression, gesture and spoken intonation for multiple conversational agents. In Proceedings of ACM SIGGRAPH '94 (pp. 413-420).

Castillo, E., Gutierrez, J. M. & Hadi, A. S. (1997). Expert systems and probabilistic network models. New York: Springer Verlag.

Castillo, E.,& Alvarez, E. (1991). Expert systems. Uncertainty and learning. London and New York: Elsevier Applied Science and Computational Mechanics Publications.

Catarci, T., Di Mascio, T., Franconi, E., Santucci, G., & Tessaris, S. (2003). An ontology based visual tool for query formulation support. In R. Meersman, & Z. Tari (Eds.), *OTM Workshops* (LNCS 2889, pp. 32-43). Springer.

Ceri, S., Fraternali, P., & Bongio, A. (2000). *Web Modeling Language (WebML): A Modeling Language for Designing Web Sites*. Paper presented at the Ninth International World Web Conference (WWW9), Amsterdam, The Netherlands, May 15-19, 2000.

CGISecurity.com. (2002). The Cross Site Scripting FAQ. Retrieved February 2, 2006 from http://www.cgisecurity.com/articles/xss.faq.shtml

Chang, Y.-S., & Park, H.-D. (2006). XML Web service-based development model for Internet GIS applications. *International Journal of Geographical Information Science, 20*(4), 371–399. doi:10.1080/13658810600607857

Charif, Y., & Sabouret, N. (2005). An Overview of Semantic Web Services Composition Approaches. *Electronic Notes in Theoretical Computer Science, 85*(6), 1–8.

Chatterjee, S., & Webber, J. (2004). *Developing enterprise Web services: an architect's guide*. Upper Saddle River, NJ: Prentice Hall PTR.

Chen, H., et al. (2004). Crime data mining: A general framework and some examples. *IEEE Computer, 37*(4), 50-56.

Chen, L., Shadbolt, N. R., Goble, C., Tao, F., Cox, S. J., Puleston, C., & Smart, P. R. (2003). Towards a Knowledge-based Approach to Semantic Service Composition (LNCS 2870, pp. 319-334).

Chen, S., Alahakoon, D., & Indrawan, M. (2005). *Background knowledge driven ontology discovery*. Paper presented at the 2005 IEEE International Conference on e-Technology, e-Commerce and e-Service (EEE '05) (pp. 202-207).

Chen, T.Y., & Yu, Y.T. (2002). A decision-theoretic approach to the test allocation problem in partition testing. *IEEE Transactions on Systems, Man, and Cybernetics, Part A: Systems and Humans, 32*(6), 733-745.

Cheng, K.T., & Kumar, A. S. K. (1983). Automatic functional test generation using the extended finite state machine model. *Proceedings of the 30th international Conference on Design Automation (Dallas, Texas, United States, June 14 - 18, 1993). DAC '93* (pp. 86-91). New York, NY: ACM Press.

Chermack, T. J. (2002). The mandate for theory in scenario planning. *Futures Research Quarterly, 18*(2), 25–28.

Chermack, T. J. (2003). A Methodology for Assessing Performance-Based Scenario Planning. *Journal of Leadership & Organizational Studies, 10*(2), 55. doi:10.1177/107179190301000206

Chevalier, A., & Kicka, M. (2006). Web Designers and Web Users: Influence of the Ergonomic Quality of the Web Site on the Information Search. *International Journal of Human-Computer Studies, 64*(10), 1031–1048. doi:10.1016/j.ijhcs.2006.06.002

Childers, D. G. (1999). *Speech processing and synthesis toolboxes*. New York: John Wiley & Sons.

Chipchase, J. (2005) Understanding non-literacy as a barrier to mobile phone communication. *Nokia research center*. Retrieved August 15, 2006, from http://research.nokia.com/buesky/non-literacy-001-2005/index.html

Cho, J., & Rajagopalan, S. (2002). A Fast Regular Expression Indexing Engine. In *Proceedings of 2002 International Conference on Data Engineering.*

Cockburn, A. (2007). *Agile Software Development: The Cooperative Game* (2nd Ed.). Addison-Wesley.

Cohen, P. R., & Levesque, H. J. (1987). Persistence, intention and commitment. In Proceedings of the 1986 Workshop on Reasoning about Actions and Plans (pp. 297-340). San Mateo, CA: Morgan Kaufmann Publishers.

Cohen, P. R., & Levesque, H. J. (1990). Intention is choice with commitment. Artificial Intelligence, 42(3), 213-261.

Cohen, P., Johnston, M., & McGee, D. (1997) Quickset: Multimodal interaction for distributed applications. In Proceedings of the Fifth ACM International Multimedia Conference (pp. 31–40). ACM Press.

Collier, K., Carey, B., Sautter, D., & Marjaniemi, C. (1999). A Methodology for Evaluating and Selection Data Mining Software. In *Proceedings of the 32nd Hawaii International Conference on System Sciences.*

Conallen, J. (2003). *Building Web Applications with UML* (2nd Edition). Addison-Wesley.

Constantine, L. L., & Lockwood, L. A. D. (1999). *Software for use: A practical guide to the models and methods of usage-centered design*. New York: Addison-Wesley.

Consumer Reports WebWatch. (2005, October 26). *Leap of faith: Using the Internet despite the dangers. results of a national survey of Internet users for consumer reports WebWatch*. A Consumer Reports WebWatch Research Report.

Coplien, J. O., & Harrison, N. B. (2005). *Organizational Patterns of Agile Software Development*. Prentice-Hall.

Cornelius, R. R. (1996). *The science of emotion: Research and tradition in the psychology of emotion*. Upper Saddle River, NJ: Prentice-Hall.

Cosmides, L. (1983). Invariance in the acoustic expression of emotion during speech. *Journal of Experimental Psychology: Human Perception and Performance, 9*, 864-881.

Cowles, P. (2005). Web service API and the semantic web. Web Services Journal, 2(12), 76-82. Available online at: http://webservices.sys-con.com/read/39631.htm

Crnkovic, F., J. K., Larsson, M., & Lau, K. K. (2000). Object-oriented design frameworks: Formal specification and some implementation issues. *Proceedings of 4th IEEE International Baltic Workshop, Vol. 2*, (pp. 63—77).

Crovella, M., Taqqu, M. S., & Bestavros, A. (1998). *Heavy-tailed probability distributions in the World Wide Web. A practical guide to heavy tails: Statistical techniques and application*. Boston: Birkhauser.

Cusinato, A., Della Mea, V., Di Salvatore, F., & Mizzaro, S. (2009, April 20-21). *QuWi: Quality control in Wikipedia*. Paper presented at the Third Workshop on Information Credibility on the Web (WICOW 2009), Madrid, Spain.

CyberNeko (2006). The CyberNeko HTML Parser. Retrieved February 27, 2006 from people.apache.org/~andyc/neko/doc/html/index.html

Danielson, D. R. (2006). Web credibility. In C. Ghaoui (Ed.), *Encyclopedia of human-computer interaction*. Hershey, PA: IGI Global.

Decker, S., Erdmann, M., Fensel, D., & Studer, R. (1998). *Ontobroker: Ontology based access to distributed and semi-structured information.* Paper presented at the The IFIP TC2/WG 2.6 Eighth Working Conference on Database Semantics-Semantic Issues in Multimedia Systems (pp. 351-369). Deventer, The Netherlands: Kluwer.

Deerwester, S., Dumais, S. T, Furnas, G. W., Landauer, T. K., & Harshman, R. (1990). Indexing by latent semantic analysis. *Journal of the American Society for Information Science, 41*(6), 391-407.

Dhyani, D., Ng, W. K., & Bhowmick, S. S. (2002). A Survey of Web Metrics. *ACM Computing Surveys, 34*(4), 469–503. doi:10.1145/592642.592645

Diryo, A. D. (2006). Prospek Bisnis Telekomunikasi Di Indonesia. *Economic Review,* 204.

Dolog, P., Henze, N., Nejdl, W., & Sintek, M. (2003). *Towards the adaptive Semantic Web.* Paper presented at the International Workshop on Principles and Practice of Semantic Web Reasoning (LNCS 2901, pp. 51-68). Springer.

Doong, R.K., & Frankl, P. (1991). Case Studies in Testing Object-Oriented Software. *Testing, Analysis, and Verification Symposium, Association for Computing Machinery,* (pp. 165 – 177). New York.

Doong, R.K., & Frankl, P. (1994). The ASTOOT approach to testing object-oriented programs. *ACM Transactions on Software Engineering and Methodology, 3*(2), 101-130.

Dou, D., LePendu, P., Kim, S., & Qi, P. (2006, April 3-7). Integrating databases into the semantic Web through an ontology-based framework. In *Proceedings of the 22nd International Conference on Data Engineering Workshops (ICDEW'06)* (Vol. 00, p. 54). Washington, D.C.: IEEE Computer Society.

Drew, A. W. S. (2006). Building technology foresight: using scenarios to embrace innovation. *European Journal of Innovation Management, 9*(3), 241. doi:10.1108/14601060610678121

Dromey, R. G. (2003). Software Quality - Prevention Versus Cure? *Software Quality Journal, 11*(3), 197–210. doi:10.1023/A:1025162610079

Dumas, M., van der Aalst, W. M., & ter Hofstede, A. H. (2006). *Process-Aware Information Systems: Bridging People and Software through Process Technology.* John Wiley and Sons.

Dumitrescu, C., & Foster, I. (2005). Gangsim: A simulator for grid scheduling studies. *In Proceedings of the IEEE International Symposium on Cluster Computing and the Grid (CCGrid'05)* (pp. 1151-1158), Cardiff, UK.

Eden, A. H., & Hirshfeld, Y. (2001). Principles in formal specification of object oriented design and architecture. D. A. Stewart and J. H. Johnson (Eds.), *Proceedings of the 2001 Conference of the Centre For Advanced Studies on Collaborative Research (Toronto, Ontario, Canada, November 05 - 07, 2001).* IBM Centre for Advanced Studies Conference. IBM Press.

Edgsim (2003). A simulation of the European datagrid. Retrieved from http://www.hep.ucl.ac.uk/pac/EDGSim/index.html.

Egenhofer, M., & Herring, J. R. (1991). High-level spatial data structures for GIS. In D. J. Maguire, M. F. Goodchild & D. W. Rhind (Eds.), *Geographical information systems: principles and applications* (Vol. 1, pp. 227-237). London: Longman Scientific Publications.

Ekman, P. (1973). *Darwin and facial expression: A century of research in review.* New York: Academic Press.

Eldrandaly, K. A. (2006). A COM-based expert system for selecting the suitable map projection in ArcGIS. *Expert Systems with Applications, 31*(1), 94–100. doi:10.1016/j.eswa.2005.09.008

EPA. (2007). *Brownfields cleanup and redevelopment.* Retrieved January 2007, from http://www.epa.gov/brownfields/

Epstein, J. H. (1998). Scenario Planning: An Introduction. *The Futurist, 32*(6), 50–51.

Ermolayev, V., Keberle, N., Kononenko, O., Plaksin, S., & Terziyan, V. (2004). Towards a Framework for agent-enabled semantic web service composition. *International Journal of Web Services Research, 1*(3), 63–87.

Espinoza, F. (2003). Towards individual service provisioning. In Proceedings of the 2003 International Conference on Intelligent User Interfaces (IUI 2003) (pp. 239-241). ACM Press.

Espinoza, F., & Hamfors, O. (2003). ServiceDesigner: A tool to help end-users become individual service providers. In Proceedings of the Thirty-Sixth Annual Hawaii International Conference on System Sciences (IEEE) (Track 9, Vol. 9, pp. 296.1-10).

Faloutsos, M., Faloutsos, P., & Faloutsos, C. (1999). On the power-law relationships of the Internet topology. In *Proceedings of ACM SIGCOMM* (pp. 251–262).

Feenstra, R. W., Janssen, M., & Wagenaar, R. W. (2007). Evaluating Web Service Composition Methods: the Need for Including Multi-Actor Elements. *The Electronic . Journal of E-Government, 5*(2), 153–164.

Feiner, S., & McKeown, K. (1991). Automating the generation of coordinated multimedia explanations. IEEE Computer, 24(10) 33-41.

Fenton, N. E., & Pfleeger, S. L. (1997). *Software Metrics: A Rigorous & Practical Approach*. International Thomson Computer Press.

FIPA Architecture Board. (2008). Foundation for Intelligent Physical Agents, FIPA Communicative Act Library Specification. Retrieved on Feb 12, 2008 from http://www.fipa.org/specs/fipa00037/SC00037J.html.

Flahive, A., Rahayu, J. W., Taniar, D., & Apduhan, B. O. (2004). A distributed ontology framework for the grid. In *Proceedings of the 5th International Conference on Parallel and Distributed Computing: Applications and Technologies (PDCAT'2004)* (pp. 68-71).

Fodslette, M. M. (1993). A scaled conjugate gradient algorithm for fast-supervised learning. *Neural Networks, 6*, 525-533,

Fogg, B. J. (2003a, April 5-10). *Prominence-interpretation theory: Explaining how people assess credibility.* Paper presented at the ACM CHI 2003 Conference on Human Factors in Computing Systems (CHI 2003), Fort Lauderdale, USA.

Fogg, B. J. (2003). *Persuasive technology: Using computers to change what we think and do.* Morgan Kaufmann Publishers.

Fogg, B. J., & Tseng, S. (1999, May 15-20). *The elements of computer credibility.* Paper presented at the ACM CHI 1999 Conference on Human Factors in Computing Systems, Pittsburgh, USA.

Fogg, B. J., Cueller, G., & Danielson, D. (2008). Motivating, Influencing, and Persuading Users: An Introduction to Captology. In A. Sears & J. A. Jacko (Eds.), *The Human-Computer Interaction Handbook: Fundamentals, Evolving Technologies, and Emerging Applications* (2nd ed., pp. 133-146). Lawrence Erlbaum Associates.

Folmer, E., & Bosch, J. (2002). Architecting for usability; a survey. *Journal of Systems and Software, 70*(1), 61-78.

Folmer, E., Gurp, J. v., & Bosch, J. (2003). A framework for capturing the relationship between usability and software architecture. *Software Process: Improvement and Practice, 8*(2), 67-87.

Folmer, E., Gurp, J. v., & Bosch, J. (2004). Software architecture analysis of usability. In *Proceedings of the 9th IFIP Working Conference on Engineering for Human-Computer Interaction* (pp. 321-339).

Folmer, E., Welie, M. v., & Bosch, J. (2006). Bridging patterns—an approach to bridge gaps between SE and HCI. *Journal of Information and Software Technology, 48*(2), 69-89.

Foster, I., & Kesselmann, C. (2004). *The Grid 2: Blueprint for a new computing infrastructure.* Elsevier Series in Grid Computing. Morgan Kaufmann Publishers.

Foster, M. J. (1989). Avoiding latch formation in regular expression recognizers. *IEEE Transactions on Computers, 38*(5), 754–756. doi:10.1109/12.24279

Fowler, M., Beck, K., Brant, J., Opdyke, W., & Roberts, D. (1999). *Refactoring: Improving the Design of Existing Code.* Addison-Wesley.

Fowler, M., Rice, D., Foemmel, M., Hieatt, E., Mee, R., & Stafford, R. (2003). *Patterns of Enterprise Application Architecture.* Addison-Wesley.

Fowler, S., & Stanwick, V. (2004). *Web Application Design Handbook: Best Practices for Web-Based Software*. Morgan Kaufmann.

Fraternali, P., Matera, M., & Maurino, A. (2002). *WQA: An XSL Framework for Analyzing the Quality of Web Applications*. Paper presented at the Second International Workshop on Web-Oriented Software Technology (IW-WOST 2002), Malaga, Spain, June 10-11, 2002.

Freire, A. P., Fortes, R. P. M., Turine, M. A. S., & Paiva, D. M. B. (2008). *An Evaluation of Web Accessibility Metrics based on their Attributes*. Paper presented at the Twenty Sixth Annual ACM International Conference on Design of Communication (SIGDOC 2008), Lisbon, Portugal, September 22-24, 2008.

Friedman, G., Hartman, A., Nagin, K., &Shiran, T. (2002, July 22 - 24). Projected state machine coverage for software testing. Proceedings of the 2002 ACM SIGSOFT international Symposium on Software Testing and Analysis (Roma, Italy 2002). ISSTA '02 (pp. 134-143). New York, NY: ACM Press..

Gachet, A. (2004). *Building Model-Driven Decision Support Systems with Dicodess*. Zurich: VDF.

Gálvez, A., Iglesias, A., & Corcuera, P. (2007). Representation and analysis of a dynamical system with petri nets. In Proceedings of International Conference on Convergence Information Technology, ICCIT'2007, Gyeongju (Korea) (pp. 2009-2015) IEEE Computer Society Press.

Gamma, E., Helm, R., Johnson, R., & Vlissides, J. (1995). *Design patterns elements of reusable object-orientated software*. New York: Addison-Wesley.

Gaudel, M.C. (1995). Testing can be formal, too. *Theory and Practice of Software Development (TAPSOFT '95): Proceedings of 6th International Joint Conference of CAAP/FACE, P.D. Mosses, M. Nielsen, and MI. Schwartzbach (eds.), Lecture Notes in Computer Science,* Vol. 915, (pp. 82-96). Berlin: Springer-Verlag.

Geoffrion, A. (1987). An Introduction to Structured Modelling. *Management Science, 33*(5), 547. doi:10.1287/mnsc.33.5.547

Georgeff, M. P., & Ingrand, F. F. (1989). Decision-making in an embedded reasoning system. In Proceedings of the International Joint Conference on Artificial Intelligence (pp. 972-978). Detroit, MI.

German, D. M., & Cowan, D. D. (2000). *Towards a Unified Catalog of Hypermedia Design Patterns*. Paper presented at the Thirty Third Hawaii International Conference on System Sciences (HICSS 2000), Maui, USA, January 4-7, 2000.

Gerrard, P., & Thompson, N. (2002) *Risk-Based E-Business Testing* (1st ed.). Artech House.

Gold, R. (2008). HTTPUnit. Retrieved April 18, 2008 from httpunit.sourceforge.net

Gomez-Perez, A., Gonzalez-Cabero, R., & Lama, M. (2004). Framework for design and composition of SWS based on Stack of Ontologies. American Assn. for Artificial Intelligence (www.aaai.org), 1-8.

Goncalves, L. M., Kallmann, M., & Thalmann, D. (2001). Programming behaviours with local perception and smart objects: An approach to solve autonomous agent tasks. In Proceedings of SIGGRAPI'2001 (pp. 143-150).

Goodchild, M. F., Hanning, R., & Wise, S. (1992). Integrating GIS and spatial data analysis: problems and possibilities. *International Journal of Geographical Information Systems, 6*(5), 407–423. doi:10.1080/02693799208901923

Goseva-Postojanova, K., Mazimdar, S., & Singh, A. (2004). Empirical study of session-based workload and reliability of Web servers. In *Proceedings of the 15th International Symposium on Software Reliability Engineering* (pp. 403–414).

Graham, I. (2003). *A Pattern Language for Web Usability*. Addison-Wesley.

Granieri, J. P., Becket, W., Reich, B. D., Crabtree, J., & Badler, N. I. (1995). Behavioral control for real-time simulated human agents. In Proceedings of Symposium on Interactive 3D Graphics (pp. 173-180). ACM Press.

Grossman, J. (2004). Thwarting SQL Web Hacks. *VAR Business*.

Grzeszczuk, R., & Terzopoulos, D. (1995). Automated learning of muscle-actuated locomotion through control abstraction. In Proceedings of ACM SIGGRAPH'95 (pp. 6-11).

Grzeszczuk, R., Terzopoulos, D., & Hinton, G. (1998). NeuroAnimator: fast neural network emulation and control of physics-based models. In Proceedings of ACM SIGGRAPH'98 (pp. 9-20).

Guéhéneuc, Y.-G., Guyomarc'h, J.-Y., Khosravi, K., & Sahraoui, H. (2007). Design Patterns as Laws of Quality. In J. Garzás & M. Piattini (Eds.), *Object-Oriented Design Knowledge: Principles, Heuristics and Best Practices* (pp. 105-142). Hershey, PA: IGI Global.

Guha, R., & McCool, R. (2003). TAP: A Semantic Web platform. *International Journal on Computer and Telecommunications Networking, 42*(5), 557-577.

Gurp, J. v., & Bosch, J. (2002). Design erosion: Problems and causes. *Journal of Systems and Software, 61*(2), 105-119.

Gutiérrez, M., Vexo, F., & Thalmann, D. (2003). Controlling virtual humans using PDAs. In Proceedings of 9th International Conference on Multi-Media Modeling (MMM'03) (pp. 27-33). Taiwan.

Guttag, J. V., & Horning, J. J., Garland, S.J., Jones, K.D., Modet, A., & Wing, J.M. (1993). Larch: languages and tools for formal specification. *Texts and Monographs, Computer Science series* NY: Springer-Verlag.

Hachey, B., & Grover, C. (2005, June 6-11). Automatic legal text summarization: Experiments with summary structuring. In *Proceedings of the 10th International Conference on Artificial intelligence and Law* (ICAIL '05), Bologna, Italy, (pp. 75-84). New York: ACM Press.

Hackos, J. T., & Redish, J. C. (1998). *User and task analysis for interface design*. New York: John Wiley and Sons, Inc.

Haddad, C., & Slimani, Y. (2007). Economic model for replicated database placement in grid. In *Proceedings of* Seventh *IEEE International Symposium on Cluster Computing and the Grid (CCGrid'07)* (pp. 283-292). Rio de Janeiro, Brazil.

Hadjerrouit, S. (2005). Designing a pedagogical model for Web engineering education: An evolutionary perspective. *Journal of Information Technology Education, 4*, 115–140.

Hafiz, M. (2006). *A Collection of Privacy Design Patterns*. Paper presented at the Thirteenth Conference on Pattern Languages of Programs (PLoP 2006), Portland, USA, October 21-23, 2006.

Halfond, W. G. J., & Orso, A. (2005). Combining Static Analysis and Runtime Monitoring to Counter SQL-Injection Attacks. *Workshop on Dynamic Analysis* (pp. 1 -7).

Halfond, W., Orso, A., & Manolios, P. (2007). WASP: Protecting Web Applications Using Positive Tainting and Syntax-Aware Evaluation. *IEEE Transactions on Software Engineering, 34*(1), 65–81. doi:10.1109/TSE.2007.70748

Han, J., & Kamber, M. (2006). *Data mining, concepts and techniques* (2nd ed.). Morgan Kaufmann.

Hansen, K. M. (2002). *Agile Environments - Some Patterns for Agile Software Development Facilitation*. Paper presented at the First Scandinavian Conference on Pattern Languages of Programs (VikingPLoP 2002), Højstrupgård, Denmark, September 20-22, 2002.

Hardwick, J. C., Papaefstathiou, E., & Guimbellot, D. (2001). Modeling the performance of e-commerce sites. In *Proceedings of the 27th International Conference of the Computer Measurement Group* (pp. 3–12).

Harold, E. R. (2008). *Refactoring HTML: Improving the Design of Existing Web Applications*. Addison-Wesley.

Harold, M. J., Gupta, R., & Soffa, M. L. (1993). A methodology for controlling the size of a test suite. *ACM Transactions on Software Engineering and Methodology, 2*(3), 270-285.

Harrold, M.J., McGregor, J.D., & Fitzpatrick, K.J. (1992). Incremental testing of object-oriented class structures. *Proceedings of the 14th International Conference on Software Engineering* (pp. 68 – 80.

Haykin, S. (1994). Neural networks. A comprehensive foundation. Englewood Cliffs, NJ: Macmillan Publishing.

Heffter, A. P., (1997). Specification and verification of object-oriented programs. Habilitationsschrift, Technische Universitaet Muenchen, 1997. Retrieved from the URL http://wwweickel.informatik.tu-muenchen.de/persons/poetzsch/habil.ps.gz.

Heflin, J., & Hendler, J. (2000). *Searching the Web with SHOE*. Paper presented at the AAAI Workshop (pp. 35-40). AAAI Press.

Heidemann, J., Obraczka, K., & Touch, J. (1997). Modeling the performance of HTTP over several transport protocols. *IEEE/ACM Transactions on Networking, 5*(5), 616–630.

Henderson-Sellers, B., Lowe, D., & Haire, B. (2002). OPEN Process Support for Web Development. *Annals of Software Engineering, 13*(1-4), 163–201. doi:10.1023/A:1016549527480

Hendler, J. (2001). Agents and the semantic web. IEEE Intelligent Systems, 2(16), 30-37.

Hendler, J., Berners-Lee, T., & Miller, E. (2002). Integrating applications on the semantic web. Journal of the Institute of Electrical Engineers of Japan, 122(10), 676-680.

Hendler, J., Lassila, O., & Berners-Lee, T. (2001). The Semantic Web. *Scientific American, 284*(5), 34–43. doi:10.1038/scientificamerican0501-34

Henninger, S., & Corrêa, V. (2007). *Software Pattern Communities: Current Practices and Challenges*. Paper presented at the Fourteenth Conference on Pattern Languages of Programs (PLoP 2007), Monticello, USA, September 5-8, 2007.

Hertz, J., Krogh, A., & Palmer, R. G. (1991). Introduction to the theory of neural computation. Reading, MA: Addison Wesley.

Hevner, A. R., March, S. T., Park, J., & Ram, S. (2004). Design Science in Information Systems Research. *MIS Quarterly, 28*(1), 75–105.

Hix, D., & Hartson, H. R. (1993). *Developing user interfaces: Ensuring usability through product and process*. New York: John Wiley and Sons.

Hoang, H. H., & Tjoa, A. M. (2006). *The state of the art of ontology-based query systems: A comparison of current approaches*. Paper presented at the IEEE International Conference on Computing and Informatics.

Hoang, H. H., & Tjoa, A. M. (2006). *The virtual query language for information retrieval in the SemanticLIFE framework*. Paper presented at the International Workshop on Web Information Systems Modeling - CAiSE06 (pp. 1062-1076). Luxembourg.

Hoang, H. H., Andjomshoaa, A., & Tjoa, A. M. (2006). *VQS: An ontology-based query system for the SemanticLIFE digital memory project*. Paper presented at the 2th IFIF WG 2.14 & 4.12 International Workshop on Web Semantics - OTM06 (LNCS 4278, pp. 1796-1805). Montpellier: Springer.

Hoare, C. A. R. (1969). An axiomatic basis for computer programming. *Comm. ACM, 12*(10), 576-583.

Hoare, C. A. R. (1972). Proof of correctness of data representations. *Acta Informatica, 1*(4), 271-281.

Hofmeister, C., Nord, R. L., & Soni, D. (1999). *Applied software architecture*. New York: Addison Wesley Longman.

Hofstede, G. (n.d.). *Geert-HofstedeTM vultural dimensions*. Retrieved January 23, 2007, from http://www.geert-hofstede.com/ hofstede_indonesia.shtml

Hokstad, P.(1978). Approximation for the $M/G/m$ queue. *Operations Research, 26*(3), 510–523.

Holcomb, R., & Tharp, A. L. (1991). What users say about software usability. *International Journal of Human-Computer Interaction, 3*(11), 49-78.

Horowitz, E. & Singhera, Z. (1993). A Graphical User Interface Testing Methodology. *Technical Report No. USC-CS-93-550*, Department of Computer Science, University of Southern California, Los Angeles, CA.

Horowitz, E.& Singhera, Z. (1993). XTester – A System for Testing X Applications. *Technical Report No. USC-CS-93-549*, Department of Computer Science, University of Southern California, Los Angeles, CA.

Horowitz, E.& Singhera, Z. (1993). Graphical user interface testing. *In proceedings of the Eleventh Annual Pacific Northwest Software Quality Conference.*

Hower, R. (2008). Software QA/Test Resource Center. Web Site Test Tools and Site Management Tools. Retrieved April 18, 2008 from http://www.softwareqatest.com/qatweb1.html

Hsu, M. H., Tsai, M. F., & Chen, H. H. (2006, October 16-18). Query expansion with ConceptNet and WordNet: An intrinsic comparison. In *Proceedings of the Third Asia Information Retrieval Symposium*, Singapore, (LNCS 4182, pp. 1-13).

Hu, S. (1999). Integrated multimedia approach to the utilization of an Everglades vegetation database. *Photogrammetric Engineering and Remote Sensing, 65*(2), 193–198.

Hu, Y., Nanda, A., & Yang, Q. (1999). Measurement, analysis and performance improvement of the Apache Web server. In *Proceedings of the IEEE International Performance, Computing and Communications Conference* (pp. 261–267).

Huang, J., Dang, J., & Huhns, M. N. (2006, September 18-22). Ontology reconciliation for service-oriented computing. In *Proceedings of the IEEE International Conference on Services Computing* (pp. 3-10). Washington, D.C.: IEEE Computer Society.

Huang, S. C., Chou, I-F., & Bias, R. G. (2006) Empirical evaluation of a popular cellular phone's menu system: Theory meets practice. *Journal of Usability Studies, 2*(1), 91-108.

Huang, S., & Tilley, S. (2003). *Towards a Documentation Maturity Model.* Paper presented at the Twenty First Annual International Conference on Documentation, San Francisco, USA, October 12-15, 2003.

Huang, Y., Yu, F., Hang, C., Tsai, C., Lee, D., & Kuo, S. (2004). Securing Web Application Code by Static Analysis and Runtime Protection. In *Proceedings of the 13th international conference on World Wide Web, May-2004* (pp. 40–52).

Hübner, S., Spittel, R., Visser, U., & Vögele, T. J. (2004). Ontology-based search for interactive digital maps. *IEEE Intelligent Systems, 19*(3), 80-86.

Huse, S. M. (1995). *GRASSLinks: A new model for spatial information access for environmental planning.* Retrieved from http://www.regis.berkeley.edu/sue/phd/

Huss, W.R., & Honton, E. J. (1987). Scenario Planning: What Style Should You Use? *Long Range Planning*, April.

Huynh, D., Karger, D., & Quan, D. (2002). *Haystack: A platform for creating, organizing and visualizing information using RDF.* Paper presented at the International Workshop on the Semantic Web.

Hyvönen, E., Saarela, S., & Viljanen, K. (2003). *Ontogator: Combining view- and ontology-based search with Semantic browsing.* Paper presented at the XML Finland Conference: Open Standards, XML and the Public Sector.

IEEE Architecture Working Group (1998). Recommended practice for architectural description. Draft IEEE Standard P1471/D4.1, IEEE.

Iglesias, A., & Kapcak, S. (2007) Symbolic computation of petri nets. Lectures Notes in Computer Science, 4488, 235-242.

Iglesias, A., & Luengo, F. (2004). Intelligent agents for virtual worlds. In Proceedings of CyberWorlds (CW'2004) (pp. 62-69). IEEE Computer Society Press.

Iglesias, A., & Luengo, F. (2005). New goal selection scheme for behavioral animation of intelligent virtual agents. IEICE Transactions on Information and Systems [Special Issue on "CyberWorlds"] E88-D(5), 865-871.

Iglesias, A., & Luengo, F. (2007) AI framework for decision modeling in behavioral animation of virtual avatars. Lectures Notes in Computer Science, 4488, 89-96.

Ingrand, F. F., Georgeff, M. P., & Rao, A. S. (1992). An architecture for real-time reasoning and system control. IEEE Intelligent Systems, 7(6), 34-44.

Internet World Stats (n.d.). World Internet Usage and Population Statistics. Retrieved October 25, 2008 from http://www.internetworldstats.com/stats.htm

ISO 9126-1 (2000) Software engineering—Product quality—Part 1: Quality Model.

ISO 9241-11 (1994). Ergonomic requirements for office work with visual display terminals (VDTs)—Part 11: Guidance on usability.

Ivory, M. Y., & Megraw, R. (2005). Evolution of Web Site Design Patterns. *ACM Transactions on Information Systems, 23*(4), 463–497. doi:10.1145/1095872.1095876

Iyengar, A., Challenger, J., Dias, D., & Dantzig, P. (2000). High-performance Web site design techniques. *IEEE Internet Computing, 4*(2), 17–26.

Izard, & Carroll, E. (1977). *Human emotions.* New York: Plenum Press.

Jankowski, P., & Nyerges, T. (2001). *Geographic information systems for group decision making:Towards a participatory geographic information science.* New York: Taylor and Francis.

Jeschke, S., Pfeiffer, O., & Vieritz, H. (2009). Using Web Accessibility Patterns for Web Application Development. The 2009 ACM Symposium on Applied Computing (SAC 2009), Honolulu, USA, March 9-12, 2009.

Jin, S., & Bestavros, A. (2005). *Generating Internet streaming media objects and workloads* (chap. 1, Recent advances on Web content delivery). Kluwer Academic Publishers.

Jones, M., & Taylor, G. (2004). Data integration issues for a farm decision support system. *Transactions in GIS, 8*(4), 459–477. doi:10.1111/j.1467-9671.2004.00196.x

Junior, P. T. A., & Filgueiras, L. V. L. (2005, October 23-26). *User Modeling with Personas.* Paper presented at the 2005 Latin American Conference on Human-Computer Interaction (CLIHC 2005), Cuernavaca, Mexico.

Kagal, L., Paolucci, M., Denker, G., Finin, T., & Sycara, K. (2004). Authorization and privacy for semantic web services. IEEE Intelligent Systems, 19(4), 50-56.

Kaluscha, E. A., & Grabner-Kräuter, S. (2003). *Towards a Pattern Language for Consumer Trust in Electronic Commerce.* Paper presented at the Eighth European Conference on Pattern Languages of Programs (EuroPLoP 2003), Irsee, Germany, June 25-29, 2003.

Kamra, A., Misra, V., & Nahum, E. (2004). Controlling the performance of 3-tiered Web sites: Modeling, design and implementation. In *Proceedings of SIGMETRICS 2004/PERFORMANCE 2004* (pp. 414–415).

Kamthan, P. (2007). Towards a systematic approach for the credibility of human-centric Web applications. *Journal of Web Engineering, 6*(2), 99–120.

Kamthan, P. (2008). A Situational Methodology for Addressing the Pragmatic Quality of Web Applications by Integration of Patterns. *Journal of Web Engineering, 7*(1), 70–92.

Kamthan, P. (2008). Ethics in software engineering. In M. Quigley (Ed.), *Encyclopedia of information ethics and security* (pp. 266-272). Hershey, PA: IGI Global.

Kamthan, P. (2008). A methodology for integrating patterns in quality-centric Web applications. *International Journal of Information Technology and Web Engineering, 3*(2), 27–44.

Kamthan, P. (2008). A Framework for the Active Credibility Engineering of Web Applications. *International Journal of Information Technology and Web Engineering, 3*(3), 17–27.

Kamthan, P. (2008). Towards High-Quality Mobile Applications by a Systematic Integration of Patterns. *Journal of Mobile Multimedia, 4*(3/4), 165–184.

Kamthan, P. (2009). A model for characterizing Web engineering. In M. Khosrow-Pour (Ed.), *Encyclopedia of information science and technology* (2nd ed., pp. 2631-2637).

Kamthan, P. (2009). A Framework for Integrating the Social Web Environment in Pattern Engineering. *International Journal of Technology and Human Interaction, 5*(2), 36–62.

Kant, K., & Sundaram, C. R. M. (2000). A server performance model for static Web workloads. In *Proceedings of the IEEE International Symposium on Performance Analysis of Systems and Software* (pp. 201–206).

Kappel, G., Pröll, B., Reich, S., & Retschitzegger, W. (2006). *Web Engineering*. John Wiley and Sons.

Karger, D. R., Bakshi, K., Huynh, D., Quan, D., & Vineet, S. (2005). *Haystack: A general purpose information management tool for end users of semistructured data.* Paper presented at the 2nd Biennial Conference on Innovative Data Systems Research (pp. 13-26).

Karvounarakis, G., Alexaki, S., Christophides, V., Plexousakis, D., & Scholl, M. (2002). *RQL: A declarative query language for RDF.* Paper presented at the Eleventh International World Wide Web Conference (pp. 591-603). ACM Press.

Kazman, R., Abowd, G., & Webb, M. (1994). SAAM: A method for analyzing the properties of software architectures. In *Proceedings of the 16th International Conference on Software Engineering* (pp. 81-90).

Kazman, R., Klein, M., & Clements, P. (2000). *ATAM: Method for architecture evaluation (CMU/SEI-2000-TR-004).* Pittsburgh: Carnegie Mellon University.

Kazman, R., Klein, M., Barbacci, M., Longstaff, T., Lipson, H., & Carriere, J. (1998). The architecture tradeoff analysis method. In *Proceedings of the International Conference on Engineering of Complex Computer Systems* (pp. 68-78).

Kerievsky, J. (2005). *Refactoring to Patterns*. Addison-Wesley.

Kerschberg, L., Chowdhury, M., Damiano, A., Jeong, H., Mitchell, S., Si, J., et al. (2004). *Knowledge sifter: Ontology-driven search over heterogeneous databases.* Paper presented at the 16th International Conference on Scientific and Statistical Database Management.

Khan, A., & Balbo, S. (2005). *Agile versus Heavyweight Web Development: An Australian Survey.* Paper presented at the Eleventh Australian World Wide Web Conference (AusWeb 2005), Gold Coast, Australia, July 2-6, 2005.

Khan, L., & Luo, F. (2002). Ontology construction for information selection. In *Proceedings 14th IEEE International Conference on Tools with Artificial Intelligence* (pp. 122- 127).

Khaslavasky, J. (1998). Integrating culture into interface design. *ACM CHI*, 365-366.

Khaslavsky, J. (1998). Culture and international software design. *ACM CHI*, 387.

Khomh, F., & Guéhéneuc, Y.-G. (2008). *Do Design Patterns Impact Software Quality Positively?* Paper presented at the Twelfth European Conference on. Software Maintenance and Reengineering (CSMR 2008), Athens, Greece, April 1-4, 2008.

Kidani, Y. (1999). Video communication system using portrait animation. In *Proceedings of the IEEE Southeastcon '99* (pp. 309-314).

Kiesler, S., & Sproull, L. (1997). Social human-computer interaction. In Human Values and the Design of Computer Technology, 199, CSLI Publications, Stanford, CA. 191.

Kim, J. H., & Lee, K. P. (2005). Cultural difference and mobile phone interface design: Icon recognition according to level of abstraction. *Mobile HCI*, 19-22.

Kimura, T. (1983). Diffusion approximation for an $M/G/m$ queue. *Operations Research, 31*(2), 304–321.

Kingston, R., Carver, S., Evans, A., & Turton, I. (2000). Web-based public participation geographical information systems: An aid to local environmental decision-making. *Computers, Environment and Urban Systems, 24*(2), 109–125. doi:10.1016/S0198-9715(99)00049-6

Kleinrock, L. (1976). *Queueing systems, Volume 1: Theory.* New York: John Wiley & Sons.

Koda, T., & Maes, P. (1996). Agents with faces: the effects of personification of agents. In Proceedings of Fifth IEEE International Workshop on Robot and Human Communication (pp. 189-194).

Kohavi, R., & Parekh, R. (2003). Ten supplementary analyses to improve e-commerce Web sites. In *Proceedings of the 5th WEBKDD Workshop* (pp. 29–36).

Komiya, R., Mohd Arif, N. A., Ramliy, M. N., Gowri Hari Prasad, T., & Mokhtar, M. R. (1999). A proposal of virtual reality telecommunication system. In *Proceedings of the WEC'99* (pp. 93-98).

Kondratova, I., & Goldfarb, I. (2005). Cultural visual interface design. In *Proceedings of the EDMedia, World Conference on Educational Multimedia, Hypermedia & Telecommunications*. Montreal, (pp. 1255-1262).

Kruchten, P. (2004). *An Ontology of Architectural Design Decisions in Software-Intensive Systems.* Paper presented at the Second Gröningen Workshop on Software Variability Management: Software Product Families and Populations, Gröningen, The Netherlands, December 2-3, 2004.

Kruchten, P. B. (1995). *The 4+1 view model of architecture. IEEE Software.*

Krunić, T., Ružić-Dimitrijević, L., Petrović, B., & Farkaš, R. (2006). Web Design Curriculum and Syllabus Based on Web Design Practice and Students' Prior Knowledge. *Journal of Information Technology Education, 5*, 317–335.

Kumar, K., & Welke, R. J. (1992). Methodology Engineering: A Proposal for Situation-Specific Methodology Construction. In W. W. Cotterman & J. A. Senn (Eds.*), Challenges and Strategies for Research in Systems Development* (pp. 257-269). John Wiley and Sons.

Kumar, S., & Mishra, R. B. (2008). A Hybrid Model for Service Selection in Semantic Web Service Composition. *International Journal of Intelligent Information Technologies, 4*(4), 55–69.

Kunert, T. (2009). User-Centered Interaction Design Patterns for Interactive Digital Television Applications. Springer-Verlag.

Kungas, P., & Matskin, M. (2006). Semantic Web Service Composition through a P2P-Based Multi-Agent Environment (LNCS 4118, pp. 106-119).

Kvaloy, T. A., Rongen, E., Tirado-Ramos, A., & Sloot, P. (2005). Automatic Composition and Selection of Semantic Web Services (LNCS 3470, pp. 184-192).

Labs Semantic Web Programme, H. P. (2008). *Jena- A Semantic Web Framework for Java.* Retrieved on March 01, 2008 from http://jena.sourceforge.net/.

Landauer, T. K. (1995). *The trouble with computers: Usefulness, usability and productivity.* MIT Press.

Lassila, O., & Hendler, J. (2007). Embracing "Web 3.0". *IEEE Internet Computing, 11*(3), 90–93. doi:10.1109/MIC.2007.52

Lassing, N., Bengtsson, P. O., van Vliet, H., & Bosch, J. (2002). Experiences with ALMA: Architecture-level modifiability analysis. *Journal of Systems and Software,* 47-57.

Lauesen, S., & Younessi, H. (1998). Six styles for usability requirements. In *Proceedings of REFSQ'98,* (pp.155–166). Presses universitaires de Namur.

Laurikari, V. (2001). *Efficient Submatch Addressing for Regular Expressions.* M.Sc. thesis, Dept. of Computer Science and Engineering, Helsinki University of Technology

Lazar, J., Meiselwitz, G., & Feng, J. (2007). Understanding Web credibility: A synthesis of the research literature. World Scientific.

Lea, D. (1994). Christopher Alexander: An Introduction for Object-Oriented Designers. *ACM SIGSOFT Software Engineering Notes, 19*(1), 39–46. doi:10.1145/181610.181617

Lecue, F., & Leger, A. (2005). *A formal model for semantic Web service composition.* Paper presented at the 5th International Semantic Web Conference, Athens, Georgia.

Lee, Y.S., et al. (n.d). *Usability testing with cultural groups in developing a cell phone navigation system.* Retrieved August 10, 2006, from uweb.txstate.edu/~yr12/Papers/HCII2005_Submission_Cultural.pdf

Lester, J. C., Voerman, J. L., Towns, S. G., & Callaway, C. B. (1997). Cosmo: a life-like animated pedagogical agent with deictic believability. In Proceedings of IJCAI'97.

Levine, J., Mason, T., & Brown, D. (1992). *Lex and Yacc*. O'Reilly

Li, Y. & Lan, Z. (2005). A survey of load balancing in grid computing. *High Performance Computing and Algorithms* (LNCS 3314, pp. 280-285).

Ling, Y., Mullen, T., & Lin, X. (2000). Analysis of optimal thread pool size. *ACM SIGOPS Operating System Review, 34*(2), 42–55.

Lipsky, L. (1992). *Queueing theory: A linear algebraic approach*. New York: McMillan and Company.

Liu, L., Kong, X., & Chen, J. (2006). *An Economic Model of Software Development Approaches*. Paper presented at the Twelfth Australian World Wide Web Conference (AusWeb 2006), Australis Noosa Lakes, Australia, July 1-5, 2006.

Liu, S., Liu, F., Yu, C., & Meng, W. (2004, July). An effective approach to document retrieval via utilizing wordNet and recognizing phrases. In *Proceedings of the 27th Annual International ACM SIGIR Conference*, Sheffield, UK, (pp. 266-272).

Liu, X., Heo, J., & Sha, L. (2005). Modeling 3-tiered Web applications. In *Proceedings of the 13th IEEE International Symposium on Modeling, Analysis and Simulation of Computer Telecommunications Systems* (pp. 307–310).

Luengo, F., & Iglesias, A. (2003) A new architecture for simulating the behavior of virtual agents. Lectures Notes in Computer Science, 2657, 935-944.

Lung, C., Bot, S., Kaleichelvan, K. K. R., & Kazman, R. (1997). An approach to software architecture analysis for evolution and reusability. In *Proceedings of the 1997 Conference of the Centre for Advanced Studies on Collaborative research* (p. 15).

MacEachren, A. M. (2001). Cartography and GIS: Extending collaborative tools to support virtual teams. *Progress in Human Geography, 25*, 431–444. doi:10.1191/030913201680191763

MacEachren, A. M., Pike, W., Yu, C., Brewer, I., Gahegan, M., & Weaver, S. D. (2006). Building a geocollaboratory: Supporting human-environment regional observatory (HERO) collaborative science activities. *Computers, Environment and Urban Systems, 30*(2), 201–225. doi:10.1016/j.compenvurbsys.2005.10.005

Maedche, A., Motik, B., Silva, N., & Volz, R. (2002). *MAFRA: An ontology mapping framework in the Semantic Web*. Paper presented at the 12th International Workshop on Knowledge Transformation.

Maedche, A., Staab, S., Stojanovic, N., Studer, R., & Sure, Y. (2001). *SEAL: A framework for developing Semantic Web portals*. Paper presented at the 18th British National Conference on Databases (pp. 1-22). London: Springer.

Maes, P. (1994). Agents that reduce work and information overload. Communications of the ACM, 37(7), 31-40,146.

Mandala, R., Tokunaga, T., & Tanaka, H. (1998). The use of WordNet in information retrieval. In S. Harabagiu (Ed.), *Use of WordNet in Natural Language Processing Systems: Proceedings of the Association for Computational Linguistics Conference*, Somerset, NJ, (pp. 31-37).

Mandala, R., Tokunaga, T., & Tanaka, H. (1999). Complementing WordNet with Roget and corpus-based automatically constructed thesauri for information retrieval. In *Proceedings of the Ninth Conference of the European Chapter of the Association for Computational Linguistics*, Bergen.

Manolescu, D., & Kunzle, A. (2001). Several Patterns for eBusiness Applications. The Eighth Conference on Pattern Languages of Programs (PLoP 2001), Monticello, USA. September 11-15, 2001.

Manolescu, D., Kozaczynski, W., Miller, A., & Hogg, J. (2007). The Growing Divide in the Patterns World. *IEEE Software, 24*(4), 61–67. doi:10.1109/MS.2007.120

MapInfo. (2007). *miAware2.0 documentation library*. Retrieved May 2007, from http://reference.mapinfo.com/common/docs/mapxtend-dev-web-none-eng/

MapServer. (2007). *MapServer*. Retrieved May 2007, from http://mapserver.gis.umn.edu/

Marcus, A. (2001). Cross-cultural user-interface design. In M. J Smith & G. Salvendy (Eds.), *Proceeding of the Human-Computer Interface Internat (HCII) Conference* (Vol. 2, pp. 502-505). New Orleans: Lawrence Erlbaum Association.

Marick, B. (1999). New models for test development. *Proceedings of International Quality Week, May, 1999.* Retrieved from http://www.testing.com/writings/ new-models.pdf

Marks, M., & Hong, D. (2006). Web Design Patterns Collection Technical Design. Center for Document Engineering (Technical Report CDE2006-TR09). University of California, Berkeley, USA.

McDonald, A., & Welland, R. (2001). *Agile Web Engineering (AWE) Process* (Tech Rep TR-2001-98). University of Glasgow, Glasgow, Scotland.

Mcgilloway, S., Cowie, R., Douglas-Cowie, E., Gielen, C. C. A. M., Westerdijk, M. J. D., & Stroeve, S. H. (2000). Approaching automatic recognition of emotion from voice: A rough benchmark. In *Proceedings of the ISCA Workshop on Speech and Emotion* (pp. 207-212).

McGregor, J.D., & Korson, T.D. (1994). Testing the polymorphic interactions of classes. *Technical Report No. TR-94-103*, Clemson University.

McGuinness, D. L., & Harmelen, F. V. (2008). *OWL Web Ontology Language Overview.* Retrieved on Feb 13, 2008 from http://www.w3.org/TR/owl-features/.

McIlraith, S., & Son, T. C. (2002). Adapting Golog for composition of Semantic Web services. *In Proc. of the Eighth International Conference on Knowledge Representation and Reasoning (KR2002),* Toulouse, France (pp. 482–493).

McIlraith, S. A., Son, T. C., & Zeng, H. (2001). Semantic Web Services. *IEEE Intelligent Systems, 16*(2), 46–53. doi:10.1109/5254.920599

Menasce, D. (2003). Web server software architecture. *IEEE Internet Computing, 7*(6), 78–81.

Mendes, E. M., Mosley, N., & Counsell, S. (2001). Web Metrics - Estimating Design and Authoring Effort. *IEEE MultiMedia, 8*(1), 50–57. doi:10.1109/93.923953

Mendes, E., & Mosley, N. (2006). *Web Engineering.* Springer-Verlag.

Mercay, J., & Bouzeid, G. (2002). *Boost struts with XSLT and XML.* http://www.javaworld.com/javaworld/jw-02-2002/jw-0201-strutsxslt-p1.html

Mercury Interactive, Mountain View, CA., http://www.mercury.com

Meszaros, G., & Doble, J. (1998). A Pattern Language for Pattern Writing. In R. C. Martin, D. Riehle, & F. Buschmann (Eds.), *Pattern Languages of Program Design 3* (pp. 529-574). Addison-Wesley

Microsoft Corporation (n.d). *Internet information services (IIS).* Retrieved June 9, 2008, from http://www.microsoft.com/WindowsServer2003/iis/default.mspx

Miller, J., Reformat, M., & Zhang, H. (2006). Automatic Test Data Generation Using Genetic Algorithm and Program Dependence Graphs. *Journal of Information and Software Technology, 1*(2), 1–24.

Minsky, M. (1985). The society of mind. New York: Simon and Schuster Inc.

Moldovan, D. I., & Mihalcea, R. (2000). Using WordNet and lexical operators to improve Internet searches. *IEEE Internet Computing, 4*(1), 34-43.

Moltenbrey, K. (1999). All the right moves. Computer Graphics World, 22(10), 28-34.

Monzani, J. S., Caicedo, A., & Thalmann, D. (2001). Integrating behavioural animation techniques. In Proceedings of the Computer Graphics Forum (EUROGRAPHICS'2001) 20(3), 309-318.

Morishima, S., & Harashima, H. (1991). A media conversion from speech to facial image for intelligent man-machine interface. *IEEE J. on Selected Areas in Comm., 9*(4), 594-600.

Morville, P. (2005). *Ambient Findability: What We Find Changes Who We Become.* O'Reilly Media. 2005.

Mozilla.org. (2008). *Rhino: JavaScript for Java.* Retrieved April 18, 2008 from http://www.mozilla.org/rhino

MSDN (2004). Injection Testing. Retrieved January 22, 2006 from msdn.microsoft.com/msdnmag/issues/04/09/SQLInjection

Murphy, G.C., Townsend, P., & Wong, P.S. (1994). Experiences with cluster and class testing. *Communications of the ACM, 37*(9), 39 – 47.

Myers, B. A. (1993). Why are human-computer interfaces difficult to design and implement? *Technical Report CS-93-183,* Carnegie Mellon University, School of Computer Science.

Myers, B. A., Olsen, D. R., Jr., & Bonar, J. G. (1993). User interface tools. In proceedings of ACM INTERCHI'93 Conference on Human Factors in Computing Systems, Adjunct Proceedings, Tutorials, (p. 239).

Nabney, I. (2001). *Netlab: Algorithms for pattern recognition, advances in pattern recognition.* London: Springer-Verlag.

Naik, K. (1997). Efficient computation of unique input/output sequences in finite-state machines. *IEEE/ACM Trans. Netw, 5*(4), pp. 585-599.

Nakatsu, R., Nicholson, J., & Tosa, N. (1999). *Emotion recognition and its application to computer agents with spontaneous interactive capabilities.* Paper presented at the International Congress of Phonetic Science (pp. 343-351).

Narayanan, & S., McIlraith, S. (2003). Analysis and simulation of web services. Computer Networks, 42, 675-693.

Narayanan, S., & McIlraith, S. (2002). Simulation, verification and automated composition of web services. In Proceedings of the Eleventh International World Wide Web Conference-WWW2002. ACM Press.

Neal, J. G., & Shapiro, S. C. (1991). Intelligent multi-media interface technology. In Proceedings of Intelligent User Interfaces (pp. 11-43). ACM Press.

Nelson, H. J., & Monarchi, D. E. (2007). Ensuring the Quality of Conceptual Representations. *Software Quality Journal, 15*(2), 213–233. doi:10.1007/s11219-006-9011-2

Nguyen, H. Q. (2001). *Testing Applications on the Web: test Planning for Internet-Based Systems.* John Wiley & Sons

NIC (2004). *Mapping the Global Future.* Report on the National Intelligence Council's 2020 Project, December 2004.

Nielsen, J. (1993). *Usability engineering.* Boston: Academic Press, Inc.

Nielsen, J. (1994). Heuristic evaluation. In J. Nielsen & R. L. Mack (Eds.), *Usability inspection methods* (pp. 25-64). New York: John Wiley and Sons.

Nielsen, J., & Loranger, H. (2006). *Prioritizing Web usability.* New Riders.

Nigay, L., & Coutaz, J. (1997). Software architecture modelling: Bridging the worlds using ergonomics and software properties. In Formal Methods in Human-Computer Interaction, Springer-Verlag, ISBN 3-540-76158-6, 1997, Chapter 3, 49-73.

Norman, D. A. (1988). The design of everyday things. New York: Currency- Doubleday.

Norman, D. A. (2004). *Emotional design: Why we love (or hate) everyday things.* Basic Books.

Nossenson, R., & Attiya, H. (2004). The N-burst/G/1 model with heavy-tailed service-times distribution. In *Proceedings of the International Symposium on Modeling, Analysis, and Simulation of Computer and Telecommunications Systems* (pp. 131–138).

Nunamaker, J. F. Jr, Chen, M., & Purdin, T. D. M. (1991). Systems Development in Information Systems Research. *Journal of Management Information Systems, 7*(3), 89–106.

Nyerges, T., & Jankowski, P. (2001). *Geographic Information Systems for Group Decision Making.* London: Taylor & Francis.

O'Reilly, T. (2005,, September 30). *What Is Web 2.0: Design patterns and business models for the next generation of software.* O'Reilly Network.

Oatley, G. C., Zeleznikow, J., & Ewart, B. W. (2004). Matching and predicting crimes. In *Proceedings of the 24ᵗʰ SGAI International Conference on Knowledge Based Systems and Applications of Artificial Intelligence (SGAI'2004)* (pp. 19-32).

Offutt, J., Wu, Y., Du, X., & Huang, H. (2004). Bypass Testing of Web Applications. *15ᵗʰ International Symposium on Software Reliability Engineering* (pp. 187-197).

Offutt, Liu, J., Abdurazik, S., & Ammann, P. A. (2003). Generating test data from state-based specifications. *Software testing verification and reliability, 13*(1), 25-54.

Ofuonye, E., Beatty, P., Reay, I., Dick, S., & Miller, J. (2008). How do we Build Trust into Ecommerce Web Sites? *IEEE Software, 25*(5), 7–9. doi:10.1109/MS.2008.136

OGC. (2007). *OpenGIS. Geography markup language (GML) implementation specification*. Retrieved May 2007, from http://opengis.net/gml/

OGC. *Web map service interface* (No. 03-109r1): OGC.

Oinas-Kukkonen, H., & Harjumaa, M. (2008, February 10-15). *Towards deeper understanding of persuasion in software and information systems*. Paper presented at the First International Conference on Advances in Computer-Human Interaction (ACHI 2008), Sainte Luce, Martinique.

Ordonez, C., & Omiecinski, E. (1998). *Image mining: A new approach for data mining* (Tech. Rep. GIT-CC-98-12). Georgia Institute of Technology, College of Computing.

Oviatt, S. (1999). Ten myths of multimodal interaction. Communications of the ACM, 42(11) 74-81.

Padgham, L., & Lambrix, P. (2000). *Agent Capabilities: Extending BDI Theory*. American Association for Artificial Intelligence.

Paolucci, M., Kawamura, T., Payne, T., & Sycara, K. (2002). Semantic Matching of Web Service Capabilities. In *Proc. Of Int. Semantic Web Conference (ISWC, 2002), Italy*.

Paxson, V., & Floyd, S. (1995). Wide area traffic: The failure of Poisson modeling. *IEEE/ACM Transactions on Networking, 3*(3), 226–244.

Pechoucek, M. (2003). *Formal Representation for Multi-Agent Systems. Gerstner Laboratory*. Czech Technical University in Prague. Retrieved from http://agents.felk.cvut.cz/teaching/33ui2/bdi.pdf.

Peng, Z.-R., & Tsou, M.-H. (2003). *Internet GIS: Distributed geographic information services for the Internet and wireless networks*. Wiley.

Peng, Z.-R., & Zhang, C. (2004). The roles of geography markup language (GML), scalable vector graphics (SVG), and Web feature service (WFS) specifications in the development of Internet geographic information systems (GIS). *Journal of Geographical Systems, 6*(2), 95–116. doi:10.1007/s10109-004-0129-0

Perry, M., & Kaminski, H. (2005). *A Pattern Language of Software Licensing*. Paper presented at the Tenth European Conference on Pattern Languages of Programs (EuroPloP 2005), Irsee, Germany, July 6-10, 2005.

Perzel, K., & Kane, D. (1999). Usability patterns for applications on the world wide web. In *Proceedings of the Pattern Languages of Programming Conference*.

Petrushin, V. A. (1999). Emotion in speech recognition and application to call centers. In *Proceedings of the ANNIE '99*.

Pirolli, P. (2007). *Information foraging theory: Adaptive interaction with information*. UK: Oxford University Press.

Pistore, M., Bertoli, P., Cusenza, E., Marconi, A., & Traverso, P. (2004). *WS-GEN: A Tool for the Automated Composition of Semantic Web Services*. Paper presented at the Int. Semantic Web Conference (ISWC, 2004).

Plutchik, R. (1980). *Emotion: A psycho-evolutionary synthesis*. New York: Harper and Row.

Polson, P. G., & Lewis, C. H. (1990). Theory-based design for easily learned interfaces. In *Proceedings of the SIGCHI Conference on Human Factors in Computing Systems: Empowering People* (pp. 235-242).

Ponsel Masih Lebih Banyak Untuk Telpon. (2006, December 11). *Kompas*. Jogja edition, 1.

Porter, R., Coplien, J. O., & Winn, T. (2005). Sequences as a Basis for Pattern Language Composition. *Science of Computer Programming, 56*(1-2), 231–249. doi:10.1016/j. scico.2004.11.014

Power, D. J. (2001). Supporting Decision Makers: An Expanded Framework. *Informing Science Conference*, Poland.

Power, D. J. (2002). *Decision support systems: concepts and resources for managers*. Westport, CT: Quorum Books.

Power, D. J., Sharda, R., & Kulkarni, U. (2007*). Understanding Decision Support Systems for Global Enterprises*. 9th International Conference on Decision Support Systems (ICDSS 2007), Kolkata, India.

Preece, J., et al. (2002*). Interaction design: Beyond human-computer interaction*. New York: John Wiley & Sons.

Preece, J., Rogers, Y., Sharp, H., Benyon, D., Holland, S., & Carey, T. (1994). *Human-computer interaction*. New York: Addison Wesley.

Pressman, R. S. (1992*). Software engineering: A practitioner's approach*. New York: McGraw-Hill.

Prevost, S., Hodgson, P., Cook, L., & Churchill, E. F. (1999). Face-to-face interfaces. In Proceedings of CHI'99 (pp. 244-245). ACM Press.

Prudhommeaux, E., & Seaborne, A. (2008). *SPARQL Query Language for RDF*. Retrieved March 1, 2008 from http://www.w3.org/TR/2008/REC-rdf-sparql-query-20080115/

Putz, S. (1994). *Interactive information services using World-Wide Web hypertext*. Retrieved 2006 from http://www2.parc.com/istl/projects/www94/mapviewer.html

Quan, D., Huynh, D., & Karger, D. R. (2003). *Haystack: A platform for authoring end user Semantic Web applications*. Paper presented at the 12th International World Wide Web Conference (pp. 738-753).

Rabiner, L. R., & Schafer, R. W. (1978). *Digital processing of speech signals*. Eaglewood Cliffs, NJ: Prentice-Hall.

Rack, C., Arbanowski, S., & Steglich, S. (2006, July 23-27). *Context-aware, ontology-based recommendations*. Paper presented at the International Symposium on Applications and the Internet Workshops.

Ramirez, R. G., Ching, C., & St Louis, R. D. (1990). Model-Data and Model-Solver Mappings: A Basis for an Extended DSS Framework. *ISDSS Conference Proceedings*, (pp. 283-312).

Ranganathan, K., & Foster, I. (2002). Decoupling computing and data scheduling in distributed data-intensive applications. *Eleventh IEEE Symposium on High Performance Distributed Computing (HPDC)* (pp. 138-145). Edinburgh, Scotland.

Rao, A. S., & Georgeff, M. P. (1991). Modeling rational agents within a bdi-architecture. In Proceedings of the Third International Conference on Principles of knowledge Representation and Reasoning (pp. 473-484). San Mateo, CA: Morgan Kaufmann.

Rao, M., Fan, G., Thomas, J., Cherian, G., Chudiwale, V., & Awawdeh, M. (2007). A web-based GIS decision support system for managing and planning USDA's conservation reserve program (CRP). *Environmental Modelling & Software, 22*(9), 1270–1280. doi:10.1016/j.envsoft.2006.08.003

Rapps, S., & Weyuker, E. J. (1982, September 13-16). Data flow analysis techniques for test data selection. *Proceedings of the 6th international Conference on Software Engineering. International Conference on Software Engineering (pp. 272-2780)*. Los Alamitos, CA: IEEE Computer Society Press.

Raupp, S., & Thalmann, D. (2001) Hierarchical model for real time simulation of virtual human crowds. IEEE Transactions on Visualization and Computer Graphics, 7(2), 152-164.

Ravden, S. J., & Johnson, G. I. (1989). *Evaluation usability of human-computer interfaces: A practical method*. New York: Ellis Horwood Limited.

Richardson, D. J., & Clarke, L. A. (1981, March 9-12). A partition analysis method to increase program reliability. *Proceedings of the 5th international Conference on Software Engineering (San Diego, California, United States,). International Conference on Software Engineering. (pp. 244-253).* Piscataway, NJ: IEEE Press.

Richardson, R., & Smeaton, A. F. (1995). *Using WordNet in a knowledge-based approach to information retrieval* (Tech. Rep. CS-0395). Dublin City University, School of Computer Applications.

Richter, J. (2000). *Programming server-side applications for Microsoft Windows 2000.* Microsoft Press.

Rieh, S. Y., & Danielson, D. R. (2007). Credibility: A multidisciplinary framework. *Annual Review of Information Science & Technology, 41,* 307–364. doi:10.1002/aris.2007.1440410114

Ringland, G. (1998). *Scenario Planning- Managing for the Future.* John Wiley & Sons.

Ringland, G. (2002). *Scenarios in business.* New York: John Wiley & Sons.

Rising, L. (2000). The Pattern Almanac 2000. Addison-Wesley.

Ritson, N. (1997). Scenario Planning in Action. *Management Accounting, 75*(11), 24–28.

Robson, C. (1993). *Real world research.* Oxford: Blackwell Publishing Ltd.

Rossi, G. (2001). *Patterns for Personalized Web Applications.* Paper presented at the Sixth European Conference on Pattern Languages of Programs (EuroPLoP 2001), Irsee, Germany, July 4-8, 2001.

Rossi, G., Pastor, O., Schwabe, D., & Olsina, L. (2008). *Web Engineering: Modelling and Implementing Web Applications.* Springer-Verlag.

Rossi, G., Schwabe, D., & Lyardet, F. (1999). *Improving Web Information Systems with Navigational Patterns.* Paper presented at the Eighth International World Wide Web Conference (WWW8), Toronto, Canada, May 11-14, 1999.

Rubinstein, R., & Hersh, H. (1984). *The human factor: Designing computer systems for people.* Bedford: Digital Press.

Rüping, A. (2006). *Web Content Management - Patterns for Interaction and Personalisation.* Paper presented at the Eleventh European Conference on Pattern Languages of Programs (EuroPLoP 2006), Irsee, Germany, July 5-9, 2006.

Rusu, L. I., Rahayu, J. W., & Taniar, D. (2005). A methodology for building XML data warehouses. *International Journal of Data Warehousing and Mining, 1*(2), 23-48.

Sahil, T. (2006). Robust Testing for Web Applications. Retrieved from http://www.Weberdev.com/ViewArticle-341.html

Saito, Y., & Shapiro, M. (2005). Optimistic replication. *ACM Computing Surveys, 37*(1), 42–81. doi:10.1145/1057977.1057980

Sakasegawa, H. (1977). An approximation formula $L_q = \alpha\rho^\beta/(1-\rho)$. *Annals of the Institute of Statistical Mathematics, 29*(1), 67–75.

Sayar, A., Pierce, M., & Fox, G. (2006). Integrating AJAX approach into GIS visualization Web services. In *Telecommunications, 2006. AICT-ICIW '06. International Conference on Internet and Web Applications and Services/Advanced International* (pp. 169-169).

Scheinblum, J. (2006). Test entire Web applications with HTTPUNit. Retrieved February 20, 2006 from builder.com.com/5100-6370-1046258.html

Scherer, K. R. (1986). Vocal affect expression: A review and a model for future research. *Psychological Bulletin, 99,* 43-165.

Schoemaker, P. J. H. (1993). Multiple Scenario Development: Its Conceptual and Behavioural Foundation. *Strategic Management Journal, 14*(3), 193–213. doi:10.1002/smj.4250140304

Schoemaker, P. J. H. (1995). Scenario Planning: A Tool for Strategic Thinking. *Sloan Management Review, 36*(2), 25–40.

Schölkopf, C. J. C., Burges, A. J., & Smola (1998). *Advances in kernel methods: Support vector learning.* Cambridge, MA: MIT Press.

Schueler, T. (1999). Microbes and urban watersheds. *Watershed Protection Techniques, 3*(1), 551–596.

Schumacher, M., Fernandez-Buglioni, E., Hybertson, D., Buschmann, F., & Sommerlad, P. (2006). *Security Patterns: Integrating Security and Systems Engineering.* John Wiley and Sons.

Schümmer, T., & Lukosch, S. (2007). *Patterns for Computer-Mediated Interaction.* John Wiley and Sons.

Schuurman, N., & Leszczynski, A. (2006). Ontology-based metadata. *Transactions in GIS, 10*(5), 709–726. doi:10.1111/j.1467-9671.2006.01024.x

Schwabe, D., & Rossi, G. (1998). An Object Oriented Approach to Web-Based Application Design. *Theory and Practice of Object Systems, 4*(4).

Schwartz, P. (1991). *The Art of the Long View.* Doubleday.

Segerståhl, K., & Jokela, T. (2006). *Usability of Interaction Patterns.* Paper presented at the CHI 2006 Conference on Human Factors in Computing Systems, Montréal, Canada, April 22-27, 2006.

Segue Software Inc., Newton, MA, http://www.segue.com

Sell, D., Hakimpour, F., Domingue, J., Motta, E., & Pacheco, R. (2004). Interactive Composition of WSMO-based Semantic Web Services in IRS-III. In *Proc. of the AKT workshop on Semantic Web Services* (AKT-SWS04).

Shackel, B. (1991). Usability—context, framework, design and evaluation, in *human factors for informatics usability.* Cambridge University Press.

Shanks, G. (1999, September 29). *Semiotic approach to understanding representation in information systems.* Information Systems Foundations Workshop, Sydney, Australia.

Sharp, H., Galal, G. H., & Finkelstein, A. (1999). *Stakeholder Identification in the Requirements Engineering Process.* Paper presented at the Tenth International Conference and Workshop on Database and Expert Systems Applications (DEXA 1999), Florence, Italy, August 30-September 3, 1999.

Shaw, M. (2002). What makes good research in software engineering? *International Journal on Software Tools for Technology Transfer (STTT), 1-7.* Springer Berlin / Heidelberg.

Shneiderman, B. (1998*). Designing the user interface: Strategies for effective human-computer interaction.* Reading: Addison-Wesley.

Shneiderman, B. (2007). Web Science: A Provocative Invitation to Computer Science. *Communications of the ACM, 50*(6), 25–27. doi:10.1145/1247001.1247022

Sikder, I. U., & Gangopadhyay, A. (2003). Distributed data warehouse for go-spatial services. In G. Grant (Ed.), *ERP & data warehouse in organizations: Issues and challenges* (pp. 132-145). IRM Press.

Sikder, I. U., & Gangopadhyay, A. (2004). Collaborative decision making in Web-based GIS. In M. Khosrow-Pour (Ed.), *Advanced topics in information resources management* (Vol. 3, pp. 147-162). Idea Group Publishing.

Sikder, I., & Gangopadhyay, A. (2002). Design and Implementation of a Web-based collaborative spatial decision support system: Organizational and managerial implications. *Information Resources Management Journal, 15*(4), 33–47.

Simon, H. (1996). *The sciences of the artificial* (3rd ed.). The MIT Press.

Sirin, E., Parsia, B., & Hendler, J. (2004). Filtering and selecting semantic web services with interactive composition techniques. IEEE Intelligent Systems, 18(4), 42-49.

Siyuan, F., Griffiths, T., & Paton, N. W. (2007). GML for Representing data from spatio-historical databases: A case study. *Transactions in GIS, 11*(2), 233–253. doi:10.1111/j.1467-9671.2007.01043.x

Slothouber, L. (1996). A model of Web server performance. In *Proceedings of the 5th International World Wide Web Conference.*

Smeaton, A. F., & Berrut, C. (1995). Running TREC-4 experiments: A chronological report of query expansion experiments carried out as part of TREC-4. In *Proceedings of the Fourth Text Retrieval Conference (TREC-4)*. NIST Special Publication.

Smith, & Davis (2008). *Foundation for Intelligent Physical Agents. FIPA Contract Net Interaction Protocol Specification*. Retrieved on Feb 12, 2008 from http://www.fipa.org/specs/fipa00029/SC00029H.html.

Smith, M.D., & Robson, D.J. (1992). A framework for testing object-oriented programs. *Journal of Object-Oriented Programming, 5*(3), 45 – 53.

Sommervill, I. (2001). *Software engineering* (6th ed.) Addison Wesley Publishers.

Song, H., Liu, X., Jakobsen, D., Bhagwan, R., Zhang, X., Taura, K., & Chien, A. (2000). The microgrid: a scientific tool for modeling computational grids. *In Scientific Programming*, volume 8, 127-141.

SPI Dynamics (2002). SQL Injection: Are Your Web Applications Vulnerable [SPI Dynamics Whitepaper].

Sproull, L., Subramani, R., Kiesler, S., Walker, J., & Waters, K. (1996). When the interface is a face. In Proceedings of Human-Computer Interaction (Vol. 11, pp. 97-124).

Squillante, M. S., Yao, D. D., & Zhang, L. (1999). Web traffic modeling and Web server performance analysis. In *Proceedings of the 38th Conference on Decision and Control* (pp. 4432–4439).

Stamper, R. (1992). *Signs, organizations, norms and information systems*. Paper presented at the Third Australian Conference on Information Systems, Wollongong, Australia, October 5-8, 1992.

Statistik Indonesia. (2007). Retrieved February 28, 2007 from www.datastatistik-Indonesia.com

STATUS deliverables, http://lucio.ls.fi.upm.es/status/results/deliverables.html

Stoimenov, L., & Djordjevic-Kajan, S. (2005). An architecture for interoperable GIS use in a local community environment. *Computers & Geosciences, 31*(2), 211–220. doi:10.1016/j.cageo.2004.09.017

Stollberg, M., & Haller, A. (2005). *Semantic Web Services Tutorial*. Paper presented at the 3rd International Conference on Web Services (ICWS 2005).

Taibi, T., & Ngo, C. L. (2002). *A Pattern for Evaluating Design Patterns*. Paper presented at the Sixth World Multiconference on Systemics, Cybernetics and Informatics (SCI 2002), Orlando, USA, July 14-18, 2002.

Tait, M. G. (2005). Implementing geoportals: applications of distributed GIS. *Computers, Environment and Urban Systems, 29*(1), 33–47.

Takefusa, A., Matsuoka, S., Nakada, H., Aida, K., & Nagashima, U. (1999). Overview of a performance evaluation system for global computing scheduling algorithms. In *Proceedings of the 8th IEEE International Symposium on High Performance Distributed Computing (HPDC-8)* (pp. 97-104). Redondo Beach, California.

Takeuchi, A., & Nagao, K. (1993). Communicative facial displays as a new conversational modality. In Proceedings of ACM/IFIP INTERCHI '93 (pp.187-193). ACM Press.

Takeuchi, A., & Naito, T. (1995). Situated facial displays: towards social interaction. In Proceedings of CHI'95 (pp. 450 – 455). ACM Press.

Tappenden, A., Beatty, P., & Miller, J. (2005). Agile Security Testing of Web-Based Systems via HTTPUnit. *Agile, 2005*, 29–38.

Teevan, J., Alvarado, C., Ackerman, M. S., & Karger, D. R. (2004). *The perfect search engine is not enough: A study of orienteering behavior in directed search*. Paper presented at the SIGCHI Conference on Human Factors in Computing Systems (pp. 415-422). New York: ACM Press.

Thalmann, D., & Monzani, J. S. (2002) Behavioural animation of virtual humans: What kind of law and rules? In Proceedings of Computer Animation 2002 (pp. 154-163). IEEE Computer Society Press.

The DAML Services Coalition. (2008). *DAML-S: Semantic Mark-up for Web Services*. Retrieved on Februrary 13, 2008 from http://www.daml.org/services/daml-s/2001/10/daml-s.pdf

The Open Web Application Security Project. (2006). *OWASP Top Ten Most Critical Web Application Security Vulnerabilities*. Retrieved January 7, 2006 from www.owasp.org/documentation/topten.html

Thorisson, K. (1996). Communicative humanoids: A computational model of psychosocial dialogue skills. MIT Media Laboratory PhD thesis, MIT, Cambridge, MA.

Tidwell, J. (1998). Interaction design patterns. In *Proceedings of the Conference on Pattern Languages of Programming*.

Tidwell, J. (2005). *Designing Interfaces: Patterns for Effective Interaction Design*. O'Reilly Media.

Tosa, N., & Nakatsu, R. (1996). Life-like communication agent-emotion sensing character MIC and feeling session character MUSE. In *Proceedings of the IEEE Conference on Multimedia* (pp. 12-19).

Tsou, M. H., & Buttenfield, B. (2002). A dynamic architecture for distributing geographic information services. *Transactions in GIS, 6*(4), 355–381. doi:10.1111/1467-9671.00118

Tuchyna, M. (2006). Establishment of spatial data infrastructure within the environmental sector in Slovak Republic. *Environmental Modelling & Software, 21*(11), 1572–1578. doi:10.1016/j.envsoft.2006.05.014

Tucker, K. (1999). Scenario Planning. *Association Management, 51*(4), 70–75.

Tweedale, J., Ichalkaranje, N., Sioutis, C., Jarvis, B., Consoli, A., & Phillips-Wren, G. (2007). Innovations in multi-agent systems. *Journal of Network and Computer Applications, 30*(5), 1089–1115. doi:10.1016/j.jnca.2006.04.005

Vallee, M., Ramparany, F., & Vercouter, L. (2005). A Multi-Agent System for Dynamic Service Composition in Ambient Intelligence Environments. In *Proc. Third International Conference on Pervasive Computing, PERVASIVE* (pp. 175-182).

van der Heijden, K. (1996). *Scenarios, The Art of Strategic Conversation*. Wiley.

Van der Mei, R. D., Hariharan, R., & Reeser, P. (2001). Web server performance modeling. *Telecommunication Systems, 16*(3–4), 361–378.

Van Duyne, D. K., Landay, J., & Hong, J. I. (2003). *The Design of Sites: Patterns, Principles, and Processes for Crafting a Customer-Centered Web Experience*. Addison-Wesley. Vigo, M. Arrue, M., Brajnik, G., Lomuscio, R., & Abascal, J. (2007). *Quantitative Metrics for Measuring Web Accessibility*. Paper presented at the 2007 International Cross-Disciplinary Workshop on Web Accessibility (W4A 2007), Banff, Canada, May 7-8, 2007.

Van Duyne, D. K., Landay, J., & Hong, J. I. (2007). *The design of sites: Patterns for creating winning web sites* (2nd ed.). Prentice-Hall.

VanderBrug, G. J., & Minker, J. (1975). State-space problem-reduction, and theorem proving—some relationships. *Commun. ACM, 18*(2), 107-119.

Vatrapu, R., & Perez-Quinones, M. (2006). Culture and international usability testing: The effects of culture in structure interviews. Unpublished masters' thesis. *Digital library and archives: Formerly the scholarly communication project*. Retrieved August 11, 2006 from http://scholar.lib.vt.edu/theses/available/etd-09132002-083026/

Vijayaraghavan, G., & Kaner, C. (2002). *Bugs in your shopping cart: A Taxonomy*. Paper presented in San Francisco QW2002 Paper 4I.

Voorhees, E. M. (1993, June 27-July 1). Using WordNet to disambiguate word senses for text retrieval. In R. Korfhage, E. Rasmussen, & P. Willett (Eds.), *Proceedings of the 16th Annual international ACM SIGIR Conference on Research and Development in information Retrieval* (SIGIR '93), Pittsburgh, (pp. 171-180). New York: ACM Press.

Voorhees, E. M. (1994, July 3-6). Query expansion using lexical-semantic relations. In W. B. Croft & C. J. van Rijsbergen (Eds.), *Proceedings of the 17th Annual International ACM SIGIR Conference on Research and Development in information Retrieval*, Dublin, Ireland, (pp. 61-69). New York: Springer-Verlag.

Vora, P. (2009). *Web application design patterns.* Morgan Kaufmann.

Wallace, D., Raggett, I., & Aufgang, J. (2002). *Extreme Programming for Web Projects.* Addison-Wesley.

Walther, J. B., Wang, Z., & Loh, T. (2004). The effect of top-level domains and advertisements on health web site credibility. *Journal of Medical Internet Research, 6*(3), 2004. doi:10.2196/jmir.6.3.e24

Wang, B., & Brookes, B. R. (2004). *A semantic approach for Web indexing* (LNCS 3007, pp. 59-68).

Wathen, C. N., & Burkell, J. (2002). Believe it or not: factors influencing credibility on the Web. *Journal of the American Society for Information Science and Technology, 53*(2), 134–144. doi:10.1002/asi.10016

Weinstein, B. (2007). Scenario planning: current state of the art, Manager Update. *Henley-on-Thames, 18*(3), 1.

Weiss, M. (2003). *Patterns for Web Applications.* Paper presented at the Tenth Conference on Pattern Languages of Programs (PLoP 2003), Urbana, USA, September 8-12, 2003.

Welie, M., & Trætteberg, H. (2000). Interaction patterns in user interfaces. In *Proceedings of the 7th Conference on Pattern Languages of Programming (PloP).*

Wendorff, P. (2001). *Assessment of Design Patterns during Software Reengineering: Lessons Learned from a Large Commercial Project.* Paper presented at the Fifth European Conference on Software Maintenance and Reengineering (CSMR 2001), Lisbon, Portugal, March 14-16, 2001.

Wentzlaff, I., & Specker, M. (2006). *Pattern Based Development of User Friendly Web Applications.* Paper presented at the Workshop on Model-Driven Web Engineering (MDWE 2006), Palo Alto, USA, July 10, 2006.

Wesson, J., & Cowley, L. (2003). *Designing with Patterns: Possibilities and Pitfalls.* Paper presented at the Second Workshop on Software and Usability Cross-Pollination, Zürich, Switzerland, September 1-2, 2003.

Westerdijk, M., & Wiegerinck, W. (2000). Classification with multiple latent variable models using maximum entropy discrimination. In *Proceedings of the 17th International Conference on Machine Learning* (pp. 1143-1150).

Weyuker, E. J., & Jeng, B. (1991). Analyzing partition testing strategies. *IEEE Trans. Softw. Eng., 17*(7), 703-711.

Wieringa, R. (1998). A survey of structured and object-oriented software specification methods and techniques. *ACM Comput. Surv., 30*(4), 459-527.

Wing, J.M. (1983). A two-tiered approach to specifying programs. *Technical Report TR-299,* Mass. Institute of Technology, Laboratory for Computer Science.

Wittel, W. I., Jr. & Lewis, T. G. (1991). Integrating the mvc paradigm into an object-oriented framework to accelerate gui application development. *Technical Report 91-60-D6,* Department of Computer Science, Oregon State University.

Wixon, D., & Wilson, C. (1997) The usability engineering framework for product design and evaluation. In M. G. Helander, T. K. Landauer, & P. V. Prabhu (Eds), *Handbook of human-computer interaction* (2nd ed.). Englewood Cliffs, N.J.: Elsevier Science.

Wong, B. (2006). Different views of software quality. In E. Duggan & J. Reichgelt (Eds.), *Measuring Information Systems Delivery Quality* (pp. 55-88). Hershey, PA: IGI Global.

Worboys, M., & Deen, S. M. (1991). Semantic heterogeneity in distributed geographic databases. *SIGMOD Record, 20*(4), 30–34. doi:10.1145/141356.141366

World Telecommunication/ICT Indicators: Cellular Subscribers. (2006). *International telecommunication union.* Retrieved August 10, 2006, from http://www.itu.int/ITU-D/statistics/at_glance/cellular05.pdf

Wright, A. D. (2000). Scenario planning: A continuous improvement approach to strategy. *Total Quality Management, 11*(4-6), 433–438. doi:10.1080/09544120050007742

Wu, D., Parsia, B., Sirin, E., Hendler, J., & Nau, D. (2003). Automating DAML-S Web Services composition using SHOP2. In *Proc. of the 2nd International Semantic Web Conference, ISWC 2003, Sanibel Island, Florida, USA.*

Wu, Z., Ranabahu, A., Gomadam, K., Sheth, A. P., & Miller, J. A. (2006). *Automatic Semantic Web Services Composition.* Retrieved from http://www.cs.uga.edu/~jam/papers/zLSDISpapers/zixin.doc

www.conceptnet.org

Xu, D., & Bode, B. (2004). Performance study and dynamic optimization design for thread pool systems. In *Proceedings of the International Conference on Computing, Communications and Control Technologies.*

Xu, J., Li, B., & Li, D. (2002). Placement problems for transparent data replication proxy services. *IEEE Journal on Selected Areas in Communications, 7,* 1383–1398.

Yagoubi, B. & Slimani, Y. (2006). Dynamic load balancing strategy for grid computing. *Transactions on engineering computing and technology, 13,* 260-265.

Yan, Z., Li, Q., & Li, H. (2006). *An ontology-based model for context-aware.* Paper presented at the 1st International Symposium on Pervasive Computing and Applications (pp. 647-651).

Yao, D. (1985). Refining the diffusion approximation for the *M/G/m* queue. *Operations Research, 33*(6), 1266–1277.

Yoder, J., & Barcalow, J. (1997). *Architectural Patterns for Enabling Application Security.* Paper presented at the Fourth Conference on Pattern Languages of Programs (PLoP 1997), Monticello, USA, September 3-5, 1997.

Zaiane, O. R., et al (1998). Multimedia-miner: A system prototype for multimedia data mining. In Proceedings of the *1998 ACM-SIGMOD Conference on Management of Data.*

Zdun, U. (2007). Systematic Pattern Selection using Pattern Language Grammars and Design Space Analysis. *Software, Practice & Experience, 37*(9), 983–1016. doi:10.1002/spe.799

Zeleznikow, J., Oatley, G. C., & Ewart, B. W. (2005). *Decision support systems for police: Lessons from the application of data mining techniques to 'soft' forensic evidence.* Retrieved December 20, 2007, from http://www.aic.gov.au/conferences/occasional/2005-04-zeleznikow.html

Zheng, G. (2008). A Historical Perspective of Web Engineering. In G. D. Putnik & M. M. Cunha (Eds.), *Encyclopedia of Networked and Virtual Organizations.* Hershey, PA: IGI Global.

Ziefle, M., & Bay, S. (2004). Mental models of a cellular phone menu. Comparing older and younger novice users. In Brewster & Dunlop (Eds.), *Mobile human-computer interaction.* Berlin: Springer.

Ziemer, S., & Stålhane, T. (2004). *The Use of Trade-offs in the Development of Web Applications.* Paper presented at the First International Workshop on Web Quality (WQ 2004). Munich, Germany. July 27, 2004.

Zipf, A., & Jost, M. (2006). Implementing adaptive mobile GI services based on ontologies: Examples from pedestrian navigation support. *Computers, Environment and Urban Systems, 30*(6), 784–798. doi:10.1016/j.compenvurbsys.2006.02.005

About the Contributors

Ghazi Alkhatib is an assistant professor of software engineering at the College of Computer Science and Information Technology, Applied Science University (Amman, Jordan). In 1984, he obtained his Doctor of Business Administration from Mississippi State University in information systems with minors in computer science and accounting. Since then, he has been engaged in teaching, consulting, training, and research in the area of computer information systems in the US and gulf countries. In addition to his research interests in databases and systems analysis and design, he has published several articles and presented many papers in regional and international conferences on software processes, knowledge management, e-business, Web services, and agent software, workflow, and portal/grid computing integration with Web services.

David Rine has been practicing, teaching, and researching engineered software development for over thirty years. Prior to joining George Mason University, he served in various leadership roles in the IEEE Computer Society and co-founded two of the technical committees. He joined George Mason University in 1985 and was the founding chair of the Department of Computer Science and one of the founders of the (Volgenau) School of Information Technology and Engineering. Rine has received numerous research, teaching, and service awards from computer science and engineering societies and associations, including the IEEE Centennial Award, IEEE Pioneer Award, IEEE Computer Society Meritorious Service Awards, the IEEE Computer Society Special Awards, IEEE Computer Society 50th anniversary Golden Core Award, and historical IEEE Computer Society Honor Roll and Distinguished Technical Services Awards. He has been a pioneer in graduate, undergraduate, and high school education, producing computer science texts and leading establishment of the International Advanced Placement Computer Science program for the nation's high school students, co-designer of the first computer science and engineering curriculum (1976), and the first masters in software engineering curriculum (1978). He has been an editor of a number of prestigious software-oriented journals. During his tenure, he has authored over 300 published works and has directed many PhD students. Complementing his work at GMU, he has worked on many international technology and relief projects in various countries and made many life-long international friendships. His past students are the most important record of his technical achievements.

* * *

Hanh Huu Hoang. Since 1996 Hanh Huu Hoang has been a lecturer of the Department of Information Technology, Hue University. He received his PhD in Information Systems from Vienna University of Technology, Austria in 2007. He was awarded the Outstanding Students Award at Hue University.

He has published many peer-reviewed papers in learnt international conferences and workshops such as IEEE/WIC/ACM WI, iiWAS, SWWS-OTM, WISM-CAiSE. His current research focus areas include the Semantic Web and Ontologies, Personal Digital Memories, Personal Information Management Systems, Business Processes Modeling, Business Intelligence Systems, Knowledge Discovery and (Semantic-) Web Services. He is co-author of two books published in Vietnamese.

Tho Manh Nguyen received his PhD in Information Systems from the Vienna University of Technology in September 2005 and currently keeps a Postdoctoral Research Fellowship. He has been awarded Microsoft Student Travel Awards, IBM Europe Student Event Recognition, and Outstanding Students Award. He is PC member and organizer numbers of international conferences and workshops and has several publications in international conferences and journals in the field of data warehousing and knowledge discovery. His research areas of interest include Data Warehousing, Data Mining and Knowledge Discovery, Business Intelligence Systems, Grid-based Knowledge discovery, Service-Oriented Computing, Ontology and Semantic Management.

A Min Tjoa. Since 1994 A Min Tjoa is director of the Institute of Software Technology and Inter-active Systems at the Vienna University of Technology. He is currently also the head of the Austrian Competence Center for Security Research. He received his PhD in Engineering from the University of Linz, Austria in 1979. He was Visiting Professor at the Universities of Zurich, Kyushu and Wroclaw (Poland) and at the Technical Universities of Prague and Lausanne (Switzerland). From 1999 to 2003 he was the president of the Austrian Computer Society. He is member of the IFIP Technical Commit-tee for Information Systems and vice-chairman of the IFIP Working Group on Enterprise Information Systems (WG 8.9). He has served as chairman of several international conferences including the IEEE Int. Conf. on Distributed Computing Systems (ICDCS), European Software Engineering Conference (ESEC), ACM SIGSOFT Symposium on the Foundations of Software Engineering (FSE), the International Conference on Database and Expert Systems Applications (DEXA), the International Conference on Electronic Commerce and Web Technologies (EC-Web). He is Honorary Chairman of the International Conference on Very Large Databases (VLDB 2007). His current research focus areas are e-Commerce, Data Warehousing, Grid Computing, Semantic Web, Security, and Personal Information Management Systems. He has published more than 150 peer reviewed articles in journals and conferences. He is author and editor of 15 books.

M. Indrawan is a senior lecturer of Computer Science in the Faculty of Information Technology, Monash University. She received her PhD in Computer Science from Monash University. Her current research focuses on pervasive computing, information retrieval and context-aware systems.

S. Loke is a senior lecturer of Computer Science in the Department of Computer Science, La Trobe University. He received his PhD in Computer Science from University of Melbourne. His research inter-ests are pervasive computing, smart containers, social devices and context-aware pervasive systems.

Andrés Iglesias is Associate Professor at the Department of Applied Mathematics and Computational Sciences of the University of Cantabria (Spain). Since Nov. 2005, he is also the Post-graduate studies coordinator at his department. He has been Visiting Researcher at the Department of Computer Science of the University of Tsukuba (Japan) for the period 2004-05. He holds a B.Sc. degree in Mathematics

(1992) and a Ph.D. in Applied Mathematics (1995). He is Associate Editor of the journals "Transactions on Computational Science", "Int. Journal of Computer Graphics and CAD/CAM", "Int. Journal of Computational Science", "Advances in Computational Science and Technology" and "International Journal of Biometrics", member of the Editorial Board of the journals "Journal of Convergence Information Technology" and "Int. Journal of Digital Content Technology and its Applications" and member of the International Reviewing Board of the journals "Int. Journal of Information Technology and Web Engineering" and "Int. Journal of Computational Intelligence Research". He has been the chairman and organizer of 24 international conferences in the fields of computer graphics, geometric modeling and symbolic computation, such as the CGGM (2002-08), TSCG (2003-08) and CASA (2003-08) annual conference series and co-chair of ICMS'2006, VRSAL'2008 and ICCIT'2008. In addition, he has served as a program committee and/or steering committee member of 70 international conferences such as 3IA, CGA, CAGDAG, CGIV, CIT, CyberWorlds, FGCN, GMAG, GMAI, GMVAG, Graphicon, GRAPP, ICCS, ICCSA, ICICS, ICCIT, ICM, ICMS, IMS, IRMA, ISVD, MMM, NDCAP, VIP, VRSAL and WSCG. He has been reviewer of 76 international conferences and 18 international journals. He has been guest editor of some special issues of international journals about computer graphics and symbolic computation. He is the author of over 100 international papers and four books. His personal web page is available at: http://personales.unican.es/iglesias

Sandeep Kumar is with the Department of Computer Engineering, Institute of Technology, Banaras Hindu University (IT–BHU), Varanasi, India. He has done his BTech in Information Technology and Gold Medal of the university and has completed his PhD course work in Computer Engineering with highest possible grade point. He has many years of experience as a Software Engineer as well as a teacher. He has published several papers at national and international levels and has also authored several books. He is a member of the review and editorial committee of various international publications, such as WASET, WSEAS, and ORS. His current areas of interest include the semantic web, web-based systems, Multi-Agent Systems (MAS), knowledge-based systems and software engineering.

Kuldeep Kumar is with the Department of Computer Science and Engineering, University Institute of Engineering and Technology (UIET), Kurukshetra University, Kurukshetra, India. He has also worked as a summer trainee in the Department of Computer Engineering, Institute of Technology, Banaras Hindu University (IT–BHU), Varanasi, India. His current areas of interest include semantic web, automata theory, compiler design and statistical models.

Ankita Jain is with the Department of Electronics and Communication Engineering of National Institute of Technology, Kurukshetra, India. She has done B.Tech in Electronics and Communication Engineering from Kurukshetra University, Kurukshetra. Her areas of interest include image processing and semantic web.

David Taniar received his PhD in Computer Science from Victoria University in 1997. He is now a Senior Lecturer at Monash University, Australia. His primary research is in database processing. He is a founding editor-in-chief of the International Journal of Data Warehousing and Mining and International Journal of Business Intelligence and Data Mining. He can be contacted at dtaniar@gmail.com. His publications can be found at the DBLP server at http://www.informatik.uni-trier.de/~ley/db/indices/a-tree/t/Taniar:David.html

Torab Torabi is currently senior lecturer in Department of Computer Science and Computer Engineering, La Trobe University. He worked as Lecturer in Auckland University of Technology. Between 1997 to 1999. Dr. Torabi worked more than 10 years in industry as developer and project manager. He is has been collaborating with more than 30 organisations in research and development of medium-size projects. His research interests include Software Engineering, Software and Business Process Modelling, Software Quality, Location Based Services, Context-Aware Mobile Services, Mobile Service Integration, and Model Driven Architecture. He is a member of IEEE and IASTED. He can be contacted at t.torabi@latrobe.edu.au.

Wei Sun completed his Bachelor of Business Systems by Honours from Monash University, Australia.

Pankaj Kamthan has been teaching in academia and industry for several years. He has also been a technical editor, participated in standards development, and served on program committees of international conferences and on the editorial board of international journals. His teaching and research interests include Knowledge Representation, Web Engineering, and Software Quality.

Lucia Dwi Krisnawati is a lecturer at the department of Informatics, Duta Wacana Christian University (DWCU), Yogyakarta, Indonesia. Her research interests include Natural Language Processing, spoken dialogue technology, Discourse, Human Computer Interaction, and semantic network. She earned a SS (BA) in English Literature from Gadjah Mada University, and an MA (Magister Artium) in Computational Linguistics - Natural Language Processing from Ludwig-Maximilian University, Munich, Germany. Contact her at krisna@ukdw.ac.id.

Restyandito was graduated from Duta Wacana Christian University (DWCU) and achieved a degree of S.Kom (BS in Informatics). After completing his Master of Science from University of Pittsburg, he began to teach in DWCU. He was also teaching as a guest lecturer at several other universities in Yogyakarta. In 2004 & 2006 he received grant as visiting lecturer at Christ College, in Bangalore, India & Augustana College in Rock Island, USA. His teaching and research interests include multimedia, HCI, software and Website Engineering. At present, he also has strong interest in the study of the effect of IT and social transformation. In 2001-2005 he was given responsibility as the head of Instructional Technology & Multimedia Development Center at DWCU. Since 2005 – present he has been appointed as the vice dean of academic affairs at the department of Informatics.

Aishah Abdul Razak received the B. Eng. degree from Multimedia University, Malaysia in 2000. In 2005 she completed her Master by research degree entitled "Voice Driven Facial Expression Reconstruction for Virtual Reality Telecommunication" in Multimedia University, Malaysia. She is currently a lecturer in the Faculty on Information Technology, Multimedia University, Malaysia.

Mohamad Izani Zainal Abidin received the B.A. and M.A degrees from Multimedia University, Malaysia, in 2000 and 2003, respectively. He is currently a lecturer in the Faculty of Creative Multimedia at Multimedia University, Cyberjaya and pursuing his Ph.D. study in the area of digital animation.

Ryoichi Komiya received the B.E. and Ph.D. degrees from Waseda University, Tokyo, Japan, in 1967 and 1986, respectively. Since 1967, he joined the Electrical Communication Labs of NTT and he has been engaged in the development of the PCM repeatered line, digital data terminal equipment, video coder/decoders, stuff multiplexers, ISDN subscriber loop transmission systems and fiber optic remote multiplexer systems. In 1992, he joined Siemens, in 1995 joined Nippon telecommunication consulting, in 1998 joined NTT Advanced technology and in 2002 he joined Distribution and Economics University in Japan. Since 1998 he has been with Faculty of Engineering and Faculty of Information Technology of Multimedia University, Malaysia, where he has been responsible for research and development of next generation telecommunication systems, services, terminals, IP network, virtual education environment, e-commerce terminal, Intelligent Transport System, and smart home. He is currently at National Institute of Information and Communication Technology, Japan where he is promoting R&D on medical ICT. Professor Komiya is a member of IEEE and IEICE.

Zafar U. Singhera has been working in the software industry for the past 15 years. His areas of interest include software and system architecture, non-functional and architectural aspects of distributed enterprise applications, multi-modal and multi media interfaces, and virtualization. He has published more than 30 journal and conference papers. In addition to working in software industry, Mr. Singhera has also been teaching as visiting faculty at various Computer Sciences institutions. He has also served as a full time faculty member at Kind Saud University, Riyadh, Saudi Arabia. He holds a Ph.D. in software engineering from University of Southern California, Los Angeles, CA. He earned his Master degrees in Computer Science, Computer and Systems Engineering, and Electrical Engineering from United States; and bachelor's degrees in Electrical Engineering and Economics from Pakistan.

Abad Ali Shah is a Foreign Professor of Higher Education Commission (HEC) of Pakistan, and placed in the Department of Computer Science & Engineering of University of Engineering & Technology (UET), Lahore, Pakistan. He spent 12 year at computer science department, King Saud University, Riyadh, KSA before joining HEC on July 2004. He received his B. Sc. in Mathematics and Physics from Punjab University, Lahore, Pakistan in 1967, a M. Sc. in Applied Mathematics from Quaid-I-Azam University, Islamabad, Pakistan in 1981 with Quaid-I-Azam Award, a MS in Computer Science from Rensselaer Polytechnic Institute, Troy, New York in 1986, and Ph. D. in Computer Science from Wayne State University, Detroit, Michigan, USA in 1992. His current research interests include object-oriented databases, temporal databases, web databases, Web services, information retrieval (IR) software engineering, semantic web, web engineering and Bioinformatics. He has more than ninety (00) research articles on his credit including three book chapters including this. Currently, he is supervising many Ph.D. and MS dissertations. He is a member of ACM.

Ellis Horowitz received his Ph.D. in computer science from the University of Wisconsin. He was on the faculty there and at Cornell University before assuming his present post as Professor of Computer Science and Electrical Engineering at the University of Southern California. He has also been a visiting Professor at M.I.T. and the Israel Institute of Technology (Technion). Dr. Horowitz has held numerous academic administrative jobs. At U.S.C. he was chairman of the Computer Science Department from 1990 to 1999. He is the author of ten books and over seventy journal articles and refereed conference proceedings on computer science subjects ranging from data structures, algorithms, and software design to computer science education. He has been a principal investigator on research contracts from NSF,

AFOSR, ONR, and DARPA. He is a past associate editor for the journals Communications of the ACM and Transactions on Mathematical Software. He was an IBM Scholar from 1989-1993. Dr. Horowitz was appointed Director of Information Technology and Distance Education in USC's School of Engineering. As Director of the Distance Education Network (DEN) he oversaw an operation that offers more than 150 graduate engineering courses per year to more than 1,000 students. Courses are delivered across the United States by satellite broadcast and Internet webcast. Dr. Horowitz is an active consultant to the legal community, specializing in intellectual property issues. He was the founder and CEO of Quality Software Products, a California Corporation, from 1983 - 1993. The company designed and developed UNIX application software.

Jan Bosch is VP, Engineering Process at Intuit Inc. Earlier, he was head of the Software and Application Technologies Laboratory at Nokia Research Center, Finland. Before joining Nokia, he headed the software engineering research group at the University of Groningen, The Netherlands, where he holds a professorship in software engineering. His research activities include software architecture design, software product families, software variability management and component-oriented programming. He is author of a book "Design and Use of Software Architectures: Adopting and Evolving a Product Line Approach", an editor of Science of Computer Programming and (co-)author of many research papers.

Eelke Folmer is an assistant Professor at the University of Nevada. His research interests lie in the area of interaction design and software engineering focusing on the domain of games and virtual worlds. He is specifically interested in making games and virtual worlds accessible to users with disabilities. His past research involved software architecture assessment of usability.

N. Gupta received his B.Tech. in CS&E from BIET Jhansi (U.P.) and M.Tech. degree in Computer Science & Technology from IIT-Roorkee in 1998 and 2002 respectively. Since 1998, he has been actively engaged in teaching and research. Currently he is attached with Birla Institute of Technology and Science, Pilani (Rajasthan), India in CS/IS Group. He is also pursuing his Ph.D. from Birla Institute of Technology and Science, Pilani. His main professional interests are in Software engineering, Software Testing, Object oriented Technologies. Contact: nirmal@bits-pilani.ac.in

D. Saini received his Ph.D. in software Systems, Prior to that he has done his Masters of Engineering in software systems. He is member of major professional bodies. He has been actively engaged in teaching and research. Currently he is attached with King Saud University, Riyadh as Assistant Professor. His main research interests are in Mathematical Modeling, Simulation, Cyber Defense, Network Security, Intelligent Techniques, software testing and quality. Contact: dksaini_bits@yahoo.com

H. Saini received his B.Tech. in CS&E from NIT Hamirpur (H.P.) and M.Tech. degree in Information Technology from the Punjabi University Patiala, Punjab in 1999 and 2005 respectively. Since 1999, he has been actively engaged in teaching and research. Currently he is attached with Computer Engineering and Information Technology Department of Higher Institute of Electronics, Libya a more than 30 years of old institute which gives graduate and post graduate engineering degrees. He is also pursuing his Ph.D. from Birla Institute of Technology and Science, Pilani. His main professional interests are in Mathematical Modeling, Simulation, Cyber Defense, Network Security, Image processing and Intelligent Techniques.

James Miller received the BSc and PhD degrees in computer science from the University of Strathclyde, Scotland. In 2000, he joined the Department of Electrical and Computer Engineering at the University of Alberta, Canada as a full professor and in 2003 became an adjunct professor at the Department of Electrical and Computer Engineering at the University of Calgary, Canada. He has published over one hundred refereed journal and conference papers on software and systems engineering.

Liyun Zhang received a BSc in communications engineering from Jilin University, China and a MEng from the University of Alberta, Canada in Computer Engineering. She currently works as a software quality assurance professional with IBM, Canada. Ejike Ofuonye is currently a computer engineering MSc student at the University of Alberta, Canada with research interests in the areas of software protection systems, secure software development and software quality assurance. He worked for some years in Socketworks Limited as a software engineer in the Technology Innovations group, pioneering and architecting portal technologies that service a broad industry base. He holds a bachelors degree in electronic engineering from the University of Nigeria.

Michael Smith obtained his PhD in physics from the University of Alberta, Canada. After a number of years teaching science and mathematics in secondary schools, he returned to academia as a professor in electrical and computer engineering at the University of Calgary, Canada. In 2003, he became an adjunct professor with the Department of Radiology, University of Calgary, Canada. His major research interests involve the application of software engineering and customized real-time digital signal processing algorithms in the context of mobile embedded systems and bio-medical instrumentation.

Jijun Lu is a PhD student in Department of Computer Science and Engineering at the University of Connecticut. He received his BS and MS in Computer Science from University of Science and Technology of China (Hefei, China) in 2000 and 2003 respectively. His research interests include: performance and availability analysis of multi-tiered Web applications, service-oriented computing, and QoS assurance of next generation network.

Swapna S. Gokhale is an Assistant Professor in the Dept. of Computer Science and Engineering at the University of Connecticut. She received her M.S. and Ph.D. in Electrical and Computer Engineering from Duke University in 1996 and 1998 respectively and her B.E. (Hons.) in Electrical and Electronics Engineering and Computer Science from the Birla Institute of Technology and Science, Pilani, India in 1994. Prior to joining UConn, she was a Post Graduate Researcher at the University of California, Riverside, and a Research Scientist in the Applied Research Division of Telcordia Technologies, Morristown, NJ. Her research interests lie in the areas of software reliability, software performance, QoS assurance of wireless and wireline networks, and application-level intrusion detection. She is a Senior Member of the IEEE. She received the CAREER award from the National Science Foundation in 2007 for her research in the area of architecture-based software reliability assessment.

M. Daud Ahmed is a senior lecturer in the School of Computing and Information Technology, Manukau Institute of Technology, Auckland, New Zealand. He has varied academic background such as B.Sc. Engineering in Electrical and Electronics, MBA on Development Management, Post Graduate Diploma in Management Science and Information Systems (MSIS), Masters of Commerce in MSIS, completed PhD study on sustainable business transformation. He has received a number of research awards such as Annual Premier Research Award 2008 and one of the two finalists of the annual research award 2007 of the Manukau Institute of Technology, Special Research Award 2008 of the New Zealand Centres for IT Research, and Performance Based Research Award for the period of 2006-12 of the New Zealand Tertiary Education Commission. He has a long experience on management consultancy, systems analysis, design, development and implementation, and planning and management of a number of engineering and social development projects. He serves as a member of the international review board, and an associate editor of several journals, conferences, books and encyclopaedias. He has research publications on framework and architecture of decision support systems, software project management, sustainable business management, sustainability modelling, triple bottom line reporting, and systems development.

David Sundaram is an Associate Professor in the Department of Information Systems and Operations Management, Business School, The University of Auckland. He has a varied academic (B.E. in Electronics & Communications, PG Dip in Industrial Engineering, and Ph.D. in Information Systems) as well as work (systems analysis and design, consulting, teaching, and research) background. His primary research interests include the 1) Design and Implementation of flexible and evolvable Information, Decision, and Knowledge Systems 2) Process, Information, and Decision Modelling 3) Triple Bottom Line Modelling and Reporting 4) Enterprise Application Integration with a focus on ERP-DSS integration.

Ghalem Belalem graduated from university of Oran, Algeria, where he received PhD degree in computer science in 2007. He is now a research fellow of management of replicas in data grid. His current research interests are: distributed systems, grid computing and data grid, placement of replicas and consistency in large scale systems.

Belabbes Yagoubi graduated from university of Oran, Algeria, where he received PhD degree in computer science in 2007. He is currently leading a research team on the management of resources in grids. His main research interests are in the grid computing, distributed systems, load balancing and resource management challenges in Grids.

Samah Bouamama is a Master candidate in Department of computer science, Faculty of Sciences, University of Oran, Algeria. His research interests are replication strategies and consistency management.

Iftikhar U. Sikder is assistant professor of computer and information science at Cleveland State University. He holds a PhD in computer information systems from the University of Maryland, Baltimore. His research interests include spatial data warehousing and data mining, uncertainty management in spatial databases, collaborative spatial decision support systems. He has authored numerous articles in peer-reviewed journals, book chapters.

Aryya Gangopadhyay is an associate professor of information systems at the University of Maryland Baltimore County (UMBC). He has a PhD in computer information systems from Rutgers University. His research interests include privacy preserving data mining, OLAP data cube navigation, and core and applied research on data mining. He has co-authored and edited three books, many book chapters, and numerous papers in peer-reviewed journals.

Nikhil V. Shampur holds MS degree in computer & information science from Cleveland State University. His research interest includes distributed GIS and Web Services. Currently, Nikhil is involved in ArcGIS Server .NET team at Environmental Systems Research Institute (ESRI).

Index

A

Active Credibility 243, 247, 248, 249, 250, 251, 252, 253, 254, 256
Agile Web Engineering (AWE) 101, 126
algorithmic level 203
ambiguities 1, 2, 6, 7, 8, 16
architecture design 177, 178, 180, 184, 187, 191, 194, 197, 198, 199
artificial intelligence 39, 40, 42, 43, 44, 46, 47, 49, 53, 57, 58, 59
auction 272, 276, 277
authorization bypass 214

B

BPEL 43

C

case-based reasoning (CBR) 101
cell phone users 129, 130, 131, 133, 134, 141, 142
class level 203, 204, 209
class level testing 209
class specification 203, 204, 205, 209
clear requests 1, 11
cluster images 92
clustering 83, 84, 86, 87, 88, 89, 90, 92, 93, 94, 95
cluster level 203, 204
cognitive parameters 63, 64, 65, 67, 68, 69, 76, 77, 80
cold anger/irritation 146
collaboration 243
collaborative GIS 282

collaborative modeling 281, 283, 289, 293, 294
command pattern 178, 181, 183
composer 52
conceptual distance 30
consistency 269, 270, 271, 272, 273, 274, 277, 279, 280
constructors 207
content language 43
context awareness 24
context-aware querying 1, 2, 7
"context-based" querying 2, 13
continuous human voice 148
conversational models 40
credibility 243, 244, 245, 246, 247, 248, 249, 250, 251, 252, 253, 254, 255, 256, 257
credibility engineering 243, 244, 245, 247, 248, 255
crime data mining 95

D

data distributing 270
data expression 44
Data Grids 269
data mining 83, 95, 96
data sources 2, 6, 7, 8, 9, 10, 11, 12, 13
data storage 1
decision making 259, 260, 264, 267
Decision Support Systems 259, 264, 268
default-deny 214
default value manipulations 227
deliberative agents 46
Desire 71, 72
destructors 207